CONFLICT AND AGREEMENT IN THE CHURCH

Volume One

CONFLICT AND AGREEMENT IN THE CHURCH

by

T. F. TORRANCE

Volume One

ORDER AND DISORDER

Wipf & Stock
PUBLISHERS
Eugene, Oregon

To
KARL BARTH

Wipf and Stock Publishers
199 W 8th Ave, Suite 3
Eugene, OR 97401

Conflict and Agreement In the Church, 2 volumes
By Torrance, Thomas F.

ISBN: 1-57910-006-6
Publication date 11/16/1996
Previously published by Lutterworth Press, 1959

CONTENTS

Part 2

PROBLEMS OF FAITH AND ORDER

PREFACE

DURING the last ten years I have found myself involved more and more in ecumenical discussions, through the *Scottish Journal of Theology*, through participation in the work of the Faith and Order Department of the World Council of Churches, and through engagement, at the request of my own Church, in conversations with the Church of England. The essays, articles, and article-reviews that make up these volumes have all arisen directly or indirectly out of that work, which to a large extent explains their character as well as the kind of questions that are raised and discussed in them. They do not, however, represent my main theological work or interest, which continues to be in the field of Christology and Soteriology. The contributions to this volume represent rather the *parerga* to that major task in spite of the fact that they have occupied so much of my time.

Some of the material in these volumes has already appeared in various journals in Scotland, England, and Ireland, in Germany, Switzerland, France, Canada, and the United States of America. I am grateful to the editors of the Journals concerned for allowing me to republish that material here. Some of it, however, has never been published before: papers read or lectures delivered to various audiences in churches and universities. For the most part they are now printed in the form in which they were delivered, but some of the addresses were delivered only from notes and now that they are written out in full they have naturally suffered some change or extension (perhaps even curtailment!). Most of them were not intended for publication. Now that they are gathered together into two volumes it is inevitable that there should be some repetition, but because the themes they cover are fairly closely related the repetition is not a little. Instead of abridging them, however, I have felt it better to give them in full as they were originally conceived and written.

I am particularly grateful to the S.C.M. Press for allowing me to publish the essay on *Eschatology and the Eucharist* written for the volume on *Intercommunion* (edited by D. M. Baillie and John Marsh) in preparation for the Third World Conference on Faith and Order held at Lund;[1] and also to the Working Committee of the Faith and Order Department of the World Council of Churches, under the chairmanship of Dr. Oliver S. Tomkins, which allowed me to reproduce here the longer draft of the "working paper" on *Our oneness in Christ and our disunity as churches* which they asked me to write in the course of their preparation for the Evanston Assembly.

It is one of the great advantages of biblical and theological study in ecumenical encounter that one learns how often one's own reading of the Bible and understanding of theology have been conditioned by looking at them through the spectacles of one's own Church tradition. That is always salutary. The tension created between different traditions is also of great advantage in understanding the history of theology and the problems it has left to us. I should like, therefore, to take this opportunity of thanking all those with whom I have engaged in theological discussion and even controversy, for there are few from whom I have not learned. Some of that learning is reflected in these different essays, particularly of course in those of later date. If the reader should find some inconsistencies between earlier and later essays, I would beg of him to think of me as but a scholar in the school of Christ who does not count that he has attained but who still presses on in apprehending that for which he was apprehended by Christ Jesus.

For the benefit of some readers I would like to add that when I speak of "sacramental incorporation" I am using what the Reformers called "the sacramental mode of speaking" and am not suggesting that there is a second incorporation performed in the Sacraments in addition to that wrought by Christ Himself.

In reading through the proofs I have been reminded again of how much I owe to the teaching of Karl Barth, that great doctor of the Church Catholic, and not least to his understanding of the history of theology. The Church's debt to him is immeasurable.

[1] This essay will appear in Volume Two.

The gathering together of these essays has been undertaken at the suggestion of the Rev. Cecil Northcott of the Lutterworth Press. To him and to the Lutterworth Press I wish to express my deep gratitude for the great kindness and patience they have shown to me throughout.

T.F.T.

New College,
Edinburgh.
Christmas, 1958.

ACKNOWLEDGMENTS

Acknowledgment is made to the following journals, etc., for permission to reproduce articles in this book:

Scottish Journal of Theology, for "The Apostolic Ministry", "Catholicity", "The Fulness of Christ", "Problems of Reunion", "The New Mariological Dogma", "Amsterdam—The Nature and Mission of the Church", "Where Do We Go From Lund?" "The Atonement and the Oneness of the Church".

The Presbyterian World, for "Our Witness Through Doctrine": *The Ecumenical Review* for "What is the Church?": *The Presbyterian Record*, Toronto, and *Biblical Theology*, Belfast, for "A New Approach": the editor of *The Scotsman* (Mr. A. M. Dunnett), the Rev. James Quinn, S.J., and the Very Rev. Mgr. H. Francis Davis, for correspondence reprinted from that paper: and *Interpretation* and *Judaica* for "Israel and the Incarnation".

INTRODUCTION

In the *Report of the Third World Conference on Faith and Order*, held at Lund, Sweden, in August, 1952, the section entitled "Christ and His Church" began with these words:

> We believe in Jesus Christ our Lord, who loved the Church and gave Himself for it, and has brought the Church into an abiding union with Himself. Because we believe in Jesus Christ we believe also in the Church as the Body of Christ.

Then the Report went on to show that the relation between the Church and Christ is grounded on and derives from the saving work of Christ.

> For He, in His incarnation, death and resurrection, has entered into oneness with man in his estrangement and in his existence under the judgment of God, and by making atonement for man's guilt has consecrated a new and living way in which man, reconciled to God, may live in union with Jesus Christ. Through Him God has given to lost humanity a new beginning, for in that Jesus Christ died and rose again, all who believe in Him die and rise again to a new life.

The union thus forged between Christ and His people created the Church, in which Jesus Christ through His Spirit so lives and dwells that He refuses to be without His Church, and His Church has no existence apart from Him.

> Thus Christ is never without His Church; the Church is never without Christ. Both belong inseparably together, the King and His people, the keystone and the temple, the Head and the Body. As members of His Body, we are made one with Him in the fellowship of His life, death and resurrection, of His suffering and His glory. For what concerns Christ concerns His Body also. What has happened to Christ uniquely in His once-and-for-all death and resurrection on our behalf happens also to the Church in its way as His Body. As the Church is made a partaker in the crucified Body of Christ, so also it is given to be partaker in the risen Body of the same Lord. This means that the Church is

called to continue the mission of Jesus Christ to the world, so that the way of Christ is the way of His Church.

That I believe to be the proper theological procedure in any approach to the doctrine of the Church and the many problems that confront us to-day in regard to our understanding of its nature and mission, provided that at every point we remember that the Church is subject to Christ and can never usurp His place, and provided that, even when we say that the Church is called to continue the mission of Christ, we do not mean that it is prolonging His atonement or continuing His redeeming work, but that it is sent out into the world to serve Him who only is Saviour by proclaiming the Word of reconciliation: "We beseech you in Christ's stead, Be ye reconciled to God."

That is not only the proper procedure for a doctrine of the Church but for all theological doctrines. For the way that God has taken with us in the Incarnation of His only Son, the way in which He has willed to reveal Himself and to save us, is not only the only way of our salvation but the only way of all our knowing of Him. That way has been revealed to us in the Holy Scriptures, so that we must turn to the way of the Incarnation as set before us in the witness of the New Testament, and follow carefully the way of God's revealing and reconciling work in Jesus Christ, if we are to cut behind our errors and conflicts and find again the way to truth and unity in the one Lord. That was well put long ago by Hippolytus writing against the heresy of Noetus:

> There is, brethren, one God, the knowledge of whom we gain from the Holy Scriptures, and from no other source. For just as a man, if he wishes to be skilled in the wisdom of this world, will find himself unable to get at it in any other way than by mastering the dogmas of the philosophers, so all of us who wish to practise piety will be unable to learn its practice from any other quarter than the oracles of God. Whatever things, then, the Holy Scriptures declare, at these let us look; and whatsoever things they teach, these let us learn; and as the Father wills our belief to be, let us believe; and as He wills the Son to be glorified, let us glorify Him; and as He wills the Holy Spirit to be bestowed, let us receive Him. Not according to our will, nor according to our own mind, nor yet as using violently those things which are given

by God, but even as He has chosen to teach them by the Holy Scriptures, so let us discern them.

Hence the Lund Report adopted the only right and proper theological procedure when it went on to say:

> On the ground of the apostolic witness to Jesus Christ, the Lord of the Church, and in obedience to Him, we seek to penetrate behind the divisions of the Church on earth to our common faith in the one Lord. From the unity of Christ we seek to understand the unity of the Church on earth, and from the unity of Christ and His Body we seek a means of realizing that unity in the actual state of our divisions on earth.

That is surely the Christian way, and the profoundest way, to deal with our disagreements. But let us note what it involves. To approach the problems in this way means that our disagreements must come under the judgments of Christ, for the very oneness of Christ condemns division; but if the doctrine of Christ includes His Cross, as indeed it does, then in the very heart of Christology we are provided not only with judgment upon our divisions but with the mighty act of God which assumed upon Himself the sin that separates and divides and contradicts in order to overcome it and set it aside in reconciliation and recreation. It is in the saving work of Christ as well as in His Person that we must look for the oneness which God bestows upon us, and which alone can solve our theological and ecclesiastical divisions, for in the heart of those divisions there is sin, and not least the sin of refusal to acknowledge it.

Now if common agreement in the doctrine of Christ as Saviour and Lord is to be the basis for the agreement that is to be realized in the midst of our present disagreements, then we must set to work again in a major way to wrestle with the profound issues of Christology and Soteriology. That is surely what the Ecumenical Movement is driving us relentlessly to do, and as it does that it reveals that there are two major errors and temptations against which we must do battle: (1) the dissolution of Christology and the displacement of Christ by man; and (2) the mythologization of the Church and the obscuring of Christ by the Church.

Both these errors have assumed powerful expression and

command wide allegiance in our day. The first has its most obvious expression in the movement from Schweitzer and Harnack (in their very different ways) to Bultmann, which lays the axe to the very root of the Incarnation as the coming down to earth of the Son of God Himself for us and our salvation. For all his disavowal of it, in Bultmann the Liberalism of the nineteenth and early twentieth centuries that set aside the Being and Person of Christ, as not of central importance, in favour of an inwardness of spirit and a modern way of life, has reasserted itself in a form that is a direct menace to the Apostolic and Catholic faith in Jesus Christ. This dissolution of Christology results also in the dissolution of the Church (*Entkirchlichung*) and in the rise of a detached and aesthetically-minded secularism. The other error has its most obvious expression in downright mythologization of the Church as a *Christus prolongatus* so characteristic of modern Romanism, but also so rampant in the Baroque spirituality of many Anglo-Catholics. In the Roman form this error is hitched to the mythologization of the Virgin Mary, and in the Anglo-Catholic form it is part of a new mystique that has its supreme expression in the episcopate. But this is by no means confined to these, for it flourishes in many of the so-called "Free Churches", especially in the new world where it assumes very different forms. But, wherever this error is found, the pre-eminence of the Person of Christ as Saviour and God is obscured by the Church, whether in its institutional forms or in its social manifestations.

Both these errors lead to the same result: the displacement of Christ by man. That is just as clear in the Roman form in which through the direct identification of the Church and Christ it is finally man's desire and man's voice that predominates, as it is in the Protestant form in which through the identification of the decisive act of God and man's existential decision Christology is ultimately replaced by anthropology. Karl Barth was therefore fundamentally right in pointing out the close parallel and kinship between the thought of Bultmann and that of Rome. Rome identifies Revelation with its own subjectivity just as much as the Protestant individualist—indeed it was from mediaeval Romanism that this modern subjectivism so rampant in the Neo-Protestantism of the nineteenth and early twentieth centuries derived, as Harnack frankly admitted; not through the Reformation, but through Anabaptism and kindred movements that emerged out of the mystical pietism of the Roman Church.

History will surely reckon the road that Neo-Protestantism has taken from Lessing to Bultmann as the *reductio ad absurdum* of this pietistic element in Protestantism. Certainly the Ecumenical Movement has made it impossible for the Evangelical Churches to take that road, for the Ecumenical encounter forces the Churches to think through their agreements and disagreements in the light of the whole history of the Church, and therefore directs the Churches back more and more to the central dogmas of the Apostolic and Catholic Church. Schweitzer and Bultmann will always be regarded where they actually are now, on the fringe of the Church. That is not to say that their challenge is to be set aside, for demythologization has more and more point when we face the mythologization of Roman theology or the new mythologies of modern science. It is from that angle that the real danger lies in the Ecumenical encounter to-day, which more and more forces us to face our differences in the doctrine of the Church, and to seek to reach agreement. We must undertake that, but never, surely, in such a way as to allow the Church to displace the Person of Christ or to obscure His Face, and never in such a way as to allow the sacramental enactments in the Church to assume priority over the mighty acts of God in Christ, which is what they always tend to do when they are thought of as something in addition to, and therefore in some sense as other than, the finished work of Christ. Besides, that involves a strange failure to realize that Jesus Christ clothed with His Gospel is ever really present in the midst of His Church on earth, so that His finished work is abiding and effective reality in it from generation to generation. He does not need to be made "present", and His work does not need to be made "real".

It is very necessary for us to-day to wrestle with the doctrine of the Church in the same way that the early centuries wrestled with the doctrine of Christ, but we must not yield to the temptation to think of the Church as an independent hypostatic reality. It was not the Church that was pre-existent and became incarnate; it was not the Church that was assumed into hypostatic union with the Deity; it was not the Church that was crucified for our salvation and raised for our justification; it was not the Church that ascended to the right hand of God the Almighty (which is what the Roman dogma of the assumption of Mary implies)—but Jesus Christ alone, the Only-Begotten Son of God. We must formulate the doctrine of the Church therefore as His Body, and His Servant, not in any sense as an *alter Christus*.

Now it is precisely because this danger has been noted, the danger of a masterful ecclesiology, that the suggestion has been made that we must seek rather to emphasize the doctrine of the Church as the manifestation in humanity correlative to the gift of the Spirit, the sphere described by God's people where God's Spirit is at work. And that is a fundamentally true aspect of the doctrine of the Church, and certainly no doctrine of the Church can neglect the doctrine of the Spirit. But this is also the very point where Roman and Protestant theology have in the past been led into serious error, both of them, in different ways, in identifying the Holy Spirit with the human spirit: in the Roman Church with the "uncreated soul" of the Church, in Neo-Protestantism with the man's "higher nature". That is why there came about such an astonishing approximation between the views of both in the late nineteenth century: in regard to the spiritual consciousness of the Church as the vehicle of Revelation and as indeed Revelation itself at work in the soul of the Church, and therefore in regard to the nature of theology as the systematic expression of the mind of the Church in its awareness of the divine. But when there is added to this the historical consciousness of the Church, then it is difficult to escape the conclusion that the *Heilsgeschichte* (salvation-history or redemptive history) is identical with the developing mind of the Church throughout the centuries. In that way again Neo-Protestant ideas coincide pretty closely with Roman ideas.

Now the decisive fact in the doctrine of the Church in relation to the Spirit is the *filioque* clause of the Creed, which asserts that the Spirit does not speak of Himself but only reveals what Christ had already taught His disciples; that Revelation was fully complete and whole with the Incarnation, Resurrection, and Ascension of Christ, and that nothing could be added to it;

and therefore that throughout the history of the Church the Revealing work of the Spirit is bounded by the particularity of the Incarnation and the form of the Incarnate Word, the historical Jesus. A doctrine of revelation and inspiration in the Old Testament Scriptures must doubtless work with the correlativity of the people of God with the work of His Spirit, so that Revelation is bound up with the history of that people, and the *Heilsgeschichte* with the acts of that people. In the Incarnation, however, the Spirit uttered the One and only Word of God, and that was a full and final Revelation. Thus in the New Covenant a doctrine of revelation and inspiration has to work with the fundamental and absolute importance of the Humanity of Jesus Christ, for with the Incarnation the *Heilsgeschichte* is bound up exclusively with Him. All the mighty acts of God have taken place in Christ, and we await only His final Parousia; the Church lives between the penultimate and the ultimate acts of the *Heilsgeschichte*.

Thus Church history cannot be identified with the *Heilsgeschichte*, although all through the history of the Church the *Heilsgeschichte* is effective and operative, being identical with Christ clothed with His mighty acts. The doctrine of the Church must be formulated therefore as a correlate of the doctrine of Christ, for the Church is the Body of Christ, not the Body of the Spirit—it was not, after all, the Spirit but the Son who became incarnate and gave Himself for the Church and affianced it to Himself as His very own. Moreover, if we take the *filioque* seriously, as the Roman Church has never really done, then we cannot intrude into the faith of the Church extraneous elements, natural theology and mythology, derived not through the Incarnate Word or Son of God (*filioque*). In the last resort it has always been a "second source" of revelation or knowledge that has corrupted the Church or led it astray. Here once again the Roman tradition as a second source of Revelation (and its natural theology) and the Neo-Protestant "spirit of man" as a source of natural theology (and its historical consciousness) coincide, while the rank growth of mythology in Roman Mariology has its Protestant counterparts in the mythologies of the Pentecostal sects and "the German Christians". If the Church is thought of only as the Community of the Spirit then it is impossible to inhibit the idea of a continuing revelation in the Church, and difficult to prevent the Church from deviating seriously from its apostolic foundations. Only if the Church's relation to the Spirit is through the Incarnate Word or Son, only if we take in utmost seriousness and with the fullest rigour the doctrine of the Church as the Body of Christ, can we prevent that, and preserve the integrity of the Church in Christ.

On the other hand, the doctrine of the Spirit has its indispensable place, for when it is allowed to be superseded or dropped out of sight the Church comes to be more or less identified with a hierarchic institution operating with a false objectivity, and the whole conception of the Church as a communion of love, a fellowship of people living the reconciled life, is suppressed. It is the doctrine of the Spirit that inhibits the imprisoning of the life of the Church in a *codex iuris canonici*, that destroys the idea that the grace of God is bound to the sacramental elements, that makes impossible the conception that divine mysteries can be controlled and manipulated by man, and therefore that keeps the Church open to the renewal of its mind and lifts it above the downward drag of the spirit of the times. But this is the Spirit of Truth poured out upon the Church by its ascended Head and Lord, and He it is who directs the Church away from itself to find its true life and being above in Christ alone.

It is thus the doctrine of the Church as the Body of Christ that must engage our attention, but that means the subordination of the Church at every point to Christ Himself; it does not mean that the Church occupies the centre of our attention but Christ alone. It is not therefore ecclesiology that is of primary importance, but Christology. That is why it is more and more imperative that the doctrines of the person and of the work of Christ should engage our full attention, even when pressing problems of ecclesiology bear down upon us. Nothing must be allowed to decentralize the Gospel—the Church is but a poor earthen vessel bearing the heavenly treasure, and it is the heavenly treasure that counts, not the earthen vessel. The great Apostle Paul, for all his high consciousness of his apostolic office, was profoundly aware of that. God intended that Paul's converts should see him as a blear-eyed man of mean appearance, just in order that they might not be tempted to confound the heavenly treasure with the earthen vessel; God kept him in the weakness of the flesh, therefore, that though death worked in him, life might abound in those to whom he preached the inestimable riches of Christ. There we have the supreme picture in the pages of the New Testament of the attitude and behaviour of the apostolic Church in Christ. Only if we are prepared to take the same line in the Church to-day, refusing at any point to exalt the Church as an end in itself, that Christ may have the pre-eminence in everything, can we reach agreement where we are so deeply divided: in the doctrine of the Church. But this means that behind that must lie full and deep agreement in the doctrine of Christ Himself.

Unfortunately the traditional confrontation of the Churches in the Ecumenical Movement has thrown the doctrine of the Church, comparatively speaking, into too great a prominence. We are learning again that the Church is part of the Creed, and that the doctrine of the Church can be formulated as an article of saving faith only within the context of faith in the Father, Son, and Holy Spirit; but we are trying to deal with it before we have gone deeply enough together into the second member of the Creed, faith in Jesus Christ. In the whole field of Christology, however, we have been given a magnificent lead in the teaching of Karl Barth, especially in his *Church Dogmatics IV*, "The Doctrine of Reconciliation". We have behind us also more than a century of the most exhaustive examination of the New Testament documents with the most phenomenal recovery of a vivid faith in the historical Jesus Christ—surely one of the great facts of all Church history—and now we have the rising tide of theological exegesis and a rigorous and constructive biblical theology. Ours must be the task of learning together again how to confess, like the early Church, faith in Jesus Christ as Saviour and God in all its breadth and length and height and depth, and therefore in the overflowing love of God. Only in that glorification of God the Son and in actual engagement in the mission of the Gospel can we produce, as a *parergon*, a doctrine of the Church in which our differences are lost sight of because they are destroyed from behind by a masterful faith in the Saviour of men.

Part

1

DISCUSSIONS WITH CHURCHES

DISCUSSIONS WITH CHURCHES

I. WITH ANGLICANS

(a) *The Apostles and the Ministry of the Church*

DISCUSSIONS with certain groups of Anglo-Catholics have regularly to reckon with a powerful non-theological factor at work in their outlook, a deep-seated inferiority complex over against the Roman Church which repudiates the validity of their orders. It is this which leads them to lay such an unbalanced emphasis upon narrow theories of the episcopate in their restless efforts to justify the Catholicity of the Church of England by its orders rather than to understand the orders of the Church of England in the light of its Catholicity. This is of course quite un-Anglican as well as un-theological; in fact it is a definitely sectarian approach. But that is precisely the approach adopted in the notorious volume, *The Apostolic Ministry*, edited by the late Kenneth E. Kirk. Unfortunately the re-publication of this volume under the editorship of Dr. A. M. Farrer does nothing to modify that approach, for the new foreword shows very little understanding of the theological positions of those within and without the Church of England who have opposed it; all that Dr. Farrer has been content to do is to attempt to rebut a few arguments abstracted from their main theological basis and to oppose a figment which he calls a "Yes-or-No Protestantism" with a manifestly sectarian spirit and a little logic-chopping that he characteristically mistakes for theology! Why is it that these Anglicans are so unsure of themselves, and of the gift of the Holy Spirit to the Church of England, that they must always be casting round for some novel theory of the episcopate as something which secures to them the Holy Spirit? Fortunately this is very far removed from the position of the Church of England itself, which does not hold that episcopal succession guarantees the Holy Ghost, and which has a far profounder and more theological understanding of the Apostolicity and Catholicity of the Church. It is time that the Church of England reasserted its historic position. Ever since the publication of *The Fulness of Christ*, there are signs that it has begun to do so with a powerful scholarship and a profound theology. That is to be welcomed everywhere, for Anglican witness without an adequate positive theology behind it cannot play a very constructive role in the world-Church to-day. Indeed, in the last ten years the situation in the Church of England has changed so much that the republication of *The Apostolic Ministry* appears like an anachronism.

It remains true, however, as Dr. Farrer avers, that that volume did throw out a challenge to rethink the doctrine of the apostolic ministry. And that must be done both within and without the Churches of the Reformation, not least by the Church of England, especially with regard to the place and significance of the apostolate itself.

The apostolic Church means the Church that is created in the apostolic mission of Christ from the Father, and of the apostles from Christ. "As the Father hath sent me, so send I you." The sending of the apostles is dependent on the sending of Christ by the Father, but is also correlative to the sending of the Holy Spirit in the Name of Christ upon the apostles and the Church. It is the Spirit who is Christ's Apostle in the strict sense in which the apostle or one sent is identical with the one who sends. Christ is Apostle in this absolute sense, for He wholly represents God in His person and work, and is the God whom He represents or manifests. The apostles, however, are sent to represent Christ in such a way that while their message is Christ's own Word, they are not personal representatives of Christ; that office is fulfilled by the Holy Spirit, the Apostle-Spirit, who is Christ's personal Representative and in whose presence it is Christ Himself who is present in Person. We have to think of the apostolate, therefore, in a twofold way: It is the mission of the apostles from Christ, but, along with that historical mission in handing on the Word of Christ, there is the Mission of the Holy Spirit from Christ who confirms that Word and through whose presence the Finished Work of Christ is really present and operative in the Church. The Church on earth is founded historically upon the apostles commissioned by Christ, but founded supernaturally by the baptism of the

Spirit sent by Christ at Pentecost; so that the Church has a double relation to Christ, historically through the apostles, and supernaturally through the Holy Spirit.

These two missions, of the apostles and of the Holy Spirit, are not to be thought of as running only in dialectical relation to one another, but as grounded in the *New Covenant* which Christ established in His Body and Blood. In this New Covenant the people of God are made one Body with Christ and the Holy Spirit is poured out upon their hearts, for God's New Covenant is not only cut into the flesh of the Body through the crucifixion of Christ but cut into the innermost beings of His people in the heart and mind of the Church. That marks the difference between the Old Testament Church and the New Testament Church, for in the New Testament Church the Word of God incarnate in Christ is incorporated into our humanity, and it is in that incarnate Word that the Church is given to participate through the Spirit. In other words, the Church is given to participate in the Covenant as it is fulfilled in Jesus Christ in His incarnation, life, death, and resurrection. The apostles were given a special place in that New Covenant at its inauguration at the Last Supper and it is through their unique relation to the Incarnate Word and the Spirit that they are constituted the foundation of the New Israel, the People of God filled with God's Spirit and incorporated into Christ as His Body. Here in the foundation of the New Covenant the apostolic obedience is knitted into the obedience of Christ, or rather, the obedience of Christ in fulfilment of the Covenant draws into itself the obedience of the apostles, so that the apostolic obedience to Christ is given a basic pattern and structure in the New Covenant as fulfilled in Christ Jesus. Because this is grounded in the New Covenant it is not a pattern and structure of obedience that rests upon its own persistence, but reposes upon the faithfulness of God in the Covenant which undergirds the apostolic obedience to Christ, sanctifies and secures it in Christ, and gives it an architechtonic function in the foundation of the Church on earth. As such it is caught up into the authority of the incarnational revelation of God in Christ, and the incarnational obedience of our humanity in Christ to the Father.

That bond of the New Covenant remains steadfast and sure,

and nothing can prevail against it. It is that covenanted faithfulness of Christ which undergirds the whole foundation of the Church and the whole of its continuity throughout all the changes and chances of history. But as part of the Covenant, and in fulfilment of the promise of the Covenant, God bestowed upon His Church the Holy Spirit through whom the Church as founded upon the apostles is given to have communion with Christ really and supernaturally, as well as historically, to share in His obedience, His love and His divine life. Now the outward form that this Covenant takes in the life of the apostolic Church is found in the Holy Sacraments, the pledges of God's faithfulness in Christ, the signs and seals of His fulfilled promise. The inward form which the Covenant takes is the communion of the Spirit through which the apostolic Church is given to share in the love and life of the Father, the Son, and the Holy Spirit. It is that communion in the very life and love of God, that continuity through communion of the redeemed life of the Church in Christ, that is the inner substance and heart of the apostolic succession or continuity in the apostolically-founded Church.

The whole continuity of the Church in its apostolic foundation depends upon the unique character and function of the apostolate. The apostles were the chosen vessels appointed to be with Christ, to receive His Revelation and to assimilate it in their obedience to Christ and to be assimilated to it, and in that way to pass it on to the Church. But they did that as special instruments in the hand of God under the inspiration of the Holy Spirit, for through the Spirit Jesus Christ Himself returned to them clothed in His Spirit, the Spirit of Truth, and gave Himself to be fully known, the same historical Jesus but now shining forth in the glory of the resurrection. As such He was appropriated by the apostles in His own Spirit, in His own Truth, and in His own Light, and in all that it was Christ Himself who returned to fill out all things and to fulfil in the apostolate His own Self-Revelation and Reconciliation. That was the apostolic mission, and the primary function of the apostolate. In it we do not have the initial stage of a continuous process, but the perpetually persisting foundation of the Church and its grounding in the incarnational Revelation and Reconciliation.

In this sense there can be no talk of apostolic succession, for that apostolic function cannot be transmitted. That is made very clear in the New Testament, in the separateness of the apostles from the other ministers in the Church. The apostles never had hands laid on them, and even when Matthias was appointed to take the place of Judas he had no hands laid on him. As Dr. Arnold Ehrhardt has pointed out, the apostles do not belong to the succession of the ministry, for they are not within it—the whole succession *depends* on them and is entirely subordinate to them. That is also clear from the fact that when the apostles died no attempt was made to fill their place, and so to give them successors in their apostolic office. (The idea that bishops are successors of the apostles was of late invention and entirely unknown to the apostolic Church itself.) Moreover, the very fact that the apostles appointed other ministers by the rite of laying on of hands—an essentially "lay-rite"—showed in unmistakable terms that they were not appointing successors to themselves but ordaining a ministry dependent upon them but of quite a different character and order, and without their judicial or magisterial authority. Only the apostles were appointed by Christ to sit upon the twelve thrones judging the twelve tribes of Israel; only apostolic witness is Holy Scripture, for their word is of judicial and magisterial authority through assimilation by Christ to His own Word. It was as such that they built up the Church, ordered it and gave it shape in its ministry and its ordinances, and above all by supplying it with the authoritative oracles of the New Testament. It was as such that they commanded the Church to be followers of them as they were of Christ, and as such that they instituted a continuing ministry different from but entirely dependent on their own.

There is therefore a secondary sense in which we can speak of "the apostolic ministry"—in relation to a succession; and this is twofold. It refers first to the Church that continues to be obedient to the apostolic teaching and commands from generation to generation. This Church continues to be apostolic when it moves out into history shaped and moulded by the apostolic tradition both in doctrine and in ordinances, and so continues to proclaim the apostolic *kerygma* and to be ordered by the apostolic *dogmata*, as the early fathers called their commands.

The Church has not only been grafted into or rooted in Christ through the apostles, but is built up and compacted together by them, and as such it multiplies and increases and is extended throughout history. And so apostolic succession means that the Church as the living Body apostolically begotten through the incorruptible Word of God continues in being in history, in reliance upon the Covenant-promises of Christ. This Church continues to be apostolic in that it continues throughout its movement and change from age to age to be schooled in the apostolic tradition, and determined by the apostolic Gospel. It is therefore a succession through the Spirit in obedience, in mission, a succession of service, of faith and doctrine, all in the continuity of the redeemed life of the people of God.

Within this apostolic succession we have also to speak of the apostolic ministry, that is of a ministerial succession within the apostolic succession of the whole Church grounded upon the apostles. That does not mean that we can think of the ministry of the historical Church as a self-perpetuating continuity, or simply as the handing on of powers apostolically delegated, but that we are to think of the ministry above all in terms of what is ministered, namely Word and Sacrament. The New Testament conception of *kerygma* takes its importance not from the preaching but from what is preached and from the source and authority from which it is derived; likewise the New Testament conception of *baptisma* takes its importance not from the rite but from the objective Christological event behind it in Christ and therefore from His Name as the source and authority for its administration. So it is with the ministry in the historical succession of the apostolic Church. The ministry of the Word is inseparable from the Word, and from the command and promise of the Lord attached to its proclamation to all nations.

The continuity of the ministry is to be understood in dependence entirely upon that living Word and within the whole continuity of the Church begotten by Him and maintained in covenant relation with Him through the apostolic Word handed on in the ministry of the Church. It is a fundamental error to abstract the ministry from that wholeness and to make it an essential and self-sufficient line of ministerial succession either of presbyters or of bishops upon which everything else is grounded from generation to generation. To isolate ministerial succession into an independent principle is to make it demonic, for it is to make it usurp the place of Christ Himself in Word and Sacrament. There is a ministerial succession, and it is necessary for the life of the Church in history, but it is only a succession within the Body where it is used and honoured by the Lord in the freedom of His Spirit and in His *creatio continua* of the Church as His Body throughout history. It is not upon the faithfulness of the ministry or of the ministry's unbroken succession that everything depends—all that is involved in the relativity and fragmentation and contingency of our fallen world—but upon the Covenant-faithfulness of Christ Himself.

This ministerial succession within the Body of the whole apostolic tradition, which is undergirded and upheld by Christ's own faithfulness, is "the power of the keys". That is, it is a ministerial succession in relation to the power of Christ's own Word and Spirit, and the faithfulness of His own promise in sending out His apostles and the apostolic Church on its mission of proclaiming the Word of reconciliation: "Whosesoever sins ye remit they are remitted, and whose soever sins ye retain they are retained." "All things are of God, who hath reconciled us to himself by Jesus Christ, and hath given to us the ministry of reconciliation; to wit, that God was in Christ, reconciling the world unto himself, not imputing their trespasses unto them; and hath committed unto us the word of reconciliation. Now then we are ambassadors for Christ, as though God did beseech you by us: we pray you in Christ's stead, be ye reconciled to God." Here the stress falls not upon the ministers of the Word of forgiveness but upon the objective Word and its divine enactment above and beyond, and, thank God, in spite of the ministers and their inadequacy and faltering faithfulness. This is the focal point in the continuation of the Church from generation to generation, namely, that it is the Word through the power of the Spirit which is mightily active to effect that which God has sent it to do, so that it does not return to Him void. The continuity of the ministry depends entirely upon that Word which is Christ's own Word and which He will unfailingly fulfil.

Now in order to understand this apostolic succession in the ministry, or rather the succession of the ministry within the whole apostolic succession of the Church, we have to note how the Church went out from the apostles into history. The apostles were the wise master-builders, the architects, of the Church's pattern of life, faith, and ministry in conformity to the pattern of the obedience of Christ. What were the basic traditions which the apostles gave to the Church? What were the fundamental things they did in order to equip the Church for this historical mission? Here we are concerned with three things which are ultimately inseparable from one another, and they all emerge into the open toward the end of the second century as the expression of the apostolic ordering of the life and faith of the Church, but they go back to the apostles themselves. These are (1) the canon of Holy Scripture; (2) the Rule of Faith, that is the canonical structure of doctrine and worship; and (3) the apostolic ministry.

We make a big mistake if we separate the doctrine of the Scripture from the doctrine of the apostolate, and so from the apostolic foundation of the Church, but we cannot separate it altogether from the rise of the Rule of Faith either, which came eventually to have the form of the Apostles' Creed, for it was partly through the Rule of Faith that the canonical Scriptures were set aside and others rejected, and the apostolic tradition was sharply differentiated as normative and authoritative from all other tradition; while it was again the regular and responsible devolvement of the ministry from the apostles, in obedience to the apostolic commands, and within the apostolic tradition, that attested and secured the faithful keeping and handing on of the apostolic Scriptures and the Rule of Faith. While we certainly must accord the canon of Holy Scripture its supreme place, we cannot truthfully separate it either theologically or historically from its integration with the Rule of Faith and the apostolic ministry. All these three factors are inescapably intertwined and have to be considered together, and one must not be isolated from the others. That applies above all to the apostolic ministry and its continuity in the life and mission of the Church. That means, as we can see at once, that if the ministerial succession is separated from continuous subordination to the apostolic Word in the Holy Scriptures, and from sound doctrine as attested in the Rule of Faith, it is a false succession, no matter how historically unbroken the links may be. But it is also true that even if ministerial succession is broken here and there historically, if it is knit into the togetherness of the other two great apostolic gifts, and especially with the supreme gift of the Holy Scriptures, its defects are more than amply made up in the coherent succession of the whole apostolic tradition.

But in order to see this more clearly, let us see how it actually began in the times of the apostles themselves and under their supervision. The ministry that continues in the Church has a twofold source:

(a) It has a source in the functions exercised by the apostles themselves, who appointed others to do some of the things that they did in the ministry. That is apparent in the appointment of the seven so-called deacons in the Acts and their ministry of tables, while the apostles gave themselves to the special ministry of the Word, which I take to mean their specific apostolic function in authoritative gathering up and handing on the *kerygma* and the *didache* of Christ, and in building up the Church on that basis. The apostles had unique functions which they could not and did not pass on; but they did also act as presbyters in ministering the Word and Sacraments and exercising a pastoral oversight in the Church. These functions as administered by the apostles themselves were necessarily fulfilled in a unique way in conjunction with their unique authority in the Word, and when separated from the apostles' unique ministry, they inevitably assumed another and subordinate character. There was no direct extending of the apostolic ministry into the continuing ministry of the Church. Some of their functions, however, came to be exercised by others, and underwent a change of character appropriate to ministers who were not themselves apostles, that is, who had no authority in the direct mediation of Revelation and in forming the New Testament witness. That then is one source of the ministry, on the historical plane going back through the apostles themselves to the historical Jesus and the historical founding of the Church. But let us be perfectly clear about the fact that this is a ministry dependent upon the apostles and is no more an extending of their ministry than an extending of their revelationary functions into the Church, although that is quite falsely what the Church of Rome seems to claim for Catholic instinct and the teaching office of the Roman Church.

(b) The ministry has a transcendent source in the gifts of the Holy Spirit sent down by the ascended Lord upon His Church, distributing them severally to its members according to His Will. These are gifts for the ministry and for the edification of the Church. Even here in the list of gifts recorded by the New Testament the prime gift was that of the apostle, differentiated from the others; but wherever the other gifts of the Spirit are given or manifest they are brought within the sphere of the apostolic commission, and it is clear that they are only exercised rightly within that sphere of the apostolic authority. That sphere of apostolic authority, as we see clearly in the Acts of the Apostles, is marked by the laying on of hands in different ways with regard to baptism and with regard to ordination. Thus even when the Spirit fell upon believers who had not already been baptized, although they then had the reality of their baptism, they were nevertheless duly baptized by the apostolic command; whereas on other occasions where people were baptized in the evangelistic mission of the Church that work was brought within the apostolic authority and commission by the laying on of hands. In that growing period of the Church, in which its pattern of orderly life and ministry was being built up, great care was taken to bring the whole expanding life and mission of the Church under apostolic authorization, and that carried with it the transmission through competent and authorized witnesses of the authentic oral tradition of the Gospel—hence the important place of the prophets and teachers in the New Testament Church.

This is not the point to discuss who these ministers were who worked under the apostles and were the first in the line of the ministerial succession; presbyters and bishops, prophets and teachers, and shepherds and leaders, are all names that are used. The point to be noted and emphasized here is that although the risen and ascended Lord gave the gifts of the ministry to the Church and only He empowered them and made them efficacious, they were given to be exercised within the apostolic foundation of the Church and under the apostolic commission which the apostles received from Jesus Christ while on earth before and after His resurrection. Thus the exercise of the spiritual gifts was rightly carried out within the sphere of the apostolic commission, and under apostolic authorization.

The sign that marked out that sphere and delimited it was the laying on of hands. Thus the succession in the apostolic ministry was the orderly passing on from generation to generation of ministerial responsibility and authority in reliance upon the command and promise of Christ given to His apostles in the foundation of the Church. That is the sign given by the apostles to be used in attesting the faithful transmission of the *kerygma* and *didache* of Christ, and in attesting the reliance of the Church and its ministry upon the faithfulness of Christ who remains true to His promises and fulfils them all in spite of our weakness and sinfulness. But this is only the sign of the real thing, namely the communion of the people of God in the divine life and love which they receive from Jesus Christ Himself through His Word and Spirit. It is not to be looked upon as a sacrament, for it was not instituted as a saving ordinance; it was an apostolically appointed sign which appropriately attests the continuity of the Church in the authentic ministry of the Word and Sacraments and in the Rule of Faith, all under the authority of the apostolic Revelation handed on to us in the New Testament. It is this apostolic authority that attaches to and governs the necessity of historical succession in the Church's ministry from age to age. But because it is the apostolic authority that is paramount, what is paramount is obedience to the Word of God in the Holy Scriptures, and to the doctrinal content of the Word unfolded according to the Rule of Faith.

It is of manifest importance that neither the apostolic tradition as enshrined in the New Testament nor the Rule of Faith has a word to say about the precise form of the ministry with which the historical Church is equipped, although both make it quite clear that this is not the apostolic ministry but a ministry dependent upon the apostles, other than theirs but deriving from them and subordinate to them in everything. That fact alone prevents us from giving to the ministry of the historical Church an absolutely fixed pattern (and certainly from rationalizing such a fixed pattern in a fixed theory) especially when there is no warrant for it in the apostolic tradition of the New Testament.

This means that no ministry in the historical Church can be judged apostolic except that which conforms to the apostolic revelation as given to us in the New Testament Scriptures.

That is the ultimate source and norm of the Church's continued existence throughout history. The apostolic Church is the Church that lives by the New Testament as its canon of life and faith, and the apostolic ministry is the ministry that remains entirely subject to that canonical life and faith. It is this fact that gives the Church its image and form as the Body of Christ on earth, shapes its mission and orders its ministry as Christ's instrument in the Gospel, so that by listening to the apostolic testimony, by the study of the New Testament and by the obedience of faith to its revelation, the Church lives throughout the changes and chances of history and throughout all temporal succession in such a way as not to be conformed to this world but to be transformed by the renewing of its mind and so to be conformed to Christ, the Apostle and High Priest of our confession. Nothing can be judged apostolic which is not in accordance with the apostolic foundation and norm, and therefore any claim to the apostolic ministry which is manifestly not agreeable to the apostolic revelation calls for repudiation by all who hold dear the integrity of the Apostolic and Catholic Faith.

That is the criterion by which we must faithfully test the claims made in *The Apostolic Ministry.*

(b) *The Apostolic Ministry*[1]

A critical review of the issues raised by *The Apostolic Ministry, Essays on the History and the Doctrine of Episcopacy,* prepared under the direction of Kenneth E. Kirk, Bishop of Oxford. (Hodder and Stoughton, 1946.)

The Apostolic Ministry is a volume of outstanding importance, not only because of its wealth of learning but because in many respects it represents a change of front on the part of Anglicans in the realization that it is ultimately upon theological grounds that a true conception of the ministry must rest. At the same time it cannot but be of extreme interest to the Reformed Churches in that it approaches their view that the ministry is creative of the Church. Nevertheless the precise interpretation given to that doctrine in these pages throws out a real challenge

[1] From the *Scottish Journal of Theology,* 1, 1948, pp. 190–201.

to the Reformed Churches which must be taken seriously, particularly as it has been thrown out in view of the widespread movement for reunion. I have no hesitation, therefore, in adding a further discussion particularly of the more theological issues raised.

At the very outset something must be said about the methods employed by the various scholars who contribute to this book. It is refreshing to find here the combination of biblical and historical research with dogmatic construction or reconstruction. That is a method of investigation which I, for one, welcome, as being a great advance even upon the impartial scholarly method of men like Lightfoot, Hort, and Swete, and I find myself in definite agreement with them against many of their predecessors in this field in their insistence that, apart from a doctrine of the ministry, no real progress can be made through the criss-cross tradition of Church history on this subject. Let it be recognized, however, that this is a method of investigation that can play only too easily into the hands of presuppositions and prejudices entertained by the scholars themselves. That alas is what happens too often in this volume, vitiating its conclusions. All learning is not scholarship. A great deal of the evidence that has been advanced in this book is "evidence" based only upon "evidence" already re-moulded by the presuppositions of the writers themselves and set forth as already proven. Against such wilfulness and inexactitude one must register a vehement protest. One welcomes the way in which Fr. Thornton and Dr. Farrer treat the Bible as a unity, which, thanks to the immense scholarship associated with the name of Kittel, and to the work of New Testament scholars like A. M. Hunter, we are beginning to realize afresh to-day, but the exegetical acrobatics of both Thornton and Farrer are not worthy of the name of true scholarship.

There is much also in the able essay of Dom Gregory Dix that one cannot let pass without calling its method in question. To one who does not know his patristics very well the Dixian evidence appears convincing, but no one who has really studied carefully the fathers he cites can fail to be amazed at his temerity in picking out bits of evidence here and there, and his wilful overlooking of disturbing facts, and sheer neglect of other facts. That is nowhere more patent than in his handling of the *Didache* and even of 1 *Clement*, not to mention a great deal in Hippolytus that smites his views down to the ground again and again, but which apparently he dares not look in the face. But perhaps more important than all this is the way in which he starts off with the schismatic Hippolytus, and "believes" that what he finds there is the key to the interpretation of the earlier less developed form of the ministry and later and more developed form of the ministry. This is to suppose that all this is a *legitimate* development of the New Testament doctrine and practice, and entails a quite uncritical handling of Church history. In the end it really means that all the Dixian evidence is based upon a mere inference which allows him to read into the New Testament notions and practices that are simply not there.

In rejecting the evidence of the *Didache*, Dix gives as his reason that it proceeds from a *milieu* so different from that in which Pauline evidence is found. He refuses therefore to interpret Pauline language from the angle of the *Didache*, but insists in interpreting the New Testament language from the angle of Hippolytus! It is not, however, from Hippolytus as a whole that he takes his cue so much as from certain liturgical selections from Hippolytus considered in almost entire abstraction from the theology of Hippolytus and his background in the Roman Schism. Incidentally, Dix seems to be ignorant of the work done by Cullmann in Strasbourg on the intimate relation between 1 *Clement* and Paul's *Epistle to the Philippians*, which has thrown a flood of light on the situation in Rome; a split between Jewish and Gentile Christians which had brought down upon both Peter and Paul the sentence of death. It is that situation which Clement holds up as a warning to the Corinthian Church who have in their midst a like schism. All the evidence goes to show that it is in the light of this Roman schism between Jewish and Gentile elements, complicated by the introduction of Gnosticism, that the *milieu* of Hippolytus is to be understood, and further that it was precisely because Hippolytus was a schismatic that he laid deliberate claim to apostolicity. That puts an entirely different complexion upon the situation, and upon the material Dix uses. But Dix prefers to shut his eyes, apparently, to all the facts, and *believes*, as he says, that the evidence he gets out of Hippolytus originates from a period before Hippolytus became a schismatic. And so all the Dixian evidence rests upon this blind inference! Had Dix taken the trouble to investigate the theology and particularly the Christology of Hippolytus, he might have been forced to a different conclusion in spite of himself. It seems extraordinary, to say the least, that a scholar who professes to take such a firm stand with his colleagues on the principles of Nicaea and Chalcedon should take some of his leading ideas from one so heretical in his Christology as Hippolytus.

The plain facts to anyone acquainted with this early patristic literature seem to be these: Particularly after A.D. 70, and until the Pauline corpus received general circulation, Judaistic and Gnostic trends of thought corroded the faith of the early Church. These elements embedded themselves in the stream of the Tradition, and were not dislodged even when St. Paul's Epistles were widely read. From people like Celsus and one of the two unknown writers of the composite *Epistle to Diognetus* one learns that there was a genuine understanding of the Pauline Gospel, but almost all the extant literature of the post-apostolic period bears witness to serious defection from the New Testament Gospel in these two ways. The struggle between these heretical elements and the Gospel became so intense that eventually at Nicaea and Chalcedon a handful of forceful bishops pressed the Church to make up its mind in dogmas which ever since have generally been recognized as binding upon the whole Church. But the fact of supreme importance for the present question is this: that although the Church gave correct formulation to its doctrine of Christ, it did not proceed to carry out this Christological correction in the form of the ministry and the shape of the liturgy. Both of these, as is most evident in Hippolytus, for example, are essentially grounded upon or mixed up with Christological heresy, partly Ebionite on the one hand, and partly Docetic on the other hand. The astonishing fact that confronts us in this volume, therefore, is that Dom Gregory starts out in his views with a form of the ministry and a shape of the liturgy that are as yet uncorrected by the Christology of Chalcedon, and tries to make them normative. This means that the major weakness of this volume is Christological. Indeed it is Christological heresy of the first magnitude.

In order to make that clear we shall have to deal with the king-pin of the whole thesis: the idea of *Shaliach*, for it is at this point that we have Judaistic heresy on the one hand (Ebionitism) and Mandaean, Gnostic heresy on the other hand (Docetism). At the root of these lies the perverse Dixian translation of the words: שְׁלוּחוֹ שֶׁל אָדָם כְּמוֹתוֹ׃ (*Ber.* 5. 5; for further examples see Strack-Billerbeck, 3. 2). Dix persistently translates this as "A man's *shaliach* is as it were himself", though, with perhaps a twinge of conscience, he adds, on the first occasion, in brackets, "like himself". The overwhelming evidence in Rengstorf's article (in Kittel's *Woerterbuch*) indicates that *shaliach* does not carry a religious or mystical relation of identity between a man and his *shaliach*. It is a purely legal relation or a legal representation—a clear example is given by Rengstorf in the instance of the man who uses a *shaliach* in order to become engaged to a girl by proxy. That is to say, the relation envisaged is a relation of proxy in function, not of personal identity. It is also pointed out, however, that *shaliach* may gain in certain associations (e.g., in Mandaean and Manichaean contexts) the sense of mystical relation. In Jewish Gnostic circles this was what sometimes happened, and there can be not a shred of a doubt that it was *shaliach* in that form (Judaeo-Gnostic) that influenced the conception of the ministry in the third century, if not earlier. There are in fact traces of it already in Ignatius where such a relation is persistently interpreted in terms of Gnostic ἕνωσις. Now that is precisely what the New Testament is concerned to avoid, and therefore, as Rengstorf points out, when in the Gospels the idea of *shaliach* appears to underlie the thought, they deliberately lay all the emphasis upon the verbs, ἀποστέλλειν and πέμπειν, and are shy about using the noun, ἀπόστολος, so that in the mission and commission of the apostles the emphasis is on the function of the disciples as eye-witnesses of the resurrection empowered by the Spirit, and *not on the persons of the apostles*. The whole New Testament doctrine of *shaliach* (if we are to use this word) is one in which the person of the *shaliach* retreats into the background, so that the living person of the risen Christ comes to the fore. A Diotrephic love of personal pre-eminence (cf. also Matt. 23: 8–12) is the very thing the New Testament avoids, but which Dr. Kirk and his confederates try their hardest to resurrect and justify, an attempt in which they appear to succeed only by resorting to "evidence" from Judaizers and schismatics!

The application of the *shaliach*-relation to the New Testament throws light upon two things.

(1) In regard to the apostles the idea of *shaliach* is used only in regard to their function as witnesses of the resurrection, and as the locus of the New Testament revelation. The rabbis used to speak of several of the Old Testament prophets as *sheluchim*: Moses, Elijah, Elisha, and Ezekiel. They restricted the term to those prophets who not only spoke the Word of God, but were obviously authorized by certain miraculous deeds as bearers of that Word. *Shaliach* referred to the man who speaks for God and acts for God in σημεῖα. It is supremely in that sense that Christ is the Apostle: He is the Word of God and the Act of God in an absolute sense. In him the Word and Deed of God are identical, identical with His own Person. Christ was sent not only to forgive sins, but to heal; not only to speak of pardon in a parable, but to enact that pardon in our flesh and blood. It is supremely at the Cross that He is God's Word and Deed. That, as Paul says, is God's testimony, *logos* and *dynamis*. In the Synoptics this Christ sends out the disciples and the seventy to proclaim the Word of God, *and to heal*. He sends them out in a special mission in which their word is accompanied by *semeia*, therefore as *sheluchim*, though the Evangelists hesitated to use that expression. Later on when the word *apostle* came to be used, it was always in that sense. They were men who had been with Jesus, who were eye-witnesses of His resurrection, and whose witness and proclamation were accompanied by special evidences of *dynamis*. Hence St. Paul defends his position as an apostle, by insisting that he too has the apostolic *semeia*. What this means we shall determine more precisely when we come to discuss *kerygma*. According to the evidence brought forward by Rengstorf, therefore, the disciples are to be thought of as sent out in their mission with this Hebrew idea of *sheluchim* in the background, in the sense that as they preached and exercised their function as bearers of the Word of God, the *semeia* bore evidence to the fact that it was God Himself who spoke their *kerygma*, and acted upon the hearers; at least upon those who had ears to hear. In this the *persons* of the apostles retreated into the background, while in the foreground there was the living Word of God. All this was reinforced by the resurrection, for

in the recommission of the apostles by the risen Christ they were sent forth to do greater works, such that in their proclamation the word of men should become the very power of God creative of the Church.

(2) But this brings us to the other fact which we must note. In the New Testament it is supremely the Holy Ghost who is the *shaliach* of Christ, and here the legal relation (Advocate-paraclete) is caught up in the relation of identity between Christ and His other Self, the *Shaliach-Spirit*. Thus John records: "But the Paraclete whom the Father shall send in my name, he shall teach you all things, and bring all things to your remembrance, whatsoever I have said unto you." "Be not afraid . . . I will come unto you", etc. In the strict sense it is only the Holy Spirit who is Christ's *Shaliach*—and even he is *Shaliach* in such a way that He does not draw attention to Himself or speak of His own Person, but speaks only of Christ. That is the inner meaning of the apostolic witness, and the apostolic function is defined in terms of this *Holy Ghost-Shaliach*: "And ye also shall bear witness, because ye have been with me from the beginning." The argument of John's Gospel is quite clear. Only the Holy Ghost is *Shaliach* in the sense of being the personal representative of Christ, and identical in person with Him. To call a bishop a *shaliach* in this personal sense, to call him *Alter Christus*, is to quench the Holy Ghost, and really amounts to blasphemy. When you ask the Fourth Gospel: What then is the relation of the apostles to Christ and His *Shaliach-Spirit*? it answers consistently by the thought of "abiding", an abiding through the Word. Thus between the announcement of the *Spirit-Shaliach* and the description of the relation of the apostles as witnesses to Him, Christ discourses on abiding in His Word and Love. Of all this there is hardly a word in *The Apostolic Ministry*. The doctrine of the Holy Spirit is almost entirely neglected, except at incidental points. The *Holy Spirit-Shaliach* is dethroned, and in His place there is substituted a doctrine of *Bishop-Shaliach* who in very person and deposit, nay in personal identity, represents Christ Jesus. The Holy Ghost is treated as a mere *paradosis* which bishops can pass on from hand to head. The index alone shows how little this huge book has to say about the Holy Spirit. That is only another indication of how Christologically false the whole

structure of its thesis is. In Christology the relation between the Father and the Son is the Holy Ghost as *communio quaedam consubstantialis*, and the relation between the Lord and Jesus is also the Holy Ghost, and so on this Christological pattern (which Fr. Hebert tries to follow) the relation between the Church and its ministry, and Christ Jesus, should also be the Holy Ghost—but no: there is substituted a quasi-psychological, mystical relation of identity called *shaliach* and interpreted in terms of Gnostic Judaism.

What is the New Testament doctrine of the *Spirit-Shaliach* relation of Christ to the apostle? This is contained in the doctrine of *kerygma*, so grievously misunderstood by every writer in this volume. *Kerygma* may be defined in modern terms as objective sacramental preaching with an eschatological result, such that the original event, Christ incarnate, crucified and risen, becomes event all over again in the faith of the hearer. It is supremely in the apostolate created by Christ as the human end of the New Testament revelation that the original unrepeatable event of the resurrection takes place as a human word empowered by the Holy Ghost. When the apostles proclaimed Christ, through them acting as mere stewards or earthen vessels, or as ambassadors speaking in Christ's stead, the amazing thing happened: the crucified and risen Christ miraculously encountered men, and there was, so to speak, an eschatological "repetition" of the Incarnation, Death, and Resurrection in them. Of that we have two sacraments, one in which the once-and-for-allness of that event is enshrined, and one in which its constant eschatological "repetition" is enshrined ("as often as . . . ye proclaim the Lord's death till He come"). This is the great mystery manifest in the flesh, the treasure which we have in earthen vessels, and of which we are stewards. That is to say, the relation of the Essential Ministry (as the Bishop of Oxford calls it) to Christ is not one of *shaliach*-identity or personal-mystical-identity, but one through the *kerygma* as the instrument of the Holy Ghost in the mouth of those called to be apostles. It is this ministry which creates the Church—but in all cases the relation is essentially an eschatological relation through the Word and Spirit. A bishop has *shaliach*-relation in this secondary sense only through the primary *shaliach*-relation of the Word-Spirit becoming event in the midst of the Church, creating the Church, becoming actual among men so that the Church becomes on earth what it eternally is, the Body of Christ.

In this doctrine of the ministry the original apostleship must be thought of as particular and unrepeatable, in the first instance, like the particularity of Jesus, or the particularity of the New Testament revelation. They form the actual place within the Church where the original event of the *Spirit-Shaliach* becomes once and for all incarnate in the language of the Church (that is, in the New Testament). Just as there can be no succession of Incarnations, no succession of New Testaments, so there can be no succession of apostles in this primary sense. But there can be a succession of the ministry, as there can be repeated celebrations of the Eucharist: "For I received of the Lord that which I also delivered." The *paradosis* continues to be *kerygma*, for the Holy Ghost who is Christ's *Shaliach* lives on in the midst of the Church, and through the witness of men so speaks that it is Christ Himself speaking and creating. Every ministry whose *kerygma* becomes God's own testimony, *Logos* and *Dynamis*, is essential, is creative.

It is precisely because this volume omits the doctrine of the Holy Spirit that it really fails to understand the eschatological nature of *kerygma* and *paradosis*. Consequently the apostolic succession is interpreted in terms of temporal repetition, and the celebration of the Eucharist tends also to be interpreted in terms of a temporal repetition of the original sacrifice of Christ, while the Christian cleric becomes the one who temporally repeats in person and function the priesthood of Christ. There is a profound truth which the Roman Mass enshrines in its doctrine of repetition, but when that is translated into temporal terms, it amounts to nothing but a travesty of the truth. In the teaching of the New Testament it is only Holy Ghost or "eschatological" repetition.

It is in the article by Fr. Hebert that we get down to the real pith of this book. He defines the position in true reformed style in these words:

> We must look at the office of the Christian ministry in the relation of man to God which has been established in Christ; we must begin with the ministry of our redemption itself and with Him as the Head of the Church.

He goes on to say, again in true reformed style (as if he had been reading Launcelot Andrewes!), that parallel to the union of God and man in Christ (two natures in one person, as the Creeds put it) we must think of the divine and human elements in the Church, for it too has a double nature, and is as such a mystery, a sacrament.

> The two natures of the Church have been joined together by God, and men cannot put them asunder; they must be distinguished, but not either confused with one another or forced violently apart. It is disastrous to merge the divine element in the human, and invest the earthly and visible Church with the perfection that belongs to the divine element, thus in fact dragging down the divine element to earth and soiling it in the mud; we shall see later that this is the root of a fatal perversion of the idea of the Christian ministry. It is equally disastrous to make a separation, banishing the divine element up to heaven under the name of the Invisible Church and leaving the earthly community as a mere human organization. We must hold fast to both sides, and grasp firmly the double truth that as a Church of God is at once divine and human, so in its earthly condition it is at once perfect and imperfect.

Apart from the implied equation of perfect with divine, and imperfect with human, this is the true doctrine of the Church. What does Hebert mean by divine? According to Chalcedon the humanity of Christ is truly human, and His Deity truly divine. We cannot therefore think of the human element as divine in any sense. Is Hebert not giving a subtle twist to Chalcedonian Christology here, parallel to the same subtle twist given by the Cappadocians through their doctrine of *krasis* to the humanity of Christ? Even after the resurrection the humanity of Christ is perfectly human, never divine. There is such a thing as Docetic heresy *post resurrectionem*!

There is no doubt that the Roman doctrine of the divinization of the priest through grace so that (as the *Lateran Council* puts it) he becomes *divus*, is Docetic heresy parallel to the transubstantiation of the worldly elements in the sacrament which is a Docetic denial of the analogy inherent in the sacrament. Similarly their doctrine of the assumption of the manhood of Jesus into God ultimately means its divinization. Seeds of this heresy are even to be found in the great Athanasius—and it had to be corrected at Chalcedon. If we take Chalcedon seriously, as these writers profess to do, particularly the definition of the hypostatic union by the words ἀσυγχύτως, ἀτρέπτως, ἀδιαιρέτως, ἀχωρίστως, then we admit that between the divine and human elements in Christ there is no fusion, no conversion, no division, no separation. This book on the Apostolic Ministry sins against the ἀσυγχύτως in no half-hearted fashion. Hebert is quite right in saying that we must think of the Church as involving two natures, a divine and a human. But the divine is no Arian nature, nor any divinizing of the human element. The divine element is the Holy Ghost, or rather Christ Himself the Head of the Church. The human element is the body which composes all creatures who believe and are incorporated into Christ, sacramentally incorporated, but are never anything else in themselves but human and creaturely.

To get ourselves clear about the principle involved here, let us take the words: *Hoc est corpus meum*. That is neither a proposition of identity, nor of difference. It is an analogical proposition of a unique sort. It is in the Incarnation that we have created for the first time in the union between God and Man in Christ (not finally at Bethlehem, but at the Cross and Resurrection also) a relation which we now know as *unio hypostatica sive personalis*, as the Reformed Anglican divines used to put it. And that relation we believe to be grounded upon the immanent relation within the transcendent Trinity. But that same relation, the *unio hypostatica*, is, as it were, projected through the Holy Ghost on to the third level to form the relation between Christ and His Church, between the real presence and the bread and the wine in the Eucharist, between the divine Word and the human speech in the *kerygma*: and that relation St. Paul calls *koinonia*. When we examine this relation in the light of Chalcedon, the classic definition of it, we see that on the one hand it is not a relation of identity, but on the other hand it is not one of difference. It is a *sui generis* relation grounded upon the act of the Trinity in Christ Jesus, and is manifest in the Church. It is upon this that the eschatological relation in the New Testament is also grounded: the very relation that forms the content of the doctrine of the Holy Spirit (see K. L. Schmidt, *Eranos Jahrbuch* for 1945). It is the doctrine of the relation of the personal presence of God to the Church such that the gift of the

Spirit is identical with the Giver; such that the Spirit cannot be possessed any more than one person can possess another. It is possession in terms of *koinonia*, that is, in terms of the hypostatic union.

Now it is the whole thesis of *The Apostolic Ministry* that this is not the case. Instead they dare to posit a relation of identity, mystical identity, personal identity, between the bishop-apostle and Christ Himself. It is such an identity that the Holy Ghost can be passed on, as if He were not the Giver of the Gift, but only the Gift. Consequently it unbends the hypostatic or Holy Ghost relation into a straight line, and turns eschatology into temporal succession on the ground of this relation of identity. The parallel in the doctrine of the sacrament is of course the temporal repetition of the sacrifice of Christ, and the transubstantiation of the worldly elements in such a way that the analogical relation is denied, as Calvin argued so cogently in the *Institutes*, and a relation of identity put in its place. This is sheer Arianism in the region of the sacrament and the ministry. That is most apparent in the Roman doctrine of the Mass which is an extremely low doctrine inasmuch as it does not teach a doctrine of the real presence. Christ's presence comes only half-way, and the worldly element is divinized or raised up by transubstantiation to meet it. This was precisely what Nicaea denied in the doctrine of Christ itself, but the Church did not go on to apply that correction to the shape of the liturgy or the form of the Church. It is to such a mis-shapen liturgy and mis-formed doctrine of the Church that this volume reaches back for justification of Anglo-Catholic doctrine.

It is Fr. Hebert who sees these issues most clearly. In the passage cited he warns us against dragging the divine element down to earth and soiling it. But what else is that but the doctrine that the bishop-apostles are invested in their human persons with a relation of identity to Christ, and with the gift or the *paradosis* of the Holy Ghost which they can pass from bishop to bishop? What else is this but a denial of the eschatological relation in which the divine is present, really and fully present, but not tied to institutions of space and time? The thesis of this book is in basic contradiction to the teaching of the New Testament which so clearly tells us, for example, in the Gospel stories of the Transfiguration and of the Emmaus manifestation that by our human institutions, even if dominically appointed, we cannot perpetuate in the continuity of space and time the risen Jesus Christ. He inevitably vanishes out of our sight at that point, for His Parousia is both a *presence* and a *coming*. It is this eschatological doubleness (Chalcedonian doubleness) in sacrament and *kerygma*, and in the ministry, that this volume ultimately leaves out. Its sin is a desire for continuity in space and time of possession of God, so that the eschatological, Kingdom-of-God-event in the Gospel which is creative of the Church is imprisoned in a human institution, in the unbroken continuum of space and time they choose to call Apostolic Succession.

It would appear that these points are not unrecognized by Hebert. He sees the danger of Arianism when he says it would be monstrous to think either of the apostles or of the ministry as a sort of third element, mediating between Christ and the Church, His Body, but he promptly falls into the more subtle error of Eutychianism. In the same way he sees the danger of Nestorianism in repudiating the idea that the cleric has vicarial relation, as if he were acting on behalf of an absent Christ. Almost in the same breath he sees the fatal mistake of identifying the Word of God with the word of man, but does not see the equally fatal mistake of identifying the Person of Christ with the person of the bishop. The fact is, that when he comes to relate this true doctrine of the Church to the doctrine of the episcopate that is advanced in these pages, he fails miserably. He does not succeed in finding a single dogmatic argument on Chalcedonian principles to prove that the bishop belongs to the very *esse* of the Church, or to prove that this doctrine of the Essential Ministry is one of the articles of saving faith. In the last resort, all he can say is that "there *needs to be* an office in the Church", and so falls back lamely upon an argument of expediency which he himself castigates in others!

There is one other major point at which we see the perversity of heresy manifesting itself. Hebert sees it too, and he is careful to avoid it. He maintains in true Pauline fashion that the Church is both perfect and imperfect on earth, what the Reformers indicated in their expression *justus et peccator*. But Dom Gregory Dix denies this outright, because he has a much crasser idea of the mystical relation of identity. He says: "It is a difference about the nature of man's fall and the process of his union with God; that is, it is admittedly a difference about the very notion of 'religion' itself." It is quite plain that Dix has never come to grips with the doctrine of justification, else he would not have enunciated a position so contradictory to Chalcedon, particularly to the "without conversion". It must surely be evident that on the showing of these men themselves the principles of Christology must be applied to the relation of the Christian to Christ, to the relation between *peccator* and *justus*, particularly if we see that we must carry the thought of the hypostatic union through Christ's Death and Resurrection. The Christian, like the Church, has two "natures", the "I yet not I" of Gal. 2: 20. There is, so to speak, a hypostatic relation between these two—*so to speak*, for the hypostatic relation is unique, but as in the sacraments so here we must by its light think out justification and sanctification. Thus the Christian must be regarded as perfect in Christ, and as such he is hid with Christ in God; but as a visible psychological personality, he is still *peccator*. To attempt to resolve this quasi-hypostatic or eschatological relation into a process of union in which man is gradually made more and more just and divine, is to flout the "without fusion and without conversion" of Chalcedon. It is the essence of the Reformed doctrine of justification by grace alone that it insists on teaching the virgin birth of faith, and a relation sacramentally and eschatologically created, parallel to the hypostatic relation, between justification as a once-and-for-all act (sacramentally, Baptism), and the constant renewal of sanctification (sacramentally, the Eucharist). Once again, had Dom Gregory Dix read his Anglican divines properly, he would not have been ignorant of this, nor would he have proclaimed himself to be convicted of a doctrine so unbiblical, un-Christological, and un-Anglican.

I have had hard things to say about this book, but I believe that if you strike out the Christological heresy which gives its exposition a fatal twist, much of its teaching will fall into astonishingly true form which could provide a common ground on which Reformed and Anglican theologians and scholars might draw nearer to one another than ever before.

(c) *Catholicity*[1]

The pamphlet of forty-six pages entitled *Catholicity* (Dacre Press, 1947) is sub-titled *A Study in the Conflict of Christian Traditions in the West*, being a report presented to the Archbishop of Canterbury and bearing a foreword by him. Its sponsors are a group of well-known Anglo-Catholics who aim to show that "the problem of reunion is that of the recovery of the *wholeness* of tradition" (p. 17). It has importance far beyond its slender proportions and ought to be read by all who are engaged in the Ecumenical Movement.

They begin by grounding their conception of catholicity in an idea of *wholeness* which they find in the biblical and Christian tradition, and speak of it as "the *wholeness* wherein the Gospel of Redemption rests upon the groundwork of Creation, and supernatural Church stands over against the order of Nature, which, no less than the Church, is of God" (p. 16). There is no doubt that here we have a profounder attempt than any hitherto contemplated by Anglicans to get to grips with the objective and theological basis of catholicity, and here too there is some attempt to understand this in its biblical eschatological context. It is a similar conception of *wholeness* that lies at the heart of the Reformed Faith, and Reformed Churches will therefore welcome this shifting of the discussion on to ground where they have always felt the important decisions must be made.

There is a great deal in the first chapter that we may gladly endorse: the insistence that the Church is the Body of Christ, and as such is prior to the Church as a visible society—though there still lurks here the Roman confusion between the Kingdom of Heaven and the Church; givenness both of the unity of the Church and the sanctification of the individual in a context of eschatology not of evolution, of growth not of progress; the inevitable tensions between the divine nature of the Church and the sinfulness of its members, between the historical once-for-allness of the Church and its abiding union with the divine life; the participation of the local Church in the whole heavenly congregation and the Church of the First-Born. Our

[1] From the *Scottish Journal of Theology*, 2, 1949, pp. 85–93.

only quarrel with the substance of the first chapter is that it is not thought through radically enough on biblical lines. The greatest single weakness is a failure to grasp properly the basic eschatological tension in which the New Testament doctrines of the Church, the new creation, election, justification, sanctification, etc., are cast, and therefore the confusion between eschatological fulfilment and temporal continuity. In regard to the relation between creation and redemption they do not see, for example, as the late Professor H. R. Mackintosh used to point out, that Christ's function in creation is proleptically conditioned by His function as Redeemer; nor do they see that the order: Christ-the Church-faithful individuals may be just as wrong as the order: Christ-faithful individuals-the Church, because such temporal sequence, one way or the other, impugns the eschatological wholeness of the Church, as does the division of baptism into two *moments* of salvation (where confirmation either injures the completeness of baptism in its once-for-all character or anticipates its fulfilment in the Parousia).

The essential eschatological doubleness which in the New Testament receives its decisive expression in the giving of *two sacraments only* is destroyed by the admission of other sacraments, such as the sacrament of penance—which shows a radical misunderstanding of the New Testament teaching about eschatological once-for-allness and eschatological continuity which come together in realized *wholeness* only when the teleological end (*telos*) and the eschatological end (*eschaton*) are fulfilled in one another at the Second Advent of Christ. These two sacraments have been given to us precisely in order that we may realize here and now through baptism the *wholeness* of Christ, and the *wholeness* of our salvation (e.g. Col. 2: 10 f.) and yet that we may understand through the Eucharist, in which we communicate again and ever again in the body and blood of the whole Christ until He come, that the fulness of Christ is the final goal of the Church (e.g. Eph. 4: 13). To introduce a third or other sacraments is to strike at the very heart of the New Testament Gospel and its whole teaching about creation and redemption.

There are several other points that need further clarification:

(1) What do they mean by "primitive *wholeness*"? The only primitive wholeness that the Reformed Churches recognize is

the once-and-for-all *wholeness* of Jesus Christ in whom God and man are at one, and the gathering together in Him of heaven and earth, things visible and invisible in the new creation, all understood on the analogy of the hypostatic union carried through the Cross and Resurrection into an abiding perfection. Is that what the pamphlet means by "primitive *wholeness*" or does it confound it, as it would appear to do, with a primitive historical *wholeness*? Should we not rather think of *wholeness* as Christ Himself, Christ the Truth, and insist that the only way toward reunion is to seek earnestly the absolute Lordship of Jesus Christ?[1] Truth is One in Christ, and there is a dogmatic *wholeness* which may be gained only as every doctrine is thoroughly criticized and corrected Christologically. For this reason the Reformation stands for a thoroughgoing critique of all doctrines, especially the doctrines of the Church, justification, and the sacraments, in terms of Christological dogma formed on the basis of Scripture. It seeks the *wholeness* of Christ on the basis of the New Testament Revelation and sees the problem of reunion to-day as the recovery, under the Lordship of Christ, of a dogmatic *wholeness* at the centre of which is the doctrine of Jesus Christ.

(2) What does *Catholicity* mean by the uniqueness of the apostolate and by tradition? We readily agree that the apostolate was integral to the existence of the new Israel, but as such it belongs to the ἐφάπαξ of the New Testament Revelation and indeed of the Incarnation. Upon this rock, apostolic witness (i.e. upon the apostles themselves as witnesses of Christ the Son of God) the Church is built, and to this apostolic witness are given the keys of the Kingdom so that in the apostolic witness Jesus Christ crucified and risen completes the revelation of Himself. And so St. Paul said: "Ye are built upon the foundation of the apostles and prophets, Jesus Christ Himself being the chief corner-stone" (Eph. 2: 20). That the apostolate was unrepeatable, and belonged to the ἐφάπαξ of the Incarnation, was recognized by the early Catholic Church when it decided to subordinate tradition to Scripture in the formation of the canon about the year A.D. 150, and so to make a decisive distinction between the *apostolic tradition* and later tradition.

[1] Cf. Visser 'tHooft, *The Kingship of Christ*, p. 77 f.

The seriousness and strictness with which the Reformed Churches take that decision does not mean that they deny the continuance of a tradition, but that they insist on the sole supremacy of Scripture as the substance of the apostolic witness and tradition regarded as part of the ἐφάπαξ of the Revelation of Jesus Christ. Because, like the early Church, they insist in interpreting *paradosis* in terms of *kerygma* and not *kerygma* in terms of *paradosis*, they hold that the Scriptures of the New Testament witness to Jesus Christ Himself *kerygmatically*, that is in such a way that He Himself, by the power of His Spirit, speaks to men through them, confirming the apostles in their power of the keys, the keys of the knowledge and interpretation of His own Person and Work.[1]

(3) What do the authors of this pamphlet mean by the Body of Christ, and by the statement that the Supernatural Church is over against the order of nature? Is there not a confusion in their thought between the Body of Christ as the Body of the Risen Lord, and the Body of Christ regarded mystically as the Church? The New Testament takes care by speaking of Christ as the Head of the Body as well as saying that the Church is the Body of Christ to make it clear that there can be no question of a proposition of identity here. The relation between the Church and the Body of Christ is one of *koinonia* and *abiding*, and is eschatologically conditioned. It is thus that the Church participates in the *wholeness* of Christ, but because that *wholeness* is already whole there can be no talk of an extension of the Incarnation or historical continuity of the Body of Christ. That ought to have been clear to our authors through the doctrine of the Eucharist, but alas they interpret the Eucharist so as to leave out the essential eschatological element given to it in the New Testament.

The Reformed Churches do not deny the continuity, but it is because they take so seriously the New Testament teaching that the Church is already the Body of Christ, and is already the new creation whole and complete, and yet on the other hand take seriously the fact that Christ now reigns through the Word of the Gospel calling His elect Church out of the world, that they formulated their doctrine of continuity in terms of

[1] Cf. Mark 4: 11; Luke 8: 10; Matt. 13: 11; Luke 11: 52; Matt. 18: 18; cf. also Cullmann, *Christus u. die Zeit* (E.T. *Christ and Time*), p. 147 ff.

election, so as to steer clear of the idea that there can be an extension in the time of this fallen world of the risen Body of Christ Jesus or of the New Creation. No doubt we successors of the Reformation may disagree with the form they gave to the doctrine of predestination, which relegated it to some still point behind history and beyond time, and prefer to interpret it dynamically as the action of the eternal God in Christ in time and through time, but the essential truth remains. By election or predestination the Reformed Churches teach that the New Creation is hid with Christ in God and at present is veiled behind the likeness of sinful history, nevertheless it is a New Creation in time involving soul and body, heaven and earth. That is to say, by means of the doctrine of election we refuse to identify the living continuity of the Church as the New Creation, participating in the wholeness or fulness of Christ, with the continuation of this present sinful world. It is a reality existing here and now, but yet to be revealed. In other words, we take in deep earnest the teaching of the Eucharist that every time in the fallen world we partake of Holy Communion, we communicate in the real presence of Christ in time, but we receive also the judgment of the Cross upon the forms and fashions of this passing world, and that includes the forms and fashions of the sinful historical Church. All that is contained in the doctrine of justification, as Calvin showed so clearly, which has on one side the doctrine of sacramental incorporation into the Body of Christ; but just because it teaches the wholeness of Christ, the wholeness of our sanctification as already given in this eschatological context, it refuses to teach a doctrine of justification as a process in sinful history. Had these writers really done justice to the eschatological cast of New Testament teaching they would have grasped this profound element in the doctrines of salvation and the sacraments, and the principle of the Reformation which insists that the Church lives in time essentially as the repentant Church, although in Christ she is already the Church triumphant. The error of the Roman Catholic Church in this respect is twofold: it refuses to criticize its doctrine of the Church in terms of the Chalcedonian doctrine of the hypostatic union, and refuses to carry the thought of the hypostatic union beyond the static conception of the Greek Fathers, and to interpret it through the Work of Christ in

Death and Resurrection. This cardinal error lurks in the pages of *Catholicity*, but we refuse to believe it is genuinely Anglican. On the other hand the great error of the Reformed Churches lies in the arresting of repentance, in the refusal to take justification *by faith alone* seriously enough, and therefore in their worldly and ecclesiastical self-justification. In the Church of Scotland, for example, this means such a hardening of the Presbyterian system of orders and government that it constantly becomes an obstacle to the renewing of the Church.

When the authors proceed to discuss the contribution of "Orthodox Protestantism" they try to present a general description such that Protestants themselves may recognize to be truthful and fair-minded. Certainly this part of the document ought to be read and pondered by all the Churches concerned if only to incite the theological penitence of which we all stand in such need. And yet it must be said quite plainly that we do not recognize our Reformed convictions here. They have cast Protestant teaching into such subjective terms and have failed woefully to understand the objective depth which the Reformation gave to the doctrines of the Church and Salvation particularly, while the suggestion that the Reformers neglected Nicaea and denied the doctrine of the incorporation into Christ, shows how little these scholars know about Reformation theology. A great deal of this we can pass over, but when it comes to their handling of what they choose to call "two radical errors" we are amazed!

(1) It is astonishing that scholars of reputation have allowed their names to go forward attached to a document which speaks of the catastrophic pessimism of the Reformed doctrine of man, and the retreat from history which it involved! In regard to the Reformed doctrine of sin which is couched in total terms, they ought to have known, as all the writings of the great Reformers make clear (e.g., Luther in *De Servo Arbitrio*) that a true doctrine of total depravity is a corollary of the doctrine that Christ died for all men, and for all of each man. It is because salvation and grace are *total*, involving a new creation, that Christian theology must speak of sin in *total* terms. This is part of the New Testament doctrine of *wholeness*. These writers deny this *wholeness*, and assert a very sectional and inadequate doctrine of sin. It is evidence again that their statement of New Testament *wholeness*

is radically defective. Here we recall the words of a former Archbishop of Canterbury: *Nondum considerasti quanti ponderis sit peccatum.*

It was because the Reformers viewed the fall of man as a fall from nature to de-nature, and not, as Romanism held, from something superadded to nature to pure nature, that they affirmed an optimistic view of human nature, and denied the contemptuous slur cast upon God's handiwork by the Roman equation of man as he is with the *pura naturalia*, a slur which is evident in such practices as world-denying monasticism and celibacy. What could be more pessimistic than to view sin as that which can be naturally propagated by sexual concupiscence? It was precisely because the Reformers thought of sin as defection from the will of God, the will of God for men—therefore from the high dignity of human nature, as Calvin put it—that they revolted from mediaeval pessimism and other-worldly quietism and escapism, and liberated the greater part of Western Europe for the most progressive advances in the whole of human history.

There is one other small point which ought to be mentioned. On page 24 the statement is made that "the discipline of rational thinking can never be shirked without disaster". That is true indeed, but it is hardly for these Anglicans to develop that into a charge against their Reformed brethren! What work of repute in dogmatic theology has there been produced in Anglicanism between Pearson and Quick that can begin to be compared with the immense literature of the Lutheran and Reformed Churches, not to mention the other Protestant Churches? Of all Western Churches is it not the Anglican that has shirked most the discipline of systematic theology? Of all modern Churchmen are not the Anglo-Catholics (with several notable exceptions) the most afraid to look in the face modern critical philosophy (particularly since Kant), the most ready to take refuge behind the mediaeval ramparts of scholasticism? I can think of no greater disaster within the Anglican Communion than the dominance in it of men who refuse to discipline their liturgical and patristic studies both by the rational thinking of modern critical philosophy and by the arduous work of systematic theology!

(2) The other alleged error is the dissociation of justification

from sanctification. One can understand how this mistaken interpretation of Reformed teaching has arisen in the minds of those who cast that teaching into subjective terms, but the whole significance of Reformed teaching on justification and sanctification is that *Christ Himself* is our sanctification and our justification, and that therefore these are *given* to us—that is, some doctrine of imputation is unavoidable, unless one adopts a crassly heretical doctrine of identity. Just because Christ is our sanctification and justification our possession of these is through incorporation into Christ and union with Him, as no one has insisted more strongly than Calvin. But just because Christ is sanctification and justification, these are gifts in the sense in which the gift is identical with the Giver, and so appropriation of them can no more be a temporal process than Christ Himself. In other words just because in Christ we are given sanctification and justification in the form of the *whole Christ*, we cannot add to them. It is a matter of *tota gratia*, and *tota gratia* both in the sense of *data*, and in the sense of *danda*—hence once again the two sacraments of Baptism and Holy Communion. This *tota gratia* is precisely the *wholeness* which the Roman Church has so deplorably lost.

At the start of this pamphlet we are reminded of the words from St. John, "Sanctify them in the truth; thy Word is truth", which Anglo-Catholics apparently are apt to forget. This is, however, precisely what the Reformed Churches have tried to stress: the experience of sanctification through the Word. It is in obedience of heart and mind to the Word proclaimed and made flesh, through which the whole Christ communicates Himself to us, that we exercise ourselves in sanctification, for that living Word acts creatively upon us and gives us constantly to feed upon Christ (John chs. 6 and 15). The sponsors of this pamphlet remark that the Reformed stress upon the Word has a detrimental effect upon right relation to worship. That criticism ought to apply equally to St. John's Gospel which stresses more than any of the others the Word, and yet gives the fullest place to worship—precisely because it is through the Word that Christ comes to us personally and worship reaches its focal point and culmination in personal encounter with the living Christ. It is then that Holy Communion has its rightful place crowning faith with vision and enacting in our flesh and blood the real presence of Christ. The Eucharist as the sacrament of the Word made flesh contains the Reformed doctrine of sanctification.

It is a wonder that these Anglicans so easily ignore their own great Anglican heritage in teachers such as Cranmer, Hooker, Pearson, Andrewes, Hall, and indeed of their own *Thirty-nine Articles* where a Reformed doctrine of justification and sanctification is taught. If, however, they are unwilling to read their own theologians, one would like to suggest to them that they might listen to one who is more authentically "Catholic" (in their sense) than they themselves are, such as Professor Ernst Gaugler of the Old Catholic Faculty in Bern who gives an admirable exposition of justification and sanctification in his recent *Römerbrief* (where they will find too a sound doctrine of *shaliach*!).

There is no space here to dwell upon the failure in these pages to make any real approach to the Reformed doctrine of the Church, or the discussion of Liberalism, and the post-Tridentine Papal Communion, throughout which there emerges again and again a fundamental failure to grasp the meaning of the eschatological element so thoroughly purged from Catholicism at the Council of Trent. There follows, however, a valuable discussion of fragmentation and synthesis of Christian truth in which there is real evidence of theological penitence, so rare in these days, and a desire to achieve a synthesis at a level profounder than that which usually occupies the discussion of reunion. There is much in this chapter that those engaged in the Ecumenical Movement could well lay to heart, not to speak of the several Churches involved. Nevertheless it is difficult to escape the conclusion that this sort of synthesis which has to do with fragments of truth and a desire to seek an underlying and primitive unity fails to take account of the differing attitudes of approach to the truth which characterize East and West, Roman Catholicism, and the Churches of the Reformation, and fails also to recognize that, in the most basic sense of the Incarnation, Christ Himself is the Truth, Truth in the form of personal Being. There can be no synthesis therefore of fragments but a synthesis of a different sort will arise out of a fresh orientation to Christ Himself. He is the *wholeness* which we seek, who gives Himself to us now through the Scriptures and the

Sacraments. No approach to that *wholeness* along the line that thinks of revelation or tradition as mediating truths will ultimately avail, for it will always result in fragmentation. It is not therefore the *wholeness* of tradition, but the *wholeness* of Christ which we seek, and to do that, as St. Paul said, we must even forget the things that lie behind, making ourselves of no reputation, being renewed in the spirit of our minds: that is what we mean by Reformation. The movement for synthesis envisaged in this book will be as much a patchwork remedy as those it repudiates.

The concluding section of this inquiry is informed by rather a naive belief that in the Providence of God it is through Anglicanism that such a synthesis may be achieved, for it is in the Anglican tradition more than anywhere else, they hold, that the diverse elements are brought together. However incomprehensible this is to many, and perhaps offensive to some, it is a sincere belief which in some quarters of the Church of England almost attains a messianic fervour. There can be no doubt whatsoever that the great Anglican Communion has much to offer the rest of the Christian world, and many valuable contributions from their heritage are thrown out in these pages, but only when it begins to take biblical and dogmatic theology seriously will other Churches in the West be more inclined to learn from it. How far this particular document, in spite of the foreword by the Archbishop, really represents the genius of the Church of England is rather doubtful, but as a member of another communion equally in need of theological penitence this reviewer would like to beseech his Anglican brethren ἐν σπλάγχνοις Χριστοῦ Ἰησοῦ to forget the things that are behind, even the great Anglican tradition, and press on toward *the wholeness of Christ Jesus*. Surely only when we all acknowledge that we are unprofitable servants even when we have done our duty will we be ready for that renewal by the living Christ in which reunion will at last be possible.

(d) *The Fulness of Christ*[1]

The Fulness of Christ. The Church's Growth into Catholicity: being a report presented to His Grace the Archbishop of Canterbury, with a foreword by the Archbishop of Canterbury. S.P.C.K., 1951.

[1] From the *Scottish Journal of Theology*, 5, 1952, pp. 90–100.

In this notable document, at the invitation of the Archbishop of Canterbury, a group of Anglican Evangelicals under the chairmanship of the Archdeacon of Sheffield have made an irenic attempt to account for the contrasts of "catholic" and "protestant" theology, parallel to the attempt already made by a group of Anglo-Catholic scholars who presented their findings to the Archbishop in the document entitled *Catholicity*. This is not a studied reply to *Catholicity*, but rather an independent and constructive approach to the problem of unity, based upon the double belief that "our Lord's identification with the Church, which is His Body, and His Lordship over it, are the foundation-truths underlying alike the Church's unity, her holiness, and her catholicity". In the preface, these scholars go on to say:

> Though in every age she has only imperfectly apprehended and expressed the mind of Christ, yet by His Spirit she has been promised and, when obedient, has been given, throughout her history, a growing apprehension of the revelation of God in Christ of which the apostolic testimony in Holy Scripture is the abiding record. We cannot, therefore, draw any line across history and seek simply to return to the standards of an age when the visible unity of the Church was unbroken; nor regard visible unity as guaranteeing loyalty to the gospel which the Church is meant both to preach and to embody. It is the whole history of the Church, including that of its disrupted life, which πολυμερῶς καὶ πολυτρόπως has reflected the glory of her Lord, and the distortions of that image are not confined to the age of the divided Church.

With the same theological balance and a deep understanding of the fulness of the Gospel these Churchmen discuss the development of the Church and her doctrine in the biblical perspective of God's saving acts in history. Without any wilfulness or prejudice in their interpretation of other views and churches, "catholic" or "protestant", they give a convincing exposition of their findings that the Church's unity is to be apprehended only in the fulness of Christ which is the destiny of the Church, and to be realized by growth into that fulness. In five successive chapters they discuss The Growth of the Church into Fulness; Growth towards Fulness at the Reformation; Tension, Schism and Modification; Towards Resolution of the Conflict; the Road to Fulness: Unity in Tension. The great point maintained throughout is that while the Church is at once "the given community" (the creation of God in Christ) and "the willed community" (of those who are called and surrender themselves to God's purpose), the given unity of the Church is to be realized only by growth through tension. This tension is grounded not simply upon a variety that comes from richness of experience, but has as its deep underlying cause sin and rebellion against the will of God. Tension within the Church is not therefore a good thing in itself, yet it can be overruled by the providence of God for good. Thus in the actual circumstances in which the Church lives, in history with its admitted failures and sin, tension is made to play a vital part in the growth of the Church.

> Both the heightening of tension and its resolution seem to be indispensable, in our human situation, to the progress of the Church. The new insights help forward the development of the Church through variety. The resolution of tension through conflict safeguards that unity of the Church, within which alone the varieties can be both safe and significant.

The great tension that has characterized the history of the Church is that which broke out into conflict at the Reformation, when there was a decided growth towards fulness in Christ—although the Roman Church drew back and declined to accept that growth, thus bearing the major responsibility for the schism. But if the full gain of that growth toward fulness is to be conserved and increased both sides of the tension must be reunited—without however in any way being disloyal to the Gospel. In such a reunited Church tensions will be inevitable, and could only be avoided at the expense of growth. Such a reunion could be possible only at a very high level of spiritual life in which both "catholic" and "protestant" sides of the tension must be guided by the Holy Spirit speaking through the biblical witness.

The relation between the Church of Evangelical Christendom and the Church of Rome is not within the immediate perspective of this document. What we have set forth here is the relation between the "catholic" and "protestant" theology within the perspective of the Churches of the West which all belong to the movement that stemmed from the Reformation, and particularly within the perspective of the Church of England itself, where these contrasting tensions have long been evident, and where, it is claimed, an experiment of unity in tension is being carried out. Upon the merit and outcome of that Anglican experiment these scholars do not claim to be able to express any final verdict, but they say quite emphatically:

> We believe that only by accepting the spiritual challenge of unity in tension can the two traditions resolve their differences and open the way for a new growing of the Church into a fuller apprehension of the truth as it is in Jesus. And if this be so, the resources of the Spirit are covenanted to those who seek to do His will and follow His leading.

Here we have more than anywhere else in contemporary Anglicanism the authentic voice of the Church of England, the Church which in her great Elizabethan days stood forth as the Champion of the Churches of the Reformation, exercising a conciliatory influence in her balanced and comprehensive outlook, the Church which in her Caroline divines expounded a theology which was at once catholic and evangelical, within which certainly the pendulum swung at times from one extreme to the other, but the Church also which has not refused to learn from a Calvinist, a Wesleyan, or a Tractarian theology. There are still extremes within the Church of England, ranging from bitter Anglo-Catholicism to bigoted Ultra-Protestantism, but without any doubt *The Fulness of Christ* speaks with the authority of a great proportion of the Church of England behind it and expresses the genuinely Anglican mind in its growth through many new insights since the Reformation and through tension to its present condition. That is all the more highly significant when it is remembered that those who have combined to present this comprehensive and representative statement belong to the Evangelical Tradition in the Church of England, a tradition which, it is clear from this document, has learned more from the *whole* history of the Church of England than any other group within its bounds, and which now at last holds forth the promise of a great theology which is both dogmatic and living, with due appreciation of the Anglo-Catholic and Non-Conformist emphases in the English Church.

If this review now turns to criticism, let it be said right away that it is meant to be constructive. Far from detracting from the significance of this really great publication, what follows is intended as a contribution toward the growth through tension into fulness of which the document speaks, as well as a contribution toward a deeper understanding between Anglican and Reformed theology, as represented by the Church of England and the Church of Scotland in particular.

There is no doubt about the fact that the theology of *The Fulness of Christ* stands within the tradition of the Reformation and its rediscovery of the living God of the Bible and of the fact that the whole history of the Church is contingent upon His creative will. Whereas the Anglo-Catholics in their document *Catholicity* work with a structure of catholicity embedded in the stream of history and interpret the development of the Church and understand her unity in terms of that ideal pattern which they claim to discern in the undivided Church of the early centuries, these Evangelical Churchmen interpret the development of the Church in terms of her divine destiny which is only imperfectly apprehended in history, and understand her unity in terms of her growth into the fulness of Christ. To be sure, the Church has an unalterable and static element which is her apostolicity, the faithful standing upon the teaching of the apostles, but her faith is always proleptic, looking forward to a fulness which has not yet been made manifest. "The over-emphasis on the static and the unalterable, the loss of the sense of pioneering in the understanding of Christ, has hindered the Church in its attempt to realize its own nature."

This position is based upon the teaching of the New Testament in the Epistle to the Ephesians, the very title of the document being taken from Eph. 4: 13, and its idea of growth mainly from the second, third, and fourth chapters of the same Epistle—but there is this significant difference, that here the idea of growth is interpreted more as *biological* development than as *eschatological* fulfilment. That is apparent from the very first page, while throughout the whole discussion the *destiny* or *end* of the Church is interpreted almost entirely in the sense of *telos* to the neglect of *eschaton*. In the New Testament both aspects of *end* are to the fore and are understood in terms of each other, for the Word which governs the growth of the Church is both συντελῶν and συντέμνων. In other words, it is the notion of divine judgment that is lacking in the view of growth expounded here. They say quite explicitly that the growth of the Church through tension is not simply a growth through imperfection as the lack of completeness, for imperfection exists also under the aspect of sin and rebellion against the will of God; and indeed it is partly because they recognize that sin and ignorance marked the primitive Church as well as the Church of later days that they cannot agree with the "catholic" position. And further, they say very rightly:

> We turn back to the Word of God, to find there the nature of the Church, as it is set forth in the will and purpose of God. In so far as we penetrate to deeper understanding of that will, we shall be able to establish criteria by which the Church in history can be judged, and by which true growth can be distinguished from perversion.

Nevertheless, they do not appear to recognize or at least do not expound the biblical teaching that the development of the Church has *as its essential pattern in history the death and resurrection of Christ.* That was one of the great insights of the Reformation. The Reformers used to point to the fact that the messianic community in Old Testament times was always subject to judgment and being plunged into disaster and death, but that God intended that in order to show by the destruction of the Temple, by the abrogation of the cult, and the break in the continuity of the priestly succession, that the Kirk in all ages has her life and continuity in a marvellous preservation, in being constantly called out of death into life. If the essential pattern of the Incarnation, *death and resurrection,* was manifest in the Church before the Incarnation, how much more after it, when the Church as the Body of Christ goes out into history bearing about in her the dying and the rising of the Lord Jesus? That is the pattern which is sacramentally enacted in Baptism and Holy Communion, and which has its counterpart in the historical life and experience of the Church in judgment and resurrection; a pattern which already anticipates the final judgment and resurrection at the Parousia when the Fulness of the Church will be, and be revealed as, the Fulness of Christ Himself.

There can be no question about the fact that the authors of this document have deliberately based their teaching upon the biblical witness and sincerely tried to follow its direction, but one would have liked to see them apply more thoroughly, as in the New Testament, the eschatological perspective to their interpretation of the growth of the Church. A more deeply biblical understanding at this point would go very far to solving many of the difficulties and tensions which they see in the history of the Church. The Church which is at once under judgment and risen again with Christ can only live her life by putting off the old man and putting on the new, by ever refusing to be conformed to the pattern of this world and through her participation in, and her conformity to, the death of Christ, by being renewed in the power of His resurrection. If we take with full candour and seriousness the teaching of the New Testament that the Church is the Body of Christ, then we can only think of the progress of the Church in history on the Christological analogy of the miraculous birth from a virgin, and in the death and resurrection of the Son of Man. The deepest difference between "protestant" and "catholic" theology in regard to the Church is to be found here, in the insistence that the Church, her life in the tensions of history, her growth toward Fulness, are to be understood exclusively in terms of Christology, while eschatology is simply a thoroughgoing application of Christology to history—history understood in terms of *ὁ Πρῶτος καὶ ὁ Ἔσχατος καὶ ὁ Ζῶν*.

The weakness of their doctrine of the growth of the Church comes out again in their account of justification and soteriology. The exposition of justification as the completely free restoration to fellowship with God is acceptable as far as it goes, though they clearly misapprehend the use of forensic terms in the theology of the Reformation, interpreting them legalistically rather than eschatologically. They are wholly right in rejecting a notion of righteousness as a static attribute and in grounding justification upon the saving activity of God, but here justification is set forth so entirely in terms of relationship as to make one wonder whether they have not missed the *substance* of justification. It is true that justification entails such a radical change in the sinner's relationship with God that his whole existence is involved, but they fail to grasp the point upon which Calvin laid such great stress, that the substance of justification is a *real and substantial union with Christ*. Justification has ontological content. They are right in rejecting with Calvin the Roman notion of an infusion of righteousness, for, as Calvin saw, such a notion was Christologically untenable and even heretical, because it entailed (contrary to Chalcedon) a confusion between the divine and human natures; but to state justification only in terms of a new relationship is to leave the doctrine very vague. Moreover, because they think of justification only in terms of relationship or fellowship with God, they think of sanctification only as the spontaneous response of man to the change which this relationship with God involves for the sinner, for it is so glorious, so astonishing, they say, that he cannot be unmoved by it. Cut out of justification its heart, our ingrafting into Christ or our union with Him, and this idea of sanctification becomes rather Pelagian. That is perhaps realized, for later on pains are taken to point out that "our righteousness will never be our own achievement. It is the righteousness which we lay hold of by faith in Christ. We shall be like Him because His righteousness has been made our own." But *how*? To that question no clear answer is given. So long as the doctrine of justification is left vague like this, there will always be room for "catholic" misunderstanding and reaction against it.

It would appear that the answer of these Evangelical Anglicans is Lutheran at this point: *Der Glaube ist die Verneuerung*. The new relationship of faith is the new life. Calvin's answer was much profounder: faith is an empty vessel and the relationship of faith has no saving or regenerating significance in itself, but faith is the vessel which holds the living reality, union with Christ, which grows and increases, for "Christ not only unites us to Himself by an undivided bond of fellowship but by a wondrous communion brings us daily into closer connexion, until He becomes altogether one with us" (*Inst.* 3.2.24). Thus Jesus Christ is not only the agent of our justification, but He is in Himself its whole substance—but Calvin is careful to point out that this means that in justification we are given a new human righteousness which is the righteous humanity of the risen Jesus. It is the whole dimension of the risen humanity of Christ, and of our actual participation in it, which is left out here when these theologians expound justification only in terms of a relationship between God and the forgiven sinner without the *tertium datur* of a new righteousness which cannot be understood only in terms of the mighty acts of God in vindication and deliverance, or in terms of a human response to that divine activity, but in terms of the concrete righteousness of the new Man, the *eschatos Adam*, who dwells in our heart by faith and whose Epiphany waits for the last day. In other words, what this document has left out of its purview is the New Testament emphasis that *Christ was raised* for our justification (cf. *Inst.* 3.25.3).

It is worth while studying carefully Calvin's exposition of this whole matter in the third book of the *Institutes*, and not least his actual procedure in that exposition. He begins with the doctrine of the Holy Spirit and faith as union with Christ through the operation of the Spirit. But this union with Christ involves us in His death and resurrection, for we cannot become one with Him without participating in His death and resurrection, that is without mortification and regeneration. It is only after a long discussion of regeneration as an actualization in the believer of the risen life of Christ, and as an anticipation in conditions of time of the final resurrection, that Calvin feels he can go on to discuss justification, for then he is in a position to show that justification entails all this at its heart and as its substance. Justification is thus expounded only in strictly Christological terms and on the analogy of Christ's death and resurrection. That is followed up at the end of the third book by two corollary doctrines, election and the last resurrection, which are doctrines emphasizing the eternal foundation of our union with Christ and its future blessedness when its full reality will be revealed. Then in book four he goes on to expound the same teaching in terms of Baptism and Eucharist, for justification and baptismal incorporation into Christ are essentially counterparts, and sanctification and Holy Communion as our continuing and deepening union with Christ are essentially counterparts. As he who is sacramentally incorporated into the body of Christ is in Holy Communion continually nourished and maintained in the Body of Christ, so sanctification is the continual unfolding and maintaining of our justification. Sanctification is not a response of man that must be added to justification, but it is the continual renewing and re-enacting in the believer of a justification that is once and for all. The experience of sanctification is such an exercise in Word and Sacrament that the believer is ever being nourished with the new humanity of Christ, and being clothed with His new divine-human righteousness which is the fundamental reality of his Christian being. Apart from this whole doctrine of union with Christ and incorporation into His body, says Calvin, justification means nothing to us. It was because the theologians of Trent failed utterly to understand the Reformed teaching on Christology and our union with Christ that they spoke of the Reformed doctrine of justification as a legal fiction. The same failure is a marked characteristic of many Anglo-Catholics, and is not wanting in these pages either.

When we examine their doctrine of the Church we find that these Anglican theologians have exercised a strange consistency, for, quite in line with their omission of the substance of justification, they define the Church mainly in terms of the means of grace, rather than in terms of Christ Himself, that is, as His Body. To be sure the visible marks of the Church are the preaching of the Word and the right administration of the sacraments, along with true discipline, but the Church can never be defined in terms of its marks. Failing to get at the real heart of the Reformed doctrine here, they go on to misinterpret the distinction between invisible/visible in terms of inner/outer aspects of the Church, which is certainly quite alien to the teaching of Calvin, for it gives the whole idea a foreign subjectivist bias; though it is in line with mystical ideas inherited from Roman Catholicism and German Pietism. If we begin again with the Church as the Body of Christ, and remember that Christ has removed Himself in Ascension visibly from history, and will be seen in like manner only when He comes again, then we have the key to Calvin's use of "invisible", for as the Body of Christ the Church becomes an object of faith: *credo* (not *video*) *sanctam ecclesiam*, and faith is the evidence of things not seen. "Invisible" thus stands for the ontological and eschatological reality of the Church which will be manifested only in its fulness at the Parousia, but which becomes sacramentally visible in the Church in history as often as she baptizes her children and ever becomes in the Holy Eucharist the Body of Christ.

It is to be remembered that the men who have written *The Fulness of Christ* go back to a tradition in the Church of England which has long stressed evangelical experience to the neglect of Church and sacraments. Though one notes in these pages a very welcome and for evangelical Anglicans a new coincidence of *evangelical experience* and the *sacramental event* within the Church and its corporate worship, their understanding of "protestant" theology is still governed somewhat by their traditional outlook. On the other hand, Continental "protestantism" has stressed overmuch the sacramental event and thought of evangelical experience too meagrely in terms of faith's acknowledgment of the objective work of Christ. Some *rapprochement* and interaction between these two emphases would be extremely healthy for both. However, had the authors of this document a more Reformed understanding of the Church and sacraments, their discussion of the resolution of the conflict between "protestant" and "catholic" teaching would have been rather different. Again and again the Reformed theologian finds in these pages thrust into the "catholic" side of the tension stresses and doctrines which he has been accustomed to hold as quite central and basic in his Reformed theology, so that the discussion particularly in the last chapter is to him rather baffling and even at cross-purposes. When he comes to the conclusion and reads the account of the six fundamental truths which any scheme of reunion between "catholic" and "protestant" would have to affirm, three from the "protestant" emphases and three from the "catholic" emphases, he finds that he has always held five of them, and that his difference on the sixth, "the historic episcopal ministry", has to do with a corporate rather than an individualistic understanding of the episcopate, not with the rejection of the episcopate as such. At first sight that looks as if there is a far closer kinship between Reformed and Catholic theology than these theologians, who have not come out of a Calvinist tradition, have ever realized; but in actual fact it means also that the tensions between "protestant" and "catholic" theology must be taken down to a much deeper level than they envisage here, before any real approach can be made toward their resolution.

The whole drift and the major point of this document is

clearly influenced by what is called "The Anglican Experiment" in which "catholic" and "protestant" traditions appear not only to be in inevitable and necessary tension within the Church of England, but to be pointing a way ahead toward the resolution of this tension. This leads many Anglicans to feel that the Church of England can become the great *Via Media* in the Ecumenical Movement, and that indeed it is her divine calling in history to be just that. I believe that such an interpretation of the Anglican Experiment as is given in these pages, in the whole notion of unity in tension as the road toward the Church's Fulness in Christ, is a major contribution to ecumenical thought, of far greater significance than anything of this kind that has yet appeared; but a clear note of warning ought to be sounded. The Anglican Experiment has far greater significance and far greater possibilities within the Anglican Communion than it will ever have outside of it, for the issues between "protestant" and "catholic" theology are much profounder both in tension and kinship than those between Anglo-Catholics and Evangelicals within the Church of England. Anglican comprehensiveness has always, in Elizabethan days as in *Catholicity* or in *The Fulness of Christ*, involved a somewhat superficial understanding of the theological issues and differences. Only a failure to understand the profounder elements of Lutheran and Reformed theology could encourage in Anglicans the hope that their intra-Anglican and indeed insular experiment of unity in tension could be effective between the great Churches of the West and the Eastern Church or the Church of Rome. The theology of Calvin, for example, was more catholic and more patristic than anything in the history of the Church of England, and yet the differences between his theology and that of Rome go down to a deeper level than is generally understood in England. In these circumstances to push forward unduly the Church of England with her comprehensiveness as the *Via Media* may prove a greater obstacle than help in the whole Ecumenical Movement. Nevertheless, I believe that the Church of England, as interpreted through a document like *The Fulness of Christ*, has more to offer the Ecumenical Movement than ever before, while, if her theology were deepened, she would have more to offer to our growth toward reunion than any other single Church.

(e) *Problems of Reunion*[1]

Problems of Reunion, by A. E. J. Rawlinson. Eyre and Spottiswoode, 1950.

Our generation has seen many books on the subject of reunion, but this is one that is more than a book, for in it the hand of reconciliation is definitely and sincerely held out by a prominent Anglican, the Bishop of Derby, to other Churches. It is a powerful work which, besides presenting its theological argument in a clear and even exciting way, succeeds in evoking penitence, and stirring the conscience as few publications of this kind actually do. Here is a most earnest attempt to reach understanding by one who is able to appreciate the other point of view and who is prepared for a sincere give-and-take in the urgent duty of reunion without in any way sacrificing principle or glossing over real differences. It will be welcomed in ecumenical endeavour everywhere, but particularly by those who are engaged in friendly discussions in our own country, and who are concerned not merely with concrete proposals for reunion with with the profound theological questions which are thus raised.

In a striking preface Dr. Rawlinson points out that divisions or schisms between Christians are to be taken as discords within the family of the Church which is as widespread as Christendom. But to adopt this view that schism is within the Church, and not from the Church (which is apostasy), is to take up a position the effect of which is to include all Christians, of whatever "Church" or ecclesiastical allegiance, under sin. Reconciliation therefore must be pursued with a deep sense of sin and shame, and with sincere contrition and forgiveness on both sides, although ecclesiastical and theological divergences must be taken seriously. That will not be easy, and so the Bishop of Derby suggests that "for a considerable period yet there may well be continuing need for the work of theologians, whose vocation and duty it is to converse on these high matters across the ecclesiastical frontiers as in very truth to reach out towards fuller understanding, purging themselves in the

[1] From the *Scottish Journal of Theology*, 4, 1951, pp. 427–33.

process mutually of error, learning best how to correct false emphases, renewing lost insights and in humility finding the way, by God's grace, to recovered balance of truth and wholeness of catholicity".

After a helpful opening chapter on the Church and the Churches, Dr. Rawlinson goes on to state the position of the Church of England. That is not easy to do, for the Church of England has nowhere formulated her position clearly in these matters—which is perhaps her greatest handicap in ecumenical discussions, while at the same time it leaves the door open for Churchmen to imply that their own views are those of their Church. There can be little doubt that the statement of the position of the Church of England given here admirably represents the views of many of our Anglican contemporaries; but it would appear to me that although he is trying to be fair and is anxious not to be biased Dr. Rawlinson underestimates the Lutheran and Calvinist influence upon the Church of England. Certainly he has the courage to state the plain fact that "the Church of England itself, as a reformed Church, broke continuity in the sixteenth century with the Church system of which it had until then been a part: that is, it reformed itself at the cost of schism" (p. 36)—although it retained institutional continuity in the episcopate (at least on the Anglican, if not on the Roman claim). At the same time much that is said here about the Anglican Reformation will be challenged by others in the same Church who have fuller sympathy for the heritage of the Reformation.

This raises a point of supreme importance which must be faced sooner or later by those who lead the Church of England in her task of reunion. How are other Churches to understand the position of the Church of England, and to take their measure of Anglican teaching? By trying to get a general concensus of Anglican thought to-day, by studying the *Doctrinal Report of the Church of England* (which God forbid!), by seeking to estimate the predominant tradition in the last hundred years, or by assessing the theological position of the Church of England throughout the four hundred years of her life since the Reformation? One fact is perfectly plain, that on the whole many leading Anglicans to-day appear to shut their eyes to the three hundred years of Anglican tradition before the Tractarian Movement, or if they do not shut their eyes altogether to that great tradition, they read it and often misread it in the light of current prejudices. No one who has examined the *Thirty-nine Articles* and noted that its doctrine of the Church is literally Lutheran, its doctrine of justification Calvinist, or examined the *Ordinal* only to discover that this, which was to a large measure the work of Martin Bucer of Strasbourg, has a non-sacerdotal view of the ministry, or remembers that the King at the head of the Church of England has vowed to defend the Protestant Reformed Religion, can but wonder whether after all those Anglican Churchmen who stress their "catholic" character are not really disavowing a great deal of their own great tradition.

Where does the Church of England stand to-day? Does she still hold with Hooker that ordination without a bishop is sometimes to be allowed, as when God extraordinarily raises up a Reformer, or with Archbishop Laud who wrote: "Much evident it is, that the 'succession' which the Fathers meant, is not tied to place or person, but is tied to 'verity of doctrine'. . . . So that if the doctrine be no kin to Christ all the 'succession' become strangers, what nearness soever they pretend of"? Does the Church of England still agree with the position adopted by representative divines like Cosin and Mason, or agree with the verdict of at least (as numbered by H. H. Henson) seventeen archbishops and forty-six bishops (including many whose works are in the Anglo-Catholic Library) who admitted the validity of Presbyterian orders? Does the Church of England repudiate to-day two significant moments in her relations with Scotland when in 1610 and 1661 at her advice the Scottish Episcopal Church accepted a whole clergy in Presbyterian orders, *without reordination*, while she herself entered into full communion with the episcopalized Church of Scotland in *that* condition? There can be no doubt that the other Churches with which the Church of England discusses reunion want from the Church of England a plain and unambiguous answer to questions like these, an answer which takes into account the *whole* of her tradition, and not one which expresses the views of a minority at one period in Anglican history. There is, for example, little point in asserting that there is no particular theory of episcopacy the acceptance of which is obligatory in Anglicanism (p. 53), if at the same time the Bishop of Derby insists that in discussions on reunion an episcopate would have to be accepted, capable of being interpreted in the form which stricter Anglicans hold it (p. 57, but cf. pp. 168 f.). So long as the Church of England allows a small if powerful minority to hold a pistol to the whole tradition of the Church of England ranging over four hundred years, serious hopes of reconciliation cannot be entertained. It is with the Church of England, not with the straitest sect within the Church of England, that we wish to discuss reunion.

Although we may complain that even the Bishop of Derby's sincere and unprejudiced discussion has not done justice to vast stretches of Anglican history, we are none the less grateful to him for powerful contributions to questions of the hour. He has given us a penetrating critique of that notorious book, *The Apostolic Ministry*, and has replaced the question of continuity in the corporate setting which it always had in the Church of England until the Tractarians, to the horror of High Churchmen and Low Churchmen alike, sought to isolate the episcopate from the whole continuing body of the Church and to rest continuity on it alone. Most Anglicans then felt that such an idea struck at the root not only of the essential unity in continuity of Church and community and doctrine for which the Church of England had always stood, but it struck at the root of her teaching on the corporate priesthood of the whole Church as the Body of Christ. Thus even a man like Laud had earlier insisted that the real continuity of the Church rested upon baptismal incorporation into the Body of Christ rather than upon a line of priestly succession, important as he felt that to be. This is the direction in which the thought of Dr. Rawlinson moves, though one would like to push it even further. Advocates of episcopacy in its Anglican form have yet to advance a single and truly theological reason why the corporate episcopate *must devolve upon individuals only*. Presbyterians do not think that in the nature of the case this can be done, but they on their part have not to my knowledge offered a single purely theological reason why the corporate episcopate, which they hold as firmly as Anglicans, *may not devolve upon individual men*. However, it is precisely this *individualism* in the notion of the episcopate, an individualism made essential (the dotted line of the succession of bishops as opposed to the real continuity of the whole Body), which Presbyterians find questionable, and difficult as a *de fide* matter. Presbyterianism stands for a doctrine of the ministry as the expression of the corporate priesthood of the Body of Christ, and of collegiate courts as the expression of the corporate episcopate of the Church.

The whole notion of validity is also discussed in a fresh and illuminating manner in these pages. "The question may be seriously raised", says Dr. Rawlinson, "as to whether the traditional doctrine of validity, developed and formulated in days prior to the Reformation and reflecting inevitably an outlook for which Protestantism as yet did not exist, may not need to be thought out afresh, and with greater realism, in relation to the much more complex ecclesiastical situation of to-day" (pp. 71 f.). Following a line suggested by the Bishop of Oxford (without, however, falling into his shocking position which really holds admittedly efficacious acts of the Holy Ghost to be invalid), the Bishop of Derby points the way to a view of the validity of orders in relation to a divided Christendom as being, in an important sense, a matter of degree. Without doubt this is a line that will prove helpful and profitable, though at its deepest level it still leaves untouched the question whether any juridical notion, which validity inevitably involves, is compatible with faith in the Holy Ghost.

When we turn to questions of Intercommunion and Christian Initiation we find a candid discussion of confirmation. It is admitted that upon the origin of laying on of hands, as a rite associated or linked with baptism, the New Testament throws no light at all, and it is insisted that teaching about confirmation should not be such as to lead to the disparagement of Baptism, and that indeed episcopal confirmation should not be pressed as indispensable in talks on reunion. This is most wise and salutary, for it has seemed evident again and again to many outside the Church of England that exclusively episcopal confirmation interpreted as the completion of Baptism, leads straight to a usurpation of lordship over the Eucharist, lordship which by right belongs to Christ alone. Once episcopal confirmation is exalted to the function of completing Baptism and Holy Communion is thus brought under the exclusive control of the bishop, the problem of intercommunion is created which ought not to be there at all. Let it be said here quite bluntly that the problem of intercommunion is quite a false problem and those who have created it bear before God the responsibility of removing it from the face of the Church. Dr. Rawlinson, however, has pointed a way to a deeper and a more biblical understanding of Baptism as the full act of the Spirit whereby we are incorporated into the Body of Christ (though he does not seem to recall that the fathers, Athanasius for example, regard Baptism as itself *teleiosis*, cf. p. 122). But that makes the question of intercommunion all the more acute. Who has the authority to deny those already fully incorporated into the Body of Christ the right to feed on the Body? And who dares to partake of the Eucharist in such a way as not to welcome all who are admittedly incorporated through Baptism into the Body of Christ, that is to say, in such a way as not to discern the Lord's Body? It is for this cause, St. Paul reminded the Corinthians, that many were weak and sickly among them—and may that not be equally true of us to-day? Dr. Rawlinson realizes the gravity of such questions when he declares that in coming negotiations between Anglicans and non-Anglicans with a view to reunion the questions about Baptism implicitly posed by Tertullian will have to be faced (p. 142).

One further point we may notice here—the prominence of the questions of priesthood and sacrifice in recent Anglican thought. Once again we are reminded of the teaching of Hooker that as sacrifice is now no part of the ministry of the Church of England, the priesthood must be understood accordingly, in a non-sacerdotal sense. Even when the classical High Anglicans of the seventeenth century spoke of Eucharistic sacrifice it is clear that they were speaking of it in much the same way as Peter Martyr in his debates at Oxford with Gardiner and Tresham, drawing from his great patristic learning on this question. Sacrifice and priesthood are essentially ambiguous terms and cannot be used univocally of Christ and His Church. The prime question to be faced here is this: how can the Eucharist be an offering of that which by its very nature was done in our stead and on our behalf? It is without doubt an *echo* of the one all-sufficient sacrifice of Him who eternally intercedes for us before the Father, but the Eucharistic sacrifice is not *identical* with that as such. There is a great deal of confusion here which can only be straightened out when Anglicans are prepared to think their Christology and their soteriology more carefully into their doctrine of the Sacraments, while many who hold the doctrine of the Eucharistic sacrifice in the Anglo-Catholic form ought to be frank enough to acknowledge, like Darwell Stone in the 1927 volume of the Anglo-Catholic Congress (in which Dr. Rawlinson also has a contribution), that here they are taking up "a different position from that of the long succession of great and good men in the English Church". Meantime, I cannot think that the Bishop of Derby really helps matters by the idea that "It is the Last Supper which makes Calvary sacrificial" (p. 133). Surely what *made* Calvary sacrificial, if we are to use these terms, was the self-offering of Christ in Gethsemane, His will to lay down His life freely. It is entirely a Latin and indeed an artificial idea to understand liturgical *sacrificium* as *making* something different. Far better were it for Anglicans to return to the teaching of their own great Caroline divines!

This review has been somewhat critical for I have dealt with several of the salient points which raise questions in the minds of non-Anglicans, but let it be said that this is a work which non-Anglicans must study carefully, for it has a great deal to say to them which will be wholesome and which ought to stimulate a penitential rethinking of their own historical traditions in several respects. After reading this book several times I for one am convinced that our theological thinking together must be conducted at a much profounder level than hitherto, and am sure therefore that the recommendation of the *Joint Report on Relations between the Church of Scotland and the Church of England* is perfectly right—that as well as a short-term policy a *long-term policy* should be adopted, in which representatives of both Churches will be able to go into the whole matter on a deeply theological basis and which will allow time for the theological discussions and conclusions of the conferences, published from time to time, to react upon both Churches with a view to drawing them as a whole into a penitential rethinking of our historical achievements and into a consideration before God of such moderations of our respective traditions as will bring us at last to sit down together at the Holy Table and be healed of our divisions.

DISCUSSIONS WITH CHURCHES

2. WITH PRESBYTERIANS

(a) *What is the Reformed Church?*

THE Reformed Church is the Church reformed according to the Word of God so as to restore to it the face of the ancient Catholic and Apostolic Church. It is not in any sense the founding of a new Church, but on the contrary the rebuttal of the innovations and improvisations that grew up unchecked through the Dark Ages and then received rationalization in the mediaeval Church at the hands of the great scholastic theologians. By that time the whole piety of the Western Church had grown so far away from its origins in the apostolic Church and had become so powerfully entrenched in the life and thought of people and clergy that it succeeded in resisting all demands for reform from within the Church and demanded instead careful systematization. And that was done with the aid of the late Augustinian theology and newly discovered Aristotelian categories. But the Church could hardly go on growing farther and farther away from its origins by way both of addition and subtraction without putting a severe strain upon the whole life of the Church—sooner or later it had to reach a breaking point. That first came when the Western Church through its innovations broke off relations with the Eastern Church, and then it came within the Western Church when its own inner life began to be renewed at the original sources of the Church in the apostolic Scriptures and in the teaching of the early Catholic Church.

Thus what happened at the Reformation was the result of the deviation of the Roman Church in which it so widened the gap between itself and its apostolic foundation that in point of fact it shattered the continuity of the Church even before the Reformation took place. When the inner life of the Church as the redeemed people of God reasserted itself only to find it shackled and fettered by a hardened and rationalized institution, it could only bear suffering witness against the scandal of a Church institutionally at variance with its own deepest life. The climax began to come when the renewed understanding of the Church in the living Creator God of the Bible, who actively intervened in history to redeem His people, began to call in question the whole Latin-Stoic conception of God as *Deus sive Natura* inherent in the mediaeval Theology. That clearly threatened the rationalization of the Roman aberrations, and Roman reaction was determined and fierce, as it sought to crush out the renewal of its own inner life at every point where that indicated a need for reform in the institution as well as in the means of conveying the Gospel of salvation to the needy multitudes. However, behind this renewing of the life of the Church there were all the ancient forces of the Church's life in the Apostolic and Catholic Church and it could not be crushed out, but rather forged ahead the more it was obstructed and persecuted. Then when the movement for reform was excommunicated by the Roman Church it grew and developed rapidly and with such power that the whole history of the world has ever since revolved round the Reformation of the Church in Europe in the sixteenth century.

This was the Church Reformed according to its own catholic norms and standards acting against the new-fangled ideas and conceptions invented and imposed by Rome upon the Western Church. The Reformation was not a movement to refound the Church, or to found a new Church; for the whole reforming movement would undoubtedly have continued within the Roman Church had it not been for the bigoted and arrogant recalcitrance of its hierarchy, which insisted in binding the movement of the Word and Spirit by the traditions of men and making it of none effect, and, when that failed, in throwing it out altogether, just as the early Christians were thrown out of the synagogues and followed with maledictions and anathemas. Thus in wide areas of Europe the Church as the redeemed people of God moved on in obedience to its apostolic foundation and left the opposing hierarchy behind to harden in its bitter reaction to the Gospel of Grace. There were areas of Europe where the hierarchy behaved very differently—notably in Sweden and England; but elsewhere in the lands of the

Reformation, and nowhere more clearly than in Scotland, the whole Church moved on and left the hierarchy high and dry as an empty ecclesiastical shell saying, "The Temple of the Lord, the Temple of the Lord", when the glory of God had departed from it and taken the humble people of the land under its wings, where they found shelter in the Gospel of justification by grace and in sacraments rightly and sincerely administered by servants whom God raised up to lead His people back into the fold of the One Shepherd of the sheep.

It is true that the Roman Church did its best to gather its strength and even set about half-heartedly to put its own house in order, but in point of fact it became even more reactionary, and with the decrees and anathemas of the Council of Trent barricaded itself behind irreformable decisions that have effectively isolated and cut off the Roman Church from the rest of Christendom, and made it impossible for it without the greatest internal upheaval to regain fellowship with the rest of Christendom on the ground of the apostolic revelation and tradition.

But what about the Church Reformed, and particularly that part of it known as the Reformed Church? How did it pursue its course of obedience to the catholic and apostolic tradition? It acknowledged the priority and supremacy of the apostolic tradition as enshrined in the Holy Scriptures, and subordinated all other tradition to it, subjecting thereby the whole history of the Church to its foundation in Jesus Christ. But in so doing it did not condemn or neglect the historical Church. Calvin realized how much the hearing and the understanding of the Word of God was conditioned by and dependent upon "the fathers", although he realized too that the teaching of the fathers had to be brought to the test of the Word of God in the Holy Scriptures. There is much in the New Testament itself, notably about its sacraments and ministry, that requires help for its understanding from the teaching and practice of the early Church outside the New Testament. Moreover the doctrines of the Faith had under God received elucidation and articulation in the early Catholic Church which were of authority for the succeeding generations of the Church, but of authority because they were faithful to the Word of God. Thus under Calvin's leadership the Church sought to reform itself according to the Word of God in the Scriptures and according to the teaching of the ancient Catholic Church.

How far into history did the Church extend without notable corruption? At times Calvin was ready to say, perhaps in line with a late mediaeval tradition, for the first thousand years, but at other times he preferred to return rather to the Church of the first six or seven centuries, and even to the pre-Nicene Church only on some matters. As a rule, however, he professed his readiness to seek reform according to the Canons of the Ancient Councils. "Although the bishops of those times published many canons, in which they seemed to express more than is expressed in the sacred volumes, yet they were so cautious in framing their economy on the Word of God, the only standard, that it is easy to see that in scarcely any respect they departed from it." That outlook, which Calvin shared with so many of his Reforming colleagues such as Zwingli, Bullinger, Oecolampadius, Bucer, and Peter Martyr, accounts for the enormous output in new editions of the fathers from Zürich, Basel, Geneva, and Strasbourg in the sixteenth century. The ancient Catholic Church was called in to redress the deviations and disobedience of the modern Church, and the teaching of the fathers was resurrected against that of the schoolmen. Thus the Reformed Church stood for "the restoration of the face of the ancient Catholic Church", as Calvin put it, for in that way it was the face of Christ Himself which came to be reflected and seen again in the historical Church which is His Body on earth.

How was this Reformation conceived?

(1) Theologically the reformation was carried out through Christological correction of the doctrines of the Church, notably the doctrines of the Church, ministry, and sacraments, but also of the doctrines of God, salvation, and of the last things. The early Catholic Church had been forced to work out a true doctrine of Christ and to safeguard it in Conciliar decisions or dogmas, but the doctrines of the Church, ministry and sacraments had just grown up, and during long ages had grown unchecked so that they had deviated from the centralities of the faith. But even the doctrine of Christ had come to suffer in this way in the Roman Church, evident even under Pope Honorius I who was anathematized by the Council of Constantinople

for his monophysite error in regard to the will of Christ. The Reformers realized that officially the Roman Church held to the Ecumenical decisions, but they found that in the applied areas of the faith Christological heresies abounded: Eutychianism in the doctrine of transubstantiation, Arianism in the notion of created grace, etc. Christological correction was needed in all these areas, and in regard to the inveterate Pelagianism that generally infected Roman soteriology. Nowhere more noticeably was this correction applied than in regard to the doctrine of the Church. Mediaeval Romanism had come to think of the Church as twofold, an invisible mystical body, and a hierarchical institution on earth, while there were many who regarded the latter as a replica of an eternal hierarchy in the heavens. Against this Calvin led the way back in formulating the doctrine of the Church as the Body of Christ in history and on earth, that is, in thinking of God's people on earth as formed by His Word and Spirit to be the Body of Christ. It was this doctrine of Christ and His Church, of Christ as the Head and the Church as His Body or Spouse, above all, that demanded that every aspect of the life and tradition and thought of the Church be subject to Christ and be shaped according to His image and likeness once again.

(2) This meant a movement of reform through the integration of faith and order. The Church is the object of faith, as the Creed declares, and that refers to the visible Church which is our mother, which has nourished us in the faith and taught us the truth which it has received from the apostles and transmitted to us. But because this visible Church is an object of faith, its order is necessarily a matter *de fide*. That does not mean that all the details of Church order and life have to have direct doctrinal warrant or explicit biblical justification, although nothing must be allowed which is in any way opposed to biblical teaching; but that the essential elements of Church order derive from doctrine and are doctrinally related to the order of the new creation revealed in Jesus Christ. Calvin had the strongest sense of the fact that redemption and creation belong together, that redemption is the restoration of the order of creation, and that wherever redemption is operative in the Church there will be manifested the true order and image of God's creation.

It is at this point that the Reformed Church stands out in comparison with the Lutheran and Anglican Churches. For Lutherans church order, discipline, liturgy, etc., all belong to what they call the *adiaphora*. They are to be held and used, therefore, only in the freedom of the Gospel, and as tools of the Gospel; but they are not to be regarded as doctrinally determined or shaped, and as if they needed to be justified by biblicist arguments and sanctions. For Anglicans on the other hand church order has been normally regarded as something belonging to the historic tradition of the Church from the earliest and even from apostolic times, and therefore to be preserved and reverenced as part of the Church's historical inheritance from the beginning. But traditionally Anglicans have not regarded order and discipline as matters *de fide* or *de jure divino*, except where they began to be influenced by Presbyterian teaching, especially by "high", that is by *de fide*, Presbyterian conceptions of discipline and polity.

For Calvinist Churches, however, the integration of faith and order meant that we must take in earnest the work of Christological correction of the form and order of the Church. The primary fact to be faced here is that the Church in history shares in the humiliation of Christ in the form of a servant. There are two conditions of the Kingdom, or correspondingly two conditions of the Church, as Calvin put it: the condition of humiliation and the condition of glory, which correspond to the humiliation of Christ in His first advent and the glory and power of Christ which He will manifest in His second advent. The Church is sent out by Christ to bear His Cross, to serve Him in the humble form of a servant as the Church militant, but not yet as the Church triumphant except through faith. This Church under the Cross already partakes of the power of the resurrection and shares in the reign of Christ, so that Church on earth and Kingdom of Christ are identical, but Christ now rules through His humanity as the Mediator and does not yet reign in the unveiled glory and power of His Majesty. The Church reigns on earth only as it proclaims the Gospel of the crucified Christ, for it is through that Word of the Gospel that Christ rules over the nations until He comes again in glory and power. The Church must therefore order its life and ministry in conformity to Christ as the "subministration" which He, the

Mediator and High Priest, uses to rule and shepherd His people on earth. Within this condition of the Church as the servant of the Cross, order is doctrinally determined, and discipline is doctrinally shaped in all essential respects; but this shaping and ordering of its life in the form of a servant is determinative even for all the other minor details which have their part in the Church's mission and ministry.

(3) The form of the Church is made to appear above all in form of its regiment and ministry. This is worked out in terms of two governing conceptions which we have noted: the Church as the Body of Christ on earth, and as sent to fulfil its mission in the form of a servant. This means that the Church's ministry is fundamentally corporate in form and ministerial in nature. It was on this basis that Calvin taught a doctrine of the corporate priesthood of the Church and of "the corporate episcopate"—the consistorial or collegiate character of the ministry in the Reformed Church.

There are two elements here that we may do well to note. (a) The bishopric was scaled down in the Reformed Church from its mediaeval enormity to the size of a parish according to the pattern visible over wide areas of the early Church, in Cyprian's time in North Africa, or in Cappadocia in the time of Basil and the Gregories. (b) These parish bishops were regarded as holding their episcopates *in solidum* under the one universal bishopric of Christ. The minister who dispenses the Word and Sacraments in his parish and exercises the office of pastor over his flock is exercising a fundamentally episcopal office, not different at all from that which bishops exercised in the early centuries of the Christian Church. But these bishops hold their office only in a fraternity of common sharing in the one ministry of Christ, and are pastors sent by Him who is the Chief Shepherd of the sheep, to minister *in persona Christi* and to fulfil *vicaria opera* as Calvin put it. But they are subordinate to the Word and Sacraments which they minister because they are subordinate to Christ, and He sends them and commissions them yet in such a way as not to resign to them His authority but to preside Himself in all their decisions and actions in the ministry in His Name.

Two distinct tendencies in regard to this are apparent in the history of the Reformed Church: (a) an emphasis upon the parish episcopate and not on Presbyterial superintendents or bishops, e.g. in the Reformed Church of France; and (b) an emphasis on Presbyterial superintendents or bishops, e.g. in the Reformed Church of Hungary, the largest of the Continental Reformed Churches.

Scotland has seen a mixture of these two emphases, due to the influence of John Knox on the one hand and to that of Andrew Melville on the other hand. The old Reformed view was given its clearest statement by Erskine of Dun, the superintendent or bishop of Angus and Mearns, in his long letter to the Regent Morton in 1572.[1] In that letter Erskine of Dun argued that a bishop and superintendent fulfilled the same office.

> This office is spiritual and therefore belongs to the Kirk which alone has the distribution and ministration of spiritual things. So that by the Kirk spiritual offices are distributed, and men admitted and received into them. And the administration of the power is committed by the Kirk to bishops or superintendents.

Then with reference to the teaching of Paul's Epistles to Timothy and Titus and the sixth chapter of the Acts of the Apostles, Erskine added:

> Thus we have plainly expressed by Scripture that to the office of bishop pertains examination and admission to spiritual cure and office, and also to oversee them who are admitted, that they walk uprightly and exercise their office faithfully and purely. To take this power from the bishop or superintendent is to take away the office of a bishop, so that there would be no bishop in the Kirk, which would be to alter and abolish the order which God has appointed in His Kirk. There is a spiritual jurisdiction and power which God has given unto His Kirk, and to those who bear office in it; and there is a temporal power given by God to Kings and civil magistrates. Both powers are of God, and they agree very well in fortifying one another, if they are used rightly.

At that point Erskine went on to protest against the confounding of these offices, and particularly against unlawful acts of the civil authorities in "passing beyond the bounds of their office" and "meddling with such things as pertain to the ministers of God's Kirk". When that happens the servants of

[1] Calderwood, *History of the Kirk of Scotland,* III, pp. 156 ff.

God cannot keep silence but must withstand it. He who does otherwise is unworthy to bear any office in God's Kirk.

> A greater offence or contempt of God and His Kirk can no prince do than to set up by his authority men in spiritual office, as to create bishops and pastors of the Kirk; for so to do is to conclude that there exists no Kirk of God, for the Kirk cannot exist unless as it has its own proper jurisdiction and liberty, with the ministration of such offices as God has appointed.

Therefore Erskine protested against any bishops intruded upon the Kirk against its own appointment.

> They may be called bishops, but they are not bishops but idols, as the prophet says (Zech. 11: 17). And therefore the superintendents who were called and placed in an orderly way by the Kirk have the office and jurisdiction (of bishop); and other bishops, so-called, have no office nor jurisdiction in the Kirk of God, for they enter not by the door, but by another way, and therefore are not pastors, as Christ says, but thieves and robbers . . .

I have cited these passages from the Laird of Dun because they indicate very clearly the problem with which the Church of Scotland began to be faced after the Reformation when the Regent and then the King wanted to intrude their own bishops, invested with civil authority and appointment, upon the Kirk, to take the place of the Kirk's bishops who were subject to the authority of the Presbytery and the Assembly. In repudiating the King's bishops the Church of Scotland never repudiated the teaching of Calvin, Knox, and Erskine of Dun, but repudiated every Erastian form of episcopacy. It was in reaction to the Erastian bishops which King James VI and I intruded upon the Kirk that the Kirk under the leadership of Andrew Melville reacted and deliberately employed novel expedients, unknown before in Presbyterian polity, in order (as far as possible) to safeguard the freedom of the Kirk. It is to Andrew Melville that we owe much in the Church of Scotland of the place which the Presbytery has long come to occupy, as the corporate episcopate; for the Presbytery as a whole came to take over the functions exercised by the superintendents or bishops in the years following the Reformation. In Scotland we have therefore a form of Presbyterian polity in which the parish minister exercises an episcopal office in the ministry of Word and Sacrament and in the oversight of his flock, but in which he shares conjointly with his compresbyters the episcopal oversight over the whole presbytery. It is this corporate episcopate or presbytery that fulfils the function of ordination and superintendence, guardianship of doctrine, and pastoral discipline which are performed by individual bishops in Anglican Churches, although they do that with the association of their presbyters. It is worth noting that Presbytery and Kirk Session functioned very well under Presbyterian bishops such as Patrick Forbes of Aberdeen. Indeed it was probably due to episcopalian influence that the local Kirk Sessions (i.e. as attach~~ed to~~ the individual parish) came to be firmly established instead of the town kirk-sessions (from several parishes) which still function in the Swiss Reformed Church.

(4) The doctrine of ministerial order and succession. True to its fundamental position the Reformed Church has always refused to divorce the order of the ministry from the truth and doctrine of Christ, and opposed therefore an institutional continuity separated from continuity in the apostolic teaching. That was a basic error in the Roman Church, the separation of the truth of the Gospel from the government of the Church. But when a government of the Church is to be found in essential unity with the truth of the Gospel it is to be honoured and accepted, even if it is "episcopal". Thus Calvin wrote:

> Let them show us a hierarchy in which bishops are distinguished, but not by refusing to be subject to Christ, in which they depend upon Him as the only Head, and act solely with reference to Him, in which they cultivate brotherly fellowship with one another, bound together by no other tie than His truth, then, indeed, I will confess that there is no anathema too strong for those who do not regard them with reverence, and yield them the fullest obedience.

That was precisely the difficulty however with which the Reformers were faced: the claim to an institutional continuity which lacked the decisive content in the truth, but where institutional continuity was divorced from continuity in the truth, it could no longer be regarded as a true continuity. It was not only that they were devoid of continuity in the truth but that such a lack affected also their institutional obedience to the forms of the early Church. Calvin claimed, for example, that in reintroducing the laying on of hands and giving it its canonical place he was bringing back what had been ousted (at least in the Gallican Church) by other ceremonies for which there was no warrant in the early Catholic Church.

When Calvin wrote his long letter to the King of Poland in 1554 offering him guidance in the reformation of the Church, he pointed to the true and canonical succession in which orderly and responsible devolvement of the ministry in the laying on of hands is not divorced from the faithful transmission of the apostolic doctrine.

> There must be a legitimate succession of persons to give due sanction to the ordination of pastors. . . . Here I confess it were to be wished that an uninterrupted succession lent us its sanction that the function itself were transmitted as it were from hand to hand. But let us keep it in mind that since purity of doctrine is the soul of the Church, it is vain to look for the peculiar properties of a Church, and whatever depends on the state of its purity, among those who are beyond all question avowed enemies of the Gospel. But because by the tyranny of the Pope, the continuous line of ordination has been broken, a new expedient for the restoration of the Church is required. . . . But God Himself brings the remedy in raising up fitting and upright teachers to build up the Church, now lying deformed among the ruins of popery. And this office, which the Lord laid upon us, when He made use of our services in collecting Churches is one that is altogether anomalous. . . . Once things are fairly ripe, by royal authority and the suffrages of the Diet, a more definite manner of ordaining pastors might be established for the future.

Scotland could never agree, however, to the suggestion that this must be done with "royal authority" or by act of parliament! It was precisely that, and not episcopacy as such, that roused the opposition of the Kirk through the centuries! This is a point where we must still side with Melville against Calvin.

But it is important to see more deeply into this question of the ministerial succession, which we can perhaps do best by comparing the attitude of the Church of Scotland with that of the Church of England. Traditionally the Anglican Church has been more interested in, and more concerned to defend, the outer shell of the apostolic tradition, rather than the real kernel or substance of it. Traditionally the Reformed Church has been more interested in, and more concerned to defend, the inner kernel and substance of the apostolic tradition, and has therefore been interested in its outer shell in its *de fide* character, that is theologically, rather than in its historical and institutional character. It has been interested in that also but not primarily. The difference between these two attitudes also reflects the difference in the reference that each makes to validity, which to the Anglicans is more a question of institutional conformity, and to the Reformed more a question of doctrinal conformity, to the apostolic teaching and ordinances.

When, however, the Reformed Church finds a stress on the outer shell of the apostolic tradition with little understanding of its dogmatic substance, it can only view it with suspicion and even with opposition. The shell without the proper substance is defective and deformed; but where the outer and inner aspects are in full agreement with one another, even if that be found to be in an episcopalian Church, the Church of Scotland can have no grounds for disagreement—where disagreement does arise, as it often does, it must be frankly admitted that it is on non-theological grounds of prejudice. The Scottish Church barricaded itself behind a firm tradition in order to resist the encroachment of an Erastian episcopacy, but to resist a reformed episcopacy divested of Erastian error, episcopacy as such, on the ground of that Presbyterian tradition is simply to lapse back into the bondage to tradition from which we were mercifully delivered at the Reformation. A true Reformed Church is subject only to the Word and is therefore the lord over its tradition because the Word is lord over its tradition. It is, therefore, an abject betrayal of the Reformed position to exalt even the Reformed tradition to a place of irreformability like that of Rome.

Now the basic fact that lies behind this is that the ministry cannot be separated from "the oracles and the ordinances of the New Testament", as our Westminster Standards call them; for these three, "the ministry, the oracles, and the ordinances of the New Testament, are given by Jesus Christ to the general Church visible, for the gathering and perfecting of it in this life, until His second coming". The oracles and ordinances of the New Testament derive from Christ through the apostles who received them from Him and handed them on, in and with the foundation of the Church which they laid.

Several things here have to be made clear. (a) The apostles exercised their ministry in "the House and Family of God" in a unique way inseparable from their unique ministry in mediating to the Church the New Testament Revelation. The apostolic ministry of the Word in that unique sense was incorporated within the New Testament Revelation, and it was as such that the apostles delivered to the Church the apostolic and prophetic witness and tradition in the Holy Scriptures of the Old and New Testament. (b) Apostolic succession in the ministry is certainly a succession in the ministry of the Word in "the House and Family of God", but it is not a ministry that is incorporated within the New Testament Revelation. It is a continuing ministry in dependence upon the apostles, and therefore and in that sense in succession to them, a succession in subordination to the apostolic Revelation. Apostolic tradition is acknowledged by the Church to be normative, and all other tradition, including the whole succession in the apostolic ministry, is subjected to the apostolic authority and norm, that is to the Holy Scriptures. (c) Thus the succession in the pastoral ministry in "the House and Family of God" cannot be abstracted from the apostolic Revelation and considered independently as if it had inherent authority in itself—that would be "fundamentalism" in the ministerial institution, parallel to "fundamentalism" in the letter of the Scripture. The continuing pastoral ministry of the Church has authority, but it is authority in the Word from which it is derived and upon which it reposes; it is authority in inseparable relation to the Word.

That is evident with regard to the continuing ministry of the Word and the continuing ministry of the Sacraments. The ministry of the Word in the Church from age to age is not separable from the Word any more than the ministry of the apostles themselves; but whereas the apostles were specially chosen instruments to mediate the Word to us, and were therefore "the wise master-builders", as Paul called them, the ministry in succession to them and on that foundation does not have an architectonic relation to the Word, but only an obedient relation. Likewise the ministry of the Sacraments, of the Lord's Supper, for example, is not separable from the

Supper itself, but it inheres in it and yet dispenses the Supper in that inseparable relation. But the continuing ministry does not have a revelational function in "the ordering" of the Lord's Supper in the way that St. Paul had. The ministry in the apostolic succession is a service (*diakonia*) and a stewardship (*oikonomia*) which is obedient to that which it serves and dispenses.

Thus we have to think of the continuity of the ministry in the succession of the apostles as a following of the apostles in their following of Christ, and as subject to the apostolic ministry and tradition, as they were subject to Christ. But within that subjection to the apostles, to the apostolic Revelation delivered to the Church in the Holy Scriptures, the ministry is inseparably bound to what it ministers in Word and Sacrament, and cannot be regarded as having any independent authority inherent in itself, apart from the Word and Sacraments. This unity of inner content and outer form, the mutual involution of faith and order, must never be forgotten, especially when an essential part of the healing in breaches of unity between Churches is the reintegration of the pattern of the ministry in the historical continuity of the Church; for apart from the inner integration in content and substance through subjection and conformity to "the oracles and ordinances of the New Testament" the integration of the ministry cannot be achieved in truth and therefore cannot be truly achieved. But if such integration is carried through in entire subordination to the Gospel, that is to the Word and Sacraments, so that these are never brought under the dominance of a ministry arrogating independence and authority to itself but the ministry thus reformed and reintegrated is made to serve the freedom and majesty of the Gospel, then, to use Calvin's strong language, no anathemas can be too severe for those who oppose or despise it.

(b) *Our Witness through Doctrine*[1]

The Calvinist Reformation stands for the Christological criticism of the doctrines of Salvation, Church, Ministry, and

[1] Address given at the Seventeenth General Council of the World Presbyterian Alliance, Princeton, 1954. From *The Presbyterian World*, Sept.–Dec., 1954, pp. 314–26.

Sacraments, and for their reshaping in terms of the Church as the Body of Christ. That was the primary and predominant emphasis in this Reformation—and not predestination, as is so often declared.

This Christological reforming of the Church and its teaching had to be fought out and maintained on a double front:

(a) Against Rome, where the doctrine of the Mass was the supreme issue, along with the false notions it involved about salvation and continuity in Church and Ministry;

(b) Against the Anabaptists and sectarians, where the doctrine of Infant Baptism was the central issue, and had to be maintained against the false notions of discontinuity involved in fanatical teaching about the Spirit.

Calvin's teaching on both these fronts is as instructive and important for us as it was in the sixteenth century. It is my firm belief that the witness of the Reformed Churches in the world to-day must be grounded upon a reassessment of that teaching in terms of our biblical and historical studies, and that it is along this line that we can make our biggest contribution to the Ecumenical Movement. The recovery of that theological perspective and task is certainly needed in the Alliance of the Reformed Churches. A strong Alliance, theologically rehabilitated, could only contribute toward the aims of the World Council of Churches because the very essence of Reformed theology concerns the unity of the Church as the one Body of Christ. No stronger emphasis is to be found in the writings of Calvin, and nowhere are his emotions more deeply stirred, than in his constant insistence that the unity of the Church is the will of God, and that to seek manifest unity is obedience to the blood of Christ by whom we are reconciled to God and redacted into one Body. The injection of this Reformed emphasis into the Faith and Order activities at Lund has succeeded in carrying the Ecumenical Movement forward in a definite and promising way. But it is supremely important for the Alliance of Reformed Churches to recover theological depth and unity in order that this may be done effectively. Nothing could be healthier for this Alliance than the initiation and carrying through of some theological task through which its own life and purpose could be renewed as a whole and by means of which it could engage with far greater effect in the

Ecumenical Movement—for example, the clarification of the doctrine of holy Baptism, or of the participation of the eldership and deaconate in the ministry of the Church.

My duty here and now is to speak about the *Witness of the Reformed Churches through Doctrine* in the context of our main theme. I would like therefore to examine more carefully the two main issues in the Calvinistic Reformation I have mentioned and then to speak of four ways along which this witness may be enunciated and worked out to-day in the world Church.

(1) All Calvin's teaching and preaching have to do with salvation through union with Christ in His death and resurrection. That is very clear in the *Institutes* in which the central message is worked out more and more clearly and fully from book to book, and is given most magnificent form in book four. In the history of theology Calvin represents the movement to bring the doctrine of the Person of Christ into the centre. In that he stood consciously in the tradition of Augustine and Bernard (the two fathers he cites more frequently than any others) in their emphasis upon personal Christological truth, but in Calvin it is more biblical, more dynamic and eschatological, than mystical—and certainly much less individualistic than it was in Bernard. Calvin, for example, would have nothing to do with Bernard's notion that the individual soul is the Bride of Christ. It is of the whole Church that we must speak in that way, and union with Christ is essentially the corporate union between Christ and the Church as His Body.

It is around this doctrine of *union with Christ*, then, that Calvin builds his doctrine of faith, of the Church as the living Body of Christ, and his doctrines of the Christian life, Baptism, and the Lord's Supper. Apart from *union with Christ*, Calvin says, all that Christ did for us in His Incarnation, death, and resurrection, would be unavailing. An examination of the structure of the *Institutes* makes it clear that this forms the main substance of his theology, and that the idea of predestination is not given a central place. Predestination or election is important, but Calvin speaks about it as a rule in connexion with certain controversies (notably with Castellio and Pighius) but never as a basic doctrine in itself—except in so far as Christ is Himself the Beloved Son and the mirror of our election. And so right in the heart of his Christology Calvin devotes a small chapter to that fact, the really central point in election. (A good account of this is to be found in the *Collected Works* of Jonathan Edwards, where there is preserved his teaching on Christ as the Head of election and of the corporate election of the Church in Christ the Head of the Body.) Rather, then, does Calvin give predestination a place on the circumference of his theology, where it acted like a protecting wall for the central emphases of grace and adoption or sonship in Christ. In the 1559 edition of the *Institutes* it is particularly evident that Calvin relegated predestination to the position of a corollary to his main teaching enshrining the mystery of union with Christ.

Nothing has done more harm to Calvinism than the invention and perpetuation of the myth that Calvin's theology was a severely logical structure. That notion grew up on French soil and was perpetuated by the great succession of Calvinist Schoolmen on the Continent, eminently in Holland. Modern research, however, makes it indubitably clear that Calvin's whole theology was formulated in a very definite reaction against the arid logical schematisms into which the doctrines of the Church had been thrust by "the frigid doctors of the Sorbonne", as he called them, and that again and again he was content to leave the ends of his theological thinking loose for the precise reason that theology runs out always to the point of wonder where we can only clap our hands on our mouth and remember that we are humble creatures. The whole inner substance of Calvin's teaching (as he shows for example in his debates with Westphal and Hesshusen), enshrines *mystery* and resists rationalistic schematization—so that it is a great disservice to interpret him as above all a logician.

That is not to say that his theology is not amazingly consistent, as it is. It is consistency, however, that derives not from formal logic but from the thoroughness with which he stated his theology in terms of the analogy of Christ. In his prefatory letter to the King of France, in the 1559 edition of the *Institutes*, Calvin pointed out that, following the Apostle Paul, Christian theology must operate with the analogy of faith, and that when doctrine is tested by this its victory is secure. By the *analogy of faith* Calvin meant both that all doctrine must be based upon the exegetical study of Holy Scripture in which Scriptural passages are interpreted in terms of each other, and more basically, that all doctrines are to be thought out thoroughly in terms of the death and resurrection of Jesus Christ. Thus, for example, in regard to *repentance*, which was such an important issue at the Reformation, while the Roman Schoolmen divided repentance into three parts, *contrition*, *confession*, and *satisfaction*, Calvin, following the analogy of faith in Jesus Christ, showed that repentance has two essential parts, *mortification* and *vivification*, corresponding to the death and resurrection of Christ. It was in carrying that Christological analogy through all the doctrines of the faith that Calvin achieved such an astonishing consistency, but it is consistency determined not by logical relation or by some kind of Calvinistic philosophy (so-called), but by the principle of Christological analogy—i.e. Christology applied to the whole of our life and work and thought.

It is just here that the Reformed Churches have a witness to give and a contribution to make of great significance to the situation of the world Church to-day: in picking up again the Reformed integration of the different doctrines of the faith and in thinking them into each other more thoroughly than ever before. Take, for example, the relation of the Church and Ministry to the doctrine of Christ which so concerns the Ecumenical Movement:—by its very principle of procedure the Reformed Church has refused to divorce the ministry from the articles of saving faith, so that for us the ministry is a *de fide* concern. The Church and Ministry themselves belong to the articles of saving faith. *Credo unam sanctam ecclesiam.* The doctrine of the Church as the Body of Christ is part of Christology, so that the ordering of the Church as the Body of Christ on earth cannot be divorced from the dogmatic discipline through which the mind of the Church grows up into mature conformity to the mind of Christ. That was why in Calvin's view *doctrina* and *disciplina* belonged together and overlapped, for *disciplina* is such learning and discipleship in the Christian faith that it shapes and orders the whole of the Christian life. The dogmatic and ecclesiastical forms of the Church, the inner and outer, so to speak, may well be distinguished but they cannot be separated. The Church is one Spirit and one Body with Christ the Word made flesh. The New Testament knows nothing of the Church as one Spirit except in its bodily existence in our flesh and blood which Christ assumed and in which we are united to Him through the Spirit. Because of this biblical emphasis upon the unity of the Church in Body and Spirit, the Reformed Church sought from the very beginning to allow the dogmatic and ecclesiastical forms of the Church's life and ministry to interpenetrate each other in obedience to the Word of God, and so to restore the doctrinal and ecclesiastical face of the Ancient Catholic Church. In our Reformed Church we will not have a doctrine of the ministry or of succession that cannot be fully integrated with the doctrines of the Person of Christ or atonement; but on the other hand, we will not have formulations of other doctrines which do not contribute to the growth or edification of the Church as the living Body of Christ, to the Church as *Ecclesia semper reformanda.*

This means, of course, that theology and the life of the Church are inseparable, and theological activity belongs to the strenuous work and daily living of the Church, but it also means that the Reformed Church will not have a liturgy or engage in worship which is invigorated by theology and a theology which ministers to the worship of the Church. The greatest theological utterances of John Knox are to be found in his prayers, and that is as it should be. Liturgy and theology go hand in hand. Theology divorced from worship is not divine, but liturgy that is divorced from theology is not true service of God. Such is the integration of doctrine and discipline, of faith and order, of worship and theology so characteristic of the Calvinistic Reformation.

As I see it, that is our greatest contribution to the theology of the world Church—the carrying through into the Ecumenical situation of an integration born out of the centrality of the doctrine of Christ, and therefore the Christological criticism of the doctrines of the Church, Ministry, and Sacraments, in order that as we seek to come together in Christ the doctrine of Christ may be allowed to reshape all our churches so that we may grow up together into the fulness of Christ. Only as in the World Council of Churches we are prepared for the strenuous task of reformation together and the joint criticism of our several traditions can we come together in such a way as to be the one flock of the one Shepherd. We in this Alliance must therefore engage in the World Council of Churches as the

Ecclesia semper reformanda, in order to let the Word of God speak to us in the context of the joint study of the Holy Scriptures, in order that we may be more and more reformed by it and in this continuous reforming be shaped and armed for the great mission of Christ, the mission of reconciliation, in which we are engaged as servants.

(2) This has already carried us into the field of the other main contribution of Calvin to the Reformed Churches about which I would like to speak: the doctrine of the continuity of the Church and its ministry which was asserted against the sectarians, mainly over the question of Infant Baptism. I believe it to be extremely important for us to recover again in all its magnitude the biblical and early Christian teaching about Baptism. In the New Testament there are whole books which have nothing to say about the Lord's Supper, and a great deal to say about Holy Baptism; while in the early Church it was Baptism that was the prime mystery of the Church, and the Eucharist had its significance within baptismal incorporation into Christ. It is our weakness in regard to Baptism, and our reducing it to a rite of small and even petty dimensions, in which its supreme significance is betrayed, that gives rise to so many of our difficulties—particularly in questions like intercommunion, marriage and divorce, as well as evangelism and Christian nurture. Let us have again the full biblical teaching about Baptism as involving death and resurrection in Christ, and incorporation into His living Body, the sphere where the mighty salvation-events are operative by the power of the Word and Spirit for our salvation, and we shall strike at the heart of many of our difficulties and divergencies, not least in regard to the nature of the Church and Ministry, and their continuity.

Here again later Calvinism tended to diverge from its greatest teacher, in regard to the notion of the *Covenant*. Like Zwingli and Bullinger Calvin also taught that there is but one Covenant which is the same in substance in both the Old Testament and the New Testament, but not the same in form. By that doctrine they asserted the continuity of the Church in unbroken perpetuity from the beginning of God's dealings with the race—but whereas the Federal Theology tended to isolate the covenant idea into a historical principle in itself, Calvin refused to think of the Covenant except in terms of the *Regnum*

Christi on the one hand and the doctrine of the Church as the Body of Christ on the other hand—and before both of those concepts which gave the substance of the Church's continuity, the Federal idea was given a secondary place. The elimination of *Regnum Christi* from the covenant idea meant the loss of eschatology; and the disappearance of the *Corpus Christi* from the covenant idea meant the transmutation of the Presbyterian Church into a hardened and too often a legalist institution.

I believe that the Reformed Churches have a notable witness to offer here too, but only if we are prepared here also to be the *Ecclesia semper reformanda*, ever ready in obedience to the Word of God to call in question the growing legalism and bureaucracy of our Church Courts, and indeed the whole concept of "Practice and Procedure", that is to say of government by the dead hand of historical precedent rather than by ever fresh obedience to the Word of God.

There is a passage in one of the fathers (Hermas) who lived about the end of the first Christian century which I like very much. In it he speaks of a vision he had of the Church as an old lady—the *Ecclesia presbytera*, he called it (translate it, if you like, as the Presbyterian Church). In his vision the old lady appears grey and wrinkled and spotted, but as he looks again something happens. Her hair gets whiter and whiter, but in point of fact she is getting younger and younger, until her flesh is restored like that of a virgin or a little child, the *Ecclesia neotera*. That is the biblical doctrine of the Church. Let the Church of Rome boast of its antiquity and its ancient vestments but the Church of Jesus Christ gets younger and younger, for if the outward man perish the inward man is renewed day by day, as we bear about in our body the dying of the Lord Jesus that the life also of Jesus may be manifest in our body, in our very mortal flesh. That is what we must learn again. Our tragedy is that we become tied up with human tradition and precedent, bound hand and foot in the graveclothes of the past, instead of living as the Church that has died and risen with Christ, and is alive in the midst of history because it is His living Body on earth. It is only as we allow the Word of God to slay us and make us alive, to criticize us and our ever hardening tradition and legalism ruthlessly, that we can live in the power of the resurrection. Let the Presbyterian Church, the *Ecclesia presbytera*, become again *Ecclesia neotera*, the Church that grows up in the renewing power of the resurrection into the full stature of the manhood of Christ.

In the Ecumenical situation in which we find ourselves I am not concerned at the moment so much with the concept of Church law as with the continuity and ordering of the Church as the Body of Christ. And here I believe we can do no better than return to the teaching of Calvin. Like Bucer, Viret, Martyr, Knox, and other colleagues in Reform, Calvin turns for his doctrine of the Church and ministry to two prime documents, and characteristically one is from the New Testament and one from the early fathers: St. Paul's *Fourth Chapter of Ephesians*, and Cyprian's *De Unitate Ecclesiae*. St. Paul gives Calvin his doctrine of the Church as the Body of Christ and of the ministry as the membering of that Body under the disposition of Christ, the sole Head of the Body; and Cyprian drawing that out gives Calvin his doctrine of the ministry as the corporate episcopate held *in solidum* by all alike who are called to the holy ministry as pastors of the flock, an episcopate which involves the parity of all before God but allows of what Calvin called "political distinctions". Here are some words from one of Calvin's latest writings, his *Commentary on the Harmony of the Pentateuch* (on Num. 3: 5), which we would do well to think over again.

> The political distinction of ranks is not to be repudiated, for natural reason (*sic*!) itself dictates this in order to take away confusion; but that which shall have this object in view, will be so arranged that it may neither obscure Christ's glory nor minister to ambition or tyranny, nor prevent all ministers from cultivating mutual fraternity with each other, with equal rights and liberties.

That was not the view of Beza or Andrew Melville, but it is fully consistent with Calvin's teaching elsewhere and with his view of what should be the order in Poland, England, Scotland, and Hungary (where there are Reformed bishops to this day), and it was certainly on those lines that John Knox had John Spottiswood and others ordained as the Superintendents or Reformed bishops in Scotland, but in such a way that they had to take vows against tyrannical jurisdiction and be subjected to the authority of their fellow presbyters in the Church Courts. That doctrine of the ministry has nowhere been better stated than by Erskine of Dun, the Superintendent of Angus, in his long letter to the Regent Morton in 1572.[1] There you see Calvin's doctrine of the corporate episcopate set out in remarkably careful and pungent terms.

That brings to a close my sketch of the constitutive ideas arising out of Calvin's doctrine of union with Christ which we must take up again and rethink in our present situation. I cannot undertake that here; but there are four lines which we may well think about, as they are so pertinent to our immediate needs. It is to them I wish to devote the rest of this address.

(a) The doctrine of *the Christian hope* was unquestionably one of Calvin's chief concerns, although it is so often misunderstood.

Calvin's main teaching can be formulated by saying that eschatology is the application of Christology to the work of the Church in history. It was on the ground of Christology, for example, that Calvin attacked the Chiliasts or Millennarians because they took such a low view of the glorious majesty of the risen Lord. Calvin's teaching pivots here once again upon the doctrine of union with Christ. Because we are united to Christ who is bone of our bone and flesh of our flesh, and participate in the risen humanity of Jesus, eschatology is essential to our faith. Union with Christ means union with the Christ who rose again from the dead, who ascended to the right hand of the Father and who will come again; and therefore union with Christ here and now carries in its heart the outreach of faith toward the resurrection of the dead and the renewal of heaven and earth at the Second Advent of Christ. The crucial issue in Calvin's eschatology is *the humanity of the risen Christ*, and our actual participation in His humanity through Word and Sacrament.

This is a supremely important question to-day: in my view it is the main issue which divides all theologies and strikes them apart to the one side or to the other. Are we to take the humanity of the risen Jesus seriously or not? Or are we to teach a Docetic view of the risen and ascended Jesus? To demythologize the resurrection of the Man Jesus, and the ascension of the Man Jesus, and the Parousia of Jesus as Man as well as Lord and

[1] Calderwood, *History of the Kirk of Scotland*, III. *Vide supra* pp. 83 ff.

Saviour, is to dehumanize Christ, and to dehumanize the Church which is His body. The main reason why so many people cannot see the importance of eschatology is because they divorce it from the doctrine of Christ, and dehumanize Him. If He who rose again and ascended to the right hand of God is no longer *Man*, flesh of our flesh, and bone of our bone, then we are of all men most miserable: we have no hope. The Christian hope is irreparably bound up with the fact that Christ is *Man* at the right hand of God, Man as well as Lord and God Himself; if our humanity is not forever joined to God in Christ, but is to be demythologized, then we are faced with no future for humanity other than inhuman elimination. That is why the central teaching of Calvin on eschatology is bound up with such passages as Col. 1 : 27 : "Christ in you, the hope of glory"; and Hebrews 6: 18 f.: "We lay hold upon the hope set before us, which hope we have as an anchor of the soul, both sure and steadfast, and which entereth into that within the veil; whither the forerunner is for us entered, even Jesus, made an High Priest for ever after the order of Melchisedec." Because we are united to Christ, anchored to Jesus who in our flesh has risen from the dead and now lives on the resurrection side of death and wrath and darkness, we are eternally anchored to hope. That is the cardinal fact upon which eschatology hinges. But in Calvin's teaching this stress upon the humanity of Christ has a double reference, which it is most important for us to-day to see clearly. On the one hand union with Christ in His risen Humanity means that we are so anchored already to the new creation, and are so joined to the new humanity, that our faith inevitably reaches out in hope toward the renewal of humanity, to the renewal of the whole earth, of heaven and earth; but on the other hand, union with the humanity of Christ means that here and now we must live out that humanity from day to day in the midst of the earth—that is why Calvin's sermons are always pressing home to the Church the need to be concerned with *humanité* in every aspect of its life and work.

Take for example that great passage from the fourth book of the *Institutes* (identically the same in 1559, as it was in 1536) in which Calvin insists that it is the duty of the magistrates and of the State to make room for humanity and by the exercise of justice and even the sword to maintain freedom for humanity on the earth. That exposition comes after the long sections in book four on the Holy Sacraments in which Calvin has been expounding the doctrine of union with Christ through Baptism in which we are incorporated into Christ, and the Lord's Supper in which we feed upon Christ's risen humanity, or feed, as Calvin puts it, so dramatically, upon the *vivifying flesh* of Jesus Christ. It is *humanitas* that provides the middle term between the life of the Church in its sacramental nourishment and growth, and the function of the State. The Church that feeds on Christ, is nourished by Him, grows up into the full stature of His manhood, increases in union with His risen humanity, but that Church must manifest this humanity upon the earth in day to day living, so that the Church that goes to the Lord's Table, and is renewed there in the humanity of Christ, must live and act according to His humanity in the midst of the inhumanity of the world. It is the business of the State to make room for that increase and growth of humanity through the Church, so that the State as well as the Church has a place in what Calvin calls the Kingdom of Christ. That is why eschatology in Calvin is concerned not only with the future manifestation of our new humanity in Christ, and indeed the future unveiling of the new heaven and the new earth, but eschatology by its very nature injects into the Christian Church on earth and in the midst of history the power and the imperative to live out that humanity, and so to extend among men, as Calvin puts it, the Kingdom of Christ. That is why the eschatology of the Lord's Prayer, as Calvin points out again and again, has a double reference: "Thy Kingdom come, AND Thy will be done on earth, as it is done in heaven." The Christian hope is the only hope for the world, not only because it tells us that the world is anchored to Christ and will be renewed entirely, but because here and now through the Church, in Word and Sacrament, that new humanity is already operative among men, and it is only through the operation of that new humanity that this wild and inhuman world of ours can be saved from its own savagery and be called into the Kingdom of peace and love. That is the way in which, as Calvin says, the Kingdom of Christ is extended to the ends of the earth, through the mission of the Church or the Body of Christ. Here, then, is the chief point of controversy, both with the demythologizers and with the millennarians: a weak and Docetic view of the humanity of the risen and ascended Jesus. Weakness at that vital point destroys the Christian hope both for the future and for the present. Let the Reformed Churches of the Alliance learn again the meaning of the *Word made Flesh*, and the *Resurrection of the Body*.

(b) The doctrine of the ministry based upon the Pauline doctrine of the Church as the Body of Christ is thrown into sharp relief by the attempts being made to-day by some Anglicans and Lutherans to give their conception of the ministry a doctrinal formulation. Sometimes they try to show that the functions exercised by Christ in His ministry are of two kinds, those which are unique to Him and those which can be passed on. And so they think of the ministry of the Church as extending certain functions in the ministry of Christ, and therefore of a relation of continuation and even of identity between the ministry of the Church and the ministry of Christ. The latest attempt in that direction is to be found in a book issued by a group of Lutheran scholars in Uppsala and edited by Fridrichsen, called *The Root of the Vine*. Calvin would never have agreed to that. He made a distinction between certain unique functions of the apostles bound up with their part in the New Testament Revelation and their part along with the Prophets in being the once and for all foundation of the Church, and other apostolic functions which were passed on through the laying on of hands of the Presbytery. But even the apostles could not be thought of as extending or continuing any of the functions of Christ's ministry. Calvin thought of the matter in quite a different way. The ministry of the Church is essentially corporate: in it the Church as Christ's Body participates in His whole prophetic, priestly and kingly ministry by serving Him. Christ exercises His ministry as Prophet, Priest, and King uniquely, vicariously, substitutionally, but the Church which is ingrafted into Him as His Body participates in His whole ministry in a way appropriate to the Church as the Body of which He is the Head. The Church is essentially and only *servant*, and yet in its servant-way it is given to participate in Christ's prophetic, priestly, and kingly ministry, because through baptism the Church is inserted into the functioning of His Body. Here then the Reformed doctrine of the ministry is at once so high that Calvin can speak of the ministers as exercising *vicaria opera* and yet as *repraesentant personam Christi*, and yet there is no hint at all of any relation of identity or prolongation between the ministry of the Church and that of Christ, and no thought of the Church as the extension of the Incarnation.

(c) Here too we have a doctrine of the continuity of the ministry as grounded upon the continuous growth of the whole Body, and of the continuity of the ministry as absolutely essential to that growth. Take away the ministry and the whole Church will collapse, Calvin said. And yet St. Paul in the Fourth Chapter of Ephesians uses two distinct words of the Church; its *edification*, and its *growth*. The ministry is utterly essential to the building up of the Church, and belongs to the *esse* of the Church in history, but it is essentially the scaffolding which God uses, for it is He and He alone who gives growth and increase by His Spirit; so that in the fulness of the Church in Christ the external scaffolding will be taken away so that the complete Church will stand to view as the very Body of Christ. If it is in these terms that the succession of the Church in history is thought out, then the false notions of continuity which so trouble inter-Church relations lose their power.

(d) Here too the Reformed Churches must think again about Calvin's notion of the corporate episcopate held *in solidum*, and recall that he could hold this in such a way that the full parity of ministers within the episcopate was conserved and yet in such a way that political distinctions, that is to say, distinctions in the administering of the Polity of the Church, were not to be done away. I have no doubt that a rethinking of this position in our own situation would demand from us a union of the presbyterian and episcopal ministries in such a way that each would be strengthened by the other. But let us be clear, *it must be a reformed episcopate*, in which the corporate episcopate is given collegiate or corporate expression and in which the presbytery is the prime locus of *episcopatus*, although *episcopatus* might be administered *in presbyterio* by a presiding Presbyter.

What I have said is entirely consonant with Calvin's teaching and also with that of Peter Martyr and John Knox, not to mention Bucer. But let us remember that Calvin and his colleagues did not have any access to some of the most important documents of the early Church which they revered so highly and the canons of which they sought so hard to put into practice in their reforming of the Church and the ministry. I refer to documents like the *Didache*, and to some of the ancient liturgies of the Eastern Church which only began to be published in the latter part of the sixteenth century. I have no doubt at all in my mind that had he realized that these liturgies came to be framed at the same time as the episcopate came to receive general form and the canon of Scripture began to take shape, all in one comprehensive settling down of the Church, Calvin would have been even more outspoken on some of these questions than he was, and, were he alive with us in our situation to-day, that he would unhesitatingly recommend the Reformed Churches while maintaining their witness undaunted to seek union with the Episcopal as well as the Lutheran Churches and so to fulfil the desire of our one Lord for one Church. It belongs to the very nature of the Church which Christ loved and for which He died and rose again to make it one Body with Him, that it should be one, in Body and in Spirit. It belongs thus to the very essence of the Reformed Church in ever fresh obedience to the Word of God and to the blood of Christ to live and work out that unity in the flesh and bone of history, that, as Calvin says, when Christ comes again there may be one flock to greet the One Shepherd.

DISCUSSIONS WITH CHURCHES

3. PRESBYTERIAN—ANGLICAN RELATIONS

By way of a short preface to what follows I would like to cite the "Ecumenical Statement" adopted by the General Assembly of the Church of Scotland in May, 1954, as a guide to its attitude in *rapprochement* with other Churches:

> The Church of Scotland, believing in one Holy Catholic and Apostolic Church, and acknowledging one Baptism for the remission of sins, affirms its intention of seeking closer relations with every Church with which it stands in fundamental doctrinal agreement, but from which it is separated in matters of government and the ordering of the ministry.
>
> In its approach to other Churches in which it discerns the one Body of Christ, the Church of Scotland would desire to look beyond the divisions of history to the ultimate fulness and unity of the Church's life in Christ, and to affirm its readiness to consider how the contributions of all such Churches may be embraced within that unity and fulness; always, however, in agreement with the Word of God and the fundamental doctrines of the Christian faith.
>
> In such approaches the Church of Scotland would seek to join, humbly and penitently, with its sister Churches in fulfilment of Christ's prayer that all who believe in Him might be one.

(a) *What is the Church?*[1]

The Church is the Body of Christ. The Holy Scriptures use many names and images with which to speak of the Church, and none of them is unimportant: Temple, Building, Vine, Bride, Flock, Israel, New Jerusalem, City, Holy Nation, Royal Priesthood, People of God, Household of Faith, Family of God, etc. All of these have to be taken into account in a full exposition, for they all modify and qualify each other, and it is only

[1] Address given to the Theological Colleges Union, November, 1956, at New College, Edinburgh; published in *The Ecumenical Review*, October, 1958.

in the whole rich complex of meaning which they provide that we can understand the Church in all its dimensions. But I believe that the most significant of them is this expression, the Body of Christ, because it is more inclusive than any of the others, provided that we understand it aright. But let it be said right away that this is not a term to be understood and expounded in biological language as "organism". The New Testament does use some biological language in speaking about it, but at those very points it deliberately uses language that is unnatural and un-biological, as when St. Paul speaks of the Body as growing from the head as well as into the head, and when he balances it with the image of the building which contrary to normal procedure is built down from the coping stone. It is only when we allow the other analogies and images to play their part in opening up and enriching this concept of the Body that it can serve its purpose in declaring the nature of the Church.

But this analogy is of primary importance also because it is the most deeply Christological of them all, and refers us directly to Christ Himself the Head and Saviour of the Body. That is apparent from our Lord's words at the inauguration of the New Covenant on the night in which He was betrayed. "This is my body which is broken for you". It is that Holy Covenant which binds the people of God so closely together with Christ that He makes them His own Body, giving them to feed upon Him, to eat His Body and drink His Blood, and to have union and communion with Him. The term "Body" is of particular importance because it can be applied to Christ and to His Church. That is not true of all the images. It is true of the word "Temple" and of the word "Vine", but perhaps not in the sense that the Church is the Vinestock. It is true of the word "Israel", for it is Christ who is Israel, and yet the Church is the Israel of God, but none of these words would be appropriate substitutes for the word "Body" at the Holy Supper. It is the Body that is broken and distributed and eaten, not the Vine, nor the Temple, nor Israel. When we look at some of the other images, they also prove to be narrower than "Body" and not so rich in Christological application. Christ is not the Bride, nor is He the Flock, for example, so that these images are the poorer because they cannot be applied both to

Christ and to His Church, and yet they are not for that reason unimportant. It is the term "Body" that seems to gather up most richly the fulness of relationship to Christ, provided that we do not use it merely figuratively or in too restricted a sense, but use it with the depth and fluidity that the New Testament uses.

But the word "Body" is most important, for in the expression "the Body of Christ" it directs us at once to Christ Himself in such a way that we have to lay the emphasis upon "of Christ" and not upon "Body". That is most important, for immediately we begin to spend much time and effort in thinking about the Church, somehow the Church tends to come in between us and Christ the Lord and that is just what the New Testament never does. The advantage of this expression is that it does not focus our attention upon the Church as a sociological or anthropological magnitude, nor upon the Church as an institution or a process, but upon the Church as the immediate property of Christ which He has made His very own and gathered into the most intimate relation with Himself. It also reminds us that the Church is *only* the Body of which He is the Head, and is therefore to be subject to Him in everything. That is what we need to learn again to-day, with or without emphatic use of this expression; that when we think of the Church our eyes must travel at once to Christ the Lord Himself, for it is He who is the essence of the Church. It is only in Him that the Church is Church, only in Him that it coheres and has its principle of being and unity, and only in and through Him does it have its function and mission in the Gospel.

Christ is Himself the essence of the Church, its *Esse*. That fact immediately relativizes and makes ultimately unimportant the endless and tiresome discussions about what is of the *esse* or the *bene esse* or the *plene esse* of the Church. "I am Jesus whom thou persecutest", said Jesus to Saul of Tarsus. "That Church you are persecuting is ME. I am the Church. The Church is My Body"—so St. Paul understood the words of Jesus and they became determinative and normative for him ever afterwards. That is the place to begin in our understanding of the nature of the Church, and in all discussions with one another regarding reunion, for it must be reunion only in Christ, in His Body, in obedient subjection to His Headship and Lordship over the

Body. But if we begin here the words of Jesus, "I am Jesus whom thou persecutest", have another reference. If we make them milder we can see that reference at once: "I am Jesus whom thou criticizest". In discussions with one another we must be prepared to discern the Body of Christ in one another, for it is into that Body that we have been baptized, but Baptism is rather the sign and seal that Christ in His grace and mercy has been pleased to gather us into Covenant-union with Him as members of His Body and therefore as members of one another. As we each look out from our own Church upon the other and are tempted to criticize it, perhaps even to call in question its doctrine or orders, do we not hear Jesus saying to us, "I am that Church you are criticizing; in criticizing it you are criticizing Me, for in spite of all its faults and weaknesses I have identified Myself with it and made it My very own Body."

It was part of the sin and schism of the Church in Corinth that they ate the Lord's Supper in division and failed to discern the Lord's Body in it and surely in one another, and so ate and drank very unworthily. But if we see the reference of these words, "I am Jesus whom thou criticizest" to the other Church and allow ourselves to overhear them as in that Church the bread is broken and the wine is poured out in the communion of the Body and Blood of Christ, surely our whole attitude will be different and the spirit in which we regard that Church will be one which is mastered and hallowed by the Spirit of Christ Jesus Himself. If we ourselves are in Christ, how can we fail to discern His Body in others whom He is pleased to call His own and whose celebrations of the Sacrament He is pleased to honour with His own real Presence and Spirit? If we fail to discern it in others the first question we must ask is whether we have ourselves learned to regard the Church as Christ's very own Body, as the Body of which HE is the Head and Lord and Saviour and Husband. Thus we must learn to make the Christological reference paramount in all our thinking and understanding of the Church, and at no point allow anything in the Church to obscure Christ Himself, to stand in His way, to set Him aside, or to subordinate Him to another interest or end, even momentarily. Christ clothed with His Gospel is the essence of the Church. There is no Church except that which participates and lives in Him and loves and obeys Him.

We are now in a position to enunciate two propositions about the Church as the Body of Christ.

(1) *Christ is the Church*, for the Church is Church only in Him. Christ the incarnate Son of God is the Church because He embodied Himself in our humanity and as such gathered our humanity in Him into oneness with God. He identified Himself with us, made Himself one with us, and on that ground claims us as His own, lays hold of us, and assumes us into union and communion with Him, so that as Church we find our essential being and life not in ourselves but in Him alone. Christ is the Church, but that proposition cannot be reversed, so as to make Christ the predicate of the Church, the predicate of its being and existence. Nothing could be further from the truth than that; and nothing could turn the whole Gospel upside down so quickly or so radically as to assert that the Church is Christ. That is partly why it is really so very wrong theologically to speak of the Church as the extension of the Incarnation as if it could be the prolongation of Christ Himself. That Christ is the Church means that He is also the Head and Lord of the Church, and that the Church is only His servant and yet—and this is His amazing grace—His friend and dear partner upon whom He freely bestows His own royal inheritance as the Son of God.

(2) *The Church participates in Christ* and draws its life and nature from Him, sharing in all He has done for it and sharing in His very life as the Son of the Father in the communion of the Holy Spirit. Everything that the Church is as Church it owes to Christ and derives from His grace, so that everything that it does or says or thinks must be in the Name of Christ and to His honour and glory alone. It is only through participating and sharing in Christ that the Church is to be regarded as His Body, as His image and likeness among men, as the expression of His love and truth, as the reflection of His humility and glory, as the instrument of His Gospel, as the earthen vessel that holds His heavenly treasure and holds it forth for all men to share freely. Only on the ground of this participation in Christ Himself is the Church a community of believers, a communion of love, a fellowship of reconciliation on earth.

We must therefore speak of the Church with a double reference to participation or communion in Christ; one which we may describe as vertical, and one which we may describe as horizontal. It is only through vertical participation in Christ that the Church is horizontally a communion of love, a fellowship of reconciliation, a community of the redeemed. Both these belong together in the fulness of Christ. It is only as we share in Christ Himself, that we share in the life of the Church, but it is only as we share with all saints in their relation to Christ that we participate deeply in the love and knowledge of God. Participation is a conjoint participation, a participation-in-communion, but the communion is above all a communion-in-participation in Christ.

We must consider that more fully.

(1) The Church in its *vertical* dimension. The New Testament word *koinonia* refers primarily to our participation in Christ, and only secondarily to our communion with one another in Christ. Primarily it refers to our union with Jesus Christ, and to such a union that the Church is one body (*synsoma*) with Him, and as such is conform (*symmorphon*) to Him. This Church that is the Body of Christ reflects in itself the nature of Christ Himself, for it shares in His New Humanity. Christ Himself is one Person in whom two natures, the divine and human, are united in such a way that they cannot be separated from one another, converted into one another, or confused with one another. The divine and human natures remain distinct but united in the One Person of the Son. The Church which participates in Christ and is "conform" to Him reflects that in its own relationship with Christ—but there is here a fundamental difference. The union between the divine and human natures in Christ is what we call hypostatic, for they are united in the one *hypostasis* or person of the Son; it is therefore a "personal union" in the sense that the two natures are united in One Person, and have their *hypostasis* or subsistence in that *One Person alone*. But that is not a "personal union" of the kind which we know, for example, in marriage where two persons are one flesh, but are one only in a union between *two persons*. We have personal union with Christ, but our personal union with Him is deeper and profounder by far than that which even a husband and wife have with one another, for in our personal

union we share in the Humanity of Christ which in Him is united to His Deity. It is in that way that we are surely to understand the New Testament word about our being "partakers of the divine nature". This does not mean that the Church has a human nature and a divine nature in the same way that Christ has, but that as in Christ the divine nature and the human nature are hypostatically united in one Person without separation and without confusion, so in a parallel way and on another level the Church is united to Christ through a personal relation of communion (*koinonia*) in which Christ and His Church are neither to be separated from one another nor to be confused with one another.

Moreover, in Jesus Christ the union between the human nature and the divine nature is a union brought about only by the amazing condescension of the Son of God who freely and out of pure grace assumed human nature into oneness with Himself, so that apart from that amazing act of grace there would have been no Jesus. Jesus was not an independently existing human being adopted to be the Son of God, but Jesus as Man came into being only with the act of the Incarnation. But there is a parallel to that also in the relation of the Church to Christ. The Church owes its existence as Church solely to the gracious act of Christ in condescending to identify Himself with it, and to assume it freely and very wonderfully into union with Himself, giving it to share in His life and love, and through Him to be a communion of people who are adopted into co-sonship with Christ, and are therefore by grace sons of the heavenly Father. The whole life and being of the Church depends entirely upon the gracious decision of Christ to be our Saviour, to gather us into union and communion with Himself and to form us into one Body by sharing in One Spirit and having One Baptism and One Faith in Him, so that we have one God and Father who is Lord of all.

The Church is united or affianced to Christ in His New Covenant and lives its life within the faithfulness of Christ who has laid hold upon the Church in His love and who will not let it go. Jesus Christ will not divorce His Church; even if she becomes unfaithful to Him, He will remain faithful and will bring her at last to perfect purity and holiness, presenting her to Himself as a chaste virgin, as St. Paul put it in his letter to the Ephesians. The Church is distinct from Christ and must never, never be confounded with Christ; it must never try to usurp His place and give itself out to be another Christ (*alter Christus*), and so stand between men and Christ arrogating to itself what belongs to Christ alone. The Church is only the Body of Christ, an alien body graciously assumed by Him into unity with Himself, but it remains other than He, a purely human Church, a communion of human believers who are marvellously given to share in His divine Life and Love because He loved the Church, gave Himself for it on the Cross, bought it with His own Blood and appropriated it to Himself as His own. But just because He has brought the Church into such union and communion with Him through the New Covenant in His Body and Blood, He remains faithful and will not break His Covenant. Once and for all He has accomplished the work of His atoning love, and nothing can undo it. How can God go back on the death of His dear Son? There is nothing that can now separate us from the love of God in Christ Jesus. Jesus Christ will never divorce His Church, and therefore the Church cannot be separated from Him.

That does not mean that the Church is perfect and without sin among its members or even in its corporate earthly life. The Church is a body of sinners who have been redeemed and justified by Christ, who have been washed and sanctified and have been given to share in Christ's own Self-sanctification on their behalf. In that sense the Church is perfect and sinless, because justified and holy. That is not just a legal or forensic declaration; it does not simply mean that the sins of the Church are not imputed to it. It does mean all that, but it means more than that. When Jesus Christ declares that our sins are forgiven, they *are* actually forgiven; He has put them completely behind His back, and forgotten them. When Christ has forgotten them, they *are* forgotten, and no one can resurrect them and bring them against us in order to accuse us. Who shall lay anything to the charge of God's elect? It is Christ that died, yea rather that is risen again! He was raised for our justification, and in His resurrection the Church has already been given to participate in His Humanity, in the perfection of the New Creation. But the Church on earth is still the pilgrim people, composed of men and women who are sinners, saved by grace and forgiven and cleansed, as their Baptism testifies, and as Holy Communion reaffirms, but they still wait for the redemption of the body, for the day when Christ will change the body of their humiliation and made it like unto His glorious Body, as Paul put it. The Church on earth as a whole, as a corporate unit, cannot dissociate itself from the sinners who make up its membership or reckon itself untarnished by their sin and so separate itself from them. The Church does not stand on the side of the Redeemer who died and rose again for all men, but stands on the side of these for whom Christ died, who come under the total judgment of the Cross and who are called to deny themselves and take up the Cross and follow Christ. But it is precisely because the Church stands in the sinful world (which God loved in spite of its sin) and shares in its guilt, that the Cross is its salvation, its hallowing and sanctifying, and its cleansing. It is only sinners who need the Saviour and are forgiven. It is because the Church continues to need the Saviour that it is given the Sacrament of Holy Communion and is commanded to celebrate it frequently, and is commanded to take upon its unclean lips daily the words: "Forgive us our trespasses as we forgive them that trespass against us", for in that way the Church partakes daily of the divine forgiveness freely granted to sinners through the mediation of Christ.

It is the two Sacraments of the Gospel which enshrine so marvellously this twofold fact, that the Church is forgiven and wholly justified, and yet daily needs cleansing and forgiveness. The Sacrament of Baptism declares that the Church has once and for all been cleansed and justified and made perfect in Christ, but Holy Communion declares that the Church needs daily to be cleansed, to have its feet washed, as it were, as Jesus so dramatically showed at the Last Supper, and that as often as the Church has communion in the Body and Blood of the Saviour so often is it renewed in its cleansing and sanctification through participation in Christ and His Self-sanctification on its behalf. It is there too that the Church which has been incorporated into Christ once and for all through His incarnation and atonement, of which Baptism is the sign and seal, is ever renewed in its membership of Christ as His Body, so that the Supper sets forth the fact that He reckons the Church to be bone of His bone and flesh of His flesh, and as such He presents it before the Face of the Father in His own Self-oblation on its behalf. It is only by taking shelter in His Name, and only through continuous renewal in the mediation of Christ, through taking refuge in His advocacy of it, that the Church can draw near to God and find grace and favour in His sight and a very present help in its need.

We can expound this in another way, by speaking of the Church as the Body of the crucified, risen, ascended, and advent Christ. Certainly we cannot do justice to what the New Testament has to tell us about the Church unless we think of it in this manifold relation to Christ. The Church is the Body of the crucified Christ—that is, it is "the body of sin", and "the body of death" which He assumed from us when He incorporated Himself into our mortal humanity and was "made in the likeness of the flesh of sin" in order that He might condemn sin in our flesh, submit our fallen humanity to the divine judgment on the Cross, and so make expiation for our sin and guilt by bearing it all vicariously in the sacrifice of Himself, He the Just for the unjust, that we might be made righteous in Him. As often as the Church celebrates Holy Communion it remembers that Christ identified Himself in utter solidarity with it in its body of sin and death, and broke His Body and shed His Blood to cleanse and heal the Church, that is, all people who take refuge in His Name and receive Him as Lord and Saviour.

But this Church is also the body of the risen Christ—that is, "the spiritual body" of Him who rose again on our behalf, and in whom we are already risen. The ancient fathers, and following them Luther and Calvin, used to describe this by using the analogy of physical birth. A baby is born head first, so that when once the head is born the whole body inevitably follows. Similarly, Christ the Head of the Church has already risen from the dead, the First-born of the New Creation, and therefore the Church which is His Body will surely and certainly follow Him in the resurrection. He has gone before and opened up the Kingdom for all believers, and therefore the Church that is united to Christ has in His resurrection both the first-fruit and the pledge of its own resurrection. In a real sense the Church is already risen with Christ—in the Epistles to the

Ephesians and Colossians that is put in the past tense, for it is already an accomplished reality in Christ. The Church enters even now into that wonderful inheritance through the Spirit, and is therefore commanded to live as having died to the past and as having risen with Christ. The Church is even now the Body of the risen Christ, and therefore shares already in the risen Body of Christ. How much that has to say about the way in which the Church should regard its own history in this world, always shot through and through with sin, and handle its own tradition, especially practice and procedure in the past that have acquired the binding force of legal enactments! As the Body of the risen Lord the Church should triumphantly live "on top", above the sinful snares of its past mistakes, untrammelled by the downward drag of the past, yet gathering up its history and tradition in Christ to be used in the freedom and power of the resurrection. But too often the Church lives as though it were still bound hand and foot by the grave-clothes of the past, and were shut behind closed doors for fear of men.

The Church is the Body of the ascended Christ, the Body whose Head has withdrawn Himself from sight, and ascended to the right hand of God the Father Almighty, who from there pours out His Spirit upon the Church anointing it as His servant in history, and rules over the nations through the Word of the Gospel which He puts into its mouth. The ascension speaks in no uncertain terms of the distinction between the Church and Christ, and yet the gift of the Spirit declares in no uncertain terms that Christ refuses to be separated from His Church. The ascension also does two other things. It points the Church back to the historical Jesus; for the risen Christ has withdrawn His present glory from view, that the eyes of the Church may be directed back to the Babe of Bethlehem, the Shepherd of the lost sheep, the Physician of the needy and the Man of Calvary who gave His life a ransom for many. That is the place where the risen and ascended Lord chooses to meet His Church and to keep Covenant with it, in the historical Jesus crucified for the world's salvation. But the ascension also directs the eyes of the Church forward to the day when Christ will keep His promise and return to judge the quick and the dead and reign in glory.

The Church is thus also the Body of the advent Christ, and

as such is directed to look ahead, beyond all history, to find the fulness of its life in the coming Lord and in the unveiling of the new creation. He will come again as Judge, and judgment will begin at the House of God, i.e. with the Church. Therefore the Church is summoned to cast itself under His judgment, to bring all that it has done and failed to do before God in humble confession that it may be cleansed and forgiven, and all its wrong may be put away. The Church is also summoned to cast all its hope upon the advent of Christ, for He will come not only to judge the quick and the dead but to renew His creation and to present the Church to Himself at last as a pure and spotless bride. It is the advent which reminds the Church that although it is already one Body with Christ through the Spirit, it has yet to be made one Body with Him in the consummation of His Kingdom. Until then the Church is the Bride of Christ waiting for the great Marriage Supper of the Lamb, and can only live in that expectation and hope. When that takes place, much that belongs to the life of the Church in history will be done away, not only its sinful past and the pattern of its life in the world determined by it, not only its adulterations of the faith, but even the institutional ministry which, God-given as it is, is but the scaffolding of the Habitation of God which is being built up in the time of mission and waiting. Then too there will be no need of Bible or Sacrament, for the Word and the Lamb Himself will be in the midst of His Church, and He will be its Light and Glory, and His servants shall serve Him day and night. The Church that lives in that advent expectation will not take less seriously the divinely-given provision for its earthly pilgrimage, "the ministry and the oracles and the ordinances of the New Covenant", but it will use them as they should be used by the Body of the crucified, risen, ascended and advent Christ, altogether and only to His glory.

(2) The Church in its *horizontal* dimension. The New Testament word *koinonia* refers also to the communion and fellowship which we have with one another as well as to our participation in Christ; it is a conjoint participation in Christ and therefore a corporate fellowship in Him which we have on earth. We have already had to refer to this horizontal communion of the Church in history just because it is inseparable from the Incarnation and from communion with the risen and heavenly

Lord. All through its history the fellowship of the Church on earth is only maintained as the Church participates in the fellowship of heaven as well as of earth, i.e. in the great communion of saints, the whole company of heaven and earth of all who are named with the Name of Christ. At no point in their earthly pilgrimage can the pilgrim people think of their life apart from the fellowship of that unseen host, or think of their mission as the Church Militant apart from unbroken communion with the Church triumphant. The Church that is sent out into history to struggle with evil, to proclaim the Gospel, to work and suffer, is the worshipping Church, the Church that ever draws near to God and enters through the veil by the new and living way that has been opened up in the flesh of Jesus Christ its High Priest and Mediator. Just as He Himself when on earth constantly withdrew for His seasons of prayer, and was ever found in His Father's House, and fulfilled His mission of obedience as He was strengthened by the ministry of angels, so the Church is the Temple of the Spirit, the Habitation of God, the Royal Priesthood, where prayer is made, where adoration and praise are continually offered, the sanctuary of God on earth where Christ dwells through His Spirit, and where there is a great ladder spanning heaven and earth (the presence of the Son of Man) upon which ascend and descend the angels of God. It is here then that we come to "Mount Zion, and unto the city of the living God, the heavenly Jerusalem, and to innumerable hosts of angels, to the general assembly and church of the first-born who are enrolled in heaven, and to God the Judge of all, and to the spirits of just men made perfect, and to Jesus the mediator of a new covenant, and to the blood of sprinkling that speaketh better things than that of Abel." It is in that perspective and in the light of that communion that we must consider the Church in its horizontal dimension in history.

This Church is a communion of love. It represents that area within humanity where the love of God is poured out by the Holy Spirit and where men and women are given to share together in their life on earth, and within the social cohesions of humanity, in the overflow of the divine Life. That is remarkably set forth in the early chapters of the Acts, where the Christian community translated this love into a communal sharing of their possessions in a way that reminds us outwardly of the Jewish "Community of the new covenant" at Qumran, although in reality it is very different. In the Christian Church there dwells the personal presence of Jesus Christ and it is His love that masters the community and binds them into unity. This love was such a new and masterful thing, divine love in its overflow into the lives of men, that a rare word had to be used to describe it—*agapé*. It was in such *agapé*-love that the early Church shared the bread and wine of the Covenant and celebrated communion in the Body and Blood of Christ. It was through constant communication with Christ the Fountain of *agapé*-love in this way that the flow of love continued and inundated all their living and doing. That is what is meant by the Body of Christ on earth. This is one of the places where the word "body" has to be enlarged and filled out and made to refer not to an exclusive coterie of the few but to an ever-widening communion in which the Body (*soma*) presses out in expansion toward a fulness (*pleroma*) in the love of God in all its height and depth and length and breadth which more and more gathers into itself men and women from the ends of the earth.

As such the Church is also a fellowship of reconciliation, not only a fellowship of those who have been reconciled to God in Christ and those who have therefore been reconciled with one another, but a fellowship sent out into the world in order to bring healing and reconciliation to the great multitudes who are alienated from God and divided from one another in estrangement and conflict. God has made the world to contain a wonderful and manifold diversity of life and form, so that every family has its own distinctiveness and richness, and every race and society its peculiar character. That diversity in creation is expressed also throughout the whole life of the Church. But the sin that entered into God's creation, has entrenched itself in the diversities of nature; it has corrupted them and suborned them to serve its own malignant purpose of division and destruction in God's creation. It was into that world alienated from God and divided and torn within itself that God sent His Beloved Son to take upon Himself the conflict of sin against God and His creation, to draw its contradiction upon Himself and in the fraction of His own Body to overcome the divisive power of sin, and so to provide healing for mankind, reconciling man to God and man to man in Himself. And Jesus Christ has sent His Church out among the nations to be a fellowship of reconciliation, bearing the divine Word of reconciliation to all men, and bringing healing to it in all its conflict and strife. That is what the Church is meant to be as the Body of Christ, a community of reconciliation bringing to men the healing of the Cross, and living out in their midst the reconciled life, drawing them into its own fellowship of peace with God and with all men.

The tragedy is that the Church has allowed the same sin that divides and destroys God's creation to invade its own fellowship and to disrupt it, creating division where there should be unity, discord where God gave healing and concord. In this way, as Professor Skydsgaard has recently pointed out, the Church has come to live in disagreement with its own innermost nature and purpose. Where it is sent to proclaim reconciliation and to live that reconciliation out in a communion of love and faith in the One Lord, it presents to the world a divided Church, and thus resists and misrepresents the very Gospel which it is sent to proclaim and which it is called to live out in the world. Were it not that God in His great mercy refuses to be baffled and dismayed, but still makes use of His Church in spite of the fact that it has so tragically sabotaged itself as an instrument for peace and love in His hands, the world would surely tumble to pieces in self-destruction. God who made the Cross to serve His redeeming purpose of love, by that same Cross is able to make even the wrath of man to praise Him. Because His mercy is greater than our unfaithfulness, His grace reigns and abounds over our sinful divisions, so that He continues to call men and women to Himself and give them the shelter of His wings and the confidence of His love—but that is no reason why the Church should continue in the sin of division, that grace may abound.

The Church that partakes of Holy Communion seeks to be renewed in it as a fellowship of reconciliation, but for that very reason it must be prepared to act out that which it receives at the Holy Table, and to live the reconciled life refusing to allow the sinful divisions of the world to have any place in its own life. The Church that nourishes its life on earth by feeding upon the

Body and Blood of Christ must live out in its own bodily existence the union and communion in which it participates in Christ. Holy Communion by its own innermost nature and by its whole intention and purpose requires the Church to work hard to eliminate its division, to resolve to seek reconciliation with all from whom it is estranged. It is just because unity is God-given that the Church cannot throw it down in the dust or allow it to be trampled upon but must cultivate it as a holy gift and as of the very essence of its salvation in Christ. The Church that allows itself to be divided thereby allows also its relation with Christ to be menaced and called into question. The divisions in the Church thus attack the Church's participation in reconciliation and threaten to snap the life-line between it and God Himself. How can the Church be the Church and not be the Church? How can it be the Church and not be a Fellowship of Reconciliation? How can it be the Body of Christ and be divided, because Christ is not divided? These are serious questions that the Holy Spirit is putting to the Churches in our day, and we have to give Him an account not in words only but in obedient acts of reconciliation.

It belongs to the function of the Church, then, to enter into history in the service of reconciliation, to live out its divine life in the midst of the world's dividedness, and by living as well as witnessing, to bring men into the fellowship of healing and peace with God. In that service, resolutely and deeply performed, the Church will suffer. It is sent to suffer, because it is sent to take up the Cross and follow in the steps of the Suffering Servant, not in order to be a co-redeemer with Christ (how could it do that?), but to identify itself with the world in its guilt and to bear it up in prayer and intercession before God, and in sympathy and compassion born of the overflowing love of God in Christ, to spend itself in the service of the Gospel until all men are confronted with the Saviour, and all nations and peoples are brought within the active reign of Christ clothed with His Gospel of reconciling grace. One day this Church will have to give an account at the judgment seat of Christ of how it has employed its gifts and undertaken its mission—that is why those seven letters to the seven Churches are recorded in the Apocalypse, that the Church may take heed, put its house in order, and be obedient to its Lord who already knocks at the door and waits to lift the latch and celebrate the final repast of communion with those who are His own.

But this Church is more than a servant, more than a fellowship of reconciliation; it is already the community that shares in the new creation and tastes the powers of the age to come. As such the Church on earth and in history is the provisional manifestation God has given to mankind of the new creation which will be revealed when Christ comes again. As the society of the redeemed it is already the New Jerusalem, the City of God in the midst of the Babylons of this earth; it is already the Kingdom of Christ in the midst of the kingdoms of this world, and therefore it is engaged in the great apocalyptic strife between the Kingdom of Light and the kingdom of darkness. It is not about that apocalyptic strife that we are concerned at the moment, but about the fact that right in the midst of the chaos and disorder of this world, right in the midst of its tensions and conflicts, right in the midst of all the cosmic patterns of its life that are schematized to sin and selfishness, God is at work in the Church manifesting His ultimate purpose, the order of the new creation in Christ Jesus, the community of love, the Body of Christ. No doubt the true visage of the Church is marred and mutilated sometimes beyond all recognition, not only because it suffers for its witness but also because it resists its true calling. Nevertheless, because it is the community where the faithfulness of God in Christ is both manifested and actualized, it is the one place on earth and throughout history where the Covenanted Communion of men and women with God points beyond to the eternal City and the New Heaven and the New earth. It is in the Church that the voice of the Good Shepherd is to be heard, and there too those who hear His voice can discern His Face. It is thus that the Church takes on the lineaments of the Kingdom of Heaven, and points a way ahead through all history to the great Consummation when even faith and hope will pass away but love will endure as the abiding reality of the Church in the life of God, when that which is in part shall pass away, and we shall see our Lord face to face and know Him as we are known. Until that day comes the Church exists and lives among men as the "fellowship of the mystery of Christ", where even though as yet we see only through a glass darkly, we do see the Lord nevertheless, and long for the day when we shall so see Him as to be wholly like Him.

There are two ways in which a minister can look at his congregation. He can look at it in the light of all that he has sought to set before it in the teaching of the Word of God, in the grace of the Gospel, and he cannot but be heavy at heart again and again when he sees how much he and his congregation fall short of the Will of their Lord. Then he may seek to draw some comfort from those who have heeded the Gospel, the converted or the reborn, the changed who have allowed their profession of faith to alter their lives, and who witness by deed as well as by word. But he can also look upon them as God's little ones, poor halting human beings, frail in their grasp of God, hesitating in their faithfulness, but who in spite of all cast themselves at the feet of the Lord and come humbly to the Table to take in their hands the pledges of the divine faithfulness. If the minister looks with the eyes of His Lord upon them He will surely discern the very Body of Christ among them, for it was for such that Jesus Christ came to give His life a ransom; it was such and still is such that He gathers round Him, freely bestowing upon them His love and even His Name and reckoning them as His very own. At last when He comes again He will take away the veil of their sin and shame and reveal the new creation which He has been fashioning out of their lives, and they will be astonished that He has been able to make something so wonderful out of such poor clay as we faithless human beings present to Him. That is not to say that He will not reject some and cast them into outer darkness, for all that Jesus has told us of the Last Day reveals that there will be a final judgment and a final division between the children of light and the children of darkness. But His parables reveal that when He calls us to account His judgments will take us by surprise; it is that element of surprise, as Professor J. S. Stewart has said, which means that His judgments will be justifications by grace alone, not according to our works, but according to the abundance of His atoning love.

Will that not be the way in which the Great Shepherd of the sheep will regard His flock, when at last He comes to divide the sheep from the goats? Happy then the Church, however poor and needy, that has learned to cast itself entirely upon His mercy and judgment, and woe to that Church that persists to the end in justifying itself by its own claims or orders or orthodoxy or good deeds, and in living in disagreement with His merciful love or in contradiction to His reconciliation. The Last Judgment will force the Churches to be what they have always been, fellowships of reconciliation and communions of love living only by the grace of God, or sources of division and estrangement and bitterness living upon their own tradition and pride.

(b) *Intercommunion and the Union of the Church*[1]

I believe that in the move toward the reunion of the Churches we have still to give much fuller consideration to the place of Intercommunion than we have done so far, and that we can do so because of the decisive change in our ecumenical conversation that took place at the World Conference of Faith and Order at Lund. It was hoped by many that at Lund itself the question of Intercommunion would have received profounder treatment and that serious steps toward Intercommunion between the Churches could then have been envisaged. At first sight those hopes were dashed at Lund, for the promise of progress at this point was not fulfilled—and that had an unfortunate repercussion upon the Evanston Assembly of the World Council of Churches where the whole question of Intercommunion fell almost entirely out of the picture. And where that happens it is difficult to see that there has been a serious engagement with the problem of reunion or a deep appreciation of the scandal and agony of division so manifest in disunion at the Lord's Supper.

But the situation is rather better than that, for what took place both at Lund and at Evanston enables us to grapple with the question of Intercommunion in a profounder way than was apparently possible before Lund. At Lund we found we could not profitably go much farther along the road of understanding

[1] Lecture delivered to the Faculty of Theology, Heidelberg University, July, 1956; German text published in *Kerygma und Dogma*, July, 1957, pp. 240–50. See *Relations between Anglican and Presbyterian Churches* (Edinburgh St. Andrew Press; London, S.P.C.K., May, 1957). It was out of the discussions which preceded this Report that this lecture was originally written. To earlier drafts I am particularly indebted on pp. 126 f. and 131 f.

and *rapprochement* by careful comparison of our diverse traditions and frank discussion of our differences. A new way was sought, which can be expressed thus: "Our major differences concern the doctrine of the Church, but let us penetrate behind the divisions of the Church on earth to our common faith in the one Lord. Let us start from the central fact that Jesus Christ loved the Church and gave Himself for it, and by His Spirit made it His own Body. From the oneness of Christ we will try to understand the unity of the Church in Him, and from the unity of Christ and His Body we will seek a means of realizing that unity in the actual state of our divisions on earth." At Evanston we found ourselves led to acknowledge before the face of our given unity in Christ the sinful nature of division both because division calls in question the Oneness of Christ and because it obscures from men the sufficiency of Christ's atonement, inasmuch as the Gospel of reconciliation is denied in the very lives of those who proclaim it. We must cast ourselves, therefore, at the foot of the Cross in repentance for the sin of division, and because the Cross tells us that where the dividing power of sin is most manifest there God has gained the victory, we must plant the Cross in the midst of our divisions praying that God will both heal us of our divisions and overrule their sin, even making them to serve His purpose of unity.

Those forward steps taken at Lund and Evanston, far from taking us away from the question of Intercommunion, bring us face to face with it in a new way, for it is precisely in Holy Communion that we have to do with the centrality of Christ and His atonement directed to the faith and order of the Church. It is there in our participation in the Body and Blood of Christ that the reconciling Cross is applied to our sin and division and we are given to share anew in the one Body of the one Lord. And it is from Holy Communion that we are sent forth to proclaim reconciliation to all men and to live it out in Church and world until He comes again. How can we do that without unity in the ordering of the Lord's Table, and without unity in the Mission of reconciliation? Because it is above all in Holy Communion that faith and order, *doctrina* and *disciplina* are brought together, in Holy Communion also faith in the one Lord requires of us reconciliation in the ordering of the life of faith, and the doctrine of Christ and of the Church as His Body requires of us a Christological correction of unnecessary divergence and an essential measure of assimilation in discipline. It is in seeking Intercommunion that these doctrinal and spiritual requirements in order and practice become most apparent, and it is through a sincere engagement in Intercommunion and in acting it out in our Churches that the appropriate measures of reconciliation in order and practice are to be undertaken.

Let me now discuss this with reference to the two Churches which I know best, the Church of England and the Church of Scotland. Both these Churches would like to have full Intercommunion, involving fully authorized interchange of communicants and of ministries between the two Churches, but each Church looks upon Holy Communion and therefore upon Intercommunion in a somewhat different way. As I see it, the Church of England thinks of the Lord's Supper as expressing the prior unity of the Church as well as renewing us in that unity. It is not a rite that stands alone as if by itself it were a bond of unity. The Eucharist reposes upon a prior unity and is set in the midst of an institutional continuity and cannot be abstracted from that continuity and unity. The visible and efficacious sign of that continuity and unity is the historic episcopate, and so Anglicans would normally refuse to celebrate the Lord's Supper outside its jurisdiction. In their case, therefore, *full* Intercommunion would be impossible without raising the question of episcopacy as a thing deemed requisite for the fulfilment of Intercommunion between Churches. It would probably be unfair to say of the Church of England that for it the Lord's Supper is only relative to, and is subordinated to, a particular pattern of church order, but nevertheless it is true that *practically* the whole question of Intercommunion is subordinated to that of episcopacy. And yet even here certain limited measures of Intercommunion are deemed proper in the context of Ecumenical conversation and activity, which suggests that where unity is actively intended, the practice of Intercommunion is proper and relevant.

The Church of Scotland, on the other hand, is deeply conscious that Holy Communion is the Lord's Supper, and that He invites to it whom He will. Certainly the celebration of the Lord's Supper is ordered by the Church through its ministry and it is embedded in the institutional continuity of the Church, but by its very nature as the Sacrament of the Real Presence of Christ it ultimately stands above the institutional continuity of the Church and can never be made relative to it, for that would make the Church the master of Christ's presence and not Christ the Master of the Church. The Sacrament is the Lord's Supper and not a private rite, so that at the Sacrament all ecclesiastical authority must be subordinated to the Lord Himself who is really present in the midst ordering the Church through His Word and Spirit. Moreover, the Lord's Supper is the Sacrament of reconciliation bringing unity as well as expressing it. It expresses a prior unity given in Baptism through which we are incorporated into the Body of Christ, and it requires of us accordingly sincerity in faith and life. But it is effective as well as cognitive, healing us and renewing us in the unity of Christ. On the other hand, because Holy Communion is the Sacrament of reconciliation and unity full and unrestricted Intercommunion should not be entered upon without solemn resolve to achieve reconciliation and unity.

Thus although both Churches differ somewhat in the way they regard Holy Communion in relation to unity, both are faced with the same problem. On the one hand it is clear that they cannot go on proclaiming the Gospel of reconciliation without acting a lie against it by refusing to be reconciled to one another in the Communion of the Body and Blood of Christ. On the other hand it would be a dishonour to Christ for the two Churches to pretend together at the Lord's Table that they are one when they are not; and it would be difficult to consider formally instituting Intercommunion between the two Churches if they were to be content with Intercommunion alone and were to refuse to act out the deep implications of Intercommunion. To eat the Body and drink the Blood of Christ sincerely is to resolve to act out that Communion in the body; to engage in Intercommunion obliges the Churches to work out their reconciliation, seeking how unity in faith and order may be achieved between them.

In view of all this it would seem to me that the way toward reunion between two Churches, such as the Church of Scotland and the Church of England, would involve three undertakings:

(1) First of all the Churches concerned should declare

formally before God their solemn readiness to seek reconciliation or reunion, and their intention to find a means of realizing that in the life of the Churches. In view of such a willingness of the Churches to seek reconciliation the whole question of Intercommunion would be put on an entirely new basis; and it would be altogether proper, indeed a solemn duty, for such Churches to come together without restriction at the Lord's Table even before they had worked out fully in faith and order the essential details of unification. Within such Intercommunion and through the corresponding fellowship of the Churches for the work of the Gospel, mutual appreciation and understanding would increase, and different ways towards fuller agreement and indeed mutual assimilation would become increasingly clear.

(2) Following the procedure suggested at Lund, the Churches should penetrate behind their ecclesiastical divisions and behind their doctrinal differences in relation to the Church and the ministry, to their common faith in Jesus Christ. Then starting from the central doctrine of Christ and of the Church as His Body they should undertake together a Christological criticism of their differences in faith and order, particularly of the doctrines of the Church, ministry, and sacraments, seeking to act out their unity in Christ obediently in the ordering of their Churches and in their ministry of Word and Sacraments. In our time the great revival of biblical theology and the fresh understanding of the early Church has made this a very hopeful procedure by providing us with increasing agreement in the following points of doctrine (1957 *Report* pp. 17 f., 23):

(a) "The Church as the Body of Christ participates in His threefold ministry as Prophet, Priest, and King, by serving Him as Lord. Sent from God it is rightly described as apostolic not only in its faith, doctrine, and mission, but also in its order."

(b) "All ministry in the Church is to be interpreted as a ministry of Christ to the Church, that is from the Head to the Body as a whole"; and all ministry in the Church is to be exercised within the corporate priesthood of the whole Church.

(c) "Within this wider exercise of ministry there is the specific ministry of Word and Sacraments to which by ordination some are set apart. Among the functions of the ordained ministry is that of exercising *episcope* or oversight in the Church."

(d) Such *episcope*, far from being exclusively concerned with administration, involves these different aspects: "apostolic mission and authority, the pastoral office, the continuance of the ordained ministry through ordination, guardianship of truth and exclusion of error, representation of the Church in its unity and universality."

(e) "The unity and continuity of the Church includes the unity and continuity of the whole Body as baptismally incorporated into the royal priesthood of Christ, and the unity and continuity therein of the ministration of the Word and Sacraments as means of grace in the Church."

(3) Guided by this Christological understanding of the Church and its ministry, the Churches should then undertake to act out their Intercommunion in reconciliation with one another in essential matters of order and practice. It is altogether important that they should look beyond the divisions of history and beyond the *status quo* of each Church to the fulness of the Church in its life and ministry which is promised to it as the Body of Christ. No doubt the Churches would be constrained through mutual criticism and learning to seek a considerable measure of adaptation and assimilation to one another in the cause of reconciliation; but the appropriate changes in each Church should not be regarded as accommodations in different forms of church polity but as "the spiritual and doctrinal requirements in order and practice to which the Churches must give heed if they are to move forward in fuller participation in the true wholeness of the one Church of Christ." "In modifications of this kind each Church must fully respect the conscience of the other while seeking at the same time to urge the acceptance of all that it regards as essential in the form of the order and practice of the Church it has itself received. Moreover, each Church must allow the other a measure of freedom in interpreting the changes proposed and seek itself to interpret them not in accordance with the *status quo ante* in its own tradition but in accordance with the plentitude of faith and order in the enriched Church of the future." This whole movement forward in a Christological reordering of the Church and its ministry should be undertaken by both Churches together in a united waiting upon God, and in the acknowledgment that they depend for their justification

and efficacy not upon valid tradition and correct action, necessary as they may be, but upon the grace of God in Christ.

At this point we must pause to ask; How far is such a scheme for reunion, through Intercommunion and Christological re-ordering of the Church, possible between a Reformed and an Episcopal Church, such as the Church of Scotland and the Church of England? There should be no difficulty between the Church of Scotland and the Evangelical wing of the Church of England, for the Evangelical Anglicans subordinate the whole question of order, including the episcopate, to the Gospel. Their whole attitude to Intercommunion is much the same as that of the Church of Scotland, though they would naturally like to see Intercommunion sincerely accompanied by a suitable measure of mutual adaptation between the two Churches. For many High Church Anglicans, on the other hand, acceptance of the historic episcopate is a *sine qua non* of reconciliation and full Intercommunion; and they have so strong a voice in the Church of England that it would be impossible for the Church of England to act without them. But with the High Churchmen a new factor has entered into the situation, which they have taken over from the Reformed Church and which makes the future full of promise and hope. It is the conviction that doctrine and order cannot be separated from one another, and that order is essentially a *de fide* concern. Thus a true conception of the episcopate must cohere with the whole body of Christian truth, and a true form of the episcopate will manifest doctrinal truth. As long ago as Archbishop Laud, for example, we find these words:

> Most evident it is, that the "succession" which the Fathers meant, is not tied to place or person, but it is tied to verity of doctrine. So that if the doctrine be no kin to Christ, all the "succession" become strangers what nearness soever they pretend of.

It was shortly after the time of Laud that the High Church Party arose in England, which was regarded as "high" because it applied the Calvinist conception of discipline to the Anglican episcopate. It was, however, only with the Oxford Movement that there was any wide and profound attempt to advance a doctrinal justification of the historic episcopate; but then the doctrine deployed to account for the episcopate was drawn not from the coherent body of Anglican teaching but from a re-pristinated catholicism and romantic idealist philosophy. In our own day this is being radically changed by the growth of biblical theology and by a desire for biblical dogmatics, so that as Anglican understanding of the episcopate comes to be thought out afresh in integration with a truly biblical and dogmatic theology, there is every ground for increasing confidence in ecumenical understanding between the Church of Scotland and the Church of England.

To show that that is not a vain hope I would like now to discuss three points at which doctrine applied to order can result in changes which would enable the two Churches to enter into full communion with one another.

(1) If all members of the Church are through baptism incorporated into the royal priesthood of Christ, then laymen should be given full and appropriate participation in the government of the Church in fulfilment of the doctrinal requirement that decisions of the Church must be made by the whole Church, by the Body of Christ in its entirety. That is the theological truth which the Church of Scotland seeks to express through its eldership, so that elders join with presbyters equally in all the sacral courts of the Church. In the Church of England, however, lay persons have no place in the doctrinal and spiritual government of the Church, with the result that the clergy tend to be divorced from the people, and the spiritual continuity of the Church reposes upon the clergy alone and not upon the whole Church as the Body of Christ.

It would therefore be on important doctrinal grounds that the Church of Scotland would urge the Church of England to bring the laity fully into the life, work, and government of the Church that their membership of the Body of Christ requires. This might well be undertaken by the Church of England through a reform of the diaconate as a means of giving "order" within the Church to the services rendered by laymen. The office of deacon would thus be regarded not as a step toward the presbyterate as it is now, but as an office representing the participation of the laity in the ministry of the Church. As it would be the function of the presbyter to minister the Word and Sacraments, it would be the complementary function of the deacon to assist the congregation in its reception of the Word and Sacrament and in the appropriate responses in worship and life. Such a modification in the polity of the Church of England would bring a very great change in it, for by providing in this way a connecting link between the clergy and the people it would not only inhibit clericalism but enable the Church of England to achieve an independence in such spiritual things as the reform of its liturgy or the appointment of its bishops.

(2) If we start again from the fact that the Church is the Body of Christ corporately participating in His threefold ministry, then it is difficult to avoid the conclusion that the ministry within the Church must be given a fundamentally corporate expression. It is for this reason that in the Church of Scotland the episcopate is exercised corporately through the Presbytery. The Presbytery is regarded, in fact, as the "corporate episcopate". In the Church of England, on the other hand, there is the distinctive office of the bishop, the essence of which is the coalescence of certain functions in a single person. Although the Church of England can offer no theological reasons why the episcopate should devolve upon individuals only, it claims that the succession of bishops is the historic and ecumenical sign of the continuity and unity of the Church from the earliest times after the apostles. The great danger of this conception, so apparent in the Church of England since the Oxford Movement, is the tendency to isolate the episcopate from the corporate priesthood of the whole Church as if it were by itself a bond of unity and so to rest continuity upon it alone. Against this it would seem proper to repeat the argument Anglicans use regarding the Eucharist as a rite of unity. The episcopate may well express the unity and continuity of the Church, but it also reposes upon a prior unity in the whole Body of Christ and is set in the midst of a sacramental continuity, and cannot be abstracted from that and considered independently as if it had inherent authority in itself.

However, if some assimilation between the "historic episcopate" of the Church of England and the "corporate episcopate" of the Church of Scotland could take place, the "historic episcopate" would not only be preserved from these corruptions but be deepened and enriched through fuller integration with the corporate participation of the Church in the ministry of Christ; and the "corporate episcopate" of the Church of Scotland on its part would gain much in ecumenical recognition without losing its essential character. If such a mutual adaptation of presbytery and episcopate were only an accommodation in systems of polity, it is doubtful whether it would be possible or advisable; but where it could be undertaken in obedience to a Christological understanding of the Church and its ministry, it would not only represent a decided advance in ecumenical *rapprochement*, but would be the occasion for real growth toward the fulness of the Church.

(3) What does the Christological understanding of the Church have to say to us about the question of continuity or historical succession? If the Church as the Body of Christ is, as Karl Barth has put it, Christ's own *irdisch-geschichtliche Existenzform* (earthly-historical form of existence), and this Church is to remain ever the same Church, identical with itself in its apostolic foundation, historical continuity is a necessary and important element in the doctrine of the Church and ministry. Moreover such continuity is an essential ingredient in the unity of the Church, for the unity of the Church is not only concerned with space but with time—that is why genuine ecumenical discussions are also historico-dogmatic discussions.

I believe that in the ecumenical perspective we may restate the whole question of the apostolic succession, in this way.[1] The apostles were given a unique place in the inauguration of the New Covenant, and had a unique function in the formation of the New Testament Revelation and in transmitting it through authoritative witness to Jesus Christ. As such they were the master-builders who gave form and order to the Church which is built upon their foundation and which continues to be apostolic as it continues to be subject to the apostolic witness and tradition enshrined in the Holy Scriptures. In regard to the apostolic office and its unique functions there can be no succession, other than a succession of obedience to their testimony. But the ministry of the apostles included a pastoral shepherding of the flock of Christ, a leadership in the evangelical mission of the Church, and a ministry of Word and Sacraments in the congregation. Through apostolic institution this ministry

[1] See 1957 *Report*, p. 19 f.

was given a permanent form in the historical Church, so that from generation to generation other servants of Christ have successively been sent into this ministry and have exercised a pastoral and missionary ministry of the Word and Sacraments in subjection to the apostolic ordering of the Church and in obedience to the apostolic teaching. Thus when the risen and ascended Lord continues to give gifts of ministry to His Church on earth, He calls men into a ministry which He has already founded in and through the apostles, and which He uses as the instrument whereby He Himself, the King and Head, ever builds up the Church on earth as His Body, and rules and guides it by His Word and Spirit.

It is not difficult to see that in the Church as the earthly-historical *Existenzform* of the Body of Christ earthly and historical continuity in the ministry of the Word and Sacraments and in the pastoral responsibility for the Lord's household is an important element in the historical existence of the Church, and an essential part of the unity of the Church through time, helping to relate each generation to every other and above all to the foundation of the Church in the apostles and prophets. At the same time the Christological understanding of the Church teaches us that the being and reality of the Church, and therefore of the continuity of the Church as Church, are not to be found in the earthly-historical forms of the Church as such, but in Jesus Christ Himself who loved the Church and gave Himself for it, who graciously assumed it into oneness with Himself in the new Covenant and who by His quickening Spirit ever renews it as His Body. But because it is the earthly and historical Church that Christ graciously assumes into covenanted union with Himself and ever renews as His Body, the earthly-historical form of the Church's existence and life from one generation to the next is involved in the covenanted union between Christ and His Church and given, as it were, a sacramental function in pointing beyond itself to the continuous life of the Church in Christ and attesting the continuity of the Church in its apostolic foundation in the Lord. Within this, it is the orderly transmission of ministerial responsibility and authority from one generation to the next which, in reliance upon the promise of the Holy Spirit, duly attests and serves the transmission of the apostolic Gospel and doctrine in the Holy

Scriptures, together with the tradition of mission, of worship and of corporate obedience in the life of the historical Church. These together constitute in the Church what is generally called "the apostolic succession" and which is brought to a head in the succession of the ministry.

At this point it is supremely important to remember that the ministry is inseparably bound to what it ministers in the Word and Sacrament and cannot be regarded as having any independent validity in itself, apart from the Word and the Sacraments. Similarly pastoral stewardship over the Lord's Household cannot be abstracted from the apostolic revelation and foundation and considered independently as if it had inherent authority in itself. The continuing pastoral ministry has authority, but it is authority in the Word from which it derives and upon which it reposes. It is authority in subjection and in inseparable relation to the apostolic Word. Thus the historical devolution of the ministry of the Word and Sacraments and of pastoral responsibility cannot have more than the signification of a sign. It is because the historical succession points away from itself, signifying and attesting the real succession of the Church in Christ, that it cannot be employed by any Church, no matter how orderly and ecumenically acknowledged its ministry is, as a principle of justification. On the other hand, where the outward devolution of the ministry through a historical succession of ecclesiastical representatives serves and is controlled by the substance of the apostolic tradition, as enshrined in the Holy Scripture, it must never be treated lightly or condemned as unessential.

All this throws not a little light upon the nature of our divisions. Where the unity of the Church of Christ, at least in its earthly-historical *Existenzform*, has been broken, it would appear to be through infidelity to the wholeness of the apostolic succession, as described above, and through a separation between the outward devolution of the apostolic tradition and its inner substantive continuity. Sometimes the ministerial succession of the apostolic tradition has been maintained without the substance of the apostolic faith. Sometimes, on the other hand, the orderly ministerial succession has been broken in an effort to maintain continuity in the inner substance of the apostolic faith. Thus traditionally the Anglican Church has been more interested in, and concerned to defend, the outer form of the apostolic tradition than the real substance of it. And traditionally the Reformed Church has been more interested in, and concerned to defend, the inner substance of the apostolic tradition, and has therefore been interested in the outer form in its *de fide* character, that is, theologically, rather than in its historical and institutional character. But if the Anglican Church acknowledges that the function of the outward ministerial succession is to serve the substance of the apostolic Gospel, and if the Reformed Church acknowledges the mutual involution of faith and order, then it should not be at all impossible for these Churches to come together and, under the guidance of biblical theology and a Christological understanding of the Church, to find agreement even on the vexed question of historical succession in the Church and its ministry in a new and profounder understanding of the continuity of the Church as the Body of Christ.

(c) *A New Approach*[1]

Let it be said right away: this Report on Inter-Church Relations cannot be understood in the light of Presbyterian and Episcopalian controversies in the past. Those controversies were always in the last resort concerned about the questions of authority and freedom in the life and ministry and worship of the Church, and Scotland has consistently repudiated every conception and every scheme that detracts from the fact that Jesus Christ is the sole King and Head of the Church, and that under Christ the Church itself is the sole judge of its faith and order. The whole constitution of the Church of Scotland laid down in the *Declaratory Articles* and the Acts of Parliament relating to the relation of the Church to the State and to the Crown, make that indubitably clear. Thus the old controversies about authority and freedom about which we struggled in two long phases, over bishops invested with civil authority, and over patronage, are quite dead and are impossible to revive. It would be just as impossible to restore authoritarian bishops to the Church of Scotland as it would be to tear up the whole

[1] *The Presbyterian Record*, Toronto, July–Aug., 1957, pp. 19, 36–37; and *Biblical Theology*, Belfast, January, 1958.

constitution of Church and State. The Church of Scotland, by its very constitution, which is protected by the State, has full authority over its faith and order, and full power, subject to no civil authority, to determine matters of faith and order, to modify and add to its constitutional articles, in agreement with the Word of God and with the subordinate standards of the faith, while under the *Declaratory Acts* the Church subordinates its formal standards to the Word of God and retains full right to interpret and modify them always in agreement with the Word of God. Moreover, through the *Declaratory Articles*, the obligation to seek and promote union with other Churches is written into the Constitution of the Church of Scotland and lodged in the vows of ordination. This was recently reaffirmed and interpreted by the act of Assembly in *The Ecumenical Statement* of 1953 to make plain not only the full freedom of the Kirk but the spirit in which it sought to enter into closer relations with other Churches.

A Reformed Church must be a Church Reforming

This means that the Church of Scotland insists on being a Reformed Church, a true Reformed Church that always requires to be reformed from generation to generation according to the Word of God. Therefore the Church of Scotland refuses to allow its past tradition to become the sole master of its life, and so to hinder fresh obedience to the Word of God to-day. Accordingly, it renounces a "fundamentalist presbyterianism" that refuses to face the criticism of the Word of God and to face the truth revealed in objective scientific research into the history of the Church, and so insists on sticking to the "verbal inspiration" of seventeenth-century Presbyterianism. The Church that really lives by the Word of God and is ever being reformed into the image and likeness of Jesus Christ cannot be bound by the grave-clothes of the past, but must seek from age to age to subordinate its life and work, and the whole pattern of its mission and ministry to the content and control of the Gospel of Jesus Christ. It is only in this way that the Church of Scotland seeks reunion with other Churches, in entire subordination to the Gospel of reconciliation through the blood of Christ, and in joint obedience to His Word alone, as it is revealed in the Holy Scriptures.

Christological Character of this Report

By far the most important thing about the Report is its doctrinal section, and the fact that it is biblical doctrine alone that is allowed to be the determinative guide to all its suggestions for closer relations between the Churches concerned. And by "doctrine" is meant here above all the doctrine of Christ. That alone makes this Report utterly different from anything that has appeared before in past relations between the Church of Scotland and the Church of England, and sets the whole discussion on quite a new basis—*in Christ.* This immediately brings into the Report two revolutionary facts:

(a) The first concerns *the spirit of the Report*, in the insistence that all the relations of these Churches to one another *must be considered in Christ.* In Christ you do not look down on the other but look up to him; you acknowledge gladly that you are not perfect without him, but that you need him as well as he needs you, and that it is only together with him, and "with all saints", that you can really know the love of God that passes knowledge. In Christ you do not stand upon your own strength; but consider the weakness of your brother and go to his help, offering to share the gifts that God has given to you for his benefit in such a way that you are also strengthened through him. In Christ you do not ask the other to capitulate to your demands any more than you can compromise the truth that He has given you to apprehend, but in Christ you seek to understand and respect the other's conscience even when you may consider it weak at certain points, and are ready to learn from the other as one to whom Christ has also communicated His Gospel and upon whom He has poured out His Holy Spirit. In Christ all self-sufficiency and arrogance, all recrimination and self-justification are given up. That is the spirit in which this Report is written. It is only by learning to respect one another's convictions sincerely in Christ, only by treading the road of reconciliation in full mutuality and obedience, and only by allowing one another in measured degree the right to different interpretations of what we do together, that we can find a way through our scandalous divisions into spiritual and physical obedience to our "one Lord, one faith, one baptism," and so into a sincere manifestation of the unity we are given in Christ.

(b) The second concerns the subordination of all doctrines of the Church and ministry to the doctrine of Christ, of all ecclesiology to Christology. This is the most far-reaching fact of the whole document, for it means that the Churches concerned are not seeking to call in question one another's orders, but are seeking together to submit their orders to Christ as the sole Source and Head of all order and life, and as the One before whom all our ministries and orders are imperfect and defective. When we stand before Christ we cannot justify ourselves or cast doubts upon others, but can only acknowledge that, even when we have done all that it is our duty to do, we are unprofitable servants. So it is with Churches who stand together before Christ and seek a way of reconciliation in Christ—far from casting doubts upon one another, they submit themselves to the judgment of Christ, for it is from Him alone that the Church derives its very essence, its essential form, and its principle of unity. It is not sufficient, however, for Churches simply to submit their forms of life and ministry to the judgment of Christ, they must seek to work out constructively and together a way of fresh obedience to Christ in the whole region of faith and order until outward behaviour sincerely corresponds to inner belief. In this way they can cut behind their differences, for by bringing their doctrines of the ministry into full conformity with the doctrine of Christ, a way is laid open for practical reforms which will not only allow the Churches to participate more and more in the fulness of Christ, but in so doing make possible a fulness of sacramental communion between them which their present differences in Church-discipline tend to inhibit.

Particular Doctrinal Issues Involved

In this light let us now turn to the particular doctrinal issues involved in the Report, their practical implications in regard to reunion, and the problems these raise for Presbyterians.

I

The Report is concerned chiefly with the doctrine of the Church as the Body of Christ, and with the theological requirements of Intercommunion.

(a) The doctrine of the Church as the Body of Christ not only demands the unity of the Church, but declares the nature of that unity. Jesus Christ was not just a spiritual experience in the hearts of the disciples, He was the Son of God incarnate in our flesh and blood, who had come to take our humanity upon Himself and to redeem it. The Church that is rooted and grounded in this Jesus Christ can no more be content with "a spiritual unity" than it can be content with a Christ who was only "spiritual" and did not have a physical body. Thus because the Church is rooted and grounded in the bodily incarnation of Christ and lives by His atoning death in our flesh and blood and by His physical resurrection, the Church can be content with nothing short of physical and visible unity in Christ. To be content only with a "spiritual unity" is to transfer the menace of Docetic heresy to the Doctrine of the Church.

But when we take the doctrine of the Church as the Body of Christ seriously several other doctrines inevitably follow. First, it follows that the ministry of the Church belongs to the *whole* Body of Christ and the special ministries within the Church necessarily have a *corporate* nature which has to be expressed in the collegiate character of the Church's councils or synods. Second, this corporate nature of the Church and its ministry determines also the nature of the Church's continuity which the Report describes as threefold, as mediated through baptismal incorporation into Christ, through the ministration of the Word and Sacraments, and through the "episcopate" as the ecumenical sign of the continuity given in the other two. This fully Christological interpretation of the continuity of the Church and its ministry cuts away from the bottom those false ideas and false notions of apostolic succession which we in Scotland have always opposed on the ground of the biblical faith, and enables us to recover a true doctrine of apostolic succession in which both the "corporate episcopate" and the "historic episcopate" are given their proper place, as well as the "priesthood" of the whole baptized membership of the Church. Third, it follows also that the ministry of the Church must be conformed to the image and likeness of Christ who came into this world in *the Form of a Servant.* Because the ministry of the Church, in obedience to Christ, must be in the form of a servant, all notions of worldly power, lordly rule, disparity, and pomp, etc., can have no place at all in it. It is safe to say that if this doctrine of *the Suffering Servant* is not only made central in our doctrine of Christ, but is made normative for our doctrine of the form and order of the Church, then most of the major differences between the Churches can be cut clean away.

(b) It was at the Last Supper that Jesus washed the disciples' feet and showed them how they should minister to one another. It is, therefore, at the Lord's Table that we must learn how Churches are to minister to one another and how their ministries are to be related to each other in obedience to Jesus Christ. That is why the question of Intercommunion belongs to the heart of this Report not simply as its goal, but as an essential part of reconciliation. What the Report does is to think out the basic doctrinal requirements of Intercommunion and to give them practical expression. It is no use talking about having Intercommunion unless we are ready to put it into practice not only at the Lord's Table, but in the whole life and work of our Churches and in their several disciplines. It is a sin against the Lord and the Lord's Supper simply to want a "spiritual Intercommunion" and not to work it out across our actual divisions. On the other hand, when Churches resolve before God to seek a way out of their divisions, then the whole question of Intercommunion is put upon a new basis—the basis of downright *sincerity*. That is why on these proposals Intercommunion would begin right away when the Churches concerned are sincerely ready not only to sit down together at the Lord's Table, but to try to work out among themselves the unity that is set forth and enacted in the Lord's Supper. Then at last these Churches could proclaim to all men reconciliation through the blood of Christ without giving the lie to it by their own sinful divisions.

II

What then are the main practical proposals in the Report?

No Capitulation on Either Side

The aim of the practical proposals is *not one Church, nor is it by any means uniformity of ministry and worship* between the Churches, but a *fulness of sacramental communion* in which there can be a ready interchange of communicants and of ministers between them. Schemes of Church union in the past in England and Scotland have all had in them some element of capitulation of one to the other, but in this Report that way is wholly set aside. Episcopalian and Presbyterian Churches are asked to come together only in such a way as to forge a bridge between them, but in such a way that none is asked in any way to deny its own heritage, its own ministry, its own constitution, or its own worship. That gives us both the greatness of the suggestions and their difficulty. When Churches with such different disciplines as Presbyterian and Episcopalian Churches are asked to come together, without denial of anything in their own heritage, there are bound, at first, to be paradoxes and contradictions or conflicts between them. But here, in Christ, each Church is asked to respect and honour the other in its whole order and tradition, and to step forward with it in an act of mutual learning in Christ, looking to the fulness of the Church which neither possesses by itself but in which each has much to learn from the other. There is no suggestion, therefore, that Presbyterians are to become Episcopalians or that Episcopalians are to become Presbyterians, but that both are to seek together fuller obedience to Christ in the light of what He has taught and now teaches both of them. Thus the proposals leave the whole doctrinal and constitutional position of the Church of Scotland entirely intact, that is the whole Presbyterian system of Kirk Session, Presbytery, Synod, General Assembly, Barrier Act, Westminster Confession, Westminster Directory, etc. The Church of Scotland is not being asked to deny its orders or to cast doubts on its God-given ministries. Similarly, the Church of England is not asked to deny its heritage. The whole system of the Church of England in Prayer Book, Thirty-nine Articles, Ordinal, etc., is left intact. The proposals are, however, that we in the Church of Scotland ask the Church of England to add to it elements which we have received from and learned in Christ, but they must be allowed to assimilate these elements in their own way, as will be appropriate to their own heritage. We in the Church of Scotland, on the other hand, are not asked to take "the Anglican form of the episcopate" into our system, but are only asked with regard to our "corporate episcopate" to add those elements in the "historic episcopate" which Anglicans have received from and learned in Christ, but we must be allowed to assimilate them in our own way, and in a manner appropriate to our own Presbyterian heritage.

Presbyterian Bishops and Episcopalian Elders

In this the concrete suggestions concern two things:

(a) An assimilation of the "corporate episcopate" in the Church of Scotland and the "historic episcopate" in the Church of England to each other. In the Church of Scotland "the bishop" is not an individual, but the Presbytery in which ministers, assisted by elders, act conjointly in a sacral court. And so we speak in Scotland of "The Rev. the Presbytery". In the Church of England, however, the bishop is an individual, who represents the coalescence of many functions in one office. The proposal is that both these should be assimilated to each other in such a way that Presbytery would not be denied in Scotland nor episcopacy in England, but that the *new form* toward which the two Churches would move would include what each already had with additional elements from the other. Thus, in the Church of Scotland the Presbytery would remain as before, with its full authority and status, but it would have a permanent Moderator as "bishop-in-presbytery" presiding over it, while in England the bishop would be assimilated to his Presbyterate in the Synod and be "more like the chairman of a committee," as the Bishop of Derby has put it. In such an assimilation, however, there would have to be a mutual commissioning in authority. Episcopalians have no authority to minister in Presbyterian Churches and Presbyterians have no authority to minister in Episcopalian Churches, so that between the bishop in the Episcopalian Church and the Presbytery in the Presbyterian Church there would have to be a mutual commissioning of authority in order to forge an interconnexion between the disciplines of the two Churches, so that those under the bishop in the Episcopal Church and those under the Presbytery in the Presbyterian Church could receive due authorization to minister in both Churches. This mutual commissioning in authority between the Episcopalian bishops and the Presbyterian Presbyteries would not mean the reordination of any ministers but the setting apart of the Moderator in a

Presbytery to be a bishop-in-presbytery in such a way that he would enter the responsible development of ministerial authority and discipline of the other as well as his own Church; and it would involve not the reconsecration of an Episcopalian bishop but an act by the Presbytery in prayer and laying on of hands in which he would enter the responsible development of ministerial authority and discipline of the other as well as his own Church.

On the Presbyterian side this would mean the additional fact of setting apart of a Moderator as permanent bishop-in-presbytery, and on the Episcopalian side it would mean the additional fact of integrating the bishop closely with presbyterate and laity in his synod, so that he would become a bishop-in-synod.

(b) An assimilation into the Church of England of laymen set apart like the Presbyterian elders for a measure of pastoral responsibility in the local Church, with appropriate participation of laymen in all the courts of the Church, synods, and convocations, etc. This might well take the form of a reformed diaconate in the Episcopalian Churches, so that they might have "deacons" more after the fashion of the Early Church corresponding to our "elders". Clearly this introduction of laymen into the Church courts and into due share in the doctrinal and constitutional decisions of the Church would be a very big and far-reaching step for the Church of England to take. It might well prove to be the most revolutionary step since the Reformation, even leading to a new form of establishment in the State and full freedom over its own affairs of constitution, doctrine, and worship.

Suggestions to the Four Churches immediately Involved

The proposals actually concern four different Churches: The Church of England and the Presbyterian Church of England, the Church of Scotland and the Scottish Episcopal Church. The Report does not go into detailed application of its proposals to each case, but is content to set forth the main principles, leaving it to each of the four Churches to apply them in its own case in a way appropriate to its own constitution and heritage. It is recognized that here due allowance must be made both for divergent applications and also for their divergent interpretations, but each Church must sincerely trust and respect the others and refrain from judging their actions in terms of the *status quo ante* in its own tradition, looking only to the richness and fulness of the Church in the future.

It is suggested that the proposals, if adopted, should be put into effect in three stages: (a) A solemn resolve by the Churches concerned to seek a way of reconciliation in Christ through mutual learning and adaptation always in subordination to the basic requirements of the doctrine of Christ; (b) the immediate beginning of Intercommunion between the Churches leading to fulness of sacramental communion; (c) the building of a bridge between the disciplines of the several Churches, enabling fulness of sacramental communion to be possible, including free interchange of ministers. The steps taken by the different Churches initiating appropriate acts of assimilation to each other should be taken as far as possible at the same time, so that they could go forward together in full mutuality.

III

Unprecedented Advance by the Church of England

The publication of these proposals has raised problems in the minds of both Presbyterians and Episcopalians, but I submit that these problems arise mainly from a misunderstanding of the other Church or from an attempt to judge the proposals in terms of what Presbyterians or Episcopalians often have been in the habit of holding apart from the thorough Christological criticism of their positions put forward by this Report. Let it be said quite frankly that the adoption of this Report by the Church of England would represent an unprecedented advance on their part in ecumenical relations in such things as the acceptance of Christological criticism of the form and order of the Church in the Anglican tradition, the concept of the corporate episcopate and the assimilation of the individual bishop to it, the readiness to begin Intercommunion right away when the Churches resolve to seek a way of reconciliation in Christ, the introduction of laymen into synods and convocations, etc. We must not allow previous and one-sided conceptions of the Anglican tradition and the practice to come into view and to exacerbate us at this point, but seek to go forward with them in full mutuality. Likewise Episcopalians must not seek to allow their previous conceptions of Presbyterian tradition and practice to come into view and to exacerbate them, but seek to go forward with us in full mutuality at every point.

Authority of Presbytery Enhanced

Let me take one example of what Dr. A. C. Craig has called an element of "unresolved tension" in the Report—the suggestion that decisions on doctrinal and constitutional matters might well have to require the consent of the bishops-in-presbytery. Anglicans do not hold that bishops in virtue of their consecration have some special chrism of truth attached to their persons, but that the office of bishop includes that of having a watching brief over questions of doctrine. In the Reformed Church, following Ephesians 4: 11, we recognize the special office of teacher or doctor or professor as fulfilling this watching brief in doctrinal matters. But, as with Anglicans, the bishop does not exercise this office in his own person, but the bishops exercise it together in a collegiate way, so in the Reformed Church the professors do not exercise this office in their own person but in the corporate decisions of Presbytery and General Assembly. In the Church of Scotland the ultimate authority rests with the General Assembly, together with the Presbyteries acting under the Barrier Act, so that no Assembly can take a decision on a doctrinal or constitutional issue without having the consent of two-thirds of the Presbyteries. Thus the Presbyteries in the Church of Scotland acting under the Barrier Act function in much the same way as the bishops in the Church of England on such matters. But on these proposals for the assimilation of the "individual bishop" with the "corporate bishop" (i.e. the Presbytery), the bishop-in-presbytery could not act as an individual alone, but could only act together with his Presbytery. Decisions could not be left to the bishop as an individual, for they rest with the whole Presbytery over which he presides as its permanent Moderator. The bishop would then give voice in the General Assembly to the common mind and corporate decision of the Presbytery which it had reached under his presidency. Whereas before on the Episcopalian model the bishop would be left to make his decision alone, and to voice it in conjunction with other bishops, on these suggestions he and his fellow-ministers in Presbytery or Synod would act conjointly, reaching a common mind through prayer and discussion. This could only mean a great strengthening to the Barrier Act in Scotland, and would have the great additional advantage of giving the Presbytery, *as Presbytery*, immediate representation and voice in the General Assembly regularly, whereas it now has this only on certain special occasions. The present practice in Scotland is greatly to the disadvantage of the Presbytery, for it allows the whole centre of gravity and power to shift from the Presbyteries to the Committees of Assembly and their officers—which is a serious menace to our Presbyterian system. But far from inhibiting the majesty of Presbytery, this suggestion could only enhance it, and be a real curb against the arrogation of power to the hands of bureaucrats and committee-prelates!

I believe that all these initial problems and difficulties that are being raised can be fully met if we work hard and patiently at these proposals. They would doubtless need some amendment on actual application and it would take a long time for them to be put into effect, but I believe they lay down the only possible lines of advance to fulness of sacramental communion between Presbyterian and Episcopal Churches, and at the same time open up the field for ecumenical advance among all the Evangelical Churches. So long as we are apart from one another, and refuse to sit down together at the Lord's Table, we can only interpret one another in the distorted light of our estrangement. But if we go forward resolved to act out our Intercommunion with one another in the whole sphere of understanding and practice we will be able to overcome our conflicts and tensions, although they are bound to be very acute particularly at the beginning of closer relations. I believe very firmly that this can be done, and that once we begin Intercommunion He who has given us the Supper as a sacrament of reconciliation and unity will Himself heal us of our divisions in new ways and lead us into paths of corporate obedience to His Gospel.

DISCUSSIONS WITH CHURCHES

4. WITH ROMANS

(a) *The Problem of Discussion with Rome*

OF all the Churches in Christendom, the Roman Church presents the greatest problem so far as discussion with it is concerned, for the simple reason that it has immured itself within its own peculiar developments and its own private conceptions, so that it is constitutionally unable to look beyond itself. Just because the Roman Church does not acknowledge anything within its own tradition greater or higher than its own tradition, it is unable to transcend itself, and is therefore unable to take up a position where ecumenical discussion is really possible. When all this applies even to the terminology which the Roman Church uses, terminology of its own making, it is apparent how extremely difficult it is even to get within talking distance of Romans; they are so turned in upon themselves that they are unable really to listen to others, for they cannot hear anything except in and through their own language. Very rarely does one find a Roman theologian with sufficient patience or sympathy, not to speak of sufficient capacity for self-transcendence, really to listen, for example, to the statements with which they disagree. That is clear even of those friendly Roman theologians who wrote in *Istina*, *Irenikon*, or *Foi et Vie* about the document produced by the Faith and Order section at the Evanston Assembly of the World Council of Churches—they all insisted on interpreting its ecclesiology in terms of what they had long imagined they understood as "Lutheran anthropology", and in so doing they completely missed the real import of the document. It is difficult to blame them, for this attempt provoked by the Ecumenical Movement to look again at the Evangelical Churches is a new venture for them, and has to work with four hundred years of Roman misunderstanding of the teaching of the Reformation—a misunderstanding made definitive by the Council of Trent.

Let us examine the problem of discussion with Romans in regard to such important terms and concepts as grace and sin. Romans mean by grace something vastly different from what the Evangelical Churches mean, and certainly from what the biblical documents mean. For them, grace is construed in essentially ontological and causal categories, and is therefore assimilated to the language of nature. Behind this radical change and departure from the apostolic tradition there lies of course the assimilation of grace to the conception of *charis* rampant in the heathen literature, piety and mysteries of the ancient Mediterranean world, the remarkable assimilation—e.g. in Tertullian—of the Christian conception of Spirit and substance to those of Stoic philosophy, and the Augustinian amalgam of all this with powerful elements of Neoplatonism. When all this was carefully and wonderfully rationalized in the mediaeval theology under the dominance of Aristotelian categories "grace" became something very far removed from what was meant by St. Paul or St. John. And because the whole of theological activity is concerned with grace, theology itself suffered a vast change, for it came to be concerned with the metaphysical relations of the divine Being as Cause to a divine creaturely being as operation, that is, with divine grace as flowing from the divine nature into human nature where it can be spoken of as created grace. Grace is thus assimilated to the concept of being and there is a graduated infusion of grace corresponding to a grand hierarchy of being. In this way the whole of Roman soteriology and sacramentalism is built up round the basic conception of the deification of creaturely man.

There is not of course a fully consistent interpretation of saving grace in the Roman Church, for the differences between Thomist and Molinist-Jesuit conceptions are sometimes very radical—St. Thomas could not have objected, for example, to the concept of justification by grace alone, although he would have understood "grace" differently; but at any rate his view is distinctly "evangelical" as compared with that which has been usually adopted by Rome. But to Thomists and Jesuits alike the Evangelical Church has to insist that grace is Jesus Christ Himself, that is, God's own direct act of pure love personally at work in Jesus Christ. In Him God has bestowed

Himself upon us and gathered us up into fellowship with His own divine life and love, but not in such a way that there is any transubstantiation of human nature into the divine or any commingling of the divine with the human. Our conflict with Rome at this point is therefore above all a conflict in Christology, and we insist that Roman theology operates here with a basically monophysite error.

When we turn to the term "sin", we can more or less say at once that for Romans sin means "want of grace". Sin is defined in essentially negative terms, under the influence of the Platonic conception of evil, as the negation of the good or privation of being, as it came to be called in mediaeval theology. But against all this we must say again, with the great Anselm, *Nondum considerasti quanti ponderis sit peccatum.* When grace and sin are defined as they are in Roman theology it is clear that to say of a person that he is full of grace is to say that he is full of deity, and to say that the Church is sinful is to say that God has not bestowed all His grace upon it, or alternatively to say that it is not fully Church for it lacks in being—hence we have the Roman doctrine of Mary and of the perfection of the Church.

Once again there is no ultimate consistency in the Roman position in regard to the meaning of sin, although here too it is on the whole the shallower view of the Jesuits that has been generally adopted. But there are real problems, and subtle distinctions in terminology (such as formal and material, subjective and objective sin, sin through analogy, etc.) are invented to get round them. Romans to-day, for example, are distinctly uneasy about the fact that although they hold that the Church as a whole is perfect and without spot or stain, they are forced to acknowledge that its members are not without sin. Such a view appears to Evangelical believers as rather hypocritical or as a contradiction in terms, or, to give it a more generous interpretation, as the Roman equivalent of the Lutheran *justus et peccator*—that is, it is a way of saying that the sins of the Church in its members are not imputed to it, which is precisely what *justus et peccator* means! On the other hand, this is a point that Protestants do not often understand. Since Romans, with all their characteristic *distinctiones*, speak of sin mainly in judicial terms, to claim that the Church as such or as a whole is without sin is a form of the doctrine of justification by grace alone, that the Church has been wholly justified and sanctified in Christ. And yet although there is a real area of agreement here, in spite of the different terminology used, the difference in terminology does mean that there is a more radical divergence than appears even on a second look. Once again it is a Christological difference.

The Roman Church repudiates the idea that in the Incarnation the Son of God assumed our fallen humanity, and it has barricaded itself behind this aberration from the Apostolic and Catholic faith by the dogma of the immaculate conception. The Eastern Church goes much farther toward the Roman Church than ever the Evangelical Church could go, but it could not possibly teach that Mary had been redeemed before the Incarnation took place, that she was altogether without original and actual sin and was sinlessly mother of Jesus, so that He did not take upon Himself that which needed to be redeemed, the flesh of Adam, but some neutral flesh of which we know nothing. The Eastern Church has departed, at least in its later fathers, from the profundity of great fathers like Irenaeus and Athanasius, and even perhaps from the Cappadocians in this matter; but it does not separate Mary, and therefore does not separate the flesh which Christ assumed from Mary, from the fallen race of men. We must hold that Christ took flesh of our flesh, humanity from our fallen humanity, in order to heal it, but we hold that in taking it His atoning work began, and that His very taking of it was the sanctification and hallowing of it, and therefore also the condemning of sin in our flesh. Our difference with the Roman Church, therefore, lies in its repudiation of the Pauline teaching that Christ took our "body of sin", our "body of death". It was in that body of ours in which He, the Just, was made sin for us that He made atonement for our guilt and consecrated us in His self-offering to the Father. In other words, we hold that the Son of God incorporated Himself into our fallen humanity in its alienation from God, was made in the likeness of our flesh of sin, although He was entirely without sin, and through that incorporation fulfilled in the Cross and resurrection He incorporates us into Himself. The Church is grounded upon the act of God the Son in incorporating Himself in our humanity under the divine judgment, and therefore in His act of reconciliation in assuming our humanity into oneness with Himself. Jesus Christ loved the Church and gave Himself for it that He might sanctify it and present to Himself a glorious Church, without spot or wrinkle or any such thing, that it should be holy and without blemish.

It is on the ground of this act in the Incarnation, death and resurrection of Christ that the Evangelical Church understands the meaning of sin. Sin is to be understood, measured, and defined, not primarily in moral, psychological, or judicial terms, but in the light of the death of Christ and His condemnation of sin in our flesh. He died for the whole man, and therefore the whole man, with his "good" and his "evil", comes under the total judgment of the Cross. But Christ died for the whole Church, and gave Himself for it, and therefore the whole Church comes under the judgment of the Cross, for it is precisely that judgment which is the atoning sanctification and justification of the Church. That is what Roman theology with its essentially Latin mind seems constitutionally unable to apprehend, and that is why it is next to impossible for the Roman Church to be penitent and to agree that as a Church it can really pray: "Forgive us our debts as we forgive our debtors". We must agree and indeed insist that the Church is utterly holy and pure in Jesus Christ, for it is once and for all washed and cleansed in His Blood and clothed with His purity and perfection—that is the doctrine of justification—but the Church waits for the redemption of the body, waits for the day when Christ will return to change the body of our humiliation and make it like unto His glorious Body—which does not just refer to individuals but to all who are one body in the Body of Christ. Christ alone has risen and ascended, and Christ alone in that bodily sense is on the other side of judgment and death and corruption, but the Church on earth—and this is God's amazing grace—while still in the body awaiting redemption, still in the body of sin and still in the body of this death, is yet justified and sanctified and pure and spotless in Christ.

Of course at this point we are still divided from the Romans, for just as they refuse to believe that the Son of God came all the way to us in becoming one with us in our fallen humanity, so they refuse to believe that Christ so identifies Himself with us on earth that it is this earthly historical body which He—oh the amazing grace of God!—declares to be His own Body, the Body which He has redeemed and justified and sanctified in Himself. The Roman divergence from the apostolic tradition on this point is clearest in its Mariology, and above all in the assumption into heaven of the body of Mary, that is, in essence, of the priesthood which continues to beget the Church from age to age as the body of Christ. Add to this the Roman conception of the "fulness of grace", applied not only to Mary but to the Church, and it becomes apparent that the Roman doctrine of the Church is essentially correlative to the monophysite error in its Christology mentioned earlier. It is doubtless because of this (shades of the heresy of Honorius I!) that Romans to-day are unable to understand a conception of the unity of the Church which allows a distinctive place for the will of God and for the will of man in the nature and being of the Church, and yet sees that the hesitating will of man is grasped and undergirded by the absolutely faithful will of God in Jesus Christ, and in spite of its fallibility and error and unfaithfulness from generation to generation is yet maintained in the covenanted holiness and truth and faithfulness of Jesus Christ. That is very apparent, for example, in the baffled Roman attempts to interpret the Unity of the Church that is manifested in the World Council of Churches or in the midst of the Evangelical Church with all its diversities, because they have only an essentially monophysite conception of unity. We must admit that again and again Protestants appear to err seriously in the other direction, in an extreme dyophysite conception of the unity of the Church (that is to say, a view of the Church which is correlative to a Nestorian separation between the divine and human natures of Christ) but the evidence is that the member Churches of the World Council, at least as judged from their delegates, appear to be moving on to a view with sounder Christological backing.

So far in this discussion we have found that the conflict which we have with the Roman Church penetrates behind the differences in conceptions of grace and sin and unity to differences in Christology, and they must be taken down to that level if we are to enter into real discussion. In that event, discussion must range over the whole history of the doctrine of Christ, for it will be in careful examination of that history and of the decisions of the Church in its Ecumenical Councils against menacing heresies that we may possibly reach such unity in faith in Jesus Christ that we may then attack our other divergences from the rear, as it were. But here we are up against another major problem in discussion with Rome—the problem of history and tradition. In its simplest form this is the claim of the Roman Church that all its magisterially defined teaching arises out of the deposit of the Church's original tradition, and that even dogmas like the physical assumption which have no historical evidence to support them are invisibly and embryonically latent in the tradition. That is of course to transpose an Aristotelian biological conception of evolution into the Christian faith, and to think of the development of the doctrines of the Church only in terms of a teleological and not also in terms of an eschatological unfolding of the truth. It is also to give priority in the end to the uncritical development of popular piety over the historico-critical investigation of the Holy Scriptures and the teaching of the early Catholic Church, not to mention the fact that it makes the Apostolic and early Catholic Church rather "poorer" in its faith than the Roman Church claims to be to-day. It means, too, that the Roman Church acknowledges two sources of Revelation, that of the apostolic tradition, the so-called "passive tradition", and that of the Roman tradition, the so-called "active tradition", and just because the former is only to be interpreted in terms of the latter, it is inevitably the latter that controls the former. In this way the Roman Church makes itself the master of all tradition; but in so doing it becomes introverted, as we noted earlier. But behind all this there is something that goes down very deep and must be brought to the light—the identification by the Roman Church of Truth with its own Subjectivity.

That is apparent in the doctrine of the *analogia entis*, which was indeed meant to assert the objectivity of the truth and to give scientific character to theological knowledge, but which has in point of fact led Roman theology to the very opposite of that, viz. the appeal by the Roman Church to its own self-consciousness as the ultimate criterion of the truth. Now the extraordinary thing is that this is just the accusation that Romans lay against Protestant theology, and with some justification so far as Neo-Protestant theology is concerned, especially where it has followed Kant in his so-called "Copernican revolution". But is that not precisely what Roman theology, for all its apparent objectivity attained through the use of Aristotelian philosophy, had already achieved in the Middle Ages, and is it not ultimately out of that that Neo-Protestantism grew? namely from the inwardness of mediaeval pietism together with the doctrine that there is not only an unbroken continuity between the mind of man and the Mind of his Maker, but a pre-established harmony between the Truth in God and the image of that truth embedded in the soul of man, and above all in the sanctified soul of the Church? Was it therefore so very remarkable that it was Romantic-idealist philosophy (with its identity of subject and object) and a corresponding theology that helped the Roman Church to reach the conclusions enunciated in the Vatican Council about the infallibility of *ex cathedra* definitions of dogma, behind which there lies the identification of the spirit of the Roman Church with the Holy Spirit, the historical consciousness of the Roman tradition with the Mind of Christ? When that stage is reached, it becomes clear that for Rome truth and scientific objectivity are no longer identical—that is, that it is always the object that determines our knowledge of it, so that rationality is the conformity of reason to the nature of the object—but on the contrary truth and subjectivity are identical; that is, it is the self-consciousness of the subject that determines the nature of the object, so that what is rational and true is that which conforms to the mind of the subject, in this case the Roman Church.

It is the promulgation of the new Roman dogma about the physical assumption of Mary that has revealed the strange position which the Roman Church now occupies, and which it occupies with the consistent but extraordinary claim that it is its own intuition or instinct that must be given priority over all historico-scientific investigation of the Truth. In other words, it is the Roman Church which creates history; for history is the product of the Roman Church's self-consciousness, that is not only a subjective reinterpretation of the facts but a moulding of them according to its own will, and even the positing of historical facts on the demands of Roman self-consciousness. It is thus that the Roman Church holds to be real for itself only that which arises out of its own self-consciousness or is determined by its own decisions. Here there is a remarkable parallel between the view of history begun by Wilhelm Dilthey when he applied the Kantian revolution to his "critique of the historical reason", and which has recently been given such clear expression in the (Fichtean) ideas of Gogarten! It is not at all surprising that this development should welcome the teaching of Martin Heidegger in his transposition of the Roman conception of history and tradition to an understanding of existence. Here we have the mutual cross-fertilization of Roman and Neo-Protestant conceptions! But in this strange denouement it is certainly the Roman Church that is the outstanding champion of the idea that truth is subjectivity, in the identity of its own corporate subjectivity with divine Revelation. Could anything actually be further from the Truth?

Romans accuse Protestants of making their own private judgments the criterion of the Truth, and we must acknowledge that unfortunately this element did creep into the Churches of the Reformation first from the Renaissance (within the Roman Church), then from the adoption in the seventeenth century of Roman Aristotelianism, and later from the adoption of Roman Cartesian philosophy, into Protestant theology, scholastic and pietist alike; but Protestant theology has in it a basic and inalienable factor which is so lacking in the Roman Church, namely, the subordination of all its thoughts and judgments to the critical judgment of the Word of God, and its readiness for a repentant rethinking of all its tradition. It is here that the basic position of the Reformation keeps reasserting itself, that knowledge of the truth is known only in the conformity of the reason to the object, only in obedience to Revelation, only in the subordination of all tradition to the Word of God, and only in the subjection of the Church to Jesus Christ the Lord. That is the position to which Protestant theology is everywhere returning, and it is the position for which the Reformed Church has always stood so firmly throughout the centuries since the Reformation, although at no time since John Calvin has it had such a consistent and mighty champion as to-day in Karl Barth, not least in his implacable opposition to Bultmann's thesis that the Gospel is the product of the creative spirituality of the first Christians.

However, to-day we are faced with a surprising development

in the history of the Roman Church. It has proceeded along the line of developing its own active tradition to the point where it has come to identify the Truth with its own Subjectivity, and to protect and encase that position in Papal definitions and irreformable dogmas; yet there is being undertaken throughout the Roman Church, and particularly in Continental Europe, an increasing volume of historico-scientific research into biblical and patristic literature which is bound to have the greatest repercussions in the Roman Church of the future. Already it becomes apparent that the Roman Church is becoming more and more an uneasy *complexio oppositorum*, and that the day cannot be very far away when in the development of the Roman Church there will take place a great prophetic outburst in which the Christian and biblical (i.e. the ancient Catholic) tradition will reassert itself in spite of the fixed and immovable nature of the dogmatic institutions which have so long clamped down upon reform and inhibited the freedom of the Word and Spirit within its bounds.

Be that as it may, it ought to be clear that the only fruitful discussions possible with Romans in the future must take the line of a common front against subjectivistic piety, but that means a common front against the individualistic subjectivism of Neo-Protestantism and the corporate subjectivism of Romanism. The temptation of Protestantism is to counteract individualistic subjectivism by assimilation of its thought to empirical science, and the temptation of Romanism is to justify its subjectivism by appeal from the individual to the corporate institution; but both these are temptations to a false objectivity. The only real objectivity is that of the object, God Himself who gives Himself to us in His Word and requires of us obedient conformity to Him in Jesus Christ. That is the acknowledgment that in all our knowing of the Truth and in all our tradition of it we are confronted by a transcendent objectivity, the living Lord Himself, who refuses to be domesticated to our subjectivity individualistic or corporate.

If the Evangelical Church is to engage in this discussion it must put its own house in order, and that means it must deal radically with the menacing conception which it harbours in its own bosom that, as it was the spirituality of the first Christians that created the Gospel, so it is to-day. If the Roman

Church is to engage in this discussion it must also put its own house in order, and that means it must deal faithfully with the cancerous growth of its own subjectivity, and allow the Sword of the Spirit which is the Word of God to cut away the persistent identification of its own creative self-consciousness with divine Revelation.

(b) *The New Mariological Dogma*[1]

Under the harsh treatment of the Christian Church by the National-Socialist régime in Germany the divided Churches found themselves drawing together, the Evangelical Church (including Lutheran and Reformed) on the one hand and the Roman Catholic Church on the other. Each was more ready to listen to the witness of the other, to set aside polemical interests, and to rejoice in the working of divine grace beyond the frontiers of the respective Churches. People recognized each other as brothers in spite of the frontiers, and profound theological discussion was carried on by groups of theologians from both Churches based on the growing sense of responsibility which each held for the other in Jesus Christ.

In discharge of this brotherly responsibility, a group of theologians in Heidelberg, under the brilliant leadership of Professor Edmund Schlink, felt urged to contribute to the Roman Catholic discussion which preceded the proclamation of the new dogma of the Assumption of the Virgin Mary. Now that the *Munificentissimus Deus* has been proclaimed, and the dogma of the physical assumption of the Virgin Mary has become for Roman Catholics necessary for saving faith, Professor Schlink and his colleagues have issued the contents of their deliberations in the form of a memorandum which serves a twofold purpose. Here Evangelical theology delivers its soul and in the most brotherly spirit warns the Roman Church of the dire consequences of its action, not only for the Ecumenical Church but even for the Church of Rome itself. The document is a model of theological discussion and a notable contribution to the relations between the Roman Catholic and Evangelical Churches.

[1] Review of *Evangelisches Gutachten zur Dogmatisierung der leiblichen Himmelfahrt Mariens*, Chr. Kaiser Verlag, Munich, 1950. From the *Scottish Journal of Theology*, 1951, pp. 90–96.

The memorandum falls into three short chapters. In the first chapter there is given a critical examination of the new dogma, both of its grounds and their relation to the apostolic foundation of the Church, and of its contents and their consequences for Mariology, Christology, for Faith and the doctrine of the Church. The second chapter discusses the bearing of all this upon the relations between the Evangelical and Roman Churches; and the third chapter is devoted to the unfortunate results of the Dogma for the common Christian Front behind which both Churches stand over against an unchristian world. The purpose of this review is not to go over again the ground which Professor Schlink has covered so adequately but to single out and discuss what appear to be the questions of outstanding significance for the whole Church.

(1) Perhaps the most stunning fact about the proclamation of the new dogma is the way in which the Roman Church has sought to justify it: *on another foundation than that of the prophets and apostles upon which the whole Church is built.* That is where the memorandum from Heidelberg first comes to grips with the Papal pronouncement. After recalling the apostolic foundation of the Church and its intrinsic finality which excludes addition to it, Professor Schlink goes on to ask how the new dogma stands to this fact (which for Evangelical theology is the supreme test). Far from there being any Scriptural authority for the idea it is actually contrary to the unique eschatological character of Christ's Resurrection and Ascension, and the unique relation this bears to the resurrection of all who will rise again at the Parousia; in fact it turns the assumption of Mary into one of the saving acts of God alongside the salvation-events of Christ Himself. Far from there being any justification for the notion in the tradition of the Church, even after the sixth century the liturgy of the feast of the Assumption of Mary regularly speaks of her *dormitio*, *pausatio*, and *transitus animae*, with never a word about a physical assumption. Even as late as 1568 the Roman Church made it clear that it did not know what had happened to the body of Mary after her death. In no sense therefore can the new dogma be said to fulfil the requirements of the Vincentian canon: *quod ubique, quod semper, quod ab omnibus creditum est. Hoc est etenim vere proprieque catholicum. . . .* The horrifying thing about this dogma therefore is not only that it has no biblical

or apostolic foundation, but that here quite plainly the Roman Church claims to be able to produce at will "apostolic tradition" out of itself. In other words, here where the Pope exercises for the first time the authority given him by the Vatican Council of 1870, he both lays claim to be able to produce dogmatic truth, and to do that apart from apostolic legitimation. In explanation of this procedure we may cite the words of a Roman Catholic theologian in a recent number of the periodical *Christ und Welt.*

> The new dogma is justified not by appealing to evidence which is regarded as strictly scientific (i.e. to Scripture and Tradition which have their source in Primitive Christianity) but by appealing instead to the so-called intuitive understanding of the present-day Church for matters of faith.[1] One begins with the acknowledged fact that the present-day Church believes in the Ascension of Mary, and then explains that because of the assistance of the Holy Spirit it would be impossible for the Church to be mistaken in such a belief. From the insight thus gained into the interpretation and estimation of traditional teaching the Church works backwards to Primitive Christianity. The priority thus recorded to the intuitive understanding of the present-day Church over the results of pure historical investigation of Scripture and Tradition is the theoretical presupposition of the new dogma and at the same time the practical consequence of its "definition" through the Pope. Therein and not so much in its content lies its extraordinary *theological significance.*

Such an argument will no doubt be accepted readily by Roman Catholics who hold to the doctrine of *fides implicita*, for this really defines tradition in terms of the conscious mind of the Roman Church and enables it by some "Catholic instinct" to realize explicitly truths which are alleged to belong to the original deposit even though there is not a single scrap of historical tradition to justify it. All that the Roman Church needs to do is to declare its mind which cannot err because it is reckoned to have incorporated the Spirit of Truth. This new declaration, however, can only convince the world at large that the Roman procedure leads to *Mythologisierung*, while to the

[1] The German text has *auf den sogenannten Glaubenssinn der gegenwärtigen Kirche*. The phrase "Catholic instinct" is used by an English Roman Catholic writer—cf. *Blackfriars*, October, 1950.

Evangelical Church it makes perfectly plain the place of the teaching office of the Roman Church as represented in the person of the Pope. It occupies a place of self-sufficiency and independence and even superiority over against the apostolic foundation, and in fact makes that of secondary importance. As Professor Schlink and his colleagues point out, it means that the Roman Church both loosens its moorings from the apostolic foundation and makes itself superior to the apostles.

This inevitably has the most far-reaching consequences for ecumenical discussions with Roman Catholics. The Evangelical Church takes its stand upon the words of the Lord in St. John's Gospel which declare that the Spirit of Truth will not speak anything of Himself but recalls the Church to all things which Christ has *said*, and so leads it into all Truth. Bound thus to the Holy Spirit speaking through the Scriptures, the Evangelical Church can only be profoundly shocked both at the extent of Roman deviation from the apostolic teaching and at the fundamental renunciation of the apostolic foundation which this involves. Add to this the fact that the Vatican Council, which gave the Pope the authority he has used, declares also that such *ex cathedra* definitions of dogma are "in and from themselves irreformable", and it becomes perfectly apparent that the Roman Church can never go back to the apostolic foundation for correction and reform.

(2) The second important fact we must note about the new dogma is that it brings Roman Catholic Mariology to its crowning point. The Evangelical Church recognizes the unique place of Mary in the Gospel as the mother of Jesus Christ the Son of God, and will not separate its thought of her from the divine act of the Incarnation. But it recognizes also that Mary was a sinner who herself in the *Magnificat* acknowledged a Saviour, and it remembers that on the Cross Jesus gave Mary His earthly mother to be the mother of John, clearly declaring that with His death His relation to her was not to be continued as it was before. She stood there one with the other sinners whose sins He was bearing as the Lamb of God, and as such came under the judgment of the Cross as well as its redemption. Roman theology has, however, for long been in the process of extracting Mary from the communion of the Church of redeemed sinners, and separating her from the fellowship of the

faithful. With this dogma the Roman Church declares unmistakably that she does not belong to the Church which waits with all the faithful for the coming of their Lord and the redemption of the body.

More significant still, however, is the fact that the Roman Church has, through some *communicatio idiomatum*, been transferring to Mary the uniqueness of Jesus Christ. The Scriptures teach us that there is salvation in none other than Jesus Christ, for there is none other name given among men whereby we must be saved. He only is Mediator, is Son of God, is King. But precisely parallel with these divine attributes we find the Roman Church speaking of Mary as *Maria Mediatrix et Corredemptrix* and even as *Filia Dei* and *Dea*. Now that Mary is declared to have ascended into heaven like Christ, we have promulgated the last stage in this parallelism between Christ and the Virgin Mary.

Let us be quite fair. The Roman Catholic Church does not teach any absolute likeness or identity of being and work between Christ and Mary, for Mary is a creature who has received divine favour (cf. the papal bull *Ineffabilis Deus* of 1854). If Christ is Lord and King in His own right, Mary is regarded as Queen on the ground of Christ's work, and as His helper, but as such she so enters into the very redemptive work of Christ and so belongs to the great salvation-events that Mariology definitely becomes a part of Roman Christology. The physical assumption of the Virgin Mary means that she is taken up into the divine sphere, and that it is there that she belongs rather than to the Church that waits to see its Lord and become like Him. What confusion this brings into the apostolic faith! Such a dogma cannot stop there. Its breach with the biblical eschatology carries terrible consequences with it which we cannot elaborate here, though it may be sufficient to say that the next dogmatic step of importance which the Roman Church, to be consistent, must take, will be to deny the Second Advent of Christ and teach in deadly earnest a fully realized eschatology.

(3) The third important fact is in some ways the most ominous of all—the enormous significance which the new dogma has for the Roman doctrine of the priesthood of the Church (cf. the encyclical *Ad catholici sacerdotii* of 1935). Roman

Catholic dogmatics teaches that the great mystery of the maternity of the Church belongs to the priesthood which miraculously continues, as it were, the birth from Mary, and is indeed an extension of the mysterious maternity which she had with regard to the God-Man (cf. M. J. Scheeben, *The Mysteries of Christianity*, p. 546 f.). Thus at the Mass the priesthood gives birth to the Eucharistic Christ, and joins Him to the Church in one body. Add to this the fact that the priesthood also extends the work of Christ, repeating and perpetuating in time His propitiatory sacrifice in the sacrifice of the Mass, and it becomes apparent that the priesthood exercises such controlling power in and over the Church that it becomes a unique and divine order. The significance of the new dogma is plain: as the Virgin Mary is the symbol (and more than the symbol) for the celibate priesthood, her physical assumption into the divine sphere carries with it what amounts to the deification of the priesthood itself. This crowns the age-long Roman teaching that through the divine grace the priest is *divus*.

How different is the view of Evangelical theology which, to make use of the same analogy, may well think of the ministry at the Eucharist as occupying rather the place of Joseph! As he had no control over the miraculous virgin birth of Jesus Christ, but was commanded to take Mary unto himself as his wife, protect and guard and nourish her, according to the revelation of God, so the ministry nourishes, and leads and guards the Church of Jesus Christ. But that which makes it Church, that which makes Christ present in its midst, is the Holy Spirit, and over the Holy Spirit the ministry has no authority. Again at the holy Eucharist the minister obeys the will of God and celebrates according to the institution of Christ; but in the miraculous presence of the Word made flesh he can exercise no control, for it is the Lord's Supper (*Kyriakon deipnon*) and not his own (*idion deipnon*); he can only stand by to wonder and adore. This is one of the crucial points in the teaching of the Evangelical Church: it is the subjection of the Eucharist to the control of the priesthood here which lies behind all denial of Intercommunion. The new Roman dogma makes it plain where such a false road inevitably leads.

The Roman Catholic Church to-day stands in a most perplexing position. It is amazing to read book after book by modern Roman Catholic theologians and scholars which are so biblical that one would hardly know they were Roman except for the evidence of the *imprimatur*. Modern biblical scholarship such as the immense work of Kittel's *Theologisches Woerterbuch zum Neuen Testament* has provided inspiration for many of them, and helped them to return to the Scriptures and to the apostolic foundation of our Christian Faith. One notes for example the rediscovery of eschatology in Roman theology and the signs of a new era which that is awakening for a great many. On the other hand, the Papal definition and promulgation of this new dogma means that the powers of reaction are mighty within the Roman Church, and that under their impulse the ecclesiastical machine can only go on grinding out its dogmas to their absurd conclusions. The proclamation of the new dogma of the physical assumption of the Virgin Mary is, however, of unique significance. Here at last the Roman Church has taken a definite step which calls in question its apostolicity. The Church which has the promise that the gates of hell shall not prevail against it is the Apostolic Church. To be the One, Holy, Catholic Church means that throughout all the changes of history until the Second Advent of Jesus Christ the Church is and remains identical with itself (*ecclesia semper eadem*) in that it maintains the teaching of the apostles in the obedience of faith, and does not alter its nature by changing its foundation, by subtracting from it or adding to it other than that which has already been laid. Therein lies the apostolicity of the Church of Jesus Christ. But now that the Roman Church has taken a step which inevitably calls in question its apostolicity, Protestants are aghast. Throughout the Roman Church, particularly in Germany and France, there are great numbers of theologians and churchmen who are deeply hurt and abashed at the turn of events at Rome, and know not what to think, especially when the *Munificentissimus Deus* ends by laying it down that those who deny or dare to doubt this Papal definition have altogether fallen from the divine and Catholic faith. In our brotherly responsibility which as the Evangelical Church we bear toward them we pray for them, and pray the more earnestly knowing how great is the agony of Reformation. *Sic Deus dum vivificat, facit illud occidendo; dum in coelum vehit, facit illud ad infernum ducendo.*

(c) *Romans and Reform*[1]

During the course of this debate with the Rev. James Quinn there came into my hands the remarkable book by Professor K. E. Skydsgaard of Copenhagen entitled *One in Christ*, described on the dust jacket by the words "Protestants and Catholics, where they agree and where they differ" (published by the Muhlenberg Press, Philadelphia). This is a model of how ecumenical discussion should be conducted, for all through these pages the reader is aware of Professor Skydsgaard's deep understanding of Roman theology and his very fair and sympathetic handling of the points of conflict. It is a work from which Roman and Protestant controversialists can learn a great deal in regard to both truth and love.

By way of preface to the discussion that follows I would like to offer two citations from this work which speak for themselves.

> A genuine respect for each other will of itself lead into conflict, because genuine respect takes the other point of view so seriously that it is worthy of combat and refutation. An ecumenical theology must not become a theology without sharp teeth and without face. It cannot be content with mere ascertainment and listing of differences and resemblances in its escape from the perhaps extremely painful encounter with its opponent. Without losing itself and becoming a harmless undertaking, ecumenical conversation cannot become a theology without passion, without "anger". A theological confessional tolerance must mean a demand for objectivity and impartiality, for openness and sensitivity; for sober work in trying to understand the opponent and what he says, and for restricted readiness to give an account of one's own point of view.
>
> . . . . . .
>
> Ecumenical conversation . . . consists not merely of a two-sided exchange where attention is fastened on one's own position, but of a much deeper exchange where both parties together have their view directed toward the third party of the conversation—the Truth itself. Without the presence of this "third" the conversation becomes as salt which has lost its savour. . . . Ecumenical conversation takes place in love; that is, in mutual respect and sincere openness, in which one thinks about one's neighbour and construes all according to its best meaning, but

[1] From *The Scotsman*, Oct.–Dec., 1957.

does not on the other hand allow one's neighbour to live in peace because that is most comfortable. Love does not seek its own. It does not rightly take a stand on its own merit, but "rises above itself" in order to meet the other. It does not meet the other with a preconceived distrust, but in confidence. It does not allow any possibility for mutual understanding to be lost, and preserves hope until the last.

The Scotsman, October 23, 1957

21 South Oswald Road,
Edinburgh,
October 22, 1957

Sir,—May I be allowed to make a comment upon your report to-day of the Church Union discussions taking place in the Y.M.C.A. Theatre in Edinburgh, in case some of your readers should carry away a false impression of what I said? Your report reads: "Professor Torrance said he would not be surprised if the greatest upheaval in the Church life of the West, began within the Church of Rome. 'It may be,' he said, 'that God will use such an upheaval for the healing of the Churches. We have no right to speak of the Roman Church with antagonism, but we must hope and pray that God will lead them and us into unity in Christ.'"

As far as I can remember that is a faithful report of what I said, but it was only incidental to the main point I made, that we could only seek unity with a Church with which we are in doctrinal agreement, but that such unity in faith required to be acted out in a unity of body. Real unity in Christ must be unity in the apostolic faith, without any sacrifice of truth or principle. The Roman Church, I said, was a heretical Church in its departure from the apostolic faith, and we could not seek unity with it. Roman dogmas made that impossible. Only in Christ, in the Truth, and on the basis of biblical theology could unity be sought and worked out. Then I pointed out that although the Roman Church remained officially obdurate in its teaching, there was a great movement of reform going on in the Roman Church, evidence of which we could see in the publication of books on biblical theology. Then I went on to make the statement reported in your columns to-day.

May I add, for the sake of greater clarity, that unless the Roman Church is prepared to return to the integrity of the catholic and apostolic faith, and to subordinate its tradition to, and correct it by, the Word of God as revealed in the Holy Scriptures, no move for unity between it and Evangelical Churches could ever be contemplated? While we must not be antagonistic to the Roman Church, we must defend the Truth, expose its heresy, and pray that the Roman Church will be led back to the purity of the faith as it is in Christ Jesus.—I am &c.

THOMAS F. TORRANCE.

The Scotsman, October 26, 1957

28 Lauriston Street,
Edinburgh,
October 24, 1957

Sir,—Professor Torrance refers to the publication of books on biblical theology as a sign of "a great movement of reform going on in the Roman church." My own reading of the signs is exactly the opposite, that the study of biblical theology among Protestants is leading them not only towards a more Catholic interpretation of certain texts of Scripture but also towards a deeper understanding of the place of Scripture in the teaching mission of the Church. The concept of the Word of God is presenting itself as something richer, more dynamic and more personal than textual study of the Scriptures (necessary and vital though that is), and is being related more and more to discussions on the nature of the Church. It is becoming recognized that Scripture cannot be divorced from the teaching Church.

This newer attitude on the part of our non-Catholic friends raises greater hopes for mutual understanding. It points to the true meaning of the "integrity of the catholic and apostolic faith" to which Professor Torrance desires the Roman Church to return, viz., the unchanging Word of God delivered in its fulness within the living tradition of the Church's *kerygma*. This the Roman Church claims always to have preserved, not simply as a series of unrelated propositions but as a living and organic whole.—I am &c.

(Rev.) JAMES QUINN, S.J.

The Scotsman, November 1, 1957

21 South Oswald Road,
Edinburgh,
October 26, 1957

Sir,—For the benefit of the Rev. James Quinn, may I give a clear example of new Roman biblical theology in the two volumes of Eugen Walter on *The Coming of the Lord* (pub. by Herder, Freiburg im B., 1947)? These works are given over to theological exegesis of the principal passages in the Epistles and Gospels dealing with eschatology and they offer on the whole good Reformed teaching such as that given so long ago by Luther and Calvin, although the language used is to a large extent derived from the Protestant Theological Dictionary of the New Testament. This is far removed from the teaching of the Council of Trent or the Vatican Council!

If there has been a change in recent Protestant writing about the Word and the Church, it has been through a more faithful exegesis of the New Testament, and a direct return to the teaching of Luther and Calvin. It was the latter above all who insisted that the Church must be understood as the Body of Christ in history, and therefore that Christological correction of the teaching of the Church must be carried through by subordinating everything to the Person and Word of Christ, the sole King and Head of the Church. Because Jesus Christ is the essence of the Church, it is the doctrine of Christ that must govern the doctrines of the Church and Sacraments. Thus, for example, Calvin pointed out that the Roman notion of transubstantiation (in which the appearance or species remained the same, while the substance of the elements was changed) represents the transfer of Docetic and Eutychian heresy into the doctrine of the Lord's Supper and is in direct contradiction to the *inconfuse et immutabiliter* of the orthodox doctrine of Christ defined at the Council of Chalcedon in A.D. 451.

That is but one example of the departure of the Roman Church from the integrity of the Catholic and Apostolic faith of the Early Church. The Church that has the promise that the gates of hell shall not prevail against it is the Apostolic Church. To be the One, Holy, Catholic Church means that through all the changes of history until the Second Advent of Christ the Church remains identical with itself in its apostolic foundation in Christ, and that it maintains faithfully the teaching of the apostles as delivered in the Holy Scriptures, and does not alter its nature by changing its foundation in the faith, by subtracting from it or by adding to it other than that which has been laid in Christ. The Church which refuses to be conformed to the apostolic Scriptures, which declines to be reformed and cleansed and purged by the Word of Truth mediated through the apostles, thereby declares that it is no longer identical with its foundation in Christ, and that it is not the One, Holy, Catholic and Apostolic Church. By calling in question its Apostolicity it denies its Catholicity.

The grave charge which we in the Evangelical Church lay against the Roman Church is that it has increasingly subtracted from the sole Mediatorship of Christ and has increasingly corrupted itself through improvisations and innovations in doctrines, sacraments and ministries. The logical conclusion of that is of course the doctrine of Maria Corredemptrix, while the formulation of the dogma of the physical Assumption of Mary is the most blatant deliberate attempt by the Roman Church to invent a doctrine (out of its own popular piety) knowing that it has no apostolic foundation, and knowing that it was contrary to centuries and centuries even of the Roman Church's tradition. The fact that so-called relics of Mary's body lie scattered about in older centres of Roman piety is standing witness that the Roman Church is no longer *semper eadem*, no longer identical with the Church that taught the death of Mary. It has thus finally and decisively shattered its own continuity, and, apart altogether from the Tridentine anathemas, has made unity with the Evangelical Churches who remain faithful to the apostolic foundation in Christ quite impossible.

We cannot deny that the Roman Church, though gravely deformed through the adulteration of the apostolic faith, is part of the Church of Christ because it continues to baptize in the name of the Holy Trinity and continues to believe in Jesus Christ as Saviour and God. Although we, the members of the Evangelical Church, cannot claim that we are ever blameless, we seek to be judged and corrected by the Word of God in continuing reformation, and therefore we cannot but pray for our erring friends in the Roman Church that they may be delivered from heresy and may return to the integrity of the Catholic and Apostolic faith in Jesus Christ.—I am &c.

THOMAS F. TORRANCE.

The Scotsman, November 5, 1957

28 Lauriston Street,
Edinburgh,
November 2, 1957

Sir,—My thanks are due to Professor Torrance for the courtesy he has done me in giving "a clear example" of "a great movement of reform going on in the Roman Church". I would be still further in his debt if he were more explicit about "the good Reformed teaching" contained in Walter's book. Eschatology as it is now treated in biblical theology was unknown to Luther and Calvin. Trent and even Vatican antedate the modern problem, and they had little enough to say on eschatology as it was then understood. If Walter's use of Kittel's *Woerterbuch* implies acceptance of its theology, then I must confess myself equally at fault. Perhaps the truth is that Professor Torrance and myself have different views on what is and what is not Catholic theology. His writings, even on this precise point of eschatology, seem to bear this out.

Eschatology, however, is really irrelevant to the main issue, which concerns the relation of Scripture to the teaching Church. We have Our Lord's own words, "This is My Body." That is what He said. What did He mean? The Catholic Church takes Him at His word, in the literal meaning. Transubstantiation is a simple corollary from that meaning.

I find it hard to take seriously what Professor Torrance says about transubstantiation. To suggest that there is anything Eutychian, still more Docetist, in the Catholic doctrine of the Eucharist shows a Pickwickian sense of historical theology—or a surprising ignorance of Catholic teaching. The bread and wine are changed into the Body and Blood of Christ, but Christ Himself remains unchanged, true God and true man, and the definition of Chalcedon in 451 is completely at one with the teaching of Lateran IV in 1215 on transubstantiation.

Let me say here that the Catholic Church does not override Scripture, and is so far from twisting Scripture to her own ends that she accepts faithfully the hard sayings of Christ. It is "with equal pious affection and reverence," in the classic words of the Council of Trent, that the Church receives and venerates the written Word of God and that other Word of God which is guaranteed by her Founder: "The gates of hell shall not prevail against it"; "I will be with you all days, even to the consummation of the world." That Word of God is not something static, but alive and vital, generating fresh insight into the Revelation given once for all as the Church turns inwards and reflects upon her life and teaching. But throughout the ages it is identifiably the same teaching.

"The Church that has the promise that the gates of hell shall not prevail against it is the Apostolic Church." I agree with Professor Torrance. But where was that Church, maintaining by Christ's promise the "integrity of the Catholic and Apostolic faith," in the days of Pope Clement in A.D. 96, exercising without apology apostolic jurisdiction over the Church of Corinth; of St. Ignatius of Antioch in A.D. 110, a clear witness to the Church's belief in its unity, in the Real Presence, in the hierarchical structure of bishops, priests and deacons; of St. Justin in A.D. 150, equally clear in his belief in Christ's bodily Presence in the Eucharist and in his witness to the devotion of the Church to Christ's Mother as the sinless Eve; of St. Irenaeus about A.D. 180, proclaiming the purity of faith of the Roman Church as the touchstone of orthodoxy—right on for the millennium and a half of Papal rule?

Professor Torrance sees Catholic Mariology as a corruption of pure doctrine. But has he tried to understand its Scriptural roots? For the Catholic Our Lady is the sinless Eve, the Woman of the great promise of redemption in Genesis, her destiny inextricably linked with that of her Son, the second Adam. But she remains essentially one of the redeemed, a member of Christ's Mystical Body. When she intercedes, it is with her Son, the one Mediator, with whom she intercedes. The dogma of her Assumption is bound up with the Scriptural notion of the corruption of death as a punishment for sin, for in Catholic teaching Our Lady was by the merits of her Son preserved immaculate, the second Eve.

Finally, we are not saved by learning. If the Scriptures are as difficult to understand as modern scholars would have us believe, is there not need of a living voice to be our guide? Will it be Schweitzer or Dodd or Bultmann or Barth? Or will it be the same voice echoing down the centuries, the voice of Peter? On the other hand, if all that is necessary for salvation is contained in the plain text of Scripture, how does Professor Torrance justify his views on infant baptism, and on the necessity of the laying-on of hands on one who is to celebrate a valid Eucharist?—I am &c.

(Rev.) JAMES QUINN, S.J.

The Scotsman, November 9, 1957

21 South Oswald Road,
Edinburgh,
November 6, 1957

Sir,—May I give the Rev. James Quinn two explicit examples of Walter's "Reformed" teaching? He speaks of the ministerial offices of the Church as belonging to the form of this passing age and as not belonging ultimately to the *esse* of the Church. Again, he shows that the growth or development of the Church in history is an eschatological as well as teleological continuity. It is precisely this fact that makes eschatology extremely relevant to the main issue.

According to Roman theology, all our theological statements are analogical. "This is my body" is thus not a statement of identity, nor of difference, but an analogical statement involving something of difference and of identity. I am aware of how Roman theologians vainly try to square this with a transubstantiation which destroys the inherent analogy. Let me refer instead to the sound teaching of Pope Gelasius I. He expounded "This is my body" on the analogy of the doctrine of the divine and human natures of Christ, and even defended the Chalcedonian Christology by pointing to the analogy in the Sacrament in which the elements are neither confused with, nor converted into, the Body and Blood of Christ, just as they are not separated from His real presence. That Rome departed from this is evidence that it has repudiated its catholic continuity and is no longer *semper eadem*.

It is downright error to hint that Justin taught that Mary was sinless. But what is the relevance of these patristic references, for none of these worthy fathers believed in Mary's assumption? That "dogma" had not been invented in their day! Does not the Roman Church, in promulgating this "dogma", thereby declare that the Apostolic and ancient Catholic Church was much poorer in its faith than the Roman Church to-day? And in declaring this "dogma" necessary for salvation, does it not thereby question the salvation of the apostles and fathers, not to speak of the rest of Christendom?

I have studied the volumes of Tiburtius Gallus entitled *Interpretatio Mariologica Protoevangelii Posttridentina*, and others relating to Mary. The concept of corredemption largely rests on the aberration in the old Latin Bible which makes Gen. 3: 15 read "She shall crush your head"; whereas the alleged sinlessness of Mary is based on a false interpretation of Luke 1 : 28, where the Greek for "favoured one" is wrongly rendered "full of grace", an expression found only in John 1 : 14 of Jesus, and in Acts 6: 8 of Stephen—the latter was certainly not sinless. But I have also read the words of Jesus from the Cross recorded in John 19: 26, in which He expressly brought the mother-son relationship between Mary and Himself to an end. The whole of Roman Mariology shatters itself upon this dominical word alone.

In regard to the Roman heresy of corredemption, let me cite two terrible Papal utterances—Benedict XV: ". . . it can rightly be said that Mary herself together with Christ redeemed the human race," and Pius XI: "It was she that stepped on the head of the gruesome serpent with her foot and brought about the salvation of the world. She is . . . the mighty mediator and redeemer with her only born Son." This is such a flagrant denial of the apostolic teaching that there is only one mediator between God and man, that it is no wonder that even Roman theologians like Professor Karrer admit that these ideas upset the whole Christological balance of Roman teaching and even make us ask in what sense we can still speak of it as really "Christian".

What lies behind these diseased growths in Roman theology is a false conception of "tradition". We do not quarrel with the distinction between a "passive tradition", the treasure of the apostolic faith which passes down through the ages without changing, and an "active tradition" which constantly unfolds the changeless treasure of the apostolic faith. But we entirely repudiate the claim of the Roman Church to a creative "faith-instinct" in virtue of which it adds to the apostolic faith and even subtracts from it, and in virtue of which it subordinates the Word of God in the apostolic tradition to its own interpretation, thus exalting itself into an authority above the ultimate authority of God's Word. It is always into this *sacro egoismo* (the Roman Church is the judge of its own case) that Roman theologians retreat when they are hard pressed by biblical and evangelical Truth.

But we in the Evangelical Church cannot leave the matter there to-day, for there are multitudes in the Roman Church in severe torment of soul and conscience owing to the deep-seated schizophrenia in its tradition. It is apparent everywhere to-day, especially in Roman research into patristic doctrine and liturgy as well as into the teaching of the Bible, that the "passive tradition" and the "active tradition" are being torn far apart. But this widening gap between biblical exegesis and "irreformable dogmas" reveals that the conflict is lodged in the very heart of Roman sacramentalism, where a "liturgical monophysitism" is co-ordinated with a strange Arianism in the notion of "created grace".

In vain do theologians like Karl Adam comfort themselves by speaking of a "complex of opposites" in the Roman tradition—that is only to cover up the wound by a paper plaster. It is just because we see this agony in the Roman Church that we cannot stand aloof from it, but must seek in every way, by speaking the truth in love, and by our intercessions above all, to help our brethren in their own self-inflicted wounds.—I am &c.

THOMAS F. TORRANCE.

The Scotsman, November 13, 1957

28 Lauriston Street,
Edinburgh,
November 9, 1957

Sir,—Your patient readers might welcome a word on eschatology. Nowadays it has to do with the interpretation of the "last days" and the coming of the Kingdom. In New Testament times these "last days" could be considered as something in the future or as already realized in the Messianic Kingdom of the Church. The latest biblical theology (really a return to tradition) emphasizes both these aspects, two stages in the Kingdom, separated by the end of the world.

Professor Torrance gives two "examples" of Walter's "Reformed" teaching. Walter "speaks of the ministerial offices of the Church as belonging to the form of this passing age and as not belonging ultimately to the *esse* of the Church." Here is an ambiguity. St. Paul speaks of faith in the same way; does he mean that faith does not ultimately belong to the *esse* of the Church? Would this be "good Reformed teaching"? Would Professor Torrance hold that baptism—or his own ministry—does not belong to the *esse* of the Church? What, in fact, is meant by "ultimately"? The ambiguity is not Walter's, for he writes that the Church is the Kingdom of God in its present condition, and is not a substitute (Ersatz) for the Kingdom.

We can dismiss Professor Torrance's second "example". It means quite simply that there is identity between the Church on earth and its fulfilment in Heaven. Walter does not say that the Kingdom in Heaven is the only real Kingdom.

"According to Roman theology, all our theological statements are analogical." Professor Torrance has confused statements about God's Being with statements about the Incarnation. The analogy of being, primarily a philosophical notion, has great significance for theology, but not for the interpretation of "This is My Body", which is a strictly univocal statement. Pope Gelasius I is really a witness for transubstantiation at the end of the fifth century. The Monophysites argued from the change of the bread and wine into the Body and Blood of Christ to a similar change in the Incarnation. The Pope, agreeing with their view of transubstantiation, pointed out that after the consecration there remained a reality which was distinct from Christ, *viz.* the accidents. This is the precise point where the analogy of being has relevance in sacramental theology. Gelasius, in fact, is in the main stream of Catholic teaching on the Real Presence.

Professor Torrance, ignoring my patristic references to the Papacy, bishops, and the Real Presence, eyes with disapproval my reference to the sinless Eve in Justin. Is his chief concern to deny Our Lady any part in the Divine plan of Redemption? Let him consult the ancient writers honoured in the Church. Their verdict is against him. To be deep in history, said Newman, is to cease to be a Protestant. It was not the Latin Bible that imposed the teaching of a special role for Our Lady—in the fourth century!—but rather the teaching of the Church which made possible the acceptance of that rendering of Gen. 3: 15. Let Professor Torrance go back beyond the Latin version, to Irenaeus in A.D. 180: "Whereas (Eve) had disobeyed God, yet (Mary) was persuaded to obey God in order that the Virgin Mary might be the advocate of the virgin Eve." Let him go East, to Ephraem the Syrian, uninfluenced by Latin tradition (d. A.D. 373). "God's Eden is Mary; in her is no tree of knowledge (i.e. experience of sin), no serpent that harms, no Eve that kills." Let him go back in history and see if I misrepresent Justin in seeing continuity with the development of his teaching in Irenaeus, Tertullian, and their successors. "Eve, an undefiled virgin, conceived the word of the serpent, and brought forth disobedience and death. But the Virgin Mary, filled with faith and joy . . . answered: 'Be it done unto me according to thy word.'"

Above all, let him consult the Scriptures, where Elizabeth greets her cousin as the second Eve (Luke 1: 45) and refers to her as the Shekinah-bearing Ark of the Covenant (Luke 1: 43–44) made, in the words of Hippolytus (d. A.D. 235) "of incorruptible wood, that is, out of the Virgin and the Holy Ghost". In the Apocalypse the Ark appears in Heaven (11: 19), and then the sign of the Woman (12: 1). Who is the Woman and "the rest of her seed" (Apoc. 12: 17)? "Who is My Mother and my brethren?" (Matt. 12: 48). It is the same question. The second Adam gives us life through the second Eve, the mother of the living according to the spirit.

If "Evangelical" Christianity interprets (by what authority?) John 19: 26–27, as the severing of the "mother-son relationship", I prefer the company of the fathers, of Christian antiquity, of the Catholic Church, to this picture of an inhuman Christ disowning His Mother at the moment of her supreme unselfishness.

As for the "terrible" Papal utterances, rudely torn from their context, they only show that Professor Torrance is unacquainted with Catholic Mariology, which, let me repeat as every Catholic text-book repeats, is completely in harmony with the Spiritual doctrine of the One Mediator. The cause of Christian unity and mutual charity would surely not be hindered by a more obvious effort to understand this.—I am &c.

(Rev.) JAMES QUINN, S.J.

The Scotsman, November 18, 1957

21 South Oswald Road,
Edinburgh,
November 15, 1957

Sir,—It is very kind of the Rev. James Quinn to take trouble to reply to my letter, although his "answers" sidestep the basic issue—they are obviously meant for popular consumption in his own Church.

It is surely a sorry day for the Roman Church when its accredited representatives have to be instructed by others in the documents of their own Church! According to Walter, the ministerial offices are necessary for the Church only during its earthly pilgrimage, and do not belong to its eternal foundation. Like St. Paul, he teaches that faith which is "in part" will pass away, and that love alone remains as the ultimate reality of the Church. Has the Rev. James Quinn not heard of the Roman doctrine that faith will at last give place to "the vision of God"?

His attempt to dismiss my second example simply means that he refuses to accept Walter's reformed teaching that the continuity of the Church is eschatological, i.e., that it is not a uniformly sound development but comes under the impending judgment of Christ, and even shares in its criticism already. I can well understand that this Petrine teaching that "judgment must begin at the house of God" should be anathema to a Jesuit!

The Rev. James Quinn seems to have been particularly badly instructed when he appears not to know that, according to Roman theology, all being is "intrinsically analogical" (as Dr. Phelan has put it)—unless, of course, he wants to exclude the Incarnation and also the sacramental reality from the category of real being!

But we really are greatly indebted to the Rev. James Quinn for giving us three clear examples of the erroneous way in which Romans of his kind handle documentary sources.

(1.) In his interpretation of Gelasius I he falsely reads back into the fifth century a heretical idea only invented in the ninth, and only accepted by the Roman Church in the thirteenth century. If he had compared the teaching of the Latin Gelasius with that of the Greek Theodoret, he would have seen the matter in its true light.

(2.) Another smokescreen of patristic citations, designed to prove the sinlessness of Mary! We in the Evangelical Church believe that Jesus was born of the Virgin Mary, but to argue from the fact that she was then an "undefiled virgin" to her sinlessness is pure nonsense. There are thousands of undefiled virgins in Edinburgh, not one of whom is sinless. According to Irenaeus even Eve was such when she sinned. (In spite of claiming to go behind the Latin text of the Bible to Irenaeus, the Rev. James Quinn only cites in translation from the later barbarous Latin version of Irenaeus.)

I grant that there is something of aptness and beauty in the typological comparison of Mary with Eve, for where Eve was disobedient Mary was obedient, as the Greek and Syriac fathers said, although, in spite of their extravagant language, they did not teach the sinlessness of Mary. It is entirely perverse to make them advocates of the late Roman heresy. They (e.g., Irenaeus and Athanasius) held to the fundamental fact that the Holy Son of God assumed our mortal, corrupt humanity under the bondage of sin in order to heal and redeem it. The flesh which He the sinless Son took from Mary was in the likeness of "the flesh of sin." That principle was tersely enunciated by Gregory Nazianzen: "The unassumed is the unhealed." To deny that is to deny the very foundation of our redemption in Christ.

The Evangelical Church in the West, like the Orthodox Church in the East, teaches that in assuming our fallen humanity from Mary the Holy Son of God healed and sanctified it, and that in that healing and sanctification Mary herself shared. But at this point Roman teaching has fallen into Scotist heresy in the doctrine of "the immaculate conception". It has gone off at a tangent, deviated from the truth, and departed from the integrity of the apostolic and catholic faith. But in so doing the Roman Church has cut itself off from the rest of historic and contemporary Christendom, and isolated and marooned itself as a lonely sect.

(3.) What about the biblical references adduced by the Rev. James Quinn? This is even where the wayfaring man though a fool can see how very erroneous he is. Luke 1 : 45 has not even a hint about a second Eve. In Luke 1 : 43–44 there is not a particle about the Ark of the Covenant. (But why should a Jesuit want to justify himself at this point by a citation from Hippolytus, the first anti-Pope?) Rev. 11 : 19 has nothing to do with Mary. Rev. 12 : 1 refers to Israel, and 12 : 17 to her offspring, the Church. In Matt. 12 : 48 f. Jesus declares that those who do the will of God are His brother, sister, and mother. But what about Mark 3 : 21 f. and 31 f., where the family of Jesus think He is "beside Himself"? As to John 19 : 26 (not to mention John 2 : 4), the Rev. James Quinn simply sets it aside in a splash of sentimental rhetoric.

This unscholarly and fantastic handling of biblical and patristic texts is precisely what destroys the Roman Church and makes it more and more an agony for those in it who know that the Kingdom of Christ is not founded upon subterfuge and error.—I am &c.

THOMAS F. TORRANCE.

The Scotsman, November 21, 1957

28 Lauriston Street,
Edinburgh,
November 19, 1957

Sir,—In three letters, Professor Torrance has given two "examples" of a "great movement of reform going on in the Roman Church", both from a modern Catholic writer. His latest formulation of Walter's view is pure Catholic theology. "The ministerial offices are necessary for the Church only during its earthly pilgrimage." What Catholic writer has ever denied this? It would be the "good Reformed teaching" of the invisible (as against the visible) Church if Walter had said that the ministerial offices were not necessary for the Church during its earthly pilgrimage. On the contrary, for Walter the visible Church is necessary.

That is why I stressed the parallel of faith in St. Paul. There are differences between the Church on earth and the Church in heaven, though there is continuity between them. Nor has any Catholic writer denied that the Church embraces sinners, who are therefore under the judgment of Christ. This is precisely Catholic teaching on the visible Church, composed of good and bad, all members of the Church, though not destined equally to share in the triumph of the Church.

In fact, both quotations must be embarrassing for those who believe only in the "good Reformed teaching" of the invisible Church, composed exclusively of the elect. How can ministerial offices be necessary in any sense for them, and what need have they to be under Christ's judgment?

Analogy of being is a philosophical concept which enables us to make true (though analogical) statements about infinite Being, though all our points of reference derive from created being; and to make true statements about accidents (quantity, quality, etc.) as distinct from substance. It is an essentially comparative operation. But statements which are not comparative are not analogical. When Christ said, "This is My Body," He was not making a comparative statement, but an absolute one, not an analogical statement, but a univocal one. If Professor Torrance believes that the Catholic Church holds this statement to be analogical, he has misconceived the Catholic position.

Gelasius I gives place to Theodoret. I have read Theodoret in the Greek. Eranistes, the Monophysite in the Dialogue who argued from transubstantiation to a similar change in the glorified Body of Christ, was arguing on the common ground of Eucharistic doctrine. Theodoret (Orthodoxus of the Dialogue) admitted his Eucharistic doctrine, but denied that there was a complete parallel, because the accidents (what appears to the senses) remained. He makes a clear distinction between what is the subject of sight and touch, and what is the subject of intellect, faith, and adoration. If Theodoret had not agreed with Eranistes' view on the Eucharist, the discussion could not have arisen. In fact, in the same Dialogue Theodoret quotes with approval the Christological doctrine of Gregory of Nyssa, Chrysostom, Ambrose, and others, and may be presumed to have approved of their views, clearly expressed, on transubstantiation.

The bulk of Irenaeus' work "Against Heresies" has come down to us only in a Latin version, probably dating from before A.D. 200, less probably from the fourth century. No scholar would, I think, suggest that it was influenced in any way by the corrupt reading of the Latin of Gen. 3: 15, which crept in after Jerome's translation in the late fourth century, though it was not due to Jerome. The Latin version of Irenaeus is trustworthy and literal. But Professor Torrance seems to have missed the point of Irenaeus' comparison between Eve and Our Lady, which is part of his doctrine of "recapitulation". Eve was a virgin until the Fall, and before the Fall she was in a state of innocence, not yet lost by original sin. In the divine plan to undo the work of Eve, Our Lady also was to be a Virgin, and, if the comparison is to be exact, in a state of innocence.

This leads us to Gregory Nazianzen. Professor Torrance quotes his principle: "The unassumed is the unhealed." From this Professor Torrance deduces that "The flesh which He, the sinless Son, took from Mary was in the likeness of 'the flesh of sin.'" Gregory Nazianzen, however, did not make this deduction. He speaks explicitly of Christ as "conceived of the Virgin, who in both soul and flesh had been purified in preparation by the Spirit" (*Orat.* 38: 13).

It is not only, as Professor Torrance says, the teaching of "the Evangelical Church in the West" (is there such an entity?) and of the Orthodox Church in the East that "in assuming our fallen humanity from Mary the Holy Son of God healed and sanctified it, and that in the healing and sanctification Mary herself shared." It is also the teaching of the Catholic Church. The Immaculate Conception does not mean that Our Lady was not redeemed, but that she was redeemed more perfectly than any other, by a redemption that preserved her from every effect of sin, that was solely by God's grace, not by her own merits but by Christ's. Could a Calvinist wish for a fuller vindication of the sovereign power of God's grace?

Professor Torrance seems to be unaware of recent work on the literary relationship of Luke 1–2 and the books of Samuel, which is the basis of my reference to the Ark of the Covenant. Nor has he asked himself the reason for the appearance in A.D. 150 of a mature doctrine of Our Lady as the Second Eve. Perhaps your readers now see more clearly the difficulty of discussing Scripture without some common ground in the authority of the Church, which gave Scripture to the world, and, more pertinently, in the evidence for the Church's beliefs that is written so large in history.—I am &c.

(Rev.) JAMES QUINN, S.J.

The Scotsman, November 25, 1957

21 South Oswald Road,
Edinburgh,
November 23, 1957

Sir,—I regret that the Rev. James Quinn persists in evading the main issues I have raised by concentrating on subsidiary questions.

I would gladly deal with all these, if space permitted, showing that according to the authorities, Jordan and Souter, the Latin Text of Irenaeus dates from A.D. 370 to 420; that the authoritative Athanasius nowhere assigns to Mary any personal agency or peculiar place in the work of redemption; that the Orthodox Church, much more authoritative in interpreting its own fathers than the Roman Church, repudiates the idea that Mary was without original sin or had a human nature liberated from sin before ever the Incarnation took place; that the great fathers explicitly declare that the substance of the elements remained the same, and that they cannot without falsity be made to fit into Roman Aristotelian theories; that true analogies are not direct comparisons but only comparisons of relations, and that the Sacramental relation, even on Roman authority (e.g. M. Scheeben), participates analogically in the Christological relation; that according to Calvin the true doctrine of the "invisible Church" is that of the Creed in which it is "the visible Church" that we speak of as object of faith, for "faith is the evidence of things not seen", etc.

But now let us get back to the fundamental question of

Scripture and tradition, and the deep rift daily developing in the Roman Church. It is not out of polemical interest that I write but because I feel strongly that Evangelical theology must deliver its soul and in a sincere brotherly spirit warn the Roman Church of the fearful consequences of its false developments.

Let me cite the words of a brilliant Roman theologian (*Christ und Welt*, 1950). "The new dogma is justified not by appealing to evidence which is regarded as strictly scientific (i.e. to Scripture and Tradition which have their source in Primitive Christianity) but by appealing instead to the so-called intuitive understanding of the present-day Church for matters of faith. One begins with the acknowledged fact that the present-day Church believes in the Ascension of Mary, and then explains that because of the assistance of the Holy Spirit it would be impossible for the Church to be mistaken about such a belief. From the insight thus gained into the interpretation and estimation of traditional teaching the Church works backwards to Primitive Christianity. The priority thus accorded to the intuitive understanding of the present-day Church over the results of pure historical investigation of Scripture and Tradition is the theoretical presupposition of the new dogma and at the same time the practical consequence of its 'definition' through the Pope. Therein and not so much in its content lies its extraordinary theological significance." (Cf. also *Blackfriars*, Oct., 1950.)

That is a lucid and frank statement requiring little comment. One could point out the consequence of this view of tradition and history by showing how the ex-Roman atheist Martin Heidegger employed it in his interpretation of "existence" with all the fatal results which even Rome deplores. But I want rather to point out the dire effects of this upon the Roman Church itself. It means that the Roman Church claims a place of self-sufficiency and even superiority over against the apostolic foundation; than in virtue of its intuitive understanding it creatively controls the active tradition and is able to bring out of itself justification for any new idea it likes; that it attempts to bind the Holy Spirit to what Rome says, rather than to bind itself solely to what Christ has said, as when He promised to the Church the gift of the Spirit who would not speak of Himself but only reveal what Christ had already said. All this means that the Roman Church has not only exalted Mary to be "the Queen of Heaven", but has in actual fact usurped the teaching office of the Spirit and obtruded itself in the very place of Christ, obscuring the precious Gospel with the traditions of men "made in Rome".

That is why this is a basic issue for the Roman priest with his flock as well as for the Roman Church, for both priest and Church will have to give an account at the Judgment Seat of Christ of their stewardship of the Gospel as proclaimed in the Holy Scriptures. If Romans really believe that the See of Rome is grounded on the rock Peter, then let them listen to Peter's words, warning that "judgment must begin at the house of God" (I Peter 4: 17), and that Jesus Christ Himself will be "a rock of offence to them who stumble and are disobedient" (I Peter 2: 8).

Let Romans consider the fact that so long as there exists the Orthodox Church and the Evangelical Church, forming the greater part of Christendom, the biggest question mark is put to the Apostolicity and Catholicity of the Roman Church, for it no longer conforms to the Vincentian Canon: "what has always and everywhere been believed"; that the plain fact that the Roman Church has never been able to achieve reconciliation with them means that it has never been able to meet their challenge, but has only been able to retire more and more into itself as a self-willed authority. But now the Roman Church begins to create by its inventions upheaval within itself through tension between loyalty to the Biblical Tradition and loyalty to "Catholic Instinct". If the Rev. James Quinn will not listen to me about this deep rift, let him study the article by the Roman Professor Geiselmann ("Una Sancta", September, 1956) who, on the evidence of the minutes of the Council of Trent, points out the cleavage between it and the Vatican Council (misled by Bellarmine and Canisius) on the relation between Scripture and tradition. According to Trent, there are not two sources of Revelation but only one, insists Geiselmann. Even if that is "explained away" there still remains the fact that there are men like Geiselmann in the Roman Church alarmed at the new developments and doing their best to restore the supremacy of the apostolic tradition over all the "misunderstanding" of the Roman Church. We in the Evangelical Church will extend to all such a brotherly hand, and do all we can to help them correct error and recover the purity of the Gospel.—I am &c.

THOMAS F. TORRANCE.

The Scotsman, November 30, 1957

28 Lauriston Street,
Edinburgh,
November 26, 1957

Sir,—I leave it to your readers to judge whether I have evaded the main issue. The main issue, as I see it, is the value to be placed on Professor Torrance's statement that there is "a great movement of reform going on in the Roman Church," and so a fundamental change of attitude to Scripture and tradition. I cannot very well evade what has not yet been proved. Walter, at any rate, has disappeared from the debate.

My entry into this correspondence was by way of the main issue. I am accused of concentrating on subsidiary questions, all raised by Professor Torrance. I am still waiting to see the relevance to the main issue of the question of analogy, explained by Professor Torrance in three different ways, all contradictory. I have shown that Pope Gelasius I and Theodoret, invoked by Professor Torrance, were orthodox in regard to transubstantiation.

In regard to Our Lady, Professor Torrance has cast needless doubt on the Latin text of Irenaeus. Patristic scholars are not generally so sweeping in their assessment of Irenaeus' testimony. On the contrary, Irenaeus (c. A.D. 180) is a landmark in Church history. Professor Torrance's appeal to Gregory Nazianzen has been shown to be valueless, as Gregory himself held the very doctrine Professor Torrance sought to disprove. Athanasius, who had nothing directly to say on the Immaculate Conception or the Assumption, seems the only authority from antiquity he will admit. What would he say of St. John Damascene (died A.D. 749), the great champion of both these doctrines, and the common Doctor of the Catholic Church and the separated East?

I find it hard to see the reason for Professor Torrance's references to the "Orthodox Church" (which does he mean?). The Catholic Church cannot meet its challenge because it is the challenge of heresy and schism. Yet there would be little sympathy among the "Orthodox" for Professor Torrance's "good Reformed teaching" on the Church, on the sacraments, on episcopacy, on Our Lady. May I suggest that the whole non-Catholic world, "Orthodox" included, is less in numbers than the Catholic Church, comprising at least one sixth of the world's population and including every nation and culture? I base this on *Life*, International Edition, February 6, 1956. The Catholic Church is the greatest, and oldest Ecumenical Movement in the world.

The basis of any disagreement with Professor Torrance in regard to Scripture and tradition is our divergent views on the meaning of Revelation, and so on the nature of the Church. May I summarize my position? In matters of faith the Church has the guidance of the Holy Spirit, and is the guardian of the Revelation given to the Apostolic Church. That Revelation is not restricted to the series of statements found in Scripture, though they are part of it, but it is an organic and living whole. It is the mystery of Christ in its fulness, which words can express but cannot contain. A world of books would not be able to sound its depths, as St. John admits. Revelation was not given originally in written books: it was the Church who produced the Scriptures from her own living tradition and gave them to the world. An "invisible" Church must rely on the text of Scripture; the visible, Catholic Church claims divine authority to interpret the Scriptures in the light of her own living tradition.

Development of doctrine is not radical change. The Church has no power to add to or subtract from the original Revelation, but she does gain new insight into its meaning. Yet her teaching remains identifiably the same in every age, not with the self-identity of a material thing incapable of development, but with the complexity of a body growing towards its full stature. That is why a Catholic is at home in history, because he can see the Church in every age identical with herself.

If the Church has the promise of Christ that He will be with her all days, the Church cannot err in faith. Whatever, therefore, the Church declares to be part of Revelation, must infallibly be so. Christ has identified Himself with His Church: "He that heareth you heareth Me." This does not mean that the Church "creatively controls the active tradition" in any other sense than that in which the promise of divine assistance was given to the Church. In a word, the Revelation which she guards is her own living awareness of the mystery of Christ.

This Revelation can be described in two ways. We may say: (1) that it has two sources, viz. Scripture and tradition; or (2) that there is but one Word of God delivered to us by the Church in the written Word and in the Church's life. Both statements are orthodox. To assert the second is not to deny the first.

What promoted my first letter was the hope that this very concept of "the unchanging Word of God delivered in its fulness within the living tradition of the Church's *kerygma*" might be a window through which our non-Catholic friends might see something of the Church's view of

Scripture and tradition. The modern Protestant theology of the Word, though at many points very different from the Catholic concept of Revelation, is justly regarded by non-Catholic theologians as their most fruitful contribution to the study of Revelation. It was my hope that it might prove a meeting-point for sympathetic understanding between Catholics and Protestants in their common love of Scripture.—I am &c.

(Rev.) JAMES QUINN, S.J.

The Scotsman, December 4, 1957

21 South Oswald Road,
Edinburgh,
November 31, 1957

Sir,—Your readers must be more and more baffled by the claim of the Rev. James Quinn to meet my main charges when once again he sets aside what I have laid before him: a Roman exposition from *Christ u. Welt* of how Roman tradition operates in justifying "the new dogma," and a Roman protest against there being two sources of Revelation. The Rev. James Quinn does claim, however, that there are two sources of Revelation, and that is quite sufficient to show the cleavage in Roman opinion to-day.

But lest your readers should think I am evading his claims about the teaching of the fathers, let me say two things:

(*a*) As against his claim to show that "Pope Gelasius I and Theodoret were orthodox in regard to transubstantiation," let me give two citations from them, and let your readers judge for themselves.

Gelasius: "Certainly the sacraments of the body and blood of Christ which we take are a divine matter on account of the fact that through them also we are partakers of the divine nature, and yet the substance or nature of the bread and wine does not cease to be (*non desinit substantia vel natura panis et vini*). And certainly it is the image and likeness of the body and blood of Christ that are celebrated in the action of the mysteries. Therefore it is shown to us evidently enough that in Christ the Lord we must feel this, regarding what we in His image profess, celebrate and take, just as if they through the consecrating (*perficiente*) of the Holy Spirit were to pass into divine substance, although they nevertheless remain in their own proper nature."

Theodoret: To the argument of the inquirer that "the symbols of both the Master's body and blood are different before the priestly invocation but are changed and become something else after," Theodoret answers as the teacher: "For not even after sanctification do the mystic symbols depart from their proper nature (*oude . . . tes oikeias existatai phuseos*); for they remain in their former substance and character and form (*ousias kai schematos kai tou eidous*), and they are visible and tangible such as they also were before. But what they became is understood and believed and venerated as if they were (*hos ekeina onta*) that which they are believed to be."

The Rev. James Quinn could only "prove" his case in regard to these if he could "prove" that by "substance" and "nature" Gelasius and Theodoret did not really mean "substance" and "nature". Doubtless that is just what he will try to do, falling back upon what *Christ u. Welt* spoke of as "the priority of intuitive understanding over the results of pure historical investigation of Scripture and Tradition."

(*b*) Professor Lossky, in his "Essai sur la Théologie Mystique de l'Eglise d'Orient," declares: "The dogma of the immaculate conception is foreign to the Eastern Tradition which does not wish to separate the holy Virgin from the descendants of Adam upon whom the fault of the first parents weighs." I cannot agree with all that Lossky teaches, nor with the sometimes extravagant statements of the Greek fathers—but is there a single statement anywhere in any of the Ecumenical Councils or in any of the acknowledged Greek fathers, including Nazianzen and John of Damascus, which teaches the Roman heresy, namely, that Mary was without original sin and that she had a human nature liberated from sin before ever the Incarnation took place? If the Rev. James Quinn can discover one, why does he not produce it?

But back again to the main issue. Is it not strange that the Roman Church should advocate a conception of tradition as a second source of Revelation alongside that of the Holy Scriptures almost identical with that of the Judaism that resented and crucified Jesus because He did not fit in with its authoritative tradition and interpretation of the Old Testament? Is it not remarkable that the Roman Church should have taken this conception of tradition over from the Gnostic heretics of the second century (including a great deal of their myth and ritual) so powerfully exposed and attacked by Irenaeus on the ground that they claimed to have the true tradition in virtue of which they alone could interpret the Scriptures truly and that they alone therefore possessed "the Gospel of Truth"? But the Roman Church has gone far beyond the errors of Judaism and Gnosticism: it has dared to identify Divine Revelation with its own "awareness of Revelation", that is, with its own subjectivity, so that what the

Roman Church declares to be part of Revelation must infallibly be so!

Now I admit that Protestants cannot absolve themselves from guilt at this point, for it was to a large extent the influence of Hegel and above all of Schleiermacher upon J. A. Müller and M. Scheeben that enabled the Roman Church to take that fearful step from the Council of Trent (bad as that was) to the Vatican Council in which Revelation was identified with the historical consciousness of the Church. Yes, we admit that in a profound sense Christ has identified Himself with His Church, but we deny that that statement can be reversed so as to make Christ the predicate of the being and historical existence of the Church. That is precisely what the Roman Church has presumed to do, so that the Holy Spirit is identified with its own spirit, and the mind of Christ is identified with the mind of the Church as declared through its teaching office. That is the ultimate heresy, the *sacro egoismo* of Rome into which, as I predicted in an earlier letter, Romans always flee for refuge when hard pressed by biblical and evangelical Truth—but when that is done, discussion is at an end. That is where the Rev. James Quinn has now taken refuge.

When the Roman Church insists on making its own laws as well as being the judge of its own case, and insists on identifying itself with the source of Revelation, so substituting itself in the place of the ultimate authority of the Lord Jesus Christ, we in the Evangelical Church can only say an unambiguous and decided "No". It is the whole Gospel which is at stake, for once again the sole Lordship of Christ is being crucified by "the traditions of men." That is what must be said again to-day to the official Roman Church, but with all the people within it who love the Gospel and seek to liberate the Word of God from the ever-tightening fetters of the Roman tradition, we join in common worship of the crucified Lord, and look for the day when He, now risen and ascended, will come again to set men free and judge the quick and the dead.—I am &c.

THOMAS F. TORRANCE.

The Scotsman, December 10, 1957

28 Lauriston Street,
Edinburgh,
December 6, 1957

Sir,—Professor Torrance's original letter, dated October 22, spoke of "a great movement of reform going on in the Roman Church," by which presumably the Catholic Church was moving towards a Protestant position, especially in biblical theology. This statement I called in question. Professor Torrance then tried to prove it from individual Catholic theologians, who, incidentally, are not the authoritative voice of the Church, which speaks through its bishops and the Pope.

First he referred to Eugen Walter, whom he has now abandoned. He then instanced the Catholic Professor J. R. Geiselmann, writing in *Una Sancta*, September, 1956. Professor Torrance sees in this "a Roman protest against there being two sources of Revelation." This suggests a protest against Tradition. But Professor Geiselmann says categorically that "Tradition is the living interpreter of Scripture." He also points out, as I did in my first letter, that Protestant theologians are interpreting the *sola Scriptura* ("Bible only") principle within the framework of tradition. The Church's interpretation of Scripture, in Geiselmann's words, is "authoritative and therefore binding on the community of the faithful".

Professor Torrance's other authority is a quotation from *Christ und Welt*. But where is the "good Reformed teaching" in its insistence on the authority of the Church? Authority and a living voice are indeed "the refuge where all Romans flee". What is Professor Torrance's ultimate authority? Is it the self-styled "Evangelical Church", whose allegiance is divided among many Churches, none of which claims to speak with real authority—or is it the *sacro egoismo* of private judgment? Does Christ still speak with authority through His Church, or is Christianity meant to be a matter for debate?

"When that [the invoking of authority] is done, discussion is at an end." Does Professor Torrance think this is a bad thing? Is argument an end in itself? What do your readers think? After all, truth ends all debate.

May I suggest that Professor Torrance's translation of Gelasius makes nonsense of the argument? Gelasius is arguing from fact, not from fiction. ". . . just as [not, as Professor Torrance translates, "just as if"] they [the bread and wine] pass into the divine substance, while their characteristic activity remains, so . . ." Professor Torrance omits the conclusion, and makes the comparison hypothetical. But Gelasius says that the bread and wine do "pass into" the divine substance, i.e. are really changed. It is in the light of Gelasius's own statement, and not in that of the developed technical vocabulary of the thirteenth century, that we must interpret his fifth-century use of "substance" and "nature", and refer them to the realities of shape, colour, etc., which continue their characteristic activity upon the senses after the Consecration.

Professor Torrance mistakenly imagines Theodoret's opponent to be an "inquirer". He is a heretic, a Monophysite. Theodoret is not explaining Catholic doctrine to an inquirer: he is dealing with the arguments of a heretic. Eranistes argues from Catholic teaching on transubstantiation, the change of the bread and wine into the Body and Blood of Christ, to a heretical conclusion, viz. that in the glorified Christ there is only one nature. Theodoret accepts his premiss, the common ground between them, and shows that in Catholic teaching there is a reality which remains, viz. the accidents. That is why, in Theodoret's words, Eranistes is "caught in his own web"—he has argued from Catholic doctrine and has been refuted by Catholic doctrine. His argument is a boomerang.

If Professor Torrance would like to discuss the evidence in the early Church for the doctrine of the Immaculate Conception, I am willing to do so, too. But first I should like to ask him if he still holds that there is "a great movement of reform going on in the Roman Church." Let us settle the "main charges" first.—I am &c.

(Rev.) JAMES QUINN, S.J.

The Scotsman, December 13, 1957

21 South Oswald Road,
Edinburgh,
December 12, 1957

Sir,—I admit that the official Roman Church is not reforming itself, but is steadily getting worse and worse, going from heresy to heresy. But the strange thing is that when twice in published writings I have cited the Vatican Council to the effect that the Roman Church is "irreformable", I have had letters of protest from world-renowned Roman theologians. Only the other day a Benedictine wrote to say how much he agreed with my view (in an article in *Kerygma u. Dogma*) on the need for a reform of the diaconate, and asked me whether I knew of the twenty-year-old movement for reform going on in the Roman Church to restore the diaconate to what it was in the Early Church in an effort to heal the cleft between the clergy and laity!

The same theologian says in that letter: "We are wholly one with you in striving for a Christological understanding of the Church and in thinking through the question of orders from that perspective." How difficult that is to do in the Roman Church is clear from the papal encyclical, *Mystici Corporis* (1943), which is designed to counteract such a movement and to reassert the reactionary mediaeval notion of a twofold

Church (invisible mystical body and perfect earthly society) avoiding altogether the credal doctrine of the One Church as object of faith. But in spite of that, Roman books continue to appear with very different teaching, such as *Geschleifte Bastionen*, by H. U. v. Balthasar, and *Das Experiment Europa*, by F. Heer.

Who could be a better example than v. Balthasar of a Roman influenced by Reformed theology? Indeed, he was so strongly influenced by the teaching of Karl Barth that he contracted out of the Jesuit order and became a "secular priest", where he could have more freedom to obey his conscience in the Truth. On the other hand, poor Père Congar lives, it appears, in banishment because of his ecumenical activities and his rapprochement to Evangelical theology. I only hope that the wrath of Rome will not now descend on the head of Eugen Walter!

But let us look at several fields where reform is going on in the Roman Church. One of the most remarkable facts of modern Church history is the move of Romans back to "positive theology", in which instead of *Summae* we have "Dogmatics", which is concerned with the Word of God and obedient conformity to it in the life of the Church. That is due to the Protestant challenge, but now, after earlier moves in this direction by Braun, Bartmann, Scheeben, etc., Romans are moving even closer to Reformed theology in writing Dogmatics with a decidedly Christological orientation—e.g. Söhngen and Schmaus. Among Romans the only real dogmatician of that calibre in this country is Mgr. Davis. My only difficulty with him is that he works with too "Lutheran" a view of faith and reason!

When we turn to Roman biblical studies, we find them engaged in the recovery of *Kerygma*, again under Protestant influence. When Aquinas in a section of his *Summa* dealt with the communication of salvation, he did not mention proclamation at all. When in 1947 the Pope published his *Mediator Dei*, he mentioned it only last, and then defined it thus: (1) recalling the laws of the Master; (2) instruction in the important circumstances of His life: and (3) appropriate advice and moral teaching. But the decisive thing there is lacking: the proclamation of the joyful Good News of the Gospel, the *Kerygma*, upon which the New Testament lays such overwhelming weight. In spite of that, many Romans are reverting more and more to the biblical *Kerygma*—e.g. Daniélou, Bouyer.

But let us look at one more field—the sacraments. I need hardly mention the reaction among Roman theologians (since de La Taille's *Mysterium Fidei*, 1930) from the crude Tridentine doctrine of the immolation of Christ in the sacrifice of the Mass. But I am more interested in the debate now going on among Roman scholars about baptism, most clearly seen in Schnackenburg's book on "Baptism as Salvation-Event," in which he seeks to move away from the notion of baptism as a mystery-rite to the New Testament conception of it as eschatological event in Christ. I have been drawn into this debate myself because the Church of Scotland's Reports on Baptism are being used by some Continental Romans to help them in their fight against the Roman assimilation of Christian baptism to the pagan mysteries of ancient Greece.

But what am I to say about the Reformed view of the Word of God and tradition? We acknowledge that all our reading and hearing of the Word of God is conditioned by the previous reading and hearing of it in the historical Church. We cannot and must not escape from our God-given setting in the Church, which has nourished us in the faith and passed on to us the Bible and the teaching of the apostles. The Church is, as Calvin said, "the Spouse of Christ, the pillar and ground of Truth, the guardian of sound doctrine, who by her ministry propagates it to posterity."

But because the Church is the Spouse of Christ, added Calvin, "she must be subject to Christ." Therefore the doctrine of the Church that is handed on to us in the decisions of the great Councils, in the teaching and preaching of the Church throughout history, must be tested reverently by the Word of God and continually corrected by it. It is because Christ is really present in His Word that we can do that, for as we obey Him and subject all our tradition and thought to His Word and Spirit, we are reformed and conformed to His Word.

We in the Evangelical Church really believe in this mighty creative Word of God and believe that Christ is able to reveal Himself even to the humblest of His children, in spite of their errors and even against their traditions, when, together "with all saints," they sincerely listen to Him speaking in the Holy Scriptures. When Romans really learn to believe in God's Word and trust its supreme authority they will cease to make Truth relative to "unproven" Roman opinion (as in *Humani Generis*, 1950!), to be cynical about the receptive capacities of humble people whom God made to hear His Word, and disparagingabout the power of the Spirit to bring about their authentic understanding of the Scriptures.—I am &c.

THOMAS F. TORRANCE.

The Scotsman, December 16, 1957

Oscott College,
Sutton Coldfield,
Warwickshire,
December 14, 1957

Sir,—My attention has been drawn to a reference to my name in a correspondence you have just closed. May I be allowed, without taking part in the closed correspondence, to correct an apparent misunderstanding of my views? Professor Torrance, after kindly allowing that my theology, with that of other Catholic theologians he mentions, is centred in Christ, complains that I have too "Lutheran" a view of faith and reason.

May I simply assert that my view is that of St. Thomas? Faith itself is above reason, since it rests on God's revealing Word, and believes what He reveals because He is eminently truthful and trustworthy, and not because what He reveals can be otherwise proved by reason. Reason, on the other hand, has a far more important part than Luther would, I believe, allow. Reason's part is first to show that there are sufficient grounds for a prudent man to believe that God has spoken. After one has accepted the faith, reason has a valuable part in helping the theologian to understand more deeply what has been accepted. But here reason is the handmaid. It can never supplant or transcend the faith, but it has a most important part in helping us to understand.—I am &c.

(Mgr.) H. FRANCIS DAVIS.

Epilogue

It would be very difficult to find a daily newspaper willing to allot so much space to a discussion of this kind as *The Scotsman*. The allowance was most generous, but even so space in the correspondence columns was inevitably restricted. Within such limits it is not possible to indulge in many lengthy citations, to take up all the points raised, or to develop the argument in full. Nor is it possible to sift out the area of agreement and deal exactly with the areas of disagreement. The debate must rather take the form of focusing attention upon primary questions, bringing out into the open those fundamental issues which continue to divide the Evangelical Churches from the Roman Church, and indicating the lines which a profounder and more exact *Auseinandersetzung* should take. It is to be hoped that the re-publication of the correspondence may enable it to continue to serve that purpose.

It must be evident that the whole question of analogy requires much more careful and critical treatment than many people in the Roman or Evangelical Church are prepared to accord to it. This is a question which we in the Evangelical Church must study and in regard to which we must be prepared to press home debate with our Roman brethren. The true use of analogy in theology, as St. Thomas showed so clearly, does not involve direct comparison but only comparison of relations in the form: as A is to B on one level, so C is to D on another level. What is to be compared therefore in regard to the Sacraments is the sacramental mode of relation and union with the mode of relation and union in Christ Himself. If, as Romans hold, the elements are transubstantiated into the human nature of Christ, then they cannot deny without contradiction that they share (in analogical proportion) in the relation of the divine and human natures of Christ described by "without confusion and without separation", etc. That is, they participate in a relation which is characterized neither by identity nor by difference. But then in the face of that to assert the univocity of the sacramental relation is to make the contradiction even more tangled. If "This is my body" involves a univocal relation, there is no need for the elements to be changed into what they are not by nature—the very fact that they are regarded as changed means that a relation of identity is not presupposed but imposed where it did not exist! We must not go further into that here, but let Romans be assured that if they wish to enter into serious discussions with us they must be prepared to think out the theological problems that divide us on the ground of the doctrine of Christ. It is the Incarnation that demands that the way that God has taken in the Incarnation of the Word must be the way we are to take in all our theological understanding and thinking. Ultimately it is the refusal to take the *analogia Christi* in its full depth and seriousness that divides us.

And yet this is the very point where in spite of all that has happened in the past we may still come together, if we centre our theology in Christ and are prepared to think out our theology in such a way that at every point it is really consistent with its centre in Him. In this we must fully agree with Mgr. Davis that "reason is the handmaid. It can never supplant or transcend the faith, but it has a most important part in helping us to understand." In my reference to him I had in mind his excellent paper on "Faith and Truth" read to the Society for the Study of Theology in April, 1956 (published in the *Scottish Journal of Theology:* 9, 4, pp. 359–373). In it, with reference to the writings of St. Thomas and St. John of the Cross and others, he gave an exposition of the relation of faith to truth in a way that would command wide agreement from Reformed and Lutheran theologians. What struck me so deeply about his essay was that he put the emphasis again and again just where we have learned that the Bible puts it, instead of at the places where mediaeval Aristotelianism put it, and yet he is no less loyal to his own Church. Behind all that seemed to lie a faith and theology centred above all in Jesus Christ Himself and in the biblical Revelation of Him. With such theologians it is possible to enter into real communication and to find a deep measure of agreement. But this makes it all the more tragic that the official pronouncements of the Roman Church should more and more undermine the pre-eminence of Christ in its theology as well as its piety, and make more and more impossible genuine communication with it.

Part

2

PROBLEMS OF FAITH AND ORDER

PROBLEMS OF FAITH AND ORDER

I. AMSTERDAM

THE NATURE AND MISSION OF THE CHURCH[1]

A Discussion of Vols. I and II of the Preparatory Studies[2]

THE *Universal Church in God's Design*, and *The Church's Witness to God's Design*, the first two volumes written in preparation for the meeting of the World Council of Churches at Amsterdam, are an ecumenical event in themselves. They form the most significant attempt at combined thinking about the nature and mission of the Church that has yet taken place. The stage is now set for a fresh and exhaustive inquiry behind the present divisions among the Churches into a biblical and Christological doctrine of the Church which may yet knit into a theological unity the agreement of the Churches reached at Amsterdam. After all "the only valid argument for the union of the Churches is theological, a belief that unity is the will of God for His Church, and that the Church as the Body of Christ ought to represent on earth the mysterious unity of the God-head" (Vol. II, p. 202). The purpose of this essay is not so much to review the actual material presented in these volumes as to face the questions they raise and, if possible, to point the discussion farther along the road to that theological unity.

We are confronted at the very outset with the fact that the pressure for visible unity, for a re-catholicization of the Churches, has not come so much from the professedly "catholic" sections of the Church as from the "evangelical" movements burdened with fulfilling the mission of the Gospel

[1] From the *Scottish Journal of Theology*, 1949, pp. 241–70.

[2] Four Volumes of Studies prepared for the First General Assembly of the World Council of Churches at Amsterdam, August 22 to September 4, 1948, and the Official Report edited by W. A. Visser 't Hooft. S.C.M. Press. 12*s*. 6*d*. each volume.

to the whole world.[1] The great impetus in the Ecumenical Movement has been decidedly missionary. That is not to say that evangelical experience and action have taken precedence over theological conviction, for side by side with this evangelism and at the very heart of its obedience to Christ there is going on a renewal of the great convictions of the faith such as we have not seen since the Reformation. It is just here in evangelism, as Oliver Tomkins says, that doctrine and practice meet (I, p. 135). Nevertheless these have yet to be integrated at the ecumenical level. That means on the one hand that "the problem of the Church's world mission is the crisis of the Ecumenical Movement. If an Ecumenical Movement is not primarily a strategy of world-wide evangelism, then it is nothing but an interesting academic exercise" (II, p. 116). On the other hand it means that "there is still in much of our ecumenism a strong element of relativism and of lack of concern for the truth of God" (Visser 't Hooft, I, p. 183). Nevertheless the hope of the situation is that "the Church in the churches insists on asserting itself. Wherever two or three are gathered together, the Una Sancta is in the midst of them and demands to be manifested" (I, p. 185). When that happens as it did at Amsterdam there are signs that something new is about to take place, especially when it is evidently accompanied by the overmastering conviction that Christ far transcends all our theological formulations and that there is an essential unity of the one flock of Christ in spite of the disobedience and failures of the historical Churches.

If therefore theological unity at the ecumenical level seems to lag behind actual fellowship in the evangel, that may not mean a lack of reflection but rather that the wholeness of Christ and the given unity of His Church press so heavily upon the sundered Churches in the hour of their coming together and renewal that they are thrown into a divine uncertainty about traditional formulations of the faith, and cannot use them in order to express the essential unity of the faith. In other words it is precisely the unity of the Church in Christ Jesus conceived as an eschatological reality that both interpenetrates history and transcends it, as a given unity even in the midst of disorder

[1] "Catholic" and "evangelical" are used here and throughout as in the Amsterdam Report, p. 52.

and as a promised unity beyond it, that has brought the Churches together as far as Amsterdam and yet has prevented them from snatching too hastily at a visible unity.

That such a stage has been reached is of the greatest significance. The persistent difficulty has been that from each side of a fundamental division, such as that between "catholic" and "evangelical", people see the Christian faith and life as a self-consistent whole, while the two conceptions of the whole are actually inconsistent with each other. If the realization of the given unity is strong enough, however, it will surely entail an eschatological suspension of the confessionalism behind these conceptions of the whole, and at the same time mean a shattering of theological relativism. Then room will be created among the Churches for ecumenical thinking in the proper sense—that is to say for a corporate thinking "with all saints" of the breadth, length, depth and height of the love of Christ which passes knowledge through which the Churches may reach out to be filled with all the fulness of God in Christ. Ecumenical thinking might well be described as *Eucharistic thinking*, not that primarily in which we offer of our own traditions and efforts toward a common pool, but an ever-new and thankful *receiving together* of the Body of Christ (cf. 1 Cor. 14: 5 and Eph. 4: 12–16) "till we all come in the unity of the faith, and of the knowledge of the Son of God, unto a perfect man, unto the measure of the stature of the fulness of Christ; that speaking the truth in love we may grow up unto Him in all things who is the head, even Christ."

The thought of the Eucharist is not of the labour of our hands in producing the bread and bringing it to the altar—that would be the sacrifice of Cain—but of receiving the one Body given and broken for us. It is the thought of one loaf broken into a multiplicity of fragments of which we partake, and yet partake in such a way that we are incorporated in the unity of the one Body. In the receiving of this one sacrifice and its unity into our multiplicity healing is given for our divisions. Nevertheless it is an eschatological unity which we shall only receive fully when the sacrament yields place to the marriage supper of the Lamb in the final consummation of the mystery concerning Christ and His Church. Until He come we receive that only sacramentally in the tension of the Cross, holding together the unity of the visible and the invisible, the material and the spiritual, the temporal and the eternal, by faith, but still waiting for the redemption of the body in the resurrection. This unity cannot therefore be perpetuated in the structure of space and time, any more than the transfigured Christ or the Christ of Emmaus can be constrained to perpetual abiding in an earthly tabernacle or institution. He is, so to speak, the vanishing Christ who must be received again and ever again in the Eucharist and shewed forth in His death until He come in glory. As often therefore as the Church partakes of the Eucharist she receives judgment upon her multiplicity and divisions, and receives too the earnest of the unity that shall be and that already is. The experience of the Church cannot be anything else therefore but "as dying, and behold we live; as having nothing and yet possessing all things" (2 Cor. 6: 9, 10). The fact that we have sacraments in the Church means that unity is hidden with Christ in God, and yet that we are given participation in this unity as we receive the Word and the Body of Christ in the Gospel and Sacraments.

The full thought of the Eucharist and of the eschatological unity of wholeness which it mediates bears several important implications for ecumenical thinking.

(1) If the given unity of the Church is essentially eschatological then the validity of all that she does is conditioned by the Parousia and cannot be made to repose upon any primitive structure of unity already complete in the naturally historical realm or upon any continuity in the fallen world out of which we are redeemed. "Like the Incarnation itself, the Eucharist is the breaking into history of something eternal, beyond history, inapprehensible in terms of history alone."[1] So we must think of the validity of the Church's ministry, of her councils and theological formulations, not in terms of history alone but in terms of a divine act which entails the eschatological suspension of all earthly validity. The Church is a divine reality and cannot be demonstrated as a divine reality in the actuality of history except by a divine act. "At no time and no place is the Church an authority which upholds itself out of itself."[2] To the divine authority the Church can only bear witness by word and

[1] Ramsey, *The Gospel and the Catholic Church*, p. 107.

[2] Barth, *Dogmatics in Outline*, p. 146.

obedience and must never cite it after the fashion of the Scribes and Pharisees (II, p. 22). It is understandable that when the early Church was faced with the dangers of Gnosticism it should appeal to an actual succession of bishops to attest the historicity of its claims, a function which is much better performed to-day by historical criticism, but it is a complete misunderstanding to transmute linear or chronological sequence into a theological principle. Nor on the other hand can a tactual succession of bishops be made to usurp the function of Baptism, which is the supreme eschatological act whereby we are initiated into the once and for all historical events in the life, death, and resurrection of Jesus Christ.[1] The very existence of sacraments in the heart of the Church ought to have protected her from this misunderstanding, inasmuch as the validity of our salvation, of our ministry, and of our faith is by baptism made to rest upon the unrepeatable events of Jesus Christ on the one hand, and yet thrown into the future by the Eucharist on the other hand. True sacramental thinking entails an entirely different conception of validity from worldly or historical validity, for it is validity which is an act of God which we must receive sacramentally ever and ever again, and not a validity reposing upon the very thing that the sacraments are designed to transcend. The extraordinary thing is that because of episcopal succession the validity of baptism has been distinguished in sort from the validity of the Eucharist to the misconception of the latter. While the Eucharist is above all the sacrament in which we receive wholeness into our earthly tensions, designed as the medicine for our sinful divisions, it has been made to rest so much for its validity upon chronological sequence within history that it has actually become the great obstacle to unity among the Churches. Nothing could be more destructive of the real Eucharist than to make it separatist.

(2) If the given unity of the Church is essentially eschatological then there is ultimately no self-consistent whole in any historical tradition. Therefore it becomes the duty of each Church in the ecumenical fellowship to listen to the witness of other Churches, or as Dr. Visser 't Hooft has put it, to open herself to the truth of God that she may learn from them, and

[1] Cf. Gaugler, *Römerbrief*, 1, p. 154 f.

to be ready to let her own faith and life be enriched and corrected by this contact. "Churches cannot treat each other as if they were sovereign states which defend the integrity of their rights and territory. They must on the contrary rejoice when the ecumenical situation leads to constructive battles and beneficial invasions. The members of the one ecumenical family cannot adopt the principles of non-intervention. They let themselves be questioned by their fellow-members. They exhort each other to great faithfulness and renewal of life. They call each other back to the apostolic witness" (I, p. 192; cf. Skydsgaard, p. 165). That is indeed the great hope of the situation, that before one another the Churches have been driven back to the biblical witness and biblical theology, and that more and more there is taking place a subordination of tradition to Scripture. That even applies to the Roman Church, for example, in her rediscovery of the notion of the Church as the Body of Christ and of the eschatological element in the Eucharist (cf. I, pp. 116, 163, 171). Apart from the wide-spread revival in biblical studies and the new readiness of all branches of the Church to place themselves under the criticism of the Word, Amsterdam would hardly have been possible.

(3) In the light of the essential and given unity of faith it becomes the duty of the Churches in the ecumenical fellowship to think out every doctrine into every other doctrine. It is only thus that they will reach back to the most ultimate truths and put to a Christian test even their doctrine of God.[1] There can be no doubt that such exhaustive theological work, particularly in the English-speaking world, is greatly needed if we are to get behind the secondary questions which are the immediate cause of our divisions. The coming together of the different Churches in constructive and mutual challenge has made it very clear that different doctrines in different traditions have suffered from arrested thinking and consequent distortion. Thus, for example, eschatology has been so thrust into the background again and again that in differing degrees in the different Churches almost all doctrines have suffered accordingly. Now that eschatology is being thought into the other doctrines of the faith bringing them nearer to the promised

[1] Cf. F. W. Camfield, *S.J.T.*, 1 : 2, p. 205.

unity in Christ, great differences are beginning to disappear. That is very apparent in the contribution of Professor Florovsky on the Nature and Task of the Church. This is a doctrine which has never received dogmatic definition in any of the great councils of the Church and has suffered perhaps more than most, particularly from a failure to receive Christological correction. Indeed it was precisely at this point at the Reformation that the Roman Church remained behind and separated from the Reformed Church which insisted on Christological correction of the doctrines of the Church, the Sacraments, and the Ministry. There are signs, however, as Professor Skydsgaard has pointed out so well, that "a new attentiveness is awakening, an inner investigation, a self-criticism, not of the Church as such, but of the exact form which the Roman Catholic Church has taken in the course of its empirical development, in which restrictions and prejudices have occurred, so that truly Catholic thought (which in this connexion means the whole and undivided Christian truth) has had an incomplete development" (I, p. 166). On the other hand, if the doctrines of Christ and the Church have themselves suffered from arrested development in the Reformed Churches, that is undoubtedly due to the failure to think eschatology into the whole. Nevertheless it is the great hope of the present, manifest everywhere in the Amsterdam reports, even in regard to the Church of Rome, that these three doctrines are being brought to bear upon each other from their biblical foundations and in such a way as to raise in our breasts the expectation that the hidden unity behind the Churches may at last spring into view (cf. I, p. 168). "It is only the unity which exists that makes possible the exploration of our differences. It is only the unity which we believe that God has already given which affords hope that the honest search for biblical truth will, not create unity, but more and more reveal it" (I, p. 17).

It is highly significant that Karl Barth, who more than any other in modern times has thrust the doctrine of the Church into the forefront of our thinking, was the one to suggest the procedure for discussion at Amsterdam: to examine agreements to discover what disagreements they contain, and then to examine disagreements to uncover their concealed agreements. The outstanding fact this brought to light was that disagreements were but differences within a total unity, a unity which was both given and had somehow become *event* (*Ereignis*) in the midst of the Assembly—one of those ever-new acts of the Church's Lord about which Barth had written as creative of the Church (I, p. 67 ff.). Nevertheless the differences were wide enough and were apt to become entrenched behind the historical division between "catholic" and "evangelical", more so in the discussion itself than in the volumes written in preparation for the Council. This entrenchment, although it brings to the surface in an honest and clear light the differences that must be faced, will nevertheless mean the ultimate failure of the World Council, unless the Churches themselves undertake to take up the agreements within the total unity, and push them through the whole region of their disagreements until there is no difference left of such a magnitude as to inhibit a confessional unity. In the rest of this essay we must face some of these agreements and disagreements as they concern the nature and mission of the Church.

1. *The Nature of the Church*

All were agreed that the Church is God's gift to men for the salvation of the world; that the saving acts of God in Jesus Christ brought the Church into being; that the Church persists in continuity throughout history through the presence and power of the Holy Spirit (V, p. 53; I, p. 213). The differences that arose within this agreement were considerable, but might not have been so great had some of the ultimate problems been faced. What is meant, for example, by the divine nature of the Church? How are we to think of the divine and human elements in relation to each other? To that question only a Christological answer can be given, and yet there seems to have been no real attempt to think out the relation between the divine and human natures of the Church in terms of the relation between the divine and the human in Jesus Christ Himself. It will readily be agreed that we cannot think of the divine nature of the Church in the same way as we think of the divine nature of Christ, for in Him the union of God and Man is absolutely unique. And yet it is only on the analogy of the hypostatic union that we can begin to answer our question—that is by giving that relation an analogical extension into the sphere of the Church. The analogy runs not "as God and Man are related in Christ so the divine and the human are related in the Church", but rather "as God and Man are related in Christ so Christ and the Church are related". "This is a great mystery", but it is failure to give this adequate thought that has often led some of the Anglican group to speak of the Church as if she were a *pre-existent* ontological reality, and has often led the Orthodox group to think of the Church as if there were over against the visible Church an invisible Platonic magnitude.[1] Behind this there also lies a failure to think out the relation between the Church and creation, both the original creation and the new creation, which is so integral to the Pauline doctrine in Ephesians and Colossians. In other words the eschatological tension tends to be conceived in terms of eternity and time or transmuted into a mystical relation, instead of being thought of in terms of the new creation and the old. The New Testament knows of no Church, even in its divine reality, except in its earthly actuality.[2]

It is clear therefore that a great deal more work must be done upon the Pauline doctrine of the Church as the Body of Christ before prevailing confusions are cleared up. The "catholic" theologians will have to ask whether there is any warrant at all in the New Testament for thinking of the Body of Christ as *corpus mysticum*. Certainly the word for body (σῶμα) is never used in this way in the Epistles of St. Paul.

Two aspects in particular seem to demand attention.

(a) What is the relation between the spiritual body (σῶμα πνευματικόν) and the natural body (σῶμα ψυχικόν), or the celestial body (σῶμα ἐπουράνιον) and the terrestrial body (σῶμα ἐπιγείον), or our vile body (σῶμα τῆς ταπεινώσεως) and that which will be made like unto His glorious body (σῶμα τῆς δόξης)? If it is the spiritual or celestial body that bears the image of the heavenly (εἰκὼν τοῦ ἐπουρανίου) can we claim for the natural body anything more, as far as we can *see*, than that it bears the image of the earthly (εἰκὼν τοῦ χοϊκοῦ)? In what sense then may we speak of the believer or the Church as bearing already the image of the heavenly? If it is part of the

[1] Cf. Dr. Germanos, V, p. 59—the very thing which Florovsky tries to avoid in his eschatological conception of the Church!

[2] Cf. Schlink, *Ecumenical Review*, 1, 2, p. 159. Contrast Florovsky, I, p. 46 f.

dying and rising of the Church as the Body of Christ not to be conformed to the fashion of this world (*μὴ συσχηματίζεσθε τῷ αἰῶνι τούτῳ*) but to be transformed by the renewing of her mind, can we ever say that in her outward and historical form as we know it in a fallen world (*τὸ σχῆμα τοῦ κόσμου τούτου*) the Church bears the essential structure of a God-given catholicity? "If it is the Body of Christ no outward forms can guarantee the Church's presence" (C. T. Craig, I, p. 41). Structure there is indeed but in the unity of the Spirit (*ἑνότης τοῦ Πνεύματος*) which is also the eschatological goal of the Church. If we are really in earnest about thinking of the Church in this fallen world as the Body of Christ (and surely we ought to be) must we not think of her as in the form of Christ's humiliation (*μορφὴ δούλου*)? And is it not of the very essence of sin to transubstantiate this form (*μορφή*) into that other form (*εἶδος*—cf. *διὰ πίστεως, οὐ διὰ εἴδους*, 2 Cor. 5: 7) which is to make of the Church an idol (*εἴδωλον*—cf. 2 Cor. 6: 16)? Surely the essential form of the visible Church wherein she images her Lord is to be found in her humble service in which the great reconciliation already wrought out in the Body of Christ is lived out among men, and the Church in life and action becomes, as it were, sacramentally correlative to the life and passion of Jesus Christ. It is not only as she receives the sacrament but as she enacts it, always bearing about in her body the dying of Jesus (*πάντοτε τὴν νέκρωσιν τοῦ Ἰησοῦ ἐν τῷ σώματι περιφέροντες*—2 Cor. 4: 10), resisting unto blood (Heb. 12: 4), that she knows Christ in the fellowship of His sufferings and becomes conformable unto His death. It is thus that she fills up that which is behind of the afflictions of Christ, and thus that she shews forth His death till He come.

It is not therefore in any worldly structure or in any hierarchy conceived as belonging to the *esse* of the Church that the Form of the Church imaging the Form of Christ will be seen, certainly in no order in which "a community of the clergy claim, or permit themselves to receive, a position in the Church which separates them from lay orders" (I, p. 83; that applies quite as much to Presbyterianism as to Anglicanism!), but rather in the order in which there is only one Master and all others are servants, and in which each esteems the other better than himself and edifies the other in love. Whenever we speak of any structure or form as belonging to the *esse* of the Church, must we not go on to add that this very structure and this very form will therefore be preserved when heaven and earth pass away and the new heaven and new earth will be revealed? If we have no authority for holding that such a structure or form belongs to the Church as the final eschatological and ontological reality, have we any right to say it belongs to the *esse* of the Church? Must it not be related as *shadow* (σκιά) to the *Body* of Christ (σῶμα—Col. 2: 17, 18)? Certainly the book of Revelation mentions a heavenly presbytery ("four and twenty elders") whereas it mentions no heavenly episcopate! The prophets and the apostles remain on in the new heaven and new earth, but not the so-called hierarchy. The last chapters of the Apocalypse make it quite clear that in the New Jerusalem there will be no temple and no creaturely ministry of light, for the Lord God and the Lamb are the Temple and the Light thereof, and even the Eucharist disappears before the Marriage Supper of the Lamb. At last the forms and fashions of this world which the Church must use but not abuse (χρώμενοι τὸν κόσμον ὡς μὴ καταχρώμενοι—1 Cor. 7: 31) will have passed away (παράγειν), and the essential structure of the new creation will be revealed. Of course it is difficult indeed to draw dogmatic concepts out of the Apocalypse, and perhaps not justifiable, but it seems clear nevertheless that the more we think the biblical eschatology into the doctrine of the Church, the more our differences will tend to disappear, though doubtless not without great heart-searching in our several traditions.

(b) The other aspect of the doctrine of the Church as the Body of Christ that demands more intensive discussion is the fact that Christ is the *Head* of the Church which is His Body. This may be the point where we can transcend the antithesis between the "catholic" emphasis upon the visible continuity of the Church as a body in space and time and the "evangelical" emphasis upon the continuity as the enduring eschatological event taking place in Word and Sacrament. Professor Florovsky's statement that "only in the sacraments does the Christian community pass beyond the purely human measure and become the Church" (I, p. 47) seems to point in this direction. The way in which Professor Hodgson has put the contrast (V, p. 60) is too sharp and does not appear to understand the "evangelical" insistence on the visible continuity of the Church in history. Calvin also taught that "to those to whom God is Father the Church must also be a mother" (*Inst.* 4.1.1); and indeed that it belongs to the essential structure of the Church that "God has deposited the doctrine of eternal life and salvation with men, that by their hands He might communicate it to others" (*Inst.* 4.3.1). "If the ministry is removed the whole edifice must fall" (*Inst.* 4.1.11). But "at no period since the world began has the Lord been without His Church, nor ever shall be till the final consummation of all things" (*Inst.* 4.1.7). The difference does not lies therefore in a doctrine of an essential historical continuity but in the form and nature of that continuity.

It must be admitted that both Roman Catholic mysticism and Protestant philosophical theology have tended to cut faith adrift from the particularity of history—but that is to sin against the Incarnation. Now that the Word has become flesh, "the Absolute Fact is also historical fact",[1] a fact in the same sphere of reality as we are ourselves. God's Word has become indissolubly bound to a human and historical form such that there is no Word of God for us apart from a physical event. Therefore no doctrine of the Church based on a timeless confrontation by the Word analogous to some eternal generation of the Son can be permitted, for the Church must involve in her structure and motion the very time-relations that are involved by the Word in the birth of Jesus, and in the physical death on the Cross. To cut the link between the Church and historical particularity is not only to transubstantiate the Church into some Docetic *corpus mysticum* but to sever her from any saving act by God in our actual existence. And so we must say that just as the Word assumed human form in history, though without ceasing to be eternal, the same Word also assumes temporal form in the Church analogous on her level to the incarnational form in Christ. As the Word of God became irrevocably involved with a physical event, so in the Church the same Word is involved in a physical event. In other language, the Church extends the corporeality of the Word and mediates it to a corporeal world through such physical events as the Bible,

[1] Kierkegaard, *Phil. Fragments*, p. 84.

Preaching, the Sacraments, etc., and the physical society of those who belong to the Church. At the same time these physical events have meaning for the Church only in their sacramental character, that is, only as in and through them it is the living Christ Himself who speaks, communicates His Body and Blood, and bestows His Spirit. The important fact that concerns us at the moment however is that in His institution God designs that His Word comes to us, creating out of the world His Church, only in such a way as to entail time relations, and yet because it never ceases to be eternal in such a way as never to be lost within the contingencies of history. God has ordained that we receive His Word through the historical communication of the Word and the growth of the Church as a historical community ——mutually correlative. As this historical actuality and concrete community the Church is the Temple of God on earth. That is the reformed doctrine of the essentially historical continuity of the visible Church. It is a doctrine which finds the essential historical continuity in the *whole Body* (πᾶν τὸ σῶμα συναρμολογούμενον) and not in a hierarchical line of priests.

It is thus that the true ministry, as the New Testament views it, is maintained and preserved in the Church. On the one hand it is grounded in a bodily and personal and historical continuity with the apostolic foundation, but on the other hand it is that divinely appointed service whereby room is created within the historical continuum for the ever-new breaking in of the Creative Word of the living Christ whereby from age to age a Christian community is continuously called into being and sacramentally gathered up by incorporation into Christ. The ministry is a failure or is not the true ministry if by it the Word of God is bound by the traditions of men or made of none effect (Mark 7: 1 ff.; Matt. 15: 1 ff.; 23: 15 ff.). This is surely the prime reason for the existence of sects, the protest against a hardening of the ministry which binds the Word of God to the traditions of men. To be truly catholic therefore the Church must see to it that the Word of God is not bound, that her Church-order makes room for the living new creation which is continuous through Word and Sacrament with the Resurrection of Jesus Christ. "The task and significance of Church-order consists in so uniting the congregation on the human level that it is rendered as free as possible for all that the Lord

Himself can, and will do in her" (Barth, I, p. 73). By the ministry rooted and grounded in the whole body of the Church, the Church lives on continuously in history, but she lives on in history by such a series of ever-new acts of quickening and repentance that in spite of the hardening of history and tradition and its sinful repetition of past actions (cf. Richard Niebuhr, I, p. 79 f.) room is made for the charismatic ministry of the Spirit. The greatest danger of the Church therefore lies in such a historical series of acts as to entrap the charismatic ministry and confine it to a hierarchical line of priests. What kind of governance of history does that imply? What view of God does that entail? To commit God to a series of acts in the relativity of history, which even He cannot abrogate, seems to mean a view of God that we do not get from the Christ who died and rose again and ever lives in the midst of the Church as her only Lord and Master. It would mean a Church in which the Body is not governed by the Head but the Head is governed by the Body. That is the perpetual danger not only of Churches in the "catholic" group but also of the Presbyterian type who too readily develop a secularized ecclesiasticism which brings derangement into their orders and stands in the path of renewal and unity. How easy it is by an act of General Assembly to make the Word of none effect! But here at least there is some understanding of the sovereignty of the Word which makes it clear that Church order is never an end in itself but exists for the sole purpose of serving the *kerygma* or rather Christ Himself.

It was evident at Amsterdam, as has long been evident in discussion with High Anglicans, that there is a manifest failure to appreciate the New Testament meaning of *kerygma* as both the *thing preached* and the *preaching* of it in one (cf. Newbigin, II, p. 21). It is such preaching that the "thing preached", Christ Himself, crucified and risen, encounters men personally and acts upon them creatively. It is such preaching that men are actually arrested and addressed by Christ in His living Body as St. Paul was on the road to Damascus—though his experience had a fulness which was the exclusive experience of an apostle. It is such preaching that in it Jesus continues to do and to teach (Acts 1 : 1) what He had already begun before and after the Crucifixion. It is done through the weakness of men and human words, but nevertheless in demonstration of the Spirit and of power (1 Cor. 2: 4), and is designed to emphasize the weakness of the earthen vessel in order that the excellency of the power may be of God and not of men, and that faith should not stand in the wisdom of men but in the power of God (2 Cor. 4: 7; 1 Cor. 2: 5). In other words, just as in the Incarnation the Word was made flesh, so in *kerygma* that same Word continues to be made flesh. That is why the *kerygma* and Baptism, followed by the Eucharist, always go together. In *kerygma* it is the *Word* made flesh; in the sacrament it is the Word made *flesh*. But apart from the Word there is no sacrament, for it is the living Word and nothing else that is made flesh (John 6: 63); while apart from the sacrament the *kerygma* as act of the living Christ does not reach its proper fulfilment. The full consummation of the act is eschatological, but until Christ come, the sacrament holds together in one here and now the "*Son thy sins be forgiven thee*", and ("that ye may know that the Son of man hath power *on earth* to forgive sins") the "*Arise take up thy bed and walk*" (Mark 2: 5, 10, 11). As long as we still wait for the redemption of the body we have the sacraments, for it is the redemption of an already purchased possession that we wait for. Although considered in terms of temporal sequence (cf. Mark 2: 5 ff.) there is a teleological suspension of the union between Word and Act, that union is given to us here and now in Word and Sacrament as a finished work (τετέλεσται—John 19: 30; cf. ἐτελέσθη τὸ μυστήριον τοῦ θεοῦ—Rev. 10: 7; cf. 16: 17). The Parousia therefore will mean not so much the final consummation of the act in terms of linear time (though it must also mean that—cf. Cullmann, *Christ and Time*), as the unveiling of a new creation which already in Christ is reality.

All this lies behind the meaning of the New Testament *kerygma* as itself in the highest sense sacramental act, for it is the living Word behind the witness of the Church which sacramentalizes, so to speak, water and bread and wine in Baptism and Eucharist. It is to preaching in this sense that men are ordained by a divine institution in the Church. It is "a *de fide* doctrine of the ministry *iure divino*".[1] It is failure to understand this view of the preaching of the Word that characterizes a

[1] Professor J. H. S. Burleigh, *S.J.T.*, 1: 2, p. 184.

great deal of "catholic" and particularly Anglican thought. By "Word" "evangelical" teaching means precisely the living Christ who is the *Head* of the Church which is His Body (cf. Aulén, I, pp. 20, 23), and it would seem that a fuller understanding of the relation between the *Head* and the *Body* would clear away much of the confusion. Just as a body is gathered up into a head without which the body is nothing, so the Church is by the Word (the Mind of Christ—*νοῦς Χριστοῦ*) gathered up as His Body in Christ the Head (Eph. 1: 10—*ἀνακεφαλαιώσασθαι*; cf. Rom. 13: 9: *ἐν τούτῳ τῷ λόγῳ ἀνακεφαλαιοῦται*). Or to put it the other way round, it is through the work of the ministry, through knowledge of the Son of God and speaking the truth in love, that the Church grows up into Christ in all things who is the Head of the Body (Eph. 4: 12 f.). Thus the "gathering up" and "incorporation" are indissolubly related and are indeed of one and the same act, for it is Christ who by Word and Sacrament does both. They take place in mutual involution. It is precisely in this mutual involution that the on-going and enduring event (*Ereignis*) takes place which is dynamically constitutive of the Church (Barth, I, p. 67 ff.). Apart from the Word or the "gathering up", which lies behind the "gathering together" of the congregation, there is no event of "incorporation". On the other hand, apart from the "incorporation" the "gathering up" does not really become event, no matter how much "gathering together" there may be. It is thus that Professor Barth brings together "event" and "unification" (I, p. 72 f.) both of which presuppose "incorporation" (*Einverleibung*), though this aspect does not come out strongly enough in his essay.

All this has further implications for a doctrine of the ministry, for it means that any real distinction between what are called the "episcopal" and "prophetic" functions of the ministry entails a serious disorder, namely, the sundering of "incorporation" from "gathering up" into the Head. Such a disorder really means that in the end the "incorporation" becomes a profane event in which the living presence of Christ is displaced by a historical juridical succession.[1] This difficulty is profoundly recognized by the Roman Church in that she vests in her

[1] Cf. Barth, *Dogmatics*, 1 : 1, p. 109.

episcopal hierarchy not only the fulness of sacramental grace but also the fulness of prophetic utterance (i.e. infallibility so far as it is gathered up to a head in the "Vicar of Christ" on earth). That such a solution ultimately destroys itself is the insight of the Anglo-Catholics who see in it a view of God and presence of Christ which is more Latin than Christian. But equally impossible is the Anglo-Catholic solution which attempts to lodge only the fulness of sacramental (priestly) grace but not of prophetic grace in the bishop, confining to him only certain actions[1] with disastrous results both to the Anglican episcopate (so bogged down in administration) and to Anglican preaching. This disorder is even reflected in the splitting up of baptism into two half-sacraments.

We are now forced to face the question as to the precise relation between the continuity of the Church as the living new creation in Christ, and the continuity of the Church in all the contingencies and relativities of history. The great difficulty about this question is that while on the one hand we cannot think of the continuity of the new creation as identical with the continuity of this present sinful world, nevertheless it is a continuity which has so interpenetrated history that its reality is unthinkable except as it includes historical succession on the stage of this world. In other words it is not with a determinist view of election that we are concerned here, but with the eternal election as the living movement of God that enters our fallen world in Christ and so appropriates the Church in atonement (περιεποιήσατο διὰ τοῦ αἵματος τοῦ ἰδίου—Acts 20: 28) that in her there is an indissoluble union between the eternal action of God and the movement of time. The eternal election of God becomes the inner core of history and constitutes its real continuity in the heart of the world's contradictions and relativities (cf. I, p. 14)—a continuity which both involves discontinuity and continuity with the visible successions of the fallen world. No doubt, as Professor Florovsky has said, a true solution transcends history and belongs to the "age to come" (I, p. 57), but inasmuch as that "age to come" has already broken into this age in Jesus Christ, and continues in His actual resurrection-body, we may begin to perceive here and now an answer on the Christological analogy.

[1] E.g. Ramsey, *The Gospel and the Catholic Church*, p. 83.

The Virgin Birth tells us that we cannot understand Christ simply by placing Him in the continuity of the history of Israel, for at the Virgin Birth that continuity was broken by an invasion from above. And yet the Virgin Birth tells us also that here in Jesus we have the true Israel of God continuous with the Messianic Remnant of the Old Testament. Here is both continuity and discontinuity.[1] Accordingly one of the basic facts the New Testament has to tell us is that on the one hand the priestly continuity of the Aaronic succession was broken by another continuity that is without beginning and end after the order of Melchizedek, but on the other hand the prophetic continuity is caught up and retransmitted through Christ and the apostles in an apostolic succession, so that the New Israel is not founded upon a priestly continuity on the stage of history but precisely upon the continuity of the prophetic-apostolic witness. It is therefore a complete misunderstanding when the New Testament Church is spoken of as the "Israel of God" in such a way as to carry on the very kind of continuity from the old Israel which the prophetic-apostolic doctrine of the messianic community regards as abrogated. The New Testament Church is indeed the Israel of God, but only as she is gathered up and incorporated into Christ. The fact that Christ is now ascended (this is the fact that Ramsey neglects in his contrast, *The Resurrection of Christ*, p. 99 f.) from the visible succession of history as we know it in this world, and *as such* (Eph. 4: 8 ff.) gathers up the Church as His Body, tells us that we cannot think of the continuity of the Church in the midst of history except in terms of this new continuity. In the eyes of Calvin the whole "catholic" doctrine of episcopal succession is shipwrecked upon this rock alone, that the Church is grafted into the Israel of God "contrary to nature" (Rom. 11: 24).

All this is even more clear in the light of the Resurrection of Christ, which tells us that we cannot find Christ to-day simply by placing Him in the continuity of history as we know it. To do so would be to by-pass the Resurrection. Jesus Christ has withdrawn Himself from sight that we may know Him by concentrating through the witness of the apostles upon the Life,

[1] Cf. E. Gaugler, *Internat. Kirchl. Zeitschrift*, 3, 1947, p. 150 f.; and *Römerbrief*, I, p. 352 ff.; and Barth's powerful discussion, *Dogmatics* 2: 2, p. 215 ff.

Teaching, Death, and Resurrection of Christ, so that it is only in history and in this particular history that He gives Himself to be known. Had Jesus continued visibly in the succession of history the Cross would doubtless have been relegated to a mere incident of bygone history, perhaps to be forgotten, so the very fact of His Ascension affirms as nothing else could the essential historical foundation of faith and knowledge in Him. At the same time the Resurrection and Ascension tell us quite plainly that Jesus Christ lives on not only as Son of God but as Resurrection-Man—He is risen in Body. In Him the new creation is already a fact, and it is in Him that its continuity is a living dynamic reality, and indeed in Him there is what Barth has called *new time*: the temporal continuity of the new creation in indissoluble union with the eternal God. It is in this new creation with its new time that the original purpose of God is perfectly fulfilled and transcended in glory. It is failure to think through the relation between the Church as the Body of Christ with God's eternal purpose of creation, as St. Paul treats of it in Ephesians and Colossians, over against this present evil world and yet as gathering up all things visible and invisible, that to a large extent makes confusion of our views of succession on the stage of history—e.g. the Docetic transubstantiation of time that the "catholic" doctrine of episcopal succession ultimately involves. The Birth, Life, and Death of Jesus Christ all speak of the most complete interpenetration of history, and indeed of a desperate struggle with the terrible continuity of its sin and guilt, but they receive their truth and validity in the Resurrection where the continuity of sin is decidedly broken and yet where there emerges the new continuity in time. Here the visible continuity of history is judged as an empty husk, the worldly succession of the church as an ecclesiastical shell (I, p. 71), and yet the new is seen to be one continuous act with the first creation. Here where the iron-grip of guilt-laden history is broken we have the great salvation-events which are creative of the Church as continuous with the living Body of the resurrected Jesus Christ.

It would be idle therefore to think of the visible continuation of the Church throughout history in any other terms than of these salvation-events.[1] No doubt it is the constant temptation

1. Cf. Gaugler, *Römerbrief*, I, p. 173 f.

of a Church that must relate herself to contemporary history from age to age to barricade herself behind her own history against the invasion of the ever-new divine reality, and to overlook the fact that it is Christ and the apostles alone who are the foundation of the Church.[1] It is at this very point that Barth's essay has such relevance, for it calls the Churches back to their true foundation in a correction both of a false ontology and a false historicity. The real continuity of history itself is to be found not on the level of the contingent but in the continuing acts of Jesus Christ the Head of the Church—that is to say in the living continuity of the new creation behind the forms and fashions of the fallen world but interpenetrating it through and through in the Gospel.

2. *The Mission of the Church*

It is significant that although the second of the Amsterdam volumes is mainly concerned with the mission of the Church, in neither of the first two volumes has it been possible to discuss the nature and mission of the Church except as they involve one another. This indicates a conception of the Church as essentially dynamic, the living Body of Christ engaged in "the purpose of God to reconcile all men to Himself and to one another in Jesus Christ His Son" (II, p. 219; V, p. 64). It is thus that the Church continues in the apostolic succession, that is to say, in the mission of Christ who is Himself the Apostle from the Father, and who commissions His Church in the same apostolic mission. "As my Father hath sent me, even so send I you. And when he had said this he breathed on them, and saith unto them, Receive ye the Holy Ghost: whosesoever sins ye remit, they are remitted unto them; and whosesoever sins ye retain they are retained" (John 20: 21–23). In the Church as founded upon the Twelve, this apostleship and the receiving of the Holy Spirit are coincident, which makes the Church's witness in the highest sense sacramental, as we have seen, so that her Word in the Gospel of reconciliation and forgiveness is in fact the Word and the Power of Christ. "He that heareth you, heareth me." That is surely the real substance of the apostolic succession, continuity in the perpetual Ministry of

[1] E. Schlink, *Ecumenical Review*, 1 : 2, p. 164.

the Risen and Ever-Present Christ.[1] It is by faith and witness to this Lord that the Church is preserved and constantly recreated—by the very Word of the Gospel which she proclaims. It is thus that she has within her the well of water springing up into everlasting life. It is thus that the life-line in the power and presence of the Holy Ghost is maintained, and it is thus and thus only that she becomes the organ of the same Spirit that was breathed upon the first apostles and put them in trust with the Gospel (P. T. Forsyth). This then is the Church Catholic because and in so far as she lives by the apostolic Gospel through the power of the Holy Ghost she partakes of the fulness of Him who fills all things. To engage in the Mission of this Gospel belongs to the very nature and life of the Church, for "the relation between Gospel and Church is not merely consequential but integral and constitutive" (Dr. Hogg, cited I, p. 153). Therefore to halt that mission, to restrict or limit the Gospel, is to sever the apostolic succession, to destroy the life-movement of the Church, to deprive her of the Holy Ghost. As Bishop Newbigin puts it: "The Church cannot stand under the Cross without accepting an obligation to share with all men the redemption which was there won for it. It cannot evade that obligation without cutting itself off from the divine life by which it lives" (II, p. 32).

All this means that the mission and the ministry of the Gospel are rooted and grounded in the whole Church and must be undertaken by the whole Church or by the whole people of God. "It is the Church which must be the 'mission'. It is upon the Church that the authority and duty is laid to preach the Gospel, for the Church is the redeemed community which itself lives by the Gospel" (II, p. 33). If the mission and ministry are primarily built upon the foundation of the prophets and apostles, it is because they were constituted the actual place where the Divine Revelation became rooted in humanity, and so formed the human end of that Revelation, belonging peculiarly to its once-and-for-all nature and caught up into its finality. In its primary sense therefore the apostolate is unrepeatable. It cannot be extended in time on the stage of this world. Along with the prophets it forms the heavenly presbytery

[1] T. W. Manson, *The Church's Ministry*.

who worship the enthroned Lord for ever and ever. The earthly counterpart to this is the biblical witness of the Old and New Testaments, the unrepeatable and perpetual foundation within history of the Church of Jesus Christ.

Dr. E. L. Mascall has written some potent words in this connexion which deserve the fullest discussion.

> The twelve apostles are not the no-longer-existing initial stage of a process which is still going on; they are the perpetually persisting foundation in which the present ministry inheres. Once this point is grasped the tiresome and inconclusive discussion whether the apostolate was intended by Christ to be a permanent element in the Church is seen to lose most of its meaning; the apostolate *is* a permanent element in the Church, because in the glory of heaven the twelve apostles still exist. And unless we are to suppose the Church militant and the Church triumphant to be two mutually isolated societies, this perpetual apostolate must be relevant to us. And if it is relevant to us, how shall we expect to find it mediated if not through the ministry which has consistently claimed to be in organic unity and continuity with the Twelve? The apostolic succession, if it is a fact at all, is, of course, historically considered a chronological sequence, but its importance lies not primarily in the fact that it is a "link with the past" (that would be mere ecclesiastical antiquarianism and romanticism) but in the fact that it is the foundation of a real unity between the Church and the apostolate in heaven.[1]

Dr. Mascall has omitted to give Holy Scripture its proper setting in relation to apostolic succession—an omission which affects his view of it in the perspective of history—nevertheless he does appear to penetrate behind the present dilemma to something really fundamental. That is apparent when we consider the question of transmission (παράδοσις).

The difficulty lies in the fact that the real substance of what we call "apostolic succession" cannot be transmitted. It has to do with the Father's sending of the Son into the world, the relation between the Father and the Incarnate Son, crucified and risen, in whom the fulness of the Godhead dwells *bodily* (σωματικῶς). He is the Head of the Church which is His Body, and therefore the real substance of the apostolic succession has to do with the body of Christ as the "fulness of Him who filleth

[1] *Theology*, June 1949, p. 220.

all in all". In other words what we sometimes call "Apostolic Succession" really refers to the complete Body of Christ, the all-inclusive fulness or wholeness which, precisely because it is that, cannot be thought of in terms of the more or less of historical succession and temporal fulfilment, as something that can be added up in history or formulated in documentary lineage. Rather is it the continuing wholeness of Christ's Body into which from age to age we are sacramentally incorporated, and which can no more be a phenomenon within the time-series than the Parousia itself. It is important to note that this wholeness is constituted by Christ Himself, and would in no sense be defective if He were separated from us; nevertheless it is such a wholeness that Christ will not be without us and insists upon incorporating us into it.[1] It is significant too that in this connexion the New Testament mentions baptism rather than the Eucharist (e.g. 1 Cor. 12: 12 f.; Eph. 4: 4 f.), doubtless because it is in the once-and-for-all character of baptismal incorporation that the *whole event* of the all-inclusive Body of Christ is revealed (cf. Aulén, I, p. 24), which Paul describes so often as the active state of being "in Christ". Baptism does not only initiate us into the operational sphere of the salvation-events (*in den Wirkkreis der Heilsereignisse*) of the death and resurrection of Jesus Christ but is the primary eschatological act of the Gospel whereby we are ingrafted into the wholeness of Christ.[2] The Eucharist has sacramental significance as communion (*κοινωνία*—1 Cor. 10: 16), as continual participation and renewing in this complete event. "He that is washed needeth not save to wash his feet" (John 13: 10). Where for some reason the primary stress is laid upon the Eucharist, and a fatal distinction is made between the administering of baptism and of the Eucharist (where the latter is severely restricted to episcopally ordained men), apostolic succession almost inevitably means the adding up of something in history, and the biblical doctrine of the Body of Christ as an all-inclusive eschatological magnitude tends to be lost. If we recognize that the Church is "not merely a historical phenomenon but an ontological and eschatological reality" (Mascall, *loc. cit.*), an

[1] Cf. Calvin, *Comm. on Eph.* 1 : 23.

[2] Cf. E. Gaugler, *Internat. Kirchl. Zeitschrift*, 3, 1947, p. 151 and *Römerbrief*, I, p. 154 ff.

"all-embracing plenitude" (Florovsky, I, p. 50), which as such cannot be transmitted, then surely we may get behind the antithesis between "catholic" and "evangelical". In this case the "catholic" will have to rethink his view of apostolic transmission as somehow an extension in time of the Incarnation of Christ, and the "evangelical" will have to rethink his view of continuity as that which is concerned only with the transmission of the apostolic faith. Behind both these views there is something absolutely primary, the thought that "throughout the whole of history the Church remains identical with itself".[1]

We have however to think of "apostolic succession" in a secondary sense, and this where the expression is more appropriate. The Church has not only been ingrafted or rooted in Christ but is built up (Col. 2: 7). Here we are concerned with the fact that the Church already complete as the fulness of Him that filleth all in all, is yet multiplied.[2] Here we think of the Church as "the particular, visible, historical society in which men and women are bound together in the communion of the Holy Spirit, and which grows through history by holding up Christ before men in the Word and Sacraments, and by ministering His love to them in its common life" (Newbigin, II, p. 30). In this connexion the New Testament can actually speak of the Word itself as increasing, multiplying, and prevailing (Acts 6: 7; 12: 24; 19: 20, etc.). By that is not meant that Christ the Word increases but that this living Word acts creatively among men building up on earth a Church "concorporate" (Mersch) with the all-inclusive living Body of Christ, and extending the area of its creative operation in the transmission of the apostolic witness. Behind the transmission and continuity of the witness there is a living continuity of the Word itself. Ultimately these are one, so that St. Paul can describe the divine plan or dispensation and the Church's stewardship in the Gospel by the same word (*οἰκονομία*). The witness is integrated with the whole body of the visible Church, and it is through the whole body growing in history that the Word continues His operation.

Behind this lies the sacramental doctrine of *kerygma*, already discussed, through which on the one hand believers are

[1] Barth, *Dogmatics in Outline*, p. 144.

[2] Cf. K. L. Schmidt, in *Wesen u. Aufgabe der Kirche in der Welt*, p. 15 f.

gathered up into the Church as the living Body of Christ and on the other hand the witness of men builds up on earth a community of Jews and Gentiles in sacramental con-corporation (cf. σύνσωμα—Eph. 3: 6) with the Body of Christ. The mystery of the Kingdom, the mystery concerning Christ and His Church hid from the foundation of the world, is now revealed to the saints, and as it is fulfilled in the Church through the preaching of the Word, all who believe may share in that mystery (Col. 1: 25 f.). The mystery itself is not transmitted. It is revealed in the preaching of the Gospel, and by Word and Sacrament men are given to participate in it. Thus we think of the apostolic succession as a twofold event such as we have described in the last verses of St. Mark's Gospel or in the last few verses of the Epistle to the Romans. On the one hand there is a transmission of witness according to the Scriptures of the prophets and the apostolic Gospel, but on the other hand the Lord Himself works with His Church on earth confirming her Word with power and establishing her in the Gospel. That is the mission of the Church, the apostolic succession, the twofold but ever-new event of the Risen Christ calling the Church and empowering her to be a fellow-worker with Him in the evangelization of the world.

No doubt our minds press for a closer understanding of that holy "synergism", but human analogies are so incomplete that they help but little. One might say however that just as in a telephone conversation the voice at one end of the line has no real continuity however successive its actions may be, but may attain continuity in the gathering up of both voices into one whole communion, so we may think of the Word of Christ Crucified and Risen as breaking into the continuity of our earthly existence and giving it in communion with Him its real continuity, even though ever since the Ascension the living Christ is withdrawn from sight at the other end of the line! Another analogy we might use, but just as incomplete, is that of counterpoint in a Bach fugue, where the given *canto firmo* calls the lower melodies into added counterpoint, and where the counter subject finds its real continuity only in answer to the prime subject and in harmony with it. In such a fugue there is an uninterrupted unfolding of events already implied from the outset. So perhaps we may think of the history of the visible Church in the contingencies of history as having her real continuity in contrapuntal relation, in ever-new obedience, to the ever-new breaking in through the Word and Sacrament of the Kingdom of God. Such a continuity is the Eucharistic life of the Church through which there is an uninterrupted unfolding of the once-and-for-all event enshrined in baptism. It is because the Church on earth is already filled with Christ who Himself fills all things that the Church is empowered by an irresistible drive to carry her witness to the very end of the world (Matt. 28: 18–20). It is universal Christ (*Totus Christus*, cf. I, p. 50) who dwells in the Church and who by His death and Resurrection has appropriated the whole world. His Spirit is grieved and quenched wherever the Church fails to bear witness to the whole world. It is as she fulfils this universal mission of redemption that the Church enters more and more into her universal and catholic inheritance in Christ.

What better analogy is there than that given by St. Paul, the Christological analogy of the *Body*? The union between God and Man was in a real sense perfect at Bethlehem, and yet we believe that the Captain of our Salvation was made perfect through suffering. The union that had broken into the continuity of history at Bethlehem was carried through the heart of history and through its deepest contradictions and discontinuities, even through the *Eli, Eli, lama sabachthani* and hell itself, into the perfect union between the eternal Son of God and the New Creation in Jesus Christ risen from the dead. So may we not think of the Church as the Body of Christ, begotten of the Holy Ghost at Pentecost and carried through the world's contradictions and discontinuities, "in the likeness of sinful flesh", but reaching forth to that perfect union between Christ and His Bride at the Parousia? Therefore because the Church is already sacramentally concorporate with the Risen Body of Christ but still waiting herself for the redemption of the body, it is the function of the Church to live out the reconciliation or atonement of Christ in the world—that is, to be in the flesh the bodily instrument of God's crucial intervention, the sphere in which the great reconciliation already wrought out in the Body of Christ is realized among men, so that the life and action of the Church militant become sacramentally correlative to the life and passion of Jesus Christ, the Suffering Servant.

Baptism and Eucharist mean that though she is once and for all dead, buried and risen with Christ (Rom. 6), yet the Church dies daily and is daily renewed in the power of the resurrection (2 Cor. 4). That is why the proclamation of Christ Crucified, the power of God, is constitutive of the Church's very life. The proclamation of the Word of the Cross is not that all men are as a matter of natural fact at one with God, but that this reconciliation is achieved only in desperate and crucial action, in the death and resurrection of Christ. And so the function of the Church in realizing this at-one-ment in the world is to enter into the judgment of God in the death of Christ upon the world and humanity[1] and thereby to enter into the birth-pangs of Christ for the new humanity. The Church cannot be at one with the world, for its at-one-ment with God brings her into critical tension with the world reflecting the judgment of the Cross (hence the Eucharist), but that is the very point at which there is introduced into the world the Gospel of a new humanity at one with God. Thus the Church is the atonement becoming actual among men in the resurrection of a new humanity corresponding to the resurrected Body of Jesus. "As in Adam all die, so in Christ shall all be made alive." As Adam is correlative to the old humanity, so through the Cross and Resurrection Christ becomes the last Adam (ἔσχατος Ἀδάμ) correlative to the new humanity. It is participation in this Christ that is the life-process of the Church—an eschatological process right in the midst of the critical situation brought about by the fire cast upon the earth in the Gospel.

That is why the Church is so concerned with world-mission, for her very foundations rest upon it. She draws her life from the new humanity in Christ. She is in faith what one day she will be, and now her life-movement consists in becoming what she actually is in Christ. No doubt it is always a temptation of the Church to conquer a certain region and settle in on it and become self-contained, but that would be to forget that she can save her life as she loses it for Christ's sake and the Gospel's. It would be to forget that the Church is humanity in eschatological concentration, the whole of humanity, and

[1] Cf. Florovsky, I, p. 55; and *Evangelische Theologie*, op. cit., p. 456: "The Cross is itself the *Eschaton*".

that in and through the Church this new humanity must break forth by the power of the resurrection and cover the earth. Therefore the daily health of the Church lies in her human range, and the more expanding and missionary she is the healthier her life-process. It is when the Church inhibits that life-process by becoming self-contained and stabilized, that the Church becomes impotent and inhuman. To restrict the Gospel would be to cut the roots of the Church from the resurrected Body of Christ, and therefore to cut the roots of the Church from humanity. It would be to sin against the Incarnation, to fight against the Cross, and to rebel against the will of God to bring all men under its redeeming power.

It is because the Church lives by the Cross and Resurrection that she has an eschatological nature which makes her such an explosive and revolutionary force in the world. If therefore, as Dr. Kraemer reminds us, we live in a universally revolutionary situation (II, p. 15), we must learn that the Church can only carry out her mission by recalling more and more the revolutionary character of the Gospel. Her relevance to the world is precisely her *eschatological relevance*. That is to say her relevance lies in the fact that in Christ she is already the new humanity. It is only by bearing witness to this design of God in Christ and His Church that the Church can make her best contribution also to the order of the world. "The Church can only help in the disorder of the world, by really being the Church. Its most important duty to the world consists in allowing itself to be remade by the Word of God" (Schlink, I, p. 104). It is because the Church possesses proleptically all things in Christ, even the new heaven and the new earth, inasmuch as these are all summed up in Him, that "the Church's Gospel is not primarily the answer to men's needs" (Newbigin, II, p. 22; contrast here the whole approach of Dr. Horton who even declares that the New Testament eschatology and apocalyptic are not expressed in language which our age can comprehend—II, p. 96. How different is the report on p. 133!). It should not surprise us therefore to read: "It is being recognized that the problems of the proclamation of the Gospel in East and West are fundamentally the same, and that old distinctions are out of date" (II, p. 13). This is a significant note, for it calls us back to the fact that because of the Incarnation and the creation of a new humanity in Christ the Church is most relevant to the world as she keeps near Jesus Christ. She cannot discover her relevance by devising new methods of evangelism (needful as these may be) or by searching for points of contact, though the personal contact is of course supreme. On this whole subject nothing better has been written than the contribution of G. F. Vicedom (II, p. 178 ff.) which every minister ought to read and study. The Church must above all rediscover the Gospel, and relearn the supreme relevance which it has to every human situation. If Churches have lost their relevance it is because they have slackened their grip upon the Gospel of the Incarnation, Death, and Resurrection of Christ, made easy and comfortable terms with the world, and only succeeded in neutralizing the dynamic energy of faith.

To recover the Gospel in all its New Testament fulness will mean of course the casting of fire upon the earth. It will mean the preaching of such a message and in such a way as to throw men into upheaval and ferment, as to confront them with the necessity of accepting or rejecting Christ, as to cut through the relativism of history with the knowledge that there is a Judge of history (Pierre Maury, II, p. 98 ff.). That is to say, far from coming to terms with the world "the Church must announce God's activity in history, which in Jesus Christ and His Incarnation gives Time its divine value" (I, p. 103). "The 'relevance' of this message to the world is this *contradiction* between the 'present age' and the 'age to come'" (II, p. 111, cf. "hatred of grace", p. 105). It is the relevance to sin (II, pp. 125, 127).

The Church will be unable to carry out this divine mission and function in the world unless she recovers more and more the eschatological character of her true being. The great shame and disorder of the Church is that she has collaborated with the disorder of the world and clothed herself with so many of its forms and fashions that so often she is too committed to the world and too compromised with it to be able to deliver the revolutionary Word of the Gospel with conviction and power (cf. Stephen Neill, II, p. 72 ff.). Because her true nature is eschatological the Church ought always to be shedding her outward garments, putting off the old man and putting on the new. "In order to ensure that she remains catholic the Church must constantly be scrutinizing all these forms of her life in the light of God's Word and bringing them into subjection to Him".[1] Just as in the crucifying of the Body of Jesus the husk of Israel in which He was bodied forth into the world was rent and the Gospel released to the whole world, so the Church must be prepared as part of her dying and rising with Christ to mortify the deeds of the body, to lay her worldly form upon the altar of the Cross and in the shedding of old ways and habits, in the refashioning of her order, to release the Gospel effectively to the world of to-day (2 Cor. 4: 10–12).

It was just at this very point that St. Paul found himself involved in a controversy with Judaism because the Judaic disciples had not yet learned the catholicizing nature of the Gospel, the almighty sweep of its comprehension revealed in the Cross which set the Church on a wholly new basis. The perpetual tragedy of the Church on earth is that she allows herself to become crusted over with secularism and goes about in the shabby second-hand clothing of a transient age. So often she is outwardly an anachronism. Instead of realizing that the Body of Christ is a living moving reality, and that she is the sphere in which the new humanity breaks into the world, the Church tends to come to terms with the old humanity and even to identify herself with civilization. But if the Church is indeed the new creation she must be fundamentally revolutionary over against the fashion of this world. That is why an era of real disquietude entered the world with the coming of Christianity. The Church is called to the task of ferment and upheaval in humanity attacking the stabilization of orders fashioned to suit human selfishness.

The more the Church discovers this New Testament vision, the more profoundly relevant to the present situation she will actually be. Where the Church is regarded primarily in terms of an apostolic succession that has to do with a continuity that reaches back through an unbroken historical series for its validity, the Church becomes so bound up with the passing form and fashion of this world as to be hopelessly bogged down within its history. Where, however, the mission of the Church is conceived in terms of an extending and continuous witness to the

[1] D. T. Jenkins, *The Nature of Catholicity*, p. 57.

all-embracing eschatological reality and these two are held together indissolubly in Word and Sacrament, then the Church will indeed be *Power of God*. She is indeed the Power of God but that power has been so systematically canalized in the ever-deepening grooves of our hardened traditions that the full force of its mighty impact is yet to be felt in the world. The great lesson which we all have to learn from Germany, as Dr. Schlink has made abundantly clear (I, p. 97 ff.), and as Dr. Niemoeller has not ceased to proclaim, is that unless she repents the Church can only be renewed in judgment when under the hand of God the worldly props upon which the Church leans are taken away and the man-made traditions shamelessly endowed with absolute divine sanction are swept aside. In God's judgment and mercy that is the hour of release when the whole body of the Church (cf. the "*lay apostolate*", II, pp. 204, 223) rises up to assume the ministry of the Gospel and finds that all power in heaven and earth is given unto her through the indwelling presence of the Risen Lord.

PROBLEMS OF FAITH AND ORDER

2. LUND

Where do we go from Lund?[1]

ALTHOUGH most of the early reports of the Conference on *Faith and Order* held at Lund expressed disappointment and sometimes even depreciation of the work undertaken there, it is becoming increasingly clear that quite another verdict must be given. Lund marks the end of an old era in ecumenical theology, and the beginning of a new era in which we have the promise of a development in modern times that may well correspond eventually to the development of ecumenical theology in the fourth and fifth centuries.

The End of an Old Era

It soon became evident during the conference that theological differences were of such a kind as to cut across the face of all the Churches represented, so that no Church through its own peculiar tradition was able to exert undue influence upon the course of events, and no one Church emerged as the rallying point for the whole Conference or even promised to be a core for future integration. On the contrary, wherever churchmen and theologians tried to stress their own traditions unduly, they found those traditions along with their intransigeance elbowed into a corner. That fact caused great anxiety among some from both sides of the Atlantic, and from both sides of the Reformation, Continental and Anglican. For a while it even appeared that the effect of Lund would be to increase the denominational tensions, and yet that must be looked upon as a temporary reaction upon the part of some to the major fact that real ecumenical theology had taken the field and was asserting itself with power and spirit.

[1] From the *Scottish Journal of Theology*, 1953, pp. 53–64; German text in *Evangelische Theologie*, 1952/53, pp. 499–508 (tr. by Pfr. Dr. W. Menn).

For the first time in a conference of this kind all the great doctrines of the faith were taken for granted, in the sense that there was no serious challenge to them, to Christology or to Christological Eschatology, for example. Even the proverbial tension between American and Continental theology largely faded out before the understanding and power of men like Calhoun, Outler, Lehmann, Trinterud, and others, while representatives from the younger churches, notably from India and Ceylon, helped considerably to quicken theological sympathy and to bridge many gaps in misunderstanding, without losing the spontaneity and power which Western compromise inevitably seems to involve. There can be no doubt, however, that what really brought about this situation was *the rising tide of biblical theology*, and on that basis a deeper understanding of, and more general sympathy for, the classical theology of the first six centuries and of the era of Reformation. To find great patristic learning in Professor Calhoun, and Calvin's language on the lips of Professor Florovsky, were but two indications of the theological interpenetration that is going on among theologians, but what has made that possible is the concern of theologians to think out together the doctrines of the faith on the basis of biblical study.

It also became clear at Lund that the old methods of *Faith and Order* procedure had not carried us as far as we had hoped, though they had done yeoman service by digging out the differences between the churches and helping within certain limits to break down some of the misunderstanding between different traditions. But this continual comparison and contraposition of different ecclesiastical traditions in frank discussion of their widest and deepest differences can actually help to harden the differences, for so long as this is the major procedure in conferences of *Faith and Order* proper theological procedure and actual theological growth are suspended. Whatever conference-procedure *Faith and Order* adopts, it must allow room for a theological procedure analogous to the nature of theological truth, for only in that procedure can there emerge a real growing together of different theological traditions.

The great value and ultimate failure of the old procedure of *Faith and Order* were evident in the three preparatory volumes of the Commission. In all of them there had been a remarkably clear contraposition of the different theological traditions in regard to Church, Worship, and Sacrament, and there was little point in going over all that ground again. The Conference began by attempting to do that but soon realized that the continuation of that procedure only ends in its stultification, and then theologians sought, with varying success, to find a way of penetrating behind these differences and to adopt a theological procedure by means of which these differences might even be cut away. What was wanted was a theological method whereby we could think together our one faith in the one Christ, beginning with the very centre, with Christ Himself, and proceeding on this Christological basis seek to think through our differences in regard to Church, Worship, and Sacrament. Already the character and results of the preparatory volumes make this a clamant necessity, for in trying to adopt the traditional conference-procedure as theological procedure, they had failed to provide any real basis for discussion at Lund, and there was a good deal of anxiety on the part of the Old Guard and even accusations of despair when it was found that theologians had at times to start almost from scratch. That was most apparent in one of the commissions on the Church which found that the Report on *The Church* even under the *Mode of its Definition* had failed to define the nature of the Church in terms of its essential relation to Christ as His Body.

The same tendency, many felt, marked the preparatory material on Intercommunion, and indeed continues to mark the Lund Report, in a hesitation to get down to bed-rock, to a proper theological basis and dogmatic procedure for the whole discussion of Intercommunion as a "problem" within the one Body of Christ—although when looked at in that light it is essentially a false problem, as our Orthodox friends were not slow to point out. In regard to the volume on Worship, and here again in regard to the Lund Report, there was certainly evidence of a marked growing together of the divergent emphases, but little real penetration to the fundamental issue as to how we are to conceive theologically the relation between the heavenly liturgy and the earthly liturgy. It may well turn out that the real difference here is not a difference in Christ but a difference in Plato, that is, a non-theological factor. Certainly it was within this commission at Lund, largely under the impetus of Professor D. M. Mackinnon, that the ideas thrown out with such vigour and clarity by Obendiek and Hromadka about non-theological factors in our discussions were taken up and thought through into an important contribution. Here is an issue rising out of the Lund Conference that must be pursued with great vigour, for clearly it will yield much fruit particularly in certain fields of discussion such as that between Lutherans and Reformed in Germany where non-theological factors are a notorious obstacle to understanding, or between the Church of Scotland and the Church of England on questions of the ministry where non-theological factors going back to Tudor and Stewart roots still obscure the issue on both sides.

In looking back upon the old era of *Faith and Order* it becomes apparent that while the conferences have provided the opportunity for encounter between theological representatives of the different churches and while there has been considerable advance in understanding of, and sympathy for, other traditions, the positive advances have been achieved not primarily because of anything done within the *Faith and Order* movement but because of the massive biblical scholarship of our day and the rise of a great positive theology upon that basis. That biblical thinking has everywhere been ready to step into the yawning differences revealed by the conference-procedure, and without any deliberate programme provided by those who plan and guide the conferences, has wrought a remarkable change in spite of the increasing realization of how deep our differences really go.[1] The time has now come, however, when this must no longer be left to chance. Consciously and deliberately *Faith and Order* must adopt a proper theological procedure in discussion through which the vast material available in biblical studies can be used to enormous advantage in getting behind and undermining the differences which still divide us within the one Body of Christ on earth. The Conference at Lund marks not only the end of an old era but the beginning of a new era partly because it took the first decisive steps in this direction. That the services of Oliver Tomkins with all his remarkable foresight and wisdom are still available to the commission of *Faith and Order* is the best augury for the future.

[1] There should not be forgotten here the remarkable work done by the *Study Department* of the *World Council of Churches.*

The Beginning of a New Era

The two main suggestions which appear to have emerged at Lund are: that we should start from the centre of the Christian faith, from the doctrine of Christ, and in thoroughly Christological terms think through the doctrines of the Church, Ministry, and Sacraments; and that a serious attempt be initiated to study Church Tradition, and in that light to examine the divergent historical traditions of the different Churches.

(1) "Because we believe in Jesus Christ we believe also in the Church as the Body of Christ." That is surely a proper starting-point for a doctrine of the Church, the common faith in the one Lord. And that is now increasingly possible because biblical studies have been forcing the Churches back to deeper appreciation and fuller understanding of the classical Christology of the Ecumenical Councils. The attempt to formulate a doctrine of the Church as part of the doctrine of Christ is not new, for it was made in the fifth century, though the first great attempts had to wait till the Reformation when it was Calvin particularly who sought to give thoroughgoing expression to the doctrine of the Church in terms of the analogy of Christ. Indeed the whole movement of the Reformation may well be regarded as a Christological criticism of the notions of Church, Ministry, and Sacraments as they had developed through the Dark and Middle Ages in strange detachment from the high Christology of Nicaea and Chalcedon.

The time has come to undertake this task again, and to set forth in truly dogmatic form the doctrine of the Church as the Body of Christ. That the Church is the Body of Christ is no mere image or metaphor. It is essential reality, though there are many biblical images which must be drawn into the orbit of the doctrine of the Church as the Body of Christ, for they have been given in order to enrich and deepen and widen our understanding of "this great mystery concerning Christ and His Church", and we cannot do without them. Biblical studies during the last twenty years have yielded an enormous amount of material on this very subject which ecumenical theology will have to examine carefully, and which promises to be of the greatest help in dogmatic reconstruction. In our day too the whole question of the analogical relation between Christ and His Church has undergone the most ruthless scientific searching and criticism particularly at the hands of Karl Barth, and is yielding results of such magnitude that many are only beginning to appreciate them through works like that of Hans Urs von Balthasar: *Karl Barth, Darstellung und Deutung seiner Theologie.* When we speak of the Church as the Body of Christ we do not mean a relation either of identity or of difference between Christ and His Church but an analogical relation in which there is no relation of proportion but only of similarity (and dissimilarity) of proportion. But it is clear that no discussion of this analogical relation in itself can get us anywhere, if it is divorced from its true substance and content in the Incarnation, for in the strict sense, as von Balthasar is ready to say, it is Christ Himself who is the *analogia entis.* That means that the analogical relation between Christ and His Church must be thought out in terms of the hypostatic union of the two natures in one Person, and indeed in terms of the *inconfuse, immutabiliter, indivise, inseparabiliter* of the Chalcedonian formula.

At this point, however, we must remember that the Church is the Body of The Christ who was crucified under Pontius Pilate, who rose again and ascended to the right hand of the Father, and who will come again to judge the quick and the dead. The Church is not the Body of the Trinity, nor the Body of the Holy Spirit. There was much confusion in certain quarters at Lund about this. Certainly it is clear that no true doctrine of the Church can be formulated which is in any sense divorced from the doctrine of the Holy Trinity, or from the doctrine of the Spirit, but it is as the Body of Christ alone that it can be formulated. The relation of union between the Church and Christ is grounded on the consubstantial communion of the Holy Spirit between the Father and the Son, but the material content of that relation of union is given by the Incarnation of the Son of God. The "divine nature" of the Church is not God, nor the Spirit, but the *Word Made Flesh*, who is True God and True Man. The new humanity of the risen Christ belongs to the "divine nature" of the Church. Thus the doctrine of the Church must be thought out in terms of a triangular relation between the Church and the historical

Christ, the risen and ascended Mediator, and the Christ who will come again in His full Humanity as well as Deity.

There can be little doubt that when the Church in the fifth century began to think out the doctrine of the Church in terms of the agreed Christology of the Ecumenical Councils she was seriously hampered by the fact that full and true emphasis upon the historical Christ had not recovered after the staggering blows administered to it by the rationalistic notions of Logos, nor had the doctrine of the Spirit been given full place, though after the Nicaean affirmation of the true Manhood of Christ the doctrine of the Spirit began to come to its own. But the doctrine of the Spirit continued to suffer from the rationalist notions of Logos and tended to develop in terms of Ecclesiology and not primarily in terms of Christology. With the loss of the full emphasis upon the historical Christ went also a loosening of the Church's hold upon the doctrine of Atonement, so that even the doctrine of the Person of Christ in the Ecumenical formulations came to be affected, for it was not stated in terms that were sufficiently dynamic, in terms of the mission of Christ. That was corrected to a certain extent by the doctrine of the anhypostasia and enhypostasia of Christ, but it still remains true that the whole doctrine of the hypostatic union needs to be rethought in terms of the death and resurrection and second advent of Christ.

At no time in history has the Church been in a more favourable position to do that than to-day, if only because of the enormous recrudescence of the biblical emphasis upon the historical Christ, and His risen humanity. Along with that has come a rediscovery of biblical eschatology which is the doctrine of the Ascension and Return of the risen Christ as true Man as well as true God, which carries with it a renewed emphasis upon time-relations because of the renewed emphasis upon the resurrection of the Man Jesus, and the resurrection of the body in Him at the last day. It is this biblical theology even more than the classical Christology which will keep true our understanding of the analogical relation between Christ and His Church. Two facts in particular will have to be emphasized. (a) The relation between Christ and His Church is the *irreversible* relation between the Head of the Body and the members of the Body. That relation of irreversibility belongs to the doctrine of the Holy Spirit through whom alone the Church is given to participate in Christ and be His Body, and through whom the Church is given continued being only as servant of the Lord. (b) The relation between Christ and His Church is the relation between the First-Born of the new creation and the body which still awaits its redemption, although sealed by His Spirit and given already an earnest of its inheritance yet to be revealed. The Church on earth is still "the body of sin" although in the amazing grace of Christ it is justified and sanctified in Him. The Church is at once the Body of Christ and yet awaits the day when its union with Christ will be fully consummated, when at last it will be presented to the Lord as a chaste virgin. Until then the Church on earth is the waiting Church of sinners under judgment as well as grace, and is called to perpetual renewal through conformity to Christ, and to look beyond its historical forms to the full unveiling of its new being in the coming Lord.

If the substance or content of the analogical relation between Christ and His Church is the doctrine of Christ Himself, the relationship involved is to be formulated in terms of the doctrine of the Spirit and Eschatology. In this way I believe the Church of our day will be able to do something that has never yet been done in the whole history of the Christian Church: give full dogmatic formulation to the doctrine of the Church of Jesus Christ. The way is certainly wide open, and if *Faith and Order* is prepared to undertake this task seriously it will do something second only in theological importance to the Christology of the early fathers or the Reformation. Should this be undertaken by *Faith and Order*, now operating within the World Council of Churches, it would give the World Council of Churches an *ecumenical* significance parallel to that of the Ecumenical Councils.

(2) The other suggestion arising out of the Lund Conference is equally significant: the study of our different traditions in the light of Tradition (with a capital "T"). All sorts of questions arise here as we place tradition alongside of tradition in the historical development and divergence of the Churches. Why does the Orthodox Church ignore so many canons of the Ecumenical Councils, for surely the canons and the dogmas belong together? Why do Anglicans in their claim to revere

the fathers stress only certain canons and refuse to consider others? Out of such a comparative study there emerge many interesting facts of prime significance. For example, as Calvin sought to "restore the face of the Ancient Catholic Church" he resurrected long-neglected canons of the Ecumenical Councils and reformed the Church accordingly, so that in the Reformed Church again and again it is obedience to Tradition that makes it differ from the traditions of the Orthodox Church or the Anglican Church!

There can be no doubt that such a historical and comparative study of traditions will be of great help in the ecumenical movement, although it must be clear that if this study is to be only historical and comparative, it will not lead very far, and perhaps will only lead back into the dead-end which *Faith and Order* found in its old procedure at Lund. In certain fields such a study can be of peculiar interest and fruitfulness, as in Scotland where a joint study of the common tradition of the Church of Scotland and the Episcopal Church in Scotland, particularly during the years 1560–72, cannot but bring closer understanding, especially if this is carried through in the light of the rediscovery of Tradition at the Reformation. But the two major factors must be borne in mind here if this kind of study is to be really helpful:

(a) The whole understanding of Tradition is undergoing remarkable change in the light of modern biblical and patristic study, a change parallel to that in our understanding of *kerygma*. True *paradosis* is *kerygmatic* as well as sacramental—Calvin also could speak of the *traditio corporis* as taking place through the sacraments. But it is important to see that the *traditio corporis* takes place through the whole *kerygmatic* continuity of the Church. (b) The understanding of Tradition cannot be separated from Church dogma. In other words, this historical and comparative study of traditions must not be divorced from the dogmatic study of the Church as the Body of Christ in history; nor must the dogmatic study of the Church be divorced from the growth of the Church "in the unity of the faith and the knowledge of the Son of God unto a perfect man, unto the measure of the stature of the fulness of Christ: that henceforth we be no more children, tossed to and fro, and carried about with every wind of doctrine, by the sleight of men, and cunning craftiness, whereby they lie in wait to deceive; but speaking the truth in love may grow up into him in all things, who is the head, even Christ: from whom the whole body fitly joined together and compacted by that which every joint supplieth, according to the effectual working in the measure of every part, maketh increase of the body unto the edifying of itself in love." The growth of the Church as the Body of Christ and the growth of the Church into the Mind of Christ belong together inseparably. They may be distinguished but must never be divorced.

Two factors must be clearly stressed here. (1) The true form of the Church in history is at once dogmatic and ecclesiastical. There can therefore be no fruitful discussion of the form of the Church as the Body of Christ in history which is divorced from the dogmatic form of the Church. Through the Word of God the Mind of the Spirit gives the Church conformity, in its growth into truth, with the Mind of Christ. (2) The relation between the dogmatic and the ecclesiastical forms of the Church, the inner form and the outer form, as it were, must be thought out, not in static terms, but in dynamic terms of growth into the fulness of Christ. And that growth must be thought out and be expounded not only in terms of teleological development but in terms of eschatological fulfilment, for the growth cannot be formulated in terms of a biological organism but in terms of the death and resurrection of Christ. The pattern of the Church's life in history is essentially cruciform, for it bears about in its body the dying of the Lord Jesus that the life also of Jesus might be made manifest. In other words, the forms of the Church in dogmatic and ecclesiastical convolution and mutual criticism are also apocalyptic, for the Church grows into the fulness of Christ in the overlap of the ages, and in that overlap the perfect pattern of the Kingdom and the perfect form of the new creation act creatively and critically upon the forms of the Church in history, so that in so far as they participate in the fashion of this present evil world, they are summoned to perpetual transformation in the risen Christ.

All this is of the utmost importance for ecumenical discussion to-day both for the light it casts upon our several traditions in the light of Tradition, and for the searching questions it directs at the several traditions as Tradition itself is seen in the light of the coming Christ who says "Behold I make all things new", and so calls them to look beyond their historical forms to the perfect pattern of their life in Him the risen Lord. It is above all in the Orthodox Church that we see the unity of the dogmatic and ecclesiastical forms of the Church, but there the relation between the dogmatic form and the ecclesiastical form is, in the main, statically formulated, and the Orthodox Church does not appear in consequence to have grown much since the early centuries. That is partly due to a failure to relate the doctrine of the Spirit adequately to the doctrine of the Son as *crucified* and *coming again*, as well as risen and ascended. The Roman Catholic Church also claims to have an essential unity between the dogmatic and the ecclesiastical forms of the Church, and claims that it has grown to maturity, but in this case the development of the Church has been conceived only as teleological growth, and eschatological fulfilment is being more and more repudiated with every promulgation of new dogma. This Church claims to be *ex sese irreformabilis*, which can only mean that its pattern of development has ceased to be cruciform, that it has ceased to allow itself to be transformed through the death and resurrection of Christ by the renewing of its mind, and so has ceased to put off the old man and to put on the new man which after God is created in the righteousness and holiness that grow out of the truth.

At the Reformation these issues were subjected to Christological criticism, but again the churches of the West began to diverge. The Lutheran Church paid little serious attention to ecclesiastical form, content with the forms of the world it found ready to hand so long as they left room for the Gospel, and the result was that they concentrated so much on dogmatic form that the Lutheran Church has become the most confessionalist church in the world. The Anglican Church on the other hand left the dogmatic form almost entirely to one side and contented itself largely with clinging to the continuity of ecclesiastical form without undertaking seriously continuous dogmatic activity as strenuous obedience to the Mind of Christ. Here there is an astonishing divorce of the ecclesiastical form from the dogmatic form of the Church. The Reformed Church under the influence of Calvin sought on the other hand to allow the dogmatic and ecclesiastical forms of the Church to interpenetrate each other in obedience to the Word of God, and so to restore in doctrinal and ecclesiastical form the face of the Ancient Catholic Church. And yet it was in this Reformed tradition that Schleiermacher arose, who thought of the dogmatic and ecclesiastical forms of the Church in such immanent integration that for him theology was little more than a systematic attempt to read the Mind of the Spirit off the historical experience and living consciousness of the Church—and we have something like a return to the romantic theology of Rome.

The recent Conference at Lund has made it very clear that we can no longer remain content with any of these historical treatments of Tradition. We must take in earnest the essential unity of the Church as the unity of the *One Spirit* and the *One Body of Christ*, and seek to allow the Church as it listens again to the Word of God to be transformed by the renewing of its mind, in order that it may grow up in the unity of faith unto a perfect man in Christ. It is in our understanding of biblical theology that we must examine again the historic dogmas of the Tradition of the Church, and seek to let the doctrine of Christ criticize and reshape the whole form of the Church so that we may grow together under judgment and grace, in the power of the Holy Spirit, into the likeness of Christ and into the stature of His fulness. Only as the churches of the ecumenical fellowship seek to think into each other the dogmatic and the ecclesiastical forms of the Church in strenuous obedience to Christ from year to year, and only as they are ready to look beyond their historical forms, dogmatic and ecclesiastical, to the full unveiling of their new being in the coming Lord, will they grow in unity and in the love which remains when all earthly and historical forms, even faith and hope, have passed away. Decisive theological steps in this direction of unity in and through faith in Christ seem to have been taken at Lund. May this be the beginning not only of a new era but the beginning of actual unity among the churches. "For to what end did Christ come", asked Calvin once, in his great Commentary on the Epistle to the Hebrews (10: 25), "except to collect us all into one body from the dispersion in which we are now wandering? Therefore, the nearer His coming is, the more we ought to labour that the scattered may be assembled and united together, that there may be one fold and one Shepherd."

PROBLEMS OF FAITH AND ORDER

3.

THE ATONEMENT AND THE ONENESS OF THE CHURCH[1]

In August, 1952 the *Third World Conference on Faith and Order*, meeting at Lund, formulated its Ecumenical objective in terms like this: Our major differences clearly concern the doctrine of the Church, but let us penetrate behind the divisions of the Church on earth to our common faith in the one Lord. Let us start from the central fact that Jesus Christ loved the Church and gave Himself for it, and by His Spirit made it His own Body. From the oneness of Christ we will try to understand the unity of the Church in Him and from the unity of Christ and His Body we will seek a means of realizing that unity in the actual state of our divisions on earth. What is envisaged here is a thorough-going Christological criticism of our differences in order to open up the way for reformation and reunion of the Church in obedience to the one Lord.

That I believe to be sound theological procedure. The Church is the Body of Christ—that is no mere figure but reality—and therefore the doctrine of the Church must be formulated in the closest connexion with Christology, as the corollary of it and strictly in terms of the analogy of Christ. In other words, it would seem that the relation between Christ and His Church, and the nature of the Church, are to be interpreted in the light of the Catholic dogma of Christ, as found, for example, in the Ecumenical Councils or the Creeds and Confessions of the Churches. That does not mean, however, that a doctrine of the Church can be formulated to-day simply by application of the formulations of classical Christology, for we have to take into major account the vast material provided by modern

[1] The *Albrecht Stumpff Memorial Lecture* delivered at the Queen's College, Birmingham, on May 3, 1954. In this printed form the argument has been somewhat expanded. From the *Scottish Journal of Theology*, 1954, pp. 245–69; German text in *Evangelische Theologie*, 1955, pp. 1–22 (tr. by Pfr. Dr. W. Menn).

biblical study. It is in fact this biblical study that has drawn discussion back within the orbit of patristic Christology, but in so doing it has also made clear that the classical terminology of the Church in its formulation of the doctrine of Christ needs qualifying and reminting in the biblical studies of our day if it is to be an adequate instrument of Ecumenical theology.

Perhaps the first step to be taken in this direction is the re-examination of the relation of Atonement to Incarnation and the bearing of Atonement upon the Church. It is the purpose of this essay to raise that issue for discussion, in the conviction that the oneness of the Church is grounded in the incorporating and atoning action of Christ, and, therefore, in the persuasion that we must bring our differences to the Cross of Christ. It was there that the divisions wrought by sin were exposed and overcome, and it was there that God made peace by the blood of Christ, that through Him He might reconcile all things to Himself. The whole relation between Christ and His Church, Christ in the Church and the Church in Christ, needs to be understood much more from the perspective of reconciliation, in terms of *Christus pro nobis*. In the words of the Lund Report: "What concerns Christ concerns His Body also. What has happened to Christ uniquely in His once and for all death and resurrection on our behalf, happens also to the Church in its way as His Body . . . so that the way of Christ is the way of His Body" (pp. 7 f.).

In order to raise this question, I should like to discuss three primary conceptions of classical Christology in their relation to the death of Christ, and then to examine three ways in which an understanding of Atonement may cut behind our differences and point us to a deeper unity.

I

(a) We may begin with the conception of the *hypostatic union* of God and Man in Christ. There can be no doubt that the Chalcedonian formulation of the Union in Christ was one of the greatest and most important in the whole field of theology, and yet it was formulated in almost entire abstraction from the historical life and work of Jesus Christ from His birth to His resurrection. It is one of the most pressing needs of theology to have the hypostatic union restated much more in terms of the mission of Christ, much more from the perspective of the cross and resurrection. I do not mean that we should contemplate any change in the fundamental position adopted at Chalcedon or even in the terminology of Leo's Tome which conserves so wonderfully the whole mystery of the God-Man in the negatives *inconfuse*, *immutabiliter*, *indivise*, *inseparabiliter*, and, therefore, I can only reject the way taken by some Orthodox theologians in recent years, in an attempt to offer a positive account of the hypostatic union in terms of sophiology. What I mean is that the Chalcedonian Christology needs to be filled out in accordance with its own fundamental position, in a more dynamic way, in terms of the incorporating and atoning work of the Saviour, for the only account the New Testament gives us of the Incarnation is conditioned by the perspective of the crucifixion and resurrection.

Look at it like this: When we think of Jesus Christ in Himself, in the mystery of His own Person, the Chalcedonian formula is quite adequate, for it expresses all that we can say, warding off on each side harmful error and reminding us that here we are face to face with a mystery that is more to be adored than expressed. But when, on the other hand, we think of His mission in relation to sinful man, of His Incarnation as the incorporation of Himself into our body of the flesh of sin and the carrying of it to its crucifixion, when we think of His entry into our estrangement in the contradiction of sin, and of His working out, in the midst of our humanity and alienation, reconciliation with God, then the Chalcedonian formula does not say enough, for reconciliation is not something added to hypostatic union so much as the hypostatic union itself at work in expiation and atonement. Following the Epistle to the Hebrews, we must give the hypostatic union more dynamic expression in accordance with Christ's learning obedience and His bringing His relations with sinners to their *telos* through suffering. We must think of Christ entering upon His active ministry as true God and true Man in one Person, in a union which penetrated into our sinful humanity and created room for itself in the midst of our estrangement, at once gathering sinful man into one Body with the Saviour, and opening up a new and living way into the Holiest. That movement gathered intensity until it reached decisive enactment in the crucifixion and fulfilment in the resurrection and ascension. Throughout the whole life and mission of Christ, hypostatic union and reconciliation, incorporation and atonement, involved each other in redemption and new creation. It is in that mutual involution that the Church is grounded as the one Body of the one Lord.

And yet while we cannot separate hypostatic union and atonement we can see that there are distinct "moments" in that movement. That is apparent when we see the actual way in which Jesus Christ founded the Church. The first thing He did as He entered upon His active ministry was to be baptized in a crowd of sinners—that was His identification in the body of His flesh with the whole mass of sin and death. By Baptism He made Himself one with us all. He spoke of that Baptism later in terms of the Cross, for it was in the Baptism of blood that by crucifixion He was incorporated wholly with us in judgment. Meantime Jesus chose twelve disciples out of the baptized multitudes to be with Him in His ministry, to continue with Him in His tribulations, and even to watch and pray with Him at last in the Garden of Gethsemane. As long before Elijah had gathered together twelve stones representing the twelve tribes of Israel to build an altar for sacrifice, Jesus gathered twelve living stones, such as the rock Peter, and built them round Himself the Lamb of God to be offered in sacrifice. Upon this Twelve, the reconstituted Israel, He was to build His Church, and so He formed and fashioned them into a foundation, in a profound sense, one Body with Himself. Their Baptism into one Body was to be worked out in self-denial and crucifixion, such that each was a member of Christ, each renounced his own name and lived in the name of Christ. That is why at Caesarea Philippi, when Peter confessed the name of Christ, Jesus immediately initiated them all into the inner mystery of the Kingdom, the union of God and Man in atonement on the Cross. The Twelve were thus the Many inhering in the One. They had one name in the Son of Man who came to give His life for the Many. In the co-inherence of the One and the Many, involving self-denial and crucifixion, the nucleus of the Church received shape and form, and together the little flock went up to Jerusalem where it was to be given the Kingdom. Then there took place the Last Supper, where Jesus in covenantal action appointed to the disciples a Kingdom, and they were made a royal priesthood, to sit on twelve thrones with Christ in His Kingdom, i.e. on the basis of communion in the Body and Blood of Christ, for the Son of Man gave them to eat His Body and drink His Blood, and to become one with Him. There followed immediately the crucifixion and resurrection.

On that ground the Church was inaugurated at Pentecost, but the movement of union creating and founding the Church involved a dual "moment". After Baptism we see the Church as the Body of sin or sinners, into which Jesus Christ incorporated Himself in order to be the Saviour of the Body. After the Last Supper where that union is confirmed, He immersed Himself in sacrificial death for sin, that the Body of sin being destroyed He might raise it again, a glorious Body in His Resurrection. It was then that the hypostatic union, carried through crucifixion to its *telos* in the Risen Christ, was through the breathing of the Spirit inserted first into the nucleus of the Church on Easter evening, and then, after Christ's Ascension to fill all things, into the whole Church at Pentecost. In other language, through *koinonia* the Church, for which Christ died and rose again, was given to participate in the hypostatic union, in the mystery of Christ. Before the crucifixion Jesus Christ came as the Son of Man who joined Himself to the Many in order to give Himself for them, the One representing the Many, but after Pentecost and on the ground of the work on the Cross the Church was sent out as the Many to represent the One Son of Man, the Saviour Lord. Thus the relation of the One to the Many carries with it and begets the relation of the Many to the One. The One and the Many is the doctrine of Christ. The Many and the One is the doctrine of the Church, the Body of Christ.

(b) We have now overtaken the point where we must consider the conceptions of *anhypostasia* and *enhypostasia*. By *anhypostasia* classical Christology asserted that in the *assumptio carnis* the human nature of Christ had no independent *per se* subsistence apart from the event of the Incarnation, apart from the hypostatic union. By *enhypostasia*, however, it asserted that in the *assumptio carnis* the human nature of Christ was given a real and concrete subsistence within the hypostatic union—it was enhypostatic in the Word. *Anhypostasia* and *enhypostasia* are inseparable. In the Incarnation the eternal Son assumed human nature into oneness with Himself but in that assumption Jesus Christ is not only real man but a man. He is at once the *One* and the *Many*.

This is of supreme importance in application of the atonement. When we interpret a term like ἱλάσκεσθαι in this light we must say on the one hand that God is the Subject of the whole atoning action: "*God* was in Christ reconciling the world unto Himself", and yet on the other hand Jesus Christ is Himself the ἱλασμός, for within the divine act of atonement Jesus as Man has a particular place in obedience, Reconciliation is God's supreme action, but within it, it is the concrete action of Jesus Christ that reconciles us. It is appropriate therefore that the middle voice should be used: ἱλάσκεσθαι. Because *anhypostasia* and *enhypostasia* are inseparable we cannot speak of two actions in the Cross, but of the act of the God-man.

The significance of that is apparent when we consider a view of atonement such as that advocated by Aulén in *Christus Victor*. If *anhypostasia* alone were to be applied to the atonement then Aulén's view would be right and proper, but that would mean that the deed of atonement would be a pure act of God over the head of man, and not an atoning act involving incorporation. Certainly the atonement is act of God, supremely act of God, but that act of God is incarnated in human flesh, giving the human full place within the divine action issuing forth out of man's life. On the other hand, if *enhypostasia* alone were to be applied to the atonement without *anhypostasia* then atonement would have to be understood as a Pelagian deed placating God by human sacrifice. The inseparability of *anhypostasia* and *enhypostasia* in application to the death of Christ is thus supremely important for it means that while atonement is throughout act of God for us, we are to understand it as act of God done into our humanity, wrought out in our place and as our act.

This has been very well put by the late Dr. F. W. Camfield in the *Scottish Journal of Theology*:

> What we could not accomplish, Christ accomplished on our behalf. The infliction and judgment which we could not bear, He bore for us. He took our place and on behalf of us all He made satisfaction for our sins and for the sins of the whole world. It

> was not Godhead *qua* Godhead that atoned; it was the God-manhood. And that means not simply God *in* man but God *as* man. The manhood was integral and essential and not merely instrumental. And that means, in the concrete sense, substitution.[1]

If this is right, that the manhood of Christ was "integral and essential and not merely instrumental" in atonement, that is to say, in the language that I have been using, that it was enhypostatic and not merely anhypostatic, then we must give the element of concrete *substitution* much greater place in our understanding of atonement. It is this aspect of substitution that needs to be added throughout to our understanding of the movement of the One and the Many we considered in terms of the hypostatic union.

The Incarnation is the movement of the eternal love of God, in which He gives Himself to man and reconciles man to Himself. This movement into our actual flesh and history of the gracious will of God to be one with man in spite of his sin involves the meeting of God and man in the very situation caused by sin. That is the life and work of the Son of Man. He was the love of God incarnate, pouring Himself out in utter compassion to man, penetrating into his existence and need, and gathering his life into the Life of God. In this ultimate self-giving of God to man in Christ man is confronted with the ultimate things, the last things before which all the secrets and intents of his heart are revealed. And so the very union of God and man which the Incarnation involved actually intensifies the state of enmity between man and God. By uniting God to man the judgment of God is brought to bear on man as never before; by uniting man to God man is brought under the divine judgment as never before. The Incarnation of the Son of God means the gathering of this intensification into the one Son of Man, but in Him the Incarnation takes the form of substitution as well as incorporation. It is not as a third party that Jesus intervenes in our human situation where God judges man and man contradicts God. The Incarnation means that God the Son entered into our human alienation from God and stood in the flesh and place of man in subjection to law and judgment. He stepped into the conflict between the covenant

[1] *S.J.T.*, vol. i, p. 292.

faithfulness of God and the unfaithfulness of man and took that conflict into His own flesh as the Incarnate Son and bore it to the very end. He shared in it from both sides, from the side of God who is offended by man and from the side of man who is under the divine judgment of death. Within our flesh He was thus act of God the Judge condemning sin in the flesh, and within our flesh where man has no justification before God, He the Just in the place of the unjust stood under judgment and rendered to God the answer of complete obedience, even to the death of the Cross.

In Him who stood in our flesh and place like that, where God's heart beats for man and man is placed under the majesty of God, there is a substitution where the guilty does not shelter behind the innocent, but such a substitution that the guilty is faced with the Light, that man is dragged out of his self-isolation and brought face to face with God in His compassion and holiness. Because it is God Himself who here steps into man's place and takes his status upon Himself, man is not sheltered from God but exposed to His judgment, for in our place He claims to displace us and demands that we renounce ourselves for Him, in order to be one with Him.

If such incorporation and substitution are the way of the Son of Man, they are the way of the Church as His Body. The atonement began with the virgin birth of Christ, entered upon active operation at His baptism and reached its culmination in the crucifixion—the whole of Christ's life and ministry were involved in the work of reconciliation as well as His death. In birth and baptism He the sinless One incorporated Himself into our flesh of sin that through substitutionary atonement we who are sinners might be incorporated into Him as His body who was raised for our justification. If incorporation and substitutionary atonement are bound up together in this way then the only way the Church can arise and become the Body of Christ is to be ingrafted into His death and incorporated into His resurrection. The only way the Church can follow Him is by way of *anhypostasia*, by way of self-denial and crucifixion, by letting Christ take its place and displace its self-assertion; and by way of *enhypostasia*, by way of incorporation and resurrection, by receiving from Christ the life which He has in Himself and which He gives His own. It is the way of

Baptism and Holy Communion. There is no other way for the Church, and so no other way to reunion, than by the way of the Cross, for it is the Cross which is the way to the resurrection of the One Body.

(c) In order to consider the full application of this Christology to the doctrine of the Church we must make use of yet another primary conception of Catholic Christology—*the analogy of Christ.* That was raised at a decisive hour by Athanasius when a crypto-Arianism was threatening to destroy the whole analogical basis of Christian theology by compromising the true doctrine of the Son. Against the misuse of figures and analogies by the *Tropici* in their greatly impoverished doctrine of the Spirit Athanasius insisted that all analogies must be subordinated to, and criticized by, the unique Revelation of the Father in the Son, for it is solely from the Incarnate Son that they have their legitimate place in Christian theology and therefore it is only in accordance with the analogy of Christ that they are to be applied. The analogical relation between Christology and the Sacraments was expounded by Theodoret and Gelasius I and that was extended by the Reformers to the doctrine of Holy Scripture, and also to the doctrine of the Church, but this has yet to be worked out fully. We cannot attempt that here, but we may content ourselves with indicating the main aspects which the analogical relation assumes within the body of Christian theology with particular reference to the Church.

Logically, the notion of analogy has been given the closest scrutiny as a relation involving neither identity nor difference but something of likeness and something of difference *proportionaliter*. Apart, however, from telling us how analogical predication should be framed, that tells us nothing at all, until we come to the actual relationship that has been established between God and man in the Incarnation. It is on the ground of that real and substantial relation that we may speak *proportionaliter* of the relation of Christ and His Church.

Christologically, the analogy of Christ means that the terms *inconfuse* on the one hand and *inseparabiliter* on the other, which the Chalcedonian dogma applied uniquely to the two natures of Christ, may be applied in a secondary and cognate sense to the relation between Christ and the Church as His Body. In regard to the Eucharist the *inconfuse* would negate a doctrine of transubstantiation as heresy, and the *inseparabiliter* would negate a doctrine which separates the elements from the Body and Blood of Christ as heresy. In regard to the Church, the *inconfuse* would negate a Docetic conception of the Church as if it had been transubstantiated into something beyond history, and the *inseparabiliter* would negate a conception of the Church which divorced it from ontological union with Christ Himself.

Soteriologically, the analogy of Christ involves a substitutionary relation, the *mirifica commutatio*. "Ye know the grace of our Lord Jesus Christ that though he was rich yet for your sakes he became poor, that ye through his poverty might be rich" (2 Cor. 8: 9). "God made him to be sin for us who knew no sin, that we might be made the righteousness of God in him" (2 Cor. 5: 21). Thus the analogical relation between Christ and the Church reposes entirely upon what He has done for the Church by taking its place that it might be conformed to Him, and is maintained because Christ continues to live for the Church so that the life of the Church is to be found not in itself but in Him. This element of substitution between Christ and His Church involves a soteriological inversion of the relationship: "Herein is love, not that we loved God, but that he loved us" (1 John 4: 10). "Ye have not chosen me but I have chosen you" (John 15: 16). "Ye have known God or rather are known to God" (Gal. 4: 9).

Pneumatologically, the analogy of Christ tells us that as Christ was born of the Spirit, baptized and anointed in the Spirit, through the eternal Spirit offered Himself to the Father, and was raised by the Spirit of Holiness from the dead, so through the Spirit the Church is joined to Christ as the Body of which He is the Head in the irreversible relationship which that establishes—the relation of the servant to his Lord. Through the Spirit the Word became flesh; the flesh did not become Word. Through the same Spirit Christ has assumed the Church as His Body, and is free to be present in the Church and to realize the relation of the Church to Himself giving it life-unity with Him as Redeemer and Lord of its being.

Within the orbit of this whole relation between Christ and His Church and within the analogical form which it demands, we may seek cautiously to apply the conceptions of *anhypostasia* and *enhypostasia* to the Church. *Anhypostasia* would then mean that the Church as Body of Christ has no *per se* existence, no independent *hypostasis*, apart from atonement and communion through the Holy Spirit. *Enhypostasia*, however, would mean that the Church is given in Christ real *hypostasis* through incorporation, and therefore concrete function in union with Him. That is why to speak of the Church as the Body of Christ is no mere figure of speech but describes an ontological reality, enhypostatic in Christ and wholly dependent on Him.

Thus while *anhypostasia* asserts that the Church as Body of Christ has no independent existence or oneness but insists on an eschatological relation between the Church and Christ in terms of His mighty acts for and in the Church, *enhypostasia* asserts a teleological relation between the Church and Christ in terms of real continuity of being. On the ground of the substitutionary work of Christ, who incorporated Himself into our humanity and took our place in order that we might be incorporated into His new humanity, we can only speak of the ontological reality and continuity of the Church in terms of *communicatio idiomatum*, while the conjunction of *anhypostasia* and *enhypostasia* reminds us that even here we can only speak in terms of analogical unlikeness as well as likeness to Christ.

At this point we must remind ourselves that all this needs to be stated more dynamically in terms of the living movement of hypostatic union and atoning reconciliation in Jesus Christ. That is the way in which it was frequently interpreted in the Fathers (*analogia* in terms of active *anagoge*) and that is certainly the emphasis in the New Testament.

Thus when we turn to the teaching of St. Paul and hear him say: "Let this mind be in you which was also in Christ Jesus" (Phil. 2: 5), we find him insisting that the whole movement of humiliation and exaltation in Christ, His Incarnational *katabasis* and His glorious *anabasis* has to be translated into the Church as Christ's Body. We find the same argument in 2 Cor. 4, Eph. 1 and 2, and in Col. 1. The same analogical perspective is found in the Epistle to the Hebrews. Thus in the twelfth chapter the author asks his readers to look away from themselves to Christ the Author and Finisher of the Faith, who for the joy that was set before Him endured the Cross, despised the shame and is set down on the right hand of the throne of God, and then he demands that they work that out analogically in themselves.

Is it not at this point that we can attack the cleavage between a so-called "eschatological view" of the Church on the one hand and a so-called "ontological view" of the Church on the other? If here both eschatology and ontology are understood as the analogical transposition of Christology and soteriology to the Church, then the real cleavage is demolished. If we think of the Church only in terms of the Incarnation and incorporation then we tend to entertain the false conception of the Church as a *Christus prolongatus* or an extension of the Incarnation. If we think of the Church anhypostatically alone, only in terms of eschatological event, then we rob the Church of its ground in the Person of Christ and demolish the understanding of it as His Body. But if, on the contrary, we think of the Church as grounded on the atoning and incorporating work of Christ, the ontology of the Church must be thought out in terms of the substitutionary death of Christ for the Church, and the eschatology of the Church must be thought out in terms of incorporation into the risen and ascended Humanity of Christ. Only when ontology is interpreted apart from *anhypostasia*, and eschatology is interpreted apart from *enhypostasia*, can there be divergence, but when we recall that only by Christ's substitution of Himself in our place is incorporation possible, while substitution is possible only on the ground of incorporation, we are unable to regard these two as alternatives. They belong together inseparably. In other words, if we think of the Church consistently in terms of Christ who died and rose again and apply that analogically to the Church so that we understand it not only as constituted by the substitutionary work of Christ but as so incorporated into Him that it bears about in its body the dying and rising of the Lord Jesus, then we cannot have an "eschatological" view of the Church that is not also "ontological", nor an "ontological" view of the Church which is not also "eschatological". The ontology will speak of the miraculous preservation of the life and being of the Church through death and resurrection in Christ, and eschatology will speak of the real and substantial union of the Church with the Risen, Ascended, and Advent Lord.

II

We may now proceed to examine several ways in which the doctrine of atonement may be applied critically to our differences in the doctrine of the Church and so point us to a deeper unity.

(a) *The Form and Order of the Church*

If the Christological conceptions we have been discussing are to be applied to the Church, as I believe they must be, then on the analogy of Christ we must think of the Church sent out into the world from the Cross as the *suffering servant.* "As the Father hath sent me, so send I you." The Church militant is still under the Cross and it belongs to its life and mission to work out analogically in itself what happened in Christ for the Church, to fill up in its body that which is eschatologically in arrears of the sufferings of Christ and so to fulfil the Word of God (cf. Col. 1: 24 f.).

It is essentially the same point that St. Paul expounds in 2 Cor. 5, "The love of Christ *constrains* us in that we make this judgment that if he died for all then were all dead." We think immediately of those words of Jesus where the same word in Greek is used. "I have a baptism with which to be baptized, and how I am *straitened* until it is over" (Luke 12: 50). Christ was anticipating the Cross and the mighty power of the divine love in Him which kept pressing Him toward the Cross, where this love would be released to the whole world in reconciliation, was so great as to be almost unbearable. The birth-pangs of the universal Gospel were already upon Him, and He was straitened in agony until it was accomplished. That is what happens to the Church as the Body of Christ, for before the Cross it is put under the constraint of the passion of Christ. It cannot contain itself—the agony of Christ is upon it. The Love of Christ shed into the Church by the Spirit must break out in the mission of redemption. And so the Church goes out into history participating in Christ's ministry of reconciliation, bearing about in its body the dying of the Lord Jesus that the life also of Jesus might be made manifest in its mortal flesh.

This participation of the Church in the ministry of the Son

of Man must be thought out in terms of analogical difference as well as likeness. In the words of the Lund Report, "What happened to Christ *uniquely* in His once-and-for-all death and resurrection on our behalf, happens also to the Church *in its way* as His Body". Thus for example, priesthood cannot be predicated of Christ and of the Church univocally, nor can sacrifice be predicated of His work and of the Eucharistic action in the same way. Jesus Christ was Suffering Servant in a unique sense in that He had a ministry of substitutionary and vicarious atonement in which His act was act of God. The Church is suffering servant like Him but in a different sense. The Church participates in His ministry of reconciliation *by serving* Him. That is the point of supreme importance, for differences arise on the one hand where the analogical likeness between the Priesthood of Christ and the priesthood of the Church is not observed, and on the other hand where the analogical difference between them is not observed.

We must understand this analogical likeness and difference between the ministry of the Church and the ministry of Christ in terms of substitutionary incorporation into Christ or substitutionary participation in His ministry.[1] The ministry of the Church is not to be related directly to the ministry of Christ as if it were an extension or prolongation of His ministry or even an extension of certain of His ministerial functions. There can be no question of distinguishing between certain functions of Christ as primary and non-transferable and other functions which can be transferred by His authority to chosen representatives. The New Testament nowhere makes any such distinction but boldly speaks of the Church as participating in Christ's own ministry. He fulfils His ministry in a unique and unrepeatable way, as Prophet, Priest, and King. The Church's ministry as prophetic, priestly, and kingly is correlative to Christ's whole ministry but entirely subordinate to it and fulfilled *alterius rationis*, in a way appropriate to the Church as the Body of which Christ is the Head, as the servant of which He is the Lord, as the herald of which He is King.

[1] In technical terms this likeness and difference are to be stated in terms not of direct analogical attribution nor of a mutual relation of proportion, but of similarity and dissimilarity of proportion—i.e. the analogy of proportionality.

The Church exercises its ministry, then, in such a way as to allow Christ to displace the Church and be Himself through the Spirit the Lord and Master of the Church's ministry. The Church can only participate in Christ's ministry in humble obedience and self-denial, so that on the ground of substitution ("He must increase, I must decrease", "Not I but Christ") it is Christ Himself who stands forth in the midst of the Church as Prophet, Priest, and King. The Church can only be the *Vicar* of Christ not by substituting itself in Christ's place but by letting Christ substitute Himself in the place of the Church. As in atoning reconciliation incorporation in Christ is on the ground of substitution, so in the ministry of reconciliation participation in the ministry is on the ground of substitution. Thus the Church is committed with the ministry of reconciliation not in such a way that the Church reconciles the world to God, but in the sense that as the Church proclaims the Word of reconciliation in Christ's stead, it is Christ Himself who fulfils His own ministry and actually reconciles the world to God.

It is by this substitutionary incorporation into Christ and substitutionary participation in His ministry that the form of the Church is determined as the form of a servant correlative to the Son of Man. It is through baptismal incorporation, through self-denial and bearing the Cross, through Holy Communion that the Form of the Son of Man becomes the form of the Church His Body. "It is enough for the disciple that he be as his Master, and the servant as his Lord" (Matt. 10: 25).

His visage was marred more than any man's, and He hid as it were His face from us. So deep was His humiliation that He had no form nor comeliness that we should look upon Him, and there was no beauty that we should desire Him. That is the Body and Form of Christ to be discerned in the Church that is planted into the likeness of His death that it should also be in the likeness of His resurrection. As the Body of Christ, the Church is cruciform, but that has to be understood in terms of active analogy, of daily crucifixion and resurrection. Wherever in obedience to the blood of Christ the Church is found engaged in the ministry of reconciliation, pouring out its life like the Son of Man that the Word of reconciliation might be delivered to all men for whom He died, wherever the Church shows forth

His death until He comes and presents its body a living sacrifice, there the image of Christ is to be seen and His Body is to be discerned in the Church. It is as a royal priesthood actively engaged in Christ's ministry of reconciliation that the Church manifests its true form.

The understanding of the Church as suffering servant is also of profound significance for the question of order, for this means that all conceptions of order and validity have to be determined by the servanthood of the Church under the Cross. That was the significance of the temptation of Christ following upon His Baptism, the temptation to gain the authority and glory of the kingdoms of this world by avoiding the Cross. He chose the way of the Servant, and the way of Christ must be the way of the Church which is His Body.

As the Servant Jesus Christ was made *under the law* and yet through His death and resurrection He justifies the Church *apart from law*. This Church which is redeemed by Christ and through His Spirit formed into His Body is sent out on a mission into history made under the law as a servant of Christ. To see the full significance of that we may draw out the biblical comparison between Christ and Adam. Adam refused to preserve the order of Paradise, the limitations imposed on him by God, and man as Adam's child refuses to fit into the order of restoration; he will not admit that he is flesh standing under judgment and can only live by grace. But Jesus Christ entering within our existence did not want to be like God, or on an equality with Him. On the contrary He confessed before God the state of man as fallen, bearing the wrath of God as a necessary righteous wrath. He did not avoid the lowliness of this estate but humbled Himself and was made servant under the law, willingly taking its consequences upon Himself. Thus He entered our human existence in this age, with its form of law, ranged Himself beside sinners and stood with them under judgment. By His obedience He acknowledged God's judgment on sin and so condemned sin in the flesh. By His obedience He accepted the verdict upon sinful man, the limitations of the creature under law and judgment, and within those limitations wrought out the mighty deed of redemption.

The Church is called to follow Christ in that lowly way of the servant, but also to follow Him who by His obedience unto death has justified the Church apart from law and risen again for its justification. While the Church follows Christ by undertaking His mission within history and within the form of law which this age through sin and judgment involves, nevertheless the Church follows Christ as justified, reconciled, and risen with Him, and is therefore differently related to the *nomos*-form of this age. In the nature of the case the reconciliation of the Church with Christ and the Church's participation in the power of His resurrection, mean the breaking-up of the form of law and the relativizing of the historico-juridical forms of the Church, for all these forms are forms of this present age which passes away and are impregnated with human selfishness and sin and guilt. That guilt-laden and sin-impregnated history with its dire determinism has been overcome by the death and resurrection of Christ, so that the Church goes out into history on its mission at once to use the forms of this world within which it is a servant to Christ, but not to abuse them for its own ends of self-justification; not to be fettered by the *nomos*-forms of this age but freely to live within them in order to preach the Gospel to the poor and to proclaim liberty to the captives.

Within this dialectic of justification, *under the law* and *apart from law*, the old Augustinian distinction between a *valid* and an *efficacious* ministry breaks down, for that is really valid which under the law ministers to the freedom of the children of God apart from the works of the law. As St. Paul puts it, "For I through the law am dead to the law that I might live unto God" (Gal. 2: 19). Likewise the whole conception of order and authority needs reinterpretation in terms of the Son of Man. He possessed supreme authority, Lordly ἐξουσία, but He exercised it in the form of a Servant. In the Person of Christ the Lordly authority and the servant form were uniquely one, so that just when He was weakest, on the Cross, His majesty as Son of God was most apparent. The weakness of God is stronger than men. The Church follows its Lord in His servant form and by participating in His authoritative ministry, but the servant form and the authority are not identical in the person of the Church, for here the servant form is given authority precisely as the person of the Church is through self-denial and crucifixion displaced by the Person of Christ. The Church does not act in its own name but solely in the name of Christ. The Church serves an authority not its own, and serves it in such a way as not to usurp it as if it were its own but to make room for the Lord the Spirit in its midst. Authority in the Church is mediated through the weakness of the Church bearing the reproach of Christ, through its submission to the way of "the Son of man who came not to be ministered unto but to minister and to give his life a ransom for many". But this brings us to examine the relation of the atonement to the time of the Church.

(b) *The Time of the Church* (that is, the notions of succession and tradition)

We may begin by noting that the atonement has backward as well as future reference. It has retroactive effect going back to the very beginning, and so Christ in the Apocalypse is spoken of as the First and the Last, the Alpha and the Omega. In the Cross we do not have mere amnesty for sin but such a total act of forgiveness and justification that guilt is utterly undone and done away. At the Cross God puts the clock back. He restores the years that the locust has eaten, for He breaks the power of guilt and liberates man from the determinism of a guilty past. Guilt and the irreversibility of time, as we know it in our sinful world, are bound up together inseparably, but in the form of guilt what is irremediable and ineradicable in the past is present determining man's existence under judgment and binding him in its tyranny. It is that in man's *anamnesis* that works his continuous condemnation, which applies not simply or even primarily to the individual but rather to the whole Adamic race, the whole of human existence, which as St. Paul says was piling up wrath against itself in the day of judgment. In His death on the Cross Jesus Christ descended into that awful pit of man's past existence, into hell itself, and by His atonement He broke it open, leading captivity captive, and now He holds the keys of death and hell in His power. Through atonement, then, Christ broke into the kingdom of the irreversibility of time and guilt with its strength in the law, and by a complete act of expiation He has undone its power and cancelled guilt and sin. That means that in the death of Christ we have an act of justification that penetrates back to the very beginning and sets man's life on the basis of God's creative purpose. The Cross makes contact with creation. Christ the Second, the Last Adam undoes the work of the first Adam and heads the race to a new and higher glory that far transcends the old, for here the past is not only undone but suborned by the Cross and made to serve the purpose of God's redemption.

The application of this to the doctrine of the Church as the Body of Christ has real importance for our understanding of historical succession and tradition. On the analogy of Christ this must be considered in terms of the whole historical life of Jesus as bracketed between His virgin birth and His resurrection in body, both of which involve at once continuity and discontinuity, so that we are to think of the work which God does through His Work in the Church as *consummans et abbrevians*, as the Vulgate puts it, involving teleology as well as eschatology. We cannot enter fully into that here but may glance at the bearing of atonement on the *time* of the Church in history, examining by way of illustration the New Testament concept of *στοιχεῖον*.

The root meaning of *στοιχεῖον* which it never lost is *succession*, from *στοῖχος* a row or *στοιχέω* to go in a row, like a row of columns or soldiers in single file. *στοιχεῖον* thus means to be in succession like the letters of the alphabet, A, B, C, etc. or the planets in their heavenly procession. Out of this there emerges a number of secondary meanings. (a) The letters of the alphabet, and so the ABC of a thing, the elements of knowledge (cf. Hebrews 5: 12). (b) The physical elements or the ultimate indivisible elements, and so the first principles of which the visible, tangible world consists (cf. 2 Peter 3: 10). (c) The heavenly elements or the metaphysical principles which lie behind the temporal successions of the cosmos, and so the rudiments of philosophy (cf. Col. 2: 8). (d) There is also another sense of *στοιχεῖον* which refers to the shadow cast by a sun dial indicating the time of day (cf. Col. 2: 17). Behind all these there lurks the notion of succession, and succession in relation to time. That is certainly clear in the Pauline usage. In the Epistle to the Galatians *στοιχεῖον* refers to succession in terms of Judaistic Tradition which has assumed the form of *nomos* or principle of the cosmos with reference to days, months, times, and years, or in the language of the Epistle to the Colossians, a holiday, or the new moon or the sabbath as well as ordinances about meat and drink and other human traditions. Here *στοιχεῖον* appears to refer to temporal succession turned into a legal tradition or cosmological principle, and this is coloured by the derived sense of rudiments of philosophy. When St. Paul links *στοιχεῖον* to *κόσμος* he clearly has in mind temporal succession turned into *nomos*, turned into a theological or legal principle, but as such the *στοιχεῖα* become demonic, for, like the renegade *ἐξουσίαι* and *ἄρχοντες* and *παραδόσεις τῶν ἀνθρώπων*, they seek through *nomos* to usurp the power of God. They belong to the tyrant forces from which we are redeemed by the blood of Christ for He has robbed them of their usurped authority and power. And so St. Paul says to the Galatians: "You were once enslaved to the *στοιχεῖα*, but now that you have known God or rather are known of God, how is it that you turn back to the weak and beggarly elements, whereunto you desire again to be in bondage?" (Gal. 4: 4–9). And he asks the Colossians: "If you are dead with Christ from the successions of the cosmos turned into theological principles, why as living in the cosmos do you dogmatize about them?" (Col. 2: 20). The teaching in both Epistles is the same: for the Church to walk *κατὰ στοιχεῖα τοῦ κόσμου* is to walk *οὐ κατὰ Χριστόν* (Col. 2: 8).

Now this does not mean that the Church must have nothing to do with *στοιχεῖον*, any more than it must avoid *παράδοσις* or *νόμος* or the *σχήματα* of the cosmos, but it does mean that the Church is not to be enslaved to them. By the death and resurrection of Christ succession is a poverty-stricken principle and must not be turned into a law or a dogma to enslave the Gospel. Because the *στοιχεῖα* have been robbed of their tyrant force by the blood of Christ, the Church must learn to redeem time or to buy back time out of the market of slavery and law and to use succession in Christ, in the power of His crucifixion and resurrection.

The same teaching is found in the New Testament elsewhere with regard to tradition, for when tradition degenerates into an independent principle it becomes the tradition of men against which Jesus set His face in sharp antagonism. In the language of St. Peter, it is by the precious blood of Christ as a Lamb without blemish and without spot that we are delivered from the vain conversation of the tradition of the fathers (1 Pet. 1: 18). That is not to repudiate tradition. "I delivered unto you that which also I received", said St. Paul. The true tradition of the Church is the *traditio corporis* in the Eucharist; it is tradition in terms of the crucifixion and resurrection of the Body of Christ. That carries me to my last point.

(c) *The Sacramental Life of the Church*

We have to take into more account than we do the relation that the atonement bears to the Church as the Body of Christ in terms of ἀνακεφαλαίωσις, which combines hypostatic union and reconciliation in one living redemptive movement gathering up the Church into the mystery of Christ. Here there is not only an unravelling of the skein of guilt and sin-laden time but a creative restoration of our being and its unification in Christ the Head of all things. Or, to put the matter the other way round, the mutual involution of Incarnation and atonement is to be applied sacramentally to the Church in terms of its birth and growth as the Body of Christ. If Incarnation and atonement are to be understood in terms of each other, the same is true of Baptism and Eucharist in terms of one living, saving operation of reconciliation and unification. But if Incarnation and atonement are to be distinguished as dual moments in the one movement, similarly Baptism and Eucharist enshrine a corresponding duality. Both Sacraments belong to the fulness of time and have to do with the whole Christ clothed with the Gospel of reconciliation and resurrection, but in Baptism we have to do particularly with the objective and perfected event, and in the Eucharist we have to do particularly with participation in that completed reality in the conditions of time within which the Church engages in the mission of the Cross. Baptism speaks of our justification and incorporation into Christ as an abiding reality; the Eucharist speaks of it as an eschatologically repeated event to be inserted into our flesh and blood, into time and history, as often as we partake of the Body and Blood of Christ until He come.

While on the one hand we are given the real presence of the whole Christ, on the other hand that is daily to be realized in sacramental obedience. We are concerned at every point with a reconciliation that is thrust into a world which continues in estrangement and alienation, so that in addition to Baptism, the Lord's Supper is given to teach us that while we are complete in Christ, yet we are engaged in a battle with the contradictions and divisions that mark the empirical history of our fallen world.

In terms of reconciliation as the movement of unification in Christ this means that through Baptismal incorporation the Church is given unity of the Spirit, a perfected reality which is to be kept, but through continuous Eucharistic communion in the death and resurrection of Christ the Church is given to grow up in the unity of the faith in the knowledge of the Son of God until it come to a perfect man, unto the measure of the stature of the fulness of Christ. But this growth from unity to unity in the fulness of Christ is not merely a growth. It is a desperate struggle in which we wrestle not against flesh and blood but against principalities, against powers, against the rulers of darkness of this world, against spiritual wickedness in high places (Eph. 6: 12), so that Baptism and Eucharist have correspondingly another aspect in the life of the Church.

Through the atoning and incorporating action of His Incarnation, death and resurrection, Jesus Christ has once and for all made the Church one with Him in His crucified and risen Body. In assuming our body of flesh and in carrying that to the Cross Jesus is the place at once of love and judgment, of the love that binds God and man inseparably together, and of the judgment that is brought about in that conjunction of Holy God with our humanity. The Body of Christ crucified is at once the sphere of union and judgment, and that is the Body into which the Church is baptized. To be baptized is to be planted into that judgment, to be ingrafted into the Body of death, inserted into the sphere of union where judgment and crucifixion are enacted as saving operation. It is therefore through baptismal incorporation into Christ that our sinful divisions are brought under the mortification of the Cross and are destroyed in Christ. If through this Baptism the Church participates in that action for it, is sacramentally incorporated into the one Body of Christ, then Baptism is the primary enactment and expression of the oneness of the Church. In Jesus Christ the Church is holy and perfected, for He presents it to the Father as His own Body pure and spotless, but on earth the Church is still the body of sinners waiting for the redemption of the body of sin and death, living in the midst of estrangement and the dividedness of mankind.

This Church, the Church militant, is also given the Eucharist in order to engage in the battle, and so to participate in the death and resurrection of Christ that it may daily be mortified and daily renewed, daily be healed where it is broken and reconciled where estranged. The Eucharistic communion does not add anything to the wholeness of Baptismal incorporation but it is a renewal of the Church's oneness in the Body of Christ, and such an anticipation of the fulness to come that through it the Church may live out bodily and spiritually in the midst of the broken and divided world the oneness of the Body of Christ.

In other words, the sacramental life of the Church has to be translated into the terms of the Church militant, into terms of its mission as suffering servant showing forth the Lord's death till He come. The sacred symbols of our faith, broken bread and poured out wine, are the symbols of violent death. The Church that communicates constantly through them in the Body and Blood of Christ is engaged in a mission correlative to the crucifixion, and must live out its life in this world in obedience to the blood of the Cross. Such a Church cannot conserve its wholeness or unity that it has in Christ by looking to itself or by trying to preserve intact its own life and tradition, but only by spending its life and offering its body in sacrifice for Christ's sake and the Gospel's. As the Church is empowered by the Spirit to engage in the mission of reconciliation and forgiveness, so it maintains the unity of the Spirit by engaging obediently in the activity of reconciliation. The very nature and continuity of the Church are inseparably grounded in the mission of the Cross, and the oneness of the Church in history reposes upon the oneness of that mission.

That is why the apostolic Church rejoiced in the face of tribulations which it was called upon to endure in the fulfilment of the ministry of reconciliation in the world, for they provided the actual occasions within which, through the Spirit, the Church could live out in the world the life of the servant, obedient like the Son of Man unto the death of the Cross. If it was by His atoning death that Jesus Christ wrought reconciliation and of twain, Jew and Gentile, wrought one new man, it is by entering into Christ's passion for the redemption and unification of a broken and divided world that the Church will find its unity in the crucified and risen Body of the one Lord. *The road to unity lies through atonement.*

We may conclude by noting the significance of that upon the Eucharist. The Sacrament of the Eucharist reposes upon a prior unity and takes cognizance of it, the unity we are given through Baptismal incorporation, but that is the living, growing unity of unification and reconciliation, unity engaged in victorious battle with the powers of disorder and sinful division. The Eucharist is not, however, merely a cognitive sacrament, but an effective sacrament through which Baptismal unity is ever being inserted anew into the flesh and blood of our broken and divided humanity. The Eucharist is therefore effective of unity for in it in the very fraction of the Body and the pouring out of the blood atoning unity is effectively re-enacted in the Church as the Body of Christ.

Here on the one hand the Church baptized into the Body of Christ eats and drinks mortification and judgment upon its dividedness as it eats the Body and drinks the Blood of Christ, and it is only through this reconciliation and healing of division mediated through Eucharistic communion that it participates in the oblation of Christ whereby He presents us in Him as one Body to the Father. But here on the other hand the Church, baptized into the Son of Man, renews its incorporation into the new Humanity of the risen Christ as it communicates in His death and resurrection, and it is because the Church as the Body of Christ is thus itself the new humanity in germ that the life of the Church consists in a movement of continuous expansion and growth correlative to the ascent of Christ in order to fill all things and to gather them up into Himself the Head of all. Thus the sacramental life of the Church is not only one of active reconciliation and unification but of growth into the fulness of Christ, of increase into the full stature of His Humanity. The Church is at once the sphere of reconciliation where the mighty victory of Christ on the Cross over all the forces of sin and division is savingly operative in the midst of the world, and at the same time the one Body headed by the New Adam in which the whole of the new humanity is concentrated and through which this concentrated humanity must break forth by the power of the resurrection to the ends of the earth and the ends of the age.

The Church is, so to speak, the atonement becoming actual among men in the resurrection of a new humanity. Because the Church's life is life in the power of the death and resurrection of Christ, the very life and function of the Church have to do with reconciliation in the midst of division and the resurgence in the world of the new creation in Christ. Nothing could be more destructive of the life of the Church than to limit the atonement, to restrict the range of reconciliation, by erecting barriers to Intercommunion, or would more quickly inhibit its own life-movement in the Spirit than to draw limits to the expansion of the new humanity through the power of the Gospel by becoming self-contained and stabilized and entrenched upon a partial tradition. That would be to sin against the Incarnation, to fight against the Cross, to deny the Resurrection, to quench the Holy Spirit.

In a word, the bearing of the atoning and incorporating work of Christ to the oneness and to the fulness of the Church insists that the road to the unity of the Church and to the evangelization of the world lies through *Intercommunion*, so that all who are baptized into the one Body of Christ may be healed of their dividedness through Eucharistic Communion and in the reconciliation thereby effectively enacted in their flesh and blood show forth to the whole world the death of Christ until He come.

PROBLEMS OF FAITH AND ORDER

4. TOWARDS EVANSTON

Our oneness in Christ and our disunity as churches[1]

"Christ in you, the hope of glory" (Col. 1: 27)

WE believe in one God, Father, Son, and Holy Spirit. Because we believe in one God who was in Christ reconciling the world unto Himself, because we believe in one Lord Jesus Christ who loved the Church and gave Himself for it, because we believe in one Holy Spirit poured out upon the Church at Pentecost bringing it into an abiding union with Jesus Christ, we believe also in the Church as the one indivisible Body of Christ.

In the following statement we seek:

(i) to speak of the oneness of the Church (a) as enduring reality grounded in the oneness of Christ and His Church once and for all wrought out in His incarnation, death, and resurrection; (b) as eschatological growth and fulfilment in the Church, for in spite of the divisions of the world in which it is involved the Church is ever renewed through communion in the death and resurrection of Christ and grows up in the unity of the faith into the fulness of Christ;

(ii) to speak of the oneness of the Church in the face of our actual disunity in the Church on earth, acknowledging that though there are God-given diversities in creation

[1] The original draft of this paper was written by a sub-committee of the Faith and Order Working Committee meeting at Bossey, August 11–19, 1953. The sub-committee consisted of Dr. H. Meyer, now Bishop of Luebeck, Professor Carl Michaelson of Drew Seminary, Madison, U.S.A., and myself. I was then asked to rewrite and expand the paper; Professor Georges Florovsky to write a critique of it, and then Dr. Oliver Tomkins to revise and reduce it, which after further amendment was used as the working paper by the Faith and Order Section at Evanston. It is my revised long draft that is reproduced here, but many minds contributed to it.

and in the gifts of the Spirit which are to be honoured, it is ultimately sin that divides, but believing that He who by the death of Jesus Christ has overcome the contradiction of sin will not allow the oneness of the Church to see corruption, for by the death and resurrection of Christ He triumphs over our sin and division, and gives us already an anticipation of our unity in the one Body of the one Lord;

(iii) to speak of the oneness of the Church as the commanding reality of the Church in Christ to which we must respond in the obedience of faith: (a) listening together in the midst of our disunity to the voice of the one Lord, that we may be compacted together and grow up together into Him who is the Head of the Body; (b) being ready to let the mind of Christ be in us, so that as He was obedient unto the death of the Cross, we may follow Him in denial of ourselves, even as "churches", and in taking up our cross; (c) learning to speak the truth in love with one another, and to discern in others the one Body of which we are members; (d) bearing joint witness in the Gospel, pointing away from our dividedness to the One Lord who has reconciled the world to Himself and has put all our divisions under the judgment of His Cross. In this obedience of faith we believe we shall be changed, although wherein we shall be changed we can know only in the act of faith and self-denial.

I

A

Our Oneness in Christ

There is only one Church. That means that in the manifoldness of the Church and in the diversity of the so-called "churches" there is a unique oneness (John 17: 11, 21–23). The one Church is to be found in its wholeness in each local manifestation of the one Church. When the New Testament speaks of this oneness of the Church in Christ, it does not begin with the fact that the Church is a body of people or a corporation forming one body, but with the fact that in a profound sense *Jesus Christ is Himself the Church* (Acts 9: 4 ff.; 1 Cor. 12: 12; John 15: 1 f.), i.e. with the fact that Christ is one Body and yet many members (1 Cor. 10: 16 f.; 12: 4–31; 2 Cor. 5: 14 f.; Rom. 5: 12 f.; 12: 3–8; Gal. 3: 27 f.; Eph. 2: 14 f.; 4: 1–7; 5: 23 f.; Col. 3: 3, 4, 15; John 10: 16; 15: 1 ff.; 17: 11, 22 f.; Heb. 2: 11; 10: 5, 9–14; 13: 3). Thus the oneness of the Church is not to be found in the fact that it is a spiritual or social entity and therefore to be called the Body of Christ. The oneness of the Church is derived solely from Christ Himself (Col. 1: 16 f.; 2: 19 f.; Eph. 4: 16 f.; Rom. 8: 29), is grounded upon His unique action for the Church (Rom. 5: 12 ff.; Eph. 2: 14 f.; 4: 4 ff.; Col. 1: 21 f.; 2: 10 ff.), and is maintained and secured by the fact that He alone is the Head of the Church (Eph. 1: 22; 4: 15; Col. 1: 18; 2: 10 f., 19). Because He gathers up the whole Church in Himself (Eph. 1: 10, 22), because He is the One and the Many, He alone constitutes and forms the *many* of the Church into *one*: "For as the body is *one*, and hath *many* members, and all the members of the body being many, are one body, so also is Christ" (1 Cor. 12: 12). He gives the many members to participate in His one and unique relation to the Father through the one Holy Spirit (1 Cor. 12: 13; Eph. 4: 4 f.; John 14: 20; 17: 21 f.). Apart from Christ there is no other principle of the Church's oneness, for both in spirit and body the Church is one with Him (1 Cor. 12: 12, 13; 1 Cor. 6: 16 f.). He is the source (*ex hou*, Eph. 4: 16; Col. 2: 19) and the goal (*eis auton*, Eph. 4: 13, 15; Rom. 6: 3) of the oneness of the Church.

According to the New Testament the oneness of the Church with Christ and in Christ is essentially a *mysterium* (Eph. 5: 32) that recedes into and issues out of the eternal purpose of God (Eph. 1: 9 f.; 3: 11; cf. Rom. 8: 28; 9: 11; 2 Tim. 1: 9). That mystery has been hid in God from the beginning of the world (Eph. 3: 3 f., 9 f.) but is now revealed through the preaching of the Gospel (Rom. 16: 25; Eph. 6: 19) to include not only Israel but all mankind, and indeed the whole family in heaven and earth (Eph. 2: 12 f.; 3: 1 ff.). In other words, *mysterium* refers to the union of God and man eternally purposed in God's love but now revealed and set forth in Jesus Christ the beloved (elected) Son, as true God and true Man in one person. This union creates room for itself in the midst of our estranged humanity, and through atonement and communion gathers a people of God out of the world and creates a Church concorporate with Christ. In the redemption-history of Israel that union is already set forth in the covenant people in whom the Word of God is on the road to becoming flesh, involving already, for example, in the prophecy of the Suffering Servant the mystery of the One and the Many. At last in the fulness of time the Word is made flesh, and the mystery of the Kingdom is present reality in the midst of Israel (Mark 4: 11; Luke 17: 21), in the person of the Son of Man and the twelve disciples who are to deny themselves, take up the cross, and be formed into one body in His name (Matt. 16: 13 ff.; 18: 15 ff.). Through the death and resurrection of Christ, and through the pouring out of His Spirit at Pentecost, the mystery becomes actualized in the apostolic nucleus through whom the mystery is revealed, and the Church is to grow, so that they become the foundation upon which the whole Church is built and through whom it is extended throughout all ages and unto the ends of the earth. The New Testament speaks of that *mystery of Christ* as at once present and future (Col. 1: 27), for though it is actualized in the midst through the Incarnation (Mark 4: 11; 1 Tim. 3: 16), it is yet to be fulfilled in the Parousia (Rev. 10: 7).

The Church as the Body of Christ is the concretion of that mystery here and now in history, but this means that the *oneness* of the Church is to be understood in terms of the New Testament *mysterium*, for even in the Church as the Body of Christ ("of his flesh and of his bones", Eph. 5: 30), the oneness is but partially revealed. It remains mystery which in the ascension of Christ recedes from our sight into God, and which awaits His coming again for its full revelation (1 Tim. 3: 16; Eph. 1: 17 f.; cf. 1 Pet. 1: 5 f.; 5: 1 f.). In so far as the oneness of the Church as the Body of Christ is revealed, it is to be understood in terms of "the body of the flesh" which Christ assumed to become one with us (Col. 1: 21 f.; 2: 11), in terms of the body of the Cross or the body of death through which we are reconciled to God (Eph. 2: 15 f.; Rom. 7: 4) and in terms of the body of His resurrection (cf. Rom. 6: 5 f.; Eph. 1: 20 and 2: 5 f.; 1 Cor. 15: 12 ff.; 2 Cor. 4: 10 f.; 1 Pet. 1: 3 f.). In these terms we may expound the oneness of the Church in the following paragraphs:

(a) The oneness of the Church is to be seen in the light of the fact that Christ the eternal Son of God has assumed a body through which He is become one with man, and through which He is given to be the Head over all men and all things. It is through this Body that He gathers all who believe in Him into one Body with Him, and through this Body that the whole creation will finally be renewed.

(b) The oneness of Christ with us is consummated on the Cross where He who was made in the likeness of sinful flesh makes us one with Him. He became bone of our bone and flesh of our flesh that through the sacrifice of Himself for us in atonement, He might destroy our body of sin and death, and present us to God holy and unblameable in His sight (Col. 1: 20 f.; Rom. 6: 6; 7: 4, 24; Heb. 10: 9 f.; 1 Pet. 2: 24). The oneness wrought out in atonement and reconciliation brings to its perfection or completion the oneness involved in the incarnation (Heb. 2: 10; 5: 9; 7: 19, 28; 12: 2).

(c) Through the resurrection of Christ in Body, that oneness is revealed and we are given to participate in His risen Body as One New Man, the New Creation (Rom. 5: 5 f.; Col. 1: 22; 2: 11; 3: 1 f.; Eph. 2: 15; 2 Cor. 5: 15 f.). Here we have manifested the perfect oneness in which all human divisions disappear (Col. 3: 11; Gal. 3: 28). This is the great objective reality, the mighty enduring event upon which the oneness of the Church is eternally grounded, and which is the supreme source and content of its hope to be fulfilled and revealed in the glorious coming of Christ.

(d) Through the pouring out of the Spirit upon the Church in Baptism—so that by the "One Spirit" the Church is through "One Baptism" given to be "One Body" (Rom. 6: 1 ff.; Col. 2: 11 f.; 1 Cor. 12: 12; 6: 16; Eph. 4: 4 f.)—the oneness of Christ and His Church is actualized in the Church. And that constitutes the oneness of the Church. Apart from the Spirit, the "flesh" profits nothing, for it is the Spirit that quickens (John 6: 63; 1 Cor. 15: 25), and indeed apart from the Spirit the body is dead (James 2: 26). Apart from the Spirit the Body of Christ and in Him the whole of humanity would remain in death. But the Body of Christ was not left in corruption. It was raised from the dead according to the Spirit of Holiness (Rom. 1: 4) so that it became *spiritual Body* (1 Cor. 15: 44).

As such Christ is the Last Adam and Quickening Spirit (1 Cor. 15: 44). Because this risen and ascended Christ gives His life-giving Spirit to the Church, the Church becomes *One Body* and *One Spirit* with Him.

(e) Because the oneness of the Church is grounded in Christ who has ascended to the right hand of the Father, its complete and perfect manifestation awaits the day when Christ will come again to meet His Church and to complete the work of redemption and judgment. In that glorious advent of Christ the oneness of the Church throughout all ages will be revealed and consummated. Until that promise is fulfilled the Church continues to be a pilgrim people in a strange land (cf. Heb. 11: 13) so that all its life and work on earth are incomplete, although it has already become one Body with the coming Christ. Therefore the Church is summoned to look beyond its present historical forms to find its fulness and oneness in the coming Lord. It is because the Church through the indwelling Spirit already participates in that fulness to come that it rejoices to look for the advent to come as the hope of glory, and waits and works patiently for the day when He will make all things new.

N.B.—(1) Jesus Christ and His Church are inseparably united to form one New Man, both in Body and Spirit. The union of Christ and His Church constitutes the oneness of the Church, so that the oneness of the Church is founded upon His atoning and incorporating act, and is as strong and eternal as His love (Rom. 8: 35 f.). *Because Christ and His Church are one and indivisible, the oneness of the Church in Christ is indestructible.* Division in the Body of Christ is an impossibility. "Is Christ divided?" (1 Cor. 1: 13). The oneness of the Church is grounded upon the Person of the One Incarnate Son of God, in such a way that there can no more be a plurality of "churches" than there can be a plurality of "Christs" or a plurality of incarnations, or of crucifixions, or a plurality of Holy Spirits. It follows that there is only one Faith, one Baptism, and one Communion. We have no right to speak of "Churches" in the modern way. There is only One Church, for there is only One Body of Christ.

(2) The oneness of the Church in Christ is the commanding and final truth. It is the enduring reality, the eternal indicative, the accomplished and perfected fact which is to be acknowledged in faith, for it commands our obedience. Just as the New

Testament speaks of the believer as already crucified and risen with Christ, as already eternally a new creature, and of that as the great reality that lays hold of us in the Gospel, commanding us to acknowledge it and act upon it, so the New Testament speaks of the Church. We cannot but believe and act upon it. "If ye then be risen with Christ, seek those things which are above. . . . For ye are dead and your life is hid with Christ in God. When Christ who is our life shall appear, then shall ye also appear with Him in glory. *Mortify* therefore your members which are upon the earth. . . ." (Col. 3: 1 f.). We must speak of the Church's oneness in exactly the same way. "If you are risen with Christ, then seek your oneness above. For your divisions are dead and your oneness is hid with Christ in God. When He who is your oneness will appear, then your oneness will appear with Him in glory. *Mortify therefore the divisions of your members which are on the earth.*" It is as we do that that the oneness of the Church as its final reality in Christ becomes a living and growing actuality in the Church on earth, and the lively hope to which we are begotten by the resurrection of Jesus Christ from the dead becomes the mighty force that controls the expectation of the Church and nourishes its joy.

B

The Oneness of the Church in its Earthly Pilgrimage

Through His Word and Spirit the Lord Jesus Christ calls His people out of the world, delivering them from the lordship of the powers of destruction, and forming them to be one Church, one community of persons, the justified and sanctified whose citizenship is in heaven and whose life is hid with Christ in God (Col. 3: 3). The Church is the community of believers who have been raised up together with Christ and already sit with Him in heavenly places (Eph. 1: 20 f.; 2: 5 f.). It is the Heavenly Jerusalem (Heb. 12: 22 f.; Gal. 4: 26; Rev. 21: 2 f.), the Church Triumphant. But until He comes again in glory and power Jesus Christ continues to send His people into the world to be the Church Militant, preaching the Gospel of peace through the blood of the Cross unto all nations and unto the end of the age. By His Spirit He thus empowers the Church throughout its earthly pilgrimage and mission to participate in His ministry of reconciliation and to be the one Body of Christ in the midst of a broken and divided world, so that as it bears about in its body the dying of the Lord Jesus the life also of Jesus might be made manifest in its body and even in its mortal flesh (2 Cor. 4: 10 f.).

Through the Spirit the Church on earth has become One Body with Christ, and yet in the gracious wisdom of God the Church on earth still wears "the body of flesh" and waits for "the redemption of the body". On the one hand the Church is a new creature, one with Christ in His risen Body, but on the other hand the Church on earth is still involved in "the body of sin" or "the body of death", or "the body of humiliation". The Church on earth lives in two ages; *in the new age of the resurrection* which has already overtaken us and is reality here and now through the presence of the Holy Spirit; and in *the old age* whose "forms and fashions" the Church must use if it is not to go out of the world. Although the Church lives in this present age (aeon) it is redeemed from it (Gal. 1: 4) and therefore must not be conformed to it (Rom. 12: 2). Although the Church has its conversation in the world (kosmos; 2 Cor. 1: 2; 1 Cor. 5: 10; John 17: 15) the Church is not of it (John 15: 19) and therefore it must not be subject to its ordinances (Col. 2: 8, 20; Gal. 4: 3, 9) or walk according to its lust (1 John 2: 15 f.) or even according to its wisdom (1 Cor. 1: 20 f.). The world (1 John 2: 17) and its form (1 Cor. 7: 31) pass away with this present evil age, so while we must use this world we must not misuse it (1 Cor. 7: 31) lest we be condemned with the world (1 Cor. 14: 10).

Because the Church on earth lives at once in these two ages the whole of its life and pilgrimage on earth partakes of this ambiguity (1 Cor. 7: 29 ff.; 2 Cor. 4: 8 ff.; 6: 4 ff.), but because it is already risen with Christ, this ambiguity does not belong to its essential nature in Him (Rom. 7: 4, 24 f.; 8: 1 ff.). Therefore it can only live and work in this present age by being crucified to the world (Gal. 2: 19 f.; 6: 14 f.). Only in terms of its crucifixion and resurrection with Christ can the Church manifest in the midst of these forms its essential form as the form of Christ. It is thus that the Church puts off "the old man" and puts on "the new man" (Eph. 4: 22 f.; Col. 3: 8 ff.)—that is, it "puts on love" (Col. 3: 14), it "puts on Christ" (Rom.

13: 14) as its essential and heavenly form. Because through the Spirit the Church is given to participate in the new age, all its historical forms are rendered ambiguous, but through the same Spirit it is given in love to transcend this ambiguity. Thus, it is through "the communion of the Spirit" that the Church spans the two ages, for it is the Holy Spirit who sheds into the Church the love of God (Rom. 5: 5). By the operation of the Spirit the Church is rooted and grounded in love and enabled to comprehend with all saints what is the breadth and length and depth and height and to know the love of Christ which passes knowledge, that it might be filled with all the fulness of God (Eph. 3: 16 ff.). It is through the operation of love that the Church grows up unto a perfect man in Christ (Eph. 4: 15), so that this love is the bond of its perfection or maturity (Col. 3: 14).

In the language of historic dogma, the Holy Spirit who is the "consubstantial communion" between the Father and the Son, and is Love, through whom God and man are one in the "hypostatic union" in Christ, is poured out into the Church giving it "communion" in the life and love of God and making it into a community of love. In the New Testament *koinonia* means primarily the Church's participation through the Spirit in Jesus Christ, and so in the divine Nature; but it also means a communion or fellowship in love with one another on that basis. Vertically, so to speak, the communion of the Spirit is the relation of the Church to Christ, horizontally it is the fellowship of love between believers, between members of the Church or Body of Christ. It is a communion which by its very nature transcends and denies all earthly divisions, so that active engagement in this communion through the Lord's Supper is the sacramental means whereby the Love of God heals the Church of its earthly divisions, compacts its members into one Body, and manifests itself as the perfection of the Church in Christ.

But what form does that Love take in history? How is this essential form of the Church in Christ related to the Church's participation in the form of this passing world? Throughout its earthly mission and pilgrimage the Church manifests its essential form in the *form of a servant*, for the way of Christ is the way of the Church also. "As He is so are we in this world" (1 John 4: 17; cf. John 15: 18 f.). The Church must therefore deny itself and take up its cross to follow Christ (Mark 15: 21 and par.). It must let the mind that was in Christ be its mind—the mind of the Suffering Servant obedient unto the death of the Cross (Phil. 2: 5 ff.). It must work out analogically (*analogisasthe*) in its life, even to the point of "resisting unto blood", what Jesus Christ had done for it (Heb. 12: 1–4). The mission of the Church is thus the mission of Christ (John 20: 21 f.). The ministry of the Church is the ministry of Christ (2 Cor. 5: 18 f.). It is the ministry of the Son of Man in the humble form of the Suffering Servant (Mark 10: 35–45; Matt. 20: 17–29; Luke 22: 14–30; John 13: 1–17). In the form of a servant the Church of Christ manifests the love of Christ as its essential form (John 13, 14 and 15). As the Church becomes one Body with Christ through the Communion of the Spirit (John 15; 16), through sacramental Communion (1 Cor. 10, 11, 12), Love as the essential form of the Church breaks through the pride and quarrels of men (Luke 22: 14 ff.; John 13: 1 ff.), breaks through the sinful forms of division and heresy (1 Cor. 10, 11), transcends even the necessary forms which the gifts of the Spirit assume in the ministry and order of the Church on earth (1 Cor. 12, 13, 14), and manifests itself as greater than even faith and hope. In so far as they are "in part" "they shall be done away", but Love remains on into eternity as the *Esse* of the Church in Christ (1 Cor. 13).

It belongs therefore to the essential life of the Church throughout its earthly mission and pilgrimage to walk in love according to its new life in the Spirit, but the way of Love is the way of the Suffering Servant in self-denial and self-sacrifice. Within the Church that means that each member serves the other (Eph. 4: 1 ff.; 5, 6; Col. 3, 4; Rom. 12) that together they may grow up into the perfection of Christ. Toward the world that means that the Church must bear about in its body the dying of the Lord Jesus that the Life also of Jesus might be made manifest in its mortal flesh (2 Cor. 4: 10 f.), knowing that though death works in the Church that is for the sake of all men that life might operate in them (2 Cor. 4: 12 f.): so that the language of the "servant" Paul becomes the language of the "serving" Church: "I rejoice in my sufferings for you and fill up that which is behind (i.e. what is eschatologically in arrears) of the afflictions of Christ in my flesh for his body's sake, which is the church: whereof I am made a minister according to the dispensation of God which is given to me for you to fulfil the word of God; even the mystery which has been hid from ages and from generations, but now is made manifest to his saints: to whom God would make known what is the riches of the glory of this mystery among the Gentiles: which is Christ in you the hope of glory" (Col. 1: 24–27). Within the Church it is the way of this ministering Love so to use the divine gifts for the ministry and edification of the Church that they are all subordinated to Love as the bond of perfection. Toward the world it is the way of this ministering Love so to use the forms of this broken and divided world that they are subordinated to the Oneness of the Church in Christ, and are made to serve Love as the unity of the Spirit.

How then are we to relate the oneness of the Church to its growth and mission on earth?

(a) Because the Church is already one in Christ, and exists in the midst of a broken and divided world, the oneness of the Church is to be understood in terms of a *double unity*. That seems to be expressed in the Epistle to the Ephesians (4: 3, 23) in terms of "the unity of the Spirit" and "the unity of the faith". The unity of the Spirit is a perfected reality which is to be kept, the unity bestowed upon the Church in Holy Baptism. "The unity of the faith in the knowledge of the Son of God" denotes the way in which the Church is to grow until it comes "to a perfect man, unto the measure of the stature of the fulness of Christ". It belongs to the essential life of the Church that it holds to the unity of the Spirit and through Word and Sacrament grows up into the fulness of Christ, that is, built up into complete unity in Him, and extended to the ends of the earth and the ends of the age as the Body of Christ, the fulness of Him that filleth all in all. However, this growth from unity to unity into the fulness of Christ is not merely a growth. It is a desperate struggle, in which "the flesh strives against the Spirit and the Spirit against the flesh" (Gal. 5: 17), in which "we wrestle not against flesh and blood, but against principalities, against powers, against the rulers of darkness of this world, against spiritual wickedness in high places" (Eph. 6: 12). Throughout this battle the mighty victory of Christ which He won in our body of flesh still operates in the Church that is made One Body with Him, but throughout the battle from age to age the Church needs continual cleansing and healing, continual renewal of its wholeness and its incorporation into the one Body of Christ.

That twofold incorporation corresponds to the two dominical Sacraments of the Word made flesh: Baptism and Eucharist. Through the atoning and incorporating action in His death and resurrection Jesus Christ has once and for all made the Church One Body with Him. Through Baptism the Church participates in that action for it is sacramentally incorporated into the One Body of Christ, so that it is Holy Baptism that is the primary expression of the Oneness of the Church. In Jesus Christ the Church is Holy and Perfected (Heb. 10: 10) for He presents it to the Father as His own Body pure and spotless, but on earth the Church is still the body of sinners waiting for the redemption of the body of sin and death, living in the midst of the estrangement and dividedness of mankind. From the wounds sustained in its ministry and warfare, from the baffling onslaught of spiritual wickedness, from failure and disobedience and sin the Church on earth needs healing and renewal. This Church *in via* is given the Holy Eucharist through which its incorporation into the Body of Christ may ever be renewed. Through this Sacrament it may so participate in the death and resurrection of Christ that it may be forgiven by Him and cleansed in His blood, be healed of its infirmities and reconciled from its estrangements. Having thus tasted the powers of the age to come in anticipation of the resurrection of the body the Church may be given constant strength to live out, bodily and spiritually, in the midst of the broken and divided world the Oneness of the Body of Christ.

(b) Because the Church is sent into the world, to follow "the Son of man who came not to be ministered unto but to minister and to give his life a ransom for many", the Church cannot conserve the unity of the Spirit by looking to itself or by trying to preserve its own life. "As my Father hath sent me, even so send I you. And when Jesus had said this he breathed on them, and saith unto them, Receive ye the Holy Ghost: whosesoever sins ye remit, they are remitted unto them; and whosesoever sins ye retain they are retained." The Church is empowered by the Spirit to engage in the mission of reconciliation and forgiveness, so that the Church keeps the unity of the Spirit by engaging in the mission of the Christ. The very nature and mission of the Church are inseparably grounded in the oneness of the Person and Work of Christ. The Oneness of the Church thus belongs to the oneness of the mission upon which it is engaged at the command of Christ. The Church must therefore rejoice in face of the tribulations which it is called upon to endure in the fulfilment of Christ's mission in the world, for they provide the very means whereby through the Spirit the Church can live out in the world the life of the servant, obedient, like the Son of Man, unto the death of the Cross, and so actually participate in His ministry of reconciliation. If it was by His death that Jesus Christ wrought reconciliation, and of twain, Jew and Gentile, wrought one new man (Eph. 2: 11 ff.), it is by entering into Christ's passion for the redemption of a broken and divided world that the Church will find its unity in the crucified and risen Body of the One Lord (cf. Col. 1: 20–27). *The road to unity lies through the atonement.*

II

Our Disunity in the Church

Christ's Body, the Church, is one, and yet we the members of Christ's one Body stand divided. The very fact that we call our various denominations "churches" is significant proof of the extent of this scandal in the Church on earth. That is apparent even in the title of the Assembly Topic for *Faith and Order:* "Our Oneness in Christ and our Disunity as Churches". Because the very term "churches" implies a denial of the unity of the Church, it ought to be dropped in ecumenical discussions. The title adopted here: *Our Disunity in the Church*, is intended both to follow the usage of the New Testament and to bring home to us the fact that while the Body of Christ cannot be divided, the impossible seems to have happened. That the impossible seems to have happened means that we are faced here with the same dark and terrible enigma of sin, the irrational mystery of iniquity which in its ultimate antagonism was exposed in the crucifixion of Christ, and overcome by the breaking of Christ's body and the shedding of His blood, and by His resurrection in body from the dead.

We differ from each other in race, nationality, history, sex, position, and in other ways characteristic of this world. We may even occupy different places in God's plan of salvation. The Jews, for example, for long occupied a position of peculiar privilege, for to them belonged the oracles of God (Rom. 3: 1 f.) until God made of Jew and Gentile one New Man in Christ, though even now the Jews have a distinctive part to play in God's gracious wisdom (Rom. 9–11). We differ from each other also in that God the Holy Spirit has bestowed diverse gifts upon us, and called us to diverse functions in the membership of Christ's Church. There are diversities in the order of creation, diversities in the gifts of the Spirit, and diversities in the membering of the one body (1 Cor. 12: 14 ff.). All these diversities produce a remarkable and rich variety in congregations, ministries, forms of church life and government, but they are given for the fulness of the Church and for the glory of God. They provide no justification for the divided state of the Church on earth. *The problem is not our God-given diversity but the scandal of our sinful division.*

The ultimate reason for our division is rooted in the irrational and awful mystery of iniquity, in the ungodly powers and forces which are still rampant in the whole creation, and which seek to confuse the Church and defeat its mission. Before the Cross, however, where the Body of Christ was broken for us, we cannot but confess that our disunity in the Church belongs to our guilt. Before the resurrection of Christ, where the husk of Israel was rent that the Gospel of the new creation might be proclaimed to all nations, we confess that sometimes in our divisions we could do no other, "that the truth of the Gospel might continue" (Gal. 2: 5). According to the measure of the faith given to us we have had to be faithful to the Truth as we knew it even when this faithfulness appeared to tear the garment of the Church. But even when we have done that which we felt right to do, we acknowledge that we are culpably implicated in sin not wholly of our own making, and cannot therefore dissociate ourselves from the sin of division. Our membership of the Body of Christ has given us to see not only our oneness in Him, but our solidarity in sin in "the body of the flesh" into which He the Holy One incorporated Himself that by His death in the body He might deliver us from sin. Thus our very participation in His one Body speaks of our implication in the body of sin which He carried to the Cross to be destroyed. Confession of Oneness with Christ carries with it confession of oneness with our fellows in sin. As we acknowledge that we also were guilty of the breaking of His body on the Cross, so we cannot but acknowledge that we are implicated in the guilt of rending the Church.

It belongs to our sin that we deny the sole Lordship of Christ over the Church by usurping it, by claiming the vineyard for our own, by possessing our "church" for ourselves, by regarding our theology, order, history, nationality, etc., as our own "valued treasures", thus involving them in the independence and usurpation of our sin, and involving ourselves more and more in the separation of sin. It belongs to our sin that by self-assertion even in maintaining legitimate truth we have extended division. Although we have been redeemed and become one Body with Christ, we have so yielded to the divisions and estrangements of the world in which we share as we wear "the body of sin", that we have allowed the divisive antagonisms of sin to penetrate into our membering in the One Body of Christ. Had there been no God-given diversities our sin would doubtless wear a different form, but within our divisions the God-given diversities in the Church have often been so corroded and corrupted that where under the one Spirit they should minister to the richness and fulness of the Church, under another lordship they may even minister to the extension of our divisions. Sometimes within the forms of our earthly divisions our God-given diversities may even appear (falsely) to be due to sin.

We must seek to interpret these divisions in terms of the death of Christ on the Cross, and thereby find a way of acting toward them. The Cross tells us that where sin exerted itself in utmost antagonism to the love of God, where the dividing power of sin was most manifest, there God has gained the victory by atonement and wrought reconciliation. In the death of Christ God has made the very wrath of man to praise Him and turned the crucifixion of Christ into the means of our redemption. By the same Cross He is able to make all things to work together for good—even our divisions. By planting the Cross of Christ in the midst of our divisions we believe He will overrule all their sin and make them serve His purpose of unity. That does not mean that we can in this way justify our divisions, nor does it mean that we are to continue in the sin of division that grace may abound. On the contrary, it means that we must place our divisions under the judgment of the Cross, and recognize that we are one only in the crucified and risen Body of Christ. This is a Oneness, however, which means the crucifixion and death of our old self, of our own theology, our own so-called "church", our own form of "order", for we may only live with Christ as One New Man and as One Body in that we deny ourselves and take up His Cross as our own. "If we would judge ourselves, we should not be judged. But when we are judged, we are chastened of the Lord, that we should not be condemned with the world" (1 Cor. 11: 31 f.). We acknowledge that when Christ comes again in judgment, His judgments will surprise us (Matt. 25), and they will divide us as children of light from children of darkness. But it belongs to our very hope that we cast ourselves with our divisions under the present judgment of the Cross, that through it we may already participate in the oneness of the new creation in spite of our divisions. That is why, in part, we are given the Lord's Supper. In the communion of the Body and Blood of Christ the crucifixion and resurrection become reality in the Church here and now, in such a way that we eat and drink judgment to our sin and division. In such a way we are given an anticipation of the complete Oneness which Christ will reveal when He comes in final judgment to do away with all that is sinful, and in the power of the resurrection to consummate the Oneness of Christ and His Church as the One Body, the fulness of Him that fills all in all.

In this way we may also see our divisions in the light of the resurrection of Christ—and that is where the hope of the Church triumphs over all disunity. He who by the death of Christ has already overcome the contradiction of sin will not allow the oneness of the Church to see corruption, for through the resurrection of Christ in body He gives the Church in spite of its divisions to participate already in the perfect unity that will be revealed in the coming of Christ. In face of the actual disunity of the Church on earth, we can only think of the unity of the Church as eschatologically in arrears, but according to the New Testament we cannot think of the unity of the Church only in future terms. The Church's eschatological hope involves a double relation. On the one hand it is the relation here and now between the new creation and the old, but on the other hand it is the relation between the present and the future when Christ will make all things new. "Old things have passed away and all things have become new" (2 Cor. 5: 17). Because that new life is hid with Christ in God, it does not yet appear what it will be, so that we must think of the eschatological relation as the relation between the present and the future. That future, however, will not be so much the consummation of what is yet imperfect as the revelation of what is a present but hidden reality. Indeed that future has through the communion of the Spirit been telescoped into this present age and manifests itself in the Church. The Church in history is the eschatological community that reaches out beyond this present age into the age to come and has its life there; and yet at the same time it is the community that still participates in the ongoing history of the present age. *Because its true life and unity are lodged in a future that penetrates back into the present, we must understand the disunity of the Church in history as even now under the attack of the unity that is yet to be revealed.* The very fact that in the Ecumenical Movement of our times the old divisions of the Church in history are being criss-crossed by new divisions may well betoken the fact that the outward husk of the Church on earth —that is, so far as it is schematized to the cosmic patterns and sinful divisions of this present age—is already breaking up under the impact of the one essential form of the Church that comes to meet us in the Advent of Christ. Because the oneness of the Church is already perfected reality in the once and for all death and resurrection of Christ, no division of the Church on earth can disrupt that oneness or withstand its advent impact upon the Church any more than it can undo the incarnation, crucifixion, or resurrection of Christ. That is the Church's unshakable hope in spite of the disunity of the Church on earth.

III

The Action of Faith

In the face of our divisions on earth we in the Church of Christ must affirm anew the reality of the Church's oneness revealed in the Gospel of Jesus Christ, and seek to act in "the obedience of faith" to that oneness. We must look away from ourselves and our dividedness to our one Lord in order to follow Him, seeking through His Cross and resurrection the way to let Him realize that oneness in the actual state of our earthly divisions. Before the Cross where Jesus Christ identified Himself with the world's sin in order to bear it and bear it away, we too must identify ourselves with the sin of the world in order to say "Amen" to the Father's judgment upon it and the divisions it entails. If "He who knew no sin was made sin for us that we might be made the righteousness of God in Him" (2 Cor. 5: 21) then the Church, because of its holiness and sanctification in Christ, must surely be ready to identify itself with the sin of the world, so manifest in divisions, if it is to act "in Christ's stead" (2 Cor. 5: 20) and fulfil "the ministry of reconciliation given" to it (2 Cor. 5: 18 f.).

Certainly *we in the divided "churches" of the Protestant world* ought at least to be united in this, that we think of our divisions only with repentance, not so much the repentance we may expect of others, but with the repentance we undertake—cost what it may—even when others are unwilling to follow. It belongs to the depth of this repentance before the face of the one Christ that we acknowledge that we have so sinned as to be caught in the net of inexplicable and inextricable evil, as to be unable of ourselves to heal our divisions. The sincerity of our repentance demands that we renounce the self-assertion and the usurpation of Christ's Lordship which have so often led us to perpetuate our dividedness even when we were contending for legitimate truth. But our great hope in the midst of our disunity on earth is that Jesus Christ, who alone constitutes the oneness of the Church, has already overcome the antagonism and division of sin on the Cross, and that He has the power to restore to us in our disunity the oneness against which we have sinned. It belongs therefore to "the obedience of faith" to let Jesus Christ take control over our divided and broken estate and to heal it by His grace and power.

(i) We must listen together in the midst of our disunity to the voice of our one Lord speaking to us through Holy Scripture. No doubt that is the hardest thing we can do, for there we encounter the sharp two-edged sword which proceeds out of the mouth of Christ, the Word of God which is able to divide asunder between the soul and the spirit and discern the thoughts and intents of the heart (Rev. 1: 16; Heb. 4: 12). But as we allow this Word which is the Sword of the Spirit to pierce into our divisions, it reveals to us where we have severally sinned and gone astray—some in one way, some in another—and uncovers the veil of deception which our very sins have so spread over us, that we have been unable to see a way out of our impossible dividedness. Whenever we are prepared so undertake together the study of the Word of God and are resolved to be obedient to what we are told, we are on the way toward realizing the oneness of the Church in Christ in the actual state of our dividedness on earth. As we do this through the unity of the Spirit, the one mind of Christ informs the divided and so-called "churches", begetting them again into the unity of the faith in the knowledge of the Son of God so that at last they may grow up into Him who is the Head. Unless the so-called "churches" are ready to bow together under the sole Lordship of Christ and allow His sovereign Word to rule and reshape the distorted patterns of their life, and are therefore *on the road toward unity*, they only allow their present dividedness to call in question their relation of union to Christ which is the ground of our oneness in Him.

(ii) As we listen to the voice of the one Lord and Master speaking to us, we hear Him say: "if any 'church' will come after me, let it deny itself, take up its cross and follow me." Because the oneness of the Church is grounded in the death and resurrection of Christ, it belongs to the action of faith that every so-called "church" allows Jesus Christ so to join its body to Himself in union with His death and resurrection, that the "church" is crucified with Christ in order to rise with Him one body in newness of life. As those who are baptized into the one Body of Christ, we dare not partake of the Holy Eucharist without shewing forth His death in our body, by denying ourselves as divided "churches" and taking up our cross. If the way of the Son of Man was through the cross and the resurrection to the One New Man, then the way of the divided "churches" is through Eucharistic obedience to Him, that the bread which we break may indeed be the Communion in the one Body, and the cup which we bless may indeed be the Communion in the Blood of Him who alone is the "Saviour of the Body" (Eph.

5: 23). Only as the divided "churches" dare to do this in obedience to the Lord of the Eucharist can they be on the road toward that oneness of the Church in Christ which is yet to be revealed in the Advent of Christ in glory, and which is already on the road to meet us.

(iii) Because we must affirm anew our oneness in Christ in the face of our actual divisions on earth, we must learn how to speak the truth in love with one another (Eph. 4: 15, 25), and to discern in others the one body of which we are members (cf. 1 Cor. 11: 29). Because Christ is Himself the Truth and we are members of Him we must bear witness to the Truth uncompromisingly, and yet because Christ Himself is Love, we must do that in love, refusing to be "lords over the faith" (2 Cor. 1: 24) of others. We must acknowledge that even when we have done that which it is our duty to do in the proclamation and formulation of the truth we are unprofitable servants whose proclamation and formulation fall far short of Him who alone is the Truth. If we discern in others the One Body of Christ who is the Truth, we shall refuse to pass judgment on them, for who are we that we should judge those for whom Christ has died? Rather shall we learn to listen to the voice of the One Lord speaking to us through them that we should not be perfect without each other, but that they and we speaking the truth in love together and strengthened by our mutual faith (Rom. 1: 12) may grow up into Him in all things who is the Head, even Christ.

(iv) Because we profess belief in the one Lord and affirm anew our oneness in Him, we must learn to bear witness together to Him who has already overcome our sins and divisions and who graciously uses sinners in His service. By bearing joint witness to the one Lord we point away from our dividedness to Him who by His death on the Cross has put all our divisions under judgment and forgiven them, and through the fellowship of His sufferings in the mission of the Cross we are given by His Spirit to grow together in the power of the resurrection in increasing unity with one another.

When in these several ways the divided "churches" act upon their faith in the One Lord, He opens their eyes to discern in themselves wherein they have contributed to the dividedness of the Church, and wherein they must learn to deny themselves if they are not to perpetuate division and are to follow the one Lord in the unity of the Spirit and the bond of peace. For some this may mean that certain theological demands (e.g. a particular conception of the Eucharist), true though it may be in the perspective of division, cannot be made binding for others. For some the demand for a particular kind of spiritual experience such as conversion cannot be made normative for others in whom there is to be recognized a diverse operation of the One Spirit. Others who are assured that they possess the true order in apostolic succession which they want to hold as a treasured possession will find themselves summoned to surrender their claim to Him who as Lord is the sole principle of the oneness and continuity of the Church. We cannot discern all that will be disclosed to us when together we look to Him who is the Head of the Body and affirm our oneness in Him. We know we shall be changed, but wherein we shall be changed we cannot truly know until in the act of faith and self-denial we are given to discern through crucifixion and resurrection the lineaments of the one true Body of Christ which our sinful dividedness obscures from ourselves and from the world.

PROBLEMS OF FAITH AND ORDER

5. THE HOPE OF ISRAEL

THE decision of the General Assembly of the World Council of Churches meeting at Evanston to omit any reference to the hope of Israel was manifestly due to the influence of "non-theological factors" on the minds of the delegates. This was all the more unfortunate as there are profound theological issues at stake here which must be faced if we are to be obedient to Jesus Christ, and if we are not to escape some of the most difficult problems in our divisions. Apart from that, we in the Christian Churches of the West cannot dissociate ourselves from the sin of unmentionable horror which eliminated millions of Jews in our generation within the bounds of Christendom. It was altogether fitting, therefore, that those from Europe who realized the grave nature of the refusal by the World Council even to mention the Hope of Israel in its full Report should have issued a statement and laid it before the Council. It is to be hoped that the Christian Churches will yet see that they have at this very point to face an essential element in the Gospel, and that the statement (in the writing of which I had a share) will help them to face their brotherly responsibility toward Israel.

Statement on the Hope of Israel

In view of the decision of the Assembly on Friday to omit any reference to the hope of Israel in its Statement on the Main Theme, we feel it our duty to offer an explanation of our convictions in the hope that it will help towards closer understanding with those from whom we differed.

Our concern in this issue is wholly biblical and is not to be confused with any political attitude towards the State of Israel.

We believe that Jesus Christ is the Saviour of all mankind. In Him there is neither Jew nor Greek, but we also believe that God elected Israel for the carrying out of His saving purpose. Jesus Christ as Man was a Jew. The Church of Jesus Christ is built upon the foundation of the apostles and prophets, all of whom were Jews, so that to be a member of the Christian Church is to be involved with the Jews in our one indivisible hope in Jesus Christ. Jesus, the Messiah of Israel, was accepted by Gentiles but rejected by His own people. Nevertheless God is so gracious and mighty that He even makes the crucifixion of His Son to be the salvation of the Gentiles (Rom. 11 : 11). Whether we are scandalized or not, that means that we are grafted into the old tree of Israel (Rom. 11 : 24), so that the people of the New Covenant cannot be separated from the people of the Old Covenant.

The New Testament, however, speaks also of the "fulness" of Israel, when God will manifest His glory by bringing back His "eldest son" into the one fold of His grace (Rom. 11 : 12–36; Matt. 21 : 29). This belief is an indispensable element in our one united hope for Jew and Gentile in Jesus Christ. Our hope in Christ's coming victory includes our hope for Israel in Christ, in His victory over the blindness of His own people. To expect Jesus Christ means to hope for the conversion of the Jewish people, and to love Him means to love the people of God's promise.

In view of the grievous guilt of Christian people towards the Jews throughout the history of the Church, we are certain that:

> "the Church cannot rest until the title of Christ to the Kingdom is recognized by His own people according to the flesh." (Findings of the Pre-Evanston Conference of the American Committee on the Christian Approach to the Jews, at Lake Geneva, August 8–11, 1954.)

We cannot be one in Christ nor can we truly believe and witness to the promise of God if we do not recognize that it is still valid for the people of the promise made to Abraham. Therefore we invite all men to join with us in praising and magnifying that God who "concluded them all in unbelief that He might have mercy upon all" (Rom. 11 : 32).

The Evanston Report, S.C.M. Press, 1955, pp. 327 f.

Israel and the Incarnation[1]

The Israel of God

From the very beginning the Christian Church thought of itself as Israel in the new phase of its election marked by the Incarnation. That is apparent in the favourite term employed

[1] From *Interpretation*, 1956, pp. 305–20. Reprinted in *Judaica*, 1957, pp. 1–18.

by the New Testament to designate the Church: *ekklēsia*.[1] In profane Greek ekklēsia was used to describe the assembly of citizens summoned together by a herald (*kērux*) for public duty. Something of that naturally remains in the New Testament term, particularly the calling out of the Church through the proclamation (*kērygma*) of the herald, but it is the special use of *ekklēsia* in the Septuagint that gives the New Testament its technical term for the Church. In the LXX *ekklēsia* refers to the congregation regarded collectively as a people and as a whole, rather than to the actual assembly or meeting of the people. Behind the Greek *ekklēsia* there lies the Hebrew *qahal* or some cognate word from the same root. The Old Testament as a rule employs two terms to describe Israel as the congregation of God, *'edhah* and *qahal*, and both are translated at different times by two Greek words, *synagōgē* and *ekklēsia*. More and more the Old Testament writers, in its later books, prefer the term *qahal*, usually rendered by *ekklēsia*, but Judaism came more and more to prefer the term *synagōgē*. Thus when the Christian Church came to refer to itself as the *ekklēsia* rather than *synagōgē* (with one or two exceptions), it was clearly claiming to be "the Israel of God" in distinction from the Synagogue.

Two further elements in the concept of *qahal-ekklēsia* should be noted here. (a) The fact that *qahal* comes from the same root as *qol*, the word for "voice", suggests that the Old Testament *qahal* was the community summoned by the Divine Voice, by the Word of God. It was the people of the voice of the Word of God. Of that *ekklēsia* is a very apt translation, indicating as it does the community of "the called" (*klētoi*) of God. *Ekklēsia* is Church not in any sociological or political sense of assembly, and not therefore in any sociological or political continuity with Israel. It is Church as act of God, as the community called into being and created by God's Word. (b) In line with that is the fact that the Old Testament *qahal* was first established at Sinai when God came and spoke, when His voice was heard by all Israel, and His Word founded the Covenant-Community. That was known as "the day of the *qahal*", and so *qahal* came to have a special significance as the community brought into

[1] See for the following the article on *ekklēsia* in Kittel, *Theologisches Woerterbuch zum Neuen Testament*.

covenant-relation with God for sacrifice and worship, and for the special end of revelation. *Qahal* denotes the Old Testament Church actively engaged in God's purpose of revelation and salvation, that is caught up in the mighty events whereby God intervenes redemptively in history, and involved in the forward thrust of the Covenant toward final and universal fulfilment. *Qahal* is the community expecting eschatological redemption. In that sense it is appropriated in the New Testament to denote the community in which the Covenant promises of God to Israel are fulfilled in Jesus Christ and in the pouring out of His Spirit. Far from being an off-shoot of Israel, the Christian Church is Israel gathered up in Jesus Christ, who recapitulates in Himself the historico-redemptive service of Israel and, after fulfilling and transcending all its hopes, launches it out again in its servant-mission laden with the Word of Reconciliation for all mankind.

What place are we to assign to God's ancient people, the old Israel, under the light of the Gospel of Jesus Christ?

The Old Israel and the Incarnation

(1) The whole historico-redemptive movement revealed in the Old and New Testaments is to be regarded as essentially one. The Old Testament speaks of the Coming One, and the coming Kingdom; the New Testament speaks of the One who has come, and of the Kingdom as having arrived in Jesus Christ Himself. The Old Testament is the revelation of the *verbum incarnandum*; the New Testament is the revelation of the *verbum incarnatum*: the centre of gravity in both is the Incarnation itself, to which the Old Testament is stretched out in expectation, and the New Testament looks back in fulfilment. This one movement throughout the Old Testament and the New Testament is the movement of God's grace in which He renews the bond between God and man broken and perverted at the Fall, and restores man to communion with Himself. God does that by giving Himself to man in such a way as to assume human nature and existence into oneness with Himself. That is what took place in the Incarnation of the Word, in the midst of Israel, in the midst of mankind.

(2) Throughout the pre-history of the Incarnation, which was itself in a profound sense part of the movement of the

Incarnation, God prepared a way, manifested His truth, and assumed man into a life-relation with Himself. This triple activity of grace God carried through in Israel. In Israel He prepared a way of covenant-love in which He established a union between Himself and Israel; within that covenant relation of love God manifested Himself as the Truth, bringing Israel into communion with Himself; through union and communion God bound Israel to Himself as the Lord, the Giver of Life, and so set up His Kingdom in the midst of estranged humanity. He began to open up through Israel a new and a living way for the redemption of mankind, that was to find its fulfilment in Jesus Christ, the Way, the Truth, and the Life.

(3) The activity of grace within the covenanted people of God involved the self-giving of God and the assuming of Israel into oneness with God in terms of Prophet, Priest and King. According to the Old Testament's understanding of itself, the Covenant was established in the once-and-for-all events at Mt. Sinai in which God decisively revealed Himself and enacted His revelation in the midst of Israel. He gave Himself to the people of Israel to be their God and He took Israel to be His people. What God did He give to Israel? The God who proclaimed His Name to Israel in these terms: "The Lord, the Lord God, merciful and gracious, long-suffering and abundant in mercy and truth, keeping mercy for thousands of generations, forgiving iniquity and transgression and sin, and that will by no means clear the guilty, visiting the iniquities of the fathers upon the children and upon the children's children, unto the third and fourth generation" (Exod. 34: 6 ff.). God gave Himself to Israel without any diminishment in His nature as Holiness and Love—that is why Sinai occupied such unsurpassable significance in the history of Israel. Such a Self-giving of God which is the Self-giving of the Self-affirming God, *I am that I am*, was made in the unity of law and cult, i.e. the unity of Word and Mediation, of Truth and Reconciliation. And so the Covenant came to rest upon the twin foundation of the Sinaitic law and the Levitical liturgy, as represented supremely in Moses and Aaron, prophet and priest in essential complementarity and unity. Once this covenantal basis was consolidated in Jerusalem, God manifested His coming Kingdom through the Davidic line of kings, and the messianic Kingdom

came to overarch the covenantal relation of Word and pardon, prophet and priest. Together prophet, priest, and king were made to point forward to the Messiah, the archetypal Prophet, Priest, and King. He was the King of the Kingdom who provided in Himself the way, the truth, and the life, and so provided the way of restoration to the Father.

(4) This triple activity of God's grace and Self-revelation was not static but was carried through the most harrowing and profound historical experience the world has ever known, in the whole life and agony of Israel. The three modes of divine activity and grace had to be worked into the innermost existence and being of this people if it was to become the instrument of God's ultimate Self-giving to man. This nation was a beggarly and despised people, and it proved itself to be the most stiff-necked and rebellious of peoples, but it was chosen out of pure love and on that basis alone was brought into covenant relation with God. The keeping of the covenant did not depend on Israel's worth, but, on the contrary, was conditioned by the pure outflowing love of God in the continuous act of grace, of grace for grace. What a magnificent account of that covenant-love is given by the prophet Hosea! But it became very clear that God could only keep faith and truth with this rebellious people by judgment, by punishment, as well as by mercy. He held on to His purpose of love, binding the covenant-people to Himself, refusing to divorce it in spite of persistent rebuffs. The covenant grounded in mercy (*ḥesed*) and truth (*'emeth*) was maintained by God in utter faithfulness, that is, in the utter consistency of truth and in the utter steadfastness of love. In that covenant-relation of truth and love Israel had to suffer, for it shattered itself on the unswerving persistence of the divine purpose of love. Israel suffered inevitably from God, for God would not let His people go.

(5) God used the historical experience of Israel to reveal Himself more profoundly and to give Himself more completely to Israel. He used the suffering and the judgment of Israel to reveal the terrible nature of sin as contradiction to God's love and grace, to uncover the enmity of man, in his persistent self-will, toward God in His Self-giving. But transcending all, God used this nation in the ordeal of history and suffering to reveal His own infinite love and the undeflecting persistence of His

will to bring forgiveness and reconciliation, until His love achieved its purpose of final union and communion of man with God in Jesus Christ. In that ordeal the Word and the cult were not mere letter and liturgy, but were worked out into the very existence of Israel: that was surely the great prophetic burden of Deutero-Isaiah and Jeremiah. Law and cult have no place in God's will merely as such; they have their place as they are kneaded into the very existence and understanding and life of Israel. That was the reason for the suffering of Israel, for word and truth and love had to be wrought out in the breaking and making of Israel as the Servant of the Lord. The whole conception of the Suffering Servant represents the activity of God whereby He begins to draw together the cords of the Covenant in which He had bound Israel to Himself as His partner; it represents the activity in which He began to narrow down His assumption of Israel into union with Himself toward the point of the Incarnation where, in the midst of Israel, He was to assume man into oneness with Himself in the ultimate act of reconciliation. The great sign of the Covenant made with Abraham and Isaac was circumcision, for in it the Covenant was cut into the flesh of this people and remained throughout the generations as the sign that the promises of God could be fulfilled in the life of this people only as the Word of God could be translated into its flesh, into its very existence. It was the sign that at last the Covenant had to be written into the heart, in the "crucifixion" of self-will, in the putting off of "the enmity of the flesh". But once the Covenant came to be enacted so deeply into the existence of Israel that it was written into the "inner man", its whole form would change. It would be a New Covenant. Such a "total circumcision" was fulfilled at last in the flesh of Christ, for through His crucifixion, the New Covenant was inaugurated, and the new and living way was opened up in the Humanity of the Son of Man.

(6) Israel suffered most throughout its history as bearer in its existence and life of the divine Revelation. It suffered from the mighty arm of the Lord, that is, at the hands of the Word of God, because it had ever to be broken and remade, reshaped, and re-aligned with the Covenant-will of God. Thus the very covenant-relation of Israel to God through which it became *laos*, God's people, *klēros*, God's inheritance, entailed political

and national disaster for Israel in its will to be *ethnos*, a nation like the other nations of the earth. That was part of the deepest agony of Jeremiah. The astonishing thing here is that the more God gave Himself to this people, the more He forced this people to be what it was in its sin and self-will, to be in truth what it actually was, a rebel. The very Self-giving of God in holy love not only revealed Israel's sin, but intensified it; it intensified the enmity between Israel and Jahweh and intensified the contradiction between Jahweh and Israel—hence "the Suffering Servant". God insisted on giving Himself to Israel in spite of its enmity to Him, and insisted on assuming Israel in its sinful contradiction into partnership with Himself—hence the profoundest agony of the psalmist and prophet alike, and hence also "the identity by assumption" of the suffering of Israel with the suffering of Messiah so poignantly described in Isaiah 53. Moreover, in the intensification of the relationship between Israel and God, in a profound sense God's Self-revelation had to blind Israel, and His Self-manifestation had to hide Himself from Israel. *Eli, Eli, lama sabachthani?* How could it be otherwise when God entered into the heart of Israel's estrangement in order to make atonement, when the assumption of refractory Israel into oneness with God intensified judgment upon Israel's self-will as well as fulfilled the Self-giving of God to Israel in love? To us, no doubt, as we look back from the Incarnation, the experience of Israel becomes clearer and clearer, but Israel itself became blinder and blinder—"Who is blind but My servant?"—as God's Self-giving pressed toward the ultimate act of Incarnation and atonement.

(7) In the ultimate act of union between God and Israel, and in the ultimate conflict which that entailed, in Israel's refusal of the Messiah, the rejection of Israel had to take place. God gave Himself to Israel and assumed Israel into covenant-partnership with Himself—and that covenant provided in the midst of humanity a revelation of God's will to be man's God in spite of his sin. It was therefore with Israel in its sinful existence and indeed in its refusal of God that God bound Himself in the Covenant of love, while Israel, on its part, was unable to escape the decision of God's love that had overtaken it in the covenant of grace gathering it into partnership with God. Israel suffered from the Covenant, but suffered because

of its persistent refusal of grace, suffering more and more until in the ultimate act of God's Self-giving in the Incarnation, Israel rejected it in the crucifixion of the Messiah, and in so doing shattered itself on the Cross—theologically, the complete destruction of Jerusalem and the Temple in A.D. 70 had to follow upon the crucifixion of the Son of Man. But at the very heart of that great darkness it was supremely revealed that God had given Himself to man at his very worst in his ultimate rejection of grace, and in spite of man's ultimate rejection of grace God had joined Himself to man for ever. The ultimate refusal of God which took place in Israel was the very means whereby the holy love of God achieved its final victory over sin, for by it (the crucifixion of Christ) man was brought into reconciliation and communion with God. That took place in the Mediator, who as true God and true Man had chosen Israel as the people in whose midst He penetrated into the innermost existence of man in his estrangement from God, and in the heart of that estrangement He consummated an eternal union between God and man in Himself.

This Man was Himself the Way, the Truth, and the Life, the Mediator: henceforth all men come unto the Father by Him. The miracle was that just when man shattered himself against the judgment of God, he was called out of death into resurrection, out of destruction into life, out of darkness into light, out of bondage into freedom; just when Israel destroyed itself in the crucifixion of the Son of David, just when the vine of God's choosing and planting was cut away down to the ground, there sprang up out of the earth a new shoot, a new vine; for He who has willed to be Israel and was crucified rose again as a root out of the dry ground to be the true Vine. That meant also, as we shall see, the resurrection of Israel, the Israel of the Covenant, but here we must note that the crucifixion and resurrection of Jesus revealed the pattern of experience adumbrated all through the long ordeal of Israel's suffering. In its completion the pattern is seen to be essentially cruciform; but now, in the light of its full manifestation, it is not difficult to see how the pattern of the recurring death and resurrection of Israel throughout its history was bent forward by the finger of God to point to the crucifixion and resurrection of Jesus, the Israelite in whom there was no guile but the

Israelite who took upon Himself the role of Israel, recapitulating in Himself the ordeal of the Servant in order "to stand in the gap", to be made a curse for the atonement of Israel, and in the midst of Israel for the atonement of all mankind.

(8) But now it is possible to look back and see something else: that the activity of grace which selected one particular people and one particular course of history in that human and historical particularity enacted a covenantal relation of union and communion with God that was essentially universalistic from the very beginning. It was essentially dual in its nature: particular and universal. That was apparent in the choice of Abraham, one particular man, but the covenant-promise was given that in him and his seed all nations would be blessed. In the enactment of the Covenant between one particular people and Jahweh at Sinai, the bond of the Covenant was the Decalogue which was essentially universalistic. The movement was paradoxical in character—the more particular it became, the more universal it also became; the deeper the bond between God and man was driven into the human existence of Israel, the closer redemption made contact with creation; the more intimately Israel was tied to the one and only God, the God of all, the more the activity of grace broke through the limitations of national Israel and reached out to all the world. That was particularly apparent in the election of Israel to be God's *laos* upon which Israel's aspirations to be *ethnos* were shattered again and again, for to be bound to God as Israel was, was essentially to become the *qahal* or the *ekklēsia* of God, and so to transcend the sociological and political husk of Israel to become the one people of the living God. It was characteristic of the whole activity of God's grace that it should suborn the very refusal of Israel to be *laos* to minister to its purpose of universal blessing and redemption. And so, the more like a single particular *ethnos* Israel became, the more it had to be scattered in *diaspora* over the face of the whole earth. At last, in the acute particularization of the covenantal bond between Israel and God in Jesus, it became absolutely universal for all men.

That was already apparent in the suffering servant portrayed by the cult-prophets. The suffering servant was Israel assumed into oneness with the Word of God, and it is in that duality that "the Servant Songs" are surely to be understood. But even there it is evident that as the Word became one with Israel, it became more and more one Israelite, for that is the only way in which the Word assumes human nature and existence into oneness with itself. Thus while in one sense the suffering servant was Israel assumed into oneness with the Word, it is primarily to be understood as the Word identifying Himself with Israel, and becoming one particular Israelite, an individual personal Messiah. Thus the ultimate Self-giving of God to Israel in its historical particularity narrowing down to one particular Jew meant the universalization and the transcendence of the Old Testament form of the Covenant, and the setting of the relation of God and man on a wholly new basis in which redemption was more than the restoration of Israel, more than an event that penetrated back to the foundations of creation; it was a new creation in which the fulness of the eternal purpose of God was to be realized in an altogether transcendent way.

(9) Now it is also possible to see more clearly than anywhere in the Old Testament itself that the life and ordeal of Israel were the election of one people as the instrument of divine love for His redemption of all creation. The election of one for the salvation of all characterized the whole story of God's dealings with Israel. But within Israel that activity of grace reached its climactic fulfilment in a singular event, in the Incarnation. In Jesus Christ, the incarnate Lord, the election of one for all has become ultimate fact within our human existence; in Him election and substitution combined in the most unique, most intense and personal concentration, with a view to universal redemption. It is in Christ, who is the real meaning and substance of the life of Israel, that we are to understand Israel's ordeal in history and place in the divine purpose. In Jesus Christ it is revealed that the election of one for all becomes salvation for all in the rejection of one for all. What took place on the Cross revealed what was happening to Israel in the election of God: because it was an election of man in his enmity to God, and acceptance of man in his sinful existence, election involved the reprobation of man's will to isolate himself from God and of his refusal of God's grace. The election of Israel as an instrument of the divine reconciliation, an instrument which was to be used in its very refusal of grace that in its

midst the ultimate Self-giving of God might take place, meant, not only that Israel was elected to be confronted with the ultimate events, the last things, before which its refractory self-will was to be exposed to the full judgment of God, but also that Israel was elected to act in a representative capacity for all peoples in its rejection of Christ. The consequent rejection of Israel is to be understood in the light of the substitution of Israel for all other peoples.

(10) How can we express this, for human words are too inadequate here? On the one hand, it is clear, the election of Israel to be the instrument of God and the sphere within which the Son of God should come not only as the divine Judge of men but as man judged by God, peculiarly involved Israel in the ultimate wrath of God. On the other hand, we cannot but acknowledge that the election of Israel to be the sphere in which the Son of God willed to let Himself be condemned as a sinner and to be put to death on the Cross, meant that Israel could only fulfil the gracious purpose of God by rejecting Christ and condemning Him to a sinner's death. The Jews carried that out in fearful wickedness, in the ultimate refusal of grace that sin involves, but throughout it all the Son of God remained in sovereign control. Surely that was a great part of His unspeakable agony, that He was in control: how could He, the incarnate love of God, let men become guilty of the ultimate wickedness, of putting the Son of God to death? And yet He came in love to do this, to penetrate into the blackest heart of evil, to expose it and to take it all upon Himself. And so at the last He pressed hard upon Israel with the finger of God, shutting it up to becoming infinitely guilty of the rejection and murder of the Son of God. It was not that He made the Jews more guilty but that He exposed the infinite guilt of man's hatred of grace, drawing it out in all its enmity that He might bear it and bear it away as the Lamb of God in holy and awful atonement.

As such He bore that infinite guilt, not only of Israel but of all men revealed in the guilt of Israel, that He might acquit and justify the ungodly. In that, He bore the guilt of those who standing in a representative relation to all others carried out the crucifixion of Jesus. He bore to the full the guilt of Israel that He might acquit and justify Israel. "Father, forgive them, for they know not what they do." "Who is blind but my servant?"—wilfully blind, no doubt, but blinded in the role for which Israel was chosen. It was chosen as the sphere of revelation and of atonement, and as such Israel was regarded by God as His first-born son. It was as such too, God's servant, God's beloved son, that Israel was involved by election in the rejection of the Messiah and therefore in the ultimate wrath of God. But the wrath that has come upon Israel through the Cross has to be understood as the chastening wrath of the heavenly Father. There is an outpouring of the wrath of God which is not the chastening of a son but the banishing of the disowned and disinherited into the outer darkness upon which God has for ever turned His back, and Jews and Gentiles alike may bring themselves under that curse. But the judgment and wrath in which Israel as a people is involved mean not the final casting off of man, but God's descent within the relation of existence between the Creator and the creature perverted by the fall of man, and His negation of the contradiction we have introduced into it by our sin.

God's wrath here means, therefore, in unmistakable terms, that what He has created He still affirms as His own handiwork and that He will not curse it or cast it off into nothingness. Even in wrath God wills to remain man's Creator and man's God. His wrath against Israel does not mean that He banishes Israel from His covenant of love and truth but that He affirms that covenant, negating everything that threatens to dissolve it. God's wrath against Israel does not mean His abandonment either of His eternal purpose or of His covenant-promises, but on the contrary it is the act of His holy love within the Covenant in which He asserts Himself as holy and loving Creator in the midst of man's perversity, in the midst of his refusal of grace. God's wrath is judgment of sin, reprobation of our refusal of God, but as such it is already part of atonement, part of recreation, for His wrath is in fact His reaffirmation of His creature in spite of his sin and rebellion—certainly, it is reaffirmation in judgment against sin, but it is a reaffirmation that the creature belongs to God and that He wills to remain its God. God's wrath insists that we remain His children, and that we belong to Him body and soul and it is within that belonging that judgment takes place.

(11) It becomes clear then that the rejection of Israel is not its abandonment but the reaffirmation of Israel in the fulness of the Covenant and its promises. The Covenant remains. God keeps His promises, and His faithfulness is not made of none effect by the faithlessness of His ancient people. The rejection of Israel as a people is only to be understood in the light of the substitutionary nature of the Cross, for Israel's rejection is bound up by God with the atoning rejection of the Man on the Cross, or rather in His acceptance of the sentence of our rejection.—*Eli, Eli, lama sabachthani?* Paul did not hesitate therefore to speak of the rejection of Israel as the reconciling of the world in almost identical language with His assertion that by the death of His Son we were reconciled to God. But it is precisely on the same ground that Paul can speak of the restoration of God's people Israel. "For if when we were enemies, we were reconciled by the death of his Son, much more being reconciled, we shall be saved by his life" (Rom. 5: 10). "For if the casting away of them (i.e. Israel) be the reconciling of the world, what shall the receiving of them be but life from the dead?" (Rom. 11: 15). Three facts of supreme importance emerge here.

(a) While Israel's fall, and blindness, and rejection, resulted from its refusal of grace, from its crucifixion of the Messiah, nevertheless its rejection was involved in the substitutionary work of the Cross, for God used that very refusal and crucifixion in order to bring forth salvation for all. Thus the rejection of Israel worked out to the riches of the Gentiles. That must determine our whole outlook upon the Jew—he was blinded for us, that we might see; he was stripped and deprived that we might become rich with the Gospel. We can only see him where he is still held by God in the shadow of the Cross. We are his debtors in Christ. (b) But the very substitutionary nature of Israel's rejection means also the restoration of Israel, for it is already involved in the resurrection of Jesus of Nazareth, the rejected Son of Man. Thus the restoration of God's ancient people will have a part in the eschatological events of the consummation, and even the full blessing of the Gentiles depends upon the fulfilment of the Covenant-promises to Israel. If the rejection of Israel brought reconciliation and riches to the world, what will the restoration of Israel involve? (c) The restoration of Israel, however, takes a way as unique as Israel's instrumental place in the redemptive purpose of God, and is to be looked for along the line of the representative capacity which it still has in the election of God. The way to Israel's salvation, therefore, lies somehow through rejection; the way to its enlightenment lies through its blindness; the way to its fulness lies through its impoverishment—these are ways of God past finding out, for they belong to His unsearchable judgments, to the deepest mystery of the Cross. But this much is revealed, that through darkness God's ancient people will come into the light of the resurrection, and all Israel shall be saved. That does not simply mean that Jews will eventually become Christians and members of the One Holy Catholic Church, but that within the one Church of Christ, the Israel of God, there will be a special place for Israel as a people, and that even in its present blindness or rejection Israel has a unique mission in the world, for by His election of Israel God has once and for all bound the salvation of mankind with Israel.

The New Israel and the Old

We have now to consider the place and function of Israel in the Christian era, particularly in relation to the Christian Church as the New Israel.

(1) Although Israel was like a tree cut down to the stump, it remains to remind the Church of its origin and root, for the Church of the Gentiles is grafted on to the stump of Israel, like branches cut out of a wild olive tree and grafted contrary to nature into a good olive tree (Rom. 11: 16–24). That is a fact of such supreme importance that the Christian Church inevitably goes astray when it forgets it: that the Christian Church has no independent existence over against Israel. It is the root that bears the branches, not the branches the root. It is Israel that bears the Church, not the Church Israel. But have we any right to use the term "Church" in this way, over against Israel? The Old Testament *qahal* was already the Church of God, although it existed under a different form and it was on to that one Church, the true Israel, that the Christian Church was grafted. The grafting was done in Christ who willed to be Israel and who gathered up and recapitulated the whole life

of Israel in Himself and was as such the true Vine. And the grafting of the Gentile Church was carried out through the apostles, who represented the twelve branches of Israel or rather who replaced them in the new growth of the Church in the Gentile world. The apostles belonged both to the Old Israel and to the New and as such they, together with the prophets, formed the basis of the New Testament Church, and provided it with its essential continuity with the one Church of God throughout the historico-redemptive activity of God's grace among men. This Hebrew rooting is an indispensable element in the proper conception of the Church's apostolic succession.

(2) The historical particularity of Israel covenanted with God persists throughout the Christian era. God has not cast off His ancient people (Rom. 11: 1 f.), for the Covenant with Israel as God's people remains in force, and cannot be "spiritualized" and turned into some form alien to the stubborn historicity of its nature without calling in question the whole historical foundation of God's Revelation in Old Testament and New Testament. No doubt the historical persistence of Israel, maintained by act of God throughout the Christian era, has often proved an "offence" to the Gentile Church, but that is part of the "offence" of Jesus the Jew from Nazareth who insisted that not one jot or tittle of the Law would pass away unfulfilled. The fact that the Covenant made with historical Israel remains in force and presses toward historical fulfilment reminds the Gentile Church that it cannot arrogate to itself alone the claim to be the Church of God, and poses for the Gentile Church the problem of schism within the one Church, as schism between the Old Israel and the New Israel. The Christian Church (i.e. of Gentiles and Jewish proselytes) cannot be perfect, cannot reach its fulness apart from Israel (i.e. the historical people of the Old Covenant). So long as Church and Israel are divided, each is impoverished. No doubt, as we have seen, initially the impoverishment of Israel in its peculiar election as one people for all peoples, meant the enrichment of the Gentiles, but the fulness of the Gentiles depends upon the fulness of Israel. As St. Paul saw it, the grafting in of the Gentiles as wild olive branches into the good olive tree served to quicken the old stock. Its dead branches had been pared away and were replaced by the Gentile Church, so that it

partook of the root and fatness of the olive tree, but the resuscitation of the old tree would mean even greater enrichment to the Gentiles.

(3) What then is the hope of Israel? The hope of Israel can only lie ultimately in the acknowledgment of the crucified Jesus as the Messiah of Israel, as Son of David and Son of God, but the way of Israel toward that goal lies evidently along the line of its election to fulfil a representative function in shattering itself against the mercies of the Covenant. Not only in the era of the Old Testament but also in the era of the New Testament, Israel has had to undergo an ordeal of unparalleled suffering and rejection—and no doubt it is through that ordeal that Israel is to recover its sight. Two possible lines of recovery are perhaps discernible today. (a) For the first time since the days of Deutero-Isaiah and Jeremiah the concept of the Messiah as the suffering spirit of Israel has emerged into the open, particularly out of the concentration camps of Europe. And now in the State of Israel that conception of the Messiah wrestles with the other conception of the hero-Messiah, the mighty Deliverer that will come out of Sion: but these two conceptions wrestle with one another in an arena where the ubiquitous cross points to the Crucified as the only One in whom these two conceptions of the Messiah come together. When we recall the remark of C. G. Jung that in the majority of his Jewish patients analysis has revealed that the root causes of their mental illness have been associated with the crucifixion of Jesus Christ, we may well ask whether the Spirit of God is not working with Israel in a decisive way, pressing it to the point of looking upon Him whom it had pierced.

(b) The creating of the new State of Israel is surely the most significant sign given in God's dealings with His covenanted people since the destruction of Jerusalem in A.D. 70, for here once again the ancient struggle between Israel and its Lord is renewed in the conflict between the "ethnic" aspirations of Israel and the "laic" nature of the Covenant. May it not be that our best way to help Israel is to help it toward a "laic" criticism of its "ethnic" aspirations? And may it not be that Israel's representative function is to be the one people among all the peoples of the earth where there will be manifested the pattern of a new kind of "ethnic" life which would be the result of serious acknowledgment of its "laic" nature? Whether this is so or not, there can be no doubt about the fact, that the Gentile Church will not be able to serve God's purpose for Israel and so help Israel, until it acknowledges far more profoundly and sincerely that it is a debtor to Israel, that it can only exist as Church grafted on to the stock of Israel, and at the expense of Israel.

(4) It belongs to the perpetual need of the Church that it should perceive its root in Israel, and acknowledge that the Church does not bear the root, but the root the Church. Israel remains the servant of the Lord and He uses it to bear witness to the nations, unwilling witness though it be. Only when the Church listens to that witness can it understand and participate in the revelation and in the reconciliation that have reached it through Israel, and only then can the Church properly understand itself. There can be no doubt that the grafting of the wild olive branches upon the good olive tree resulted in rich fruit for the Church; this through the grafting of Greek modes of thought upon the Hebraic tradition enabled the divine Revelation to reach a fulness of expression in Christian theology that would hardly have been possible otherwise.

But here Christian theology must remember that it does not bear the root, but the root bears it; and that once theology detaches itself from its rooting in Israel it turns into an alien and sterile philosophy. The long ordeal of Israel out of which God has delivered to us His Self-revelation represents the struggle of the Word of God with the mind and will of man, and the preparation for the work of reconciliation between God and man wrought out at last in Jesus Christ in the midst of Israel. Thus the biblical modes of thought have a sacrosanctity not because they are Hebraic but because they represent both the way which God's revelation and reconciliation have taken within the mind of man, and the covenanted patterns of response and obedience to that revelation and reconciliation. Apart from that prepared sphere of revelation and reconciliation no one could have grasped the bewildering miracle of Jesus or begun to understand the Incarnation and the atonement. It is still necessary to be schooled in Israel, to be disciplined through the Old Testament Revelation, in order truly to apprehend the reconciling revelation of God in Jesus Christ. Our Gentile ways of thought cannot by-pass the ordeal of Israel, for even though Israel went through that ordeal as one people in substitution for all other peoples, we cannot enter into its rich inheritance apart from being refashioned in the mould of the biblical Revelation and a sharing in the ordeal of Israel as it was continually being broken and remade in the hands of God. Far from meaning that Gentiles have to become proselytes to Judaism, this means that Gentiles grafted on to Israel in Christ bear a fruit as Gentiles which would have been otherwise wanting. It is not the substitution of Jewish for Gentile modes of thought that is to be envisaged here, but a "learning obedience" to the Word of God which Gentile modes of thought can only gain in the midst of Israel where the Mind of God and the mind of rebellious man have at last been brought to reconciliation, after long discipline in the history of Israel, in Jesus Christ.

This continues to be one of the main ways in which Israel serves the Church, for even in Israel's persistent refusal of the Messiah, God uses Israel to summon the Church back from its temptations to detach itself from the historical covenant, and to call it back from its abstract and impersonal philosophies to the biblical way of knowledge, to a personal Lord who encounters us face to face in His Word, and to a rational obedience to His Will. On the other hand God uses the fact that Israel, in spite of being the root and stock of the Church, has become blind in the study of the oracles and hardened in the ordinances of grace, to remind the Church that even as Church it can refuse God's grace, become blind and hardened without knowing it by becoming wise in its own conceits, as St. Paul puts it. Not only of the events in the history of Israel in the Old Testament era, but of the events in the history of Israel in the New Testament era, may we say that all these things happened to them for our admonition upon whom the ends of the world are come.

(5) It is surely clear that it belongs to the Christian Church as one of its greatest tasks to wrestle with Israel in the prayer for understanding and reconciliation. Only through the Church that enters into the fellowship of Israel's sufferings can Israel find its way through the *Eli, Eli, lama sabachthani?* into resur-

rection and new creation. So long as Israel persists in unbelief the Church itself is denied its fulness both in regard to Revelation and in regard to Reconciliation. The Church needs the enlightened eyes of Israel to discover for it the full riches of the Gospel of grace, and it may well be that apart from Israel the Christian Church will never be able to find its way out of the present divisions into true wholeness and unity. God has coupled together the hope of Israel and the hope of the Church for ever.

PROBLEMS OF FAITH AND ORDER

6. CHRIST THE HOPE OF THE WORLD

Christ the First and the Last[1]

It may serve us as a beginning in this discussion if we try to see the contrast between the eschatology of the apostolic Church and Greek idealism on the one hand and Jewish eschatology on the other hand.

Greek thought is not characterized by eschatology, but by a concern for an ideal world, a world of ideas. To be sure, in classical Platonism the ideal world was not conceived in the modern subjectivist sense but rather in a most real way; nevertheless it was concerned with a world of ideas and not of actions.

It is worthwhile pausing here to contrast the two languages, Hebrew and Greek, for they appear to reflect the two contrasted outlooks. No doubt Greek was originally as concerned with the verb as Hebrew, but it certainly came to be more concerned with substantives and abstract conceptions and adjectival relations. Hebrew on the other hand never seems to have grown out of its early verbal emphasis, for its nouns and adjectives are ad-verbial in form and character. The fundamental relation is verbal, and therefore, as Martin Buber has taught us, it is action that is primary in Hebrew thought, and that means the kind of action that takes place between persons.

Now doubtless this contrast cannot be wholly maintained when we examine linguistic details between the two languages, but for all that it remains true that the Greek language belonged to a way of life and involved a whole web of meaning basically different from that of the Hebrew language. It was not accidental, for example, that it was out of Greek that formal logic emerged; for Greek is much concerned with abstract conceptions and their formal logical relations, but

[1] A lecture delivered in Edinburgh, October, 1953, in a post-graduate course on the history of eschatology.

not much with dynamic action. Indeed formal logic eliminates the active verb and translates propositions into forms of the verb to be and that in the present tense. Hebrew language and thought, on the other hand, were not concerned with abstract conceptions and their logical relations but with action and personal relation. Thus Hebrew thought about God is not concerned with ideas such as His infinitude, omnipotence, omnipresence, omniscience and the like. These are essentially Greek ideas derived from finite existence and abstractly raised, as it were, to the *n*th degree and then posited as attributes of the Infinite. That whole way of thinking was foreign to the Hebrews, although they had expressions corresponding to those just mentioned, but they were conceived rather as the properties of God in action in creation and history and among men. He is the living God and we know Him not as we know ideas but as we know people in love and meeting.

Perhaps the difference between the two ways of thinking and speaking comes out most clearly when one takes the vivid dramatic sentences of the Hebrew, with its images and daring analogies and intense activity, and translates them into Greek which, beautiful and accurate as it is, robs the Hebrew of its dramatic imagery and tones down its activism and tends to substitute, in the place of its dynamic temporal movement, static relation between ideas and conceptions. And yet it was the Greeks who taught us how to write history and not the Hebrews—this is where the contrast tends to cut across any schematized comparison between them; but after all the Hebrews were concerned to speak of the acts of God in history and the Greeks were not, and ultimately it is Hebrew and not Greek thought that takes time seriously.

I do not for a moment mean that we can do without Greek, or even Latin, for in the divine providence it was when Hebrew thought came to be translated into Greek that the great doctrines of Christ and the Trinity began to emerge into something like clarity or at least to be given clear statement. On the other hand Theology cannot rest content with purely Greek, and certainly not with purely Latin, formulations: that is, partly at any rate, the meaning of the Reformation. The theology that gained so much from the precision and clarity of Greek and Latin had to be reminted in the Hebraic world of thought in order to regain its dynamic and living character, and so biblical studies and biblical theology have ever since played a fundamental role in the Churches of the Reformation.

Let us consider for a moment the Hebraic conception of election; a most intensely personal choice by God of a personal community, a choice that was actively being fulfilled in the history of that community. But when we translate that loving election of the living God into the abstract categories of Greek and Latin thought, it is very difficult indeed to avoid determinism, for the whole notion of election is translated into terms of logical relation; but logical relation means necessary relation, and necessary relation means deterministic predestination. Hebrew thought in Judaism shows the same tendencies when it enters the world of European thought—and yet, once again, this is where neat comparisons break down. It is the theology of Islam which is so thoroughly deterministic. But is not the reason for that precisely what lies behind Greek thought, and played such a prominent and at times such a disastrous role in the fathers, namely "the immutability of God"? The Muslim God is a prisoner in His abstract Deity and is not free to enter into active relations with men, and in that respect is far more Greek than Semitic and certainly far removed from the living active God of the Old Testament and God the Son who became incarnate in Jesus Christ. It is ultimately the doctrine of God that stands behind the great contrasts in eschatology.

But to return to an earlier point; Hebrew thought is concerned not with logical, timeless relation but with action and with time, or rather with God acting in time, God acting among men in history. Therefore the end of God's action is also an historical end as well as an eternal end. It must be concerned with an eternal end, for it is the action of the eternal God; but it is the action of the eternal God in time and history, an action that reaches throughout history to future fulfilment and perfection. Greek thought, on the other hand, is ideal, and reaches out not to an historical end but to an ideal end, a timeless end. There is therefore a vast difference between the Greek notion of end and the biblical notion of end, and the biblical notion of end is precisely the core of the Gospel. If the end is ideal, no matter how much a man strives to realize it, i.e. to be what he ought to be, the end is still ideal and beyond his attainment. But in the Christian Gospel this end has broken into the present and is even now operative in the world. Because that final end has already entered history, the whole of Christian thought and action can no longer be construed in terms of idealism but in realistic terms of history and time, in terms of a new creation, a new heaven and a new earth.

A further characteristic of biblical eschatology is that the divine action which intervenes in the lives of men in history, bodies itself forth concretely in human history, embodies itself in humanity. Hence the place of the Messianic Community in the heart of biblical eschatology. The action of the living God is intensely personal as well as historical, and creates a community of persons as the sphere of divine operation in the world. That is the significance of Israel—but more and more that divine action becomes acutely personalized as it presses toward the Incarnation, and reaches its end and fulfilment in Jesus Christ in the fulness of time.

It is here that we come to see the contrast between Christian eschatology and Jewish eschatology—by Jewish eschatology I mean the late Judaistic eschatology which diverged somewhat from the prophetic teaching of the Old Testament. The characteristic way in which Judaism stated its view was through the contrast between the two ages or realms, between the present age (αἰών οὗτος) and the future age (αἰών μέλλων). This present age, the historical cosmos as we know it day by day, will pass away and it will be replaced by a new age entailing a new heaven and a new earth, and entailing a community which is both continuous with the old in lineage, and yet radically new. But the second of these ages follows hard upon the heels of the first, so that as long as we are still in this present age which passes away, the new age is entirely future. The Christian Gospel, however, is synonymous with the exciting news that the future age has already come upon us, telescoping itself, as it were, into the present age. This present age still goes on; history continues in the same old way, but the whole framework is altered, for the final goal of history has come into the midst of time and is now lodged in the very heart of it. That is the eschatological significance of the Incarnation, and that is what Jesus preached. "Repent! for the Kingdom of God is at hand; it has come upon you." In Jesus the King of the Kingdom, the Judge of all the ages, is actively present among men.

But with the death and resurrection of Jesus Christ, the apostles came, as Jesus predicted, to a deeper realization of what had happened and was still happening. In the death of Jesus Christ the final judgment of the world had precipitated itself into the present; the final, ultimate conflict between God and evil had taken place on the Cross. That was the great decisive point in the ages, the turning-point between the old age and the new age. With the resurrection of Jesus from the dead the apostles realized that not only had the decisive event taken place, but the new age had already dawned; the new creation was already revealed in its transcendent perfection and glory in the risen Man, Jesus—the Firstfruits of the resurrection, the New Adam, the Last Adam, the earnest and pledge of our inheritance.

Apostolic eschatology was therefore breathless with excitement and wonder, for the ends of the world had come upon mankind, and the final victory of God over the forces of evil lay behind. The apostolic age is on the resurrection side of the Cross, advancing into the promised land.

With Pentecost, the outpouring in fulness of the Holy Spirit, the apostles realized that not only was Jesus Himself the beginning of the New Creation, but by participating in the Holy Spirit the apostles themselves were already participating in the powers of the age to come, and were already living in the new age. The New Community was inaugurated in the Church and as such it advanced into history increasing and growing and expanding; beginning with the nucleus of the twelve disciples and the one hundred and twenty on the day of Pentecost, it reached out in ever widening dimensions under the command and promise of the Lord which directed them to the ends of the earth and the ends of the age.

But now to be more precise, let us try to summarize the main features of this eschatology in several sections.

(1) The basic fact is the Person of Jesus Christ, the risen Lord ascended to kingly rule over all in heaven and earth. The resurrection and ascension mean the completion of His work and include the certainty of His advent in glory. At the heart of the apostolic eschatology, therefore, lies the emphasis

upon the present Lordship of Christ, a Lordship asserted by His death and resurrection over all principalities and powers, and all dominions. The assertion of that sovereignty is an accomplished fact in the complete triumph of the Cross and Resurrection, and therefore the Kingdom has already come with power in the very first generation of the followers of Jesus Christ. The full unveiling of that triumph is still awaited, when Christ will make an open show of His power and exhibit the spoils of His victory.

(2) Eschatology concerns the Parousia of Jesus Christ the King of the Kingdom. That Parousia comprises His birth, life, death, resurrection, ascension and second advent as one extended event, the great inclusive event of Immanuel, God with us. From the aspect of on-going history, however, the Parousia is both the decisive intervention of the Kingdom in time, in the incarnation of the Son of God in Jesus Christ, and also the final advent in glory. The link between the two advents is the Parousia of Christ through the Spirit, the abiding Parousia. It is this trinitarian understanding of Parousia that is of the very essence of eschatology in the apostolic age, as we see with particular clarity in the Apocalypse: Christ the *Protos*, the Alpha who was, Christ the *Eschatos*, the Omega who is to come, but also the Christ who is here and now in the midst of His Church on earth. It was not till the middle of the second century that the Church started to speak of two advents of Christ and so to use the word parousia in the plural—at least I am not aware of any earlier use of it. The Parousia is strictly one inclusive coming-and-presence operating with different modes of revelation.

(3) The two great moments in the eschatological economy are the death and resurrection of Christ, and the final apocalypse of His Glory. It was in the incarnation, death and resurrection of Christ that the perfect work of redemption was accomplished. The work of the Kingdom in Jesus Christ was final, once for all. To that finality belongs the outpouring of the Spirit at Pentecost, the New Testament Revelation, and the constitution of the apostolate and so the foundation of the Church. That final deed in Christ was also regarded as having cosmic import and cosmic effect, the significance no doubt of the witness recorded as to the cosmic disturbances when Jesus

died on the Cross. The Cross was the great *kairos* when the Sovereignty of God struck into the heart of the world, and it is still by that Cross that He draws the whole world into the sphere of His redeeming operation. All history is now placed under the power of the Cross, while in the Resurrection the new age already dawned overlaps this present age, the age of on-going empirical history. The full manifestation or unveiling of the new age, the perfection of Christ's work of redemption and its full power, are yet to be revealed in the final *kairos* when Jesus Christ will come again in glory. Then this present age, the cosmos as it is now constituted, the world in its present conditions with all its forms and patterns suited to human selfishness and sin, will pass away, and the new age, the new creation, will stand revealed. Meantime all that happens on earth and in time, within or without the Church, is conditioned proleptically by the coming of Jesus Christ as Judge and Saviour.

(4) Between those two eschatological moments or *kairoi*, the first advent and the second advent, the Parousia refers to the abiding presence of Jesus Christ. He is the *Protos* who was, the *Eschatos* who will be, but He is also *Ego Eimi* the "I am", *Ho On*, "He Who is". It is here that we must see the place of the ascension in apostolic eschatology. The ascension means on the one hand that Christ has ascended to the throne of God Almighty, and from there rules over all things and fills all things; it means on the other hand the pouring out of His Spirit in fulness upon the Church on earth—so that while He is above, the Lord of the ages, King of the aeons, yet He is present in the midst of His people on earth and in history. How is the Parousia of Christ here and now connected with the Parousia of His Kingdom in the fulness of glory? Clearly, Jesus Christ has withdrawn Himself from sight, from on-going empirical history, withdrawn Himself from contemporaneous contact within history for reasons of mercy. Full manifestation of the risen Lord now in all His glory and majesty would mean the immediate end of this age, the end of the world, the final judgment—only fleeting glimpses of that glory did He give to His disciples after His resurrection, sufficient to show them that He had risen indeed, in body and in the fulness of His humanity.

Moreover, by withdrawing Himself from sight the ascended Lord sends the Church back to the historical Jesus, to the Gospel story of the incarnation, public ministry, death and resurrection as the only *locus* where He may be contacted. If Jesus had continued to be with His Church all through history as the contemporary of every generation, the Cross would have been relegated into the past and treated as a passing episode, and not as the fact of final and supreme and central import. The whole historical life and revelation of Jesus would have lost much of its significance. But He has veiled His present glory, so that if we would find Him we must go back to the historical Jesus. That is the only place where we may meet Him, but there we make contact with Him through the Cross at the point where the final act of God regarding sin has been accomplished. There is no other road to the Parousia of the risen Jesus, the Lord of Glory, except through the Jesus of Humiliation, the Jesus of Bethlehem and Judaea and Galilee and Calvary.

But even when we turn to the historical Jesus we can no longer make contact with Him as did the disciples before His crucifixion and resurrection. We must seek to contact Him, therefore, not after the flesh but after the Spirit. We go back to the historical Jesus, to the Gospel story, but there it is with the risen and ascended Lord that we make contact. We look back at the historical Jesus from the perspective of the resurrection and we encounter the risen Christ in His abiding Parousia. We find that Parousia only as the Jesus of history is transfigured before us; that is partly the significance of the way in which the Fourth Gospel presents Christ, but it is clearly the import of the Johannine presentation of Christ in the opening chapter of the Apocalypse: the familiar figure of Jesus clothed with His transcendent majesty and glory, and yet for all that still the same Jesus.

The ascension means, therefore, that we who live between the times, between the first advent of Christ and His second advent, can only encounter the risen Lord if we go back to the first advent, to Jesus as He was; that is, if we go back to the historical witness, to the word of the Gospel. But on the other hand, the ascension means that we who live between the times have the gift of the Spirit, and yet we have that gift only as we go back to the historical Jesus, for the Spirit is sent not to speak of Himself but to take of the historical Jesus, the life and words, the death and resurrection of the historical Jesus, and to reveal them to us in their full significance and reality. Thus between the two advents of Christ, eschatology is concerned with the double movement: the thrusting into history by the witness of the Church, the Word of the Gospel, but as that Word of the Gospel is proclaimed in all the world, by His Spirit it is Christ the Lamb of God who reigns over all things, making all things to serve His purpose of redeeming love. That means that eschatology and world-mission belong together, as Jesus made clear in His final commands to the apostles before He ascended. In other words, eschatology is concerned with the relation between the Word and the Spirit, whether that be within the fellowship of the Church in Word and Sacrament, or in the witness of the Church unto the ends of the earth that Jesus is Lord and Saviour, or in the disturbance and upheaval caused among the nations by the proclamation of the Gospel; that is, apocalyptic tension and conflict.

(5) We come now to the Church in history as the eschatological community, the community that reaches out beyond this present age into the age to come, and derives its life from there, even though it still participates in the on-going history of this present age. The Church lives in the midst of that eschatological tension, but that tension is itself dual—this is the difficult thing about the eschatology of the New Testament, but its very heart. The tension is twofold: (i) tension between the new and the old here and now, and (ii) tension between the present and the future.

The tension between the new and the old is created by present participation through the Spirit (in Word and Sacrament) in the new creation. Therefore the Church, already in the new creation and tasting its powers, inevitably feels that the thinnest veil of sense and time divides it from the full experience of the new. The new is absolutely near through the Spirit, and its impact on the old means even now the break-up of the old. The tense awareness of the new age, of fellowship in the power of the resurrection here and now carries with it the imminence to faith of the epiphany of Christ, His final unveiling in glory. That eschatological expectation, the hope of Christ's appearing just round the corner, so to speak, is essential to faith in Jesus Christ, for He is there already present waiting to unveil His majesty. That is why the writers of the New Testament are acutely aware of the pressure of the Parousia upon them, the knocking of the advent Christ already on the door.

But faith exists not only in hope in the epiphany of Christ; it is bound up with the veiling of Christ, with the ascension, and here we come back to the other reason for the ascension or the purposed withdrawal of Christ from sight. Faith can exist only where there is a gap, an eschatological reserve, between the present and the future, between actual participation in the Kingdom here and now and the future manifestation of its glory. Let us consider it like this. If Jesus on earth had manifested His full divine glory so that men were confronted face to face with the ultimate majesty of God, then they would have been damned on the spot; they would have been face to face with the final judgment. But the veiling of His ultimate glory meant that Jesus was giving men a chance to repent; He was holding them at arm's length away, so to speak, giving them time to repent, room for decision. He came veiling His glory, yet revealing Himself obliquely, so as to give men enough light to believe but not enough finally to blind them or judge them. That is why He refused to give a compelling demonstration of Himself, but sought to evoke faith. Faith is not sight, but faith answers to revelation that is yet only in part, for faith exists in the gap between partial and final manifestation. Faith is, therefore, essentially eschatological in its inner nature.

Now the ascension means that Jesus Christ has withdrawn Himself from sight and history in order to allow the whole world time for repentance. He holds back the final unveiling of His glory and majesty, holds back the final judgment, when, as the Apocalypse puts it, he that is filthy will be filthy still. That gap between the times is the eschatological time when this present age is already interpenetrated by the age to come, but it is time when the new age in all its glory is as yet veiled from sight, in order to leave room to preach the Gospel and give all men opportunity for repentance and faith. Thus the world-mission of the Church is part of God's grace, for it is God's grace alone that keeps back the dissolution of this age.

(6) We have seen that it is the Church's participation through the Spirit in the new age that involves it in that situation of eschatological tension, but now we must see that the involvement of the Church in this present age gives particular form to that tension. The real life of the Church lies in its participation in the resurrection, in the new creation, and so in its detachment from the forms of this present evil age.

Therefore the Church is warned in the New Testament against systematization or schematization to the patterns of this cosmos; for it lives through being transformed and renewed in Christ, and it must not live in disagreement with its essential nature. That contrast is also of the essence of eschatology. In Pauline language it is the contrast between law and Spirit, between works and grace. The form of this present world is law, but the essential character of the Church's life is freedom in the Spirit. The Epistle to the Galatians, therefore, from this point of view, is the most eschatological of all Paul's epistles. Christian freedom in the Spirit is grounded in justification—by grace and not by works—therefore we are made free from the law of works. God's grace has set our life on a wholly new basis in which love and gratitude operate on the ground of what Christ has completed in His death and resurrection on our behalf. In Johannine language this is the contrast between death and eternal life, between darkness and light, between the lie and the truth; and here too, one must say, from this perspective, the First Epistle of John is a thoroughly eschatological piece of writing. In the language of the Apocalypse, this is the clash between the perfect Kingdom of God and the kingdoms of this age, between the perfect pattern of the new creation and the bestial and brutal images thrown up out of the sea of the nations in defiance of God's love and grace.

(7) The Church that is launched into this situation in history is the suffering servant, the Church under the Cross, and to all outward appearances the weak and helpless, the despised and down-trodden Church, but it is also the Church of the victorious King. The shout of a King is in its midst! A new song is in its mouth, the song of final and complete triumph, a song of indescribable joy and confidence in Jesus Christ. The apostles of this Church were essentially the ambassadors of the King of Kings, sent into all the world as heralds of the new era, already

inaugurated, and soon to be revealed. They were eye-witnesses of the resurrection, of the fact that the Last Day had already dawned, and they were heralds of its coming in power. That is why the *kerygma* of the New Testament is eschatological through and through, because it is exultant with the glad news of the Kingdom.

INDEX

I. Biblical References

INDEX

II. Names

INDEX

III. Subjects

CONFLICT AND AGREEMENT IN THE CHURCH

Volume Two

CONFLICT AND AGREEMENT IN THE CHURCH

by

T. F. TORRANCE

Volume Two

THE MINISTRY AND THE SACRAMENTS OF THE GOSPEL

Wipf & Stock
PUBLISHERS
Eugene, Oregon

To

ANDERS NYGREN

and

EDMUND SCHLINK

Wipf and Stock Publishers
199 W 8th Ave, Suite 3
Eugene, OR 97401

Conflict and Agreement In the Church, 2 volumes
By Torrance, Thomas F.

ISBN: 1-57910-006-6
Publication date 11/16/1996
Previously published by Lutterworth Press, 1959

CONTENTS

ACKNOWLEDGMENTS

Acknowledgment is made to the S.C.M. Press for permission to reproduce the essay on *Eschatology and the Eucharist* written for the volume on *Intercommunion* (edited by D. M. Baillie and John Marsh) in preparation for the Third World Conference on Faith and Order held at Lund; and to the editors of *Theologische Zeitschrift* (Basel), *Revue d'Histoire et de Philosophie Religieuses* (Strasburg), *The Church Quarterly Review* (London), *The Canadian Journal of Theology* (Toronto), *The Expository Times* (Aberdeen), *The Scottish Journal of Theology* (Edinburgh), and *Verbum Caro* (Taizé), for permission to reproduce articles printed in their Journals.

INTRODUCTION

It is increasingly evident to-day that the lines of conflict and agreement in the Church coincide less and less with the frontiers of the historic Communions. That appears to be due in considerable measure to the resurgence of biblical theology and Christology in all the Churches, and may well be taken as an indication of the way ecumenical advance will take in the future. Thus new alignments are cutting through the membership of the existing Churches in a way that is bound to undermine denominational barriers and to bear positive fruit in growing reunion.

On the other hand, it still remains true that the conflict is most acute and agreement is most difficult in regard to what is called "the means of Grace".[1] The reason for that probably goes back to a distinctively Western habit of mind that grew up in the Dark and Middle Ages when undue prominence was given to practical and institutional questions and Latin pragmatism and Christian Gospel came to be compounded together in the daily life and mission of the Church. Thus the traditional Faith tended to be codified in the rational structures of the Church and Grace tended to be institutionalized in canonical forms for its easy ministration to the multitudes. In this highly pragmatic consciousness the Church was regarded as the Ark of Salvation equipped with the means of Grace for the salvation of souls, and in it the ancient Roman genius for organization, administration and deployment of resources found new scope for expression and development.

It was thus that the Roman Church grew up, but it grew up in such a way that the content of the faith was permanently tied to modes of thought deriving from the ancient world, and

[1] The very expression "means of Grace" is difficult and misleading, for it brings Grace into the realm of *means and ends* where some object is to be attained or some result achieved, and so it opens up the thought of its administration. In the New Testament Grace is never related to Baptism or the Lord's Supper, and is only once associated with the Spirit (Heb. 10:29).

the evangelical ministrations of the Church were channelled in dogmatically defined ways and means in accordance with unchangeable patterns in the institutional structure of the Church. Thus when the Church came under pressure from within for the renewal of its life and faith in the Gospel, the tension was most severe wherever the renewed life and faith broke through its encasement in the dogmatized and canonized patterns of thought and ministry. The tragedy that came over the Roman Church was that it failed to realize that the mediaeval modes of thought and patterns of life, which had served their purpose for centuries, had only a limited range of applicability, and when absolutized or invested with final authority could quickly become demonic like the principalities and powers or the ἐξουσίαι of which the New Testament warns us, and from which we can be redeemed only by the Blood of Christ.

The Reformers found themselves faced with an extremely difficult situation in their attempt to restore the face of the ancient Catholic Church, for the complete intransigence of Rome, culminating at last in the Council of Trent, left no alternative to a break in which each side found itself forced to barricade itself behind a total exclusion of the other. The fact that the Reformers had to do battle with the Roman Church over the means of Grace, that is, at the point where the Gospel had been tied down in the tradition to inflexible institutional forms, meant that the whole question of the means of Grace was given a place of undue prominence in the Evangelical Churches themselves, so that they were tempted over against the Counter-Reformation and over against one another to seek and claim justification for themselves in their practical manifestations and in the modifications and changes they introduced into the mediaeval institutions they had inherited. Thus the theological issues came to be confused with *post hoc* rationalizations of historical events, and justification by Grace alone was denied in practice by a form of self-justification.

That is what happened in the late sixteenth and in the seventeenth centuries when comparatively peripheral questions, significant though they were, were thrust right into the centre and given a distorted importance in the Evangelical Churches, and they settled down into hardening institutional structures over against one another. What could be more revealing in this respect, as we look back upon it, than the action of the Westminster Assembly which sought to impose by Parliament a uniform pattern of faith and ecclesiastical government upon the Churches of the United Kingdom? Is it any wonder that the Church of England on its part has barricaded itself behind institutional structures that have become increasingly adamant, and that this in turn continues to provoke hardening reaction on the part of its sister Churches? On all hands we have repeated the failure of the mediaeval Church to see the limited nature and sanctity of many institutional patterns, and in claiming to fight for essentials we have often betrayed them by confounding them with time-conditioned forms that rarely have historical support from the New Testament or even the Early Church.

In view of the present state of inter-church relations among the Evangelical Churches there are three questions, among others, for which I would like to press for immediate and more careful consideration.

(1) *Fundamentalist notions of the ministry.* By "fundamentalism" I do not refer to loyalty to the Gospel and the Word of God as delivered to us in the Holy Scriptures, but to the binding of this to fixed forms or set modes of interpretation that in themselves have no essential relation to the Gospel or the Word of God. There is, for example, a "fundamentalist" interpretation of Holy Scripture that is tied to rationalist, philosophical forms of thought deriving from the seventeenth century, but there are also "fundamentalist" notions of the ministry that are tied to man-made traditions and time-conditioned notions of the seventeenth century or earlier. There are Churchmen, for example, who appear to believe in the verbal inspiration of seventeenth century Presbyterian conceptions of the ministry, in spite of the fact that they do not stand up well to criticism on the ground of biblical exegesis or historical evidence now available from the Early Church. But perhaps nowhere is this intransigent "fundamentalism" more in evidence than in some of the champions of Anglicanism, who are prepared to accept exact, scholarly handling of the Scriptures, but who are not prepared to extend that treatment to their peculiar notions of "the historic episcopate".

(2) *Justification by Christ alone.* Justification means that we are

put in the right with God solely through Jesus Christ, that only in Him are we clothed with righteousness. Therefore it calls in question and relativizes all else that claims to be righteousness. Because we believe in justification by Christ alone, we believe that He and He alone constitutes the Church His Body, that He alone sanctifies it in Himself, and gives it Truth and Grace, and that He alone gives it the Ministry of the Gospel. Only in Him may we look for justification anywhere in the Church's life and work. Therefore we can never justify ourselves or demand justification from one another without betraying Christ or usurping His prerogative. But when one Church calls in question the orders of another, is it not seeking to justify itself over against it? and when the other demands recognition of its orders, is it not renouncing justification by Christ alone and seeking honour of man rather than of God? This is the *damnosa inheritas* of Latin Mediaevalism that is still with us—by tying the ministry of the Gospel to time-conditioned institutions, we give pragmatic questions a dominant place which distorts and obscures the Gospel. When debate takes this form, justification by works replaces justification by Grace, and the whole Gospel is at stake. Justification by Grace means that pragmatic considerations cannot be put in the centre, either through insisting on them or through opposing them unduly, without disastrous betrayal of Grace.

Justification by Christ alone means that in all ecumenical discussions Jesus Christ must be allowed to occupy the central place, that we begin only through unreserved committal to Him and allow ourselves to be guided throughout by what such committal may involve.

(3) *Intercommunion.* Nothing can be more heart-rending than the way advocates of so-called "open Communion" or of "reunion before Communion" seem to be manipulating division at the Lord's Table in order to achieve their own ends. On both sides of this issue there is apparent a deep failure to understand the nature of division at the Sacrament of the Body and Blood of Christ, and the outrage to Christ it involves. If we are really ready to seek reconciliation in Christ we cannot but enter upon Intercommunion as soon as possible, and, in and through the forgiven and healed relation to Christ which it mediates, work together towards *fullness* of Communion be-

tween the Churches. How can we sit down at the Lord's Table and then refuse to act out in our body and blood what we have received in communion with the Body and Blood of Christ, that is, refuse to act out reconciliation in the whole of our physical life and work in the Church? Therefore how can Churches sit down separately at the Lord's Table to proclaim the death of Christ till He come, when by their very separation they are acting a lie to reconciliation through the Blood of Christ?

On the other hand, the argument given by so many of our Anglican brethren seems equally to indicate failure to feel deeply enough the outrage of schism in the Eucharist. Thus it is argued against engaging in Intercommunion as part of the way to unity that "since the Eucharist is an offering in history of the memorial of redemption, it can only be offered by those who are historically at one". But does that not mean (except perhaps to the wilfully blind) that no Church which is separated from another Church can offer the memorial of redemption in its separation? To use such an argument against Intercommunion, while not using it against Communion, can only be a form of sinful pretence, while to insist on this argument and yet to hold separated Communion is only to eat and drink judgment. Surely we must recognize frankly that on both sides of this question we are deeply involved in sin, and that arguments advanced from out of that sinful separation are inextricably intertwined with self-justification and with rationalization of disunity.

What is absolutely imperative is that we repent, without waiting for repentance on the part of the other, and resolve together, without laying down conditions for the other, to seek reconciliation in Christ, and so take into our hands the holy means He has provided for repentance, forgiveness, healing, reconciliation, and unity; and then and ever after resolve to work out, in obedience to reconciliation in the Body and Blood of Christ, all that it entails for those incorporated into Him. Anglicans and Presbyterians alike might do well to study the illuminating work on unity in Communion, called *Brotherly Reconcilement*, written by Egeon Askew in 1605 and presented to James I as a contribution toward healing division—that in the seamless coat of Christ schism may be sewed up, men in orders brought into order, that God may be served in verity by His Church, and the Church be preserved in unity until the coming of His Son Christ Jesus unto judgment.

It is with the same prayer that the essays collected in this volume are offered to the Church, and with the desire on my part to learn more and more from my brethren through their criticism of these pages. These essays are not controversial, but are meant to be irenic and constructive, in the hope that they may help to clear some ground for agreement. Nothing like a systematic account is given in them of the Ministry or the Sacraments, so that perhaps I may be permitted to direct any who are interested to the new edition of *A Manual of Church Doctrine* by Wotherspoon and Kirkpatrick for an interpretation of Church, Ministry and Sacraments, as held in the Church of Scotland.

1

THE MINISTRY

(a) *The Meaning of Order*[1]

ORDER is the co-ordinating of the life of the Church in its fellowship, worship, and mission in the service of the glory of God. The order of the Church's ministry is the ordering of its life and work through participation in the obedience of Christ. Let us elucidate that in a number of paragraphs.

(1) In the biblical revelation the whole concept of order is viewed over against disorder and chaos. Apart from the ordering of God's creative Word the world is without form or void, but into the ordered cosmos there has broken the disorder of sin. It belongs to the very nature of sin to divide, to disrupt, to be anarchic—sin is lawlessness, *anomia*. The opposite of all that is order, harmony, communion. When God made the world He made it in order and everything was set in its due proportion. But through the lawlessness of sin the world fell out of proportion, out of order, and was threatened with sheer chaos. Were it not for the persistent fact of God's purpose of love the world would destroy itself; but in His Covenant mercy God holds the world together in spite of its chaos, and to that end He has promulgated His law which restrains and contains disorder and chaos, and reduces it to a measure of proportion, even while it is in the grip of *anomia*, or lawlessness. But God's Covenant contains the promise of a new order, of a new creation when all things will be restored to their obedience and perfection in the divine Will. Meantime wherever there is *anomia* it is met by the divine *nomos*, and there is conflict between disorder and order.

(2) The biblical revelation does not work with a concept of natural law, that is, of an order immanent in natural processes capable of being brought to its self-expression. There is an order of creation (*ordo creationis*) but that is not discernible by observing the creation (*cursus naturae*) but only by observing the

[1] Reprinted from *The Church Quarterly Review*, vol. CLX, Jan. 1959, pp. 21–36; French text in *Revue d'Histoire et de Philosophie Religieuses*, No. 2, pp. 129–142.

creative Will of God. This creative Will of God will restore to creation its lost order, and restore to creation its true form and harmony in the Word of God. That is shadowed forth in the divine law promulgated in the Old Testament, the revealed law of God, but as yet that law set over against the lawlessness of the world is revealed mainly in its negative aspect of judgment upon disorder, and of restraint upon lawlessness. It is through the judgment of disorder that order is maintained, and laws are formed to make life in the disordered world possible at all. But the ultimate function of that law is to point beyond itself to the new law, the new order of the new Covenant. Under the old Covenant there was a divine form of administration or economy given in the law of Moses; but that points ahead to the new Covenant when the Covenant Will of God will bring and manifest a new form of administration or economy. This will be inserted into the world and written into its inner being—the new law to be inscribed upon the heart through the Spirit. As such it is a new order that comes from without and is planted within.

(3) That new order, the new economy, or rather the eternal Economy of God for His creation, came into the world in Jesus Christ. In the Incarnation the Word of God entered into His own disordered world; the Light shone into the darkness; the divine economy entered within historical and creaturely existence. In other words, the Covenant Will of God broke into our world and is completely fulfilled in Jesus Christ both from the side of God and from the side of man. That is the economy of which St. Paul speaks, when he describes its work as that of gathering up all things into Christ the Head, things visible and invisible, and their ordering in the eternal purpose of the divine love and fellowship. *OIKONOMIA* describes literally the ordering of a house, household administration. God is the great Householder who has come to take control of His own house and family and order it according to His Love. He does that in and through the Incarnation, in which His *OIKONOMIA* is not imposed upon the world from without but enters into it and operates from within it. *OIKONOMIA* represents the great condescension of the divine Will to work out His purpose of love without violence within the alienated will of man, to work out His divine economy within the disordered existence of the world. Now the *mode of that economic condescension* is the way of

Jesus Christ the Servant, the way of obedience even to the death of the Cross, and it is through that mode of economic condescension that He is exalted to be the Head of all things, and especially the Head of the Church, His Body.

(4) In Jesus Christ, therefore, in His Incarnation and in the whole course of His obedience, there has taken place in the divine economy a restoration of alienated man to fellowship with God, a conversion of rebellious humanity to the obedience and love of God. In other words, in the whole human life of Jesus the order of creation has been restored; in the midst of our disordered, sin-disrupted existence, there has been lived a human life in perfect order and proportion to the Will of God. The Covenant purpose of God in creation has been fulfilled and more than fulfilled. Here we have the divine economy entering into our creaturely and human existence and ordering it from within *against* our human nature, that is, against the consequences of sin in all its disorder, chaos, and lawlessness entrenched in fallen human nature. This is the order of redemption which reaches back to the original order of creation and far transcends it in the amazing purpose of the divine love, as the order, of the new creation. Here in the new Humanity in Jesus Christ nothing is out of order, or out of proportion. Everything has its proper order, proper time, proper place, proper sequence, and proper end. From beginning to end the whole life of Jesus in obedience to the Father is directed to His praise and glory, so that the new order of creation established and revealed in the Humanity of Christ can be spoken of as the praise of creation for the Creator.

(5) Order in the new creation is to be regarded as a third dimension. We are not concerned here simply with the Will of God and the obedience of man, with the Law of God, and the conformity of man to that divine law, but with a *third dimension*, with a divinely provided fulfilment of the divine Law. In the Old Testament we have a situation in which God gathers His children into Covenant relation with Himself, and within that Covenant He declares: "I will be your God, and you will be my children. . . . I am holy, therefore be ye holy. I am God, walk before me and be perfect." But God knows that His children are unable to be holy or obedient or perfect before Him; they are unable to fulfil the requirements of His Covenant Will, so that within the Covenant and as part of its Covenant

mercies He graciously provides a way of response to His Will, a way of obedient conformity to His Covenant which He is pleased to accept as from His people in the Covenant. That was provided in Israel's Cult or *leitourgia*. But that cultic pattern of response had to be acted out in obedience, while it pointed beyond itself to God's promise of a way of obedient fulfilment of it in the actual existence and life of His people. That was the theme in the Servant Songs, which was fulfilled at last in Jesus Christ, who in His obedient Humanity is our God-given way of response to the divine Will. God's Covenant Will is fulfilled for us, on our behalf, and in our stead, and through our participation in the obedient Humanity of Christ we are given to share in the fulfilled economy of the new Covenant, indeed of the new creation. That then is the third dimension. We are not simply concerned even in the Christian Church with the Will of God in love and grace, and then with the obedience of man in love and fellowship. We are concerned with these two, but with the two as fulfilled and completed in Jesus Christ, in the obedient ordering and perfection of His human life as an oblation of all praise and thanksgiving to God the Creator and Father, and therefore of our sharing in His obedience through the power of the Spirit. Thus *order* in the New Testament refers to the concrete ordering of our human life and being in the obedient Humanity of Jesus Christ. All order in the Christian Church is a participation in His obedient Humanity—whether that order be an ordering of its daily life, daily worship, or daily fellowship, or daily mission. The whole of the Church's life is ordered through participation in the ordered life of Jesus Christ, the New Adam, the Head of the New Creation.

(6) The form which this re-ordering in Jesus Christ takes is the form of a Servant. It was through His obedience within our disobedient humanity that He restored us to order and peace in God. But in that He the obedient Servant is given to be the Head of all creation, all creation is now re-ordered in obedience to Him, for He gives it to share in His obedience to God. Because Christ is the Head of creation, chaotic, lawless creation is restored to order in Him, and because He restored order through obedience to the Father, He restores order to the creation through bringing creation into obedience to Himself, by granting it through the Spirit to share in His own obedience.

Thus as Jesus was obedient in the Father, who sent Him to fulfil His Will, so the Church is ordered in its obedience to Christ who sent it to fulfil His Will. The obedience of the Church to Christ is not simply an imitation of His obedience but a fulfilling of God's Will through participation in Christ's obedience.

(7) It is through the Spirit that the Church is given to share in Christ's obedience, and so to be ordered in and by and through His obedient Humanity. Christ is the Law of the Church's life, the Law according to which its life and work are to be ordered, but that Law is fulfilled not simply by external obedience and conformity but by inner and outer sharing in His Life, so that *through the SPIRIT* the Church is in-the-law to Christ (*ennomos Christou*), conformable to Him through communion with Him. It is the Spirit who is the Law of the Church's ordered life; not the Spirit as a new law of nature, not the Spirit as the soul of the Church, not the Spirit as a new immanent norm in the development of the Church through history, but the Spirit who gives the Church to share in the obedience of Christ the Head of the Body and who is other than the Church, its Lord and King but who in economic condescension has come to be obedient to the Father from within the Church, that the Church may share in an obedience not its own, and in an order that is new to it, indeed against its own nature; an order from beyond the Church's own being but in which it is given to participate by the Spirit.

(8) This being so, *actual order* as we see and have it in the historical Church on earth is essentially ambiguous. Its basic order is the obedient new humanity in Christ. The Church shares in that through the Spirit, so that its life is ordered through the Communion of the Spirit. But the Church that shares in that order of the New Creation is the Church that is sent by Christ out into history, to live its life in the physical and temporal existence that awaits redemption in the second advent of Christ. The Church in the midst of the old creation and all its disorder shares in the new creation and its new order. By sheer participation in the empirical life of this fallen world which comes under the divine judgment, and therefore the divine law, the Church participates in worldly forms and laws and cannot escape from them. It is sent to have its mission right there under law, but under law to share in the new order in-the-law to

Christ through the Spirit. Just as the Son of God Himself condescended to be made under the law and through obedience to fulfil the Will of God, and as such was exalted above all, so the Church which is given to share through the Spirit in the new Humanity of Christ is sent into history to live out its new life in the form of a servant under the law—not to be fettered by the law, not to be schematized according to the forms and patterns of this age, that is, not to be legalized in its life, but to use the patterns and forms of the law of this age in the service of its new life in the risen and ascended Lord. Thus all order in the historical Church is essentially ambiguous because it is order in the overlap of the two ages, this present age that passes away and the new age which through the Spirit already overlaps it in Christ.

Another way of putting that is to say that all order in the historical Church is essentially eschatological. By "eschatological" here two things are meant: (a) that order carries within it the tension between the new and the old; and (b) the tension between the present (including the past) and the future. True order in the Church of Christ is order that points above and beyond its historical forms to its new order in the risen Christ, and points beyond its present forms to the future manifestation of its order in the new creation. All order in the Church is thus ambivalent and provisional: it is order that visibly reflects its life hid with Christ in God, and order that exercises a provisional service in time, until Christ comes again. The outward order is like the scaffolding of a building which is to be torn down and cast away when the building itself is complete. In history God has given the Church its historical order and structure which participates in the forms of this passing world, but when the building of the Church as an habitation of God is complete, and its new order is revealed in the advent of Christ, the historical forms of order and structure will be cast away. Or to put it another way: all order is at once juridical and spiritual. It is at once participant in *nomos* and participant in *Pneuma*, that is, in Christ through the *Pneuma*. The validity of orders in the Church partakes of that ambivalence. Validity is at once a juridical term relative to the particular nomistic structure of a Church, relative to the law of a Church, but validity is also a spiritual term referring to the sharing of the

Church in the authority of Christ through His Spirit, a sharing in the *exousia* of the Son of Man. It is that essential ambiguity in validity that makes it such a difficult term, and forgetfulness of it that causes persistent confusion.

Now in the light of all these eight paragraphs we have to think of the *order* of the Church's ministry with reference to its actual life in the space and time of this world. The ordering of the Church's life through sharing in, and therefore according to, the obedient Humanity of Christ, is an ordering within the physical and temporal life of this world. Order has therefore to be thought out in terms of *space* and *time*.

(1) *Order in regard to Space*

Because the Church is the Body of Christ, it has a physical and spiritual life in which the physical and the spiritual are not to be separated, though they may be distinguished, from one another. The Church as Body of Christ in history has therefore space. It has its place in this world, the place which it has been given by Christ, and into which He has sent it. It is in its place in the physical world that its life is to be ordered. Let us look at that in this way. Jesus Christ, the Man Jesus, is the place in this physical world where God and man meet and where they have communion with one another. The Temple in the Old Testament was the place where God put His Name, where He kept tryst with His covenanted people, and where they kept covenant with Him. Jesus Christ is that Temple on earth and among men where God has put His Name, and where He has appointed us to meet Him. It is the place where heaven and earth meet, the place of reconciliation. Jesus Christ is Himself God's mercy-seat, God's place in this world where He is really present to us in our place. But Jesus Christ ascended and He is in heaven—that is, He has a heavenly place far beyond anything that we can understand and far beyond our reach, but Jesus Christ through His Spirit has also bestowed His presence upon us in the Church, so that the Church on earth is the place of Christ.

The place of the Church in history is the place where Christ's presence is to be found. That is His real presence. It is of course above all in the Sacrament of the Lord's Supper, in the midst of the Church on earth, that we are given the real presence of

Christ. That is the place of Christ in the place of the Church on earth. That is the place where heaven bends down to earth, and where man on earth is made to sit in heavenly places in Christ. Here we are concerned with two places, as it were: the heavenly place of Christ and the spatial place of the Church. The place of the Church is to be defined with regard to that heavenly place of real presence of Christ on the one hand, and with regard to its participation in the spatial context of the physical world on the other. The Church's life, worship, fellowship, and ministry are all ordered in regard to that twofold place, heavenly and earthly place. No adequate understanding of the order of the Church can neglect that twofold involvement in space enshrined so clearly in the Sacrament. Order will concern the indicating or defining of the place on earth where the heavenly place of Christ makes contact with it, but that earthly place cannot be so delimited and defined as thereby to define and delimit also the heavenly place of Christ. Christ the risen and ascended Lord is in a place that is beyond definition and delimitation. It is through the Sovereign Spirit that He graciously condescends to be really present in the appointed space of the Church and to make that His place on earth. But He does not thereby bind Himself to that place on earth; rather does He bind us through that place to His own real Presence, to His heavenly place, and so from that appointed place on earth He exalts us to sit with Him in heavenly places. All this means that the Church's *order* in space is concerned with the ordering of its physical fellowship and worship in the Spirit. Order serves the proclamation of the Word and the Eucharistic fellowship on earth, but orders it in such a way that it makes room in it all, makes a place in it all, for the Sovereign presence of the Spirit, for the heavenly place of Christ—that is, for His real presence. The Christian Church as the Body of Christ on earth knows nothing of a spaceless ordering of its life.

(2) *Order in regard to Time*

Because the Church is the Body of Christ, it has a temporal and eternal life in which the temporal and the eternal are not to be separated, although they may be distinguished, from one another. The Church as the Body of Christ in history therefore has time as an essential ingredient of its reality. It has its time in this world, the time which it has been given by Christ, and into which He has sent it. It is in the time-form of this world, in historical existence that its life is to be ordered—to be ordered as Christ's Body in time. Now Jesus Christ in His historical life is the area in the time of this creaturely world where God and man, eternity and time, meet and have communion with each other. Israel through its history was the area within world-history into which God intervened with His redeeming purpose, in order to work into our time and from within our time toward that area in the fullness of time when God would become man and gather man into the life of God, when the Eternal would come into the passage of time, and gather time into union with the eternal. In Israel God bound our time into Covenant-relation with Himself, but all that is completely fulfilled in Jesus Christ where time is not only the sphere of the eternal event, but time is sanctified, redeemed, reconciled, and given new reality in union with Eternity, once and for all.

In Jesus Christ, therefore, the Eternal Son of God has lived His life within our time; He became time, and has in Himself elevated time into abiding communion with the eternal God. In Jesus Christ God has recreated time, redeemed it from its vanity, from its guilt and irreversibility, its decay and corruption, and given it a new reality in the new Humanity of the incarnate Son. But Jesus Christ has ascended and He is in heaven, in Eternity—that is, He has an eternal time far beyond anything that we can understand, or can measure by the kind of time we have in this passing age. It is not a timeless time, or a timeless eternity, but eternal time in which our time, redeemed new time, is eternally real in union with Eternity itself. That is the new time of the Kingdom manifested in the forty days of the risen Jesus Christ upon the earth, and within the lapses of our temporal history; but now that Jesus Christ has ascended, He has withdrawn that new time of His New Humanity from sight, from the visible succession of passing time on the plane of history.

And yet Jesus Christ bestows Himself upon us in time, and in such a way that our faith and worship are not timeless, any more than they are spaceless. It is within our passing time that He has time for us, that He makes time for us, makes time for communion, for faith, for worship, for growth, for development, for advance. It is in the Church in history that Christ has time for us, for by the very act of His ascension He waits for us and makes time for us, in which we can hear the Gospel, time in which we can repent, time for decision and faith, time in which we can preach the Gospel to all nations.

This was a frequent element in the teaching of the historical Jesus, in His parables of the householder or the king who went into the far country and waited till the right time to return, but in that period of waiting he gave his servants time, and then returned to call them to account for the time he had given them—the word sometimes used to describe that is *chronizein*, but it has also associated with it the word *chorein*, to make room, that is room for freedom to believe, freedom to decide, and freedom to be obedient (within time) until the return of the householder or king. It is in that light that we are to understand Christ's ascension, and the fact that by the very act of ascension, and His heavenly waiting until the right time for Him to return, Jesus Christ establishes the Church in history with temporal form within the passage of time where it has time to work, and time to obey Him. It is in that time that the Church has time to exist and carry out its mission, within the succession of history where there is time between revelation and decision, time between decision and act, time between present and future, time for the Gospel. Thus the existence of the Church as bound up with its mission is inseparable from time. The Church as the Body of Christ in history is the area within the time-form of this world where God and man meet in the Gospel, and where man is reconciled to God and united to Him in Jesus Christ.

But it is *IN Jesus Christ* that God gives the Church that time, and that place in time—and that means in the historical Jesus, and in the risen and ascended Jesus. Just as Jesus Christ is the place where heaven and earth meet, and God and man are reconciled, and the only place where that takes place, so Jesus Christ is the one place within time and the only place within time where God has provided time for the reconciliation of man, and man finds time for forgiveness and redemption. Jesus Christ is Himself the fullness of time. Therefore the order of the

Church in time means the ordering of the Church's life and mission in relation to the time of Jesus Christ, the historical Christ, and the risen and ascended Christ. In all Church order we are concerned with *the time of Jesus on earth* when God's Son condescended to enter within our fallen time in order to redeem it, but also with *the time of Jesus ascended into Eternity* who yet bestows Himself upon us in time through His Spirit. The time of the Church will therefore be defined by the relation of the Church in history to the historical Jesus Christ, and to the ascended and advent Jesus Christ; the Church's life, worship, fellowship, and ministry are all ordered with regard to that twofold time, heavenly and earthly, historical and eternal time. No adequate understanding of the order of the Church can overlook that twofold involvement in time.

Look at it like this. On the one hand, Christ by His ascension has withdrawn Himself from the visible passage of time on the plane of this earth in order to send us back to the one time in all history where in the fullness of time the Son of God became incarnate—that is the time of the whole historical life of Jesus, culminating in the "hour" of His death and breaking out into the new time of the resurrection. The Church is for ever bound to the historical Jesus, for the Truth and the Life of God have become historical fact in Jesus and are now historically communicated and transmitted. The Church exists in that history stemming from the historical Jesus, and lives by the Word historically communicated through the apostles. Therefore all the life and ministry of the Church has to be ordered in time, according to the nature of that divine event in time, the time of the historical Jesus. By withdrawing Himself from the visible succession of history, and by refusing to abrogate our existence in time by sheer immediacy, Jesus Christ gives us time, enables us to take time with the historical Jesus and the historical Word communicated by and from Jesus. Thus, far from abrogating our existence in the on-going time of this world, by His ascension Jesus Christ sends us into the time of this empirical world, and commands us within it to focus our attention on the time of the historical Jesus, to be bound by it, and to be obedient to it; for it is by that time and through it that Jesus continues to rule the Church and order it according to His Word in actual history. Hence throughout all its life on earth, throughout all its continuity in history, the Church lives its life in historical attachment to the fullness of time in Jesus, and in historical continuity with it. It is out of that one time in Jesus that the Church lives from age to age, and from it that the Church derives its own time in history. It cannot in any circumstances detach itself from the historical Jesus, or depreciate its historical attachment to Him in the fullness of time, for it is precisely by its being bound and obedient to the historical Jesus Christ in the tradition of the apostolic Church that Christ continues to rule over the Church by His Word and Spirit, making it His own Body and Servant in history.

Church order is therefore the ordering of the Church's life in history in relation to that one time in all history, the time of Jesus; for that is the only place in time where eternity and time have really met, and where they are for ever joined, and it is in and through that union of eternity and time in Jesus that the Church lives its life on the plane of history. On the other hand it is in that time of the historical Jesus that the Church, from age to age, still meets with the eternal God and is gathered up "into" eternal time. It is only within the time of the historical Jesus that the new time of the risen Jesus breaks in upon the Church in history, and gives it to share and abide in the new time of the new creation. It is in the historical Jesus that the new time overlaps with the old time in our history, and only there, so that it is as the Church lives there in that overlap of the two times, that it is given to share in new time above and beyond the time of this passing age on the mere plane of earthly history. The Church continues to live within the time of this on-going world, but it finds its life above and beyond it in the risen and ascended Lord, not in some timeless eternity, but in One who has Himself descended into our time, redeemed it and gathered it up in Himself into union with Eternity. The Church is therefore bound to the succession of time by relation to the historical Jesus, but it is precisely in the historical Jesus that it knows its true life to be hid with Christ in God, and to be found beyond the passing and successive forms of this age. This does not mean the abrogation of the Church's historical existence, but it does mean that the historical existence of the Church, its continuity within the succession of time on earth, is determined by relation to the new time of the risen Lord. Hence the Church within the succession of time on earth is given a new orientation within the limitations of time; so that instead of being fettered by the bonds of time, bound by the sheer irreversibility of time that is laden with guilt, instead of being determined by the temporal processes of this world, the Church within time has freedom to meet with eternity, to rise above its past and to live a new life from age to age in Christ.

It may help us to understand that by thinking a little naïvely of the "two times" of the Church, as *horizontal time* on the plane of history in which it is bound to, and ordered in relation to, the time of the historical Jesus, and as *vertical time* in the Spirit in which the Church shares with Christ the time of His new Humanity. If the Church had only horizontal time, then the Church would only be a construct of historical succession, having only its temporal origin in Jesus but actually being fettered and determined by its place within the temporal process. Then the Church would not be free to have real meeting with the risen Lord; it would be enslaved to history, enslaved to its own past and all the errors and sins of its past; it would not be free from all the limitations and determinisms of history. But the Church within history is the Church of Jesus Christ in whom the Eternal has broken into our sin-determined and guilt-fettered time, and brought freedom and redemption from bondage. Jesus Christ is the area in our fallen time where the Eternal has broken through the limitations of this passing age to which we are in bondage, and where God acts freely upon men through His Word and Spirit, confronting them with His own Person and enabling them to respond freely in spite of all the downward drag of sin, in spite of all the piled-up determinisms of our guilty past, in spite of our bondage in the time of this world. The Church is therefore the place within time where that free meeting with the Eternal is possible, where within time men are delivered from the tyrant forces of bondage and are made free for God, so that real meeting in faith and love is not only possible but actual.

In the light of all that, then, the order of the Church's ministry in time is to be regarded as the ordering of its life within the on-going time of history and its succession which makes time for meeting with the risen and ascended Lord. It is an ordering of the historical and temporal life of the Church that binds it to that one place in history and time in the historical Jesus, but because in Jesus the Eternal breaks into our history and time giving us, through the Spirit, freedom to meet with the living God within time and history, it is also an ordering that will not allow the life of the Church to be tied down to the temporal framework of mere succession on the stage of this world. The ordering of the Church's life and ministry in time means giving it such a new orientation within on-going time and all its limitations, that the time-forms of the Church's historical existence become the signs of the new divine order that already breaks in upon the Church in history. Thus for example the historical succession in the ordering of the ministry, far from involving the Church in bondage to the past, attests the binding of the Church to the historical Jesus and so becomes the sign of the new ordering of the Church's life in Jesus Christ. Historical succession does not secure or guarantee the binding of the Church in Christ, for He, the risen and ascended Lord, is not bound by the forms of fallen time; for by His resurrection He has triumphed over them. Historical succession, however, binds the Church to that one time within our fallen history where the risen and ascended Lord keeps tryst with us as the Lord of all time and history, and where alone we may freely meet Him. It attests the fact that, through relation to the historical Jesus, Christ binds us to Himself on the ground of the historical incarnation, atonement and resurrection, and declares that we cannot find any life or salvation in detachment from the historical Jesus.

All this is wonderfully enshrined in the Lord's Supper. "This do in remembrance of Me. As often as ye do this, ye do proclaim the Lord's death till He come." In the Supper the Church's life and ministry is so ordered that it is bound to the historical Jesus, to His death on the Cross, but at that very point in time the Church is given to have communion with the risen and ascended Lord and to share in His New Humanity, and from the Supper it is sent out to proclaim that until He comes again. Thus the ordering of the Church's life and ministry should follow the pattern enshrined in the Lord's Supper. "For I have received that which I also delivered unto you. . . ." It is celebrated in that succession or tradition, and it is ordered within that continuity, but within that continuity it is the risen Christ, the Lord of the Supper, who comes through closed doors, through all the limitations of our fallen time and sinful history, and gives us to eat and drink with Him in the new time of the Kingdom of God. While the Supper is to be ordered therefore within the historical continuity of the Church, it is such an ordering that room is left within it for the new time of the Kingdom, and in the presence of that new time all the historical time-forms of the Church are relativized and given new orientation—they are taken under the command of the risen and ascended Lord, are made obedient to His real presence, so that instead of being mere limitations to the Church's life and ministry they are the signs pointing beyond to the reality of the new time of the new creation. In so doing they are themselves transcended, and made subordinate to communion with Christ in the time of His New Humanity.

(3) *Order in regard to Space and Time*

Space and time cannot be separated in the Church. The Church on earth and in history is inescapably involved in space and time and in all the machinery of physical existence, for it is sent out to minister the Gospel in space and time. It is in that involvement with space and time that lies the significance of its order. The Church's very bodily and historical existence and mission require spatial and temporal order if it is to perform its divine purpose in space and time, but it can only live its life and fulfil its work in space and time, if its place on earth is ordered in obedience to its share in Christ's heavenly place, and if its time on earth is made obedient to its share in Christ's heavenly time. Church order concerns the ordering of the Church's life and ministry in the meeting of heaven and earth in the place of the Church, and in the intersection of historical continuity and immediate unity with the risen and ascended Christ. The place that the Church has in the space-time form of this world is not abrogated, but in that place the Church is given to share in the real presence of the New Man and real time of the New Creation. Until Christ comes again to change the space-time form of this fallen world (not to eliminate it but to change and renew it) the Church shares in the real presence of the New Man and the real time of the New Creation, under the form of space and time as we know it in this on-going world, as under a veil, as in a mystery. The actual space of the Church, its physical place in this world, has to be regarded as the trysting place of Christ on earth; and the time of the Church, its historical actuality, has to be regarded as the time appointed by Christ for meeting with Him. This space and this time have to be used therefore in obedience to His appointment, in subordination to the space and the time of the historical Jesus, that is, the actual founding of the Church upon the rock of the apostles, and to the actual tradition of the historical Jesus which we have received from the apostles, for it is in that obedience within the space-time form of the Church on earth to the historical Jesus that the Church goes into history as His servant, the obedient Body of which He is the Head. Only as that Body is it His Church. Therefore the ordering of the Church in space and time is concerned with its obedience to Christ, to the risen Lord in the space and time of the historical Jesus alone. Then it is, however, that through the Spirit Christ keeps tryst with His Church in history and bestows upon it His real presence, so that the time and place of the Church become Christ's own time and place among men. Then it is that the Church lives and works as the earthly and historical form of Christ's Body (as Karl Barth has called it), obedient to Him, its risen Head and Lord, and as such it is the instrument He is pleased to use to proclaim His Word to all nations and to manifest Himself to all who believe.

In all this the Church looks upon itself as covenanted with Christ, and as gathered into union and communion with Him as His covenant-partner. Just as its historical succession in time and space does not secure or guarantee its unity with Christ, but only serves to attest its binding to Him in the time and space of the historical Jesus, so the Church's obedience to the time and space of its foundation in the apostles and to the apostolic tradition does not secure or guarantee that it is the Body of Christ. Throughout all its succession in the relativities and contingencies of our sinful history, throughout all its life of faith and obedience, in which the Church cannot but acknowledge its unfaithfulness and disobedience, the Church relies upon the New Covenant which Christ has made with it in His Body and Blood. It is only in that Covenant undergirding all its historical relativity and all its unfaithfulness that the Church's security rests. In obedience the Church relies not upon its own obedience but upon the obedience of Christ, and acknowledges that it is given a ground of faith and reliance beyond all the changes and chances of this passing world and all its own unworthiness. The Church can never justify itself, therefore, by claiming historical succession or doctrinal faithfulness, by reference to its own place and time on earth and in history, but must cast itself upon the justification of Christ's grace alone, and rely upon His covenant-mercies who promised that the gates of hell would not prevail against His Church, and that He would be in its midst until the end of the world. The ordering of the Church can never be allowed to assume a role of independence and authority, as if the duly ordered Church, even in its obedience to Christ, could be anything more than an unprofitable servant. Order must always be maintained in ever renewed amazement at the grace of God, and in ever renewed thankfulness for His undeserved grace and justification.

To sum up. The Church is ordered in its life and ministry on earth:

(a) By being obedient to the historical Jesus Christ in space and time in the tradition of the apostolic Church, in which He, the risen and ascended Christ, comes to rule and order the Church by His Word and Spirit, making it His Body and Servant in history;

(b) By sharing in the obedience of Jesus Christ in space and time through the communion of the Spirit in which He, the New Man, gives it to share in His New humanity as He, the Lord, undergirds it in all its frailty and weakness by His New Covenant, so that already it is given to abide in the life and time and order of the New Creation;

(c) By looking beyond the historical and institutional forms of its ordering in space and time to the fullness of its life in Christ, who comes to meet it in mercy and judgment, and who at His Parousia will unveil the full reality of the Church in the glory of the Son of Man.

In this threefold way the Church looks upon its ordering in the space and time of this on-going world as the required form of its obedience to Christ, or the attestation of its reliance upon the new Covenant founded for ever in the historical Jesus, as the sign that points to the new divine order of the Church's life communicated to it even now through Word and Sacrament in the Spirit, and as the provisional form given to it, until the redemption of the body, of the order of the new creation which will be revealed only at the final advent of Christ.

(b) *Consecration and Ordination*[1]

In order to understand the New Testament teaching about consecration and ordination we have to examine the rites and language of the Old Testament tradition. The rites were not carried over as such into the Christian Church, for they were fulfilled in Christ and abrogated; but the New Testament does use the language of the rites to speak both of Christ and His Church, and it does adapt some of the Old Testament rites for its own use, but with entire freedom and with quite new significance. The basic line we have to consider is the consecration of the priest, and king, and prophet in the Old Testament, and see how they are fulfilled in Christ, and then see how *in this Christ* the New Testament thinks of the ministry as consecrated and ordained.

The Consecration and Ordination of the Priest

The main passages that concern us are Exod. 28 and 29; Lev. 6, 7, 8, 9; and Num. 8. It is worth remembering right away that the Leviticus passages fell in the Jewish Lectionary for the Passover week, and are clearly reflected in the Gospels, especially in John 13–17.

To get the proper perspective we have to remember that Israel was consecrated in the Covenant to be a holy people, a kingdom of priests to God (Exod. 19: 6; Lev. 20: 26; Deut. 7: 6 f.; 14: 21; 26: 19; 28: 9; cf. Is. 62: 12). As such, too, Israel was God's "first-born son"; that is, it occupied among the human family the part of "the head of the house" (the *ben-bayith*, the householder or steward of God's holy purposes, reflected in several of Jesus' parables). Within Israel it would appear that the primitive priests were the first-born sons, the heads of the house which is preserved in the Passover rite where the ceremony is conducted by the head of the house. But the first-born

[1] Prepared for the use of the *Aids to Devotion Committee* of the Church of Scotland, November, 1957, and reprinted from *S.J.T.*, vol. 11/3, 1958, pp. 225 ff.

were "redeemed back" for life among the people and their place was taken by the tribe of Levi (Num. 3: 12 f., etc.). Thus within Israel as a priestly nation, one tribe is set aside for priestly functions instead of the first-born, and within the tribe of Levi the "sons of Aaron" are set apart for special functions as liturgical priests. The Old Testament priesthood has thus an interim institutional character, and its importance lies in its functions and in obedience to the divine ordinances. It was the business of the Levites and priests to teach the Law to Israel, and so they lived scattered through the twelve Tribes. The sons of Aaron came to be divided into twenty-four courses, twelve functioning in the Temple and twelve in Israel, although all twenty-four came up to Jerusalem for the great festivals.

How then were *the priests* consecrated and ordained? This is very fully described. The whole congregation (*ekklesia*) assembled at the door of the Tabernacle where they were addressed by Moses and told they were about to act in accordance with God's ordinance. Then he "brought forward" or "brought near" or "presented" Aaron and his sons. They were solemnly washed at the Laver, and clothed with priestly garments. Aaron was anointed with oil by pouring, but his sons were only sprinkled with his anointing oil. Aaron only was called "the anointed", the *christos*. Then there followed sacrifices, the most significant of which was the "consecration offering" or "fill-offering". Some of this along with unleavened bread was offered for the consecration of Aaron and his sons, some of it was broken up into portions, and portions of flesh and bread were put into the hands of Aaron and his sons who offered them as "peace-offerings". Then Aaron and his sons repaired to the door of the Tabernacle and in the presence of the congregation partook of a sacred meal of what remained of the flesh of the fill-offering and bread of the consecration offering—that was called "a sacrifice of praise and thanksgiving". This was repeated for seven days, during which they stayed within the Tabernacle.

It is to be noted that in this rite the chief and proper subject is Aaron the high priest, although his sons are consecrated through association with him, and have their hands filled too and share with him in the sacred meal of consecration. But Aaron alone is the *christos*. (In an extended sense of cause all Israel is spoken of as *messiah* = anointed, Ps. 84: 9; Hab. 3: 13; Ps. 89: 38, 51.)

That act takes place only once and does not need to be repeated. The *Minhah* that Aaron offers avails for himself and the sons of his house. On his death, his eldest son was clothed with his high-priestly garments and was consecrated with his priests in the same way—but the anointing was apparently not repeated, except to recover a break in the priestly line (2 Chron. 13: 9). It has also to be noted that although the priests were consecrated only once, every time they went in and out of the Tabernacle or Temple they renewed their consecration through washing their hands and feet, while the high priest renewed his consecration through solemn and total baptismal ablution once a year in preparation for the renewal of the Covenant on the Day of Atonement. It should also be noted that the consecration of Aaron and the sons of his house to the priesthood was called "*the covenant of salt*".

What about *the Levites*? In Num. 8 we are told that all the Levites were cleansed and "separated" within Israel, cleansed by the sprinkling of the water of expiation (used at circumcision and in cleansing the leper to restore him to membership in the priestly race) and then they were "presented" to God with the same offerings as Aaron and his sons; but in addition all the Levites *had hands laid on them* by the Children of Israel (doubtless acting through their elders) gathered at the door of the Tabernacle, who offered them up to their holy use as their representatives. Then Aaron took the Levites and offered them before the Lord as an oblation on behalf of the people that they might do the service of the Lord. Here the laying on of hands indicates the representative part played by the Levites, but as such they are offered unto God. Thus in their case ordination is twofold: laying on of hands and commissioning by the whole priestly people, and offering to God as consecration for His service.

What about *Moses* in all this? As Augustine pointed out long ago, Moses stands above all this without any ceremonial consecration. It is he who offers the sacrifices for Aaron and his sons, offers them to the Lord, and consecrates them. He himself had no other consecration than that of his supreme relation to the Word of God alone. Moses did not therefore pass on a consecration he had himself received; he acted only as "the servant of the Lord", and the entire validity of the consecration of the priesthood depended on God's command and grace alone—not on any "priestly grace". The priesthood is represented as God's "gift" (Num. 18: 7) and rests on its "givenness". Hence the Hebrew word to give, *nathan*, is frequently employed for ordaining to the priesthood; it is an appointment of grace.

The Language of Consecration and Ordination in the Old Testament

The general term used for consecration and/or ordination in the Septuagint is *hagiazo*, meaning "sanctify" or make holy. The emphasis here is always upon the fundamental fact that God will be sanctified or hallowed in the midst of His people (Exod. 31: 13; Lev. 20: 8—cf. also the incident of Nadab and Abihu in Lev. 10: 1, 2, etc.). All consecration or hallowing is a sharing in God's hallowing of Himself in the midst of His people, and has its significance only within the Covenant in which He is Holy and requires His people to be holy too.

Three distinctive terms are used, however, to describe this sanctification or consecration of the priest in holy things:

(a) To clothe with priestly garments—"to put on" (including baptismal ablution, etc.);
(b) To anoint with holy oil (the preparation of which was a secret) given along with sprinkling of blood;
(c) "to fill the hands", which was accompanied by a special sacrifice of consecration.

Of these three it is the third that is the distinctive term for consecration or ordination—the priest has his hands filled: *mille' yadh* (מִלֵּא יָד Exod. 28: 41; 29: 29; 35: 35; Lev. 8: 33; 16: 32; 21: 10; Num. 3: 3; Judges 17: 5,12; 1 Kings 13:33; 2 Chron. 13: 9; cf. 2 Chron. 29: 31; Is. 43: 26). The offering of consecration was called "filling" (*millu'im*).

What "filling the hands" means exactly is not clear. Generally it means that the priest has the priesthood committed to him; he receives it as a gift. Specifically it means that the act of consecration is brought to its fulfilment or completion when his hands are filled with the holy oblations. It can also be applied in an extended sense to the consecration of the altar through having the oblations laid on it. Its meaning is thus twofold, which comes out very well in the Greek of the LXX in its twofold translation of *mille' yadh*:

(a) *pleroun tas cheiras* (πληροῦν τὰς χεῖρας). Cf. Lev. 7: 29; Exod. 32: 29.
(b) *teleioun tas cheiras* (τελειοῦν τὰς χεῖρας) or simply *teleioun* as applied to the priest as object or in the passive with the priest as subject. It is almost equivalent to *hagiazein*. Cf. Exod. 28: 41; 29: 33.

These words are used, then, to describe the act of the consecration of the high priest in whose self-consecration the sons of his house are also consecrated; that consecration is brought to its completion in the filling of the hands with the oblations and in the sacrificial meal of flesh and bread, "the sacrifice of praise and thanksgiving".

The Language of Consecration in the New Testament

Although in the Old Testament "to fill the hands" was the more technical term, it does not make very good Greek when translated literally. It is natural therefore that in the Greek the word *teleioun* should be preferred to *pleroun tas cheiras*. The latter expression is, perhaps, to be detected lying behind John 3:35, which has reference to Christ's baptismal consecration in the Jordan and His anointing of the Spirit. If so, the underlying Aramaic has been turned into smooth Greek, and the "filling of the hands" is not very recognizable except to one familiar with the Old Testament rite. Along with this should be compared John 17: 2–4; cf. also John 4: 34; 5: 36. Possibly the Pauline *pleroma* hints of this too sometimes, cf. Eph. 1: 23 ff.; 3: 19.

It is, however, the word *teleioun* that is prominent in the New Testament especially in the Fourth Gospel and in the Epistle to the Hebrews. The verb *teleioun* is of course often used in the New Testament with no relation to the conception of priestly consecration, but when it is found in John 17, Christ's high-priestly prayer, which clearly reflects the reading of Lev. 7–8, we must see it in a different light. The evangelist also uses the other word *hagiazein*, e.g. 17: 17–19: "Sanctify them in the truth. Thy Word is truth. As thou hast sent me into the world, even so have I sent them into the world, and for their sakes I sanctify myself, that they also might be sanctified through the truth." Then in verse 23 Jesus prays that the disciples might be consecrated in one (*teteleiomenoi eis hen*).

When we turn to the Epistle to the Hebrews there are several instances of *teleioun* which refer to the consecration of the high priest, while the word *hagiazein* is used in a sense parallel to the usage, both in the Old Testament and in John 17. Thus Heb. 2: 11: "For both he who sanctifies (or consecrates) and those who are sanctified are all of one, for which cause he is not ashamed to call them brethren." In Heb. 7: 28 and 9: 9 the other word, *teleioun*, is used of the consecration of Christ the High Priest. In the tenth chapter the writer uses both terms, *hagiazein* and *teleioun*, to describe the fact that through Christ's own self-offering once and for all we are consecrated. By consecration the author of this epistle meant what Paul meant by justification through the blood of Christ and sanctification through His Spirit. It is Christ's own consecration of Himself on our behalf which both justifies us and sanctifies us as His holy servants, giving us to share in His consecration in such a way that through Jesus Christ our High Priest we all, with our bodies washed with clean water and with our consciences sprinkled with His blood, draw near to worship God, that is as priests in the House of God. It is interesting also to note that in this Epistle the institutional priesthood of Aaron is set aside because fulfilled and abrogated in Christ, and that He is High Priest as God's First-Born Son, and therefore we are all first-born sons in Him, while the Church is the Church of the first-born. That is to say, here where the institutional priesthood is done away all God's children are priests after the fashion of the first-born in Israel. Just as we are given to share in Christ's Sonship, so we are given to share in His Priesthood. In Christ sonship and priesthood are the same.

The Consecration of the King

The classical passage about this is found in 2 Kings 11: 12, 17 which describes the consecration of the king by Jehoiada, and which reposes upon Deuteronomy 17: 18–20. It is also based on the rites formed under King David and carried out with regard to Solomon (1 Kings 1: 33 ff.; 1 Chron. 29: 22 f.; cf. 2 Chron. 6: 42). The main elements here are as follows:

(a) Anointing, possibly along with washing in the Gihon. David and Saul were the first to be anointed, and the anointing was accompanied by the gift of the Spirit (1 Sam. 10: 1; 16: 13;

cf. 1 Sam. 26: 11; Ps. 2: 2 (Acts 4: 26)). David himself was anointed three times. (Cf. 2 Sam. 2: 4; 5: 3. This was regarded in the Old Testament as indicative of the Messiah; cf. Ps. 45: 7 and Hab. 3: 13.)

(b) The kings were enthroned and crowned—the royal insignia of David were apparently used in later times.

(c) The putting of the "Testimony" into the hands of the king. According to Deuteronomy the king had to copy out the book of the Law with his own hand, so as to remember it and rule by it.

(d) A covenant was made between the king, God and the people. In the case of God's covenant with David it was known as "a covenant of salt", like the covenant made by God with the house of Aaron. In the case of Solomon's consecration we know that there was also prayer and sacrifice—see 1 Chron. 29: 22 f.

Here, then, in the consecration of the king the fundamental pattern of consecration was similar to that of the consecration of the priest, involving: anointing, filling of the hands, and affirmation of the covenant relation. The difference lies chiefly in that to which the king is consecrated, kingship, not sacrifice, and that the king's hands are filled therefore not with oblations but with the Law. He is crowned and enthroned, which does not apply to the priests.

The Consecration of the Prophet

We have even less information about this, but a clear instance of the consecration of Elisha by Elijah is given in 1 Kings 19: 16. It was by anointing followed later by investment with the prophet's mantle. In Ps. 105: 15 "the anointed" and the prophets are synonymous. The anointing of both Saul and David gave them prophetic gifts, and presumably that meant that the anointing of kings was an extension of the anointing of prophets through whose Word proclaimed and enunciated God ruled as King.

In Is. 61: 1 the Servant of the Lord speaks of himself as anointed to preach the Gospel, which Christ claimed to be fulfilled in Himself, Luke 4: 18; John 10: 36.

In addition to this Old Testament tradition, it should be noted that in the Judaean Scrolls the Anointed of the Lord, the Messiah, is regarded apparently as deriving both from the

House of David and from the House of Aaron—the anointed priest-king. The members of the community initiated into the new covenant are spoken of as "anointed ones" and as forming a holy and "priestly" messianic community. That may have some influence on the New Testament, e.g. on 1 Peter.

Summary of the New Testament Teaching

Jesus Christ is the fulfilment of the threefold consecration to the office of priest, king, and prophet in the Old Testament. We have seen something of the fulfilment of priestly consecration in Christ, but kingly and prophetic consecration was also fulfilled in Him (Luke 4: 18; Acts 4: 26; 10: 38; Heb. 1: 9). This was all fulfilled in His anointing by the Spirit, which no doubt referred to His birth of the Spirit as well as to His anointing at His Baptism in the Jordan; it was as the Anointed Son of the Father that He gathered up and fulfilled the threefold anointing of Prophet, Priest, and King. The Church which He has made His own was anointed with Christ's Spirit at Pentecost by the Baptism of the Spirit, so that through Baptism all who come to Christ are not only given the right to be sons of God but are anointed with His anointing, receive the *chrism* of the Spirit (1 John 2: 20, 27; 2 Cor. 1: 21), or are given the *seal* of the Spirit, as St. Paul puts it.

Here, then, in Christ the First-Born Son of God and our High Priest, we are restored to the priestly Kingdom, for He has washed us from our sins in His own blood and made us kings and priests unto God. Every one who is a Son of God through Christ the Son belongs to this royal priesthood, and shares in Christ's self-consecration on our behalf. Christ alone is the *Christos*, the Anointed and Consecrated One (John 10: 36), but we who follow Him in Baptism are given to share in it, putting off the old impurity and putting on Christ as our priestly garment, clothed with His righteousness, His consecration, and His holiness. Here there is no institutional priesthood like that of the Aaronic priesthood. That was an imperfect interim-measure only, necessarily done away when the true priesthood of sonship, the priesthood of the first-born, was restored in Christ. Here priesthood and sonship are the same, but when this is so, it is Baptism, through which we are consecrated as sons of God, which is our consecration to priesthood in Christ.

Consecration and Ordination of the Ministry in the New Testament

When we turn to the consecration and ordination of a special ministry as Christ's gift to His Church we find that this has its place only within the consecration of the whole membership of Christ's Body, and therefore within the ministry of the whole Body, which it has through sharing in Christ's vicarious Self-consecration. But within that there is something else. There are in fact two things: (1) The special consecration of the apostles in Christ's Self-consecration; and (2) The apostolic ordination of others through the laying on of hands and prayer.

(1) *The special consecration of the apostles in Christ.* The accounts of Christ's appointment of the apostles, His "making" of them, of His drawing them into a very private and close relation to Himself and to His teaching and His passion, and above all His special purpose for them in the Last Supper, as reflected in the Fourth Gospel as well as the Synoptics, are of special importance.

Although the Lord's Supper belongs to the whole Church, its first enactment belonged peculiarly to the apostles, who were at that point given a special place in the New Covenant and in the Kingdom of Christ, appointed to sit upon twelve thrones judging the twelve tribes of Israel, as the patriarchs of the New Israel, the Foundation of the Church. Jesus' solemn washing of their feet and His deliberate actions at the Supper clearly designed for the disciples peculiarly, and His high-priestly prayer of consecration in which He prayed above all for the disciples, make it clear that He regarded Himself, in going forth to the Cross, as the High Priest in whose Self-oblation and Self-consecration He was giving the disciples to share in a most intimate way as "the sons of His house". His Self-consecration as the *Christos*, His action as the High Priest on the Great Day of Atonement, was fulfilled once and for all, and can never be repeated. Just as when Aaron acted all Israel acted in him and through him, for he acted for all Israel, but at the same time the sons of his house had a special place in it, being sprinkled with the blood of sacrifice and with the oil of anointing, so when Christ went forth to the Cross all His people were given to share in it, for He acted on their behalf and in their stead; and yet in a special way the Twelve were given to be related to it. They alone went forth to the events of His passion after having shared with Him the consecration meal of the bread and wine of the Last Supper, and they alone, as it were, were sprinkled with His blood in Gethsemane where they were taken to watch and pray with Him in His awful agony; and they alone when He returned from His sacrifice had breathed upon them His Spirit in the Upper Room and so were anointed with His anointing. As such the apostles belonged to the once-and-for-all events of the Founding of the New Covenant in the Body and Blood of Christ; they remain for ever the authoritative witnesses of the New Covenant, the Pillars of the Church, in whom and through whom Jesus Christ made an everlasting Covenant of Salt with His Church making it a royal priesthood in Himself.

The apostle-disciples were appointed to their ministry like Moses directly through the Word, and were given to sit, as it were, in Moses' seat, or rather in Christ's seat, inasmuch as they mediated His Word to the Church and in Christ's Name were appointed to rule and order His Church; but, like the sons of Aaron, the apostles shared peculiarly in the Self-consecration and anointing of their High Priest. All that is something that cannot be repeated, and therefore cannot be extended. The apostleship can have no successors, for the apostles remain under Christ as the permanent authorities over the Church, the foundation upon which all other ministry within the Church depends. And so they were sent out by Christ with His Commission to engage in the mission of reconciliation. It was in the fulfilment of that commission and mission that they came to ordain others to the ministry, giving the sign of the laying on of hands to attest that they were sent to fulfil their ministry within the one Commission of Christ given to His apostles, and within the once and for all Consecration of His Church upon the foundation of the apostles. But in taking an entirely different method of ordination from that which they had received the apostles showed unmistakably that they were in no sense extending their office to others, but ordaining a ministry in dependence upon their unique ministry in Christ.

(2) *The apostolic ordination of others through the laying on of hands and prayer*[1] (Acts 6: 6; 13: 3; 1 Tim. 4: 14; 5: 22; 2 Tim. 1: 6;

[1] In this section I am indebted to the discussion of A. Ehrhardt, *The Apostolic Ministry*, *S.J.T. Occasional Paper* no. 7, ch. II.

cf. Acts 14: 23; 2 Cor. 8: 19). The laying on of hands is the only ceremony that is taken over from the Old Testament by the New Testament Church for the consecration and ordination of its ministry. The consecration of the Church and of its ministry in the apostles had of course already taken place, and taken place once for all, so that whenever in the history of the Church there is an ordination to the ministry that ordination is grounded upon the once and for all consecration of the Church and its apostolic ministry in Christ; it shares in it, takes place only within it, and is the means whereby that consecration is through prayer related directly and particularly to those set apart for the ministry within the sphere of the apostolic commission and mission.

It does not appear that the early Church took over the rite of laying on of hands from Judaism so much as from the Old Testament. The elders in the Sanhedrin were instituted apparently only by enthronement in Moses' seat, but later on ordination by laying on of hands took the place of this. This rite may have had earlier usage in Judaism which influenced the New Testament Church, but the evidence on the whole suggests that the apostles went back directly to the Old Testament itself for their guidance.

In a recent work (*The New Testament and Rabbinic Judaism*, p. 224 f.) Professor Daube has pointed out that three different words are used in the Old Testament for a rite of blessing or ordination with hands. (1) *Nasa* to describe the priestly blessing when hands are lifted up, e.g. in the Aaronic benediction. This was an act of prayer and blessing in which the Name of God was put upon the people—the act used by Jesus in blessing His disciples at His ascension. (2) *Sim* or *shith* which describes the act of placing hands upon someone for blessing, as in the patriarchal blessing of Joseph's sons by Jacob. It was possibly this act that was used by Jesus in healing, and perhaps by the early Church at Baptism. (3) *Samakh* which describes the solemn act of laying (literally "leaning") on of hands as applied to sacrifices when sins are symbolically transferred to a victim, or used where the transference of guilt or association in responsibility is indicated, e.g. in stoning a blasphemer or in instituting someone to responsible office. (I cannot agree with Professor Daube's psychological interpretation of *Samakh* as "the pouring of personality" from one person to another.) There is no evidence that Jesus ever used this. In Judaism the laying on of hands was not used for the ordaining of "the seven of a city" or local "elders", although their appointment to the local presbytery required the authorization of the Presbytery of the People or the Sanhedrin in Jerusalem. In the second century (and possibly in the first) rabbis were ordained by *samakh*, the solemn laying on of hands, called "the laying on of hands of the elders".

There are two instances of laying on of hands in the Old Testament important for the Christian precedent. (1) The laying on of hands through which the Levites were ordained to their office. This was an act carried out by the people, presumably through their elders, and was a lay-act in which the Levites were inducted into responsible representation of the people, appointed to stand for the first-born of the people in their ministry at the Tabernacle. That act of laying on of hands was completed when they were offered to God by the priests. (2) The other instance is the act of Moses in ordaining Joshua as his successor in the leadership of the people. In doing so Moses was commanded to "put of his honour upon Joshua" (Num. 27: 18, 23; Deut. 34: 9). With this act God bestowed upon Joshua His Spirit to enable him to fulfil his appointed task. Joshua was not of course ordained to take Moses' place either as a priest or as the mediator of the Word of God, but simply in civil and military leadership of the people. He was a lay-governor under the Kingship of God. This was in a different sense an act of *lay ordination*.

Laying On of Hands in the New Testament

The first case of laying on of hands was that of the seven elder-deacons in Acts 6. Here, as we have noted, hands were laid on the seven by the congregation, not by the apostles (except according to Codex Bezae), but they were set before the apostles, to indicate that the apostles had part in the act. It was, however, an act of lay-ordination like that of the Levites in the Old Testament. At the same time the language used in the Old Testament of Joshua's ordination is reflected in Acts, in the choice of seven men in whom there was the Spirit. But again the language also seems to reflect the appointment of the seventy elders in Numbers 11: 16, when, without any laying on of hands,

God put His Spirit upon them to enable them to fulfil their office on appointment to the Presbytery of Israel. The laying on of hands upon the seven elder-deacons in Acts was accompanied by prayer, and these ordained were given the Spirit in fulfilment of their ministry. The fact that the apostles did not lay hands on them suggests that they were not being appointed as their deputies, but only as their assistants (i.e. as Levites!).

The instance of the separation of Paul and Barnabas by the command of the Spirit and their ordination at the hands of a group of prophets and teachers to which they belonged at Antioch seems to be (as Professor Daube suggests) a case of ordination for special embassage, in which they were commissioned to carry out a particular task on behalf of the rest. They were not ordained as "Rabbinic" pupils or disciples, but rather sent out as "apostles" of the community on a limited mission. The language used here, e.g., "separate me Paul and Barnabas", also suggests that used of the Levites in Num. 8: 6 f. It does not seem to refer to ordination in the proper sense. This sort of thing was a common Rabbinic practice in the second century, but may well have been used earlier.

The most important instance of ordination by laying on of hands in the New Testament is that of Timothy, described in two verses, 1 Tim. 4: 14 and 2 Tim. 1: 6, which have to be taken together with the other passages in Timothy and Titus regarding the appointment and ordination of other ministers.

In 1 Timothy 4: 14 we read: "Neglect not the gift that is in thee which was given thee by *prophecy* with the laying on of hands of the presbytery." In 2 Tim. 1: 6, we read: "Stir up the gift of God which is in thee through the laying on of hands." Putting these together, as I think we must, I make the meaning to be as follows: Timothy has been carefully instructed in the faith and trained in the *didaskalia* which he exercises; in that training it was clear that he was called to the ministry, that God had imparted to him a gift for its fulfilment; at the same time that gift is looked on as imparted formally through the act of laying on of hands, authorizing him as an accredited teacher and minister, but used by God as the means of imparting to him a *charisma* for the ministry. The act of laying on of hands has been carried out by Timothy's teacher Paul, and by the presbytery acting together. It is possible, as Professor Daube suggests, that the laying on of hands of the presbytery (*epithesis ton cheiron tou presbyteriou*) is simply a Rabbinic term for "the ordination of elders" (*semikhath zeqenim*, *Bab. San.* 13 b). But it seems more likely that it means that the presbytery as a whole laid on hands, while Paul acted along with them and doubtless presided over them in the act of ordination. The fact that Timothy, who is put in charge of missionary churches by Paul and commanded to appoint elders in them, is not to lay hands suddenly on people, indicates that he would himself be the chief minister in ordaining presbyters in that area under his supervision, but that he should only do it after due and careful training. According to Rabbinic rules a man was not to be ordained to teach until he had reached the age of forty. It may be with that in mind that Paul exhorts Timothy not to let anyone despise his youth, for, young as he is, he is fully authorized by Paul and the presbytery to undertake his ministry.

This instance is of fundamental importance for a number of reasons:

(a) It provides us with a clear case of what even Professor Daube (who sees it, however, as parallel to Rabbinic ordination) calls "apostolic succession". Timothy is not appointed to be an apostle, but he has the full authorization of Paul the Apostle to do the office of a minister, and indeed of a bishop; and as such he is to fulfil the same office in ordaining others as Paul fulfilled in ordaining him.

(b) But this ordination is a corporate act of the presbytery. It was the presbytery that was the repository of authorization at the local level, although the presbytery had also to be acting within the sphere of the apostolic commission and mission, a link that was supplied by St. Paul. It is not suggested that it was the local presbytery that joined with Paul in ordaining Timothy. At any rate it is clear that the presbytery is the medium of ordination although Paul has a special part in it, and Timothy afterwards takes a similar place in the ordination of others. Presumably, however, he would not act apart from the presbytery, except perhaps in founding a new church and appointing and ordaining new presbyters, in which instance he would be the authorized person acting within the apostolic commission to undertake that; but once established the presbytery would act as a body with Timothy. Here both "presbyterian" and "episcopalian" elements are clearly held together.

Now in interpreting what the New Testament has to say about ordination and its adaptation of Old Testament rites, we have to remember that nowhere does the New Testament take over an Old Testament rite and develop it as such. What it always does is to lay several images or rites together, elements of which are then used in the freedom of the apostolic Church for its own purposes in forming a new image or a new rite which derives its significance not from the Old Testament ceremonies or images as such but from Christ and from what the apostolic Church makes of it. How then are we to interpret the New Testament concept of ordination?

(1) The first thing to note is that by selecting this rite of laying on of hands, which was essentially a *lay rite* both in the Old Testament and in Judaism, the Christian Church made it decisively clear that the Christian ministry was not to be interpreted in the sense of the priesthood of the Old Testament. That had been fulfilled in Christ who alone is Priest. But because all that was fulfilled in Christ, permanent elements of significance in it might well be transferred from Christ to the interpretation of the Christian rite. That is what happened.

(2) The main element in the laying on of hands seems undoubtedly to be the commissioning of ministers of the Word to proclaim the *kerygma* and teach the *didache* in obedience to the apostolic witness to Christ and in following their example and ordinances. Ordination is for those who labour in the Word and carries with it acknowledged authorization to do so, authorization that derives from the apostolic commission as an attestation of the tradition of the apostolic teaching and preaching of the Gospel. Here we recall the old rites of consecrating the king by filling his hands with "the testimony", and the consecrating of the prophet through whose Word it is God who acts and rules.

(3) But this ordination has other elements associated with it; the gift of the Spirit, the bestowal of a special *charisma* for the ministry; and it is performed with prayer. It is difficult to resist the conclusion that, while in the Old Testament three different sets of expressions are used to describe three different forms of laying on or lifting up of hands, the New Testament seems to

blend elements of all three together. That was certainly done immediately after New Testament times. Thus in addition to the strict concept of *samakh*, responsible commissioning with authority to minister the Word, ordination also draws into its orbit the concept of blessing the one ordained through prayer, and calling upon him the gift of the Spirit, who brings a special *charisma* to the one ordained for the fulfilment of his ministry. But also the other idea found in the practice of *samakh* in the Old Testament is not absent: that of offering or presenting the one upon whom hands are laid before God, symbolized by the presentation of the seven before the apostles, as Joshua was presented before Eleazar by Moses when he ordained him, or the Levites were presented before the Tabernacle and then offered to God. That is a concept which Paul applies to his missionary congregations; he offers them to God as an oblation. According to Calvin this element is a powerful ingredient in ordination, for the ordinand after the analogy of the Old Testament sacrifices is through laying on of hands offered to God for His service and so consecrated. This act of ordination takes place in the Name of Christ the King and Head of the Church, so that all the ordinand does when ordained is to be done in the Name of Christ. That Name is his sole authority; nothing is to be done apart from it. But to ordain in the Name of Christ, and to act in the Name of Christ, is to act within the Self-consecration of Christ on our behalf, as the language of the Name of God declared by Christ to the apostles in John 17 indicates.

(4) Ordination thus means ordination in the sphere where we are all consecrated through participation in Christ's Self-consecration on our behalf. We recall that the disciples were specially related to the Self-consecration of Christ at the Last Supper, for in His solemn prayer of consecration they were associated by Christ with Himself as those who would take His Word to others so that others would believe through their word and be drawn into the unity of the one Church of Christ. We cannot dissociate ordination in the Name of Christ from that fact. Those ordained are to be regarded as drawn in a special way within the sphere of Christ's Self-consecration so that it is only as they share in His Self-consecration that they can minister the Word to others in His Name. It is in this connexion then that we have to see the relation of ordination to participation in

the Lord's Supper, and see the Lord's Supper as the New Testament counterpart to the meal of consecration in which Aaron and his sons participated at their consecration, "a meal of thanksgiving and praise". That expression is reflected in an important passage in Hebrews 13 which speaks of the ministry in several injunctions and adds: "Through him then let us offer up a sacrifice of praise to God continually, that is the fruit of the lips which make confession to his name continually." It was not unnatural therefore that in very early times, as in the *Apostolic Constitutions*, the rite of ordination to the ministry was looked upon as being brought to its completion when the one ordained first celebrated the Lord's Supper, for it was when the gifts of bread and wine were put into his hands that the Lord Himself fulfilled the act of consecrating His servant to His ministry, as He consecrated the apostle-disciples at the Last Supper. It is significant therefore that all the earliest consecrations and ordinations known to us took place in a Eucharistic context. This is a practice that should still be followed. The act of the presbytery in ordination should be followed by the celebration of Holy Communion in which the newly ordained person should dispense the Sacrament for the first time. The early Church of Scotland practice of "fasting" at ordination seems to have been derived from the old rite of the consecration of the priests with its seven days of separation.

The Doctrine of Ordination

In gathering up our discussion to present a doctrine of ordination we must consider it from three aspects:

(1) The source of ordination: its derivation from Christ through the ministry of the Church.
(2) The end of ordination: that to which a man is ordained determines the nature of ordination.
(3) What the act of ordination means and how it is carried out.

(1) *The source of ordination.* Who is it who ordains a man to the ministry? In answer to that question we have to give the unambiguous answer: Jesus Christ Himself. Ordination is His act. It is His authority that stands behind it, and therefore it can be done only in His Name. But Christ ordains within His Church

which He founded upon the apostles and it is through that Church that He acts. Here we are confronted with a fundamental duality, but it is also the fundamental duality of Revelation. Revelation is the act of Christ which is brought to bear upon us directly through His Spirit, but it is Revelation which He communicates to us through the Word historically mediated in the Holy Scriptures. The risen and ascended Lord has bestowed His Spirit upon the Church, but the Spirit utters to us what Christ has already said: He does not speak of Himself and does not teach us anything new, but takes what Christ has already revealed and leads us fully into its Truth. The Church is thus bound to the New Testament Scriptures, but in and through the New Testament Scriptures the risen and ascended Lord communicates Himself directly to His Church in the communion of the Spirit. So it is with ordination. It is the risen and ascended Lord who acts directly through His Spirit ordaining His servant to the ministry, but He does that in and through the Church which He has once and for all established in the apostles and bound to the Revelation which He has committed to the Church through the apostles.

The Church is bound to act in obedience to the apostolic teaching and commands, and through them it is bound to the historical Jesus Christ. When the Church from age to age ordains men to the ministry in the Name of Christ, it does that only within that obedience to the apostolic teaching and ordinances, and only within the sphere of the apostolic commission and mission given by Christ in founding the Church. That duality is apparent already in the New Testament Church. It is the risen and ascended Lord who bestows gifts upon the Church through the Spirit, but these gifts are bestowed for exercise within the one Church founded upon the apostles and within the sphere of their commission by Christ. The apostles appointed the rite of the laying on of hands to mark out and delimit the sphere of their commission, and to attest the propriety of a ministry within that sphere. That laying on of hands cannot be regarded as determining or delimiting the sphere of the operation of the Holy Spirit, for although Christ has bound the Church to its foundation in the apostles, He is Himself sovereignly free over the apostles as the risen and ascended Lord. The laying on of hands cannot be understood therefore as securing or guaranteeing the presence or the operation of the Holy Spirit, but as the apostolically given sign witnessing to the presence of the Spirit, attesting the obedience of the Church to its apostolic origins and binding its continuance, and the continuance of its ministry, within the sphere of the apostolic commission and authority. It is Christ, not the apostles, not the Church, who bestows upon the ordained minister the Spirit and the gifts of the Spirit for the exercise of his office; nevertheless it is clear that the laying on of hands was given by the apostles with the promise of Christ to impart spiritual gifts for the fulfilment of the ministry.

Ordinarily and normatively we are to understand the laying on of hands as the apostolically appointed sign and instrument used by the Spirit in bestowing the *charisma* for the ministry. Its necessity is one of obedience to the apostolic ordinance, and it attests that the ordination of the ministry derives from the historical Jesus and His historically communicated authority to the apostles. But the historical Jesus is risen and ascended, and it is He who from generation to generation continues to bestow His Spirit upon the Church and continues to bestow the grace-gifts for the ministry of Word and Sacrament within the Church. Therefore it is Christ the living Lord who is the actual Ordainer in ordination, although He makes use of the ministers who have been sent by Him already to carry out the ordinance within the Church on earth. It is only in this togetherness of "the Risen Lord" and "the historical Jesus" who is one Lord Jesus Christ, the King and Head of the Church, that we must think of ordination. The risen Lord sends us back to the historical Jesus and sends us back always to the commission He gave to the apostles, so that ordination is through the historical communication of the apostolic Word and the apostolic commission. The historical Jesus still commissions His ministers through that external and historical succession, and therefore the historical mediation or communication of ordination is of fundamental importance as attesting the binding of the Church to the historical Jesus and the historical Revelation.

The Church which separates itself from the historical Jesus ceases thereby to be Christ's Church, for it cuts itself off from its historical rooting and grounding in the historical Revelation and Incarnation. But within that historical communication it is the risen Lord Himself who ever comes to His Church acting obediently in His Name and Himself ordains. He Himself is really present where we meet in His name to obey His command, and He fulfils what He promises, and His presence in grace and in the power of His Spirit undergirds all our actions. We rely in all ordination therefore not upon the faithfulness of the Church, nor upon the unbroken nature of the historical succession, for these are all involved in the relativities and contingencies of this fallen world; but upon the faithfulness of Christ who remains with His Church that lives and acts in His Name. It is His covenant faithfulness undergirding our weakness and faltering faithfulness, and renewing our participation in Him, that is the ground of our reliance in every act of ordination.

It is this same fundamental duality in ordination that gives the concept of the so-called "validity of orders" its elusive ambiguity. Validity must refer absolutely to the fact that it is Christ the Lord who ordains, and ordains to ministry in the Church of God. He it is who honours that ministry as His own gift to the Church and makes it efficacious through His Spirit. But validity also refers to the responsible transmission of authorization from generation to generation, attesting the obedience of the Church in all its ordinations to the apostolic teaching and ordinances. Because this involves historical communication and responsible action it involves a duly intended and orderly act of ordination. It cannot be given in abstraction from the ordering of a Church's life, from its discipline and polity. Thus validity has also a juridical aspect, in which the term is relative to the legal structure of a Church in history. It refers to the responsible authorization of a Church in history, which orders its life and discipline in obedience to the apostolic Church and therefore is bound up with the canonical way of administering life and discipline in that Church.

In the Church of Scotland we ordain a man to the ministry of the Word and Sacraments in the Church of God, because we believe it is Christ Himself who ordains, but in ordination the Church (through its authorized ministers) commits to him due authorization to minister the Word and Sacraments within the discipline of the Church of Scotland within which he also promises at ordination to be subject to the Church. But the Church of Scotland does not thereby claim that, in that sense of authorization, it has authorized its ministers to administer the Word and Sacraments in every other Church. It does not necessarily acknowledge the authorization of those ordained in other Churches as giving them authority to administer the Word and Sacraments in the Church of Scotland, but it does not for that reason question the validity of their orders in the sense that their ordination is an act of Christ and is honoured by Him in making their ministry efficacious. The Church of Scotland does claim, however, that in obedience to the teaching and ordinance of the apostles "the laying on of hands of the presbytery" is the proper and responsible way of ordaining the ministry and of transmitting in the historical communication of the Church due authorization for the ministry of Word and Sacraments within the sphere of the apostolic commission and mission. While it acknowledges that authorization for the ministry of the Word and Sacraments is inescapably bound up with the discipline of the Church of Scotland and is therefore relative to its own structure and law, it claims that its careful and orderly transmission of ordination from generation to generation is in full conformity to the apostolic ordinance and teaching, and therefore reaches beyond what is merely relative to the particular legal institutions of the Church of Scotland itself to what is valid in the Church of God.

(2) *The end of ordination.* Ordination means ordination to the ministry of Word and Sacraments, that is to dispensing Word and Sacraments. Strictly, therefore, "ordination" should be used only for the order of those who dispense the Word and Sacraments. It is using "ordination" in a somewhat loose sense to speak of ordaining deacons or deaconesses or ordaining elders, for they are not ordained to dispense the Word and Sacraments but are set apart or consecrated to assist in that ministry, even although a rite of laying on of hands may be used. A rite of laying on of hands is used also in some baptismal rites or in confirmations, but it does not therefore mean that those who have hands laid on them are ordained—what determines ordination is the end to which ordination is directed and intended by the Church. This involves two important points.

(a) That which a man is ordained to minister, the Word and Sacraments, is more important than ordination. Ordination is in order to minister the Word and Sacraments, and therefore ordination is subordinate to the Word and Sacraments which it serves. In other words, the ministering of Word and Sacraments is subservient to the Word and Sacraments themselves. The ministry is but an earthen vessel, as St. Paul put it, but it contains the heavenly treasure, and must never be confounded with the heavenly treasure. Therefore in the ministering of the Word and Sacraments, the mysteries of God, the ministering itself must be dependent upon that which is ministered and can never exalt itself over it. Ordination does not give the minister authority over the Word and Sacrament, but sets him in a servant-relation to them. They are always transcendent to the ministry and their efficacy cannot be tied to the ministry or only be relative to the worth of the ministers. The very authority which a minister has for ministering Word and Sacraments lies in the Word and Sacraments and not in himself—that is another way of saying that the ministry is at every point dependent upon the apostolic Word and Ordinances, for it is through the apostles that we have committed to us the Word and Sacraments and it is only in obedience to the apostolic ordering of the ministry that we administer them.

(b) There can in the nature of the case be no higher ministry than that of the ministry of Word and Sacraments, for that would be to suppose that there was a higher authority than that of the Word and a higher sanction than that of the Seals of the Word directly instituted and given by Jesus Christ. If ordination is defined by its end in the ministry of Word and Sacrament, and Word and Sacrament are more important than the ministering of them, it follows that there is only one order of the ministry in the proper sense; that of the minister dispensing Word and Sacraments. The order of the presbyteral ministry is not only the highest order, but in the strict sense the only order of the ministry. Other so-called orders are either for the assistance of this order or for the convenience of maintaining unity and concord and discipline among those so ordained. The fact that there is only one order of the ministry in the strict sense is the meaning of the so-called parity of ministers in a Presbyterian Church, but this does not preclude distinctions in jurisdiction either in the Church Courts to which presbyters are subject or among presbyters themselves. Thus, as Calvin says, "The political distinction of ranks [i.e. distinctions in Church polity, not 'politics'] is not to be repudiated, for natural reason itself dictates this in order to take away confusion; but that which shall have this object in view, will be so arranged that it may neither obscure Christ's glory nor minister to ambition or tyranny, nor prevent all ministers from cultivating mutual fraternity with each other, with equal rights and liberties."[1]

There can therefore be no doctrinal grounds for any distinction between a presbyter and a bishop or a presbyter-bishop, nor any ground at all for a distinction in order, though there may well be ecclesiastical or historical grounds for making a distinction in function and therefore for adding some measure of jurisdiction to one presbyter to enable him responsibly to fulfil that extra function. But such a distinction in function could not make a bishop more of a minister or give him a higher ministry in relation to Word and Sacrament than that of any other presbyter. The doctrine of parity of ministers must not therefore be confused with differences in function or relative distinctions in jurisdiction. Thus in the Reformed Church we acknowledge that some presbyters are set apart and are acknowledged to have a special *charisma* for teaching doctrine and for keeping a "watching brief" over the purity of the Church's proclamation and doctrine in obedience to the teaching of the apostles. These are the "doctors" of the Church, and they are responsibly commissioned to exercise their functions with appropriate jurisdiction, not in their case in Church or pastoral government, and so they are not given ecclesiastical jurisdiction of any kind but in the teaching and training of the ministry and in doctrine. That does not in any way do away with "the parity of ministers" in the sense that the doctors have a higher ministry or a superior order to other presbyters. The same would apply to the "bishop-in-presbytery", although in that case where his special function would be concerned with pastoral discipline he would naturally be set apart for that in the appropriate way by the Presbytery, in "the laying on of hands by the Presbytery", so keeping him under its own authority but commissioning him to act responsibly for it in the ways the Church would lay down. Here the nature of "the laying on of hands" would be determined by the end intended and determined by the Church. In

[1] *Comm. on Num.* 3:5.

this instance it would not be determined simply by the Word and Sacraments, but by something else: a function to act as spiritual counsellor and guide to his fellow-ministers, and to act in a presidential capacity or even a representative capacity for the presbytery in its solemn acts and deliberations. But because the bishop-in-presbytery could be given no higher relation to the Word and Sacrament—that is in the nature of the case impossible—he could have no higher order than that of his fellow-presbyters.

(3) *What ordination is and how it is carried out.* Ordination is the solemn setting apart to the ministry of Word and Sacraments of a man who has been called to that ministry. It is an act in which the whole Church concurs, although the act of ordination itself is carried through by those who have already been ordained, for they only are the proper instruments for "regular" association of others with the commission they have received and which they in obedience to the apostolic ordinance devolve upon others. It is not that they thus transmit "grace," or the Holy Spirit, nor that they transmit divine authority; but in so doing they attest that it is Christ alone who acts, and they make evident that they are acting only in obedience to Christ's own commissioned apostles. But, as we have already noted, the act of ordination is also the lawful act in the discipline of the Church where responsibility in office is devolved in an orderly or canonical way upon others in succession to their fathers in the same office. It is an act that takes place in space and time: in the space or place of the Church where Christ has put His Name on earth, the visible Church, and in the time or historical continuity of the Church which Christ has sent out into history to proclaim the Gospel of His Kingdom until He comes again. Thus the physical, visible, and temporal action in ordination attests the binding of the Church to the physical, visible, and temporal incarnation and the Church once and for all founded by the incarnate Son on the apostles and prophets. Just as the Church's life and worship is neither timeless nor spaceless, but in the historical and risen Jesus Christ, so the act of ordination is not a spaceless and timeless act in which the visible and temporal element is of no importance.

On the other hand, the act of ordination is not a Sacrament in the proper sense—although Calvin himself was not averse to calling it a sacrament. It is certainly not a "Sacrament of the Gospel", that is a sign and seal of a saving ordinance through which salvation is bestowed in the unity of Word and appointed Sign; but because ordination is the appointed ordinance with its accompanying and appropriate sign for the ordering of the ministry of the Word and Sacraments, it necessarily partakes of the sacramental character of the Word and Sacraments and is rightly performed only within the Church as the Body of Christ, within the Covenant-signs-and-seals of the Church's incorporation into Christ. No unbaptized person can ordain or be ordained, for no uncovenanted person can be commissioned within the ministry of the New Covenant; and no one who is not himself a communicant member of the Church can ordain or be ordained, for no one who has not himself shared in the communion of the New Covenant and in the Self-consecration of Christ, sealed upon His own at the Holy Supper, can be a consecrated minister of the New Covenant. Just because ordination has this setting within the Church's incorporation into Christ in Word and Sacrament, it must take place in the context of Word and Sacrament as well as in the context of the Church's solemn judicial action in a Sacral Court.

This dual aspect of the rite of ordination reflects its dual character. It takes place in and through an act of the Presbytery met and constituted as a Sacral Court of the Church. Ordination is not properly and validly enacted by any association of presbyters, but by an association of presbyters duly convened within and according to the discipline and constitution of the Church by a resolution of the appropriate court as a whole; for it must be an act in which the whole Church concurs and which therefore has the acknowledged authority of the Church. That is the judicial aspect of ordination, which has its appropriate ceremonies such as the interrogation and response, the taking of vows and the signing of the formula in the Church's roll, and the solemn act of laying on of hands, which in part is an essential legal act attesting the lawful and responsible bestowal of a commission or the canonical conferring of authority to minister the Word and Sacraments within the bounds of the Church and its mission. This judicial part of ordination is not carried out in and by itself apart, but only within the whole spiritual action of ordination, though it is particularly in the laying on of hands that the overlap between the judicial and the spiritual aspects of ordination is most apparent.

Ordination is primarily a spiritual act within the Church in which Christ Himself is the Principal Agent, and in which the ordained ministers (those preaching presbyters to whom it belongs to act thus in Christ's Name) act as servants of Christ and only in obedience to His commands. The whole act of ordination is therefore dependent upon the Word of God as mediated through the apostolic tradition. If ordination is by Christ in accordance with His Word, then it is carried out only in "sacramental" dependence upon His Word—it is the Word which commissions to the ministry, and the Word which is the sole repository of divine authority in the Church and which bestows that authority as the Church acts in obedience to it. The Word is the sceptre through which Christ the risen and ascended Lord continues to govern and rule His Church and continues to call men into His ministry and to command them in His service. Ordination takes place therefore in accordance with the apostolic Warrant, in solemn declaration of the Word, and in the context of the Church meeting to wait upon that Word in its proclamation through the heralds sent by Christ to the Church. Only when the royal proclamation of the Word of the King has been made does the Church through its ministers act in obedience to it in the ceremony of ordination.

The other parts of this ceremony are prayer and the laying on of hands. The *Westminster Form of Church Government* puts the laying on of hands first, but the *Second Book of Discipline*, following the order of the *First Book of Discipline* and the teaching of Knox and Calvin, puts prayer first. That indicates that the primary element in ordination is the *epiclesis*, the response of the Church to God's Word made in the prayer calling for the bestowal of the Spirit upon him being set apart to the ministry. It is Christ Himself who ordains through the sending of His Spirit, and it is entirely the divine intention and act that determines the nature of the ordinance and its effect. The emphasis upon the act of prayer as an *epiclesis* also makes clear that the formal act of laying on of hands, necessary and important as it is juridically, is not to be regarded mainly as a legal act, but as the apostolically appointed sign attesting that it is Christ who ordains, that it is the Spirit who acts, and that the rite of ordination has its root and ground beyond in the Self-consecration of Christ in His own prayerful Self-oblation on our behalf. Within that act of prayer the laying on of hands has its essential and indispensable place. But when it is taken within that act of prayer we must say with Augustine: "*Quid aliud est manuum impositio quam oratio super hominem?*" The imposition of hands is primarily the lifting up of hands in prayer, so that actual tactual laying on of hands is really secondary. On the ground of biblical teaching, however, in which it is clear that the act of *samakh* was the main ceremonial act, we lay stress upon tactual imposition as well as the laying on or lifting up of hands in blessing; for in the biblical teaching tactual imposition itself is recognized as an act offering and presenting the one who is the object of laying on of hands to God in dedication and consecration for His service. It is because of this extremely close relation between laying on of hands in prayerful offering and the lifting up of hands in prayer in blessing that many of the earliest books of Church Order omit its actual mention, for the stress was laid upon the act of prayer and was considered to be implied in it. That was the attitude of John Knox in 1560, although in 1572 (if not actually earlier) the imposition of hands was restored in detailed action and has ever since been regarded as indispensable in the Church of Scotland.

Accompanying and preceding the act of ordination there are other rites which have their proper place and are designed to attest the fact that the person ordained is acknowledged as one who has himself received a divine call to the Holy Ministry, that his own private recognition of that call is confirmed by the Church acting through its duly constituted Courts, and confirmed by the congregation which has called him to be its minister in the Name of Christ. The act of ordination thus requires the *imprimatur* of the Church as a whole and the acclaim and acquiescence of the local congregation, who also take vows in support of the minister and in obedient acknowledgment of the fact that their minister has been *sent* to them by Christ Himself. The minister himself takes vows which bind him to the continuity of the Church's obedience to the apostles in doctrines and ordinances, and in which he solemnly promises to fulfil His ministry with devotion to Christ as His servant, and, without lording it over the flock, to seek their good in the Lord. At the same time he acknowledges that the government of the Church is agreeable to the Word of God, promises to be subject to its discipline, to take his due part in its affairs, and to seek the unity and peace of the Church. But in his undertaking these vows, as in the administration of ordination to him, the Church makes it clear that the minister acts not on his own charges or on his own resources, but only on the *command* and therefore only in reliance upon the *promise* of Jesus Christ who remains the same yesterday, to-day, and for ever, and who never fails to keep His Word.

2

THE GOSPEL AND THE KINGDOM

(a) *A Study in New Testament Communication*[1]

IT is often claimed that the problem of communicating the Gospel is the major practical problem facing the Church today, as it may also be the major theological problem. This concern is a very healthy sign, but it is becoming increasingly apparent that we are apt to be so concerned with devising new methods of evangelism as to forget the one factor of supreme importance: the burden of the Gospel itself, that is, to forget that the Gospel is not simply the message of divine love, but the actual way in which God communicates Himself to us in history. No technique that forgets that the Gospel has already been made supremely relevant to sinful humanity in the Incarnation and death of Jesus Christ will ever avail for the communication of the Gospel. This is therefore an attempt to probe into what the New Testament has to say to us about this, and into the way in which, as a matter of fact, the New Testament actually communicates the Gospel to us.

We may take as our starting point the Parables in the Synoptic Gospels with the parallels in the Fourth Gospel. According to Professor C. H. Dodd, "a parable is normally the dramatic presentation of a situation intended to suggest vividly some single idea".[2] Jesus used parables to "illustrate what Mark calls the mystery of the Kingdom of God"[3]—i.e. He presented His teaching in a concrete fashion and not in abstractions. However, because "there is no mere analogy but an inward affinity between the natural order and the spiritual order"[4] the Parables are so self-luminous that "the interpretation will show through".[5] Professor Dodd goes on to say: "The

[1] From the *Scottish Journal of Theology*, 1950, pp. 225–240.
[2] *The Parables of the Kingdom*, p. 165.
[3] P. 33, Mark 4: 11.
[4] P. 24. [5] P. 20.

Kingdom of God is intrinsically like the process of nature and of the daily life of man . . . the sense of the divineness of the natural order is major premiss of all the Parables".[1]

In this view Dr. Dodd follows Jülicher in rejecting the idea that Parables are allegories where the elements are treated as mysterious cyphers or allegorical equivalents for eternal ideas, but he refuses to follow Jülicher in making "the process of interpretation end with the generalization". No doubt the Parable has the character of an argument but "the way to an interpretation lies through a judgment of the imagined situation, not through a decoding of various elements in the story".[2] "The Parables bear upon the actual and critical situation in which Jesus and His hearers stood: when we ask after the application we must look first not to the field of general principles but to the particular setting in which they are delivered. The task of the interpreter of the Parables is to find out, if he can, the setting of a Parable in the situation contemplated by the Gospel and hence the application which would suggest itself to one who stood in that situation."[3]

Unquestionably Professor Dodd has put us greatly in his debt for his exposition of the Parables, and for the astonishing light that his method of interpretation casts on them again and again. It is difficult to avoid the feeling, however, that his restricted definition of the Parable and the resulting method of interpretation are unduly narrow. A more balanced and, certainly to the preacher, a more satisfying account has been given by the Rev. R. S. Wallace in a previous number of this Journal.[4] In that article Dr. Wallace raised the question whether the relation upon which the Parable reposes is a natural or a sacramental relation. That is the point of crucial importance for a doctrine of communication. Is it really true, as Dr. Dodd maintains, that when we scrutinize the Parables and relate them to the original situation so far as we can reconstruct it, the conclusion regarding the original meaning and application follows or shines through?[5] That would mean that so far as we can reconstruct the original Jesus in His setting in history (*Sitz im Leben*), we can read off the divine Revelation because there is an inward affinity between the natural order and the spiritual order, and

[1] P. 22. [2] P. 23. [3] P. 26.
[4] 2, 1. pp. 13 ff. [5] C. H. Dodd, *op. cit.*, p. 31.

because of the divineness of the natural order. Surely that is not the message of the Synoptic Gospels, nor the teaching of the Parables. Undoubtedly the divine communication must involve analogy if it is to get across to men who can only think in terms of human and worldly analogies, but the whole significance of the Parable is that it is *analogy with a difference*, analogy which has at its heart an eschatological event which, until it actually overtakes us, nothing in the natural or historical order can begin to reveal. Even when it happens, absolutely necessary as the analogical elements are to convey the Revelation, they are unable of themselves to point to the truth. "Flesh and blood hath not revealed it unto thee, but my Father which is in heaven" (Matt. 16: 17). The extraordinary fact is that while Professor C. H. Dodd recognizes this teaching quite unambiguously,[1] he fails to carry it into the heart of his epistemology. In other words the eschatological relation upon which he has thrown such a flood of illumination is not truly realized in the depth of faith. That is the significance of the *mystery* of the Kingdom.[2]

The Synoptic passage which we must discuss here is Mark 4: 1 ff., especially 4: 11 ff. Professor Dodd's thesis is that the evangelist has misunderstood the Parables and the significance of the Parable itself, and the result is a series of interpretations attached to the Parables which he pronounces a confusion. This leads him to reject every New Testament interpretation of the Parables. In this instance Dr. Dodd's own method of interpretation does not allow him to make sense of the passage as it stands, and he is forced to mutilate and reconstruct it. In particular he lays the axe to the word *mysterion* as not being a genuine word of Jesus, in spite of the fact that an *agraphon* survives through Clement of Alexandria and the Clementine Homilies in which *mysterion* in a similar connexion is found on the lips of Jesus, apparently from a different source altogether, which makes the genuineness of *mysterion* in this passage all the more certain. However, it does not matter ultimately whether the word itself is scored out, for the thought is inextricably woven into all three Synoptic accounts as well as the Johannine, going back to Old Testament passages such as Deut. 29: 29; Ps. 78: 12; Is. 6: 9 ff.; 42: 18 ff.

[1] *Op. cit.*, p. 197.

[2] Cf. Wallace, *loc. cit.*, p. 14.

What did Jesus mean when He said, "How shall we liken the Kingdom of God?" or "the Kingdom of God is like" this or that? Surely that Kingdom or the Word of the Kingdom or the Mystery is difficult to express directly. It is like this and it is like that, and yet it is like this and like that. We cannot say, "Lo, here is the Kingdom of God" or "Lo, there is the Kingdom of God", for the Kingdom of God does not come like that. It does not come with observation. As the Fourth Gospel puts it, "Except a man be born again (from above) he cannot see the Kingdom of God."[1] "How shall I liken the Kingdom?" says Jesus. "I shall express it by a parable" (παραβολή).[2] The word of the Kingdom can be expressed only indirectly by a series of parallels on a different analogical level side by side with it. The Word of the Kingdom can be expressed to men of flesh and blood and concrete existence only by throwing a parallel in flesh and blood and in the language of humanity to the Word of the Kingdom. That means, as Jülicher and Dodd agree, that the parable is not an allegory, although to say that the parable yields *one idea* is to make it as much an allegory as if it yielded a series of ideas. Behind the parable, or rather beside it, there is the Kingdom which has broken into the midst, the *eschaton* which is here and now. Dr. Dodd agrees that it is this which gives the parables their peculiar significance. The *basileia* or *eschaton* is identified with the Word of the Kingdom. That comes out very clearly, as K. L. Schmidt points out, when we compare the Synoptic parallels. The parable therefore is the picturesque, dramatic and analogical speech thrown alongside the invisible Kingdom already in the midst, already "among you" (ἐντὸς ὑμῶν). "The Kingdom of God is come upon you" (Matt. 12: 28; Luke 11: 20: ἔφθασεν ἐφ' ὑμᾶς ἡ βασιλεία). The parable is thus essentially two-sided. It has a visible side, the analogical; but that is thrown alongside the invisible Kingdom and is, so to speak, contrapuntal to it. The parable is essentially sacramental in form and that is always its intention on the lips of Jesus. Jesus Christ, in teaching and Person, is Himself the great Parable of the Kingdom of God.

If the Word of the Kingdom is identical with Christ

[1] Cf. 1 Cor. 2: 1 ff.

[2] The Greek word used by the evangelists is particularly significant. παραβολή indicates the act of throwing alongside (παρα-βάλλω).

Himself then it is clear why the Word cannot be expressed directly in speech. Christ Jesus cannot be put into words. In Him we have the Word and the Act of the Kingdom, *logos* and *dynamis*, in one: a Person in the midst. As Professor Dodd says, the parable describes an aspect of Christ's own ministry and the developing situation and the crisis which His coming has brought upon history. But the design of the parable does not lie in itself or in any symbolic meaning to be read off the face of it or even in any single idea. It is designed to put a man into a situation in which he is confronted with God and can hear for himself the Word of the Kingdom which flesh and blood cannot reveal. Consequently the relation between the Word of the Kingdom and the parables is conceived in terms of *mysterion* or *krypton*. It will help us to understand this if we remember that *mysterion* is not used in any sense relating to the Greek mysteries. A passage such as 1 Tim. 3: 16 is helpful, "Great is the mystery of Godliness, God manifest in the flesh." That is the fundamental sense in which it is nearly always used in the New Testament, in the Synoptics, in St. Paul's Epistles, and in the Apocalypse as well.[1]

There is a very illuminating sentence from the Fourth Gospel (8: 43) which throws a flood of light upon the situation here. "Why do you not understand my speech (λαλιάν), because you cannot hear my word (λόγον)?" The Jews were unable to make anything of the speech (λαλιά) of Jesus, i.e. the parables (παραβολαί), because they could not hear or could not bear to hear His Word (λόγος). If we ask the Fourth Gospel what the relation is between the speech and the Word the answer is given in the expression "abiding" (μένειν). It is when a man abides in the Word or when the Word abides in a man that the man understands the speech and knows the Truth which will make him free. Thus the preaching of Jesus is broadcast to all who hear it as speech but only he who has ears to hear or who makes room for it (χωρεῖν), as the Synoptics say, can hear the Word. In this way the Word is broadcast to all and sundry through speech and parable, but only those who are prepared to receive it in faith actually hear it as the Word of the Kingdom. That comes out again and again in the Fourth Gospel. The voice of God speaks; the unbelieving crowds say

[1] There is, of course, a counterfeit *mysterion* of evil.

that it thunders, but the believers say that it is the voice of an angel. "Lord, how is it that thou wilt manifest thyself unto us and *not unto the world?* Jesus answered and said unto him, If a man love me he will keep my word (λόγον) and my Father will love him and we *will come unto him and make our abode with him*" (John 14: 22, 23). That is the Johannine way of putting the Mystery of the Kingdom.

This helps us to understand the teaching in Mark and the Synoptic parallels. "To you is given to know the mystery of the Kingdom of God but to them who are without all things are spoken in Parables." Then Jesus declares that the clue to all the Parables is the same—the Word (λόγος). "Do ye not know this parable? How then shall ye know all parables? He who sows, sows the word (λόγον)."[1] And so Mark goes on to say (v. 33): "And with many such parables He spake (ἐλάλει) the word (τὸν λόγον), as they were able to hear" (καθὼς ἠδύναντο ἀκούειν: recall the οὐ δύνασθε of John 8: 43). "Without a parable He did not speak unto them (χωρὶς παραβολῆς οὐκ ἐλάλει αὐτοῖς)." There is little doubt therefore that the thought of the Synoptics is close to that of the Fourth Gospel.

We come now to what is usually reckoned exegetically most difficult, the scandal of a ἵνα (Mark 4: 11 f.), "Unto you it is given to know the mystery of the Kingdom of God but to those who are without, all things are done in parables, that seeing they may see (ἵνα βλέποντες βλέπωσι) and not understand (καὶ μὴ ἴδωσι): and hearing, they may hear; lest at any time they should be converted and their sins should be forgiven them." Several things must be said here.

(1) Its very harshness is the strongest argument for the authority of ἵνα.

(2) No doubt the Greek is harsher in sound than the Aramaic. It may be that the Aramaic was capable of ambiguous interpretation as Professor T. W. Manson avers.

(3) This ἵνα must be put side by side with ἐὰν μὴ ἵνα in v. 22, which indicates that the Parables, while they concealed

[1] K. L. Schmidt points out that in each Synoptic set of parallels Kingdom and Word of the Kingdom are equated with the key of knowledge (Luke 11: 52). The hearing of the Word is the key to knowledge, the key to the Parables of Jesus. Cf. G. Kittel, *Theologisches Woerterbuch zum N.T.*, 1, pp. 581 ff.

the mystery, only concealed it with the intention of revealing it (4: 21–23), while the expression in v. 33 *καθὼς ἠδύναντο ἀκούειν* also throws a flood of light upon the passage.

Why, then, does Jesus speak in parables?

(1) He speaks in parables in order to reveal that the Kingdom of God has come into the midst in His own Person and to direct men to believe in Him in such a way that there is evoked from them full decision. The parable is chosen by Christ as the means of confronting men with Himself, the Word, in such a way that men can choose Him in love and yet not be overwhelmed by His divine majesty. The Word comes through the parable in such a way that men have to choose God in order to know Him, to surrender to His will in order to understand. The Word is so nigh that it creates room for faith and decision. Jesus consistently avoids giving a compelling manifestation of Himself for that would leave no room for faith and decision and men would be fixed in their sin by the unveiled divine majesty instead of being wooed to belief and trust so that Christ can heal them. In the parable, so to speak, the Kingdom of God comes into the midst and throws a man into the crisis of decision, and yet by its veiled form the Word of the Kingdom holds man at arm's length away in order to give him room and time for personal decision.[1]

(2) We can say with Calvin that Jesus spoke in parables not simply for the purpose of instruction but to keep the attention of the hearers awake until a more convenient time. He kept the un-understanding and the unbelieving in a state of suspense till a fitter opportunity arrived. And so in the parable Jesus accommodated the Word to men's capacity who were yet rendered inexcusable by the amount of light they got from the surface of the parable but whose final verdict is suspended because as yet they were not sufficiently prepared to receive instruction. That is the force of the words "as they were able to hear" (*καθὼς ἠδύναντο ἀκούειν*, Mark 4: 33). Above all forms of speech the parable is calculated to have the greatest propensities for suggestion in which with the light and skilled thrust of a rapier Jesus gently touches men to the quick of their soul by the two-

[1] This necessary time-element is really eliminated by a realized eschatology which holds that "the time-scale is irrelevant to the ultimate significance of history" (C. H. Dodd, *op. cit.*, p. 71).

edged Word, summoning them to decision without crushing them to the ground by an open display of majesty and might. It is by means of the parable that Jesus pierces to the heart in such a way as not to crush the bruised reed or quench the smoking flax—καθὼς ἠδύναντο ἀκούειν. In Johannine thought, this means that Jesus did not want to judge the hearers on the spot in any final fashion. The *eschaton* had broken into the present but if men were confronted openly with the *eschaton* in the Word and presence of Jesus in their unbelief, they would be finally damned on the spot. But Jesus veiled the *eschaton* so that it encountered men obliquely. "I judge you not; but the word that I speak, that shall judge you at the last day" (John 12: 48). The Word of God is always creative. It always acts upon a man whether he will or no, but in the event of a man's "no", in the event of his unbelief, Jesus intends that the judgment shall fall with a delayed action still leaving room and time for decision and faith. The Word of the Kingdom creates ferment among men and sooner or later there must be an explosion. There may be conversion now, which is an eschatological event: "Repent, for the Kingdom of God is come upon you." It may be damnation in the *eschaton*: "Depart from me, for I never knew you."

(3) Jesus deliberately concealed the Word in the parable lest men against their will should be forced to acknowledge the Kingdom, and yet He allowed them enough light to convict them and to convince them. Jesus refused to reveal Himself to men in such a way as to command their assent and still leave them unbowed in the haughtiness of their pride. He revealed Himself in a way that often involved offence (σκάνδαλον) so as to cut across the grain of human pride and demand humility and rebirth.

We make a real mistake if we imagine that the Jews simply did not recognize Jesus as the Son of God. They did indeed, and yet they did not recognize Him. They were blind, but they were wilfully blind. They had such an obstinate disposition of soul that in the very act of perceiving the truth they insisted that it should not apply to them, for they could not bear the Gospel; they could not endure the Word of Christ because it cut clean across all their proud national aspirations, their rigid ideas and desires. Thus they rendered themselves morally and spiritually incapable even of understanding the speech (λαλιά) of Jesus. In the language of St. Paul they deliberately held down the truth in unrighteousness. When a man does that, God delivers him over to a reprobate mind. That is God's punishment for the perverter and evader of the truth; and so Jesus said quite plainly, "For judgment am I come into this world, that they which see not might see, and that they which see might be made blind" (John 9: 39). That is the force, the terrible force, of the *ἵνα* in Mark 4: 11. It is not, says Calvin,[1] that the teaching of Christ by itself or by its own nature causes blindness. "Where the Word of God blinds and hardens the reprobate, as this takes place through their own depravity it belongs truly and naturally to themselves, but is accidental as respects the Word." The Word of God in its own nature is always full of light, but its light is choked by the darkness of man and it becomes a savour of death to death and a savour of life to life (2 Cor. 2: 15, 16).

That is surely the meaning of this difficult passage. As we have seen in the interpretation that follows, the Word of the Gospel is broadcast to all and sundry. Only where it is received in good soil does it bear fruit. That does not mean that the Word presupposes an esoteric aristocracy and acts selectively upon them. Professor C. H. Dodd points out that Jesus told another series of parables to show how this selective activity (if we may call it that) works. The appeal goes to all and sundry. The saved are separated from the others by their free reaction to the demands which the appeal of the Word involves.[2] This selection is itself the divine judgment, though men pass it upon themselves by their ultimate attitude to the appeal. That is very apparent in the series of *pericopae* in Mark 10: 17–22 and Luke 9: 57–62. The fact that in Mark 4: 11 we have a *ἵνα* and not just a *οἵ* means that this is a divine judgment. That inevitably happens when the Kingdom of God comes into the midst. It takes full charge of the situation and acts upon men whether they will or no. God is always subject. He is the King. This is the breaking of His sovereignty (*βασιλεία*) into the midst of men's desires and decisions and choices, throwing them all into critical ferment and giving them an essential form *vis-à-vis* the Kingdom. Had Jesus spoken openly (*ἐν παρρησίᾳ*, John 16: 29) men would have been damned on the spot, but as He

[1] *Comm. ad loc.*

[2] *Op. cit.*, p. 189.

spoke in the veiled encounter of the parables men were judged in unbelief and yet given freedom still to believe. However, because in the breaking in of the Kingdom the emphasis is laid upon the action of God, the δύναμις of the λόγος, this experience is viewed as divine act.

So far we have been dealing with the relation of Word to speech, of mystery to parable, but here is another relation which is also central to the question of communication, the relation of Word (λόγος) to power (δύναμις). It will be sufficient to say here that in the Synoptics there is the closest relation between the Word and the Act in Jesus' preaching. Word and Act are inseparable and complementary. The Kingdom is essentially God's saving intervention among men, and that takes place in the preaching and the miracles of Jesus in inseparable unity. This identity of Word and divine Act is most obvious in Mark's Gospel (cf. 9: 1; cf. 1 Cor. 4: 20), but the notable passage is that of Matt. 12: 28 (with the Lukan parallel 11: 20). "If I by the Spirit (or finger) of God cast out devils then the Kingdom of God is come upon you"; and so Jesus went about *preaching* and *healing* (Matt. 4: 23) and sent the disciples out to *preach* and to *heal* (cf. Matt. 13: 15: καὶ ἰάσομαι αὐτούς). This "and to heal" (καὶ ἰᾶσθαι, Luke 9: 2; cf. Matt. 10: 7 ff.; Mark 3: 13 ff.) is of special importance as it throws considerable light upon Mark 4: 12 (and parallels), where Jesus says, "Lest they should be converted and I should heal them" or "Lest it should be forgiven them."[1] In the eyes of Jesus the Act of healing thus appears identical with the Word of forgiveness. The classic example of that identification is found in the case of the paralytic in Mark 2. There, however, for the purpose of faith there is a lapse of time inserted between forgiveness and healing—"That ye may know the Son of man hath power on earth to forgive sins." It is precisely that lapse of time or eschatological reserve between the Word of the Kingdom and the power (even the violence—βιάζεται) of the Kingdom that Jesus is concerned to preserve in the Parable where the *Word* is spoken in such a way that full Action is still suspended, even in the case of the believer who enters the Kingdom of God.

[1] This is a quotation from Is. 6: 9 ff.; the LXX has instead of "and it should be forgiven them" the words "and I should heal them", both of which come in the Synoptics.

Jesus is not one whose Action falls short of His Word. Therefore, though the Word of forgiveness is spoken in such a parable as that of the Prodigal, that same Word is acted out in Himself on the Cross. There the Word of pardon is enacted in flesh and blood and inserted as a reality into our history and life. There the Word of forgiveness becomes an actual fact, not just a mere idea, not just a word spoken into the air, but an accomplished fact. "It is finished."

We may now see further why the Word was indirectly communicated through the parable because the Act is also part of the Word. The Word of God is not mere speech (λαλιά) but power of God (δύναμις τοῦ Θεοῦ), Christ crucified, as St. Paul said. It is because the Word is also power that it cannot be conveyed in mere speech but has to be conveyed in saving acts, in miraculous signs (σημεῖα or δυνάμεις) until the final great Act is completed. In the death of Jesus the Word and the Action are completely one. God is just and the justifier of the ungodly.

The next conception which demands our examination is that of *witness* (μάρτυς). Fundamentally there are two kinds of witness in the New Testament. First there is witness in the sense of John the Baptist, the man sent from God to bear witness to the light of the world. He was not himself the light, but pointed away from himself to another. So much did he concentrate upon bearing witness to this other that he reduced himself, as it were, to a bony finger pointing and the voice of one crying "Behold, the Lamb of God." Here the light is not mediated through himself. He himself fades out of the picture. "I must decrease, He must increase." He is witness only in the sense that he is a voice. It is in that sense that the preacher of the Gospel is witness in the act of preaching. He does not call attention to himself, but points away to the Lamb of God, so that all the focus of attention is concentrated upon Him to whom witness is borne. It is such preaching that as a result there takes place an encounter, a conversation, and an abiding with Jesus Christ (cf. John 1: 35 ff.).

Second, in the profoundest sense Christ is witness. He does not witness to a light that is other than Himself for He *is* the light of the world. Here, then, the witness and the light witnessed to are identical. Jesus Christ is in His own Person witness to Himself. That is why in the Fourth Gospel Jesus says: "I am the Truth." He is Truth in the form of personal being. He Himself is the Truth of God embodied forth in history, personally encountering man. Some of the most significant passages in the Fourth Gospel are concerned with this majestic *I am*. The most illuminating passage in this respect is that which describes Jesus before Pilate: "To this end was I born and for this cause came I into the world that I should bear witness unto the truth. Everyone that is of the truth heareth my voice. And Pilate saith unto him, What is truth?" Why did Jesus not answer Pilate?[1] Just because to ask Jesus Christ, who is Himself the Truth, a question about the Truth is to assume that He is not the Truth and that He only thinks *about* it or knows *about* it. Suppose we are talking to a man and then suddenly we say, "Do you exist?"; what can a man say if he is asked that question? He can only say something like this. "If you who stand here and talk to me cannot feel sure that I exist, what good can I do if I *tell* you that I do exist. If you do not believe that I exist you cannot believe what I say." That was the situation before Pilate. We can almost hear Jesus saying, "Pilate, if you do not hear my word you cannot understand my speech." But here we go a step deeper. "Pilate, if my person or my life does not open your eyes to what truth is, then it is utterly useless for me to *tell* you what the truth is." The word is identical with the Person of Jesus Christ. That thought comes out again in the trial with the majestic, kingly words of Jesus, ΕΓΩ ΕΙΜΙ, when the cry went up, "What need have we of further witness?" This man is witness Himself. He is a witness in which Word and Person are identical.

That event made a profound impression upon the early Church—indeed to such an extent that the fact that Jesus *witnessed a good confession* before Pontius Pilate became part of one of the earliest creeds of the Church.[2] The point is this: It is in His death that the Word and the Act of Christ, the Teaching and the Person of Christ become absolutely identical. It is there that He is supremely "the faithful and true witness" (Rev. 1: 5; 3: 14). It is there that the Captain of our salvation is made

[1] Cf. S. Kierkegaard, *Training in Christianity*, pp. 199 ff.

[2] Cf. O. Cullmann, *The Earliest Christian Confessions* (Eng. trans. by J. K. S. Reid), p. 25 f.

perfect through suffering. He is God's Truth done into flesh and blood. God's Truth in the midst of sin and guilt being true to itself. It is God's own witness in the flesh and blood of Jesus Christ, a witness consummated in His death. The New Testament calls that witness God's testimony (μαρτύριον): Christ crucified who is both Word (λόγος) and Power (δύναμις), that is, the Word made flesh, the witness who is Himself the Truth.

We must now ask in what sense we Christians are witnesses. How may we communicate the Truth by personal witness?

We are witnesses without doubt in the sense of John the Baptist when we preach, when we proclaim Jesus Christ in such a way that the person of the preacher fades out of the picture altogether and the Person of the living Christ is in the foreground encountering men face to face. But we must say more than that of Christian witness, for he that is least in the Kingdom of God is greater than John the Baptist. This Truth, to which we bear witness, is no longer a bare word but Truth in the form of personal being. The Christian has an intimate relation to the Truth such as John the Baptist did not have. Because Truth and personal being, Word and Deed are now one, the Christian does not know the Truth without being true, without in a profound sense becoming one with the Truth. That is why the New Testament uses such expressions as "doing the truth", "being true" and in particular ἀληθεύοντες ἐν ἀγάπῃ (Eph. 4: 15), and so St. Paul could say, "It pleased God to reveal His Son in me." In a profound sense the Word becomes flesh in the Christian by his incorporation into Christ, i.e. not through any extension of the Incarnation but through an eschatological "repetition" of the Incarnation in faith. And that is why real faith is always a virgin birth in the soul, for Christ, as St. Paul says, becomes formed within the believer. John the Baptist could never have said, "It pleased God to reveal His Son in me"; but now that the Word has been made flesh and the Incarnation has been completed upon the Cross, the Truth is done into our flesh and blood. It is part of the *mysterion* that "he that is joined to the Lord is one Spirit". The word that St. Paul uses here is very enlightening. It is κολλᾶσθαι, the word that is used for the marriage union when a man shall cleave unto his wife and they shall be one flesh. Behind that lies an idea that comes out more clearly in the Johannine literature, expressed in the

Hebrew word *yada* which means both to *know* and to *love.* The knowledge of the Truth is an act of the most intimate union. And so the Christian is a witness to the Truth in a profound sense because he is in the Truth and the Truth is in him. He has a relation to the Truth which Paul calls "communion" (κοινωνία) and which John calls "abiding" (μένειν). Christ alone is absolutely identical with the Truth. No one can be a witness to the Truth in that unique sense except Jesus Christ. The Christian, however, can be a witness to the Truth in a parallel fashion in so far as he is in Christ and Christ is in him.

The early Church thought of this union with the Truth as begun in baptism where the believer is sealed with the Truth and joined to Christ in death and resurrection. What he is in baptism he becomes through suffering inasmuch as through the fellowship (κοινωνία) of Christ's suffering he becomes conformable to Christ. Just as Jesus Christ began His ministry as a witness at baptism, identifying Himself with men, and completed that in His terrible baptism of blood in which He was so straitened till it was accomplished, when He became God's Testimony, God's Word-deed, God's Witness in flesh and blood, so the Christian in the thought of the early Church follows his Lord beginning with baptism when he starts to be a witness (μάρτυς) but becomes a witness in deed and in life through suffering for Christ. Thus, it is in the Christian's suffering witness (μαρτυρία) or martyrdom that he becomes conformable to Christ, and there, as far as is possible for men, he, the martyr-witness, becomes in his death and resurrection at one with Christ the Truth, who in Himself has already wrought out that atonement. He is a complete witness in word and life and seals it with his blood.[1] This is not the same as truth mediated through personality in the modern sense. It is something vastly different. How different we shall see now as we discuss the New Testament thought of proclamation.

According to St. Paul (1 Cor. 2: 1) God's testimony, *martyrion*, takes place through proclamation (κήρυγμα). God's testimony, as we have seen, is defined concretely as Christ crucified, Power of God. *Kerygma* may be defined as the straightforward

[1] There is a similar thought in the Epistle to the Hebrews in the idea of the death of the Testator where the promise is sealed with blood and where the Christian bearing witness to Christ must resist evil unto blood.

proclamation of this *martyrion* in such a way that the original *martyrion* actually takes place in the experience of the hearer. That is to say, the original event becomes event all over again through the power of the Spirit so that in *kerygma* a man encounters the living Christ, Christ crucified but risen. No doubt the *kerygma* in itself is mere speech (λαλιά or simply λόγοι) but it is not in the enticing words of man's wisdom nor with the excellency of speech, nor indeed by human or logical demonstration that the *martyrion* takes place, but in the demonstration of the Spirit and of power (ἐν ἀποδείξει πνευμάτος καὶ δυνάμεως). In other words, God bears witness to Himself as men proclaim the crucified and risen Christ. Through the power of the Spirit God's Testimony is self-authenticating. Thus St. Paul goes on to say that *kerygma* is a revelation (ἀποκάλυψις, see also Rom. 16: 25) or a mystery (μυστήριον). In itself *kerygma* is simply speech (λαλιά) but it becomes the power of God (δύναμις τοῦ Θεοῦ)—that is the great mystery (μυστήριον): God manifest in the flesh. This is the treasure that we may possess in earthen vessels. The Christian is put in trust with the Word of the Gospel, the *mysterion*, and it is in that sense that it pleases God to reveal His Son in the Christian's witness, while the Christian's sufferings in witness are the signs and the marks of Christ upon him. We may put this in our own words by saying that *kerygma* is objective, sacramental preaching with an eschatological result such that the original event (Christ crucified) becomes event all over again in the hearer.[1]

In the parable, as we saw, the action of the Word was suspended until the Crucifixion. Now the Word and Act are one, as one they take the field in *kerygma*. Whenever Christ crucified is preached in the demonstration of the Spirit there is power (δύναμις). Whether a man believes or not, the creative Word continues activity. It cannot return void. It is the Word-Deed that always acts upon man, the unbeliever as well as the be-

[1] That is why we cannot reject outright the thought of *repetition* in the Roman Mass. In the teaching of the New Testament, however, this is not temporal repetition, but eschatological event. Thus there is also an element of truth in the Roman doctrine of the *opus operatum*, for the Word-deed of God, that becomes event and becomes flesh in the sacrament, is the creative Word, the creating Word, the active Word, the original Word-deed of God (cf. John 1: 1 ff.). It is that Word that is the *dynamis* in *kerygma*.

liever. Hence it becomes a savour of life unto life or of death unto death. Some eat and drink salvation; others out of the same cup and the same plate eat and drink damnation. The Word of God is never idle. It always accomplishes its action upon man in the *kerygma.*

No doubt that is a terrible thought for the preacher (κῆρυξ), to think that through his preaching some may be damned. That is what Paul called the "terror of the Lord". But the constraint of the love of God was so heavy upon him that he was unable to resist. He was impelled to go on preaching as an ambassador of the reconciling love of God in Jesus Christ.

It is at this point that we meet again with the difficult passage of Mark 4: 11. If we score out the ἵνα, then we deny the *kerygma* its gracious and yet dread urgency, an urgency that modern preaching has largely lost. In Jesus Christ God's Word and God's Action are absolutely identical. He is the *Eschatos* who confronts men in His own Person, in His teaching and in His work, with the final Word and Act of God, and demands absolute love and obedience. The situation has the urgency of finality, of salvation and judgment. It is that eschatological urgency that lies at the heart of *kerygma. Kerygma* is not the proclamation of ideas or a bare message, but such a proclamation of Christ, the Word-Act of the living God, that by the Holy Spirit it becomes itself the actualization of the Word-Act among men in salvation and judgment.

Kerygma has thus a dual significance corresponding to the eschatological tension at its heart. It is used by God to intervene Himself in the human situation as He who once and for all has wrought out His final Act in the death and resurrection of Jesus Christ, so that through the *kerygma* the hearer is brought face to face in the present with the *eschaton* and may pass from death to life here and now. That takes place in the Church of Jesus Christ where the age to come has already overtaken this age and overlaps it. In the mercy of God, however, Jesus Christ, the *Eschatos* by whom God will judge the quick and the dead, has withdrawn Himself visibly from history, *without being absent*, and has appointed a day when He will *appear* again in glory and power. Meantime the Word of the Gospel and the final Deed of God are partially held apart in eschatological reserve until the *Parousia* or the *Epiphaneia*. This is therefore the age of grace, the age of *kerygma*, in which the Word of the Gospel is proclaimed to all, in which time and space are given for repentance and decision. But this is the age too when by the Spirit of God all who believe the *kerygma* of the Church may taste already the powers of the age to come and with her enter into the Kingdom of God. Because this Kingdom is neither an ideal nor a bare message but actuality in the midst, the *kerygma* of the Church is power of God, and through it the sovereignty of God (*βασιλεία τοῦ Θεοῦ*) overtakes men and by the passion of Christ struggles with them (Matt. 11: 12—*βιάζεται*). Those who lay violent hands upon it (*βιασταὶ ἁρπάζουσιν αὐτήν*)[1] may press into it (Luke 16:16—*βιάζεται*), but whether they will or no the grace of God will abound and reign over all.

(b) *An Aspect of the Biblical Conception of Faith*[2]

Several scholars have recently called for a reconsideration of faith as faithfulness answering to and dependent upon the Divine faithfulness. Certainly the New Testament conception of faith (*pistis*) is much more than that, for in faith the intellectual element of belief is powerfully represented, but even so this intellectual aspect of faith in the biblical context is grounded upon the basic fact of the faithfulness of God and falls within the determination of man's obedient and faithful response to the covenant-mercies of God.

The Hebrew root that concerns us here is *'mn*, with the meaning of firm, steadfast, together with the terms *'aman* and *'emunah*, with corresponding meanings, etc. As in the case of so many Hebrew words, the fundamental significance of *'mn* seems to be related closely to the intense family-consciousness of Israel. Thus, as Arthur Weiser points out,[3] the *qal*, *'aman*, is applied to a mother, or a nurse, or the guardian of a child, with reference to the faithfulness and reliability of that relationship. Thus, too,

[1] Cf. Luke 24: 29: *καὶ παρεβιάσαντο αὐτὸν λέγοντες, Μεῖνον μεθ' ἡμῶν.*

[2] Read before the Society for the Study of Theology, at Oxford, March, 1956; printed in *The Expository Times*, 1957, pp. 111–14.

[3] In the article on *pistis* in Kittel's *Theologisches Woerterbuch zum N.T.*, v. 183 f.

'ōmēn, *ōmeneth*, means a nurse, or a trustee, and *'omnah* means nursing or bringing up. And so *'ōmen* comes to refer to faithfulness in that light. Thus the vivid picture of the constancy and steadfastness of a parent to her child lurks behind the Old Testament conception of faithfulness.

This is the conception of steadfastness which in the Old Testament is applied to God in His covenant-faithfulness. For example, in Deut. 7: 9 it is used to speak of God's constancy in keeping covenant and *ḥesed* (RSV, "steadfast love") with His people, and in Is. 49: 7 it is applied to the faithfulness of God in His election of the Servant, to whom He will not only prove utterly faithful but for whom He will fulfil all His promises. Then this is described in v. 15 f. in the familiar words: "Can a woman forget her sucking child, that she should not have compassion on the son of her womb? yea, these may forget, yet will not I forget thee."

This conception of steadfastness or faithfulness is also applied in the Old Testament in a religious sense to people, such as the servant of God (Moses, Num. 12: 7), witnesses (Is. 8: 2; Jer. 42: 5), messengers (Prov. 25: 13), prophets (1 Sam. 3: 20), priests (1 Sam. 2: 35), and so on. But the conception of *'emunah* is applied above all to God.

To illustrate that, A. G. Hebert, in a recent article, cites Ps. 36: 5–7, and then comments as follows: "As the psalmist implies, the Hebrew word denoting steadfastness and firmness applies properly to God and not to man, who is repeatedly characterized as physically frail ('All flesh is as grass . . . the grass withereth, the flower fadeth: but the word of our God shall stand for ever'—Is. 40: 6–8) and as morally unstable (as in the first four verses of Ps. 36, where the ungodly man 'flatters himself in his own eyes' and his words are 'iniquity and deceit'). Hence the words 'faith' and 'to believe' (*he'emin*) do not properly describe a virtue or quality of man; they describe *man as taking refuge from his own frailty and instability in God who is firm and steadfast*. So in Is. 7: 9 the prophet says to the weak and timid King Ahaz, who is scared of the kings of Syria and northern Israel, 'If ye will not believe, ye shall not be established'—if you will not make-yourselves-firm (on God), you will not be made firm."[1]

[1] *Theology*, lviii, No. 424 (Oct., 1955), 374.

From this it is clear that we are faced with a problem when we have to translate the Hebrew into Greek, for the Greek *pistis* and *pisteuein* are not very happy equivalents for the words denoting faithfulness in Hebrew; *pistos*, however, is more applicable. Certainly the LXX is very uneasy about their use, and significant facts emerge which require far greater consideration than, I think, we have given to them. *Pistis*, for example, is never used in the LXX to signify "faith" or "belief", and *pistoi* is not used to describe the Old Testament "believers"—indeed it occurs but once in the canonical books in application to the members of the covenant-community, in Ps. 101: 6: "Mine eyes are upon the faithful (*pistous*) of the land", where clearly *pistoi* is properly rendered "faithful". The term *pisteuein* is used frequently in the LXX and used also in a strict religious sense, but this usage is dominated by the Old Testament conception of faithfulness.

The verb *'aman* has, it would appear, mainly a twofold usage. Primarily, it is used to mean "to make firm", "to establish", "to ground in the truth", and as such is sometimes translated in the LXX by *sterizein.* This meaning is apparent in many New Testament passages, of which we give two examples—

2 Thess. 3: 3: "Faithful (*pistos*) is the Lord who will strengthen (*sterixei*) you."

Luke 22: 31 f.: "Satan has desired to have you, that he may sift you as wheat: But I have prayed for you that your faith (*pistis*) fail not: and when you are converted, strengthen (*sterison*) your brethren."

The other use of *'aman* which we may note refers to "believing in" or "relying on", where the LXX translates by *pisteuein* or a compound form of it. Here we may cite two typical instances.

Gen. 15: 6: "Abraham believed (*episteusen*) God and it was counted unto him for righteousness (*dikaiosunen*)."

2 Chron. 20: 20: "Believe in (*empisteusate*) the Lord your God and ye shall be established (*empisteutheesthe*)."

In all these, and many similar instances in the Old Testament and the New Testament, the main emphasis is upon establishment or reliance upon God or upon the Truth in the Hebrew sense of the word for "truth".

That brings us to examine the concept of *'emeth*, the primary word in Hebrew for "truth". *'emeth* derives, of course, from the same root as *'emunah*, and indeed there does not seem to be a great deal of difference between *'emeth* and *'emunah*. There is a wide area, at any rate, in which they overlap in their meaning.

The usual translation of *'emeth* in the LXX is *aletheia*, but *aletheia* is not used to signify abstract or metaphysical truth, but what is grounded upon God's faithfulness, i.e. truth not as something static, but as active, efficacious reality, the reality of God in covenant-relationship. It is the steadfastness of God which is the ground of all truth. Primarily, truth is God's being true to Himself, His faithfulness or consistency. God's Truth means, therefore, that He keeps truth or faith with His people and requires them to keep truth or faith with Him. Thus the Hebrew *'emeth* is translated not only by *aletheia* but also by *pistis* and *dikaiosune*. There is no doubt that again and again where we have the words *pistis* and *dikaiosune* in the New Testament we must see behind them the Hebrew words, *'emeth* and *'emunah*, and where in the New Testament we have *aletheia* we must understand that not simply as a Greek word, but in the light of the biblical inclusion of *pistis* and *dikaiosune* in the concept of truth.

Because in the biblical context truth is grounded upon the divine faithfulness and the covenant-relation which it sets up, truth is also concerned with the event of the word through which relation between God and man, and man and man, takes place. It is in and through the word-event relationship that God's Truth is revealed and becomes efficacious reality among men. Here, of course, we have to do with the familiar Old Testament conception that when word and event coincide there is *'emeth* or truth. This is applied above all to God's Word, for when His deed corresponds to His Word, that is Truth. Truth is the faithfulness between God's actions and His Word. His Word accomplishing its purpose, actualizing itself, is the Truth with which men have to do, and it is with that Truth and Word of Truth that the prophets are burdened. The mighty Word of God enacts itself as Truth in the midst of God's people, for when through the prophets the Word of God reveals God and establishes His will, there is His Truth. Then God's Truth is fulfilled and actualized.

In the nature of the case this divine Word pressing to its Truth among men requires truth from the side of man in answer to it: man must walk before God in truth, and all his living, doing, speaking is to be a living of the truth, a doing of the truth, and a speaking of the truth. But when God's people prove unfaithful and untrue, His Truth becomes their judgment, and so *'emeth* is also used juridically or forensically. God keeps faith and keeps truth with sinners in judgment of sin, in vindication of the right, in justification. But out of this there arises the conception of God's Truth as a supreme eschatological and messianic conception, especially in Isaiah, Deutero-Isaiah, and in many Psalms. God is faithful who will bring His Word of Truth to pass in spite of all the unfaithfulness of His people, in spite of all the sin of man. When God's Word is finally established as Truth, when God has finally acted, the messianic Kingdom will be established. Truth will spring out of the earth, and a throne will be established in mercy and one shall sit on it in truth. It is this conception that forms such a powerful ingredient in the notion of the Servant in Deutero-Isaiah, for in and through the Servant the faithfulness of God both in judgment and in redemption presses toward its complete fulfilment in all the relations between God and His own.

When we turn over the pages to the New Testament and find this language being used and these conceptions being employed in the interpretation of Christ and the gospel, it becomes evident that Jesus Christ is understood as *the incarnate faithfulness of God*, the Word of God at last become event in our flesh in the fullest sense. "He is the Faithful and the True, the Amen." He is the Truth of God actualized in our midst—that is the Faithfulness of Christ Jesus (*pistis Christou Iesou*) of which St. Paul speaks so often.[1]

The New Testament conception of faith has a great wealth and variety which it is impossible to discuss here, where we are limiting ourselves to one main, fundamental aspect, but there are many passages where the usual translations are inadequate and where considerable light is brought to bear upon them from the Old Testament conceptions we have been discussing. Most of these passages have been adduced by Dr. Hebert in the valuable article referred to earlier. For our purpose here a

[1] See *The Church of Scotland Interim Report on Baptism* (1955), pp. 46–52.

selection will serve to indicate the line of interpretation that we must follow—

> 2 Thess. 2: 13: "God chose you from the beginning unto salvation in sanctification of the Spirit and faith of the truth" (*pistei aletheias*).

In Greek "faith of the truth" is an awkward expression, but it is clear from the Old Testament background that for St. Paul neither *pistis* nor *aletheia* will express fully what he is after, and so he puts both words together to convey what the Old Testament means by '*emeth* and/or '*emunah*.

> Rom. 3: 3: "Shall their faithlessness (*apistia*) make of none effect the faithfulness (*pistin*) of God?"

Difficult as the Greek is, the *pistis* of God, it expresses very excellent biblical teaching. The fundamental reality of our salvation is the divine faithfulness, and this in St. Paul's Epistles is equivalent to *dikaiosune*, righteousness, and in the Johannine writings, to *aletheia*, truth: all of these terms in the LXX may render the same Hebrew conception. Surely it is in this light that we are to translate

> Rom. 1: 17: "The righteousness of God is revealed from faith (*pisteos*) to faith (*pistin*)."

That is to say, the righteousness of God is revealed from God's *pistis* to man's *pistis*, but man's *pistis* is his implication in the divine *pistis*. God draws man within the sphere of His own faithfulness and righteousness and gives man to share in it, so that his faith is embraced by God's faithfulness. It is in precisely the same sense that St. Paul employs his favourite "*Pistos* is God who . . .", and then goes on to speak of man's salvation, or righteousness or faith in its utter reliance upon the divine faithfulness. That is the whole point of

> Rom. 3: 21–25: "God's *dikaiosune* is manifested through the *pistis* of Christ to all who believe (*tous pisteuontas*)."

Another set of significant passages we may take from the Epistle to the Galatians.

> Gal. 2: 16: "We . . . knowing that a man is not justified by the works of the law, but through the faithfulness of Jesus Christ (*dia*

pisteos Christou Iesou), even we believed (*episteusamen*) on Christ Jesus that we might be justified out of Christ's faithfulness (*ek pisteos Christou*), and not by the works of the law."

Gal. 2: 20: "I have been crucified with Christ; yet I live; and yet no longer I, but Christ liveth in me: and that life which I now live in the flesh I live in faith, the (*faithfulness*) which is of the Son of God (*en pistei te tou huiou tou theou*) who loved me and gave himself for me."

Gal. 3: 22: ". . . that the promise which derives from the faithfulness of Jesus Christ (*ek pisteos Iesou Christou*) might be given to them that believe (*tois pisteuousin*)."

In most of these passages the *pistis Iesou Christou* does not refer only either to the faithfulness of Christ or to the answering faithfulness of man, but is essentially a polarized expression denoting the faithfulness of Christ as its main ingredient but also involving or at least suggesting the answering faithfulness of man, and so his belief in Christ, but even within itself the faithfulness of Christ involves both the faithfulness of God and the faithfulness of the man Jesus. These typical passages from the Epistle to the Galatians give us the supreme difference between the Old Testament and the New Testament. Like the Old Testament, the New Testament also lays emphasis upon the faithfulness of God, and requires from man a corresponding faithfulness. But in the gospel the steadfast faithfulness of God has achieved its end in righteousness and truth in Jesus Christ, for in Him it has been actualized as Truth, and is fulfilled in our midst. Jesus Christ is not only the Truth of God but also Truth of God become man, the Truth of God become truth of man. As such Jesus is also the truth of man before God, for God, and toward God. Jesus Christ is thus not only the incarnation of the divine *pistis*, but He is the embodiment and actualization of man's *pistis* in covenant with God. He is not only the Righteousness of God, but the embodiment and actualization of our human righteousness before God. Thus St. Paul writes to the Philippians (3: 9): ". . . not having a righteousness of my own, based on law, but that which is through the faithfulness of Christ (*dia pisteos Christou*), the righteousness from God that depends on faith (*epi te pistei*)".

To expound this more fully we should have to go into the whole doctrine of the Atonement through the obedience of

Jesus Christ, and of our involvement in the whole movement of the Incarnation from the birth of Jesus to His ascension, and we cannot do that here. It may be sufficient to say that in the incarnate life of Jesus Christ, the Son of God become man among estranged men, we have the life of One who was God the Judge of man, and who was man judged by God; who was God bestowing Himself upon man in utter love, and who was man in obedient self-offering to God. In that life of union between God and man Christ manifested a twofold steadfastness or faithfulness: the steadfastness of God and the steadfastness of man in obedience to God; the steadfastness of God the Word revealing Himself to man, and the steadfastness of man believing and trusting in His Word and living faithfully upon it. Jesus Christ is God being true to Himself steadfastly and faithfully in the midst of our human estrangement, into which He entered in grace and steadfast love. Jesus Christ is man being perfectly true to God, steadfastly and faithfully obedient to God, the Amen of truth to God's truth. He is from the side of man, man's *pistis* answering to God's *pistis*, as well as from the side of God, God's *pistis* requiring man's *pistis*: as such He lived out the life of the Servant, fulfilling in Himself our salvation in righteousness and truth.

All that is remarkably summed up in 2 Cor. 1: 18 f., according to which Jesus Christ is not only the faithful *Yes* of God to man, but is also the faithful *Amen* of man to God. He offers to God for us, and is toward God in His own person and life, our human response of obedience and faithfulness. Here there are two great aspects of the Christian gospel which need to receive from us much fuller consideration than they have found in modern theology.

(a) The whole of our salvation depends upon the faithfulness of God who does not grow weary of being faithful. It is God's faithfulness that undergirds our feeble and faltering faith and enfolds it in His own. In Christ Jesus we are in fact unable to disentangle our faith from the faithfulness of God, for it belongs to our faith to be implicated in the faithfulness of God incarnated among us in Jesus Christ.

(b) Jesus Christ is not only the Word of God become flesh, He is also Believer, but Believer for us, vicariously Believer, whose very humanity is the embodiment of our salvation. In

Him who is Man of our humanity, we are graciously given to share, and so to participate in the whole course of His reconciling obedience from His birth to His death. That He stood in our place and gave to God account for us, that He believed for us, was faithful for us, and remains faithful even when we fail Him again and again, is the very substance of our salvation and the anchor of our hope.

(c) *The Mystery of the Kingdom*[1]

It is sometimes said, without much theological inquiry, that the New Testament does not use the word *mystery* in any homogeneous sense, and that it cannot rightly be applied to the Sacraments of Baptism and the Lord's Supper. Certainly the New Testament does not apply the word *mystery* directly to the sacraments, but it does, I think, use it in a fundamentally homogeneous sense appropriate to the sacraments; for it is appropriate to the life of the Church in Jesus Christ.

It is the aim of this article to seek to give a positive account of *mystery* in the biblical doctrine of Christ and His Church by drawing out the theological significance of three important words: μυστήριον, πρόθεσις, and κοινωνία. In its fullest and deepest sense, μυστήριον refers to the union of God and man eternally purposed in God but now revealed and set forth in Jesus Christ as true God and true Man in one Person, a union which creates room for itself in the midst of our estranged humanity and through fellowship or communion gathers men into one Body with Jesus Christ. In these expressions *union* and *one Body* with Jesus Christ we have described the meaning of μυστήριον. In the expressions *eternally purposed* and *set forth* we have the significance of πρόθεσις. And in the expressions *creates room* for itself, *fellowship* or *communion*, and gathering into *one Body with* Jesus Christ, we have the significance of κοινωνία. All this has to be understood from beginning to end in terms of the Incarnation, of the union of God and man brought about in the Incarnation of the Word, the hypostatic union of God and Man in Jesus Christ. That hypostatic union is a union which recedes back into the mystery of the Holy Trinity, the con-

[1] French text published in *Verbum Caro*, 1956, pp. 3–11.

substantial communion of Father, Son, and Holy Spirit; but it is set forth in the incarnate life of Jesus Christ in terms of the reconciliation of man and God, for through His atonement and through His Spirit Jesus Christ who is God and Man in Himself creates out of the world a Church concorporate with Himself, or one Body with Him.

Primarily, then, *μυστήριον* refers to the union of God and Man in the one Person of Jesus Christ. In Him that union is thrust like an axis into the midst of our Humanity, making everything to revolve around it and have significance only in relation to it. That axis recedes into eternity in the eternal election or *πρόθεσις* of God, but it also manifests itself in history in the Church of Jesus Christ. Jesus Christ is Himself the manifestation, the setting forth (*προτίθεσθαι, πρόθεσις*) of the eternal purpose (*πρόθεσις*); and it is in communion with Him, through participation in the divine *πρόθεσις*, that the Church of Christ is called into being and maintained from age to age as the sphere through which Christ continues to manifest Himself, as the community (*κοινωνία*) in which He dwells by His Spirit, and which He who ascended to fill all things will bring to its fullness in His eternal purpose; for He, the First-born of all creation, will return again to consummate His eternal purpose in the new creation. Then the *mystery* consummated already in Christ will be revealed and manifested in the new heaven and the new earth.

We may put that the other way round. *Mystery* is the secret that lies behind God's creation. In the heart of that creation God created man, in the union of male and female as one flesh, to reflect the image of God within their relation of union between man and God. But that union between man and God was sundered, and the union within mankind making mankind one flesh, was sundered: the secret was lost to man, the mystery was wholly recondite. But the eternal purpose of God remained, and so at last in Jesus Christ, after long preparation in God's purpose with Israel, the mystery of God's will became incarnate; it embodied itself in the midst of our humanity, begetting in Jesus Christ the One in whom all mankind is gathered back into communion with God. By the atonement of Christ the God-Man, through at-one-ment and *κοινωνία* in Him, mankind is restored to the lost relation with God; restored in Christ to union with God. The Church is the sphere or *κοινωνία* in history, Christ's own Body, where that mystery of the Kingdom is proclaimed, revealed, and actualized, and there is created a new humanity through participation in Jesus Christ the First-born among many brethren, the First-born of all creation.

That in compendium is the significance of *μυστήριον*, *πρόθεσις*, and *κοινωνία*, but it needs to be controlled and modified by more detailed exposition of the theological significance of these terms.

(1) *μυστήριον*

Mysterion has a twofold sense in the New Testament—and an opposite sense, the counterfeit *μυστήριον* of evil which we will not consider. Primarily *μυστήριον* is the *μυστήριον τοῦ Χριστοῦ* as Paul calls it (Eph. 3: 4), but it is also the *μυστήριον* that has become actualized among the apostles and prophets and is to be described as the mystery of Christ and His Church (Eph. 5: 32). This mystery is *Revelation* that is identical with Christ Himself—and here one thinks of the Johannine record of the majestic word of Jesus: Ἐγώ *εἰμι ἡ ὁδὸς καὶ ἡ ἀλήθεια καὶ ἡ ζωή* (John 14: 6).

In 1 Tim. 3: 16 the mystery is spoken of as "the great mystery of godliness, God manifest in the flesh, justified in the Spirit . . .". That is the mystery of the Kingdom of which Jesus Himself speaks in the Synoptic Gospels (Mark 4: 11; Luke 8: 10; Matt. 13: 11): "To you is given to know the mystery (or mysteries) of the Kingdom of God." It is significant that both singular and plural are used by the evangelists, as if one wanted to emphasize the Person of Christ as the full content of the mystery, and another the knowledge of this mystery. Christ in the midst is the real focus of the parable—so that in Johannine language the mystery is the Ἐγώ *εἰμι* of Him who is one with the Father, God with us in Christ. In Synoptic language He is Emmanuel, but that Christ is the Son of the living God is not revealed by flesh and blood, but only by the Father. This mystery of the Person of Christ, however, has the same doubleness as the word to *reveal* in both Hebrew and Greek usage in the Bible, where *reveal* means not only an unveiling or uncovering of God but an uncovering of the ear, or an unveiling of the heart, of man. Thus the Revelation of this mystery refers not only to the secret of the Person of Christ as true God and true Man, but also to the revealing of it to men. It is highly significant, therefore, that this mystery, in the records of the Synoptic Gospels, gathers round it a conclave of twelve disciples to whom it is given to know the mystery as it is not given to those without. "To you it is given to know the mystery of the Kingdom; but to those that are without, all things are done in parables" (Mark 4: 11).

Several Old Testament passages are here in view and immediately leap into the mind of the reader, such as Deut. 29: 29; Ps. 78: 12; and especially Is. 8: 16 f. which speaks of the messianic testimony and instruction out of the Torah as sealed up among the disciples. "Behold I and the children whom the Lord hath given me are for signs and wonders in Israel." This is also recalled by an *ἄγραφον* or unwritten saying of Jesus recorded by Clement of Alexandria and the Clementine Homilies, in which Jesus speaks of His *mystery* which He has between Himself and the sons of His house (Clem. *Strom.* 5.10.69; *Clem Hom.* 19.20). Jesus and His disciples build together one Temple or Body in His mystery of the Kingdom.

No doubt there is also in view here the twofold fact of the Danielic vision that the Kingdom is given to the Son of Man and to the saints of the Most High (Dan. 7: 13 f., 27; cf. also 2: 44). The mystery of the Kingdom is thus not only the mystery of the union between God and man in Christ Himself, but the mystery of the One and the Many through atonement which Paul expounds in several of his Epistles. Christ who died One for all, forms all who believe in Him into one Body with Him, one New Man enshrining at its heart in Christ Himself the union of God and man. That is the mystery of Christ, God manifest in the flesh, and the mystery concerning Christ and His Church.

This same mystery is enshrined in the apostolic revelation and *kerygma*, for through His *Šālîaḥ*-Spirit Christ Himself dwells in the midst of the apostles, leading them into all truth and making them in a unique sense stewards of the mysteries of God and able ministers of His Spirit (1 Cor. 4: 1). It is on the foundation of this oneness between Christ and His apostles that the whole Church is built up and grows up into Christ the Head as one

Body with Him. This mystery which was concealed from the ages but is now made manifest in the *kerygma* of the apostles is spoken of in a doubleness corresponding not only to the significance of revelation but also to the significance of the οἰκονομία. This term οἰκονομία refers either to the dispensation of the mystery on the part of God, or it can refer to the *stewardship* of the mysteries on the part of the apostles which is given to them for the sake of the Church (see Eph. 1: 10, and 3: 2, 9; Col. 1: 25; 1 Cor. 9: 17; 1 Tim. 1: 4; 1 Cor. 4: 1 f.). That mystery is to be fulfilled in the οἰκοδομή and αὔξησις of the Church, and belongs in that fulfilment to the great gathering together into one of all things in Christ, things in heaven and earth, things visible and invisible, through the reconciliation of the Cross. In other words, the mystery concerning Christ and His Church reaches out in cosmic significance and redemption, and will be brought to its complete consummation to which we may well apply the language of the Apocalypse: ἐτελέσθη τὸ μυστήριον τοῦ Θεοῦ (Rev. 10: 7). That is the eternal purpose of God which He has purposed in Jesus Christ, and is now revealed and proclaimed in the Church.

(b) πρόθεσις

Like the word μυστήριον, πρόθεσις has essentially a twofold sense.

(1) It refers to the purpose of God and is used by Paul particularly of the eternal election which God has purposed in Himself and wrought out in Jesus Christ. It is the eternal purpose which in Rom. 8: 28 ff. Paul speaks of as ranging from predestination on the one hand to future glory on the other hand: it is at once pre-destination and post-destination, as it were, but the emphasis is clearly on the purpose of God in Christ as reaching out into the eternal and infinite mystery of God. That eternal πρόθεσις in the fullness of time is incarnated in Jesus Christ (Eph. 3: 11 f.), and it is defined in terms of Jesus Christ by whom all things were created and through whom all things are restored to the purpose of the divine Will. Thus πρόθεσις is pre-destination, the eternal election moving into time in Christ the Elect or the Beloved One, and reaching out to fulfilment and consummation in the Church as Christ's Body, the fullness of Him who fulfils all in all, as Paul puts it in Eph. 1: 22 f.

(2) πρόθεσις, however, has another meaning as *setting forth*—προ-θέσις, where it appears primarily to have had a liturgical significance. Thus in the famous passage in Rom. 3: 24 f. where Paul speaks of our justification freely by grace through the redemption that is in Christ Jesus, he adds, "whom God set forth (προέθετο) a propitiation (ἱλαστήριον) through faith in his blood, to declare his righteousness . . .". The language of Paul recalls the language of the Old Testament in Exod. 25: 17; 37: 6 and 1 Chron. 28: 11, and the thought that it is at the mercy seat where the blood of the covenant is set forth in atonement that God communes with His covenant people. He holds communion with them on the basis of the atonement wherein His covenant-purpose is ever renewed in the midst of Israel.

It is difficult also not to see associated in the mind of St. Paul, as in the Old Testament liturgy, the significance of the shew-bread with that communion in covenant with God. By eating this bread the priests participated sacramentally in the Word of Life enshrined in the Holy of Holies: it was a kind of sacramental manna. In Hebrew this is spoken of as the bread of the face or the presence of God, and in Greek it is called the ἄρτος τῆς προθέσεως (cf. Heb. 9: 2). In Mark 2: 26 (Matt. 12: 4) we have a significant passage where Jesus asserts the authority of the Son of Man over the Old Testament regulations and in particular over the barriers the Jews had erected in worship in the House of God. Jesus deliberately broke down those barriers to inter-communion and gave as an example the act of Abiathar the high priest, who took of the sacred shew-bread of the priests and gave it to common men in their hunger. The thought here is that the Son of Man has authority to break down the φραγμός, the middle wall of partition as Paul calls it (Eph. 2: 14), dividing the Jews from the Gentiles, the inner from the outer court of the Temple. Jesus Himself spoke of this φραγμός as the fence or hedge which God had built round Israel His tender vine which He cultivated with such care (Matt. 21: 33, cf. Is. 5: 1 f.), but which had to be destroyed, while its inheritance was given to the nations of the earth (Mark 12: 1 ff.). The same word φραγμός is used in Jesus' parable of the wedding feast. God's servants are sent out to the highways and hedges or φραγμοί to compel people to come in and fill up God's house (Luke 14: 23). There they sit down to partake of the messianic meal, the heavenly manna and drink of the water of life. That is in parabolic form the counterpart to the apocalyptic description of the Great Marriage Supper of the Lamb, when the mystery will be completed and the Church will become one with the Word of God. But until then the Church is given the sacraments of Baptism and Holy Communion in which the Church as one Body with Christ continues to feed upon the Body and Blood of Christ. There in this sacramental fellowship, corresponding surely to the priestly meal at the Table of shew-bread before the face of God, the Church holds communion with God, feeding upon the heavenly manna on the very threshold of the Holy of Holies through the veil of which Christ has already entered, our High Priest.

Not all this, of course, is immediately related to the actual word *πρόθεσις* in its use in the New Testament; but it belongs to the whole context of the word in the *κοινωνία* of the Church. We may sum up the significance of *πρόθεσις* by saying: it refers both to the divine election or eternal purpose in Christ who is in Himself God and Man, and refers to the fact that the eternal purpose is set forth in the Incarnation (see also 2 Tim. 1: 8 f.), and continues to be set forth in the midst of the Church in its *κοινωνία*. Through Word and Sacrament in the Church we are ever given to have fellowship in the mystery of Christ (as one reading of Eph. 3: 9 puts it).

(3) *κοινωνία*

Like *μυστήριον* and *πρόθεσις*, *κοινωνία* has a twofold sense: a primary and a secondary sense. Primarily *κοινωνία* means participation through the Spirit in Jesus Christ, participation in the union of God and Man in Him—in the Johannine record that is profoundly given in John 17. Secondarily *κοινωνία* refers to the fellowship which is the Church, the communion which exists between members of the Body of Christ.

Primarily, then, *κοινωνία* means participation in the mystery of Christ. We have seen that *μυστήριον* is the union of God and Man in Christ, for in the eternal purpose that union was incarnated and bodied forth among men in the Word made flesh. That is the mystery of the Kingdom in its vertical dimension of *πρόθεσις* as it is inserted into human life and history, the axis of God's purpose of love. In Christ Himself that mystery is fully realized and actualized. God and Man are uniquely and finally One in Him, and in Him the Kingdom has fully and finally come. Jesus Christ as true God and True Man is the mystery of the Kingdom in His own Person. The whole work of atonement and reconciliation is already wrought out in Him. It is a finished work. κοινωνία means our participation in that completed union between God and Man, participation in the finished work of atonement and reconciliation. It is indeed only in that participation, in the κοινωνία of the mystery of Christ, that we *know* the mystery of the Kingdom.

Secondarily, however, κοινωνία means fellowship in the mystery as well as participation, but fellowship only on the ground of participation. Through the eternal πρόθεσις actualized in the Incarnation of Christ the mystery of the Kingdom is inserted, so to speak, into our fallen humanity, inserted into the midst of our flesh, into the midst of our choices and decisions, into the midst of our knowledge. The penetration of that mystery of the Kingdom, of the mystery of the union of God and Man, into our humanity means that it acts critically and creatively in the midst of our life and society creating room for itself, creating space for itself in the midst of our humanity. That is, it creates the Church, the circle of fellowship in which Christ Himself dwells. We have already seen that to belong to the mystery of the Kingdom in its secondary sense as the mystery given to the saints of the Most High, is realized first of all in the apostolate: that is the nucleus of the κοινωνία, the *communio sanctorum*. It is the κοινωνία of those who all together have κοινωνία in the mystery of Christ.

These two senses of κοινωνία are inseparable and are mutually related. There is no participation vertically in the mystery of Christ except by horizontal fellowship in the mystery, but there is no horizontal fellowship except by joint participation vertically through the Holy Spirit in the mystery of Christ who is true God and true Man. Now it is supremely in the cross and resurrection, by atonement and reconciliation, that the union of God and Man is inserted with power into our humanity, creating the Church as the Body of Christ, giving it to participate in His relation with the Father, but already that insertion had begun in the birth of Jesus; it was continued throughout His whole Incarnate life, and was enacted in the ministry of

Christ where already, therefore, the Church was founded as it was formed in the twelve disciples round the Person of our Lord, one Body with Him.

In the Incarnation the mystery of the union of God and Man, of the Oneness of God and Man in Christ, is inserted and enacted in our midst in a twofold way:

(*a*) It is inserted into the midst of our knowledge, and that takes place in the Teaching of Jesus and in the Revelation of the Father through the Son to the disciples, giving them communion or participation in God's knowledge of Himself. Thus Jesus says in Matt. 11: 25 f.: "I thank thee, O Father, Lord of Heaven and earth, because thou hast hid these things from the wise and prudent and hast revealed them unto babes. Even so, Father, for so it seemed good in thy sight. All things are delivered unto me of my Father: and no man knoweth the Son, but the Father; neither knoweth any man the Father, save the Son, and he to whomsoever the Son will reveal Him." Thus *κοινωνία* is participation in the relation of the Father and the Son, which takes place through the Holy Spirit—very clearly set out by the Fourth Gospel from ch. 14–ch. 17. It was the insertion of that mystery into the midst of Israel that created at once the band of disciple-learners and -receivers of Revelation, and yet called forth the reaction of resentment which culminated in the Cross. This is a *κοινωνία* which cuts across the face of man's knowledge of God and calls it radically into question: and men resent it. But in spite of all the contradiction of sin, the oneness of God and Man in mind is inserted into the knowledge of sinners, which is an essential part of Christ's reconciliation. The Teaching of Jesus was an essential part of the atonement, and the atonement could not have taken place apart from it.

(b) The oneness of God and Man in Christ is inserted into the midst of our being, into the midst of our sinful existence and history, into the midst of our guilt and death on the Cross. The inserting of the Oneness of God and Man into the deepest depths of man's existence in his awful estrangement from God, and the enactment of it in the midst of his sin and in spite of all that sin can do against it, is atonement. In a profound sense atonement is the insertion of the hypostatic union into the very being of our estranged and fallen humanity. That insertion of oneness by atonement results in *κοινωνία*, in the Church as the communion in which we are made partakers of the divine nature. The κοινωνία thus created by the atonement and resurrection of Christ is fully actualized by the outpouring of the Holy Spirit, and is maintained by the power of the Spirit as the Church continues in the fellowship of Word and Sacrament. We cannot here pursue the doctrine of the Church, but it is important to see that the Church is founded first not simply by the words of Jesus to Peter: "Upon this rock I will build my church", but upon the oneness of God and Man which in the birth of Jesus is inserted into our human existence, which reaches throughout the course of His life and particularly of His ministry, into the atonement and into the resurrection, and then into the ascension. The Union of God and Man which is the very life of the Son of Man is already of the essence of the atoning and reconciling work of Christ, and it is the same union which, after resurrection and ascension, through the Spirit gathers men into itself in and through the Church: that is in and through κοινωνία the divine πρόθεσις enshrining the eternal μυστήριον embodies itself horizontally in a community of those who are at one with God through the reconciliation of Christ.

We may summarize this in more dogmatic language. The mystery of Christ is the hypostatic union of true God and true Man in One Person; and as that union is enacted in atonement and in resurrection it issues in the community of the reconciled, the community of the resurrection. The πρόθεσις refers to the fact that what God is in Christ as God and Man in union, God is antecedently and eternally in Himself, and so the πρόθεσις speaks of the recession of the hypostatic union and its grounding eternally in the communion between Father, Son, and Holy Spirit. But πρόθεσις also is the setting forth of that union through Christ, through the atonement in such a way that men are given to participate in the communion of God the Father, the Son, and the Holy Spirit. Thus πρόθεσις is, as it were, the projection (προ-θέσις) of that communion in and through Christ into mankind, creating κοινωνία as its counterpart through the communion of the Holy Spirit. Indeed it seems clear that these three terms imply the doctrine of the Trinity; μυστήριον more particularly the eternal Son, πρόθεσις the eternal Father, and κοινωνία the eternal Spirit. This trinity of action is grounded eternally in the Holy Trinity of Father, Son, and Holy Spirit.

Is not baptism in the name of the Father, Son, and Holy Spirit, the sacrament of the Trinity, and in that sense a mystery, because it points to the mystery of the Kingdom? And is not Holy Communion in which we feed upon Christ a communion in the mystery of Christ? For it is here at the Lord's Supper that the Church ever becomes what it is, the Body of Christ, and rejoices in the great mystery between Christ and His Church. If we are to use the term *mystery* of the sacraments, however, it is clear that this differs *toto caelo* from the way in which mystery was used in the mystery-rites of ancient Greece. But if in this sense we can recover the setting of the sacraments in the doctrine of the Church as the communion in the mystery of Christ, and in the whole context of the Trinitarian faith, should we not use the term *mystery* rather than the term *sacrament* which lays the stress not on what God has once and for all done for us, but on our responsibilities and our vows of response? The term *mystery* used in the biblical sense would help us also to recover the biblical idea that there are not two or many sacraments but two essential "moments" in the one whole relation of the Church to Christ, one "moment" speaking of the once and for all participation in what Christ has once and for all done, and the other "moment" speaking of our continual renewal in that perfected reality in Christ Jesus.

3

THE SACRAMENT OF BAPTISM

(a) *The Origins of Baptism*[1]

It is by no means an easy matter to trace the precise origins of the rite of Christian Baptism both because there is a vast amount of material relevant to it and because the New Testament does not seem to offer any one clear line for consideration. It takes all this for granted and speaks of Baptism quite naturally, without any difficulty of communication and without any need for explanation. The derivation of the rite and the actions involved are everywhere presumed as familiar. That makes it all the more difficult for us, for we have to examine minutely the many allusions, hints, and images employed in the New Testament writings, and in particular the references, and citations (often very incomplete) from the Old Testament, in order to place ourselves as completely as possible in the position of the New Testament writers, and then from their *Sitz im Denken* as well as *Sitz im Leben* seek to unravel their presuppositions and interpret their meaning.

Perhaps one of the most difficult things for us to do to-day, after a century of exhaustive Old Testament investigation, is to get ourselves into the position from which the New Testament writers regarded and interpreted and handled the Old Testament. Take, for example, the very extraordinary passage in the sixteenth chapter of Ezekiel. The interpretations of this by Old Testament scholars appear to differ widely, but they differ radically from that found everywhere in the Rabbinic Judaism of the first three centuries A.D., e.g. in the older *Pesikta*. But how would the writers of the New Testament have interpreted it? One thing must be clear, that we cannot expect them to have understood it after the fashion of scientific Old Testament scholarship to-day. They did not have that sort of approach to the Old Testament and certainly did not have the equipment

[1] Lecture delivered to the University of Lund, October, 1956, reprinted from *S.J.T.*, vol. 11/2, 1958, pp. 158–171.

it requires. It is more likely that they would have looked at it as their Jewish contemporaries looked at it, as a parable of Yahweh's dealing with Israel after the fashion of Jewish adoption of a newly-born foundling child of heathen parents. In this way the parable was interpreted to speak of Israel as a child-proselyte from heathendom, baptized and cleansed and brought into the Covenant, and then when she grew of age assumed into the marriage-relationship. But alas! she proved unfaithful to her husband who had entered into covenant with her. Taken in that way, it is certainly a remarkable parable of Israel adopted to be the child of Yahweh, sealed with the seal of the Covenant, and then in renewal of the Covenant espoused as the Bride of Yahweh. This double sealing of the Covenant was Rabbinically discerned in the reference in Ezekiel 16 to the two "bloods", vv. 6, 9, 22, and was interpreted to refer parabolically to circumcision and passover. This very language is still used to-day in the rite of circumcision.

Now that is quite definitely typical of Judaistic interpretation of the Old Testament during New Testament times, and we know that this passage and its interpretation played a fundamental part in the understanding of proselyte Baptism. Those incorporated by baptism into Israel were adopted into the Covenant in the same way that Israel itself was adopted by Yahweh. But can we say that the New Testament writers would have regarded Ezekiel 16 in this light? We have to allow for the fact that these interpretations, repeated *ad nauseam* in the Rabbinic literature, were embedded in the Jewish tradition and conditioned the Christian reading and interpreting of the Old Testament, but on the other hand their interpretation of the Old Testament was decisively altered by the overwhelming and shattering fact of Christ, which drew to it all the lines of Old Testament teaching, fulfilling them and abrogating them in a sovereign manner.

That is what makes it so difficult to get into the *Sitz im Denken* of the New Testament writers to see precisely how they looked at particular passages in the Old Testament. They certainly looked at the Old Testament from a Christian perspective. That did not mean that their Jewish tradition of interpretation was altogether destroyed. On the contrary it was given reinterpretation and made to point forward in a new way to Christ.

But just because all lines were now seen to point forward to Christ, the many lines made to converge on Him overlapped the nearer their point of convergence. That is particularly evident in the way the New Testament writers use images from the Old Testament. They lay them on top of one another and employ several together in their use of the Old Testament to express their understanding of the salvation fulfilled in Christ. That usage extends even to Old Testament words and phrases and part-sentences, which are brought together sometimes within a single verse in the New Testament. That process of conflating images and terms was already at work in Judaism, but now in the fulfilment of the ancient promises in Christ that is done in a new way, and with a sovereign freedom in handling Old Testament citations. The reality in Christ is not bound by the ancient shadow or image; that was only a signitive pointer to the reality and now that the reality has arrived it interprets itself, not by an arbitrary handling of the Old Testament, but by a significant and sovereign use of it, bending it in subservience to the New.

In all this there is a tendency to go back direct to the Old Testament, to read it with new eyes and the new insights imparted by the mighty events of the Gospel; but even so there could be no escaping from the oral Jewish tradition which for so long had shaped the reading and understanding of the Old Testament. Rather was this Jewish tradition itself taken under control and adapted in the reinterpretation of Israel in the Church. It is only when we get inside that complicated reorientation to the Old Testament and to Jewish interpretation of it that we can discern the significance of so many of the allusions and references of the New Testament to the Old and to Jewish tradition. It is in that light, for example, that Paul appears to make use of Ezekiel 16 in Ephesians 5: 25 ff., but if so, how radically different is his employment of Ezekiel 16 from that of Rabbinic Judaism when he uses it to speak of the Baptism of the Church as the Bride of Christ.

That is but one important allusion offered in the New Testament to the origin of the rite of Baptism, but how are we to thread our way through the maze of allusions and references in this connexion? I believe that we may profitably take our cue from the Judaistic conception of proselyte baptism. By that I do not mean at all that we are to see in proselyte baptism itself the source of the Christian rite, but that proselyte baptism helps us to see a line of interpretation embedded in the Jewish tradition which throws considerable light upon what the New Testament writers took for granted in regard to the origins of the Christian rite. The firm use of proselyte baptism appears in Judaism in the middle of the second century; allusions to it appear frequently in Justin Martyr's *Dialogue with Trypho*. There are references to it also in the *Mishnah* which allude to a time when the Temple was still standing. But perhaps our oldest evidence for it comes from the New Testament, particularly from the Epistles of St. Paul who appears to use the language of Proselyte Baptism in 1 Cor. 10: 1 ff.; 2 Cor. 5: 17; 6: 14 ff.; 7: 1; Rom. 6: 15 ff.; Eph. 2: 11 f., etc. Be that as it may, it is extremely difficult to conclude that the firm practice of proselyte baptism in second-century Judaism did not go back, like everything else, to authoritative sanctions in their tradition very much earlier, and that the written teaching of the second century did not have behind it a long oral tradition.

I do not say this in order to argue that Christian baptism depends on or derives from proselyte baptism, but simply in order to make it clear that it is a legitimate procedure to examine the hints that proselyte baptism gives us of formative lines of interpretation at work in Judaism long before the firm practice of proselyte baptism was established, or its rite and meaning fully set forth in the tractate *Gerim*.

Proselyte baptism involved three main elements: circumcision, the sprinkling of sin-offering water on the third and seventh days after circumcision, and immersion. This was the rite of incorporation into the Covenant-people and of taking on the yoke of the Torah. Behind the rite lay a powerful theology of participation in the Exodus redemption out of Egypt, the crossing of the Red Sea, and of sanctificatory cleansing in the establishment of the Covenant at Mt. Sinai. This is found with particular clarity in the *Pesikta*, and is still preserved in the *Passover Haggadah*. The "proselyte" to Judaism, the *ger*, meant more than a proselyte in our sense of the word. Even the Greek sought to render the fact that he is one who may "draw near" to worship God as one of His holy people engaging in the holy things of law and cult. But the Hebrew *ger* has also a fundamental significance, as Nahum Levison has recently pointed out,[1] close to the word *hibri* or Hebrew, the one from the other side, a foreigner. Thus what was prescribed for the *gerim* in their incorporation into the *hibri* throws a good deal of light upon the Hebrews as a Covenant-people. It is in this respect that Ezekiel 16 surely has part of its far-reaching significance. On the other hand, incorporation into the *hibri* must be one of the oldest and most telling ideas governing the conception of Baptism which it eventually demanded. By looking behind these rites incorporating proselytes into the Covenant-people we can find considerable help in understanding the teaching of the New Testament.

(1) *Circumcision*

In the account offered by the Old Testament itself, this rite was given to Abraham and his family as *hibri* in ratification of the Covenant and in seal of the divine promise attached to it, the promise of a country but also of a messianic future. The promise of the land was not fulfilled for four hundred years, for the Hebrews were themselves to be *gerim* in the land of Egypt (Gen. 15: 13). It was in connexion with the first Passover and the Exodus out of Egypt that the term *ger* seems to come into prominence in the Old Testament. There it is that we hear that the *ger* was to be circumcised (and all male members of his family), if he was to take part in the Passover. He was to come under the one Law of the one Covenant (Exod. 12: 43–49). That is further elucidated in Leviticus 19, where it was prescribed that Israelites should love the *gerim* as they loved themselves, for they also were *gerim* in Egypt—"I am Yahweh, your God", it is added, for the whole worship of Yahweh was at stake.

There are two main points I would like to stress here.

(a) The relation of circumcision to the messianic promise. Until the Hebrews entered the promised land they too were *gerim*. That is a conception that came to the fore in the later literature of the Old Testament, exilic and post-exilic, when the Jews came to think of themselves as sojourners and aliens resident in a foreign country. They were essentially pilgrims expecting the messianic country, the messianic Kingdom. They were God's *gerim*, a thought particularly clear in the Psalms

[1] *S.J.T.* 10/7, p. 45. On Proselyte Baptism, see *New Testament Studies*, vol. 1/2, 1954, pp. 150 ff.

where there is a return to the idea that they were children of Abraham waiting to take possession of the promised land. At the same time the status of the non-Israelite *gerim* came to be increasingly appreciated as in Isaiah 56: 3–5, which seems to have influenced the Zadokite community of Damascus and the allied Community at Qumran. Thus at the height of the Old Testament teaching we have the important idea that the circumcised children of Abraham are messianically to be regarded as *gerim* expecting a country, expecting the fulfilment of the ancient promises of the Covenant.

(b) The Covenant cut into the flesh. In circumcision the Covenant was cut into the flesh of Israel as a sign and seal of its promised fulfilment. The Covenant was such that it had to be actualized in the whole life of Israel, enacted in its flesh, done into its existence before God. From the Deuteronomic literature on this was given a deeper interpretation in terms of the circumcision of ears, lips, and heart—the whole "inner man", so to speak, had to be circumcised. That is to say, the Covenant will of God had to be inscribed by His finger or by His Spirit upon the tablets of the heart. That idea came to prominence especially in Ezekiel and Jeremiah, but it is clear that when that took place, the writing of God's Word and will in the heart through the operation of the Spirit, then the Old Covenant would take on a new form. It would be a New Covenant.

But how was this Covenant to be fulfilled in the flesh of Israel? How was it to be cut right into the existence of Israel and so fulfilled from within Israel, wholly and completely fulfilled? The answer given by the Old Testament is found in the Deutero-Isaianic doctrine of "the Servant of the Lord", as He who will fulfil and mediate the Covenant. (I am myself convinced that while the Servant represents Israel in its ordeal it has a further significance in which, without denial of the corporate character of the Servant, one Servant in the Midst of Israel is indicated, and that here it is ultimately the figure of Moses, "the servant of the Lord", that lies behind it.) The fulfilment of God's Word and Truth, His judgment and mercy, takes place in the life of the Servant, but in him it is vicariously fulfilled for all. In the later Isaianic prophecies we hear also of the Holy Spirit. The Servant is anointed with the Spirit and through Him the Spirit is bestowed. And in this connexion we may add the prophecies of Joel fulfilled on the day of Pentecost in the Baptism of the Spirit.

We are now in a position to gather up the results of this discussion and put it into New Testament language. Circumcision is fulfilled in the New Covenant, (a) in the blood of Christ, which is the blood of the New Covenant, that is in His total circumcision or crucifixion; and (b) in His gift of the Holy Spirit. With these two facts the Old Covenant no longer remains in force in the old form, and therefore the outward sign of it is abrogated or rather displaced by a sign appropriate to the fulfilled reality of the New Covenant in Christ. Here it is the Epistle of Galatians that is most instructive. If the Covenant still stands in its old form, then argues St. Paul, what Christ has done is of no avail. But actually the whole relation between man and God has entered upon a new age, in the New Covenant made by God in Christ. This is fulfilled once and for all in the breaking of the Body of Christ and in the shedding of His Blood, and in the outpouring of the Spirit upon all flesh, that is upon all who enter into the New Covenant in the Name of Christ. Baptism is therefore given to take the place of circumcision as the sign and seal of the New Covenant.

(2) *The Sprinkling of Sin-Offering Water, or the Water of Separation*

The significance of this has been much neglected, no doubt because of its obscurity to Western minds. However, the fact that in the majority of cases, where the Greek word *baptizein* is used religiously in pre-Christian Jewish literature, it refers to this solemn cleansing by sprinkling ought to be sufficient to indicate its importance in examining the background to the rite of Baptism. The commandments regarding this rite and the traditions connected with it make it clear that it was one of the most solemn and awful rites in the Old Testament except perhaps that of the high priest entering into the Holy of Holies once a year on the Day of Atonement at the very risk of his life. It is important to realize, as Levison has pointed out anew, that the language used of it in the Old Testament is incredibly strong, viz., *chatah*, meaning to *un-sin*. The language used in the *Mishnah* indicates that in some sense it was thought of as a baptism of death, a death to sin. The rite involved the total burning by fire without the camp of a red heifer as a sin offering, and the preservation of its ashes which were to be used along with the sprinkling of water for un-sinning and sanctification on occasions of grave defilement. Some scholars, not without justification, regard the rite as an Israelite substitution for the pagan rite of "passing through fire" children in sacrifice to Moloch. That may well lie behind the incident recorded in Numbers 31 where the purification of Israel and their Midianite prisoners was to be effected through the water of separation or impurity while the gold and silver, etc. captured were to be "passed through fire". What could not endure the fire was to be made to pass through water, that is, by means of this solemn sprinkling. Whatever the origin of the rite, cleansing by sin-offering water was a "vicarious rite" in place of a kind of baptism by fire.

Be that as it may, we find that the ordinance of separation and un-sinning in this awful way applied to the *gerim* as well as to the Israelite. It was this that added awful solemnity to the circumcision of the proselyte, and made his coming from circumcision to be like "a coming from the grave" as the *Mishnah* puts it.

To see the deep significance of this it is worth looking at the rites ordained for the cleansing and readmission of lepers to fellowship in Israel. Lepers were separated and banished from common life as utterly unclean and were regarded as having no civil rights. Healed lepers, however, had to be readmitted through a double rite, a ceremony of reconsecration through a sevenfold sprinkling of the water of un-sinning, remarkably parallel to that for the consecration to priesthood, enabling them to draw near to holy things, and a ceremony remarkably parallel to that of the Day of Atonement for the annual renewal of the Covenant between God and Israel. Only thus could a leper be reincorporated into the holy nation and priestly people of Israel. Something of that undoubtedly influenced Elisha in the commands he gave to Naaman, the Syrian leper, whose sevenfold baptism (the word *baptizein* is used in the LXX) corresponded to the sevenfold sprinkling of the leper.

It is in Psalm 51, however, that we see even more deeply into its spiritual significance. David after his fearful sin regards himself as cut off from God and deprived of His Spirit, and prays for cleansing as if he had become a leper or a heathen. "Purge (i.e. un-sin) me with hyssop and I shall be clean: wash me and

I shall be whiter than snow. Hide thy face from my sins, and blot out all mine iniquities. Create in me a clean heart, O God, and renew a right spirit within me. Cast me not away from thy presence; and take not thy holy Spirit from me. Restore unto me the joy of thy salvation and uphold me with a willing Spirit." It was only then that he could draw near with the customary sacrifices to be offered upon God's altar.

It is significant that at important points in the Old Testament writings this language was used with profound spiritual and even messianic significance. It was used by Ezekiel in his spiritual reinterpretation of circumcision, and above all in the important passage in 36: 25 where the messianic gift of a cleansing and quickening Spirit is spoken of as the sprinkling of "clean waters", resulting in a new heart and a new spirit. "And I will put my Spirit within you, and cause you to walk in my statutes, and ye shall keep my judgments and do them. And ye shall dwell in the land that I gave to your fathers: and ye shall be my people, and I will be your God." Israel regarded as still waiting to enter the promised land is promised a fulfilment of God's Covenant made with Abraham, but a Covenant fulfilled in a new way through the Spirit. This passage was cited times without number in the Mishnaic and Talmudic literature of Judaism, but nowhere perhaps more significantly than at the end of the *Yoma* where it is adduced to give interpretation to the baptismal ablution of the high priest on the Day of Atonement, and to interpret that baptism messianically as "the hope of Israel".

Thus circumcision came to be reinterpreted in terms of a messianic gift of the Spirit, but the association of the sprinkling of the water of separation added to that the idea of a baptism of the Spirit which was at once un-sinning and quickening. The association of this kind of baptism or sprinkling of the water of the Spirit with circumcision, and its messianic reinterpretation, can hardly be over-estimated so far as the origins of the New Testament rite are concerned. It is of course the Epistle to the Hebrews which particularly points to this line of tradition in the origin of the rite of Baptism. The Old Testament rites are regarded as fulfilled in Christ Himself, the Mediator of a New Covenant, who, like the red heifer, suffered in vicarious sacrifice without the camp. Thus in Christ we may "draw near with a true heart in fullness of faith, having our hearts sprinkled from an evil conscience, and our bodies washed with pure water". The reinterpretation of the Old Testament rites in Christ does not mean the abolition of the use of water, but the language of the old rites is used to interpret the relation of this baptismal rite to Christ's fulfilment of the Covenant and His opening up for us a new and living way into the holy presence of God.

(3) *Immersion in Water*

Where did this rite come from and what was its significance? We know that the Near East abounded in "baptist" movements at the turn of the era, and that even within Israel there were many sects practising baptismal ablutions, the best known of which were the Pharisees who had a rite of initiation into the sect by immersion of the whole family, including women and children, but who practised frequent and daily baptisms in which they carried late-Jewish purifications to absurd lengths. In Judaism, however, all these rites of baptismal ablution and purification seem to go back to the central rites associated with the Laver in the Tabernacle or the Sea in the Temple, at which washing in water was required by priests on entering or leaving the Holy Place, and also before solemn sacrifice. Washing of the victims was also required, a fact which may be reflected in the sacrifice by Elijah on Mount Carmel. The particularly solemn act of ablution was that of the high priest at consecration (the only instance of baptism of one at the hands of another, e.g. of Aaron at the hands of Moses, unless Solomon was given a similar cleansing at the Gihon at his consecration to be king) and again on the Day of Atonement. It would appear that the placing of the Laver in the Temple was originally designed, or at least later interpreted, to represent symbolically the crossing of the Red Sea together with the sanctification of Israel for the service of God within the Covenant, just as the placing of the Tables of the Law in the Ark within the Holy of Holies appears to represent symbolically and to recall liturgically the ascent of Moses to receive the Law in the thick darkness which shrouded the holy presence of God on Mt. Sinai. At any rate the Laver did represent a liturgical extension into the worship of Israel of its sanctification and cleansing as a people taken into holy Covenant with God. When this sanctification and cleansing was applied to the proselyte, Judaism certainly interpreted it in an elaborate doctrine of the crossing of the Red Sea and the sanctification of Israel before Mt. Sinai.

Thus the application to proselytes of an act of immersion at the end of their initiation meant their participation in the mighty acts of Israel's redemption out of Egypt at the Exodus, their entry into the holy and priestly people of the Covenant, and their readiness through sanctification to receive instruction from the Law of God and to come under its yoke. It meant that they shared in God's sanctification or hallowing of Himself in the midst of His people Israel, and separated themselves from the darkness and uncleanness of the heathen world to live within the light and purity of God's revelation and appointed way of life. In this way they took shelter in the Name of God and came under the wings of His Holy Spirit; born again out of heathendom, they were new creatures, no longer aliens and strangers but fellow-citizens of the commonwealth of Israel in the family of God.

When we turn from the Old Testament and its traditional interpretation to the New Testament we are confronted right away with the Baptism of John the Baptist, and the Baptism of Jesus by John. Did this rite appear in entire independence of what we have been considering in the context of Jewish thought and practice? That is most unlikely. Then how are we to regard the distinctive characteristics of John's Baptism and how are we to interpret them over against the tradition of prior and contemporary Judaism?

Here we are offered, it would appear, some real help from the so-called Dead Sea Scrolls, both in a general way and at two particular points which seem to me to be important.

Generally these Judaean documents, and in particular the Manual of Discipline, along with the Zadokite Fragments from Damascus, use not only the language but many of the ideas we have been discussing, such as spiritual circumcision, the sprinkling of sin-offering water for atonement messianically interpreted, and the application of priestly ablution from the Temple to all initiated members of the Covenant Community. In all this circumcision itself falls into the background. Indeed there is no mention of it in the two documents named except in a spiritual sense. What is important is its fulfilment in the anointing of the Spirit and in the illumination of the Thorah, which is accompanied by sprinkling and immersion. These rites are not regarded as efficacious in themselves but as symbolic of the divine cleansing and justification. Atonement is by the Holy Spirit of God, apparently replacing the blood of the Covenant and all animal sacrifices. And of course it is supremely noteworthy that on the ground of such purification in water and Spirit admission is given to the messianic meal of bread and wine.

The attempts that have been made to draw close parallels between these ideas and practices and those of John the Baptist to prove their direct and immediate influence upon him are not convincing, but it is significant that here we have some justification for the general line of interpretation of the origins of the rite of Baptism we have been pursuing. If the documents in question are to be dated just prior to the fall of Jerusalem or even sometime within the first century, they do indicate clearly that there was within Judaism a remarkable development in reinterpreting the Old Testament similar to that which appears to lie behind the pages of the New Testament in the Jewish tradition, a development which was radically and critically reinterpreted once again in the light of the mighty acts of God in Christ. The parallels between the conceptions embedded in the New Testament and those in these sectarian communities at Qumran and Damascus help us to understand the change that took place in Jewish Christianity as it emerged out of Judaism, although they do not supply us with actual source-material governing that change.

There are two particular points that demand closer consideration.

(a) Although the *gerim* are mentioned as a distinct group of novitiates in the Covenant Community by the Damascus document, and may well be implied in the Manual of Discipline, in both of them all members of the Covenant Community admitted by baptismal lustration and covenantal oath-taking tended to be regarded as proselytes to the Lord or converts to the New Covenant. The term used is *nilwim*, taken from Isaiah 56: 3, 6, to describe "messianic *gerim*", as it were. Here Israelites are somehow looked on as polluted and unclean like lepers, so that solemn purification is absolutely necessary.

Hence the solemn cleansing applied to lepers and to those polluted by death, and to the high priest on the Day of Atonement, is applied to them. In other words, it is no longer sufficient to be a circumcised Jew. All have to undergo repentance and purification, circumcised Jews and proselytes alike; they have to become converted as members of the messianic Community and as participators in the New Covenant. (It is also interesting to note that the Damascus Document refers to the idea, common also in Rabbinic literature, that Abraham was a proselyte even in the narrower sense of the word.)

(b) Along with this there is apparent a reaction against a crude and literalist practising of the Cult in favour of an attempt to translate the priestly Cult into the actual life and existence of the Covenant people. Thus the structural pattern of the Tabernacle or Temple seems to be transferred to "the Community of the New Covenant" or "the Covenant of friendship" (*berith ḥesed*), as Brownlee has translated it. Through their initiatory rites the people were shaped into a unity and were regarded as building together a sort of living Temple of people, a "House of Holiness" with its Holy of Holies, Holy Place, and its Outer Court for Israelites, and in the Zadokite Document from Damascus also a fourth peripheral group apparently corresponding to the outer Gentile precincts of the Temple. Moreover, priestly ablution and the priestly ephod were extended to all covenanted members of the Community, now regarded as a sort of corporate priesthood of "the anointed ones". In other words, here we have an attempt by rigorous discipline to carry out what I have called the requirement that the Covenant Will of God must be done into the very life and existence of Israel.

We are of course at once reminded of the teaching of the New Testament, notably of Paul and 1 Peter, of the Church as the Habitation of God, the Temple of the Spirit, as the Holy People or House of God built up of living stones, but here in the New Testament there is a radical difference: the living Temple is above all the Body of Jesus Christ, and His Body in two senses; in reference to Christ Himself and in reference to the Church of Christ which He adopts in His grace to be His Body. In other words, the difference between the conception of the Covenant

Community in the documents of Qumran and Damascus and the Christian conception is that the Church is the people of the New Covenant only because, and on the ground of the fact that, the Covenant has actually been fulfilled in Jesus Christ, who gathers up Israel in Himself and is the beginning of a New Israel embracing all who are gathered into the Name of Christ and are baptized with His Spirit. It is in and through Jesus Christ and by the power of His Spirit that the Covenant Will of God is at last enacted into the existence of God's people. Baptism is therefore into His Name, for He is the Mediator of the New Covenant, but "into His Name" includes also the Name of the Father and the Spirit, for the Covenant He mediates is that in which God wills to be our Father and determines us to be His children; and the nature of this Covenant is spiritual, inscribed in our hearts by the Spirit of God Himself.

(b) *Aspects of Baptism in the New Testament*[1]

All the four Gospels take time to speak about John the Baptist before they offer us any account of the ministry and teaching of Christ, and they are concerned to show the very close relation between the mission of John, preparatory though it was, and the mission of Christ the Son of God and Servant of the Lord. That connexion is nowhere more evident than in regard to Baptism which had been given such a central and significant role in the ministry and message of John, as Baptism into repentant preparation for the coming of the Christ. John came to be known as the Baptizer not only because Baptism occupied such a central place, but because He administered Baptism to others. Under him Baptism was no longer to be ministered by the subjects of Baptism to themselves, but was administered to them as passive receivers. As such, John's Baptism had a radical character appropriate to his radical message, cutting through all the claims and pretensions of the Jews to the very root of their existence as a people of God, in order to clear the way for the advent of the Messiah and to prepare for Him a people ready for an entirely new situation. Therefore John summoned the Jews to uproot themselves out of their nationalist existence

[1] Lecture delivered to the University of Lund, October, 1956, reprinted from *Theologische Zeitschrift*, 14.3, 1958, pp. 241–260.

and to become a people of God again, a pilgrim people expecting to enter into the messianic country. He stood on the banks of the historic Jordan and pointed the way through the water to the messianic Kingdom, insisting that it had already drawn near and was about to break in with eschatological swiftness and urgency.

Two facts stand out in the narratives. This Baptism and message proclaimed an uprooting and a radical judgment, but also a new era of the Spirit, and both were to be fulfilled by the Messiah. He would lay the axe to the root of Israel and cleanse the Temple (the threshing floor), but He would also baptize with the Spirit and a new sort of Abraham's children would be begotten.

Then into the midst of that situation stepped the Messiah Himself, Jesus, to fulfil all righteousness: to fulfil the divine judgment and to fulfil the Covenant-Will of God, to enact the mighty acts of God and so to bring redemption. It is made clear in various ways that Jesus steps in to do that as the Servant-Son, while His life and work as Servant-Son begins right away with this submission to the Baptism of John. Thus the Baptism of Jesus is regarded as one of the mighty acts of the Gospel, one of the saving acts inaugurating the Kingdom; for with it the heavens were opened and the power of the Spirit descended upon Christ the acknowledged Servant-Son, while the language of that acknowledgment from the Father to the Son indicates the nature and character of the relationship to God which this Baptism involved. The language of the Evangelical narratives appears to recall that of *The Testament of Levi* (18): "The heavens shall be opened and from the temple of glory shall come upon him sanctification, with the Father's voice as from Abraham to Isaac. And the glory of the Most High shall be uttered over him, and the Spirit of understanding and sanctification shall rest upon him." At any rate in His Baptism, Jesus was clearly consecrated and anointed as the Christ and sent out to fulfil His mission as the Son of God on earth. He was immediately thrust into the wilderness where He, who had just been baptized in solidarity with sinners with the Baptism into repentance, fasted forty days and nights, humbling and submitting Himself (Son of God though He was) as one of us to the Will of His Father. It was then that He was tempted and entered upon His redemptive work, being obedient to the Will of God where we were disobedient, and offering throughout the whole course of His life an offering of obedience well pleasing to the Father—all on our behalf, that in Him we might be brought to the obedience of the faith and become children of the heavenly Father.

When we examine the Gospel records, the Fourth and the Synoptic Gospels alike, we discover that none of them gives an account of John the Baptist, of his message or of his baptismal rite, apart from the transformation of John's Baptism that took place in Jesus' submission to it. They all interpret John's Baptism from the perspective of Christ's Baptism by John, and indeed of His death and resurrection and His gift of the Spirit. This is much more in evidence in the Fourth Gospel than in the others, but the principle is the same in all of them. So interpreted John's Baptism is the beginning of the Gospel, and they actually use of it the distinctive word, *baptisma*, used only in Christian literature, and not used of John's Baptism outside the New Testament (e.g. by Josephus). *Baptisma* was clearly coined to speak of Christian Baptism, but was therefore applied rightly to John's Baptism; for his Baptism was not only into the name of the Coming One, the Christ, but it was the Baptism of Jesus by John which transformed John's rite of Baptism into Christian Baptism.

There can surely be no doubt about the fact that John the Baptist supplied the Church with its ritual act, the rite of initiation by water into the messianic Age and Community, into the New Covenant, while the origins of that rite lie apparently along the line we have been tracing out; but the doctrine of Baptism is determined not by any Old Testament typology, nor by ideas derived from Judaism, but by the event of Christ's Baptism and by all it involved for Him on our behalf.

To this assertion, however, a qualification requires to be made. There are points in the rite of Christian baptism in which it is modified or determined by the doctrine of the saving event in Christ, and there are points in the doctrine where the exposition of it makes fundamental use of the pattern of the rite of Baptism. Thus, for example, the Christian rite of Baptism derives from John the Baptist, but the form of that rite is determined by the event that took place in the Baptism of Jesus. He went into the water to be baptized by John, but when He did that the Spirit came down upon Him and, as Jesus claimed, anointed Him. That gave Christian Baptism a double form; not only Baptism in water from below, but Baptism in heavenly water from above, that is, in the Spirit. The Semitic language lying behind this—*mayim* = water, and *shamayim* = heaven, with all the Old Testament teaching bound up with it, particularly from Ezekiel—is reflected all through the literature of the early Church, and not without reason. This twofold character of Baptism was reinforced at Pentecost when the Spirit was poured out in Baptism upon the Church, and immediately the apostles summoned men and women, with their children, to be baptized in water, calling upon God and entering into the fulfilment of His promise to pour out His Spirit upon mankind. A typical text describing this double idea contained in Baptism which reflects the twofold character in the actual rite is found in Titus 3: 5. "According to His mercy he saved us, through washing (or laver) of regeneration and renewing of the Holy Spirit which He poured out upon us richly through Christ Jesus our Saviour. . . ."

On the other hand, the doctrine of Baptism is expounded in the New Testament after the pattern of the rite. In the ritual act of Baptism there was a descent into the water and an ascent out of it—language which really derives not from the Gnostic myths but ultimately from the Old Testament cult, but possibly immediately from proselyte Baptism. In the New Testament this language was applied to the doctrine of Christ, not only to speak of His death and resurrection, but also to speak of His incarnation and ascension—the descent and ascent of the Son of Man. There is every reason to declare that that was the primary usage of this language, found according to the Fourth Gospel, on the lips of Christ Himself in His discourse with Nicodemus. In other words, "the baptismal language" of descent and ascent applies fundamentally to the descent of the Son of God into our mortal humanity and to His ascension to the right hand of the Father. It is only by a false abstraction that this language is applied to Baptism with reference only to the death and resurrection of Christ, and not also to His incarnation and ascension, all for us and our salvation. Certainly the early Church regarded His Baptism in the Jordan not as His adoption to be the Son of God, but as His manifestation and public consecration as God's Son pointing back to His birth from above of the Spirit, and regarded His ascent out of the Jordan and His receiving of the Spirit when the heavens were opened over Him, for our sakes, as having its fulfilled counterpart in His ascension to open the Kingdom of Heaven to all baptized into His Name and to pour out upon them the fullness of His Spirit. Thus Baptism, like the redemptive work of Christ, must be related to His Person, to the whole course of His obedient life, and to the whole act of His divine condescension to our lowly estate and exaltation of us in Himself to the Father. We cannot be true to the whole teaching of the New Testament unless we consider Baptism in that its essential context.

But now we must turn to look at the word which the New Testament uses to speak of this—*baptisma*. We have not paid sufficient attention to the fact that it is a new word that is used, and not the word *baptismos* (found in the New Testament only in Mark 7: 4, and Heb. 6: 2 to describe rites of ablution). *Baptisma* must surely be understood in close proximity to *kerygma* as referring to the mighty acts of God in Christ that are proclaimed in the Word and Sacrament—the content of *baptisma* is the same as the content of *kerygma*, but while it is the Self-proclamation of Christ that lies behind the *kerygma*, it is the Self-consecration of Christ that lies behind the *baptisma*, and as in the Church's *kerygma* it is Christ Himself who acts and is mighty to save, so in the Church's *baptisma* it is Christ Himself who acts confirming His Word and sealing His work of salvation. Even in the preparatory ministry of John the Baptist *keryssein* and *baptizein* were conjoined; so it is also in the ministry of the apostles—*baptisma* follows their *kerygma* and is given, not as the seal of faith, but as the seal of the Word of the Gospel, for faith cannot be the content of the *baptisma* any more than it can be the content of the *kerygma*, although both require faith.

This interpretation is reinforced by the fact that nowhere does the New Testament offer us a description of the rite of Baptism. It is not interested in the rite as such, but in the event behind the rite; nor is it interested in the human minister of the rite but in the One who fulfilled the Will of God and ordained the rite as the seal of His command and promise. It is not of course that the New Testament regards the rite itself with indifference, but that the rite is to be used like a window through which we look to something beyond it altogether. Just as we do not normally when looking out of the window look at the window-pane (except to note on occasion how far its imperfection distorts our vision); we look through the window-pane without noticing it. So it is with the New Testament *baptisma*. Just as *kerygma* does not call attention to the preacher or the preaching but only to Christ Himself, so *baptisma* by its very nature does not direct attention to itself as a rite (that would be as *baptismos*) or to him who administers it, but directs us at once beyond to Christ Himself and to what He has done on our behalf; that is, to the objective and fulfilled reality.

This being so, it might be best for us to speak precisely of *baptismatic* rather than *baptismal* relation to Christ. We do speak of "baptismal ingrafting into Christ", of "baptismal dying and rising with Him" and of "baptismal regeneration", and in so doing we use a "sacramental mode of speaking"; but the difficulty about this language is, that no matter how much the emphasis is laid upon Christ Himself, some foolish people will always take it to mean that it is the rite of baptism which ingrafts or regenerates us, or that it is actually in the experience of the rite that we die and rise again with Christ, which can only mean that they think of this ingrafting or regenerating or dying and rising as acts in addition to what has already taken place in Christ on our behalf and therefore already been fulfilled in us in Him. The New Testament nowhere teaches us that there is a saving act in addition to that which has once and for all taken place in Christ and for us in Him. There is only one Jesus Christ, the historical Jesus Christ who does not have to be made present but who is actually present with us to the end of the world; so there is only one mighty saving event (including all the mighty acts of God that took place in the incarnation, life, death, and resurrection of Jesus Christ) which is ever present with us, availing and effective and operative for us because we have already been involved in it, for it took place on our behalf in Christ. The event is inseparable from the Person of Christ. It is Christ in His life-act, Christ with His mighty acts wrought out for us, who is always present with us to the end of the world; so that when we in His Name proclaim the *kerygma* and administer the *baptisma* it is actually Christ Himself, really and fully present, who acts savingly in His Church, revealing Himself and baptizing with His Spirit. Only when we learn to get behind the false stress upon our own subjectivity in *kerygma* and *baptisma* can we fully appreciate the teaching of the New Testament, and at the same time fully understand the royal freedom for faith that both *kerygma* and *baptisma* involve.

But now we must speak more precisely of this baptismatic event. To do that we must return to consider the Baptism of Jesus Himself, and that means to return to the start of His ministry in His submission to John's Baptism. That great event pointed back to His own birth from above of the Spirit, an aspect particularly stressed in the first three chapters of the Fourth Gospel; but it also pointed forward to His death on the Cross, an aspect also stressed by the Fourth Gospel but particularly stressed by the Synoptic Gospels. It may be better to consider the latter first.

(1) *The Relation of the Baptism of Jesus to His Crucifixion*

As we have already seen, the Baptism in the Jordan is to be regarded as the consecration of Jesus to His mission as Suffering Servant. It was Baptism into His vicarious work. It was of course His consecration both as Victim and as Priest in one act —a theme of the Fourth Gospel which speaks of Jesus as the Lamb of God bearing the sins of the world, and also as the Son consecrated and sent by the Father and endowed with the Spirit without measure. But this mission of Christ is presented primarily in the Gospels in terms of His Servant-ministry. He was baptized into a life of vicarious passion, in which He went forth to bear our sins and sicknesses throughout the whole course of His public life right up to the Cross and there above all. As such, however, it was a Baptism in His obedience to the Father's Will, obedience as the Son of God within the conditions of our estranged and alienated humanity, and obedience unto the death of the Cross. It was thus into the Cross that He was baptized, so that His Baptism came to its fulfilment in His crucifixion. But between His Baptism in water in the Jordan and His Baptism in blood on the Cross His whole servant-existence and active obedience was His Baptism, for throughout the whole course of His obedience He was enacting the Will of God in our flesh, and doing that on our behalf. "I have a baptism with which I am being baptized" (Mark 10: 38 f.), He said, with reference to the work which He was accomplishing and with which He was sorely pressed until it was finally accomplished.

It is sometimes said that by "the baptism with which He was being baptized" Jesus was speaking only metaphorically or figuratively of His death, and that His words contain no reference to Baptism as such at all. Those who say that make the mistake of thinking that by *baptisma* the New Testament means *baptismos*, and fail to see the dimension of objectivity in which the New Testament always uses this term. But they make another mistake—they give the word *baptisma* in this saying a meaning which it nowhere possesses in all Greek literature. The verb *baptizein* is used often in Greek, and several times in the Septuagint, only metaphorically, to speak of drowning or dying, but nowhere is the word *baptisma* so used. Thus, to give this use of "baptism" by Jesus only a figurative meaning, they have the impossible linguistic task of proving that in this instance only it must be figuratively interpreted while in all other instances it is used of Baptism. Of course Baptism contains a figurative element, but the association of *baptisma* with *baptizein* here is clearly more than a Semitism; it is designed to drive home, with the use of the specific and distinctive word coined by the Church for Baptism, the fact that Christ deliberately linked His Baptism in the Jordan with His death on the Cross, and with the whole course of His ministry in obedience and passion on our behalf; and thereby also to drive home the fact that our Baptism in the Name of Christ is a covenanted consociation with Him in all He did to fulfil righteousness from His Baptism in the Jordan to His crucifixion on the Cross. In our Baptism we are drawn within the range of His vicarious work in life and death, and are consecrated to God the Father in His Self-consecration on our behalf.

We must say, then, that Christ's vicarious Baptism was His whole living passion culminating in His death, His Baptism in blood, once and for all accomplished on the Cross. That is the objective event, the one baptismatic event in Christ, that lies behind every administration of Baptism, the all-inclusive *hen baptisma* that is the primary fact referred to every time the word Baptism is used by the New Testament. But this objective event has a subjective counterpart, in the Baptism of the Spirit at

Pentecost. At the Jordan, Jesus wearing our humanity was baptized and anointed for us; at the Cross, suffering in our humanity, He was baptized for us in judgment and death; and in the resurrection He was clothed with power and raised for our justification. On the ground of His whole atoning act in life and death and resurrection He ascended to pour out His Spirit once and for all upon human flesh, upon the Church, giving it to share in His One Baptism.

We have not made sufficient of the essential relation between atonement and Pentecost, and of the fact that the Spirit was poured out only after Christ had been glorified. Melito of Sardis sought to expound this by relating the shedding of blood to the release of the life or spirit, thus laying stress upon the pouring out of Christ's Spirit as well as the pouring out of His blood as His atoning action. As we have already seen, the Jewish Community at Qumran related the atonement in the New Covenant to the work of the Spirit. Whether these particular ideas played a part in the minds of the New Testament writers or not, it is clear that as they thought of the Baptism in the Jordan as one of His mighty acts bringing in the Kingdom of Heaven, so they thought of His ascension and His pouring out of the Spirit in Baptism upon the Church as a mighty act of redemption and salvation. This was not a new act or something that had to be added to what Christ had already done, as if that were incomplete, but it was rather the full actualization of His redemption in the midst of His people on earth. In the language of Melito of Sardis, the Church was not only sealed with the blood of the Covenant but sealed with the Spirit. Indeed, both these are one and the same redemptive event.

Thus we have to say that the great baptismatic event includes the once and for all Baptism of Blood on the Cross and the once and for all Baptism of the Spirit upon the Church at Pentecost. There is *One Baptism*, and *One Body*, common to Christ and His Church, but each participates in it differently—Christ actively and vicariously as Redeemer, the Church passively and receptively as the redeemed Community. This baptismatic event is essentially corporate in Christ and in His Church—it is corporate because the Church was already included as "the many" in "the One" who suffered and died on their behalf. "Except a corn of wheat falls into the ground and dies, it abides alone", but in dying this One became many for He gave His life a ransom for many. That is why the New Testament can speak of the work of Christ as a work for the Church, although it was also for the world. "He loved the *church* and gave Himself up for it, that he might sanctify it, having cleansed it by the washing of water with the word, that he might present it to himself, a glorious church, not having spot or wrinkle; but that it should be holy and without blemish" (Eph. 5: 25 f.). It is only within that One Baptism of Christ for the Church and of the Church in Himself that the administration of Baptism to individuals has its proper place. In other words, it is only through and within the Church created by the corporate Baptism of the Spirit at Pentecost, and drawn and established within the fulfilment of the Covenant-will of God in the obedient life and death of Christ, that when from generation to generation the Church in obedience to Christ's command baptizes in water, others are added to the Church that they may share in what has already taken place for them and live in the power of the Name of Christ, as members of the Body of Christ who was crucified for them and raised again in justification for them. Thus the Baptism of the individual, child or adult, is not a new Baptism, but an initiation into and a sharing in the One Baptism common to Christ and His Church, wrought out in Christ alone but bestowed upon the Church as it is yoked together with Him through the Baptism of the Spirit.

(2) *The relation of the Baptism of Jesus to the Incarnation*

Here we come to a much neglected line of teaching in the New Testament. Some people appear to have difficulty in accepting Matt. 28:19 as the authentic utterance of Christ: "Go ye into all the world and disciple all nations, baptizing them in the name of the Father and of the Son and of the Holy Spirit, teaching them to observe all things whatsoever I have commanded you: and lo I am with you always even unto the end of the world." The textual authorities for this verse are overwhelmingly strong, so that doubt about it can be only on purely *a priori* grounds, in a refusal to believe that the name of the Father, Son, and Holy Spirit could be brought together like that on the lips of Jesus. But hesitation in that way must arise from a myopic reading of the Gospels, the Synoptics and the

Fourth Gospel, for all through them we have to do with the relation of the Son to the Father and with the presence and power of the Spirit. That is nowhere more clear than at the Baptism of Jesus in the Jordan where we have the voice of the *Father* in address to the *Son*, along with the manifestation of the *Spirit*. Perhaps it is only when we fail to give the Baptism of Jesus by John its full and proper place in Christian Baptism, and so make a false abstraction of Baptism from the whole course of Christ's ministry from the Jordan to the Resurrection, that we have difficulty in thinking of Matt. 28: 19 as our Lord's own direct command. Although it has always been to that verse that the Church has looked for its dominical warrant for Baptism, Baptism is grounded upon the whole life of Christ going back to His Baptism, and even to His birth of the Spirit.

But here we must pause to think of the significance of Baptism into the Name of the Holy Trinity. It means that we are not baptized in the Name of Christ alone, but equally into the Name of the Father and of the Spirit. Therefore Baptism cannot be interpreted exclusively as Baptism into the death of Christ, for neither was the Father crucified for us, nor did the Spirit become incarnate on our behalf. Baptism in the threefold Name is a rite essentially appropriate to the trinitarian character of the baptismatic event, which includes throughout it the relation of the Son to the Father through the Spirit. Baptism is thus concerned with the act of the Father in sending His Son, with His eternal love which He has poured out upon us in the incarnation of His Son that through Him we might be adopted into sonship and assumed into fellowship with the Father. But Baptism is also concerned with the work of the Spirit through whom Jesus was born of the Virgin Mary, by whom He was anointed as the Christ at His Baptism, through whom He cast out demons and brought the Kingdom to bear redemptively upon the needs of men, through whom again He offered Himself without spot to the Father, and according to whom He was raised from the dead by the Father. It was this same Spirit whom Christ after His ascension as the Son to the right hand of the Father poured out upon His Church, renewing them in the power of the resurrection, giving them to share in all that He had done for them, and enabling them to cry, in echo of His own prayer, Abba Father. Baptism in the Name of God the

Creator and the Father is the seal of His Covenant promise to be our Father, and Baptism in the Name of the Spirit is the actualization of that promise, the sealing of us as belonging to the Father, the creative renewing of us as His children in God's image. In inseparable relation with Baptism in the Name of the Father and the Spirit, Baptism in the Name of Christ has direct reference to His birth on earth as the Son of the Father, to the whole course of His obedience, as well as to His death and resurrection, and it also has reference to the ascension of the Son to the Father where He stands in for us as our Surety and Advocate and where He confesses us as His brothers and presents us to the Father as His sons.

What I wish to stress here is the much neglected fact that Baptism has essential reference to the whole incarnational event: to the coming of the Son of God into our mortal humanity, to His whole life of obedient self-oblation well-pleasing to the Father, and to His ascension in which wearing our humanity He brought back with Him many sons to glory. As we have already noted, the language of descent and ascent, used to speak of the death and resurrection of Christ, is also used to speak of His descent into our mortal humanity and His ascent in our resurrected humanity to the right hand of God. Thus behind baptism into Christ there lies the whole incarnation and ascension of the Son of God, spoken of as the descent and ascent of the Son of Man. Ultimately the Sacrament of Baptism is grounded in the incarnation in which the eternal Son immersed Himself in our mortal human life and assumed us into oneness with Himself that He might heal us and through the whole course of His obedience reconcile us to the Father in an abiding union and communion with Him.

The significance of this will be apparent if we say that while Baptism is usually spoken of only as the Sacrament of our incorporation into Christ, it is ultimately grounded upon the fact that in Jesus the Son of God incorporated Himself into our humanity. It is indeed only because of the union with us effected in His incarnation that we can be given to share in all that He has done in our humanity on our behalf, and so have part in His vicarious death and resurrection. If Baptism as a Sacrament of the death and resurrection of Christ is detached or abstracted from this primary fact of His incorporation into us in the Incarnation, then baptism too easily becomes the sacramental mystery of a timeless dying and rising known also to the Semitic and Hellenistic religious mysteries. It was precisely this that the early Church resisted, and they did so by grounding Baptism upon the whole of the New Testament witness to Christ the incarnate Son, and not simply upon Rom. 6. That is to say, alongside the important fact that Baptism is the Sacrament of the death and resurrection of Christ they laid the important fact that Baptism is the Sacrament of the Incarnation, the Sacrament of the Nativity, as it was sometimes called.

In Baptism we are adopted to be sons of God the Father; we are born again of water and of the Spirit—but this is grounded in the Birth of Jesus of the Holy Spirit from above, for it was in and with His birth as well as in and with His resurrection that the regeneration (*palingenesia*) of our humanity was brought about. In the language used earlier there are not two acts of regeneration, incorporation, etc. but only one, that which has already been wrought out in Jesus Christ and in which we are given to share through the Spirit, so that it is in Christ that we are born again through sharing in His birth, and it is in Him that we are converted through sharing in His obedient life, and in Him that we are resurrected through sharing in His resurrection. He was not born on earth for His own sake, but for our sake. His birth for our sake was part of His reconciling and redeeming work, and Baptism is grounded primarily upon that basic event, His incorporation into our humanity, and therefore upon His obedience unto the death of the Cross in expiation of our sin and guilt, and in His resurrection out of our mortality as the New Man.

This is a favourite theme in the Johannine literature in the New Testament. It is apparent in John 1 : 12 f.: "To as many as received him to them gave he the right to become children of God, to them that believe into His name; who were born not of blood, nor of the will of the flesh, nor of the will of a husband, but of the will of God." All the patristic citations of this verse in the second and early part of the third centuries (Irenaeus, Tertullian, Hippolytus, etc.) cite it in the singular with direct reference to the virgin birth of Christ; but whether that is the original text (as seems most likely) or not, it contains a clear indirect reference to the fact that we are born again in Christ's miraculous birth. That is the point also of Jesus' conversation with Nicodemus, that our birth of water and of the Spirit is not a carnal but a spiritual event, from above, and behind it lies the primary reality of Christ's birth, for it is He who is the One born from above, who descended from heaven. Thus what is true of Christ in the reality of His virgin birth is true of us also who believe in Him and are baptized into His Name in virtue of the right (*exousia*) which He gives us. Again this is the teaching of the Johannine writer in his first Epistle, e.g. in 1 John 5: 18: "Whosoever has been born of God (*gegennemenos*) does not sin, but he who was born of God (*gennetheis*) keeps him." Christ's birth described in the aorist tense was a specific event, but the Christian's birth described in the perfect tense is rather the result that accrues from that rather than an event in itself; it is the effect or fruit of that unique event, and is not something in addition to it, but a sharing in it.

There is a very definite parallel to this in the teaching of St. Paul about our participation through Baptism in the New Man, the New Adam, the Man from Heaven, the First-Born of all creation, and so of our adoption in Christ through the Spirit who makes us to call upon the name of the Father like Christ Himself. We are adopted to co-sonship with Christ and share in His birth and resurrection. That aspect of Pauline teaching, which is particularly strong in the Epistle to the Galatians, has to be considered together with the two passages which speak of Baptism as our sharing in the death and resurrection of Christ found in Rom. 6 and Col. 2.

All this does not mean that we are to neglect the very important aspect of Baptism as the Sacrament of Christ's death and resurrection, but that we must balance that by regarding it also as a Sacrament of His miraculous birth of the Spirit, and therefore as a Sacrament of our regeneration in Him through sharing in His new Humanity. What binds these two aspects together is the simple but often neglected fact that our incorporation into Christ is grounded entirely and primarily upon His incorporation into us. It is, moreover, just because He incorporated Himself into our estranged humanity under the divine judgment, and through that incorporation fulfilled that judgment both in His holy life in condemning sin in our flesh and by submitting and offering our humanity in Himself to the final judgment of God, that Baptism also has an aspect as baptism into judgment and into repentance, into the sphere where the Spirit convicts of sin, righteousness, and judgment.

It is from this point of view that we can see in a deeper way the integral relation of John's Baptism and message with that of Christ, and understand why Christ began His ministry by proclaiming the same message as John and, it would also appear, by continuing (through His disciples) for a while at least to administer Baptism and make disciples like John. It is significant that even John the Baptist could speak of God as being able to raise up a new generation through this Baptism into judgment and repentance, just as He could raise up children to Abraham out of the stones lying in the river Jordan. In other words, what we find in the teaching of the New Testament is that the conceptions of birth and death and resurrection are all brought together. It is through Baptism that we are given to share in the death of Christ, but in that way, argued St. Paul, we are made to grow together with Him, in order that we may be resurrected unto newness of life. It is through the Cross, through atonement and reconciliation, that we are given to share in the new life of Man which began with the birth of Jesus and was completely manifested in His resurrection. Just as the atoning work of Christ reached back from His Cross to His birth, or rather reached forward from His very birth to His Cross, so our sacramental participation in the whole baptismatic event involves a sharing in the Birth of Christ and in His death and resurrection, as it reaches out also to the final Parousia when our life now hid with Christ in God will be fully unveiled. Apart from our sharing in His death and resurrection we can have no share in the new life and the new humanity begotten in Jesus Christ when He was born of the Virgin Mary, or be assumed into a life of fellowship with the Father through the obedience of the incarnate Son.

We must now address ourselves briefly to the question of our relation as individuals to the corporate baptismatic event that has taken place in Christ and is common to Christ and His Church. This is perhaps best approached from the fact that Baptism is the Sacrament of "the One and the Many", but we may expound that by using the language of the Covenant. When God made His Covenant of grace with Abraham it was none other than the Covenant of grace which He established with creation of the world, and which took on a redemptive purpose with the rebellion and fall of man. But with Abraham that Covenant assumed a particular form within history and with one race elected from among all the races of mankind in order that God might prepare a way within humanity for the fulfilment of His Covenant Will for all men. "I will be your God, and you shall be my people." "I will be a God to you and to your seed after you." With such words the Covenant was established in which God willed to be the Father of His people and willed that they should be His children, and He gave them as a seal of this Covenant and its promise of blessing, the sign of circumcision, which we have already considered.

This Covenant was re-enacted with Israel as a people after its redemption out of Egypt as God's first-born son, but now the Covenant took on more specific shape. "I am holy, be ye also holy." As Head of the Covenant God required a corresponding holiness from His covenant-partner, for He willed that His people should live in fellowship with Him and share in His own Holiness. But God knew that His people were unable to fulfil the Covenant, and so in His Fatherly mercy He provided a way within the Covenant of obedient response to Himself and a way of sacrificial worship as a witness to His readiness to cleanse and forgive His people within the Covenant. The bounds of the Covenant had already been marked out by the rite of circumcision, which also indicated that the holy Will of God had to be fulfilled in the flesh of His people and that His promises availed for their seed from generation to generation. But then within these bounds God provided in the Law a revelation of His Will, commandments to show the way of obedient conformity to Him, and along with these God provided in the Cult solemn symbolic indications of the way in which He Himself was ready to provide fulfilment of His Covenant both from His own side and from the side of Israel in all its weakness and frailty. The whole Covenant thus rested upon the divine faithfulness, and pointed ahead to a future in which this divine provision would be translated from the realm of symbolic ritual into the actual existence of His people. The worst thing that could be done with such a Covenant would be to turn the symbolic ritual into an end in itself, as a means of acting upon God and bending His will to serve the ends of men. That is precisely what Israel tried to do again and again, so that God sent the prophets to protest against their use of the Cult and to demand obedience rather than sacrifice. But with the prophets He also began to reveal more and more His purpose for messianic fulfilment of His Covenant in a Servant who would not only fulfil the Covenant vicariously but be the Mediator of a New Covenant, in which the Will of God would be written upon the hearts of His people by His Spirit.

That fulfilment we have in Jesus the chosen Servant-Son, who fulfilled the Covenant both from the side of God and from the side of man, and so mediated a New Covenant which set the relations of men with God on a wholly new basis. This is the new form of the Covenant which is freely proclaimed to all men in the Gospel. It was as a sign and seal to this New Covenant that Baptism was given, not a sign and seal like circumcision of a Covenant yet to be fulfilled in the future but a sign and seal of a Covenant already fulfilled once and for all in Jesus Christ. Hence the seal of this Covenant took on a form appropriate to the nature of that which it sealed, namely, an accomplished fact, a finished work, a completed act of pure grace. Here too the essential pattern of the Covenant remains the same. God wills to be the Father of all men, and enacts a New Covenant in which they are to be His children; but here in sheer grace, and in merciful knowledge of our frailty and unfaithfulness, He has provided us with a covenanted way of response in the obedient life and sacrifice of Jesus Christ, His righteous Servant, His beloved Son. In Jesus Christ God has not only done a work of grace for us and upon us in which He has done away with our guilt and sin and set us free, but He has also provided us in the obedient humanity of Jesus Christ with a perfected communion between man and God in which the Covenant-union is fully and finally actualized. It is in that obedient Humanity, and in that perfect communion between the Son and the Father lived and worked out to the uttermost within our human existence, that we are mercifully given to share. That is to say, in Jesus Christ the Covenant faithfulness of God has been met and answered by a Covenant faithfulness within our humanity, so that that divine-human faithfulness forms the very content and substance of the fulfilled Covenant which is the New Covenant. Thus the

Covenant relationship is now filled with the relationship or communion between the Son and the Father, and it is in that communion that we are given to share by the Spirit. We really can be given to share in it, for the Covenant Communion was wrought out and perfected in union with our humanity in Jesus Christ.

With that change in the form and content of the Covenant the sacramental seal becomes the seal of union with Christ and of communion with the Father through union with Christ. The form that this Covenant-Communion takes is the Church, the Body of Christ, and the sacrament of initiation into that communion and of participation in the relation of the Son to the Father is holy Baptism. In the nature of the case, Baptism is the sacrament of what has already been fulfilled for us and on our behalf in Christ; more specifically it is the Sacrament of the obedience of Christ offered in our stead in which He throughout His life and in His death stood in our place and gave to God an account for us, submitting to the Father's judgment upon our sin and guilt; and therefore it is also the Sacrament of the Father's satisfaction in the life and work of His Beloved Son whom He sent to carry through this redemptive work on our behalf. More briefly, Baptism is the Sacrament of the fact that in Jesus Christ God has bound Himself to us and bound us to Himself, before ever we have bound ourselves to Him.

"Before ever we have bound ourselves to Him"—that has to be emphasized. Baptism is not the Sacrament of a Covenant voluntarily made between two partners, and which is only made when both partners freely and willingly enter into contract. In that event Baptism would be partially the Sacrament of God's act, and partially the Sacrament of the individual's act—and so it has been, and still is, frequently expounded. But in the biblical teaching God's Covenant is quite a different thing from a contract, for it is wholly and graciously made by God, and depends therefore entirely upon the divine faithfulness. But in the biblical Covenant there are not only two factors, God and man, but a third, the Mediator of the Covenant, who is not a third in one sense, for He is Himself God on the one hand, and Man on the other hand. It is this divine-human faithfulness and divine-human fulfilment which is proclaimed to man in the

Gospel as the good news of salvation: namely, that God the Son become man has offered to the Father a human response and a human obedience and a human fulfilment of His Covenant Will, doing in our stead and in our place and on our behalf what we are unable to do, and doing it freely that we may freely share in it. Our part in the fulfilment has already been completed, and so Jesus Christ invites us in the Gospel to bring all our burdens to Him and to be yoked together with Him, for He has already made Himself responsible for us. When therefore Jesus had fulfilled all righteousness, as He was baptized to do, He gave His Church the ordinance of Baptism to be administered as the Sacrament of His fulfilled work and as the sign and seal of His promise extended to all men in the proclamation of the Gospel. Baptism is above all the Sacrament of that vicarious obedience of the Son to the Father which we are given to share through the Spirit; but as such it is a sharing in a finished work to which we cannot add one iota of our own, it is a participation in a righteousness not our own, in a justification which is a reality independent of our faith. Therefore we can only come to Baptism to receive and to rely upon the Mediator.

Just because in Baptism we are drawn into the covenanted communion and covenanted way of response, we are drawn into the sphere of obedience to the Father; just because we are given to share in the obedience of Jesus to the Father, we are covenanted to a life of obedience in His Name. Baptism requires faith and obedience, just because it is the Sacrament of our sharing in Christ's obedience and faith. Hence the Sacrament of Baptism tells us in unmistakable terms that it is not upon our own faith or our own faithfulness that we rely, but upon Christ alone and upon His faithfulness. Baptism is primarily and fundamentally, then, the Sacrament of Christ's obedience on our behalf, and of His faithfulness, and therefore it is the Sacrament which covenants us to a life of faith and obedience to the Father in Him. He who is baptized by that sign and seal relies not upon himself but flees from his own weakness and faithlessness to the everlasting faithfulness of God; but he also attests before men that he renounces reliance upon himself and his own works of obedience or faithfulness to God's Will. That is the faith and faithfulness in which we are baptized, the faith and faithfulness in which we baptize our children, for the promise is not only to us but to them also in the faithfulness of Christ who commands us to present them to Him.

It is when we keep this biblical perspective and refuse to let go as the very essence of the Gospel the fact that God has bound Himself to us and bound us to Himself before ever we bind ourselves to Him, that we have no difficulty about infant-baptism, for infant-baptism is then seen to be the clearest form of the proclamation of the Gospel and of a Gospel which covenants us to a life of obedience to the Father. But whether baptism is administered to children or adults it is administered with the same doctrine and with the same form, for it is only as little children that we enter into this inheritance of the Kingdom freely bestowed upon us in the New Covenant; and we enter into it relying not upon ourselves in any way but solely upon Him who has already laid hold of us by His grace, and who wills to have fellowship with us on that basis that we may be free to love and trust Him all our days.

(c) *The Meaning of Baptism*[1]

What is the meaning of Baptism? That faces us right away with serious questions of New Testament interpretation which it would not be right to set aside. It was Friedrich Schleiermacher, more than a hundred years ago, who posed for us the two main problems which are still being debated. (1) Interpreters of the New Testament have to face the fact that while the language of the New Testament comes from the Greek world, the thought of the New Testament emerges out of the world of Hebrew Religion. Thus even though the words remain the same the inner meanings are different, so that something more than a grammatico-historical interpretation is necessary. The solution which Schleiermacher offered lay in psychological analysis. (2) In regard to the actual content of the New Testament Schleiermacher drew a radical distinction between what he called the "sensuous" and the "spiritual" elements in it, and advocated the reinterpretation of the "sensuous" into the "spiritual" by means of the religious consciousness.

[1] Broadcast address on the Third Programme of the B.B.C., May, 1956; reprinted from *The Canadian Journal of Theology*, 1956, pp. 129–34.

To both these problems Schleiermacher offered a fundamentally subjectivist solution which came to exercise a dominant influence in the nineteenth and twentieth centuries, still apparent in the views of Rudolf Bultmann. Certainly the idiom has changed, but the issues remain the same, while the solution offered is still rather subjectivist. Instead of psychological analysis, we have existential analysis; instead of the distinction between the "sensuous" and the "spiritual", we have a distinction between the "mythological" and the "scientific"; and instead of the religious consciousness we have self-understanding. Yes, the idiom has changed, but it is doubtful whether Bultmann has taken us much beyond Schleiermacher.

But what of the other side of the picture? Against this whole movement of idealistic and existentialist reinterpretation of the Christian message there has been growing up a massive revolt. In its secular form this revolt is most apparent in Marxist thought and its movement down to earth and work-a-day humanity. In its Christian form this revolt is seen most clearly in the recovered emphasis upon the Incarnation and the reconciliation of man in his flesh and blood reality to the living God. It is with the latter that we are concerned here: with the return to a Christian realism, and a theological objectivity.

All this requires of us an interpretation of the New Testament at a deeper level. Schleiermacher's hermeneutical analysis went to the heart of the matter, but his solution does not meet the demands of scientific objectivity. We cannot by-pass the real problems by psychology. We have to take the speech of the New Testament with all its Hellenistic affiliations and by arduous historico-critical study of its usage in the actual life and worship of Israel and the Church build up a correct understanding of the distinctive meaning of the New Testament concepts. This impels us to think out the whole relation of the Church to Israel, of the New Testament to the Old Testament, and of theology to worship.

At the same time Schleiermacher's radical dichotomy between a realm of sensuous events and a realm of spiritual ideas must be rejected on the ground that it mutilates the actual evidence and denies the very essence of the Gospel of the Incarnation. It disrupts the whole significance of reconciliation which involves not only the reconciliation of man with God but the binding together into a new unity of the two aspects which Schleiermacher wanted to divide asunder. Much the same argument must be advanced against Bultmann's programme of demythologization.

This means that it is the doctrine of Jesus Christ who is God and Man in one person, and who wrought out in Himself the reconciliation of man to God, which comes again to assume the central role in theological interpretation which it has always had in the heart of the Gospel.

What then are some of the theological issues raised about Baptism?

The New Testament writers employ an unusual word for Baptism and attach to it a distinctive meaning. This is the term *baptisma*, which is to be interpreted in much the same way as another important New Testament term, *kerygma*. *Kerygma* refers to the proclamation of the Gospel, and yet not so much to the proclamation itself as to what is proclaimed, namely, Jesus Christ; not so much to the act of proclaiming as to the saving work of Christ. When the Gospel is proclaimed it is Christ Himself the crucified and risen Lord who is present and active for our salvation. Similarly in regard to Baptism, the New Testament is not interested so much in the outward rite as in what stands behind the rite; not so much in the subjective experience of the baptized as in the death and resurrection of Christ; and therefore it is not interested in the human minister but in the One into whose name we are baptized.

This is not to say that the outward rites are dispensable; on the contrary, they are quite indispensable; but the main focus of attention is directed on to the objective reality in the person of Christ and His finished work on our behalf. This indicates that Baptism is to be interpreted not in relation to what we do but in relation to what God in Christ has done and will do for us; its meaning does not lie in the rite itself and its performance, or in the attitude of the baptized and his confession of faith, important though they are. It lies beyond—in Christ. It was not Baptism that was crucified for us, nor was it faith that was crucified for us, but Jesus Christ. It is therefore only with the greatest reserve that we can speak, as the New Testament does occasionally, of faith or of Baptism as saving us. Certainly we are summoned to believe if we are to be saved; and we are commanded to be baptized; but Baptism tells us that though faith is required of us it is not by our believing that we are saved but by Christ Himself.

But this raises another issue. We are not baptized into the name of Christ only, but also into the name of the Father and of the Holy Spirit. This is very important, for it indicates that the meaning of Baptism cannot be determined exclusively with reference to Christ. Baptism is concerned with the eternal love of the Father and with His gracious decision to reconcile us in His Son, and to adopt us as His children; and it is equally concerned with the sanctifying and renewing work of the Creator Spirit. Thus Baptism in the name of the Father speaks of the prevenient love of God, and tells us that long before we learned to love and believe in Him He loved us and chose us to be His own; and Baptism in the name of the Holy Spirit speaks of the supernatural presence and work of God, telling us that our coming to love Him and our learning to believe in Him are the creative work of the Holy Spirit within us. It is only within that context of Baptism in the name of the Father and of the Holy Spirit that we can speak rightly of Baptism in the name of Christ.

On the other hand, because the eternal love of God was incarnated in Jesus Christ, and because the Father sends us His Holy Spirit in the name of Christ, it remains true that the significance of Baptism is essentially Christocentric. Two primary aspects of Baptism have to be mentioned in this connexion.

(1) Baptism is into the name of the whole Christ; not just into the name of the dying and rising Christ, but the Christ who was born of the Virgin Mary, who was baptized at the Jordan, in fact the whole historical Jesus. Baptism into Christ includes therefore a sharing in His birth and His human life, as well as in His death and resurrection. When were you born again? In your conversion? In your Baptism? The profoundest answer you can give to that question is, when Jesus Christ was born from above by the Holy Spirit. The birth of Jesus was the birth of the new man, and it is in Him and through sharing in His birth that we are born again. Modern theology has tended to neglect the reconciling and renewing significance of the birth of Jesus—but that is, I believe, an important element that needs to be restored to the doctrine of Baptism. If the miraculous

birth of the infant Jesus is the sign of the wonderful way in which the Love of God begins with our humanity, bringing forth out of it a new life born of the Spirit, learning obedience and growing in wisdom and grace, then is it not in sacramental likeness to the birth and growing life of Jesus, as well as His death and resurrection, that infant-baptism is to be understood as the sign of the way God deals with us? On the ground of what He has already done for us in Christ He quickens us by His Spirit and gives us to learn obedience, growing in wisdom and grace, until we grow up into the full stature of the manhood of Christ.

(2) When Jesus was baptized at the Jordan, identifying Himself with the sinners He had come to save, God the Father openly acknowledged Him as His beloved Son and the Holy Spirit manifested His descent upon Him. That not only pointed back to Jesus' birth of the Spirit as the One who had come to save men from their sins, but it pointed forward to the death of Jesus on the Cross when He was to fulfil the whole work of atonement. That is the objective reality of our Baptism which witnesses to it and shows it forth. When we are baptized in the name of Christ, we are baptized into a work that has already been completed on our behalf in the whole course of Christ's obedience, from His birth to His resurrection. Baptism is not the Sacrament of what we do but of what Christ has already done and which we could not do for ourselves. Baptism is the divinely given ordinance which directs us and our children not to something which only becomes real when we believe, but into the saving act of God's love which He has already fulfilled for us in Jesus Christ, and into which we enter as the great inheritance offered to us in the Gospel.

We must now turn to the place of faith in regard to Baptism. The fundamental significance of faith lies in the fact that in it man takes refuge from his own frailty and instability in the steadfast love and unswerving faithfulness of God. Only when we think of Baptism truly as the attestation not of our faith but of God's faithfulness, as the sign and seal not of something that begins with our human decisions but with the prior decision of Christ, can we give faith its full place. It is not enough to say that the primary emphasis is upon the initiative and the work of God, and that the subsidiary emphasis is upon the response of faith. Even if my salvation depends on God for ninety-nine per cent of its efficacy and only one per cent on me, my salvation is nevertheless as uncertain as my own frailty and weakness. The strength of the chain is to be measured by the weakest link. No, we are to think of this in another way. We are entirely dependent upon the divine decision, but that is a decision which overlaps and undergirds my decision and gives it ground and room and freedom for full personal activity. When I take my little daughter out for a walk, holding her by the hand, and she stumbles, she does not rely so much on her little grasp of my hand as on my strong grasp of her hand. It is when her little grasp is wholly enfolded in my own that it is secure and reliable.

Let me illustrate that from the Gospel account of the conversion of Zacchaeus. Some people interpret this by saying that Jesus saw that Zacchaeus had it in him to be a disciple, and that behind his wicked greed there was embedded an essential goodness, and so Jesus waited long enough in Jericho to draw it out of him and to effect his change of heart. There is no evidence in the record to substantiate that. What we are told is that this wicked extortioner wanted to see Jesus without being seen by Him; short in stature, he hid in a tree where he could observe Jesus as he liked without being noticed. But Jesus broke into the fortress of this man's security and announced His decision that He intended to lodge in Zacchaeus' house, and He told him to make haste and come down. Then the astounding thing happened. This man who did not have it in him to change his heart, who was not free to rid himself of his own selfish will, found himself free to make a decision for Christ, because Christ had already made a decision on his behalf.

That is the very heart of the Christian Gospel: that the Son of God has come into our world where men are enchained in their self-will and crushed down with the responsibility for their sins, in order to take that burden wholly upon Himself and to give an account of it to God. "Come unto me all you that labour and are heavy laden and I will give you rest", Jesus says. That is the Gospel which cannot be truly preached in such a way that the awful responsibility for our sins and for our salvation is taken off the shoulders of Christ the Lamb of God and laid back again on the head of the poor sinner. It is because Christ has already shouldered the burden of our sin and in our stead has given an account of it to God, that He makes it possible for us freely to believe in Him, to love God and our neighbour.

There is one more question we must discuss: Baptism as the sign and seal of regeneration. The whole point of this aspect of Baptism is missed if two primary facts are forgotten. (1) The concept of regeneration applies first of all to Christ Himself, to His birth of the Spirit and to His resurrection from the dead. Christ is the One in whom the regeneration of our humanity has already taken place. (2) The concept of regeneration is also applied by the New Testament to Christ's second Advent in power when He will come to judge the quick and the dead and renew His creation. Baptism as the Sacrament of regeneration is the ordinance of promise given by Christ to His Church in its life between His two Advents, between what has already taken place in the Incarnation and what will take place in the resurrection. It is not of course the rite of Baptism which regenerates, but in Baptism our regeneration in Christ is declared, and shown forth, and promised: it is *sacramentally* enacted as an image and likeness of the birth and resurrection of Christ. But our regeneration is more than a symbolic likeness of the birth and resurrection of Christ. It is their effect upon us, and yet not effect in the sense of a different and subsequent event. Our regeneration has already taken place and is fully enclosed in the birth and resurrection of Christ, and proceeds from them more by way of manifestation of what has already happened than as new effect resulting from them. It belongs to the peculiar nature of Baptism that it promises us a redemption which has already been accomplished in Christ; and therefore in Baptism the end is already given to us in the beginning. Baptism is not simply the starting of a process which we have to carry on and to which we have to make our own additions if we are to be saved. It is the initiation into a wholly new life which has been freely bestowed upon us in Christ, and which awaits His coming again for its full revelation and consummation. That is why the promise of Baptism and its fulfilment cannot be tied down to the enactment of a ceremony or be exhausted in this life. It is a promise that is valid for the whole of our life and reaches out beyond into the resurrection and the new creation.

When we look into the waters of Baptism we see our faces

reflected in it, not very clearly, but very brokenly. In the Sacrament of Baptism we see the image of our regeneration only, as it were, "in a glass darkly", in an enigma. It is essentially a sacramental mystery which under the veil of water directs us back to the work of our renewal which has once and for all taken place in Christ, and directs us forward to the day when we shall see Jesus face to face and become like Him.[1]

[1] See further *The Biblical Doctrine of Baptism*, St. Andrew Press, Edinburgh, 1958.

4

THE SACRAMENT OF THE LORD'S SUPPER

(a) *Toward a Doctrine of the Lord's Supper*[1]

THERE can be little doubt about the fact that the doctrine of the Lord's Supper as at present formulated in all the Churches of the Reformation is conditioned by reaction against the Roman aberrations and innovations which began particularly with the ninth century, but reached their culmination in the Tridentine decisions. The Churches of the Reformation sought to go behind these aberrations and in various ways to recover the teaching of the New Testament and the early Church, but they themselves were not able to escape making other innovations, if only by way of protection against the deformed conceptions from which they sought to be delivered in reform of the Mass. These Churches have developed their own characteristic traditions both in emphasis and practice, and these also need to be put to the rigorous test of the Word of God in the light of our understanding of Holy Scripture and of the teaching and practice of the early Church. This is not to say that there are to be no developments at all in the celebration of the Lord's Supper, but that such developments are only legitimate if they are in agreement with the teaching of the Holy Scripture and if they serve an important purpose in the celebration of the Supper in the differing circumstances of Churches in different ages and peoples and contexts. At the same time it ought to be manifest that simplicity should be an essential feature of the rite, in accordance with its inherent nature and pattern as manifested in the pages of the New Testament, so that elaborations should be very fully and critically examined. That is not the subject of this essay, however, but rather an examination of some of the main features in the doctrine of the Lord's Supper which require from us to-day careful thinking, if we are to go

[1] Prepared for the Creed Association of the Church of Scotland.

forward to a formulation of the doctrine in such a way that it embraces the fullness of what the Church throughout history has learned of the apostolically ordered ordinance and of the apostolic instruction upon it.

(1) *Preliminary Considerations on the Origins of the Supper*

Is the Lord's Supper to be regarded as a reinterpretation of the Passover Meal or a Covenant Meal or simply a *kiddush*; and is it to be regarded as the memorial continuation of "the Last Supper" or as an extension into the Church's history of the Messianic Meal, of which there are traces in the Gospel records? These questions raise many difficult critical and linguistic problems which we cannot go into here, although they must not be avoided in a complete and thorough examination. Some of these questions in detail at least are probably insoluble, but when all is said and done, there are certain results that stand out and (in spite of their ragged edges) demand fairly full acknowledgment.

The origins of the Lord's Supper evidently lie in the Passover Meal, to which there had already been assimilated the Covenant Meal with its cup of wine. The original Passover according to the records in Exodus is rather different, for example, from the Passover celebration that we find to-day in the Jewish *Passover Haggadah.* The latter has of course developments in detail that may or may not be legitimate extensions of the original rite, but the essential pattern found in the *Passover Haggadah* is clearly one in which the original elements of "the Passover of Egypt" (as it was called in Judaism) have been enlarged and somewhat transformed by assimilation to the Covenant Meal of the Israelites at Mount Sinai, which took account of the mighty events of Israel's redemption that transpired after the celebration of the first Passover. There was added to the Passover Meal the consumption of wine, for it was a joyful and thankful feast before the presence of God, and this was called "the Passover of the Generations". It would appear that the *kiddush* with its rite of sanctification using a cup of wine and water, observed at the beginning of the festivals, also reflects a similar tradition, so that its influence upon the Last Supper must also be taken into account. Likewise we must take into account the *chaburah* meal with its rite of thanksgiving or blessing along with the breaking of the bread at the start of the meal and along with the cup of wine at the end.

Whether or not the Last Supper was enacted through the transformation of a *chaburah* meal or not, it is difficult to exclude the influence of this upon what took place even in the Passover of the Generations. Again, we cannot leave out of account, especially in view of the early chapters of the Acts of the Apostles, the rite of *'erub*, in which the use of a common dish or of a whole loaf was employed in an act of associating together or common participation with a view to reaching a common mind at a festival or in the convocation of a court. Whether or not this was actually in the mind of Jesus as He inaugurated the New Covenant in the breaking of the bread and the distribution of the cup, we do not know, but there is every reason to believe it came to play a part in the apostolic perpetuation of the Supper.

No doubt when these various Jewish rites are set over against one another in pride of place as antecedents of the Lord's Supper, the discussion is endless, but in some way or other they all appear to have had their influence. At any rate it is clear that the act of Jesus involved the use of bread and wine with the significance of the Passover and with the deliberate intention of founding the New Covenant in His Body and Blood.

There are other elements we have to take into account which we find in the Gospel records, in the various parables of Jesus about the Wedding Feast or Royal Supper, in His own acts in feeding the multitudes, the four and five thousand, and the occasions when He deliberately ate and drank with publicans and sinners, the excommunicated and lost sheep of the house of Israel, and justified it on the ground of the great Messianic Meal of the future when they would come from the East and West and sit down together with Abraham, Isaac, and Jacob in the Kingdom of God. These distinctly Messianic acts of Jesus at meals, especially in the light of His teaching about the divine constraint put upon the outcasts to come in and fill the house and partake of the Great Supper, are very important—neglect of them in considering the institution of the Lord's Supper belongs to the general failure to give the whole historical life and ministry of Christ its proper place in His saving work.

In addition to all that has so far been adduced, there is still the supreme fact of the appearances of the risen Jesus to His disciples, notably those in the same Upper Room where the Supper was held a few nights previously. According to Luke it was at their Easter Evening meal that Jesus first returned to His disciples as a body. The incident of His being made known in the breaking of bread to the two disciples at Emmaus is likewise significant, as well as the Johannine account of the meal with the risen Jesus at the lake-side. It can be argued, of course, that these are but incidents which have no explicit reference to the solemn participation in the Lord's Supper, but even then it must be granted that after the resurrection the disciples could not participate in the Supper as if Jesus had not risen and as if He were not present with them in it. The resurrection inevitably modified the character of the meal, as it was intended to do, so that the Lord's Supper as celebrated in the Church was not just the prolongation of the Last Supper (when did this expression *Last Supper* first arise?) but was a "sacramental" continuation of the acts of Christ in the miraculous feeding of the multitudes (as with manna) and entailed the "sacramental" extension into the Church of the resurrection meals of the risen Lord with His disciples. The relation of the Lord's Supper as celebrated in the Church to the Last Supper as celebrated on the night in which He was betrayed is, therefore, not unlike the relation between "the Passover of Egypt" and "the Passover of the Generations". Thus, in distinction from the Last Supper, the Lord's Supper enshrines both the historical Supper before the crucifixion of Jesus and a celebration of the resurrection. The Lord's Supper is a historical action in remembrance of Christ, after the fashion of the Last Supper, and a Messianic Meal with the risen Lord, joined together in one. That conjunction also affects the meaning of *anamnesis* in the Supper.

That was the Eucharistic meal of the early Church, held especially on the Lord's Day, the Day of the Resurrection, and significantly, in the context of a love-feast with its mutual sharing of God's gifts. To get the full tradition regarding this Meal we have to take the Synoptic accounts of the Last Supper with the Johannine accounts of Jesus' discourses and His high-priestly intercession at the Supper, together with the Johannine and Synoptic accounts of the events of Easter Evening when Jesus came into the midst of His disciples as they ate bread together, showed them His wounds, gave them His peace, breathed on them His Spirit and recommissioned them as His covenanted apostles. "As the Father hath sent me, so send I you." Then we have to conflate that with the Pauline account of the formed tradition as he received it and delivered it to the Corinthians, and consider the whole in the light of the actual practice of the Church as reflected in the Acts of the Apostles, the teaching of the Epistle to the Hebrews, and the illuminating allusions in the Apocalypse.

(2) *The Reformation of the Roman Mass*

The Reformers reacted very strongly to the Pelagian conceptions of atonement, and the Pelagian notions of the priesthood of the Church, which they found to be embedded in the Mass. These took the form of a repeated sacrificial immolation of Christ even in a propitiatory sense, which gave the Church control over men's salvation, and the form of a sacerdotal control over the Body of Christ which through the words of consecration fetched it down from heaven and brought it to rest upon the altar. These are crude ideas. They were not held in that crude form by the best of the Roman theologians even during the period of the Reformation, but they were not repudiated. The view they represent was given dogmatic definition in the decisions of Trent in a way that has for ever involved the Roman Church in excommunion from the rest of Christendom. For the Romans a priest was a *pontifex*, one who builds a bridge and so mediates between God and man; the priest fulfilled that mediation by re-enacting the sacrifice of Christ. But for the Reformers the Incarnation had radically altered the whole conception of priesthood, for only He makes a bridge between God and man who is Himself that bridge. The unity of act and person in the One Mediator, and the vicarious fulfilment in the Humanity of Christ of our response to God in obedience and sacrifice once and for all, made any view such as the Roman quite impossible. It was in radical conflict with the apostolic tradition. For the Calvinists, it was the teaching of the Epistle to the Hebrews (which brought together in such a fundamental way the priesthood of the incarnate Son who opened up in Himself a new and living way to God, and the once and for all perfection of His priestly work) that shattered the Roman error and directed the obedient Church away from those deviations back to the apostolic teaching and ordinance. Behind this lay also the change in the conceptions of God, the recovery of a full

Christology both in the doctrine of Christ itself and in its application to correlative aspects of the faith, and a recovery of the doctrine of justification through the grace of Christ alone, or more concretely, as John Knox always preferred to put it, through the Blood of Christ alone.

In their reconstruction of the rite itself the Reformers revolted against the idea of the Mass as a timeless rite, and returned to the conception of the historical Supper. True to their whole doctrine of God and their faithfulness to the Christology of the early Church they insisted in grounding the Supper again in the action of the historical Christ, upon His inauguration of the New Covenant with the disciples on the night in which He was betrayed, and upon the once and for all act on the Cross that cannot be repeated. What was partly at stake here was the assimilation of the Eucharist to the pagan conception of the mystery of the dying and rising god and to the process of deification and transmogrification that involved. That reduced the Sacrament to a *mythos*, the counterpart in time, dramatically ritualized, of a timeless reality. Against all that the Reformers sought to get back to the historical perspective of the biblical revelation, to the historical Jesus, and the historical character of the Supper in the tradition of the apostolic Church.

The Supper thus restored to its native historical character was not separated, however, from the presence of the living Christ, the Lamb who was slain but is alive again, ascended to the right hand of God and reigning as Priest and King over His Church. Hence the element of eschatology has such a full and powerful place in the Reformed understanding of the Supper, the very element which (doubtless in sheer reaction) the new Roman liturgies that appeared after the Council of Trent did their best to eliminate. Nowhere is this eschatological element more in evidence than in Calvin's stress upon the ascension of the risen Christ, and therefore upon the *sursum corda* in the celebration of the Eucharist itself. The Lord's Supper is a communion with the risen and ascended Christ through the Spirit which He pours upon His Church, and in it He who was crucified comes to show us His wounds in His hands, feet, and side, to give us peace and forgiveness through His passion and to quicken us again by the breath of His Spirit that we may go from the Supper to fulfil our calling in obedience to His sending, meditating upon the future life, working for the extension of Christ's Kingdom, and waiting for the day when He will return to take up His power and reign.

In this Supper the Church is given to taste and experience already the powers of the age to come; it is essentially a prelude to the new creation. The Sacrament of the Lord's Supper takes place therefore in "two times", and "two kingdoms" or "two ages", as Luther and Calvin both put it, or, as we would put it to-day, in the overlap of the two ages, the present age and the new age that has overtaken us in Jesus Christ and is already actual in our midst through His Spirit. It is above all in the Lord's Supper that the new age which overlaps the old, and is therefore veiled by it, is sacramentally unveiled in anticipation of the great unveiling of the Kingdom of Christ at the final Parousia. This means that we have to distinguish in a doctrine of "the real presence" between the Eucharistic Parousia of Christ and His final Parousia in judgment and new creation. Jesus Christ is really present under the veil of the bread and wine, but in such a way that He holds back the full power and majesty of His presence to give us time on earth and in history to fulfil His Will before He comes again. Therefore, as Calvin reminds us, we pray at every celebration of the Holy Supper, "Thy Kingdom come; thy will be done on earth, as it is in heaven."

The union between these two aspects in the Reformed doctrine of the Lord's Supper is in sharp contrast to the views of the Supper which (a) look upon it merely as a memorial of the historical Last Supper; and (b) which transmute it into a timeless rite of mystical repetition. The one involves an un-Christological separation between the sign and thing signified, and treats the sign as the sign of what happened historically in the past alone; and the other involves an un-Christological confusion between the sign and the thing signified through a doctrine of transubstantiation. Calvin held very strongly that because in the Eucharistic Communion we partake of Christ our relation with Him reflects and images His own nature. In participating in Him we become conformed to Him so that we participate also in our own way in the union of the divine and human natures in Christ. Thus the mode of sacramental relation reflects the mode of hypostatic union in Christ. But transubstantiation destroys that whole analogical relation of participation and conformity to Christ, and so disrupts the basic Christological nature of the Sacrament. It destroys it in its character as a communion in the mystery of Christ. Precisely by refusing to preserve the distinct propriety of the two sides involved in the sacramental relation, it makes it impossible for it to image or reflect the image of Christ in whom divine and human natures, while remaining distinct, are joined in such a way that neither is converted or changed into the other. But Calvin opposed equally those who held that the two sides in the sacramental relation are disparate and separable, that the Supper is only a historical act in memory of the historical death of Christ carried out in obedience to Christ's command. That view, often but quite falsely attributed to Zwingli, was held by the humanists in the Reformation era both within and without the Roman Church, and notably by the Anabaptist groups, as it is widely held to this day in many Protestant Churches. Here the emphasis upon the simplicity and historical character of the Supper has been given a humanist twist which depreciates the supernatural presence of Christ and diminishes severely the Christocentric nature and pattern of the ordinance.

(3) *The Formulation of the Doctrine of the Supper*

When he wanted to give a brief exposition of the Lord's Supper Calvin frequently spoke of it under three heads, which may serve a useful purpose here: *signification*, *substance* or *matter*, *effect* or *action*.

(a) *Signification.* The terms signification and representation have each a double reference in Calvin's thought. Here we are concerned with something which is not usually admitted and then it is simply an ambiguity. Signification may be the equivalent to "meaning", but it may also refer to the "thing meant". It is doubtful whether Calvin ever employs signification with regard to the Sacraments except in conjunction with its concrete sense as the "thing signified". The same applies to his use of represent, which means more than represent or symbolize, namely, *re-present*; it represents only in the concrete act of re-presenting. This means that it is not really possible to discuss signification in abstraction from the matter or the substance of the Sacrament.

The Lord's Supper as celebrated in the Church is a sign with a meaning; it is signitive, pointing beyond itself to what Christ has done and does for us, and so it figures our union with Christ in His death and resurrection and ascension, and relates us to His future advent. A true sign, however, has in it something of that which it signifies; it is analogous to the thing signified, and corresponds appropriately to its nature. In the ordinance of Christ, through His command and promise, the outward sign and the inward reality belong together as form and content of the sacramental communion; although the form is not the content, and the participation in the outward sign as such is not the communion, nevertheless it is the form in which the content is communicated to us, so that apart from the specific form commanded and to which the promise has been attached we cannot conceive or receive the reality. Wherever the outward sign or form is neglected or repudiated the inner content inevitably goes with it.

Two things must be noted here. (1) In this sacramental signification we must think of the relation of the sign to what it signifies as involving neither a relation of identity nor a relation of difference, but of analogy involving something of identity and something of difference. (2) But this relation of sign to the matter signified depends entirely upon the nature of the matter, so that the analogical relation is determined by the nature of Christ Himself, who is the substance or the matter signified. The analogical relation by itself tells us nothing, for that is just the bare form of the sacramental relation; but the content of it is Christological, that is union with Christ, and, as we have seen, such a union that it reflects in itself the nature of Christ.

Now it belongs to the nature of Christ that He is *mystery*; that is the incomprehensible union of God and man in one Person. It is Christ alone in the strict sense who must be spoken of as *mysterion*, but the Church is given to have communion in the mystery of Christ, and it is the Sacraments which are the appropriate signs of that mystery in the life of the Church. Thus in a secondary sense we may speak of the Sacrament as *mysterion*, inasmuch as it is a sign of Christ who is Himself the thing or matter signified. Now traditional theology especially since Augustine had been accustomed to speak of this in terms of *res* and *signum*, but Calvin like others of the Reformers, notably Bucer, Martyr, and John à Lasco, felt that the term *res* was not as appropriate as the term *mysterium* to denote the reality signified, namely Christ Himself as God and Man in one Person, the Mediator. The use of the terms *res* and *signum* tended toward a static and metaphysical interpretation of the sacramental relation, but the use of the biblical terms *mystery* and *seal* had the advantage of preserving both the Christological mystery behind it all, and the dynamic character of the union and communion involved in participation in Christ. Moreover, the term mystery made it clear that the sacramental relation which reposes upon the relation of God and man in Christ can no more be explained positively and put into precise rational terms than the hypostatic union which is stated by the Church only in negatives.

Calvin was therefore rightly adamant at every point in guarding the mystery of the sacramental relation, and it was at this point as well that his stress upon the ascension and so upon the *sursum corda* played such an important part. In our participation in the mystery of Christ we must raise up our minds and hearts above and beyond our senses and our abilities to provide in rational categories an explanation of the act of communion in the Body and Blood of Christ; for this is by its very nature a union wrought by the Spirit and therefore far transcends the capacities of our minds to grasp. The only way we can approach understanding of this is to conceive of it after the pattern of Christ Himself, and therefore, in accordance with the wonderful union of divine and human natures in Christ so clearly expressed in the Chalcedonian Christology.

(b) *Matter* or *substance*. The matter or substance is not any mystical event but Jesus Christ Himself, the *totus Christus*. As He is not only the agent or instrument of our salvation but its very substance, so the matter of the Sacrament is to be found in the substance of Christ Himself. (It should be noted of course that by "substance" Calvin has reverted to patristic rather than scholastic usage, just as his use of "matter" is obviously different from that of Mediaeval Romanism.) At this point it was characteristic that he should lay the emphasis upon the *Humanity* of Christ. "The thing requisite must be not only to be partakers of His Spirit, but also to participate in His humanity in which He rendered all obedience to God His Father, in order to satisfy our debts, although properly speaking one cannot be without the other; for when He gives Himself to us, it is in order that we may possess Him entirely." There are clearly two points here: our sharing in the obedience of Christ, that is, the whole historical self-offering of Christ in obedience to the Father's Will; and our participation in and union with Christ's human nature. It is only through union with Christ's human nature that we can really and fully share in His obedience, so that justification in Christ reposes upon union with Him.

On this matter Calvin used powerful language that has often been criticized by those who fail to understand the fundamental significance of what he has to say. "We acknowledge without equivocation that the flesh of Christ gives life, not only because we once obtained salvation by it, but because now, while we are made one with Christ by a sacred union, the same flesh breathes life into us, or, to express it more briefly, because ingrafted into the Body of Christ by the secret agency of His Spirit we have life in common with Him. For from the hidden fountain of the Godhead life was miraculously poured into the Body of Christ that it might flow from thence into us." That citation is taken from the *Mutual Consent of the Swiss Churches*, and is not simply a private opinion of Calvin, but part of the basic Reformed agreement on the Sacrament.

The danger in using such language, of course, is that it might suggest a fusion or commingling between us and Christ in the sacramental union or in faith-union. That was precisely the kind of confusion that Calvin opposed in Osiander and Servetus, for it was a form of monophysite heresy transferred to the Sacraments. For all his strong language about union with Christ and participating in His "vivifying flesh" Calvin took care to guard it from metaphysical explanations of the mode of Christ's presence with us and union with us—for such explanations, he held, could only be shameless intrusions into the essential mystery of Christ which is more to be adored than expressed. But Calvin had two fundamental interests here which must not be neglected. What he wished to stress was that the Lord's Supper is the ordinance whereby Christ gives us to communicate in His sanctified and sanctifying life, that in and through Him wc may share in all the benefits of the Covenant fulfilled in the flesh of

Christ; and that through sharing in Christ's humanity we may be brought within a covenanted union with God to be thought of as enduring event or permanent reality. Christ's own human nature is risen and exalted to the right hand of the Father, and it is in that incorruptible human nature that we are given to participate so that we have perpetual reconciliation and communion with God.

That is why Calvin interpreted the discourse of Jesus in John 6 not as referring specifically to the act of Eucharistic participation but as referring to our permanent and abiding union with Christ and our continual feeding upon Him. Because in Christ human nature is everlastingly united to His divine Person we are assured of everlasting life and salvation through our sharing in His human nature, so that through Christ we share in the very life of God. "Christ Himself is in us through His flesh, and we are in Him, while that which we are in Him is in God. While He is in the Father by the nature of His Deity, we are in Him by His corporeal nativity, and He on the other hand is in us by the mystery of the Sacraments. Thus perfect union was taught by the Mediator: while we were remaining in Him, He remained in the Father, and remaining in the Father, remained in us, thus advancing us to unity with the Father, since while He is naturally in the Father, in respect of His nativity we are naturally in Him, and He remains naturally in us."

(c) *Action* or *effect.* If Christ is Himself the matter of the Sacrament, "the effect flows from this that by the sacrifice of His death our sins are expiated, by His blood we are washed, and by His resurrection we are raised to the hope of life in heaven". That is to say, the action in the Sacrament is none other than that which Christ has already accomplished on our behalf once and for all. We are not concerned here with a new or a different effect, but with the one saving action of Christ effectively extended to us and continuously operative for our salvation. It cannot be emphasized enough that here we have to think of the whole action of Christ for us, in His Incarnation, obedient life, His Self-sacrifice for us on the Cross, His Self-offering to the Father in His ascension on our behalf and His eternal advocacy of us or intercession on our behalf. Union with this Christ cannot therefore be construed in terms of metaphysical or static relationship but in terms of dynamic movement. As Calvin puts it in the *Institutes*:—"This is the wondrous exchange made by His boundless goodness. Having become one with us as the Son of Man, He has made us with Himself sons of God. By His own descent to the earth He has prepared our ascent to heaven. Having received our mortality, He has bestowed on us His immortality. Having taken our weakness upon Himself, He has made us strong in His strength. Having submitted to our poverty, He has transferred to us His riches. Having taken upon Himself the burden of our unrighteousness with which we were oppressed, He has clothed us with His righteousness."

This in turn transforms the whole conception of the analogical relation in the sacramental participation. Not only is it one which has Christological content, but it is an *active analogy*, the kind by which we are conducted upward to spiritual things, and are more and more raised up to share in the life of God. This is an elevation or exaltation into fellowship with the divine life through the amazing condescension of the Son who has been pleased to unite Himself with us in our poverty and unrighteousness, that through redemption, justification, sanctification, eternal life and all the other benefits that reside in Christ we may be endowed with divine riches, even with the life and love that overflow in Christ from God Himself.

This stress upon the action of God in the Sacrament is reflected in the actual rite itself when the emphasis is laid upon the verbs "broken for you", "shed for you", which are figured and attested by the outward action of the minister. What Christ has commanded to be figured and attested in this active way, He undoubtedly performs, giving His broken Body and shed Blood for our nourishment, and effectively applying His death and resurrection for our salvation. The Sacraments are in no sense deceiving, lying symbols; what He has promised in His ordinances He perfectly and completely fulfils.

How are we to think of this action as taking place in the sacramental relation, and how is it different from the direct action of Christ when He was here on earth or when He will come again in glory? Just as there is a sacramental mode of relation, so there is a sacramental mode of action or operation. In Christ's direct action His Word and His Act are absolutely identical and coincident, but in the sacramental mode of operation they are held partially apart in order to make room for personal relations in decision and faith and repentance, and so for the growth of personal communion in union and love. We may illustrate that from the Gospels. In the healing of the paralytic let down through the roof Jesus deliberately held apart His *Word* of forgiveness and His *Act* of healing—"in order that ye may know that the Son of man hath power on earth to forgive sins", that is, in order to make room for knowledge and faith. Similarly in a number of parables He spoke of the Householder or King going into a far country and spending time—*chronizein*—there and returning to reckon up with His servants—parables which not only have reference to Israel, but apply also to the time between the ascension and the final advent.

The very institution of the Lord's Supper was designed for the same reason, as a sacramental measure for operation between the ascension of Christ and His coming again; an institution that very clearly reveals that our Lord contemplated a long period of waiting before He returned, a long period in which the Church would have time to grow and develop in union and communion with Him. Thus in the sacramental mode of operation He not only declares His Word and truly performs what He declares, but performs it in such a way that its final fulfilment is yet to take place in the consummation of the Kingdom. That is why we have two Sacraments; one which seals His once-and-for-all work of salvation, and one which continually seals our renewal in that finished work and gives us to participate in its effective operation until He comes again in power and glory. There is then in the Lord's Supper both a sacramental fulfilment and an eschatological suspension, and these belong together inseparably, and therefore it is most important to hold Baptism and the Lord's Supper closely together; if they are allowed to fall apart, the essential relation between the finished work and the future consummation tends to be radically misunderstood, as when the whole sacramental relation and operation is divided up into seven stages of increase in "grace".

So far we have discussed mainly the action of Christ in the Lord's Supper; but what about its effect in our reception of it? The all-inclusive effect is our abiding union with Christ and through union our participation in all the benefits of Christ, which we have already considered. But here we may add that this union and communion with Christ and sharing in His benefits has two "moments". The first "moment" is that of receiving His gift of Himself in all that He has done on our behalf, and that receiving is effectuated through our communion in His Body and Blood, through which we are renewed in our membership in His Covenant and our incorporation in His Body. But this union with Christ through receiving Him in communion involves a union with Him in the whole of His obedient Self-oblation to the Father; that is to say, it engages us to participate in the prayer of His obedient life on earth (and so we pray in the Lord's Supper "Our Father which art in heaven, hallowed be thy Name, . . ."), but it also engages us anew in the eternal Covenant in which Christ stands in for us as our Advocate before God, our High Priest who ever lives to make intercession for us (and so through the Spirit we echo in the Eucharist our Lord's high-priestly prayer which we are given to overhear in John 17). Not only in word does Christ put His own prayer into our mouth, but in the communion of the Lord's Supper He takes us with Him into the hallowed place where we are asked to watch and pray with Him in His passion of intercession as He alone bears and bears away the sin of the world, and bends our will back into union with the divine: "Not my will but Thine be done".

All this is reflected in the signification and figuration of the sacramental rite. As the Son of God descended and taking upon Himself our humanity offered Himself in vicarious sacrifice on the Cross, thus giving His life for us and bestowing Himself in utter love upon us, so the Lord's Supper represents His Self-giving for us and His Self-impartation to us. As He rose again from the dead triumphant and ascended as our Mediator and Intercessor and Advocate, the Lord's Supper represents His advocacy and prayer for us. Thus the Sacrament is an action in which we receive Christ and feed upon His Body and Blood by faith, giving thanks for what He has done in the whole course of His obedience, but it is also an action in which we set forth the bread and wine and plead the merits of Christ, taking shelter in His sole and sufficient Mediation and advocacy on our behalf, and lift up our hearts in praise and thanksgiving for His triumphant resurrection and for His ascension, in which we cling to the royal intercessions of the ascended Lord who is set down on the throne of God Almighty. He has ascended to present Himself before His Father, and to present us in Himself as His brothers and as those whom He has redeemed with His Blood and given to share in His own filial relation to the Father. It is in His Name that we draw near, and worship and pray in the Lord's Supper. The Supper, therefore, has to do both with the death and with the resurrection of Christ; it is both a memorial in thanksgiving of His sacrifice once and for all accomplished, and a eucharistic memorial before God in which we lift up our hearts in responsive obedience to His ascension and are made to sit with Christ in heavenly places. It is our entering within the veil through Christ, who ever lives to make intercession for us and our consecration before the face of the Father.

(4) *The Lord's Supper as Eucharist*

The Lord's Supper is essentially a prayer and hymn of thanksgiving, dramatic prayer acted out in the broken bread and poured-out wine which Christ Himself puts into our hands through His ordinance, and bids us do in remembrance of Him. The use of the words "blessing" (*eulogia*) and "thanksgiving" (*eucharistia*) from New Testament times indicates that this is a primary aspect of the Lord's Supper deriving from our Lord's own words in blessing and giving thanks at His institution. In the old custom of the Church of Scotland the "Communion season" lasted several days, and the "Communion" itself lasted throughout the whole of the Lord's Day, although it came to be broken up into "Communion" at the morning service and the "Thanksgiving" at the evening service. That has tended to have the unfortunate result of separating the eucharistic aspect of the Supper from the communion. Therefore this aspect requires further and deeper consideration by us to-day, lest it be allowed to slip away from us, especially in reaction to modern misunderstandings of "the eucharistic sacrifice".

Calvin and Knox both drew a very clear distinction between the "propitiatory sacrifice" and the "eucharistic sacrifice". Christ alone has offered to God a propitiatory sacrifice in the sacrifice of Himself in obedient life and obedient death once and for all, and we can only offer to God praise and thanksgiving for what He has done and finished for ever on our behalf and in our stead and for our sakes. Because Christ is our High Priest who has taken our place and offered once and for all an all-sufficient sacrifice on our behalf, it is only "by the right hand of Christ" that we can offer anything to God at all, as John Knox put it. Or, to put it otherwise, Christ's high-priestly prayer recorded in John 17 is perpetual in its virtue and ever obtains mercy for us in the presence of His Father; it is that intercession of Christ that stands behind our prayer when we approach God in the Name of Christ and plead His passion on our behalf, and offer ourselves to Him as sinners whom Christ has redeemed by His Blood, adopted as His own and covered by His righteous Name. It is therefore under the cover and shelter of Christ's sacrifice that we draw near to God in the Holy Supper, bringing nothing in our hands but clinging only to Christ's Cross, in order to pray and to offer intercessions in the Name of Christ the Mediator.

But sincerely to pray to God means that we present our bodies to Him as a living sacrifice, holy and acceptable unto God as our reasonable service; and sincerely to intercede for others for Christ's sake means that we pour ourselves out in the service of others for whom Christ died. Thus "under the sacrifice we call eucharistic are included all the offices of charity by which while we embrace our brethren, we honour the Lord Himself in His members; in fine; all our prayers, praises, and thanksgivings, and every act of worship which we perform to God. All these depend on the greater sacrifice with which we dedicate ourselves, soul and body, to be a holy temple to the Lord. For it is not enough that our external acts be framed to obedience, but we must dedicate and consecrate first ourselves and secondly all that we have so that all which is in us may be subservient to His glory, and be stirred up to magnify it." In those words of Calvin we see that eucharistic sacrifice ultimately means directing ourselves and all that we have and do in the Name of Christ *to the Glory of God*, which is accompanied by the fruit of our lips in praise and thanksgiving to His Name. "This kind of sacrifice", Calvin continues in his *Institutes*, "is indispensable to the Lord's Supper in which, while we show forth His death and give Him thanks, we offer nothing but the sacrifice of praise. From this office of sacrificing, all Christians are called 'a royal priesthood', because by Christ we offer that sacrifice of praise of which the

Apostle speaks, 'the fruit of our lips, giving thanks to His name' (1 Peter 2: 9; Heb. 13: 15). We do not appear with our gifts in the presence of God without an Intercessor. Christ is our Mediator, by whose intervention we offer ourselves and our all to the Father. He is our High Priest who, having entered into the upper sanctuary, opens up an access for us, He the altar on which we lay our gifts, that whatever we do attempt, we may attempt in Him; He it is, I say, who hath 'made us kings and priests unto God and His Father'."

In order to get Calvin's teaching about this fully before us, it may be helpful to look at his comments on Num. 19, which describes the solemn rite of the sacrifice of the red heifer without the camp and the application of that sacrifice through the sprinkling of its ashes mixed with water upon those needing cleansing. Calvin looked at the passage in the light of Heb. 13 and it led him to speak of our offering of Christ to the Father. "In order that we may be partakers of cleansing, it is necessary that each of us should offer Christ to the Father. For although He only, and that but once, has offered Himself, still a daily offering of Him, which is effected by faith and prayers is enjoined upon us, not such as the Papists have invented, by whom in their impiety and perverseness, the Lord's Supper has been mistakenly turned into a sacrifice because they imagined that Christ must be daily slain, in order that His death might profit us. The offering, however, of faith and prayers, of which I speak, is very different, and by it alone we apply to ourselves the virtue and fruit of Christ's death." Then with reference to the fact that in the Old Testament rite "the people offered vicariously by the hand of the priest", Calvin added: "In this way also at present, although we set Christ before God's face in order to propitiate Him still it is necessary that Christ Himself should interpose and exercise the office of a Priest."

Calvin thus objected to the conception in which Romans thought of the Eucharist as a propitiatory sacrifice, as in the Creed of Pius IV: "I profess that in the Mass there is offered to God a true, proper, and propitiatory sacrifice for the living and the dead." But once that is resolutely set aside, Calvin can even speak about offering Christ to the Father and setting Him before the Father's Face—that is precisely what is done in faith and prayer at the Lord's Supper, but surely not in order to propitiate God(!) as Calvin put it, but in taking shelter under Christ's advocacy and in thankful pleading of His passion in the knowledge that once and for all we have been reconciled to God in Christ, and now for ever have a place in Christ's Self-consecration on our behalf and Self-presentation before the Face of the Father in Heaven. It is in communion with that risen and triumphant and ascended Lord and by His right hand alone that we offer our worship at the Lord's Supper to the Glory of God's Holy Name.

(5) *The Corporate Nature of the Lord's Supper*

This is an aspect of the Eucharist that has always been strongly emphasized in the teaching and practice of the Reformed Church. It is the Sacrament of the communion in the Body of Christ and is therefore rightly celebrated with the whole Body of the Church in heaven and earth. That is given its active signification in the assembling of the whole congregation to Holy Communion, in which Communion is held conjointly with the Lord and therefore with one another in Him. It is in no sense a private rite of a few, it is the Sacrament of the New Covenant in which Christ gave Himself a ransom for many, and all are to eat the bread and all to drink the wine; for there is one loaf and one cup, as there is One Lord in whom the many are reconciled to God and formed into One New Man.

It belongs to the essence of the Sacrament that each is a deacon to the other at the Holy Table, and serves him in love as Christ washed the disciples' feet at the Last Supper, giving us an example of what we should do to one another both in giving to one another and in receiving from one another humble, even menial, service in the name of the Crucified. This corporate Sacrament enshrines not only the mutual relations in love of the members of Christ's Body but a two-way relationship between the spiritual and the physical, the invisible and the visible. The communion in Christ is physically acted out in the dividing and eating of the bread, in the distributing and drinking of the wine, and the participants go from it to live and act it out in their daily life and work and in all their personal relations within the Household of faith, but also to shew forth the death of Christ to all men until He comes again. The Sacrament cannot be restricted to a cultic act, for by its very nature it presses out to fulfilment in the whole life and mission of the Church in all its spiritual and bodily existence and action.

Three things here demand further consideration.

(a) In the corporate act in which all join and in which there is a conjunction between the visible and invisible, the physical and the spiritual action involved, there arises the problem of the *manducatio impiorum*, as it has been called, of those who eat and drink unworthily to their own judgment. This requires that the Table be "fenced", for it is a Holy Table, and holy things are to be given only to the holy. Each Church therefore administers the Supper within its discipline, although in so doing it must acknowledge at every point that it is the Lord's Supper and not the prerogative or the possession of the Church. But what of those who come unworthily to participate; do they too eat the Body and drink the Blood of Christ? We must surely answer this question by recalling that the action in the Supper is not another action than that which Christ has already accomplished on our behalf, and which is proclaimed in the Gospel. But even in the proclamation of the Gospel some who refuse the light are blinded by it, and others who receive the light are illuminated by it, so that the Gospel is, as St. Paul put it, a savour of death unto death to some and of life unto life to others. We may take another illustration, from the Johannine account of the prayer of Christ answered by the voice of the Father from heaven which some heard only as thunder whereas others heard it as the voice of an angel; or the Lucan and Pauline account of the encounter of Saul of Tarsus with Jesus on the Damascus road, when Paul alone discerned the Voice of Jesus while others who saw the light heard no voice. Surely it is in that way that we are to think of those who come to the Table unworthily without faith. It is the same Christ giving Himself in His Body and Blood who is extended to all; but while some receive in faith so that Christ dwells in their hearts, others are blinded and judged by the very gift of grace extended to them, by the Body and Blood of Christ, for it is only by the Body and Blood of Christ that they can be judged; Christ does not therefore dwell in their hearts, for they do not feed on Him by faith.

(b) The Church that partakes of the Body and Blood of Christ at His Table is committed to engage in His mission of reconciliation, to proclaim the Gospel to all nations and to live it out as a fellowship of reconciliation bringing healing to a divided world. The Church must see to it therefore that its daily life and work are in agreement with its communion in the Body and Blood of Christ, and that the ordering of its whole life is in worthy correspondence with the Gospel. It is pledged to that in the most solemn and awful way by the Body and Blood of Christ, and cannot resile from that without seriously damaging its own life and quenching the Holy Spirit in its midst. No doubt it is because of failure at this point that the Churches in our day are so weak and sickly, repeating the lapses of the Corinthian Church which drew upon them the rebuke of St. Paul.

(c) This brings us also to face the vexed question of intercommunion. We cannot forget that so long as the Church is divided within itself it betrays the Gospel of reconciliation, and cripples the effectiveness of its mission in the proclamation of reconciliation to the world. But how is the Church to keep holy discipline over the celebration of the Supper, to acknowledge that it is the Lord's and not its own Supper, and to find a way in which common participation between the Churches can be achieved again with sincerity? We cannot forget the parable of Jesus about the man who went to lay his gift on the altar and remembered he had a quarrel with another; he was commanded to go and *first* be reconciled with his brother and then to come and lay his gift on the altar. That applies to intercommunion, for how can we sit down at the Holy Table together and pretend that we are one there when we refuse to seek or work out a way of reconciliation in which our outer life in the ordering of our mission and ministry is in agreement with the Gospel proclaimed at the Supper? But how can we go to the Lord's Table at all if that is so? for the parable tells us that we cannot go at all until we are first reconciled with our brother.

Where is the Church that dares to take this parable seriously? Surely the very discipline that Churches profess to exercise means that they wish to celebrate the Supper only in truth and sincerity; if so, none of these Churches should go to the Table without resolving to seek a way out of our divisions and without seeking to do all it can to work out, along with others, an ordering of the ministry and mission of the Church which is in worthy agreement with the Gospel enshrined and enacted in the Holy Communion. The Unity of the Church is a gift of Christ freely bestowed at Holy Communion. Woe to the Church that receives this gift in the broken Body and shed Blood of Christ and then hides it or refuses it because it loves its own man-made traditions and prejudices more than that which has been bought with the Blood of the Saviour. Behind all the problems of intercommunion there lies deep failure to grasp the true nature of this sacrament of reconciliation, refusal to believe sufficiently that it is an efficacious Sacrament, effective as well as signitive of unity, but also a failure to enter very far into the Garden of Gethsemane and to enter into the passion of the Lord. That applies as much to those who claim to have "open communion" but refuse to respect or listen to the sincere conscience of others, as it does to those who have erected again "the middle wall of partition" (the *phragmos*) which Jesus deliberately broke down in parable and in act, and at last in His crucifixion on the Cross.

(b) *Eschatology and the Eucharist*[1]

It is a significant fact that in the last thirty or forty years the difference between the Roman Catholic Church and the Evangelical Church in their teaching on the Eucharist has been narrowed down considerably. That is most evident in the abandonment by many leading Roman Catholic theologians of the Tridentine explanation of the sacrifice of the Mass in literal terms, and in their return to a deeper understanding of the sacramental and eschatological significance of the Eucharist. The outstanding event in this movement was the publication of *Mysterium Fidei* by Maurice de la Taille after the First World War, and since then other notable works have appeared moving more or less within the same orbit of thought.[2] To the Reformed theologian much of this discussion is still hampered by unreal scholastic distinctions and a too literal approach to the eucharistic sacrifice, but he cannot but be impressed with two major elements in it: (a) the distinct sensitiveness of Roman theologians to the Protestant criticism of the pre- and post-Reformation

[1] Prepared for the World Conference on Faith and Order at Lund, and published in *Intercommunion* (edit. by D. M. Baillie and John Marsh, S.C.M. Press), 1952, pp. 303–50.

[2] Cf. the works of Baumstark, Cabrol, Guardini, Héris, Masure, Casel, Vonier, Bardy, Warnach, Söhngen, Schmaus, Jungmann, etc.

doctrine of the Mass, and the concern of all to maintain the unique character of the sacrifice on the Cross as an unrepeatable event; and (b) the fresh understanding of biblical teaching and consequently a rediscovery of the eschatological nature of the sacraments of Baptism and Eucharist. In spite of this *rapprochement*, however, we cannot blind ourselves to the fact that the difference between the Roman Catholic Church and the Evangelical Church is very deep,[1] and much deeper than anything which divides the branches of the Evangelical Church.

In the branches of the Evangelical Church, that is in the Churches of the Reformation, differences have also been narrowed down considerably. To a certain extent the modern liturgical movement has tended to harden those differences through its search for a definitive shape of the liturgy, but on the whole it has served rather to bring the Churches together by taking their differences to a deeper level and testing them by the prophetic and apostolic foundation of the Church. Here it has become apparent that difference in practice has carried divergence in belief farther than it actually is. That is a heartening discovery; for it indicates that in the Evangelical Church, where we do not have to do with irreformable pronouncements of faith, a fresh understanding of the apostolic message may so undermine our differences and correct our several traditions that intercommunion will become a compelling necessity for all who confess "one Lord, one faith, one baptism, one God and Father of all". This essay is an attempt from within the Reformed Church to engage in discussion at this stage, and if possible to penetrate below the existing principles governing intercommunion to theological foundations in the hope of laying bare the significance of the Eucharist as the divinely given Sacrament of unity, indeed the medicine for our divisions.

I

The Sacraments and Eschatology

We may begin with the word *sacrament*, and note that the New Testament does not speak of sacraments, but rather of Baptism

1 This difference is made very clear by the new Roman dogma. Instead of the Evangelical *solus Christus* at the right hand of the Father, the Roman Church substitutes *Christus et Maria*.

and the Lord's Supper. If we are to penetrate to the biblical foundations, therefore, we must avoid thinking about Baptism and the Eucharist as if they had to fulfil some man-made definition of a sacrament from Augustine, for example, or Aquinas or Calvin, helpful as they may be. When we set aside for the moment the centuries of theological discussion and turn to the pages of the New Testament Scriptures, we become aware of the fact that again and again the language it uses about Baptism is interchangeable with that it uses about the Eucharist.[1] Indeed, Baptism and Eucharist are just as parallel, and just as one, as *in Christ* and *Christ in us*. If anything, the emphasis is laid upon Baptism, as in the confession of unity cited above, "One Lord, one faith, one baptism", where the Eucharist is not mentioned, while whole Epistles such as that to the *Romans* do not mention it either. That would not be understandable were it not for the evident fact that the New Testament regards Baptism and Eucharist as two aspects of the same event, and that it is Baptism rather than the Eucharist which is all-inclusive. Both have to do with incorporation into Christ, but whereas Baptism is all-inclusive and final, the Eucharist is the continual renewal of that incorporation in time. The Eucharist cannot be understood except within the significance of Baptism, although the once-and-for-all significance of Baptism bears upon history only through the Eucharist. We may say, therefore, that strictly speaking there is only one sacrament, and that Baptism and Eucharist belong to this indivisible whole.[2] It is the sacrament of the *Word made flesh*, of the *Christ-event*, which includes the life, teaching, death, and resurrection of Jesus Christ. It is the same Word which sacramentally becomes flesh in both Baptism and the Eucharist, and it is in that action of the Word becoming flesh that they have their underlying and indivisible unity. In the action of the Church the relation between Baptism and Eucharist is through the *kerygma*: it is a *kerygmatic relation*.

[1] Cf. especially Mk. 10: 38 f.; 1 Cor. 10: 1 f.; 12: 12, 13.

[2] This is borne out very clearly by the art of the Roman Catacombs—cf. Vladimir Weidlé *The Baptism of Art*. The unity of Baptism and Eucharist has been remarkably conserved by the Orthodox Church. It became also a point of cardinal importance in the Reformation writings of Calvin and Peter Martyr, following Augustine.

In the elucidation of this we may recall the meaning of the Christ-event as the Word made flesh. It is the Christian message that in the Incarnation of the Son of God the eternal Word has entered into history, and partakes of the relativity of history, without ceasing to be God, and without at the same time destroying the continuity of ongoing history. In the historical Jesus the eternal Word is made flesh so that He is seen and heard in the flesh in history, and yet because He does not cease to be the eternal Word He cannot be seen or heard except in His eternal recession in God. That is why the Synoptic Gospels speak of the Word as *mysterion*. Jesus can be known historically as part of human flesh, but the real significance of the historical Jesus is not apparent except to faith. The Word has become flesh, and cannot be known by men of flesh and blood except in the flesh; but it is the Father in heaven alone who reveals Him, and not flesh and blood.

That, however, is only part of the significance of the Christ-event. The Word is not only eternal Truth but the act of the Eternal in time. That is why in the Gospels there is the closest relation between the Word and the act in Jesus' preaching. Word and act are inseparable and complementary. The Word of the Kingdom is God's saving intervention among men, and that takes place in the preaching and miracles of Jesus in inseparable unity. We may put the matter thus. Jesus is not one whose action falls short of His Word. Therefore, though the Word of forgiveness is spoken in a parable, that same Word is acted out in Himself on the Cross. There the Word of pardon is enacted in flesh and blood and inserted as a reality into our history and life. It becomes an actual fact, not just a mere idea or a word spoken into the air. That was why on the lips of Jesus the Word was indirectly communicated through the parable because the act is also part of the Word. The Word of God is not mere speech but power of God, Christ crucified, as St. Paul said. It is because the Word is also power or act that it cannot be conveyed in mere speech but has to be conveyed in saving acts, in miraculous signs. The parables were designed not to convey a symbolic meaning which can be read off their face but to confront men with Christ Himself as the Word of God, and the miracles were designed not just to prove the divinity of Christ but to confront men with the mighty power of God already at work among them in Jesus Christ. Both parables and miracles, however, pointed beyond themselves to the crucifixion and resurrection, where in the fullest sense the divine Word and act were one in the person of Jesus Christ.

That happened once and for all, and is absolutely decisive for all men and all time. It was not a once-and-for-all event merely in the sense in which every other historical event happens but once and is unrepeatable, but once and for all in the sense of eternal finality. As such, however, it is not merely a piece of past history, but is an enduring event with critical and decisive significance for all time.[1] Everything else will pass away, but this will not pass away. How does this unique and enduring event bear upon men in time now that Jesus Christ has withdrawn Himself from visible participation in history? It is here that the New Testament speaks about *kerygma*, and also about Baptism and the Lord's Supper.

Kerygma means both the thing preached and the preaching of it in one. It is the proclamation of the Christ-event, but such proclamation that by the Holy Spirit it becomes the actualization of that event among men. It is such proclamation that in and through it the living Christ continues to do and to teach what He had already begun before and after the crucifixion. *Kerygma* is the Word of the Kingdom that cannot be conveyed in mere speech, but is used by God to intervene Himself in the human situation as He who once and for all has wrought out His final act in the death and resurrection of Jesus Christ, so that through *kerygma* the Church is continually being called out of history to become the very Body of Christ, and by the communion of His Holy Spirit is given to taste the powers of the age to come and to stand already on the side of the resurrection. Accordingly, even after the Lord Jesus was received up into heaven and sat on the right hand of God, the disciples "went forth and preached everywhere, the Lord working with them, and confirming the Word with signs following". That is the twofold event of *kerygma*.

This means that *kerygma* is in the fullest sense the sacramental action of the Church through which the mystery of the Kingdom concerning Christ and His Church, hid from the founda-

[1] Cf. E. Brunner, "The Christian Understanding of Time", *Scottish Journal of Theology*, 1951, Vol. 41, pp. 1 ff., and his *Eternal Hope*, ch. 5.

tion of the world, is now being revealed in history. Just as in the Incarnation the Word was made flesh, so in *kerygma* the same Word continues to be "made flesh" in the life of the Church. Thus we read in the Acts of the Apostles of the Word as increasing and multiplying. By that is not meant that Christ the Word grows or increases, but that His living Word acting in and through human witness works creatively among men, building upon earth the Church which is concorporate with the all-inclusive Body of Christ. It is within this sacramental and kerygmatic activity of Church and Spirit that Baptism and the Lord's Supper are given their place in the New Testament. As such they may be regarded as bearing a relation to the *kerygma* of the Church similar to that which the signs and miracles bore to the *kerygma* of Jesus. Jesus took care in His preaching never to give a compelling manifestation of Himself, lest by an open display of His majesty and might He might crush men to the ground, leaving no room for faith or repentance or decision. In Him the *eschaton* had broken into the present, but if men had been confronted openly with the *eschaton* in the Word and Presence of Jesus they would have been faced with the final judgment. Jesus deliberately held the Word and its action apart in order to leave room for repentance and faith, but at the same time He followed up the Word with a sign which gave ample evidence of His saving power. The classic example of that is to be found in the Markan account of the healing of the paralytic, where for the purpose of leaving room for faith ("that ye may know that the Son of Man hath power on earth to forgive sins"), an interval of time was inserted between the Word of forgiveness and the act of healing. It was precisely that lapse of time or eschatological reserve between the Word of the Kingdom and its power that Jesus was concerned to preserve in His *kerygma*.

A similar relation between Word and act is to be found after the death and resurrection of Jesus, for though it is as one that they take the field in the *kerygma* of the Church, Jesus has withdrawn Himself from visible participation in history, reserving that for the *parousia* or the *eschaton*. Here, however, both the unity between the Word and action and their eschatological tension are intensified. The Church is redeemed not in Word only but also in power, and yet it waits for the redemption of the body. The new age has already overtaken it and through the Spirit it stands on the resurrection side of the Cross, and yet it still waits for the day when the form and fashion of this world will be torn aside and the new creation will be revealed. The Church lives between those two moments, between the Cross and the *parousia*, between the Word of forgiveness and the final act of healing, between Pentecost and the resurrection of the body. In the mercy of God the Word of the Gospel and the final deed of God are partially held apart in eschatological reserve until the *parousia*. This is the age of grace, the age of *kerygma*, in which the Gospel is proclaimed to all, in which time and space are given for repentance and decision. But this is the age, too, when by the Holy Spirit, who inhabits the Church and energizes its kerygmatic ministry, all who believe in Jesus Christ may taste the powers of the age to come through sacramental incorporation into the new creation.

It was said above that the relation between the sacraments and the *kerygma* of the Church is similar to that between the signs and the *kerygma* of Jesus—but there is this supreme difference, that now the death and resurrection of Jesus Christ have taken place and the great act for the redemption of the world has been completed. It is true indeed that the unveiling of the full reality of that act is still to take place, but it is equally true that with the death and resurrection of Jesus Christ the Kingdom of God and with it the new creation have already interpenetrated the age in which we live, so that this is already the fullness of time. The two sacraments of the Word made flesh, Baptism and Eucharist, are essentially *signs* belonging to this fullness of time, and as such are charged with the power of the resurrection. They enshrine in time the great *mystery* concerning Christ in His Church.

We must be clear, however, about the meaning of these two words, *sign* and *mystery*. The sign is to be understood in terms of the miraculous activity of Christ, as *kerygma* is to be understood in terms of Christ the living Word. These may be distinguished from each other in thought, but are actually inseparable. As the virgin birth and the resurrection are miraculous and active signs of the Word made flesh, so Baptism and Eucharist are miraculous and active signs of the Word made flesh in the Church as the Body of Christ. The great difficulty about the word *sign* in traditional theology is the unfortunate fact that *signum* corresponds to *res* and involves a quite unhebraic and unbiblical denotation as static matter or significant thing.[1] Even the expression *effective sign* used by the Reformers is inadequate.[2] Sign is essentially event, the worldly form which the Christ-event assumes in action, the point at which Revelation embodies itself actively in history. Sign is not, however, a complete or final embodiment, as if Revelation completely passes into or is absorbed in history, but such an embodiment in conditions of time as to point beyond itself to an infinite fullness. Before the Cross the miraculous signs were actual anticipations of the saving act of God in the death and resurrection of Jesus; afterwards they are the miraculous signs charged with the incarnate presence of the crucified and risen Lord which point beyond to a fullness which, as signs, in the conditions of our fallen world, they cannot altogether contain. In other words, the whole significance of the sign is bound up with the fact that the ascension comes in between the resurrection of Jesus Christ and His second advent. *Parousia* means both a presence and a coming. The sacramental signs are charged with the real presence, but it is a presence which is also yet to come, a presence whose full reality is yet to be unveiled and consummated.

That takes us to the significance of the word *mystery*. Here it is the Greek idea which has confused understanding. Like *sign*, *mystery* is essentially event, but event as that which is not yet fully disclosed in conditions of the fallen world. It is the event of Revelation in time in so far as it recedes into the eternal, in so far as the sign bears witness to the fullness beyond. In the New Testament, mystery is spoken of in relation to the *kerygma*, and not directly in relation to Baptism and the Lord's Supper, but its bearing upon the sacraments was inevitable. In its fundamental sense mystery refers to God manifest in the flesh, but as the great sign of that event is the Church of Jesus Christ, the relation of Christ to His Church is also spoken of as mystery. It is in that sense that the word may legitimately be applied to the sacraments. We may put it this way. Through its ministry of *kerygma* the Church is regarded in the New Testament as the great sacramental sign, for it is the visible counterpart of the

1 Cf. E. Gaugler, *Das Abendmahl im Neuen Testament*, pp. 7 ff.; K. Barth, *Die christliche Lehre nach dem Heidelberger Katechismus*, pp. 88 f.

2 This did enable Calvin, however, to teach a doctrine of *dynamic presence* in the sacraments.

resurrection-body of Christ. As such the Church can neither be fused with Christ nor separated from Him. As the God-Man Christ was Himself the embodiment in the world of the mystery of the Kingdom, but as the Church is the embodiment of the Spirit of Christ (for "he that is joined to the Lord is one Spirit"), it is also in its way the embodiment of the same mystery. The sacraments of Baptism and Eucharist are therefore the miraculous and active signs through which that mystery is embodied in the Church on earth, but, be it noted, embodied in such a way that, while they anticipate, they point to an eschatological fullness beyond. The sacraments are given to us because of the ascension and cannot be made to impugn it as if they contained a presence fully identical with that of the *parousia*. Had Christ not withdrawn Himself visibly from the world there would doubtless have been no need for sacraments, not in our sense at any rate. When Christ comes again and the Marriage Supper of the Lamb is consummated, the sacraments will give way to literal reality. Until that day comes the sacraments have to do with the breaking of the Christ-event into time here and now, and with our participation in the new creation.

To understand that more clearly we must recall the nature of the Christ-event, which, while it is once and for all in a final sense, is also an abiding or enduring event that can never pass away. The union of God and Man in the Incarnation also involves the union of eternity with time, and though that union is inserted into our history with its limitations and relativities it is a union that is carried through the contradiction of sin and death itself into the resurrection. There we have revealed the new creation in the risen Body of Jesus Christ. But just as the original creation involved the creation of time, so this new creation involves new time, time that is no longer at variance with the eternal through sin, but time that is cleansed and restored to union with the eternal. The Christ-event is absolutely unique and decisive in that through it redemption has been wrought once and for all, nevertheless it is an event that involves this new time, and as such it transcends the limitations and relativities of history as we know it from day to day, and endures for ever. It endures and abides for ever as new time just because it is indissolubly united to the eternal. That is the significance of the session at the right hand of God the Father, but it is also the significance of the continuity of the new creation in the Church, the Body of Christ.

We may say that as God and man are united in the God-Man in such a way that the two natures may not be identified with or separated from each other (we recall here the Chalcedonian formula), so the sacraments involve on another plane, in conditions of this fallen world, a like union between divine action and human action, but here let it be noted that the "divine" action is the action of *Totus Christus*, of the God-Man, and not of God *simpliciter* apart from the incarnation. There is then in the sacraments a union between the divine action and human action, between the *actio* of Christ Jesus and the *re-actio* of the Church, and *actio* and *re-actio* can neither be identified with, nor separated from, each other. Just as God and Man in Christ Jesus are united in the *communio consubstantialis* of the Holy Spirit, so here in the sacraments the divine action and the human re-action are united in *communio substantialis* through the same Holy Spirit.

This means that the sacraments do not have to do simply with a union between the present and the future, but with a union between the Church in history and the new creation as an abiding union here and now even in the heart of the world's estrangement. It is because that union is only partially revealed in the sacraments that we must talk about it in terms of mystery, and it is because that union will be fully revealed in the future that we must speak about it in terms of eschatology. The sacraments tell us, however, that the reality of the new creation is temporal fact here and now, even though its reality, veiled since the ascension of the Lord, is yet to be unveiled at the *parousia*. The New Testament emphasis upon the future is not so much the future of the reality but the future of its full manifestation, so that the eschatological tension involved in the sacraments is the tension between the time of a present but hidden reality and the time of the same reality revealed in the *parousia*.

It is because the eschatological relation involves both the relation between the present and the future and the relation between the new creation and the old, here and now, that the one sacramental relation between the Church and Jesus Christ has two particular "moments": Baptism and the Lord's Supper. Just as the Christ-event had its two supreme "moments" in the virgin birth and in the death and resurrection of Jesus Christ, although neither "moment" can be understood except as it involves the other, so here in the sacramental union where the Christ-event breaks into the historical life of the Church incorporating it into Christ as His Body, there are two corresponding "moments", Baptism and the Lord's Supper, each of which involves the other in a single whole. The doubleness of the eschatological tension is enshrined in both of them, but the emphasis upon the once-and-for-all incorporation into Christ or union with the new creation falls most heavily upon the sacrament of Baptism, while in the sacrament of the Eucharist we have emphasized most the breaking in of the new creation as the enduring event in, and in spite of, the conditions of this sinful and historical world. If at Baptism we think of our having died and risen with Christ so that we are born anew in Him, so that old things are passed away and all things are become new, at Holy Communion we think of that not only as a *datum* once and for all, but also as a *dandum* which must be given anew, day by day, in the conditions of our fallen world. Every time we communicate is eschatological time until we drink it anew in the Kingdom of God. It is just because, in the sign of Baptism, the complete event recedes into the mystery of the Eternal that we are given in the Eucharist continual participation and renewal in that complete event. In both sacraments we are told that the Kingdom of God is amongst us not in Word only with suspended action, not in Spirit only, but in deed and in power, as real act in time, as Word-deed enacted in our flesh and blood and inserted into history. But precisely because it is both, it is at once a complete reality and an eschatologically reiterated event until Christ comes.

It is important to remember that both Baptism and Eucharist are sacraments of the Word made flesh. They do not have existence or reality independently of the Word. To make them self-sufficient and independent of the Word would be to take away their sacramental character, for it would deny to them their element of mystery, or infinite recession in the Word that is in the bosom of God and is God. That is why, following St. Augustine, the Reformers insisted that it is the Word which sacramentalizes, and apart from the Word sacraments cannot exist. Apart from the Word there is only an empty sign that is nothing but a ceremony. *Kerygma* and sign go together and cannot be sundered. In *kerygma* the *Word* is made flesh. In the sacraments the Word is made *flesh.* Baptism, *kerygma,* and Eucharist together form a whole, the sacramental life and action of the Church. "And Jesus came and spake unto them, saying, All power is given unto me in heaven and in earth. Go ye therefore, and teach all nations, baptizing them in the name of the Father, and of the Son, and of the Holy Spirit: teaching them to observe all things whatsoever I have commanded you: and lo, I am with you alway, even unto the end of the world." The emphasis here is upon *kerygma* and Baptism, but in the promise of the real presence *alway* we may surely understand the eucharistic communion.

II

The Eucharist of the Lord's Supper

Before we speak more precisely about the Eucharist we must be more precise about Baptism as the primary eschatological act of the Gospel, whereby we are ingrafted into the wholeness of Christ. The Baptism of John clearly had reference to the liturgical washing at the laver in preparation for the sacrifice of the lamb, a sign which pointed to a fullness in the Spirit that was yet to come. That Baptism had its counterpart doubtless in Jesus' cleansing of the Temple in preparation for His sacrifice as the Lamb of God whereby He was to make atonement for sin, a cleansing which pointed to the sanctification of the Church, cleansed with the washing of water by the Word, a glorious Church not having spot or wrinkle, but holy and without blemish. We cannot, however, speak about the Baptism of the disciples and of Jesus in univocal terms. Theirs was a Baptism of repentance and renewal even though the power of the resurrection was not fully released until Pentecost; Jesus' Baptism was substitutionary and was completed in His Baptism of blood on the Cross when He died for all men. In the profoundest sense all men are actually involved in that Baptism of Jesus, and it is that Baptism which turns John's Baptism into Christian Baptism. After the crucifixion and resurrection Baptism has much more than parabolic significance, for now the Word and act are one event, and it is because of that unity that *kerygma* and *baptisma* are always thought of together in the New Testament.

The Word in *kerygma* presses into physical enactment, creating the bodily Church—and that happens through Baptism. It is through the *kerygma*, however, that Baptism gains its particularity and is given power as concrete event. A purely substitutionary and objective Baptism would have little reference to the life which we live in history, even though after the crucifixion all history happens within and under the shadow of the Cross and the mighty act of God wrought out there. It is through the *kerygma*, through the ministry of the Church empowered by the Holy Spirit, that the Cross exerts its power over men and history. In the *kerygma* of the Church the living Word, Christ crucified and risen, lays hold of men in their sin and weakness. The Word demands decision and through men's obedience and disobedience it acts selectively upon them, calling the Church into being, a work which will be fully unveiled at the last day when the Word will complete its judgment. But already that Word is event, for through the *kerygma* the death and the resurrection of Jesus Christ break into the present, so that all who believe are given to participate in that death and resurrection and are inserted into the operational sphere of the Christ-event. Baptism is the fulfilment of that as the particular actualization of the Christ-event, so that through it the Church called out of the world becomes the Church which is the Body of Christ. There is only one Baptism, the Baptism of the Spirit at Pentecost which corresponds to the one Baptism of Christ, and into that each believer is incorporated through water-baptism.

Parallel to the hypostatic union between God and Man in Jesus Christ there is a sacramental union in Baptism between the divine action and the action of the Church, between its manward and its Godward action. Baptism is not in any sense an independent agency whose benefit is conferred *ex opere operato*; rather is it the action of the Church in obedience to the divine ordinance, which God uses to fulfil His holy Will. In other words, the mediation of the divine act is not through the element as such but in its particular use in the action of the Church. Baptism is, on the one hand, then, the breaking in of the Christ-event, so that it is not simply an historical event belonging to the past, but as a once-and-for-all historical event it is also precipitated into the present and is active with saving power here and now in the Church. Baptism indicates that the Church is the sphere and the medium in the world whereby the saving acts of Jesus Christ are at work, invading history and subjecting all things to Christ as King and Lord. Baptism is the outworking in time of the absolutely decisive event of the Cross and resurrection of Christ, and gathers to that event the corresponding life and action of the historical Church. The Church is not therefore merely an historical institution, but is a sacramental magnitude maintained in being upon foundations that are not laid with hands, rooted and grounded in the God-Manhood of Jesus Christ.

On the other hand, as in Baptism the Church binds believers to the *Heilsgeschichte*, pledges them to faith in Jesus Christ who died for them and rose again, and offers them to Him as Saviour and Lord, the Holy Spirit uses this Godward action of the Church as the means whereby He gives believers participation in the Baptism of Christ, inserts them into the Christ-event, incorporates them into His Body, ingrafts them into the New Creation, and makes them to sit in heavenly places. This means that something absolutely decisive is wrought in Baptism. Baptism in the Name of Jesus, in the name of the Holy Trinity, means that Christians are delivered from the power of darkness and translated into the Kingdom of the Son of God. A radical change has taken place which can only be described in terms of a complete change of Lordship. The Christian is no longer under the domination of the law or the elements of this world, but is dead to sin and alive to God through the Lordship of the Spirit, so that old things are passed away and all things are become new. Outwardly Baptism is no doubt incorporation into the earthly Church, initiation into the operational sphere of the salvation-event, and outwardly the Church on earth knows itself to be embroiled in the relativities of history and the sin of mankind, but behind all that and beyond, Baptism has a dimension in depth which is its eschatological *mystery*: "Ye are dead and your life is hid with Christ in God." The really significant event in Baptism is a hidden event; it recedes from sight in the ascension of Christ and waits to be revealed fully at the last day.

However, the Lord has not simply left His Church stricken with anguish and awe at the foot of the Cross, or standing looking up into heaven from Galilee. He has provided for the renewal and maintenance of its life and faith—in the Eucharist.

Through continual communion in the body and blood of the Saviour, the Church finds that Baptism is given its complement and recurring confirmation. After the Baptism of John, Jesus had called twelve disciples and formed them round Himself into one body, the reconstituted Israel of God. They were pledged to drink His cup and be baptized with His baptism, but the mystery of the Kingdom, the New Israel incorporate in the Messianic Saviour, baffled them. They understood indeed that they were called to cast in their lot unreservedly with Jesus and to share His life, but in the crucial moment they found themselves standing not with Jesus but with the crowd of sinners who were crucifying Him and for whom He was dying. They had all forsaken Him and fled.[1] At last the Messiah was left unutterably alone under the judgment of God upon the world's sin. He was their Lord and Master. He was their Representative and their very Life, but in the agony of substitution He was unutterably alone, the Lamb whom God had Himself provided for sacrifice.[2] The disciples could only stand afar off in sin and shame and fear, and broken-hearted that the bonds between Him and them were utterly severed. Then they remembered the Last Supper. That was why He had designed it, for He meant them to remember. And they realized that within that awful separation and in spite of it He had effectuated His oneness with them in a way that nothing could break, for He had given them in the Supper a sacramental counterpart to His atoning death. And then they knew that their baptismal incorporation into one Body with their Lord had come to its stark reality in the sacrificial death and its sacramental counterpart. They understood how in that wonderful Last Supper Jesus "had definitely consecrated them for inheritance in the Kingdom of God as those who, despite their brokenness so soon to be made visible, formed one body with Himself. He had given their lives a sacramental dependence on His own."[3] In the Lord's Supper and in the enactment on the Cross the mystery of their baptismal incorporation into Christ, and into the Israel of God, actually became materialized in flesh and blood.

[1] For this and what immediately follows see W. Manson, *Scottish Journal of Theology*, 1950, vol. 3.1, pp. 38 f.; and *The Way of the Cross*, 1958.

[2] Cf. O. Cullmann, *Christ and Time*, pp. 107 ff.

[3] W. Manson, *op. cit.*, p. 39.

After the resurrection and ascension the disciples understood why, again and again, Jesus had gathered the lost sheep of the House of Israel, the cultically unclean and those debarred from the Temple liturgy of sacrifice, and although it scandalized the priests He deliberately broke down the barriers erected by the cultus, and enacted in their midst a sign of the Messianic Meal, when many would come from the east and the west and sit down with Abraham, Isaac, and Jacob in the Kingdom of Heaven.[1] That eschatological meal was not an eating and drinking between holy priests and holy people, but the marriage-supper of the Lamb, who because He had come to bear their sin, gathered the poor and the outcast, the weary and the heavy laden, the publicans and sinners, and fed them with the bread of life and gave them living water to drink. The disciples remembered also the parables of the prodigal son and his feasting in the father's house, of the bridegroom and the wedding-feast, and the final judgment which would discover those who had given or not given food to the hungry and drink to the thirsty, and they understood their bearing upon the Lord's Supper as the great eschatological meal of the Kingdom of God through which that very Kingdom is realized here and now, as far as may be in the conditions of this passing world. The disciples recalled, too, those Galilean meals of fellowship with Jesus, the miraculous feeding of the multitudes by the Great Shepherd of the sheep, and the equally wonderful words He spoke about manna and water, about His flesh and blood, and the life-giving Spirit, and they knew that what had been parable and sign and miracle then had at last materialized in the Easter breaking of bread.

They saw in His death and resurrection such fulfilment of the Old Testament oracles as gave their teaching creative reinterpretation and threw a flood of light upon the mystery of the Cross. In that Jesus had died for them and risen again, He had inaugurated a new covenant within which they could sit down together and eat bread and drink wine, assured that they were one with their Lord, given to partake of His sacrifice, to share in the power of His resurrection and to be bound up with Him in the same bundle of life. The ends of the earth had already come upon them, for by this sacramental meal they tasted its powers and were given to stand with Christ on the other side of

[1] Cf. Lohmeyer, *Kultus und Evangelium*, pp. 36 f., 80, and 90 f.

the judgment, in the new creation. The incredible mystery of Baptism was become a visible reality, and the disciples continued in the breaking of bread to commune with their Lord and to proclaim His death as the power of God unto salvation.

In order to unfold more fully the significance of the Eucharist we must return to the event of the Upper Room. The apostolic records of that night make it clear that they saw converging in the institution of the Supper both the pascal and covenantal meals of the Old Testament and the messianic meals of the wilderness of Sinai and the hills of Galilee. It was charged through and through with eschatological significance. At the beginning of the meal Jesus must have followed the Jewish custom of passing round a cup of wine in token of thanksgiving to God; but before that was done, a piece of bread and a cup of wine were set aside for the Messiah in case He should suddenly come to His own in the midst of the feast. Then at the end of the meal, fully charged with pascal and covenantal significance, Jesus took the bread and wine set aside for the Messiah, and said, "This is my body broken for you. This is my blood which is shed for you." By breaking the bread and giving it to the disciples, by passing round the cup, He associated them with His sacrifice, giving their existence in relation to Himself a new form in the Kingdom of God, indeed constituting them as the Church concorporate with Himself. When the apostolic Church looked back upon that Last Supper they recalled that Jesus had bidden them do this repeatedly in remembrance of Him, proclaiming thus His death till He should come again to drink it anew with them in the Kingdom of God. St. John records, too, that the original Supper was set in the context of our Lord's high-priestly prayer in which He consecrated Himself and interceded for His Church.

There is a great deal here which we must discuss in order to elucidate its theological structure. We may begin by noting the two fundamental moments within which the Eucharist has its place: "the night on which He was betrayed", and "till He come", as St. Paul puts them. The Eucharist is therefore at once bound to history, and related to the advent of Christ at the end of history. It reaches into the past, to the death of Christ, and sets it in the present as reality operative here and now in the Church. On the other hand, the Eucharist reaches out beyond the present into the future, and becomes the means whereby the Church in the present is brought under the power of the advent of Christ. The Eucharist thus belongs to the very nature of the Church, rooting and grounding it in the historical Christ and His saving acts, and also bringing to the Church its own ultimate reality from beyond history. By the Eucharist that ultimate reality stands not only at the end of time but impinges creatively upon the Church throughout history, for it is both the *proton* and the *eschaton* of its existence. Through the Eucharist the Church becomes, so to speak, the great arch that spans history, supported by only two pillars, the Cross which stands on this side of time, and the coming of Christ in power which stands at the end of history. From age to age the Church is grounded upon these two supports by the Eucharist, so that its very being is bound up with the essential unity of the two events, the perfected event of the death and resurrection of Christ, and the future event of the *parousia*. It is because the Church receives its being ever anew, through the Eucharist, as the new creation which is yet to be revealed at the *parousia*, that it lives in dynamic tension here and now on the very frontiers of eternity.

Once again, we must return to the thought of the hypostatic union between God and Man in Jesus Christ, in order to understand this eucharistic reality clearly. We must think of that hypostatic union, however, not in the static categories of patristic thought, but in terms of biblical eschatology, that is, in dynamic categories. As the Captain of our salvation was made perfect through suffering, we must think of that holy union inserted into our flesh and blood at the virgin birth of Jesus as carried through our human life and death, through the contradictions of sin and the relativities of history, through the passion and agony of the crucifixion to its transcendent perfection in the resurrection of Jesus from the dead, so that He lives on for ever, our Mediator and Atonement, in whom all things cohere, and in whom all things in heaven and earth will be brought back to the fullness of God. It is by the Eucharist, following upon Baptism, that that union is inserted as an abiding union into the heart of our estrangement from God the Father, and into all the conflicts of history.[1] Here we are given the perfect union between the eternal and the temporal, between the divine and the human,

[1] Cf. Karl Heim, *Jesus the World's Perfecter.*

inserted into our flesh and blood, and it is that made flesh in the Eucharist which is the inner core of the Church's reality on earth. This has several implications which we must not pass over because of their bearing upon intercommunion.

(1) The enactment of this abiding union within the world's estrangement increases the tension between the new creation and the fallen world. Just as the union between God and Man became fact and reality for us once and for all through the desperate passion and agony of the crucifixion, so the Church bound to its Lord by this sacramental union can only follow Him by taking up His Cross daily. The world continues in its estrangement from God and its contradiction to Him, but that is surely why the Church is given the Sacrament of the Eucharist in addition to the Sacrament of Baptism. It is taught thereby that while in reconciliation and justification and sanctification the Church is already perfect in Christ Jesus, yet in the broken conditions of time, in the conflicts and divisions of history, so long as it waits for redemption of the purchased possession, it is unable to realize that perfection in its wholeness here and now. The Church must nevertheless reckon that it is dead to the old life and alive in the new, for that is what actually takes place in the Eucharist. That the Church is once and for all justified and perfected in Christ is enshrined in the Sacrament of Baptism, but that its justification and perfection are also prolonged in time is enshrined in the Eucharist. The perfection of the Church's union with Christ Jesus has to be carried through the conditions of time, and how it is straitened until that is accomplished! By means of the Eucharist, so to speak, the agony of Calvary is witnessed in the ages into which the Church goes out as the suffering servant in the mission of the world's redemption. And so it learns to fill up that which is eschatologically in arrears of the sufferings of Christ as it throws itself into the heart of the world's trouble and acts out there, however costly that may be, the reconciliation of the Cross.

The Church can do that only because in the heart of its life and worship there is set the Sacrament of Holy Communion in which it is united to Christ through His sacrifice, and in which also it is given to share in the triumph of the Saviour: "Be of good cheer, I have overcome the world." In the consummation of that triumph the Church will have no need of the

Eucharist,[1] but so long as it is still the Church Militant in this world, the Eucharist is both its agony and its supreme joy. Here there is the memory of the travail and agony of Calvary as well as expectation of resurrection and the new world beyond. But it is part of the Church's agony that here in the Eucharist the wholeness of its union in Christ is received only sacramentally in the brokenness of time, and the more that wholeness presses toward its complete unveiling at the *parousia* the more evident does it become that the forms of the Church's existence in this passing world are broken up in order that the abiding reality of the new creation may appear. The Sacrament of the Eucharist, then, is the form which our sacramental union with Christ takes within the brokenness and the divisions of history, and yet mediates the wholeness of that union as such an abiding reality that the brokenness and the divisions of history, in which the Church inevitably partakes, are revealed to be but the shell of the old life which passes away. The Eucharist is the sacrament which God has given to us as the counterpart of the ascension, for while He holds apart as yet the faith and sight of the Church until the *epiphaneia* or the *apocalypsis*, He also joins them together, so that Christ makes Himself known in spite of the fraction of time. Here, as surely as the Church is given healing for its estrangement from God, it is given also healing for its divisions in history. The Eucharist speaks both of the fraction of the body on earth, evident even on the night of the Last Supper, and the "conversion" of the Church into the risen Body of Christ.

(2) The perfect union of God and Man which has broken into time in the virgin birth, and inserted into history at the Cross, is yet not held a prisoner to the relativities of time, because of the resurrection. It entails a new creation which travels through time and history inasmuch as Jesus Christ lives on. Therefore, although we must communicate again and again in the real presence of this Christ-event through the Sacrament of Holy Communion, we cannot forget the reality of Baptism, that inasmuch as through Baptism the Church is once and for all incorporated into the Body of Christ, it feeds uninterruptedly upon the flesh and blood of Christ through faith (John 6). As such the Church has eternal life abiding in it (John 15). That is

[1] Cf. Thomas Aquinas, *Summa Theol.*, III.q.61.4.

the reality which is so often misconstrued in terms of temporal repetition or continuity in the relativities of historical succession. To do so is to fall into the error of "sacramental occasionalism" and to by-pass the resurrection as the enduring reality in the heart of the Church. It is precisely because the Church lives on in the power of the resurrection that it must refuse to be imprisoned in the wrappings of by-gone history or of human systems and decisions. To give these absolute significance in its tradition means that the Church denies its ultimate reality as that which comes from beyond the relativities of history, and that it fails to realize the profound eschatological element in the Eucharist: that as often as the Church communicates in the body and blood of the crucified Saviour, it receives the judgments of the Cross upon the forms and fashions of this passing world in which the Church on earth, waiting for the redemption of the body, inevitably partakes.

The Church cannot participate in the Eucharist, and through it become the real Church, without placing itself under the impact of the *eschaton*. Whenever the Church denies that eschatological element in the Eucharist it becomes but a human Church, for then it denies that the Church transcends itself in the new creation, or rather is given to transcend its embroilment in the passing forms of this world. We must be quite clear, however, that it is because the Church is implicated through the Words and Sacraments in the ever-living continuity of the Christ-event travelling through and under the visible and historical continuities that the latter are disrupted, and will finally break up at the *parousia*.[1] The Church, which through Baptism

[1] Cf. M. Schmaus, *Aus der Theologie der Zeit* (ed. by G. Söhngen), p. 78: "Was in der Eucharistie in der Weise des Mysteriums geschieht, wird im Leiden und im Sterben im Raume der Geschichte mächtig. Der ganze Verlauf der auf Christus folgenden Geschichte wird von ihrem Anfang und von ihrem Ende bestimmt. Am Anfang steht das Kreuz, das Zeichen des schöpferischen Untergangs. Am Ende steht der völlige Zusammenbruch der jetzigen Formen der Schöpfung sowie der neue Himmel und die neue Erde. Anfang und Ende wirken in jede Gegenwart herein. Vom Anfang und vom Ende empfängt jede Gegenwart immerfort Stösse, die ihr kein Leben in ungestörter Ruhe und Sicherheit gestatten. Unsicherheit und Ungeborgenheit gehören wesentlich zu der Welt, die im Zeichen des Kreuzes und im Zeichen des neuen Himmels und der neuen Erde steht. Die jetzigen Weltformen haben keine ewige Verheissung. Es ist vielmehr gesagt, dass sie einmal völlig zusammembrechen werden."

has been planted into the dying and rising of Jesus and initiated into the new order, must learn to put off the old as often as through the Eucharist it participates in its new being. That is partly why apocalyptic is an inner necessity for faith and the sacramental life of the Church, for apocalypse is the fulfilment of history against itself, and apocalyptic images indicate the contradiction between the form and order of the Kingdom of God and the form and order of all earthly institutions. The very fact that in the Eucharist the Church is confronted with its own ultimate reality breaking into history from beyond history, a reality inexpressible in terms of history alone, reveals to the Church that it is also an earthly institution, but that it cannot perpetuate this historical form and order as essentially divine or as belonging to the *esse* of the Church, without either denying altogether or presumptuously anticipating the ultimate eschatological judgment. Inasmuch as by His ascension Jesus Christ has withdrawn from history His visible face and form, the true face and the true form of the Church remain essentially a *mysterion*. To deny that is to deny the essentially sacramental character of the Church's ministry, and to resolve it into a mere worldly institution.

We must now turn to another aspect of the Lord's Supper which requires elucidation, that concerned in the words: "do this in remembrance of me", and "ye proclaim the Lord's death till he come". These words have received a great deal of discussion in recent literature which it is not possible to go into here. It would seem, however, that memory must be understood as *anamnesis* both before God and before man, and that *proclamation* is *objective proclamation* both before God and before man. These involve each other (cf. Mark 14: 9), though we shall have to discuss first one and then the other. The fundamental fact, however, that helps to clear up many difficulties is that memory and proclamation are here set in a sacramental context and must be interpreted accordingly if they are to elucidate the theology of the Eucharist. We are concerned here, then, with sacramental *memory* which, as Zwingli insisted, is more than "historical faith". It was at that Last Supper that Jesus also said: "The Comforter, who is the Holy Ghost, whom the Father will send in my name, he shall teach you all things, and bring all things to your remembrance, whatsoever I have said unto you." That helps us to understand. Memory that is sacramental has two sides to it (we recall again the Chalcedonian formula about the two natures of Christ) which cannot be fused or separated. It is at once the action of the historical Church for which Christ died, and the action of the eternal Spirit through whom Christ offered Himself without spot to God. The *anamnesis* is both historical and eternal, and in sacramental *anamnesis* they involve each other. The Church's memory of the historical death and resurrection of Christ in itself is merely memory of the historical past, but through the eternal Spirit by whom Christ offered Himself a sacrifice it becomes such *anamnesis* that the past is made a present reality. The eternal Spirit glorifies Christ, who died and rose again and now sits at the right hand of God, and so shows the Church things to come that He makes the Church to sit together with Christ in heavenly places. The Holy Spirit does not speak of Himself but listens to Christ who ever lives to make intercession for us, and what He hears He *echoes* in the *anamnesis* of the Church.

To the Church on earth, then, it is given in its eucharistic worship to *echo* the eternal intercession of Christ. The action of the Church is the *anamnesis* of an act that is once and for all, and enduring before the Face of the Heavenly Father; but it is no more than *anamnesis*, for it is not the act itself. It is the living echo of that act which Christ alone performs as Mediator and Saviour, "the splintered reflection on earth of Christ's presentation of His sacrifice in heaven".[1] In the sacramental *anamnesis* the Church is raised by the eternal Spirit to the throne of God, made unto Him a kingdom and a priesthood, saying, "Amen: Blessing and glory and wisdom and thanksgiving and honour and power and might be unto our God for ever and ever. Amen." The Eucharist is the *Amen*, the counterpart on earth, to the eternal oblation in heaven, and the eucharistic thanksgiving the counterpoint on earth to the new song, "Worthy is the Lamb", of the saints in the Church triumphant.

We must go on to add that the *anamnesis* of Christ's atoning death and its eternal power includes eucharistic intercession. How could the sacramental memory of His sacrifice be anything

[1] D. M. Mackinnon, *Report of the Sixth Anglo-Catholic Congress*, p. 134. I have borrowed from Prof. Mackinnon his use of the word *echo* in this context.

other than prayer, the prayer that has nothing to bring but clings to the Cross of Christ and holds it up before the Father, the prayer that has nothing to offer but pleads the merits of the Saviour's oblation, the prayer that knows not how to pray, but is energized by the eternal Spirit who Himself makes intercession for us with groanings that cannot be uttered? And what can His intercession be but the echoing in the Church of the intercession of the great High Priest? And so through the *anamnesis* the Church enters into the passion of the Redeemer, and in His name travails in prayer for all mankind. We know not what to pray for as we ought, but the Spirit helps our infirmities, and through the same eternal Spirit by whom Christ offered Himself to God, we may offer our intercessions, on the merits of His sacrifice alone. And where even two or three are thus gathered together in His name, the Lord is in the midst of them. When the veil is lifted, and the mystery of that intercession is revealed, we read: "An angel came and stood at the altar, having a golden censer; and there was given unto him much incense, that he should offer it with the prayers of all the saints upon the golden altar which was before the throne. And the smoke of the incense, which came with the prayers of the saints, ascended up before God out of the angel's hand." *Anamnesis* before God. And so the early Church prayed at the Eucharist: "Remember, Lord, Thy Church" (Did. 10: 5).[1]

When we turn to the eucharistic *proclamation* of the sacrificial death of Jesus, we find the same sacramental character that we found in the *anamnesis*. That was already apparent in the *kerygma*, where the missionary preaching of the Church was sacramentally contrapuntal to the continuing work of the risen Lord, but here we have the same *kerygma* as it is intertwined with the continuing being of the Church. Here it is *objective proclamation* in the life and action of the Church on earth, which corresponds sacramentally to the eternal action of the Lamb slain before the foundation of the world and to His eternal destination of the Church as the Bride for the future marriage-supper of the Lamb. It is more than parable; it is the actual *homoioma* of the Christ-event, in which the faith of the

[1] Cf. J. Jeremias, *The Journal of Theological Studies*, January–April 1949, p. 9.

Church has to do not only with its objective ground but with its *objective duration.*[1] This eucharistic proclamation enshrines therefore as its eternal *canto firmo* the Self-consecration of the Lamb of God, the Self-presentation of the Mediator before the face of the Father in His intercession for the Church, but that is the *mysterion* which is the dimension in infinite depth behind the action of the Church in the Lord's Supper.

The Church's proclamation is not itself identical with that mystery, but it cannot be separated from it. It is sacramentally and analogically derivative from it, but as such it is analogically different. There in heaven is the ascended Lamb Himself ever before the Face of the Father; here on earth is the waiting Church of sinners, with all saints, showing forth His death and pleading His sacrifice—"Lamb of God that takest away the sins of the world, have mercy upon us"—but both are united in the *koinonia* of the eternal Spirit, through whom Christ offered Himself to the Father, and through whom we are given to participate in that oblation made on our behalf. That is the profound mystery of Holy Communion, that the Church is given to participate (*koinonein*) in Christ's substitutionary Self-consecration ("For their sakes I sanctify myself that they also might be sanctified through the truth"), as it communicates in His body and blood, proclaiming His death until He come.

"Till He come", however, reminds us that participation in His substitutionary oblation is essentially eschatological. At last the eucharistic rite, with all its wonderful liturgy, will pass away with the passing form of this world, for it will be displaced by the marriage-supper of the Lamb. But in so far as that real presence of Christ in the Eucharist is the real presence of the *Eschatos*, that future Supper in the Kingdom of God interpenetrates the present action of the Church, so that here and now the Eucharist enshrines an essential displacement of the action of the Church by the action of Christ. It is the Risen Lord Himself who is the true Celebrant at the holy table, and unless that eschatological substitution, the *mirifica commutatio*, as Calvin called it,[2] is recognized, the eucharistic sacrifice becomes but a pagan ceremony. No doubt the Church's *re-actio* to the sacrificial

[1] Cf. Karl Barth, *Die christliche Lehre nach dem Heidelberger Katechismus*, p. 99.

[2] *Inst.* 4. 17. 2, 4.

actio of Christ itself partakes of sacrificial character, but if *re-actio* is identified with the *actio*, the Sacrament is destroyed, because its derivative sacramental and analogical nature is denied. Just as the once-and-for-all sacrifice of Christ entailed the rending of the veil and the ultimate destruction of the Temple, and the undermining of its liturgical validity, so the consummation of Christ's action in the marriage-supper of the Lamb sets aside the eucharistic liturgy in which now we see through a glass darkly, for then we shall see face to face. "And I saw no temple therein," said St. John of the New Jerusalem, "for the Lord God Almighty and the Lamb are the temple of it." But in so far as that future marriage-supper of the Lamb is already present eschatologically in the Eucharist, the liturgical *re-actio* of the Eucharist is displaced by the immediate *actio* of Christ Himself, as the reality which the liturgy had proclaimed. Thus there is a "point" in the celebration of every Eucharist in which the real presence of the *Eschatos* suspends the liturgical action, and makes it point beyond itself for validity and order. The Son of Man is Lord also of the Eucharist, and He dispenses it as He wills. In such an eschatological economy the sacrifice of the Church can only participate in the Sacrifice of Christ by *mirifica commutatio*, and all order and liturgy have validity and truth only in so far as they leave room for such eschatological substitution. Where that is not so the Lord insists on cleansing His Temple.

That is why the life and being of the Church are intertwined with eucharistic proclamation, for the presence of the living Lord in the Church, which is the very essence of the Church, is not a static presence, but is the living action appropriated by the Church in its continuous action of proclamation.[1] In such proclamation the Church declares that its anchor is cast within the veil, that its being is grounded beyond itself in the ascended Lord, that its real life is a divine gift, and by such proclamation it opens the door in the Church for the incoming of that ultimate reality from beyond ("If any man open the door I will come in and sup with him and he with me"). And so the proclamation includes the *Maranatha* as an essential element in its liturgical action.

It is clear, therefore, that the bringing of the Eucharist under

[1] This is brought out with great power in K. Barth's pamphlet, *Die Botschaft von der freien Gnade Gottes.*

the rubric of proclamation excludes the idea of its being a sacrifice in itself or in its own right. Not the actual and literal offering of the sacrifice, but an action proclaiming a sacrifice once offered and eternally valid before the Father is what the Eucharist effects. In other words, by such proclamation the Eucharist becomes the sacramental counterpart to the unique sacrifice of Christ, and therefore in its own way, inasmuch as it echoes that, and is derivative from it, a sacramental sacrifice. It is thus that in the Eucharist the Church continually sets before itself and appropriates, by the power of the Spirit, the atoning sacrifice of Christ "through the eternal Spirit", because through the Spirit the proclaiming activity of the living Lord stands behind the Church's proclamation, as His intercession stands behind its *anamnesis*, so that it is really Christ in the Eucharist who represents to the Church and makes effective for the Church His own atoning deed of sacrifice.

The eucharistic proclamation, then, points to the *divine action* as the heart of it all. We may bring our best to the sacrifice, as Abraham brought his beloved Isaac, but at last God Himself provides a sacrifice in the place of Isaac, in His only-begotten and well-beloved Son, for the atoning deed is His and His alone, though it is wrought on our behalf. That is the very heart of proclamation and atonement, and it is from there that the significance of eucharistic sacrifice is determined.[1] This crucial point is too often missed by theologians of the "Catholic" type, for again and again they are found using "sacrifice" and "offering" univocally of God and the Church. That is even true of de la Taille, although he can write nobly of this fact. "Our sacrifices and that of Christ do not exist as members of one and the same genus, in the strict sense, in which the word sacrifice, used of our sacrifices and of His, would be a univocal term, but they are only in the same order by way of analogy. His sacrifice being the principle, and ours being subordinate to it. . . . Just as Christ on earth absolutely and simply offered only one sacrifice, so the duality which exists between His sacrifice and ours must

[1] It is essentially false procedure therefore to interpret the atonement from the point of view of a theology of the Eucharist, which is itself drawn from an idea of sacrifice which has not been given creative reinterpretation in Christ, rather than to interpret the Eucharist from the point of view of a true and N.T. doctrine of atonement.

be made such as not to imply any repeated sacrificial offering made by Christ, but such as to subordinate immediately our own sacrificial activity to the offering of the sacrifice made by Christ in the past, which continues for ever by its own efficacy."[1] What is it then that differentiates Christ's unique sacrifice and puts such a holy distance between it and anything that we may do even in His name? Surely that Christ bore God's judgment upon man's sin, that He did that alone on our behalf, and further, that He wrought out that atonement not only as Man but as God-Man, as God in Man.

It belongs to the essence of atonement that Christ bore man's judgment, the judgment of God upon man's sin.[2] In the Cross, God identifies Himself with man just where he is farthest from Him, that is, just where he stands under the divine judgment. Such a deed of atonement whose essence is the bearing of divine judgment cannot be prolonged in a ceremonial cultus. It can only be proclaimed and celebrated. That which distinguishes Christ's atoning sacrifice from the Church's sacrifice is the bearing of judgment. We must distinguish, then, between the propitiatory sacrifice and the eucharistic sacrifice,[3] realizing that the heart of Christ's unique sacrifice, the bearing of judgment, cannot be repeated in the latter in any sense. Its value lies mainly in its being a sign pointing to the divine action of atonement, and in its being entirely subordinate to that.

The atonement, however, was more than the bearing of the divine judgment. It was the offering to God of a perfect holiness, a holiness corresponding to that of God Himself, the holiness of perfect obedience. Both in bearing the divine judgment and in offering a perfect obedience, Jesus Christ stood absolutely alone, acting on our behalf. What we could not do, He has done for us. It was a substitutionary atonement. As the sacramental counterpart to that, the eucharistic sacrifice has not to do ultimately with our offering, but with Christ's offering on our behalf, His putting of Himself in our place, and taking upon Himself our judgment. "All that constituted atonement was wrought in our place and in our stead; wrought verily in *our* place, that is,

[1] *The Mystery of Faith* (English trans.), Vol. II, pp. 24 f.

[2] The following is indebted to an Anglican theologian, the late Dr. F. W. Camfield. Cf. *Scottish Journal of Theology*, 1948, vol. I, I, pp. 282 ff.

[3] Cf. John Calvin, *Institutes*, 4.18.12 f.

wrought *for* us and *as our act*."[1] The eucharistic sacrifice answers to that *as our act*, and involves the acceptance of Him as the One who has taken our place, the acceptance of His Self-offering as our offering to God. But in the nature of the case the eucharistic sacrifice must be entirely analogous in character to the substitutionary act of Christ, and involves its wondrous exchange. It might be called the counter-sacrifice of the Church, but never can it be said to be of the same genus as the unique sacrifice of Christ Himself. By participation in His body and blood He gives us to be associated with His sacrifice, but in such a way, as in the Garden of Gethsemane, that He removes Himself to a holy distance from us. We may indeed watch with Him, but in the awful hour of His agony we know that He dies alone and we are found among those who crucified Him.

What makes Christ's sacrifice absolutely unique is the identity between the Offerer and the Offering and Him to whom the Offering is made. In this connection the Reformers were fond of citing the famous words of the great Augustine: "Since in a sacrifice four things are considered, viz., to whom it is offered, by whom, what and for whom, the same one true Mediator, reconciling us to God by the sacrifice of peace, remains one with Him to whom He offered, made Himself one with those for whom He offered, is Himself the One who offered, and the one thing which He offered."[2] It is that identity which sets His sacrifice absolutely apart from anything else, and makes it quite clear that the eucharistic sacrifice is only the *anamnesis* or *proclamation* of that lonely sacrifice, and does not involve any identity between a sacrifice of our own and His.

It is quite certain, however, that such a unique sacrifice invokes from us a corresponding sacrifice of thanksgiving and praise, in which we turn our proclamation of Christ's death upwards to God, and not only plead the merits of Christ's sacrifice alone, but offer Him all that we have and are. How can we answer His grace except by offering ourselves up in obedience and thanksgiving? We know that we are unworthy, and can only offer Him our unworthiness, that He may make us worthy. But the worthiness which He enjoins "consists especially in faith, which places all things in Christ, nothing in ourselves, and

[1] F. W. Camfield, *op. cit.*, p. 292.

[2] *De Trinitate*, 4.24; cf. Calvin, *Inst.*, 4.18.10.

in love, love which, though imperfect, it may be sufficient to offer to God, that He may increase it since it cannot be fully rendered."[1] Thus all our sacrifices of praise, prayer and thanksgiving "depend on the greater sacrifice with which we dedicate ourselves, soul and body, to be a holy temple to the Lord. . . . We do not appear with our gifts in the presence of God without an intercessor. Christ is our Mediator, by whose intervention we offer ourselves and our all to the Father; He is our High Priest, who, having entered into the upper sanctuary, opens up an access for us: He the altar on which we lay our gifts, that whatever we do attempt, we may attempt in Him. He it is who 'hath made us kings and priests unto God and His Father'."[2]

There is a way, however, of speaking too easily about the bringing of our offerings in the Eucharist, about bringing the fruit of our labour as represented by the bread and wine, which savours rather much of the sacrifice of Cain. And then it is said that this offering and sacrifice of ours when laid on God's altar becomes identified with, and identical with, the sacrifice of Christ and we do verily offer Christ to God. Surely this *identity* involves an entire displacement of the centre of gravity, for after all, what the Eucharist proclaims is not our offering but Christ's offering on our behalf, which only in that derivative way becomes our offering. The denial of Christ's substitutionary act at this point for some doctrine of identity would mean an undermining of the atoning work of Christ. It is precisely this doctrine of identity between the bread and wine of the Eucharist with the glorified Body in the heavenly places, identity between the action of the Church on earth as it celebrates the sacrifice of Christ, and the perpetual Self-Offering of Christ Himself before the Face of the Father, which the theology of the Eucharist cannot allow, for that entails its destruction as a sacrament.[3]

Behind all this there is something deeper, an essentially Pelagian doctrine of the atonement, and certainly on a Pelagian view any substitutionary notion is impossible and abhorrent. How can Holy God allow one man to die for another, and judge the innocent man for the guilty? The doctrine of the atonement is impossible unless it is the doctrine of the divine action, of God

[1] Calvin, *Inst.*, 4.17.42. [2] Calvin, *Inst.*, 4.18.16 f.

[3] Cf. Karl Barth, *Die christliche Lehre nach dem Heidelberger Katechismus*, p. 104.

Himself coming to intervene and to save. God indeed became man and translated divine action into terms of human action. "Thus the background of the atoning deed is not the Godhead *per se*, but the God-manhood of Christ. But if that be so, then the idea of substitution is inevitable, and is constitutive of the doctrine of Atonement. . . . What we could not accomplish Christ accomplished on our behalf. The infliction and judgment which we could not bear, He bore for us. He took our place and on behalf of us all He made satisfaction for our sins and for the sins of the whole world. It was not the Godhead *qua* Godhead that atoned; it was the God-manhood. And that means, not simply God *in* man, but God *as* man. The manhood was integral and essential and not merely instrumental. And that means in the acutest sense, substitution."[1]

There are, accordingly, false ways of speaking of the eucharistic sacrifice as that which invests the deed of Christ with its sacrificial nature or validity, or as that which continually presents the sacrifice of Christ to the Father. We have seen the element of truth that lies behind such views, but we must beware of stating this in such a way as to involve a Pelagian view of the atonement as though it were not altogether a divine act.[2] A great deal of the horror of the Reformers for the doctrine of the Mass was recoil from its faulty soteriology, and its Pelagian notion of man, even if he were the Man Jesus, appeasing God. Once it is clearly seen, however, that the atonement is God's act, and that He bears in Himself our judgment, that He does in Jesus what we cannot do, then the false doctrine of identity falls to the ground, and a true doctrine of eucharistic sacrifice can be enunciated, and a true doctrine of proclamation in which the Church can share in the atoning and victorious action of Christ.[3]

We must now turn to yet another aspect of the Lord's Supper, to the words "This is my body broken for you. This is my blood

[1] F. W. Camfield, *op. cit.*, p. 292.

[2] This was evidently in the mind of D. M. Mackinnon, *op. cit.*, p. 134, when he corrects his own statement: "We consecrate the death of Christ as a sacrifice, or rather, participate in the act whereby He consecrates His Passion as the recreation of the world in Him."

[3] A crude doctrine of identity can lead to terrible extremes, as when some people insist that in the Eucharist we must will the death that we have caused. That is to turn the eucharistic sacrifice into murder.

shed for you." There can be little doubt, as Calvin used to say,[1] that "almost the whole energy of the sacrament consists in these words". The impartial exegete cannot but conclude that it was upon these verbs that Jesus Himself laid the emphasis, that here it was intended not only that by these elements the crucifixion should evidently be set before our eyes, but that the stress should be laid upon the taking and eating and drinking, that is, in communicating in the body and blood of Christ. It is a sign of serious disorder in the Church's Eucharist when Jesus' own emphasis upon our communicating by eating and drinking His body and blood is overshadowed by a disproportionate emphasis upon the Church's sacrifice. The *Summa Theologica* of St. Thomas Aquinas is surely right when it gives the space for only one *Question* to the idea of sacrifice, and some twenty to communion in the real presence of Christ. Though the Last Supper was in point of historical time prior to the Cross, it was clearly designed, as the emphasis upon *broken* body and shed *blood* made clear, to take place as the meal following the completion of the perfect sacrifice once-and-for-all enacted on the Cross. No elaboration of exegesis upon the Old Testament can alter the fact that the sacrificial meals of the Old Testament did not repeat the act of oblation, but were the means by which the benefits of the sacrifice were conveyed.[2] The corresponding emphasis here in the eucharistic communion is the Church's thankful participation in so great salvation and its unrestrained joy (*agalliasis*) in the real presence of the risen Lord.

We can only look at the Lord's Supper through the eyes of the apostles who were eye-witnesses of the resurrection, and who recalled that again and again when they were breaking bread the risen Jesus chose suddenly to come into their midst. Those Easter meals gave them their understanding of the rite in the Upper Room. Recalling again the union between the deity and humanity of Christ, and the nature of the sacramental union grounded upon that, we must understand the Lord's Supper in similar terms. There is then, on the one hand, the historical enactment of the rite which the Church is commanded to repeat in accordance with our Lord's institution, handed on to us by the

[1] *Inst.*, 4.17.3.

[2] Cf. Markus Barth, *Das Abendmahl——Passamahl, Bundesmahl u. Messiasmahl*, p. 25.

Synoptic Gospels and St. Paul. On the other hand there are the resurrection events, such as that recorded by St. Luke of the two disciples at Emmaus to whom Jesus was made known in the breaking of bread, or that recorded in the Fourth Gospel, when "Jesus came and stood in the midst, and saith unto them, Peace be unto you. And when he had so said, he shewed unto them his hands and his side. Then were the disciples glad when they saw the Lord. Then said Jesus unto them again, Peace be unto you: as my Father hath sent me, so send I you. And when he had said this, he breathed on them, and saith unto them, Receive ye the Holy Ghost: whosesoever sins ye remit, they are remitted unto them; and whosesoever sins ye retain, they are retained."

The Last Supper and those resurrection appearances belong together in one sacramental whole. Though Jesus has withdrawn His visible presence from us, there is such an intervention by the risen Lord as the invisible reality behind each celebration of the Lord's Supper. Jesus Christ is as really present in the Eucharist as He was on that Easter day to His disciples. As surely as in the Eucharist we handle bread and wine, we put our fingers into His wounds and He breathes upon us His peace and forgiveness in answer to the prayer: "Lamb of God who takest away the sins of the world, grant us thy peace." The Eucharist then is the sacramental enactment of the real presence of Christ. It is the historical action of the Church in which the historical passion of the Saviour is vividly exhibited before our eyes, but we must go on to say, with Calvin, that "what the minister figures and attests by outward action, God performs inwardly".[1]

When we say, however, that the Eucharist is the sacramental enactment of the real presence of Christ, we must make clear that it is the real presence of the God-Man. No doubt it is through the eternal Spirit, through an act issuing from the Godhead, but it is the divine enactment of the Incarnate Presence in the Church. Our Lord was not only the bearer of the divine Word of forgiveness, but He enacted that Word in our flesh and blood, the flesh and blood which He had made His own from the Virgin Mary. We may go on to say that on the ground of that supreme action, the mystery of the incarnation and the crucifixion is sacramentally "re-enacted" in those who have been baptized into Christ. When we turn to our Lord's teaching

[1] *Inst.*, 4.14.17.

as recorded in the Fourth Gospel, in His discourse on the bread of life, we find that there is an eating of the flesh and a drinking of the blood of Christ before eucharistic participation. But how could it be otherwise inasmuch as the Word was made flesh, for His words are Spirit and Life? The union of the baptized with Christ through the Word involves also a continual feeding upon the flesh and blood of Christ.[1] He who is sacramentally incorporated into the body of Christ is already participant in sacramental communion. We must allow ourselves to be reminded therefore that the Eucharist presupposes baptismal incorporation, presupposes the Church as the Body of Christ and that faith brings to the Eucharist a continuous feeding upon the body and blood of Christ. What are we then to say of eucharistic communion? Surely, as Calvin has made so clear in the Reformed Church, that while we can only eat and drink the body and blood of Christ through faith, yet, by the power of the eternal Spirit, the Church is given through the Eucharist a *relation in being* to Christ, beyond its relation to Him through faith.

Calvin was fond of discussing this matter with reference to the words of the Epistle to the Ephesians: "That Christ may dwell in your hearts by faith, that ye being rooted and grounded in love may be able to comprehend with all saints what is the breadth, and length, and depth, and height; and to know the love of Christ, which passeth knowledge, that ye might be filled with all the fullness of God" (3: 17 f.). Christ dwells in our hearts by faith, but His dwelling in our hearts is an ontological relation not identical with faith, though through faith. So we may say that in the Eucharist believing and actual communication through the bread and wine are not one and the same thing.[2] There can be no doubt that as yet we walk by faith and not by sight, nevertheless the significance of eucharistic communion lies in the fact that by the act of the eternal Spirit the believing Church is given to step over the eschatological boundary, and to partake of the divine

[1] Calvin's *Commentary on John*, 6.35, 53; *Inst.*, 4.17.5. Cf. 4.17.30: "A perpetual connection with Christ could not exist unless He dwells in us *corporeally*, independently of the use of the Supper."

[2] See, for example, *Inst.* 4.17.5. Cf. W. Niesel, *Calvins Lehre vom Abendmahl*, p. 38.

nature. As faith and hope pass away, while love endures as the eternal reality, so here already through the Eucharist relation in being in the love of God follows from faith and hope.[1]

We must pause to say that there is an infinite mystery here which completely transcends the ability of our minds to grasp, a mystery that is more to be adored than discussed. Wise indeed were the Chalcedonian fathers who formulated the *unio hypostatica* only in negatives, and wise are they who likewise are content to adore the mystery in the Eucharist without explanations of how the *unio sacramentalis* actually takes place. The Reformed Church standing upon the Chalcedonian Christology repudiates both Nestorianism and Eutychianism in its doctrine of the sacramental union, denying that there is either separation or fusion between the elements of bread and wine and the reality of the body and blood of Christ.[2] Just as the humanity of Christ remains true humanity even after the resurrection and ascension and is no docetic phantasm, so the bread and wine remain true bread and wine and are no mere species,[3] though by consecration they are converted into instruments of the real presence.[4] Through the consecrated elements the Church partakes of the very body and blood of Christ, and there is enacted a *true and substantial union*,[5] an ontological union, between Christ and His Church. Christ has become bone of our bone and flesh of our flesh, but in the Eucharist we become bone of His bone and flesh of His flesh. No union, save that of the Persons of the Holy

[1] Cf. W. Niesel, *op. cit.*, p. 95: "Die eschatologische Grenze wird durch die Tat des heiligen Geistes überschritten, und aus dem Glauben folgt ein Sein in Christus." Cf. also E. Walter, *Das Kommen des Herrn*, Vol. I, pp. 38 ff.

[2] This was the position taken up by Zwingli against Luther, by Calvin against both Romanists and extreme Lutherans, and by Peter Martyr in his notable controversy with the Bishop of Winchester at Oxford. It passed into Anglican theology and became a feature of the Caroline divines.

[3] Calvin argued that the doctrine of transubstantiation involved docetic heresy, for it undermined the analogy between the elements and the reality which they figured. "The analogy between the sign and the thing signified cannot be destroyed without destroying the truth of the sacrament." *Inst.*, 4.

[4] For a clear statement on the conversion of the elements see *The Mystery of the Lord's Supper, Sermons on the Sacrament* by Robert Bruce (edit., 1958), pp. 114 f. Cf. Calvin, *Inst.*, 4.17.14.

[5] This was Calvin's usual way of stating the nature of the union.

Trinity, could be closer, without passing into absolute identity, than that between Christ and His Church as enacted in the Holy Eucharist.

It is in the Eucharist, then, that the Church really becomes the Church, both as the ontological and eschatological reality and as the extension into history of the visible sacramental fact which is the Church's existence on earth. It is both the filling of the Church with its divine mystery, and the manifestation of that mystery within history without its ceasing to be mystery. In no sense can the Church be said to be an extension of the incarnation, though here we have to do with the re-enactment by the Word of its becoming flesh. The Eucharist, therefore, together with Baptism, involves the mystery of the incarnation, the virgin birth and the resurrection of Christ. The virgin birth and the resurrection were the miraculous signs through which the divine Word both entered history in Self-revelation, and yet ever remained identical with Himself. Parallel to that, Baptism and the Eucharist are the miraculous signs through which the divine Word enters into the Church it has called out of the world, in Self-impartation, and yet ever remains identical with Himself. Baptism and Eucharist as one Sacrament are analogically related in the Holy Spirit to the virgin birth and the resurrection as the one act of divine Self-revelation. Virgin birth and resurrection, however, involved more than Self-revelation; they involved the actual descent of the Son of God into our humanity, and the actual ascent of the Son of God in ascension bearing with Him our humanity. Likewise in the Eucharist there takes place an actual *katabasis* of the living Lord, and an actual *anabasis* in which He bears the Church up with Him to the throne of God—whether "in the body or out of the body", who can tell? But it is an eschatological anticipation both of the Advent of the Son of Man and the rapture of the Church. The Eucharist involves at its very heart the *sursum corda*, for our union with Christ in history and yet out of history is a reality that utterly transcends all our categories of space and time.

The incomprehensible fact is that God begins eternally with Himself. The Son is begotten, not made. And the ineffable mystery of the Eucharist is that in it God begins with Himself in the continuity of the Church's action in the creaturely world, but independent of it.[1] That has supreme importance for what follows in our next section, for it means that the Church through its ministry can no more exercise its authority over the Eucharist than Joseph could exercise his authority over the virgin birth. As Joseph could only stand aside at the miracle of the incarnation, so the ministry of the Church can only stand aside even in the Eucharist where it is ordained to serve. The Church can never manage the Eucharist or exercise any lordship over it unless it wishes to be like the kings of the Gentiles that exercise lordship and authority over them and are called benefactors. At the Last Supper Jesus took pains to make that clear, enacting a vivid parable before the disciples in washing their feet that they might learn to forswear all lordship. The Kingdom appointed to the Church and its ministry at the Eucharist is grounded on the abasement of Christ unto death, and is one of service (*diakonia*). The Church is joined to its Lord at the Eucharist only as a body is joined to its head. The Eucharist means the enactment of the authority of Christ the Head over the Church and over its ministry. *Ecce ancilla Domini.* Inasmuch as the mystery of the virgin birth is sacramentally present in the Eucharist, it belongs to the Church in the Eucharist humbly to *receive* (*Take ye, eat ye*) the eternal Word as the ground of the Church's being, and to be entirely subordinate to Him as Word.[2]

Further, inasmuch as the mystery of the Resurrection is sacramentally present in the Eucharist, it belongs to the Church in the Eucharist to acknowledge that its outward historical form which partakes of the fashion of this passing world is made the empty tomb out of which the new creation is raised up to enter the Kingdom of God. This means that at every true Eucharist, where there is a sacramental enactment of the mystery of the virgin birth and the resurrection of the body, there is involved an eschatological suspension of historical continuity and the order and authority which that involves.

[1] See the superb discussion by Karl Barth, *Dogmatik*, I, 2. pp. 187 ff., *Das Wunder der Weinacht*, to which I am much indebted. (E. T. pp. 172 ff.)

[2] Cf. Edmund Schlink, *The Student World*, 1950, I, p. 48: "The Church is the place, the creation and the instrument of the Lord's Supper but never its Lord. On the other hand, we find degeneration where the Church departs from its function as receiver and server of the Lord's Supper and makes itself lord of the Lord's Supper."

III

Intercommunion and Order

We must now draw the foregoing discussion to a close by working out its implications in regard to intercommunion. We may begin by recalling an incident which all three Synoptic Gospels record, the objection by the priests and scribes to our Lord's cleansing of the Temple (or reformation of the Church), and to His practice of teaching in the Temple against the priestly order. They came to Jesus and asked Him: "By what authority doest thou these things? And who gave thee this authority to do these things?" Our Lord answered first by reference to Baptism and then by a telling parable which the priests and scribes recognized as directed against the priestly and legal mind. Jesus was undoubtedly referring to cleansing before sacrifice, and to the eschatological preaching of John that the axe is laid to the root of the tree. He indicated further that one cannot ask questions about the highest authority, for that is to misconceive it—and it is upon that misconception that all rigid doctrine of orders is based.

But may we not allow His words to remind us of something else, that the authority for Reformation and the administration of the Eucharist, even against the priestly and legal notion of validity in the idea of episcopal succession, is derived from Holy Baptism? If Baptism means actual incorporation into the Body of Christ, and already means through the Word a continuous feeding upon the flesh and blood of Christ, as our Lord stated so clearly in the Fourth Gospel, who are we to deny those so baptized renewal of their incorporation in the Body of Christ, provided that they are sincere? Baptism reminds us that Christ dwells in us corporeally, independently of the Supper, for otherwise absolute continuity there could not be. Baptism reminds us that the real continuity of the Body of Christ is not to be sought on the plane of historical relativity but in the continuous act of God, which in the Resurrection is continuous temporal fact. Therefore to refuse the Eucharist to those baptized into Christ Jesus and incorporated into His resurrection-body amounts either to a denial of the transcendent reality of holy Baptism or to attempted schism within the Body of Christ. How can we hold apart the Body of Christ from the Body of Christ? How can we hold apart the once-and-for-all incorporation into that Body and its continual renewal in the Holy Eucharist? Surely a clear and high doctrine of Holy Baptism forbids us to allow any wedge to be driven between Baptism and Eucharist. If Baptism is of the living God, then who can deny those baptized the right to partake of the Eucharist? If Baptism is of men, then we disinherit the masses of common people.

We must turn to another incident, however, to see more clearly into this question of authority—to the encounter between our Lord and the Pharisees over the Sabbath-breaking of the disciples, also recorded by all the Synoptic Gospels. It is the incident in which Jesus declared: "The sabbath is made for man, and not man for the sabbath; therefore the Son of Man is Lord also of the sabbath." The context speaks about Jesus' eating and drinking with publicans and sinners, which as we have seen was an enactment of the messianic meal; then it speaks about the coming and going of the Bridegroom, the new wine of the Kingdom of God which always breaks old bottles when poured into them, and the action of Abiathar who did not refuse to give to outcast David and his hungering friends the holy bread that was reserved by sacred law for priests alone. It is in such a significant context that these words about the authority of the Son of Man are recorded. In the presence of the Son of Man the barriers to intercommunion are thrown down, the new wine of the Kingdom breaks the old bottles, the sacred bread from the altar is distributed to the hungry, and publicans and sinners are freely invited to eat and drink with the Lord. The Son of Man is therefore Lord of the Sabbath and all that it stands for, the Lord of the cult, the Lord of the sacred bread.

It is in entire keeping for us in the Christian age to say, following our Lord: "The Eucharist was made for man, and not man for the Eucharist. Therefore the Son of Man is Lord also of the Eucharist." That is to say, the Son of Man reserves the right to dispense His own Supper to whom He will, and to distribute the holy bread to the outcasts and the hungry, in spite of all priestly protestations. In the presence of the eschatological Christ, the Son of Man, all barriers to intercommunion are broken down. So it will certainly be when the Bridegroom comes, and the marriage-supper of the Lamb takes place. But in as much as there is the real presence of the *Eschatos*, of the Son of Man, in the Eucharist, the new wine which we drink in the Kingdom of God breaks down the old vessels and spills over freely to all who hunger and thirst after righteousness. So soon as we realize that the Eucharist is charged with the real presence of the Son of Man, to whom all judgment has been committed, we realize that it is the Lord's Supper (*Kyriakon deipnon*) and not our own (*idion deipnon*) and that we cannot send any Church or any sincere baptized believer away, without sinning against the majesty and grace of the Son of Man.

That does not mean that the Church is prohibited from "fencing the Table", by excluding from participation in the Eucharist the lapsed who have denied their Baptism or the impenitent and insincere, but it does mean that the Church must exercise its discipline *with the authority of the Son of Man*, and not with the authority of priests and scribes and Pharisees. It is by the Word that the Son of Man exercises His authority, and by the Word that He judges and divides between men. "Lord, how wilt thou manifest thyself unto us and not unto the world? Jesus answered and said, If a man love me he will keep my word and my Father will love him, and we will come unto him and make our abode with Him." "If any man hear my voice and open the door I will come in and sup with him and he with me." On the other hand, Jesus says also: "If any man hear my words and believe not, I judge him not: for I came not to judge the world but to save the world. He that rejecteth me and receiveth not my words, hath one that judgeth him: the word that I have spoken, the same shall judge him in the last day." It is with just such judgment, said St. Paul, that the discernment of the Lord's Body in the Eucharist is concerned. In other words, the real fencing of the holy Table is lodged in the prophetic ministry through which the holy Majesty and Grace of the Son of Man are brought to bear upon the Church. It is when the Son of Man, Christ crucified and Christ to come, is proclaimed with power in all His saving grace and judgment, that the Table is kept holy and undefiled; and it is then when His Word and authority are glorified that it is indeed the Lord's Table and the Lord's Supper, and not a private supper owned and administered on exclusive principles by the Church. It cannot be said too plainly that whenever the prophetic ministry decays, whenever the Church refuses to give priority to the ministry of the Word over the ministry of Tables, the priestly authority gets out of hand, and inevitably falls under the judgment of the Son of Man.

There is another aspect of this matter to which we must give full recognition, for it is of the utmost importance—the place of order in the Church. "The spirits of the prophets are subject to the prophets; for God is not the author of confusion but of peace, as in all the Churches of the saints" (1 Cor. 14 :32 f.). That means that the Church and its ministry cannot be indifferent to church order. There is a subjection even in the realm of spiritual gifts and *charismata.* On the other hand, St. Paul says quite plainly that "the Lord is the Spirit, and where the Spirit of the Lord is, there is liberty" (2 Cor. 3: 17). There cannot be any absolute fixity of order in the charismatic ministry of the Church. How are we to understand this order in which there is both freedom and control? That was one of the crucial problems facing St. Paul in the Corinthian Church, and the answer he gave is taken straight out of the Eucharist, though it is closely linked with Baptism.[1]

We may fill out St. Paul's thought with other New Testament teaching, and put the matter in the following way. In Baptism the Church is incorporated into the Body of Christ and puts on Christ. That is to say, the Church partakes of the form of Christ's Body. The conformity of the Church to Christ, which is once-and-for-all in Baptism, is not static, but dynamic, for it is bound up with the Church's obedience as it carries out the ordinance of the Lord to proclaim His death till He come. That concerns both missionary *kerygma* and the eucharistic proclamation, though it is above all in the Eucharist where the Church knows Christ in the fellowship of His sufferings and the power of His Resurrection that it becomes conformable unto Him. There the Church is crucified unto the world, and is transformed by the renewing of its mind into the image or form of Jesus Christ. It is in the Eucharist, too, that the Church becomes visible as the Body of Christ in history, for it is there that it becomes a membered Body under the Headship of Christ. "We being many are one body, for we all partake of the one bread." That

[1] Cf. especially for the following, E. Käsemann, *Evangelische Theologie,* 1948, 9–10; and H. Dobert, *Evangelische Theologie,* 1949, 11.

membering or ordering of the Church is the new order or the new covenant of the Kingdom, into which the Church is initiated at Baptism, but which now materializes in visible bodily fashion. It is the constitution of the Church in Jesus Christ.

Christ is Prophet, Priest, and King. Therefore the Church, which in Baptism puts on Christ and in the Eucharist becomes one Body with Him, is given to participate in that *triplex munus.* As His Body the Church manifests the form of that Body as it exercises in obedience to Him, a prophetic, priestly, and kingly ministry. We have to remember, however, that the Church is only joined to Christ as a body is joined to its head, and its ministry as Body is not the same as the ministry of the Head. To take priesthood, for example, with which we are mostly concerned at this point in our discussion: Christ's Priesthood and the Church's priesthood cannot be spoken of in univocal terms any more than Christ's sacrifice and the eucharistic sacrifice. They are not of the same genus. Once that is understood clearly a great deal of the confusion resulting from the ambiguous use of the word "priesthood" can be swept away. It should be perfectly clear right away, therefore, that the Church's priesthood cannot be thought of as having in any way control over Christ, any more than the body can control the head.[1]

Two further facts about the ministry of the Church must be noted:

(a) The Form of Christ in the Eucharist remains a mystery, and is not to be fully discerned. We see Christ by faith, only through a glass darkly, for He is veiled behind the elements as well as unveiled or revealed through them. That means that the whole question of the Church's order and ministry is bound up with the Self-revelation of Christ, and because of that the Church's order cannot come under its ultimate control. It belongs to the nature of Revelation to take concrete form as human word, human form, human ordinance. Revelation therefore conceals Christ behind word, sacrament, ordinance, as well as reveals Him. A direct reading off of the Church's form and order from the Eucharist is impossible. It belongs to the nature of the Church to bear witness in definite orders to the Form of the Body of Christ and so to manifest that Form in

[1] See *Royal Priesthood, S.J.T. Occasional Paper* no. 3, 1955, ch. IV.

historical conditions, but because that Form is the content of Revelation the Church cannot transcribe it into the conditions of time and history in any perfect or indelible or fixed structure. Every time it partakes of the Eucharist it allows its order or historical structure to be called in question by that which here comes from beyond history and is not expressible in terms of history alone. It is only in such a way that we can think of the order or the orders of the Church.

(b) In this situation it is the function of the Church's ministry to build or edify the Church on earth by Word and Sacrament, so that the form and order of the Church in history may correspond sacramentally to the true form and order that are yet to be revealed. This means that we must think of the priesthood of the Church as having an essentially sacramental character. Through Baptism and the Lord's Supper the Church is formed into a corporate priesthood, a royal priesthood,[1] but that priesthood remains essentially a mystery, and only becomes visible in a historical and membered priesthood which points to a fullness beyond itself. That is why St. Paul speaks of this membered priesthood not in terms of priesthood but in terms of *charismata*. We may distinguish then between the Church's priesthood and *charismata*, by saying that the priesthood is essentially corporate, is a whole, and cannot be broken up into parts. *Charismata* are the gifts of the ascended Lord, and are essentially fragmented. Not all are prophets, not all are apostles, or teachers or workers of miracles. There are diversities of gifts and administrations and operations, but it is the same Spirit, the same Lord, and the same God who worketh all in all, and behind all this diversity of gifts and members there is one body in Christ. The diverse *charismata* have no value in themselves, but only as they minister together to the edification of the whole body.

The Church in history, then, is related to its ascended Lord by means of these diverse *charismata*, which partake indeed of historical fragmentation and which shall therefore pass away before the ultimate reality which is the oneness of the Church to Christ in love (1 Cor. 13),[2] but which here and now are the

[1] Cf. 1 Peter 2: 5, 9; Rev. 1: 6; Luke 22: 29; 1 Cor. 11: 25; 2 Cor. 3: 6. The Church in the New Covenant is appointed at once a Kingdom and a priesthood or a ministry.

[2] Cf. E. Walter, *Das Kommen des Herrn*, I, pp. 38 f., 90 ff.

historical means that God uses to build up the Church on earth. In this situation it is the function of the ministry to edify the Church by Word and Sacrament, that its form and order may more and more approximate to and partake of the one Body of Christ. That takes place above all in the Lord's Supper, where the *charismata* are to be regarded as the signs pointing to the new divine order which is ever breaking through the eucharistic participation and being realized afresh in the Church on earth. That new divine order is only visible in orders that serve it truly and never in orders that obscure it or seek to manage it. It is the function of orders to make room in the Church and to keep that room open for the actual intervention of the ascended Lord in Word and Sacrament.

Here in the Eucharist, therefore, we are given our deepest insight into the meaning of order under the Lordship of Christ, as order which is sacramentally and eschatologically conditioned. The actual ordering of the Church partakes of the form and fashion of this passing world, and as such it can never be identified in its historical structure with the essential form of the Church or be allowed to anticipate the order yet to be fully disclosed in the *eschaton*. It can only point beyond itself. The Church that is truly ordered will possess its orders as if it possessed them not, coveting earnestly the more excellent way which abides for ever, the way of love, when all orders, however necessary and sacramental they are within history, will pass away. Such a Church will watch and pray for its Lord, waiting for His coming, when it will put off the image of the earthly, the compromised ecclesiastical shell that marks its continuing historical existence, and put on the image of the heavenly.

From all this, three conclusions follow which are important for our discussion of intercommunion.

(1) The Eucharist cannot be subordinated to any conception of order. If the Church really becomes the Church in the Eucharist, how can it bring order to the Eucharist if it is there that it receives its order with its true being? It is only because there are repeated celebrations of the Eucharist that the Church can bring order to the Eucharist, but the very repetition of the Eucharist means the relativization of that prior order and its reordering in the presence of the Church's Lord. As often as we

celebrate the Lord's Supper we proclaim His death till He come, we receive anew His death and resurrection into the existence of the Church, and so bear about the dying of the Lord Jesus in the body of the Church that the life also of Jesus may be made manifest in that body. Through the Eucharist, therefore, death worketh in the Church and its members and orders. If through the Eucharist the Spirit of Christ is in the Church, then its "body" is dead, mortified by the death of Christ—that is to say, its "body" understood as its implication in the forms of this world. It is only when through the eucharistic enactment the judgment inherent in the death of Christ is allowed to break up the hardened forms of the Church's liturgy, into which eschatology is continually being transmuted, that the Church can truly serve the Lord it worships, and at the same time hold out life to the world.

It is sometimes argued that the Eucharist does not stand alone, but is embedded in the historical continuity or the institutional continuity of the Church, including its structure of faith and order, which is part of the significance of its continual repetition in the action of the Church. Undoubtedly the celebration of the Eucharist is so embedded in the institutional continuity of the Church, but the Eucharist by its very nature, in as much as it enshrines the real presence of the Son of Man, the Lord of the Eucharist, stands above the institutional continuity of the Church and *can never be made relative to it*, for that would make the Church the master of the Son of Man and not His servant.[1] This is the crucial point in ecumenical discussion on intercommunion, for it is here that the ultimate difficulty lies, in the difference between Churches which take biblical eschatology seriously and those who are retrenched in a fixity of orders within which they involve the *Lord's* Supper as though it were their own. As Professor Manson has said so well (in the same article): "The sacrament is a catholic ordinance for catholic approach. It proclaims not the Church in the Lord but the Lord in the Church." It is one of the extraordinary facts about the ecumenical fellowship that to-day the younger Churches are everywhere feeling the pressure of the coming

[1] For a remarkably clear discussion of this fact, to which I am much indebted, see W. Manson, "Church and Intercommunion", *Scottish Journal of Theology*, 1950, vol. 4.1, pp. 4 f.

Kingdom upon them and bear evidence of a truly charismatic ministry—that is nowhere more in evidence than in the Church of South India—but some of the older Churches show, on the contrary, evidence of a marked hardening of their orders, which can only be interpreted as a sign of the last times.

(2) The Eucharist cannot be subordinated to history. The enactment of the eucharistic presence into the flesh and blood of history means that the Church can never be allowed to forget its involvement in history. We do not stand before the Son of Man as we shall do when He comes again, for His suspension of final judgment until the last day gives history its course. The Church stands to-day and all through history where the Lord's Supper takes place, between the Resurrection of Jesus Christ and His Second Advent, that is, in the midst of history. The Revelation, which calls the Church into being and recreates it from age to age, takes place within history, and it is there that the living Lord gives Himself to be known to us, within the actual ongoing historical Church and nowhere else. On the other hand, the eucharistic presence involves the power of the Resurrection, which breaks the fetters of history and tells us that the risen Lord cannot be holden in the fixity of the past.

In other words, the Eucharist means the enactment of the real presence of the living Christ to-day, and every day it is celebrated. But if we have to do with the real presence of Christ *to-day*, we may not bind that to the embodiment of Christ in His Church in the passing forms of another day—that would be to perpetuate a dead Christ and to by-pass the resurrection from the dead. If Christ had not ascended and we had continuous visible contact with Him to-day, that would doubtless mean that the historical events of His birth, ministry in Judaea and Galilee, and death under Pontius Pilate, would be relegated to the incidents of past history and perhaps forgotten, but His ascension tells us that to know Jesus Christ and make contact with Him we must concentrate upon those historical events of His birth, life, and death; that is to say, we must concentrate upon the historical foundation of the Church's faith. "I have received of the Lord that which also I delivered unto you. As often as ye do this ye proclaim the Lord's death till He come." At the same time the withdrawal of Christ by ascension from visible implication in ongoing history, and His promise to come again as the Lord and Judge of History, tells us that all historical existence is made relative to His immediate presence. It is that real presence which breaks into history in the Eucharist, from beyond history, which cannot be construed in terms of history alone, and which cannot be imprisoned in history, either in the history of a particular period such as the Catholic ages or the Reformation, or in the long sweep of Church history. The Eucharist therefore cannot be made subordinate to history, for it is creative of history.

Nor can we forget the fact that every time in the Eucharist we eat the broken body and partake of the blood of Christ we are communicating in the death of Christ, partaking of the judgment which that death involved, in order that we may also partake of the power of His resurrection. To participate in the Eucharist and its proclamation of the death of Christ until He come is to involve the Church in the final judgment upon the forms of history in order that its new life may appear. The repeated celebrations of the Eucharist do not mean that the Church is growing old with tradition and ancient glory, for its glory is yet to be revealed in the manifestation of the Son of Man, but it means that the Church is ever growing younger and younger, until at last it arrives at the great day when as a Bride it shall be presented to the Bridegroom for the consummation of its joy in the marriage-supper of the Lamb. In as much as the Eucharist is an anticipation of that day, it stands above history, and can never be subordinated to it or made relative to the fixity of its passing forms.

(3) If the Eucharist cannot be subordinated to history or to any particular conception of order, but is the transcendent manifestation of the Son of Man within history until He come in the fullness of His glory, then the Eucharist is above all the divinely given means of unity in the Church. "We being many are one body, for we all partake of the one bread." That is a fact that can never be made relative to anything outside of it, if it is not to be dwarfed and domesticated into a private rite. The very place of the Eucharist between the two Advents of Christ, in the very midst of history with all its divisions and heart-rending failures, means that it is designed to be such a means of unity

within diversity that in spite of diversity and division that unity is continually recreated in conditions of time until its full reality is disclosed in the Kingdom to come. We are unable to trace the lineaments of the Kingdom in the fragmented patterns of history so that we can say: lo here is the *Una Sancta*, or, lo there is the *Una Sancta*. But we know that we have been baptized into one Body, and that there is one Lord, one Faith, one Baptism. Supervening upon that we have been given the Holy Eucharist as the sacrament of unity in diversity to tell us that our oneness with the Lord does not depend upon our success or failure in loyalty to Him, but on His Will to be one with us and to make us all one in Him. That belongs to the heart of Christ's high-priestly intercession, and we cannot hold that the Eucharist is in any sense the counterpart on earth to that (not merely in some pious mystic hope, but in actual enactment of the mystery of our unity in flesh and blood) without believing that it is through participation in the Eucharist that we are meant *more and more* (as Calvin put it) *to coalesce in one body with Him and so with each other*.

If the Sacrament only proclaimed that unity in word and did not also serve to enact it, it would not be the Sacrament that the Church holds it to be. Here the corporeal Self-communication of Christ to the Church through the one bread and the one cup, actually enacts in flesh and blood the unity of the one Lord, and constrains us to concrete corporeal obedience in the one Body of the Lord. The refusal of intercommunion entails a failure to discern the Body of the Lord and an unworthy participation in His body and blood. St. Paul told the Corinthians quite explicitly that for groups to meet for communion separately is not to hold the *Lord's* Supper, but to turn it into a private supper, and indeed to create schism in the Church. It is for that cause that so many are weak and sickly in the Church. There can be no doubt, therefore, that Churches ought to sit down together before the presence of the Son of Man, and together eat and drink the judgment of the death of Christ upon their sinful divisions and compromised histories, in order that together they may be given anew the power of the resurrection to rise above the trammels of the past and to realize the very unity of the one Body into which they have been baptized.

This means that intercommunion should come early in the

approach of the Churches toward full unity in the ecumenical fellowship, for that unity can never be reached so long as the separated Churches refuse to give each other the divine medicine for their healing. The Holy Eucharist cannot be celebrated without the breaking of the bread and the pouring out of the wine. Let it be celebrated, then, within the fraction of the Church, wherever the Church is sincere enough to resist unto blood everything that stands between it and its Lord. Let the Church that gives communion to another remember the words of the Lord: "In as much as ye have done it unto one of the least of these my brethren, ye have done it unto me." And let the Church that refuses to give communion to another remember also those other words of the same Lord which will be spoken at the final judgment: "I was an hungered and ye gave me no meat: I was thirsty and ye gave me no drink." "Lord, when saw we thee an hungered or athirst, and did not minister unto thee?" Then shall he answer them, "In as much as ye did it not unto one of the least of these, ye did it not unto me." Those are solemn words which have direct bearing upon intercommunion.[1]

It is certain that at the last day all the barriers of liturgy and cult and order that have been erected in history around the Holy Table of the Lord will be torn down, for in that great day "The Spirit and the Bride say, Come. And let him that heareth say, Come. And let him that is athirst come. And whosoever will, let him take of the water of life freely." And St. John adds, if any man shall take away these words from the Book of Prophecy, God shall take away his part out of the Book of Life, and out of the Holy City. We cannot afford to wait until the *eschaton* to hear those words. The Eucharist is given to us here and now as an anticipation within history of the marriage-supper of the Lamb. In every true Eucharist, therefore, the Church, as the Bride of Christ, will join the Spirit, saying, *Come. Whosoever will, let him take the water of life freely*. Only when that happens can it be an eschatologically valid Eucharist.

[1] See further *Essays in Anglican Self-Criticism*, edit. by D. M. Paton, pp. 202 f.

INDEX

I. Biblical References

Genesis

Exodus

Leviticus

Numbers

Numbers (*continued*)

Deuteronomy

Judges

1 Samuel

1 Kings

2 Kings

1 Chronicles

2 Chronicles

John

Acts of the Apostles

Romans

1 Corinthians

1 Corinthians (*continued*)

2 Corinthians

Galatians

Ephesians

Philippians

INDEX

II. Names

INDEX

III. Subjects